ISBN 978-1-5280-5619-9
PIBN 10944818

1 MONTH OF
FREE
READING

at

www.ForgottenBooks.com

By purchasing this book you are eligible for one month membership to ForgottenBooks.com, giving you unlimited access to our entire collection of over 1,000,000 titles via our web site and mobile apps.

To claim your free month visit:

www.forgottenbooks.com/free944818

English
Français
Deutsche
Italiano
Español
Português

www.forgottenbooks.com

Mythology Photography **Fiction**
Fishing Christianity **Art** Cooking
Essays Buddhism Freemasonry
Medicine **Biology** Music **Ancient**
Egypt Evolution Carpentry Physics
Dance Geology **Mathematics** Fitness
Shakespeare **Folklore** Yoga Marketing
Confidence Immortality Biographies
Poetry **Psychology** Witchcraft
Electronics Chemistry History **Law**
Accounting **Philosophy** Anthropology
Alchemy Drama Quantum Mechanics
Atheism Sexual Health **Ancient History**
Entrepreneurship Languages Sport
Paleontology Needlework Islam
Metaphysics Investment Archaeology
Parenting Statistics Criminology
Motivational

THE

REVISED REPORTS

BEING

A REPUBLICATION OF SUCH CASES

IN THE

ENGLISH COURTS OF COMMON LAW AND EQUITY.

FROM THE YEAR 1785,

AS ARE STILL OF PRACTICAL UTILITY.

EDITED BY

SIR FREDERICK POLLOCK, Bart., LL.D.,

CORPUS PROFESSOR OF JURISPRUDENCE IN THE UNIVERSITY OF OXFORD

ASSISTED BY

R. CAMPBELL,   AND   O. A. SAUNDERS,

OF LINCOLN'S INN, ESQ.   OF THE INNER TEMPLE, ESQ.

BARRISTERS-AT-LAW.

VOL. XLV.

1837—1838.

2 & 3 MYLNE & CRAIG—6 & 7 ADOLPHUS & ELLIS—2 & 3
NEVILE & PERRY.

LONDON :

SWEET AND MAXWELL, Limited, 3, CHANCERY LANE.

BOSTON :

LITTLE, BROWN & CO.

1900.

BRADBURY AGNEW, & CO. D., PRINTERS,
LONDON AND TONBRIDGE.

PREFACE TO VOLUME XLV.

Three cases in this volume are classical: *Lechmere Charlton's* case, p. 68, on contempt of Court (a subject rather prominent of late); *Hitchcock* v. *Coker*, p. 522, on agreements in restraint of trade; and *Pickard* v. *Sears*, p. 538, on estoppel. In *Hitchcock* v. *Coker*, Sir William Follett's argument contains an ingenious attempt (p. 529) to explain the dyer's case in the Year Book of Henry V. —which would now be regarded as a case of quite ordinary and harmless limited restraint—by suggesting want of consideration as the real objection. But there is nothing of the kind in the book, and, moreover, the doctrine of consideration was still unformed. The truth is that the law has completely altered its point of view on this subject: exceptions introduced at first with much hesitation have practically become the rule.

Tasker v. *Small*, p. 211, is still a profitable corrective to the wild notions of equity jurisdiction and procedure which occur in many old text-books and some old decisions, and of which the traces are perhaps not yet wholly removed from books that may come into students' hands.

Millington v. *Fox*, p. 271, is an interesting early example of the questions which we are beginning to collect under the new rubric of Unfair Competition. In these cases there has been some doubt whether the plaintiff's right should be put on the ground of a kind of property in his trade mark or name, or on the ground of fraud in the defendant, or conduct equivalent, after notice, to fraud. Apart from specific rights created by statute, the latter view seems the sounder, and the better supported by recent authority, though in *Millington* v. *Fox* the conception of a quasi-proprietary right is more prominent.

Powell v. *Rees*, p. 747, introduces the subject—since much more fully discussed, and perhaps not yet finally settled—of the remedies available for a landowner whose minerals a stranger has taken by trespass.

The copyright of Smith's Leading Cases came before the Court in *Saunders and Benning* v. *Smith and Maxwell*, p. 367.

Church v. *Imperial Gas Light and Coke Co.*, p. 638, was an important and beneficent decision on the inherent powers of a trading corporation to do the necessary business of its trade without the formality of the corporate seal.

Rex v. *Davie*, p. 494, bears witness to the local pronunciation of "Crediton, otherwise Kyrton, in the county of Devon." As the rhyme has it:

> "Kirton was a market town
> When Exeter was vuzzy down."

The case may be welcome to men of Devon for that reason, though not otherwise of any great interest.

F. P.

JUDGES

OF THE

HIGH COURT OF CHANCERY.

1837—1838.

(7 WILL. IV.—1 & 2 VICT.)

LORD COTTENHAM, 1836—1841 . . *Lord Chancellor.*

LORD LANGDALE, 1836—1851 . . . *Master of the Rolls.*

SIR LANCELOT SHADWELL, 1827—1850 . *Vice-Chancellor.*

COURT OF KING'S BENCH.

LORD DENMAN, 1832—1850 . . . . *Chief Justice.*

SIR JOSEPH LITTLEDALE, 1824—1841 . . . ⎫

SIR JOHN PATTESON, 1830—1852 . . . ⎪

SIR JOHN WILLIAMS, 1834—1846 . . . ⎬ *Judges.*

SIR JOHN T. COLERIDGE, 1835—1858 . . ⎭

COURT OF COMMON PLEAS.

Sir N. C. Tindal, 1829—1846 . . . *Chief Justice.*

Sir James Alan Park, 1816—1838 . .⎫
Sir Stephen Gaselee, 1824—1837 . .⎪
Sir John Vaughan, 1834—1839 . .⎬ *Judges.*
Sir John B. Bosanquet, 1830—1842 . .⎪
Sir Thomas Coltman, 1837—1849 . .⎭

COURT OF EXCHEQUER.

Lord Abinger, 1834—1844 . . . . *Chief Baron.*

Sir William Bolland, 1829—1839 . .⎫
Sir John Gurney, 1832—1845 . . .⎪
Sir E. H. Alderson, 1834—1857 . .⎬ *Barons.*
Sir James Parke, 1834—1856 . . .⎭

Sir John Campbell, 1835—1841 . . *Attorney-General.*

Sir Robert M. Rolfe, 1834, 1835—1839 . *Solicitor-General.*

TABLE OF CASES

REPRINTED FROM

2 & 3 MYLNE & CRAIG; 6 & 7 ADOLPHUS & ELLIS; 2 & 3 NEVILE & PERRY.

Note.—Where the reference is to a mere note of a case reproduced elsewhere in the Revised Reports, or omitted for special reasons, the names of
the parties are printed in italics.

NOTE.

The first and last pages of the original report, according to the paging by which the original reports are usually cited, are noted at the head of each case, and references to the same paging are continued in the margin of the text.

The Revised Reports.

VOL. XLV.

CHANCERY.

CAMPBELL *v.* MACKAY.

(2 My. & Cr. 31—38.)

1886.
Nov. 10, 11.
1837.
Jan. 16.
———
Lord
COTTENHAM,
L.C.

[31]

The Court will not make an order, permitting its infant wards to be removed out of the jurisdiction, with a view to their residing permanently abroad, except in a case of imperative necessity; as, where it is clearly proved that a constant residence in a warmer climate is absolutely essential to their health.

Such an order, if made, ought to comprise a scheme for the education of the infants, as well as a provision for informing the Court from time to time of their progress and condition, and an undertaking to bring them within the jurisdiction when required.

THIS was an appeal by the defendants, the executors of the late Sir James Campbell, against an order of the VICE-CHANCELLOR, by which the plaintiff, Lady Dorothea Louisa Campbell, who was jointly named with them as an executor of Sir James's will, and as one of the guardians of the infant plaintiffs, was permitted to remove the infant plaintiffs, her children, out of the jurisdiction, for the purpose of establishing their residence in France or Italy.

Sir William Horne, Mr. Wigram, and *Mr. James Russell,* for the appeal.

Mr. Knight and *Mr. Parry,* in support of the VICE-CHAN-CELLOR's order.

CAMPBELL
v.
MACKAY.

The facts of the case, and the general effect of the evidence on both sides, are stated and summed up in the judgment.

1837.
Jan. 16.
——

THE LORD CHANCELLOR :

The petition, upon which the order under appeal was obtained, stated that it was necessary for the health of the children that they should reside in the south of Europe, or in some climate warmer than that of England. The original order permitted Lady Dorothea to take them " to the south of Europe, or elsewhere, out of the jurisdiction ; " but as it was subsequently altered, and as it now stands, it permits the infants to reside in France *or Italy. With this order, which goes on to direct the usual inquiries relative to the ages and fortunes of the infants, and the sums that would be proper to be allowed for their maintenance, respectively, no scheme is connected for the education and superintendence of the children ; no undertaking or security is to be given, that they shall be brought back within a limited time ; and no direction or provision is introduced, by which the Court may be informed at any future period of their actual condition or progress. [His Lordship here stated in detail the substance of the affidavits which had been read, as well in support of the appeal, as in opposition to it, and proceeded :]

[*32]

Such is the evidence upon which I am required to come to a decision which may most materially affect the future prospects of these children ; and the first question is, whether such a case is made out as to justify me in permitting the children to be kept abroad and out of the jurisdiction of the Court.

It cannot be now said that the Court will not in any case permit its wards to be taken out of the country. No doubt, circumstances may arise under which it would be most inexpedient to adhere strictly to the general rule against permitting an infant ward of the Court to be taken out of the jurisdiction ; because cases may occur in which the health, and possibly the life of the ward, may depend upon his removal to another climate. Such instances, however, are, I trust, very rare ; and so lately as in the year 1801, in the case of *Mountstuart* v. *Mountstuart* (1) Lord ELDON appears to have said that the

(1) 6 Ves. 363.

Court never makes an order for taking the infant out of the jurisdiction. Subsequent decisions show that exceptions are sometimes made to the rule, *but such exceptions are and ought to be very rare. Since I have held the Great Seal I have had reason to lament that the rule has not been more strictly adhered to. In a case referred to in a note in Mr. Jacob's Reports (1) it will be seen with what difficulty Lord ELDON was induced to permit a father to take his child, a ward of the Court, out of the jurisdiction, and with what guards he thought it necessary to protect the infant against the probable consequences of that permission; and in *De Manneville* v. *De Manneville* (2) his Lordship restrained a father from removing his child to a foreign country.

Independently of this well established rule of the Court, and the principle upon which it proceeds, I am convinced that scarcely any thing can be more injurious to the future prospects of English children, and particularly of English boys, than a permanent residence abroad. Without the proper opportunities of attending the religious service of the church to which they belong, separated from their natural connections, estranged from the members of their own families, withdrawn from those courses of education which their contemporaries are pursuing, and accustomed to habits and manners which are not those of their own country, they must be becoming, from day to day, less and less adapted to the position which, it is to be wished, they should hereafter occupy in their native land.

In addition to all these considerations I find, in the present case, the most anxious wishes expressed by the father of these children, that they should be settled in this country and receive a purely English education, and that the son should pursue that profession in which *the father had himself gained considerable emoluments and the highest honours. It is needless to observe that the law, which permits the father to appoint the guardians

[*34]

---

(1) In Jac. 264, where the case is noted without any name, as having been heard in private by the LORD CHANCELLOR, in August, 1821. The importance of the case was consequently overlooked, and a report of the case under its actual title of *Jackson* v. *Hankey*, taken from the note of Mr. Jacob (who was one of the counsel engaged in the case) will be found *post*, p. 7.—O. A. S.

(2) 7 R. R. 340 (10 Ves. 52).

of his children, will pay the highest respect to the expression of his wishes as to the mode of their education.

All these considerations, however, must yield, and the hopes, wishes, and projects of the father must be disappointed, if an irresistible necessity be proved to exist for the permanent residence of the children abroad. I say permanent, because if the grounds, alleged in this case, for the permission to leave the country be sufficient for that purpose, there is no reasonable hope that they will cease to exist during the minority of the wards. The ground on which the permission is sought is not any accidental disease, which a temporary residence abroad may help to eradicate; but supposed infirmities in the constitutions of three of the children, all of different kinds, but all supposed to lead to the unusual result of an incapacity, without danger, of living in the climate of this country.

Such being my view of the evil not only likely but, in my opinion, certain to result from the long continuance of the permission granted by the VICE-CHANCELLOR's order, I must next consider the weight and effect of the medical evidence, in order to ascertain whether the danger be such as to justify me in exposing these wards, and particularly the boy, to evils so certain and so great.

[His Lordship here entered into a minute and critical examination of a number of affidavits made by medical gentlemen, who had been professionally consulted with respect to the health of the children, and their supposed constitutional tendencies; and

[*35] came to the conclusion *that although the evidence was in some degree conflicting, it decidedly preponderated in favour of the opinion that a residence in the South of England, especially in some spot where the air was mild and dry, would in all probability be as well suited to the constitutions of the children, as any place which could be fixed upon in France or Italy. His Lordship further remarked that the apparent discrepancy in the affidavits upon this point might be explained by the circumstance that most of those medical gentlemen who were disposed to recommend a residence abroad, appeared to have founded their opinions, rather upon the statements which they had received from Lady Dorothea, with respect to her past

experience, than upon personal observation and knowledge. His Lordship next proceeded to examine the amount and value of the evidence alleged to be furnished by the experience of the past; and arrived at the conclusion that the evidence with respect to the result of that experience was far from being clear or decisive. His Lordship then continued as follows :]

CAMPBELL
v.
MACKAY.

I am therefore of opinion, that there is not in the medical testimony, or in the evidence of the result of past experience sufficient to justify me, by affirming the order of the VICE-CHANCELLOR, in sanctioning the permanent residence of these children abroad, and thereby exposing them to the unquestionable evils of such a course. To the evidence furnished by Lady Dorothea herself, I might have added, indeed, the fact that, after having obtained the order of the VICE-CHANCELLOR, upon the ground that a milder, drier, and warmer climate was required for the children, some of the medical opinions specifying the south of France or Italy, I find them passing the winter in the neighbourhood of Paris.

Having come to this conclusion upon the principal question raised by the order of the VICE-CHANCELLOR, I need do no more than mention some other matters, as to which I should have thought it necessary to vary the order, even if I had concurred in the question of residence abroad.

[36]

The effect of that order is to place the maintenance and education of the children absolutely in the hands of one of four guardians, the other three dissenting, and without any inquiry before the Master, as to a scheme for their maintenance and education ; and in permitting that one guardian to take the children abroad, it does not provide any security for their return, or make any provision by which the Court could, at any time, be informed of the state of the children, or the progress of their education, a matter which, in the case in Mr. Jacob's Reports (1), Lord ELDON thought necessary even in the case of a father. I am aware that these directions were not asked of the VICE-CHANCELLOR ; and I mention the circumstance only that the form of the order may not be drawn into precedent.

I have now gone through this most distressing case. I must

(1) *Post*, p. 7.

CAMPBELL
v.
MACKAY.

discharge so much of the VICE-CHANCELLOR's order as permits the residence abroad. The rest of the order may stand; but there must be added to it that, which cannot be dispensed with when guardians do not agree as to the management of their wards, namely, a reference to the Master to approve of a scheme for the maintenance and education of the children.

I do not mean to leave to the Master the reconsideration of the question as to residence abroad. The order, therefore must

[*37]

direct the Master, in approving of *any scheme, to consider that the future residence of the children will be in this country.

I am not desirous however of requiring the immediate return of the children. They have been taken abroad under the authority of the Court, and a hurried return must be inconvenient and, at this season of the year, might be hazardous. It will be better to let the severity of the winter pass away, and to take the first favourable opportunity on the return of the spring, to settle the journey to this country. There is nothing to apprehend from prolonging their residence abroad, until it can be conveniently and satisfactorily terminated. It is to the protracted and indefinite duration of it that the objections apply.

I cannot dismiss this subject without expressing my earnest hope that, now that the important subject of contest is disposed of, the guardians of these children will endeavour, by coming to a proper understanding among themselves, to co-operate for the welfare of their wards. Without such co-operation, the care and protection of this Court must be comparatively ineffectual.

I have no reason to doubt, but on the contrary I see much reason to be convinced of the devotion and affection of Lady Dorothea towards her children; and possibly that very devotion and affection may have led her into error. But there certainly appears from her correspondence to be much misconception as to the position in which she is placed, with respect to her children. Every attention ought to be paid to the opinions and to the wishes of a mother; but in point of authority she is upon an equality with the three other guardians. There is, therefore, nothing to justify any attempt on her part to oppose

[*38]

their interference, or to dispute their authority: *and I hope that upon reflection, Lady Dorothea will see reason to think that

Colonel Mackay and the other guardians have, under trying circumstances, shown much temper, moderation, and self-command, as well as fairness, in the execution of the delicate and important duty cast upon them by the testator. In all that they have done, they appear to have had no other object than the welfare of the children.

The Court will be desirous as far as possible, to consult the feelings and wishes of the mother, but that desire will not induce it in any particular to depart from the course which it may think most conducive to the interests of its wards.

If Lady Dorothea can bring herself to co-operate with the other guardians, and readily assist in carrying into effect such plan for the education of her children as the Court may approve, she may be assured that she will be doing that which her duty towards them requires, and that which is most likely to promote their welfare and to secure to herself the pleasure and satisfaction which can only result from their future prosperity.

CAMPBELL
v.
MACKAY.

JACKSON v. HANKEY.

(Reported anonymously in Jacob, 264—265.)

Conditions under which the Court has allowed the father of a ward to take the ward out of the jurisdiction.

[IN this case, which is reported anonymously in Jacob, 264—265, as having been heard in private by the LORD CHANCELLOR in August, 1821, the mother of infant children who were wards of Court] was possessed of a considerable property, settled to her separate use ; the mother and father were living separate, and the income of the latter was small. A petition presented by the mother in the name of herself and the infants, prayed that they might be placed with her, or that it might be referred to the Master to approve of a plan for their education, and to appoint a proper person to have the care of them, the mother offering to provide for their maintenance out of her separate income; it also prayed that the father might be restrained from taking them out of the jurisdiction. It was urged, as one of the grounds in support of the petition, that the father's income was

1821.
August.

Privately
heard by
Lord
ELDON,
L.C.
[Jacob, 264]

not sufficient to enable him to give the infants an education suitable to their situation in life and to their expectations, and that it would therefore be for their benefit that their mother's proposal should be acceded to.

[The *Attorney-General* and *Mr. Raithby* were counsel for the father ; *Mr. Heald* and *Mr. Jacob* on the other side.]

[265] His Lordship refused the application, but added, that his decision was without prejudice to any other application or proposal which might be made, in case of any permanent provision being made for the infants. As to the father taking them abroad, there was no difficulty about that; as they were wards of the Court, he must be restrained from doing that. And he had no difficulty in saying, that, as they were wards of the Court, and therefore under its protection, and recollecting that children ought to be brought up in dutiful obedience and warm affection towards both parents, he would not allow the father to take them so out of access as not to have opportunities of nourishing those feelings. If any complaint was made of want of access, that might be remedied.

The father being some time afterwards appointed to a situation in his Majesty's service, which required him to reside abroad for several years, petitioned for leave to take the infants with him. He stated that he was desirous of being reconciled to his wife, and it appeared that he had with that view made some overtures to her, which she had declined. The matter was several times mentioned before the Lord Chancellor, and his Lordship ultimately ordered that the father should be at liberty to take the infants abroad with him, undertaking to bring them, or such of them as should be living, back with him ; and he was half-yearly to transmit, properly vouched, to be laid before the Court, the plan of tuition and education for each of the infants, actually adopted and in practice at the time of such half-yearly returns, specifying particularly where and with whom they resided.

EWING *v.* OSBALDISTON.

(2 My. & Cr. 53—88; S. C. 6 L. J. (N. S.) Ch. 161; 1 Jur. 50.)

An agreement for an illegal partnership will not be enforced even if it has been partly performed.

[THIS case is reprinted only with reference to the point stated in the head-note. It is not thought needful to reproduce the facts in detail, or the arguments.]

THE LORD CHANCELLOR :

The object of the bill in this case is to establish a partnership with the defendant in the performances at the Surrey Theatre, from the 10th of December, 1831, and to have the accounts incident to such partnership taken ; to have proper articles executed for the future; to remove the defendant from the management of the theatre, and to appoint a manager in his place ; or to have the partnership dissolved and the affairs of it wound up.

[His Lordship then read the correspondence and evidence showing that the plaintiff had paid considerable sums of money (amounting to 1,000*l.*) to the defendant upon the faith and for the purposes of the alleged partnership; and he continued his judgment as follows :]

From this correspondence and this evidence it is clear, first, that the performances, as they had been carried on at the Surrey Theatre, before the contract between the plaintiff and the defendant, and as they were intended to be carried on under that contract, consisted of all the ordinary descriptions of theatrical representations ; secondly, that the plaintiff knew this before he entered into the contract, or paid his money, and knew that such theatrical representations were contrary to law ; and that the intention of both parties was to continue such representations.

Two questions only can be for consideration in this case. First, were these representations in fact contrary to law? Secondly, if they were, can the plaintiff in this suit be entitled to any decree ?

Upon the first point, his Lordship referred to various Acts of Parliament (since repealed) which prohibited certain

1836.
May 6, 9, 27.
June 1, 4.

1837.
Jan. 18.

Lord
COTTENHAM,
L.C.

1837.
Jan. 18.
—
[80]

[82]

[83]

theatrical representations, and which, in his opinion, were clearly violated by the representations which the partnership was formed to produce. And upon the second point, after referring to the authorities which had been cited, his Lordship said :]

[87] It is, therefore, impossible that the plaintiff can be entitled to any decree which shall be founded upon or growing out of this contract. But it was said that some of the purposes were legal, such as the purchase of the lease and of other articles about the theatre, and that so far as the business of the partnership was lawful, the contract ought to be carried into effect, and *Knowles* v. *Haughton* (1), was cited for that purpose ; but, in that case, the business of brokers was entirely distinct from that of insurers, whereas, in the present case, every part of the joint transaction was auxiliary to, and in execution and furtherance of, the illegal object ; besides which, the lease then existing has expired, and there is no evidence of any new lease having been granted, and the answer says that it has been refused.

In *De Begnis* v. *Armistead* (2) the plaintiff was not permitted to recover money actually paid, at the request of the defendant, in furtherance of the illegal object, such as for the dresses and

[*88] travelling expenses of the *performers, though he was permitted to recover a sum of 30*l*. paid for the personal expenses of the defendant.

It was then urged that the plaintiff ought at least to recover the money he had advanced ; and it was said that he had a lien for it upon the property purchased. If the plaintiff be entitled to recover back the money paid, and that right be a personal demand against the defendant, this is not the Court in which such a demand can be enforced ; and as to the alleged lien, it is sufficient to observe that no such case is made by the bill. If it had been, it is difficult to imagine how such a case could have been supported, consistently with the ground upon which the Court declines to give to the plaintiff the benefit of his contract ; for such, undoubtedly, would, to a certain extent, be giving him the benefit of it. The mere payment of the money can give no lien. You must, therefore, look to the contract to raise the question of lien ; and if the plaintiff be entitled to any lien,

(1) 11 Ves. 168.   (2) 38 R. R. 406 (10 Bing. 107).

it must be upon or in consequence of the illegal contract; but
I do not consider this question as before me. It is undoubtedly
a case of great hardship upon the plaintiff to have parted with
his money, and now to be denied the fruits of it; but this hardship is common to all cases of contract which cannot be enforced,
from their illegality. It was stated at the Bar, and, I believe,
stated in the answer, that the defendant had offered to return
the money advanced by the plaintiff. As an honest man, this
was, and clearly is, his duty; but in this suit I have no power
to enforce it. I think the judgment of the VICE-CHANCELLOR
supported by principle and authority; and I must therefore

Dismiss this appeal with costs.

IN THE MATTER OF JEREMIAH NEWMAN, A LUNATIC.
AND IN THE MATTER OF THE ACT FOR THE ABOLITION
OF FINES AND RECOVERIES.

(2 My. & Cr. 112—117.)

Principles by which the Lord Chancellor, when protector of a settlement in the place of a lunatic, will be guided, in giving or withholding
his consent to a deed of disposition under the Fines and Recoveries Act.

1836.
Aug. 9, 13.
1837.
Feb. 4.

Lord
COTTENHAM,
L.C.

[112]

THE petition of Charles Seale and Edith his wife, stated that
William Newman deceased, by his will, dated the 2nd of July,
1810, devised to Samuel Jones and Thomas Dowle, his messuage
and farm called Walton's Hill, and all his free lands and
hereditaments occupied therewith, situate in the parishes of
Deerhurst, Elmstone, Hardwicke, and Lye in the county of
Gloucester; and also all his lands in Artersfield and Britsfield,
and his free lands in Wickham in the parish of Deerhurst aforesaid, with all the appurtenances, or the allotment set out in lieu
of those lands under the Deerhurst Inclosure Act; to hold the
same unto Samuel Jones and Thomas Dowle, and their heirs,
to the use of his (the testator's) son Jeremiah (the lunatic) and
his assigns, for his life, with remainder to the use of trustees to
preserve contingent remainders, with remainder to the use of
all and every the children of his son Jeremiah, in equal shares
and proportions as tenants in common, and the heirs of their

respective bodies, and in default of such issue, then to the use
of all the other children whom he (the testator) should leave
at his decease, except his sons John and Samuel, in equal
shares and proportions, as tenants in common, and the heirs of
their respective bodies ; and in default of such issue, then to the
use of his (the testator's) own right heirs for ever.

[113]   The petition then stated that the testator died soon after the
date of his will, without having altered or revoked the same, and
left at his decease William Ireland Newman, his eldest son and
heir-at-law, David Newman, Mary Martha Dowle, wife of the
said Thomas Dowle, Ann Hough, wife of —— Hough, the
petitioner Edith Seale, wife of the petitioner Charles Seale,
and Elizabeth Newman, his six other children, except his sons
John Newman and Samuel Newman, who were both since
deceased. The petition also stated, that the lunatic Jeremiah
Newman, immediately after the testator's death, entered into
possession of the Walton's Hill estate and premises, so devised
to him as before mentioned, and continued in such possession
until he was found a lunatic ; since which time William Ireland
Newman had been in the occupation thereof. The petition went
on to state, that under the circumstances before mentioned the
lunatic was tenant for life, with remainder to his children,
if any, as tenants in common in tail, with remainder, as to
one undivided sixth part, to the petitioner Edith Seale in tail,
with remainder, as to the same one undivided sixth part, to the
right heirs of the testator in fee, such right heir being William
Ireland Newman ; and that by virtue of the Act for the Abolition
of Fines and Recoveries, the lunatic became and was the sole
protector of the before-mentioned settlement of the premises
called Walton's Hill, and the lands and appurtenances thereto
belonging. The petition then stated, that a commission was
issued on the 20th of February, 1821, and was executed on the
12th of March, 1821, by an inquisition taken, upon which it
was found that Jeremiah Newman was then a lunatic, and
did not enjoy lucid intervals, and had been in the same state of
lunacy for nine months then past. The petition added that no
further proceedings had been taken under the commission, and
that no person had been appointed committee of the person or

*of the estate of the lunatic ; but that William Ireland Newman had had the custody of the lunatic ever since he was found such.

The petition then stated that the petitioners had been married ten years and upwards, and had not any children, and that they were anxious to make and concur in making an effectual disposition of their undivided sixth part in remainder, with the consent and approval of the LORD CHANCELLOR, and to bar the remainders over in that sixth part, and to settle such sixth part upon the petitioner Edith Seale for life, with remainder to the petitioner Charles Seale for life, with remainder to their issue in fee ; and if no issue, with remainder to the survivor in fee ; subject, nevertheless, to a joint power of appointment by both the petitioners during their joint lives, by way of sale, mortgage, or otherwise.

The petition alleged that the lunatic was forty-three years old, or thereabouts, and had never been married, and that there were no incumbrances upon the said sixth part of the property.

The prayer of the petition was, that the LORD CHANCELLOR, as the protector of the settlement under the Act for the Abolition of Fines and Recoveries, would consent to such disposition of the undivided sixth part as was thereinbefore mentioned ; or that his Lordship would make such other order as would entitle the petitioners to make an effectual disposition of their one sixth part of the premises to the effect thereinbefore stated.

Mr. Wigram, in support of the petition.

On a subsequent day, *Mr. Girdlestone*, on behalf of William Ireland Newman, the heir-at-law of the testator, submitted that the LORD CHANCELLOR'S concurrence, as protector, in barring the entail, was by no means a matter of course ; but that his Lordship would consider himself as standing in the situation in which the lunatic would stand if he were sane.

Aug. 13.
[115]

THE LORD CHANCELLOR :

I have looked into the papers in this case, and I do not think that I can make the order prayed.

The petition came before me as protector of the settlement under the Fines and Recoveries Act, to induce me to consent to

1837.
Feb. 4

a deed of disposition on the part of the lunatic, who is tenant for
life ; to act, in fact, for the tenant for life, in order to give effect
to a recovery. The lunatic is tenant for life, with remainder to
his children. He has no children, and is not married; the
estate is limited in remainder to his brothers and sisters in tail,
with an ultimate remainder to the right heirs of the testator.
The eldest son of the testator and eldest brother of the lunatic is
the testator's heir-at-law; and he has a remainder in tail, in one
sixth, with the ultimate remainder in fee in the entirety. This
is an application by the husband of one of the daughters of the
testator, who is entitled, in default of issue of the lunatic, to an
estate tail in one sixth ; and it asks that I would consent, on
behalf of the lunatic tenant for life, to a deed, the object of which
is to bar the issue of that daughter, and of course to destroy the
remainder to the heirs of the settlor, in order to give his share
of the property to the husband and wife, to dispose of as they

[*116]   *please; for it is to be settled to such uses as they shall appoint.

As protector of the settlement, the only duty of the Court
is to see what, with reference to the interests of the family,
it would be proper for the tenant for life to do ; and the object
must be rather to protect the objects of the settlement, than to
give any benefit to one member of the family to the exclusion of
the others. Now, if nothing is done, one sixth will go to this
daughter, and her children, if she has any, and if not, to the
eldest son of the testator as his right heir : and I am asked
to consent to that which will take it away from the eldest son,
and take it away from the family, by giving it to the husband of
the daughter. That would be anything but protecting the settlement : it would be destroying the settlement ; giving the estate
to a person not a member of the family, namely, the husband of
the daughter. I should not consider that it would be a proper
act for the tenant for life to concur in a deed of disposition
to that effect.

It is not very easy to lay down any general rule on this
subject ; but there were two cases upon it before Lord Brougham.
One of them (1) was very similar to the present; the object

(1) *In re Blewitt*, 3 My. & K. 250; subsequently over-ruled, 6 De G.
M. & G. 187.

being to bar the remainders which had been limited to collateral relations, and the application there was refused: but in the other case (1), he object was to make a provision for one of the lunatic's family, his son, and Lord BROUGHAM thought that a fit case for his concurrence as protector. So that he consented, where the intention was to provide for the immediate *family of the lunatic; but declined to consent where the object was to give a benefit to one member of the family at the expense of the others.   *Order refused.*

In re
NEWMAN.

[*117]

ATTORNEY-GENERAL v. FORBES.

(2 My. & Cr. 123—135.)

1836.
Nov. 28, 29.
——
Lord
COTTENHAM
L.C.

[123]

Injunction granted, on information and bill, upon the ground of public nuisance, to restrain the magistrates of a county from cutting the timbers supporting the roadway of a bridge, which timbers and roadway, at the place proposed to be cut, were within their jurisdiction, but of which the other extremity was within the jurisdiction of a different county.

Principles on which courts of equity interfere by injunction, in cases of apprehended nuisance to the public.

THIS was an information and bill filed by the *Attorney-General,* at the relation of Thomas Tindal, the treasurer of the county of Bucks, and by the relator, on behalf of himself and all other the inhabitants of that county, against four gentlemen who composed a committee of the magistrates of the county of Berks, and also against the surveyor of the last-mentioned county, and against three other persons whom the Berkshire magistrates had authorised to proceed in the repair or re-construction of the bridge over the River Thames at Datchet.

The information and bill stated that there is a bridge over the River Thames called Datchet Bridge, one end of which is situate in the county of Bucks and the other in the county of Berks; that in the year 1810 the inhabitants of the two counties were, under an indictment, found liable to the joint repair of the bridge; and that thereupon committees of magistrates were appointed by the justices of the respective counties, to report respecting the bridge to their respective Courts of Quarter Sessions: that at a meeting of the committees in the month

(1) *Grant* v. *Yea,* 41 R. R. 62 (3 My. & K. 245).

of August, 1810, it was resolved, that it was the opinion of the committees, from the evidence they had examined, that the boundary of the respective counties at Datchet Bridge was in the mid-stream of the River Thames ; and that consequently the expenses to be incurred respecting the bridge should be borne by the two counties in equal proportions : that at another meeting of the committees *on the 9th of April, 1811, Robert Tebbott, a builder, delivered in a tender in writing to perform all the works required to restore Datchet Bridge for 4,750l. ; and that contracts were thereupon entered into, and the bridge repaired by Tebbott, pursuant to the order of the Courts of Quarter Sessions of the two counties respectively, and that the sum of 2,875l. being one moiety of the expenses thereof, was paid by the county of Bucks.

[*124]

The information and bill went on to state the mode in which the bridge was then repaired, being in substance as follows : The whole of the upper part, forming the roadway of the bridge, was re-constructed of oak timber, and consisted of corbels projecting three feet beyond the face of the piers, and also of nine joists extending over each bay or arch (except in the centre bay, where in consequence of the greater width of the roadway two additional joists were used) ; the joists were tree-nailed to the corbels, and their ends, which reached to the centre of the piers, were secured by struts. Upon these timbers was laid three-inch oak planking, tree-nailed, and the sides of the bridge were protected with posts and rails. The con-struction of the centre bay of the bridge, in which was the division of the counties, was similar in principle ; but that bay differed from the others in this respect, that one half of it was in each county, the joists reaching from the last pier on the Berkshire side of the stream to its opposite pier in Buckinghamshire.

The information and bill then stated, that the oak joists extending from pier to pier over the centre bay were paid for in equal moieties by the two counties : that in the year 1834, the bridge being out of repair, the magistrates of Bucks appointed a committee of their *number to meet a committee of the magistrates of Berks, and make arrangements for repairing

[*125]

it: that the committees could not agree upon the subject; the Bucks committee deciding in favour of adopting the plan of 1811, and the Berks committee being of opinion that the bridge should be rebuilt and constructed of iron: that finally the magistrates of Bucks resolved to repair that part of the bridge which was situated within their own county, as soon as the season of the year would admit: that other meetings, respecting the repairs, were subsequently held between the magistrates of the two counties; but in consequence of the difference of opinion between their respective surveyors they could come to no agreement: that in consequence of such difference of opinion, the Court of Quarter Sessions, held for the county of Bucks, at Easter, 1836, directed the committee to cause the repairs to be done as speedily as possible; and the clerk of the peace for that county was ordered to communicate such resolution to the clerk of the peace for Berks, with a request that the magistrates of the latter county would repair their part of the bridge at the same time: that William Mosely was appointed by the magistrates of Bucks the surveyor to superintend and direct the repair of their part of the bridge, and that Charles Parker was appointed surveyor on behalf of the county of Berks: that at the Bucks Midsummer Quarter Sessions for 1836, Mosely delivered in his report upon the state of the bridge, together with a plan and estimate of the expense of repairing the same, at the cost of 1,866*l.* 10*s.*, by placing an entirely new superstructure of timber on the present piers; but that no agreement could be come to between the magistrates of the two counties or their respective surveyors, as to the centre bay of the bridge (which required joint support from the extreme pier in each county), or upon other matters connected with the repairs; that in consequence of such disagreement, particularly *as to the centre bay, and the refusal of Parker, the surveyor   [*126] for Berkshire, to allow Mosely to rest the new joists on the pier in the county of Berks, Mosely, with the approbation of the magistrates of Bucks, altered his intended plan, and instead of laying new joists the whole length across from pier to pier over the centre bay, proposed to lay joists fifty-one feet in length, and continued through from the centre of the bridge

to the second pier on the Bucks side, and by the leverage so
obtained, and by securing their ends to the other timbers by
iron ties, and binding them together by means of rod bolts,
and also by the assistance obtained by blocking them up from
the top of the old oak joists, he proposed to render them secure :
that this proposal was adopted ; and that the bridge on the
Bucks side was well and sufficiently repaired according to this
plan, the old oak joists, which reached from pier to pier over the
centre arch not being disturbed, and the new work on the Bucks
side being dependent thereon ; and that the bridge to that
extent is now in a state of thorough repair : that on the 22nd
of October, 1836, the clerk of the peace for Buckinghamshire
received a copy of an order of the Berkshire Court of Quarter
Sessions, made on the 18th of Octoler, 1836, giving notice of
the intention of the magistrates of Berkshire, to deprive the
Bucks side of the bridge of any support from the Berkshire side,
by cutting the beams on the Berkshire side of the centre arch :
that no agreement could be entered into with the Berkshire
magistrates or their surveyor, who threatened to carry into
effect the intention of cutting the centre beams : that no
diagonal support could be obtained from the pier in the county
of Bucks on which the joists rest, as such support would
interfere with the craftway under the bridge ; and that Mosely
was therefore compelled to adopt the plan of repair already

[*127] stated : that the threatened *cutting of the old oak joists would,
if carried into effect, be a public nuisance, and an invasion
of the rights and property of the inhabitants of the county of
Bucks, and of the public at large : that the defendant Parker, the
surveyor employed by the county of Berks, and the defendants,
James Mansfield, senior, James Mansfield, junior, and George
Mansfield, the builders employed by the Berkshire magistrates,
would be the persons, or some of the persons to carry into effect
the directions of those magistrates for cutting the old oak joists.

The bill therefore prayed an injunction to restrain the defendants, their workmen and agents, from cutting the old oak joists
extending from pier to pier over the centre bay of the bridge.

The VICE-CHANCELLOR granted an *ex parte* injunction, and
the defendants, the committee, the surveyor, and the builders,

having subsequently filed three general demurrers to the information and bill, the demurrers now came on for argument
before the Lord Chancellor.

> *Mr. Wakefield, Mr. Jacob,* and *Mr. Teed,* in support of the
>   demurrers :

This suit, in point of form, is novel and unprecedented.   The
relator and plaintiff is the treasurer of the county of Bucks ;
but he is not alleged to be a ratepayer, or to have any personal
interest in the subject of the suit, or to be acting with the
sanction or privity of the county magistrates.   The powers
vested in the justices at Quarter Sessions over the bridges
within their jurisdiction are particularly fixed, defined, and
regulated by a variety of Acts of Parliament.   *   *   If any   [128]
relief can be had in such a case, the proper course would be,
to move for a writ of prohibition in the Court of King's Bench.
*   *   Why are the defendants to give way to the whim or
caprice of the magistrates of Bucks?   *   *   Should the Berk-   [129]
shire side of the centre bay be left in its present ruinous
condition, the injunction could not be pleaded as a defence to
any indictment that might be preferred against the magistrates
for leaving it in that state.   *   *   *

> *Mr. Knight* and *Mr. L. Lowndes, contrà,* were not called
> upon by the COURT.

THE LORD CHANCELLOR :

The question I have to decide is whether the record as it
stands (assuming of course every allegation in the information
and bill to be correct) does not present such a case as entitles
the plaintiff to come into this Court for relief.   In informations and proceedings for the purpose of preventing public
nuisances, the ordinary course is for the *Attorney-General* to
take it on himself to sue, as representing the public ; but it
is equally certain that individuals, who conceive themselves
aggrieved, may come forward and ask the assistance of the
Court, to prevent a public nuisance, *from which they have   [*130]
individually sustained damage (1).

(1) See *Crowder* v. *Tinkler,* 13 R. R. 267 (19 Ves. 617).

A.-G.
r.
FORBES.

[His Lordship here stated the material allegations and general effect of the information and bill ; and proceeded :]

It is said, on behalf of the Berkshire magistrates, that they will construct one half of the bridge,—as far as the limits of the county of Berks extend,—in an unexceptionable manner ; and that I take for granted they would do. But they would then leave one half of the centre bay without any bridge at all : there would be an open space reaching from the Berkshire extremity of the bridge to the outermost pier on the Buckinghamshire side, and those who had to cross the bridge would be left to pass over that open space as they best might. Nevertheless, that is represented as being the most useful way of carrying the repairs into effect ; and it is said that I am not to prevent it, because no nuisance is contemplated. It was strenuously argued that it is not for the magistrates of the county of Bucks to complain that the magistrates of Berks adopt a particular mode of repair ; but surely, it must have struck the counsel who urged that argument, that the magistrates of Berkshire, who are assuming this prerogative to themselves, by taking away and destroying that portion of the bridge which the magistrates of Bucks are bound to maintain, are virtually compelling the latter to adopt a course in conformity with the views which they themselves entertain.

I know no more effectual mode of interfering with the magistrates of the county of Bucks than by telling the Berkshire [*131] magistrates they are at liberty to cut away the *beams which support the centre arch, and to leave the magistrates of Bucks to repair and rebuild it as they best may. The magistrates of the county of Bucks have proceeded (at great inconvenience, no doubt, compared with what would have been experienced if the two counties had acted in concert) to maintain their portion of the centre arch. But it seems to me that the plan which they were recommended to adopt, and which they have, in fact, adopted, was the only one which, under the circumstances, was practicable. That plan was to employ large pieces of timber, projecting over their extreme pier ; and so, partly by the leverage and the weight of the timber, and partly by securing the extremities of the timber which projected across the centre arch, and by fastening it to the old oak joists, to complete and secure their

portion of the centre arch. The information and bill then states
that all this has been done and completed; that the old oak
joists have been used for that purpose; that the new timbers
are supported by being attached to the old joists, and that in
that way the bridge is now in a state of perfect repair and
security, as far as the county of Bucks is concerned. According
to the present proposal, however, instead of the old oak joists
assisting to bear up the new timbers which have been put in by
the county of Bucks, the magistrates of the county of Berks are
to cut them through; and so far from the new timbers having
then the support of the old oak joists, they would themselves
have to bear up those joists, which would no longer have any
support of their own. It is not pretended that what has been
done by the county of Bucks, with respect to the centre bay,
can remain or will stand, if any part of the old oak joists is
removed. The whole argument assumes that the cutting away
of these timbers on the Berkshire side will effectually open the
whole of the centre bay and compel the county of Bucks to adopt
some other course of proceeding.

Now, whether the magistrates of Berks are right or wrong in
what they propose, this, at least, is clear, that they have, under a
regular order at Quarter Sessions, given a distinct notice (a notice
quite sufficient for the purpose of maintaining an injunction)
that they intend to adopt this course, if they have a right to do
so. Neither can there be any doubt that if their intention is
carried into effect, it will occasion a great public nuisance. Why
then is the Court, with those two facts so stated on the record,
not to interfere to prevent the nuisance to the public? It was
argued that there is no appeal from the Court of Quarter
Sessions to the Court of Chancery, and that the former Court
is the only Court of competent jurisdiction in such a matter.
I am not in the least interfering with the orders of the Berkshire
Court of Quarter Sessions within their jurisdiction; but what
I am doing is to prevent an act of the magistrates of that county
which would create a public nuisance in respect of a bridge not
within their jurisdiction.

Nobody can dispute that when a bridge becomes dilapidated,
or dangerous, the public must submit to the inconvenience of

having it shut up for a certain time, in order to have it repaired :
but the defendants' object in cutting away these joists is not to
repair the bridge, but that it may remain entirely unrepaired,
or open and inaccessible to the public, or that another body of
persons, not under their jurisdiction at all, may, in order to
escape the penalties of the law for leaving the bridge out of
repair, be compelled to concur in constructing in a particular
manner that part of the bridge which, according to the argument,
is exclusively within the jurisdiction and ought to be subject to
the control of the Berkshire magistrates.   If these two counties
have been brought into a difficulty by an act, which was a

[*133]   highly proper act in the year 1811, and which one *only regrets
is not the course of proceeding adopted in 1836, namely, a
mutual agreement as to the mode in which that work is to be
carried on, no doubt it is extremely unfortunate ; and the only
question is, in what way these parties can exercise their respective rights.   But it is the duty of the Court to take care that
while these magistrates attempt to exercise their respective
rights, the public shall not sustain any injury, and that a public
nuisance shall not be occasioned.

With respect to the question of jurisdiction, it was broadly
asserted that an application to this Court to prevent a nuisance
to a public road was never heard of.   A little research, however,
would have found many such instances.   Many .cases might
have been produced in which the Court has interfered to prevent
nuisances to public rivers and to public harbours ; and the Court
of Exchequer as well as this Court, acting as a court of equity,
has a well established jurisdiction, upon a proceeding by way of
information, to prevent nuisances to public harbours and public
roads ; and, in short, generally, to prevent public nuisances.
In *Box* v. *Allen* (1), this Court interfered to stay the proceedings
of parties whose jurisdiction is quite as high as that of the Court
of Quarter Sessions over bridges, namely, the Commissioners of
Sewers.   Those commissioners possess a jurisdiction founded on
Acts of Parliament (2), and they have a right, within the due

---

(1) 1 Dick. 49.   c. 10, and the recent statute, 3 & 4
(2) 23 Hen. VIII. c. 5, 3 & 4   Will. IV. c. 22.
Edw. VI. c. 8 13 Eliz. c. 9, 7 Ann.

limits of their authority, to do all necessary acts in the execution of their functions. Nevertheless, if they so execute what they conceive to be their duty, as to create or occasion a public nuisance, this Court has an undoubted right to *interpose. The same question occurred in *Kerrison* v. *Sparrow* (1), before Lord Eldon, in which his Lordship, under the circumstances of the case, considered that he ought not to interfere; but the jurisdiction of the Court was not there denied or disputed. In *Attorney-General* v. *Johnson* (2), the objection to the jurisdiction was attempted to be raised. The defendants in that case, the corporation of the city of London, were authorised by Act of Parliament to do what was necessary to be done in the exercise of their duty as conservators of the river Thames; but, in that particular instance, they had assumed to themselves a right to carry on or sanction operations, which created a nuisance to the King's subjects; and the Court accordingly interfered to prevent them from so exercising their undoubted legal powers. To say that this Court, when it interferes in such a case, is acting as a court of appeal from the Court of Quarter Sessions, is any thing but a correct representation of the fact. The jurisdiction is exercised, not for the purpose of overruling the power of others, by way of appeal from their authority, but for the purpose of executing a salutary control over all, for the protection of the public.

The allegations of fact appearing on the face of this information and bill may be pure fiction; but I am to take the record as it stands, and finding that it represents a case where, if the act proposed to be done be carried into effect, a great public mischief will be occasioned, I think the obvious result of all the authorities is, that I am bound to interfere.

Mr. Wakefield then submitted that the demurrer of the defendants, the surveyor and contractors, ought at all events to be allowed.

The LORD CHANCELLOR (after examining the statements in the information and bill, which referred to the proceedings of the surveyor and contractors), said that in his opinion those

A.-G.
v.
FORBES.

[*134]

[135]

(1) 19 Ves. 449.   (2) 18 R. R. 156 (2 Wils. C. C. 87).

A.-G.
v.
FORBES.

defendants were all so much mixed up and identified with
the proceedings of the Berkshire magistrates, that they were
properly made parties, and that their demurrers also ought
to be over-ruled.

1886.
Nov. 22, 28.
———
Lord
COTTENHAM
L.C.

[135]

ATTORNEY-GENERAL *v.* SMYTHIES.

(2 My. & Cr. 135—144 ; S. C. 6 L. J. (N. S.) Ch. 35 ; affirming 1 Keen, 289 ;
5 L. J. (N. S.) Ch. 247.)

A decree having directed the settlement of a scheme for the regulation
of the hospital of King James in Colchester, and for the future application of its revenues, the Court, in afterwards considering the scheme,
came to the conclusion that, upon the true construction of the charter
of foundation, and of the laws and statutes of the hospital, it was intended,
and was essential to the proper performance of his official duties, that the
master should have a proper residence within the hospital, or on the lands
belonging thereto ; and a reference was accordingly directed for the
purpose of ascertaining the best mode of providing such residence ; but
the Court declined to make any specific declaration that it was the duty
of the master to reside, that being a matter falling within the jurisdiction
of the visitor.

THIS was an appeal from an order of Lord LANGDALE, whereby
it was declared that according to the true construction of the
charter, the master of the college or hospital of King James, in
the suburbs of Colchester, ought to reside in such college or
hospital, for the purpose of discharging the several duties of his
office ; and that it should be referred to the Master to inquire
whether there was a fit residence in the college or hospital for
such master ; and if the Master should find that there was not,
then it was declared that such residence ought to be provided,
and the Master was to review his scheme with reference to this
declaration.

The cause is reported upon the original hearing before Sir
John Leach, and upon the appeal before Lord Brougham, in
34 R. R. 192 (2 Russ. & My. 717).

[The LORD CHANCELLOR upon this appeal considered it abun-
dantly clear that the master ought to be resident, and he
approved of the inquiries directed with a slight variation, but
with regard to the declaration which prefaced the inquiries, his
Lordship said :]

[142]   This college is a corporation, with a visitor appointed by the

charter, who is to inspect and visit the college, and the master
and poor, and the state, order, and government of the college.
To call the master into residence, if improperly absent, to hear
and judge of the excuse he may make for his non-residence, are
properly the duties of the visitor.

[The declaration was accordingly struck out of the order
appealed from.]

LLOYD *v.* LLOYD (1).

(2 My. & Cr. 192—206; S. C. 5 L. J. (N. S.) Ch. 191; 6 L. J. (N. S.) Ch.
135; 1 Jur. 69.)

1837.
Feb. 7, 8.

Lord
COTTENHAM,
L.C.

[192]

In marriage articles or settlements containing reciprocal covenants to
settle property on the marriage the failure or default of either covenantor
is not generally any excuse or defence for the non-performance of the
reciprocal covenant by the other covenantor.

Marriage articles recited that L., the father of the intended husband,
had agreed, in case the marriage should take effect, to pay 200*l.*, and also
to settle the lands of T. in the manner, to the uses, and upon the trusts
thereinafter mentioned; and that S., the father of the intended wife, who
was an infant, had agreed to convey the lands of G. in the manner, at the
time, to the uses, and upon the trusts thereinafter mentioned, and also
to pay to the intended husband 100*l.* upon the marriage: it was then
covenanted by L. that, in case the marriage should take effect, and S.
should, as soon as the intended wife came of age, settle the lands of G.
to the uses thereinafter expressed, he, L., would settle the lands of T. to
his own use until the marriage, and from and after the marriage, to his
own use for life, with remainder upon certain trusts for the benefit of the
husband and wife, and the issue of the marriage; and it was covenanted
by S., that in case the marriage should take effect, and L. should perform
his covenant, he, S., would settle the lands of G. to the use of himself
for life, with remainder upon certain trusts for the benefit of the husband
and wife, and issue of the marriage. The marriage took effect, and the
wife came of age, but S. failed to settle the lands of G.: Held, nevertheless,
that L. was bound to perform the covenant on his part.

[THIS case turned entirely upon the construction to be placed
upon the special wording of a badly-drawn covenant in marriage
articles which was inconsistent with the intention of the parties
as plainly expressed in other passages in the same document.
The judgment of the Lord Chancellor (Lord COTTENHAM) contains
the following passage of general interest:]

With respect to marriage contracts there can be no resistance
on the part of one, because another contracting party has failed

[203]

(1) *Jeston* v. *Key* (1871) L. R. 6 Ch. 610, 40 L. J. Ch. 503, 25 L. T. 522.

LLOYD
r.
LLOYD.

[*204]

to perform his part of the agreement; and the obvious *reason
is that the parties to the contract are not the only persons having
an interest in the subject, but the contract is made by them on
behalf of the issue of the marriage. Although, therefore, in
the case of an ordinary contract, a party who has not performed
his part may not be entitled to claim the benefit of it against the
other party, it is different in marriage articles, where the two
contracting parties reciprocally enter into contracts both of
which are made for the benefit of a third party. Unquestionably, however, even in the case of a marriage settlement, the
covenants may be so framed as to be mutually dependent; and
if it be clear on the face of the settlement that such was the
intention, that intention must prevail.

[His Lordship then held that as it was impossible for each of
two covenants to be a condition precedent to the other, the intention of the parties as declared by the recital must prevail, and
that the covenants must accordingly be treated as independent
of each other.]

1837.
Feb. 2, 3, 15.

Lord
COTTENHAM,
L.C.

[207]

SOUTHBY *v.* HUTT.

(2 My. & Cr. 207—219.)

By conditions of sale it was stipulated that the vendor of an estate
which was sold in lots should deliver an abstract of the title to the purchasers, and deduce a good title; but that as to a part of the estate,
acquired under an inclosure, he should not be bound to show any title
thereto prior to the award; and it was farther stipulated that the vendor
should deliver up to the largest purchaser in value all the title deeds and
other documents in his custody, but should not be required to produce
any original deed or other documents than those in his possession and
set forth in the abstract: Held, on the construction of these conditions,
that they did not relieve the vendor from his liability to verify the title
shown upon the abstract by producing the title deeds themselves, or, if
any of them were not in his possession, by other satisfactory evidence.

If a vendor intends to deprive a purchaser of the right to the production
of any evidence necessary to verify the title beyond what the title deeds
in his own custody will supply, he is bound to make that intention
previously known to the purchaser in clear and explicit terms.

A vendor who has failed to deliver his abstract of title within the
time specified by the conditions of sale cannot object to the delivery
of requisitions by the purchaser after the time similarly specified.

THIS was a suit instituted by the vendor of an estate which,
in the month of May, 1833, was sold by auction in a great

number of lots, for the purpose of enforcing a specific performance
of his contract against the purchaser of certain of the lots.

The main question in the clause was whether, upon the true
construction of the conditions of sale, the plaintiff was or was
not relieved from the obligation of verifying the abstract of his
title by producing, for the inspection of the defendant or his
solicitor, the several documents mentioned in the abstract, or
by other satisfactory evidence.   A subordinate question, was,
whether, if that point should be decided against the plaintiff,
the defendant had not, by his subsequent conduct, and upon
the result of the dealings and correspondence which had taken
place between the respective solicitors of the parties, waived all
objection to the title.

The conditions of sale, so far as they were material to the
question between the parties, were the following :

" 4th. The vendor will, at his own expense, deliver an abstract
of the title, to the purchaser, or his solicitor, of *the first seven
lots, and Lot 33, within twenty-one days from the day of the
sale, and deduce a good title; but as to such parts of the land
as were allotted or taken in exchange under the award of the
commissioners of the Appleton inclosure, the purchaser shall
not be at liberty to require, and the vendor shall not be bound
to show, any title thereto prior to the said award, from which
period the title to such lands will be deduced.   The purchaser
shall, within the next twenty-one days after the delivery of the
extract, declare in writing, his acceptance or disapproval of the
title, after which he is to be precluded from raising objections :
and in case objections are made within that period, the vendor
shall be at liberty to vacate the sale, upon returning the deposit
with interest, auction duty, or other further compensation.

" 5th. That upon payment of the remainder of the purchase-
money, on or before the time above mentioned, the vendor will
convey the premises to the respective purchasers, who are to be
at the expense of preparing their own conveyances.

" 6th. The vendor will deliver up, to the purchaser of the
greater part in value of the said estates, all the title deeds and
copies of deeds, and other documents in his custody, but shall
not be bound, or required, to produce any original deed, or other

SOUTHBY
v.
HUTT.

[*208]

documents than those in his possession and set forth in the
abstract, or which relate to other property ; and such purchaser
is to enter into the usual covenants for the production of the
title deeds to the purchaser or purchasers or proprietor of the
remaining or other lots ; but if the largest portion in value of
the estate shall remain unsold, the vendor shall be entitled to
retain the deeds, upon entering into such covenants ; all such
[*209]   covenants *to be prepared by and at the expense of the person
or persons requiring the same, who may have attested copies of
such deeds at his or their own expense."

The decree of Lord LANGDALE, made upon the hearing of the
cause at the Rolls, declared that the defendant was not entitled
to have the abstract of the title verified, except so far as the
plaintiff could verify the same by the production of the deeds
and other documents in his possession ; and that subject to the
plaintiff's procuring the execution of a certain deed of release
(the purchaser's right to which had not been disputed), the
defendant was bound to accept a conveyance of the estate, and
should pay the costs of the suit.

The defendant appealed from his Lordship's decree.

Mr. Wigram and *Mr. R. Perry*, in support of the decree.

Mr. Tinney and *Mr. Bagshawe*, for the appeal.   *   *   *

The material facts of the case, and the principal arguments
urged [and cases cited] in support of the decree, are stated and
considered in the judgment.

Feb. 15.   THE LORD CHANCELLOR :

[210]   This was a bill by a vendor for specific performance of a
contract of purchase, and praying that the defendant might be
declared to have accepted the title.

The premises in question were put up to sale by auction on
the 7th of May, 1833, subject to certain conditions of sale. By
the fourth of those conditions the vendor was to deliver an
abstract of the title to the purchaser, or his solicitor, within
twenty-one days of the day of the sale, and to deduce a good
title ; but as to certain lands allotted under an inclosure, the

purchaser was not to be at liberty to require, and the vendor
was not bound to show any title thereto, prior to the award;
from which period the title was to be deduced. The purchaser
was, within the next twenty-one days after delivery of the
abstract, to declare his acceptance or disapproval of the title;
and if objection were made the vendor was to be at liberty to
vacate the sale and return the deposit.   The fifth condition was
that, upon payment of the remainder of the purchase-money,
the vendor should convey the premises to the purchaser.   The
sixth was to the effect that the vendor should deliver up to the
purchaser of the greater part in value of the estate all the title
deeds, and copies of deeds, and other documents, in his custody,
but should "not be bound or required to produce any original
deed, or other documents than those in his possession and set
forth in the abstract, or which relate to other property;" and
such purchaser was to enter into the usual covenants for the
production of the title deeds to the purchasers of the remaining
lots; or if the largest part should remain unsold, then the
vendor was to enter into such covenants, and retain the deeds,
and the purchasers were to have attested copies of such deeds at
their own expense.

The abstract of title was not delivered within the twenty-one   [211]
days, so that no question arises as to the time specified in these
conditions of sale.   The abstract, when delivered, stated deeds
and instruments which, it is admitted, if duly verified, showed a
good title: but the question is, whether the vendor was bound
to verify the deeds so abstracted, except so far as he had in his
possession deeds enabling him to do so.

In the margin of this abstract, against certain deeds of the 28th
and 29th of November, 1813, was a note in these words: "An
attested copy of these indentures will be produced, but not the
originals, which are not in the possession or power of the vendor;"
and in the margin of the abstract of another deed, of the 6th of
August, 1818, there was the following note: "A copy of this
deed will be produced, but not the original, which is not in the
custody or power of the vendor;" and in the margin of the
abstract of certain other deeds, of the 10th and 11th of September,
1832, there was the following note: "These deeds are not in the

possession of the vendor and relate to other property;" and there was a similar note in the margin of the abstract of a deed, dated the 11th of September, 1882.

A long correspondence took place between Mr. Baker, the solicitor for the vendor, and Mr. Leake, the solicitor for the purchaser, from the effect of which, coupled with the notes in the margin of the abstract, it is contended, that whatever may be the proper construction of the conditions of sale, the purchaser had bound himself to accept a conveyance which he had caused to be prepared, without any verification of the abstract; but the first question is, what were the rights of the parties under the conditions of sale, unaffected by what afterwards took place.

[212]   The decree has declared that the defendant is not entitled to have the abstract verified, except so far as the plaintiff can verify the same by the production of the deeds and other documents in his possession; and it then declares that the defendant is bound to accept the conveyance of the estate, executed as in the bill mentioned.

If this be the true result of the conditions of sale taken by themselves, it is obvious that, however good the title might appear to be upon the abstract, the purchaser could not be sure of having any proof whatever of such title; because, at the time of the purchase, he must be supposed to be ignorant of what deeds or documents were in the possession of the vendor, and the conditions give him no information upon the subject. The vendor might have had an abstract of a good title, and not one deed, or only some immaterial deeds, corresponding with the abstract. If, by these conditions, the vendor was protected from the necessity of verifying some of the material deeds deducing his title, he must have been equally protected from verifying any of the deeds whatever.

The case was necessarily argued for the respondent to this extent, that the conditions amounted to a declaration that the purchaser was to take such title as the vendor had, as was stipulated in *Freme* v. *Wright* (1): and undoubtedly a vendor may so stipulate; but he is bound, if such be his meaning, to make the stipulation intelligible to the purchaser. The purchaser,

(1) 20 R. R. 313 (4 Madd. 364).

in such a case, cannot object to any infirmity in the title or in the evidence to verify it; but could a purchaser so understand a contract by which it was stipulated that the *vendor should deliver an abstract and deduce a good title? It may be said that "to deduce" means to draw out and exhibit a good title upon the abstract: but if the purchaser be not bound to verify any part of it, the deducing and exhibiting a good title upon paper would be mere mockery and delusion. The subsequent words of the fourth condition, however, put a construction upon this word "deduce," and prove that it means not only to exhibit upon paper, but to deduce and show a good title; for it provides that as to certain allotted lands—and that by way of exception to the generality of the obligation to deduce a good title—the purchaser shall not be at liberty to require, and the vendor shall not be bound to show, any title prior to the award, from which period the title shall be deduced. Can it then be doubtful whether the vendor, when as to the other lands he contracted to deduce a good title, did not so contract as to give to the purchaser a right to require, and to bind himself to show a good title?

Had this fourth condition stood by itself, there could not have been any doubt upon the subject: but it is said that the sixth condition destroyed the whole effect of the contract so contained in the fourth condition, and converted a positive contract for a good title into a contract under which the purchaser might be obliged to take the estate without any title at all, and certainly without any means of proving a title. If such be the effect of the sixth condition, why contract by the fourth condition to deduce and show, thereby giving to the purchaser a right to require, a good title? Could it be the intention of the vendor to protect himself by one condition, from the obligation of performing that which, by a prior condition, he had contracted to do? Could any purchaser have so understood it?

It is to be observed that the fourth, fifth, and sixth conditions follow the usual course of proceeding in completing a purchase. The fourth relates to the title; the fifth, to the payment of the purchase-money and the conveyance; and the sixth, to the delivery and custody of the title deeds. The latter provides that

the vendor shall deliver to the purchaser of the largest portion of
the estate, all the title deeds in his custody, but shall not be
bound or required to produce any original or other documents
than those in his possession, and set forth in the abstract, and
which relate to other property.   The exception is to the contract
to deliver the title deeds.   To the contract in the fourth condition
to deduce and show a good title, there is no limitation or restriction ; but to the contract to deliver up the title deeds after the completion of the purchase, there is a restriction limiting the obligation
to produce, to such only as the vendor had in his possession.

It was said that the word " produce " has a more general
meaning than " deliver," and that it must therefore have been
intended to apply to a production for the purpose of proving the
abstract, and cannot be confined to production for the purpose of
delivery. If the word, however, had been used in that sense, it
would not have been confined to deeds in the possession of the
vendor ; because, for the purpose of proving the abstract, the production of deeds not in his possession, but of which he had the right
or the means of procuring the production, would have been equally
available.   He must have intended to give the best proof of his
title in his power ; though he might have wished to guard
against being called upon for more evidence in support of it,
than he had at his command.   He would therefore have
stipulated that the purchaser should not, for that purpose, be
[*215] entitled to call for any deeds which were not in his *possession,
or the production of which he had not the means of procuring.
With reference to the latter class, a clause confining the liability
to the producing of deeds in his possession would plainly have
been inapplicable ; though that would be the natural limit of the
obligation as to delivering up deeds on the completion of the
purchase. Apparently, the framer of these conditions did not
advert to the difficulty in proving the title, arising from the want
of some of the title deeds, and therefore did not guard against it ;
although he did think of protecting the vendor from the obligation
to deliver up any deeds except such as were in his own possession.

It by no means follows that the vendor cannot prove his title,
because he has not in his possession all the deeds necessary for
that purpose.   It could not, therefore, have been inferred by the

purchaser, that the restriction as to the liability to deliver up certain deeds, was to apply to the liability to produce them for the purpose of proving the title ; and if that inference was not obviously to be drawn from the conditions, will a court of equity compel a purchaser to take the estate without a title ?

For these reasons, I cannot think that upon the terms of the conditions alone, the purchaser was bound to complete his contract, until he had a good title deduced and proved, either by the production of the deeds professed to be abstracted, or by such other evidence as would satisfactorily prove the statements in the abstract to be correct.

Assuming that to be so, I have next to consider whether the notes in the margin of the abstract, coupled with the correspondence, deprive the purchaser of this right. The abstract professes to give the substance *of various instruments, which it was admitted, if truly abstracted, show a good title ; but the marginal notes in the abstract, when delivered, informed the purchaser that the originals of certain deeds were not in the possession or power of the vendor, but that attested copies would be produced. It by no means follows from this, that the most distinct and positive evidence might not be furnished of the existence and contents of those deeds. The earliest of them are of so late a date as the year 1813 ; the attesting witnesses may be forthcoming, and it may be known in whose possession the originals are. Much the same observations apply to the notes with respect to the ·deeds of August, 1818, and those of September, 1832. The note as to the latter merely is, that they are not in the possession of the vendor ; but they may be in his power, and they are of so recent a date, that it is scarcely possible that any difficulty should exist in proving their existence and contents. These notes certainly informed the purchaser that he was not to expect to have those deeds delivered up to him upon the completion of his purchase ; but did they inform him that the vendor was unable to give any proof of the existence or contents of documents set out in his abstract, and upon which his title depended ?

It was then said that the effect of the correspondence between the respective solicitors of the parties, amounted to an acceptance

[*216]

of the title.   If a purchaser accepts a title, he accepts it both as
to law and fact.   He agrees to take it as it stands, and he can no
more object that it is not proved, than he can that it is not good
in law.   The decree, however, does not proceed upon any such
ground.   On the contrary, it assumes that the purchaser is
entitled to have the abstract verified, so far as the plaintiff can
verify the same, by the production of deeds and other documents

[*217]   in his possession ; and although *it assumes that this verification
has not taken place, it decrees the purchaser to accept the
conveyance.   My present observation, however, is confined to
this, that the decree does not proceed upon the ground that the
purchaser had accepted the title : but that by the contract, the
vendor was bound to verify the title only to a certain extent, and
in a particular manner.   So that if it should now appear that the
letters amounted to an acceptance of the title, it will be a new
point, and one not constituting any part of the ground upon
which the decree stands.

Before I examine the letters, it must be considered in what
position the parties stood, according to my construction of the
conditions of sale.   The purchaser conceived himself entitled to
have a good title made out ; but he knew that his right to have
a delivery of the title deeds was limited by the sixth condition.
He saw upon the abstract a good title stated ; but he was told
by the notes that of certain deeds he could not have the
possession.   The question then upon the letters will be, whether
the purchaser waived all proof of the abstract, which would
amount to an acceptance of the title,—for he certainly accepted
it, if proved as stated,—or whether, according to the terms of the
decree, he waived all proof except so far as the vendor might be
able to afford such proof from the deeds and documents in his
possession.

(His Lordship here entered into a minute examination of the
various passages in the correspondence upon which the plaintiff
had relied as constituting or evidencing an acceptance of the title
by the defendant.   His Lordship then proceeded as follows :)

[218]   I cannot find any thing in these letters amounting to a new
contract as to the deeds, or to any waiver of such right as the
purchaser had with respect to the deeds under the original

agreement. It appears to me, that all the parts of this correspondence relied upon by the vendor as evidence of the purchaser having waived his right to have the abstract verified, were written under an expectation of having the abstract verified by an inspection of the title deeds, or some evidence of their existence and contents, before the completion of the purchase; and that the vendor's solicitor was fully informed, in September, 1833, of the existence of this expectation, and did not say or do any thing to remove this impression till the letter of the 9th of August, 1834, after his client had been called upon to execute a covenant for the production of the title deeds. The evidence of the defendant's solicitor confirms this, but does not carry the case further than the letters.

Such being the view which I take of the transactions subsequent to the sale, it follows that the opinion I have expressed of the effect of the contract then entered into under the conditions of sale, must regulate my judgment upon the whole case. I am satisfied that there was nothing in the conditions of sale sufficient to lead the purchaser to understand that he would have no right to have any evidence of any title to the land sold, unless the vendor should happen to be in possession of deeds sufficient for that purpose,—a circumstance of which the purchaser could know nothing.

Whether that was the intention of the vendor or not, is immaterial, if he did not take proper measures to explain such intention to the purchaser. To state in the conditions of sale, that the vendor would deliver *an abstract of title, and deduce a good title, except as to certain allotted lands, as to which he was not to be bound to show a good title prior to the award, from which period he was to deduce the title, was not the mode of informing a purchaser that he was not to require any evidence whatever of title to any part of the property, except such as the vendor might have the means of proving from deeds which might be in his possession, and which might amount to nothing.

The doctrine of Lord LYNDHURST in *Dick* v. *Donald* (1) is

[*219]

---

(1) 1 Bligh (N. S.), p. 655, in which case a vendor had agreed to execute and deliver a valid disposi- tion of certain property as described, and to deliver certain specified deeds which were described as " all the title

SOUTHBY
v.
HUTT.

much in conformity with my view of this case. It is, therefore, impossible for me to concur in the opinion, that the purchaser has no right to have the abstract of the title verified, except as far as the vendor can verify the same, by the production of the deeds and other documents in his possession. Instead of that declaration, I must declare that the purchaser has accepted the title as set forth in the abstract, subject to the same being verified, and direct a reference to the Master to inquire and state, whether the vendor can make out and verify the title set forth in the abstract delivered to the purchaser.

1836.
Jan. 30.
Feb. 9, 10.
Dec. 16.

Lord
COTTENHAM,
L.C.

[230]

THORNTON *v.* BRIGHT (1).

(2 My. & Cr. 230—255; S. C. 6 L. J. (N. S.) Ch. 121.)

A real estate was settled to the use of a father for life, with remainder to the use of all and every or such one or more of his children, for such estate and estates, and in such parts, shares, and proportions, and with such limitations over, and charged with such annual or gross sums, such limitations over and charges to be to or for the benefit of the same children, some or one of them, and in such manner and form as the father should appoint. The father afterwards appointed the estate to trustees and their heirs, upon trust to pay the rents and profits thereof to his daughter, who was a married woman, for her sole and separate use during the life of her husband, without power of anticipation: Held, that the appointment of the estate to trustees for the separate use of the daughter during the joint lives of herself and her husband was a valid exercise of the power.

BY the settlement made in contemplation of a marriage between Samuel Heywood, barrister-at-law, afterwards Serjeant Heywood, and Susannah Cornwall, afterwards Susannah Heywood, dated the 26th of December, 1780, and a common recovery duly suffered in pursuance thereof, the whole townland and hereditaments of Ballygrubane in the county of Armagh, in Ireland, were settled and assured (subject to life estates therein

deeds of the property in his custody," and the LORD CHANCELLOR (Lord LYNDHURST) observed (p. 661): "As to the condition with respect to the title deeds, I never heard that because the vendor provides by the conditions of sale that he will give to the pur- chaser only certain specified deeds the purchaser must take a bad title, or such title as appears by the deeds." —O. A. S.

(1) *In re Ridley* (1879) 11 Ch. D. 645, 48 L. J. Ch. 563.

to the father and mother of Samuel Heywood) to the use of   THORNTON
Samuel Heywood for life, with remainder to trustees to preserve,   *v.*
&c.; with remainder to the use of Susannah Cornwall his   BRIGHT.
intended wife for life; with remainder to the use of all and
every or such one or more of the child or children of the body
of Samuel Heywood on the body of Susannah Cornwall to be
begotten, whether male or female, for such *estate and estates,   [*231]
and in such parts, shares, and proportions, and with such
limitations over, and charged with such annual or gross sums,
such limitations over and charges to be to or for the benefit
of the same children, some or one of them, and in such manner
and form, as Samuel Heywood, at any time or times during his
life, by any deed or deeds, writing or writings, or by his last
will and testament in writing, executed and attested as therein
mentioned, should direct, limit, or appoint; and in default of
such direction, limitation, or appointment, and as to such parts
of the same estate whereof no such direction, limitation, or
appointment should be made, to the use of the first and other
sons of the marriage, successively, in tail male ; with remainder
to the use of the daughters of the marriage equally, as tenants
in common, in tail general, with cross remainders between
them ; and in case all such daughters but one should die without
issue, or there should be but one such daughter, then to the use
of such one surviving or only daughter and the heirs of her body,
with the ultimate remainder to the use of Samuel Heywood, his
heirs and assigns for ever.

The settlement contained a covenant by the father of Susannah
Cornwall that he would, within a month after the marriage,
transfer into the names of the trustees of the settlement the sum
of 300*l*. per annum Bank Long Annuities, upon certain trusts
for the benefit of the intended husband and wife for their
respective lives, and subject thereto, upon trust, as to 200*l*.
of such annuities, for all or such one or more of the children of
the marriage, and in such shares and proportions, manner and
form, and at such ages, as Susannah Cornwall should, if she
survived her intended husband, as therein mentioned appoint;
and as to the remaining 100*l*. of such Long Annuities, and also,
in case the husband should survive the *wife, as to the said sum   [*232]

of 200*l.* of such annuities, upon trust for all or such one or more of the children of the marriage, in such parts, shares, and proportions, and at such age or ages, and subject to such powers and limitations, such limitations to be for the benefit of the children, as the husband should by any deed or writing, or any last will and testament executed and attested as therein mentioned, direct or appoint; and in default of such direction or appointment, or as to so much of the said sums of 200*l.* and 100*l.* as should not be so directed or appointed, upon trust for all the children of the marriage equally, the shares of sons to vest and to be assigned to them at twenty-one, and of daughters at twenty-one or marriage, which should first happen, after the decease of the husband and wife; with benefit of survivorship and accruer with respect to the shares of such of the children as should die before they should have taken vested interests.

The marriage took effect; and, in pursuance of his covenant, John Cornwall, the father of Mrs. Samuel Heywood, thereupon transferred into the names of the trustees the sum of 300*l.* per annum Long Annuities, upon the trusts of the settlement. There were issue of the marriage several children, of whom three only, namely, Phœbe Augusta Heywood, Anne Heywood (afterwards the wife of William Granville Eliot), and Mary Isabella Heywood, lived to attain the age of twenty-one.

Under the will of John Cornwall, two several sums of 3,000*l.* and 2,000*l.* were afterwards laid out by the trustees in the purchase of Bank Long Annuities, and held by them upon the same trusts as the 300*l.* per annum like annuities originally settled; and the whole amount of the Bank Long Annuities included in the settlement was thereby increased to the sum of 552*l.* 1*s.* 9*d.* per annum.

[233] By indentures of settlement, dated the 4th and 5th of January, 1815, and made in contemplation of a marriage between Anne Heywood, the daughter of Samuel Heywood, and William Granville Eliot, after reciting (among other things) that Anne Heywood was entitled, under the settlement of the 26th of December, 1780, after the decease of Samuel Heywood and Susannah his wife, in case no appointment was made to the contrary, to a vested interest in one third share of 552*l.* 1*s.* 9*d.*

per annum Bank Long Annuities ; and that she was also, by virtue of the said settlement and of a common recovery suffered in pursuance thereof, and of a certain deed poll of appointment dated the 3rd of January, 1815, and duly executed by Samuel Heywood in pursuance of his power contained in the settlement, from and after the decease of Samuel Heywood and Susannah his wife, entitled to her and her heirs for ever, to one equal undivided third part of and in the townlands and hereditaments of Ballygrubane ; and reciting that, upon the treaty for the intended marriage, it was agreed that such third part of the said hereditaments and premises should be conveyed, and the said one third of the Bank Long Annuities assigned, to trustees, upon the trusts, and subject to the provisoes, declarations, and agreements after mentioned ; she, Anne Heywood, with the privity and consent of her intended husband, thereby conveyed and assured to certain trustees therein named and their heirs, all that her undivided third part of and in the townland of Ballygrubane, to hold the same with the appurtenances unto the said trustees, their heirs, and assigns (subject nevertheless to the several life estates of Samuel Heywood and Susannah his wife therein) to the use, after the marriage, of William Granville Eliot and his assigns for life, without impeachment of waste ; with remainder to trustees to preserve, &c. ; with remainder to the use of Anne Heywood, his intended wife, for life ; with remainder to the *use cf the children of the marriage, in such [*234] manner, and subject to such appointment as therein mentioned ; and in default of appointment, to the use of the first and other sons of the marriage successively in tail male ; with remainder to the daughters of the marriage equally as tenants in common in tail general ; with cross remainders amongst such daughters ; with the ultimate remainder to the use of Samuel Heywood, his heirs and assigns for ever. And Anne Heywood, with the like consent and approbation, thereby assigned to the same trustees, their executors, administrators, and assigns, all that her equal undivided third part of the sum of 552*l.* 1*s.* 9*d.* per annum Bank Long Annuities, to hold the same upon trust (after the decease of the survivor of Samuel Heywood and Susannah his wife) to pay the dividends thereof to William Granville Eliot for

THORNTON
v.
BRIGHT.

his life, and after his death to pay the same to Anne Heywood ; and after her death, to make over the same one third of the said funds and the dividends thereof to the children of the marriage in such manner and subject to such power of appointment as therein mentioned.

This settlement also contained a covenant by William Granville Eliot that in case Anne Heywood, or William Granville Eliot in her right, should, at any time during her coverture, become entitled, by survivorship or otherwise, to any further share or interest in the said townland and hereditaments, or any further sum in the Long Annuities, or to any other money, estates, or effects, by virtue of any gift, bequest, or otherwise, of any of her relations or friends, exceeding the value of 50l., he, William Granville Eliot, would, within a month after she or he in her right, should become so entitled, unless otherwise expressly ordered or appointed by the deed or will under which she should become entitled thereto, convey, assign, pay and

[*235]

make over the same to *the trustees of the settlement for the time being ; as to such part thereof as should be of the nature of real estate, to the several uses thereinbefore mentioned concerning the third part of the townland and hereditaments thereby granted and released ; and, as to such part thereof as should be of the nature of personal estate, upon the several trusts therein expressed and declared concerning the Bank Long Annuities thereby assigned. And Samuel Heywood, thereby, for himself and for Susannah his wife, covenanted with the trustees that neither he nor his wife would at any time in virtue of their respective powers, make any appointment of any part of the sum of 552l. 1s. 9d. [per annum] Bank Long Annuities that should lessen or diminish the one third share thereof to which Anne Heywood was entitled, and thereinbefore assigned by her.

The marriage between William Granville Eliot and Anne Heywood was duly solemnised ; and there were issue of the marriage two surviving children only, both of whom are infants. In the month of January, 1822, Susannah Heywood died, and was survived by her husband, and their three daughters. Mary Isabella Heywood, one of those daughters, died in October, 1822, unmarried and intestate, and her father, Serjeant

Heywood, took out administration to her estate. The trustees of Serjeant Heywood's marriage settlement, conceiving that Mary Isabella Heywood, in default of appointment, took a vested interest in one third of the sum of 552*l.* 1*s.* 9*d.* per annum Bank Long Annuities, subject to her father's life interest therein, shortly afterwards sold out that third (being 184*l.* 0*s.* 7*d.* per annum) and paid over the proceeds to Serjeant Heywood, as the administrator of his deceased daughter. The amount of the Long Annuities standing in the names of the trustees was thus reduced to the sum of 368*l.* 1*s.* 2*d.* per annum.

On the 15th of June, 1826, Serjeant Heywood made his will, which was executed and attested as required by the power contained in his marriage settlement. By that will, after reciting, among other things, that, by virtue of a deed poll, dated the 3rd of January, 1815, and executed in pursuance of the power contained in his marriage settlement, and by the settlement made on the marriage of his daughter Anne, one equal third of the townland of Ballygrubane had been settled and limited as therein mentioned, and that one third of the Bank Long Annuities to which his said daughter was then presumptively entitled was assigned to her trustees upon the trusts therein mentioned ; and further reciting the receipt by the testator of the proceeds of the sum of 184*l.* 0*s.* 7*d.* per annum Bank Long Annuities, as administrator of his deceased daughter Mary Isabella, and that 184*l.* 0*s.* 7*d.* being one moiety of the remaining sum of 368*l.* 1*s.* 2*d.* per annum Bank Long Annuities was, by virtue of his covenant in the marriage settlement of his daughter Anne, to be transferred, upon his decease, to the trustees of her settlement ; and that he had a right to appoint the remainder of the Bank Long Annuities, under the power reserved to him in his own marriage settlement ; the testator, in pursuance and execution of that power, and of all other powers in him vested, directed and appointed the remaining two thirds of the estate of Ballygrubane, to the use of Richard Bright and Benjamin Heywood and their heirs, and also appointed to the same trustees, their executors, administrators, and assigns, the sum of 184*l.* 0*s.* 7*d.* Bank Long Annuities, being the remaining third of such Long

[236]

Annuities, upon trust, out of the rents of the two thirds of
Ballygrubane, and the dividends or income of the Long
Annuities, yearly to pay unto or for his daughter Phœbe
Augusta Heywood, during her life, for her own use and benefit,
such sums of money, not exceeding in any one year 300*l.*,

[*237]   as his trustees *and his daughter Anne Eliot might think
most for her advantage. And the testator directed that the
annual surplus, if any, of such rents and dividends should be
paid to his daughter Anne Eliot for her separate use, free
from the control of her then present or any future husband,
during the joint lives of herself and Phœbe Augusta Heywood,
and that her receipt alone, notwithstanding her coverture,
should be a sufficient discharge to the trustees; and in case
of the death of Anne Eliot, during the life of Phœbe Augusta
Heywood, then such annual surplus was to be paid to such
person or persons as should be the heir of the body of Anne
Eliot for the time being. And after the decease of Phœbe
Augusta Heywood, in case Anne Eliot and her then present
husband should be then living, upon trust to pay the whole
of the rents and profits of the two-thirds of Ballygrubane into
the proper hands of Anne Eliot, or such person or persons
as she should by writing appoint, for her sole and separate
use, and free from the control of her then present husband;
and her receipt alone, notwithstanding her coverture, was to
be a sufficient discharge to the trustees; but Anne Eliot was
not to be at liberty to assign or appoint such rents and profits
by anticipation, or before they became actually due. And in
case Anne Eliot should survive her then present husband,
then the testator, from and after his decease, and the decease
of his daughter Phœbe Augusta Heywood, appointed the said
two third parts of Ballygrubane to Anne Eliot and the heirs
of her body. But in case Anne Eliot should die in the lifetime
of her said husband and of Phœbe Augusta Heywood, the
testator thereby willed that Anne Eliot should have full power
to give or appoint, after the decease of Phœbe Augusta Heywood,
the whole or any part of the two third parts of Ballygrubane
to all or any one or more of her children who might survive
her, for such *estate and estates, upon and for such trusts,

[*238]

and in such manner and form as, notwithstanding her coverture, she, by her last will and testament in writing, or any codicil thereto, executed and attested as therein mentioned, should direct or appoint; and in default of such direction or appointment, then the testator directed and appointed the same unto the heirs of the body of Anne Eliot. And the testator thereby also directed that, from and after the decease of Phœbe Augusta Heywood, the income of the Bank Long Annuities should be paid to Anne Eliot for her separate use, during the joint lives of herself and her then present husband; and in case she should survive her husband, that the capital of the Bank Long Annuities should be transferred to her for her own use; but in case she should die in her husband's lifetime, then, after her decease, the trustees were directed to transfer the capital of such Long Annuities to such person or persons and in such manner and form as Anne Eliot should, notwithstanding her coverture, by her last will and testament in writing, or any codicil, executed and attested as therein mentioned, appoint; and in default of such appointment, unto her executors or administrators as part of her personal estate. Richard Bright and Benjamin Heywood were appointed the executors of the will.

Serjeant Heywood died in the month of September, 1828, leaving his daughters Phœbe Augusta Heywood and Anne Eliot his co-heiresses-at-law and only next of kin. Phœbe Augusta Heywood died in the month of June, 1832, unmarried and intestate, leaving Anne Eliot her heiress-at-law and only next of kin.

The bill was filed by the trustees of Serjeant Heywood's marriage settlement against the trustees and executors of the Serjeant's will (one of whom had also *obtained letters of administration *de bonis non* of Mary Isabella Heywood) against Mr. and Mrs. Eliot, their infant children, and the trustees of their marriage settlement, and against the personal representative of Phœbe Augusta Heywood; and it prayed that the rights of the several parties in the property which formed the subject of the settlement of December, 1780, might be ascertained and declared.

[*239]

By the decree of the VICE-CHANCELLOR, made at the hearing of the cause, it was, among other things, declared that the settlement of the 5th of January, 1815, made on the marriage of William Granville Eliot and Anne Heywood, was a valid appointment of one third of the 552*l*. 1*s*. 9*d*. per annum Bank Long Annuities; and that the one third of the sum of 552*l*. 1*s*. 9*d*. per annum Bank Long Annuities, amounting to 184*l*. 0*s*. 7*d*., per annum like Annuities, sold out in the lifetime of Samuel Heywood, and the proceeds whereof were paid to him, was unappointed; and that one third of such last mentioned third vested in Anne Eliot, one other third in Phœbe Augusta Heywood, and the other third in Mary Isabella Heywood; and that Anne Eliot became entitled, as the next of kin of Phœbe Augusta Heywood to her said one third of a third, and that the two thirds of a third, to which Anne Eliot so became entitled, were liable to be settled under the covenants contained in her marriage settlement; and that under the appointment contained in the will of Samuel Heywood, Anne Heywood became absolutely entitled for her separate use to the remaining one third of the sum of 552*l*. 1*s*. 9*d*. per annum Bank Long Annuities; and that she was not bound to settle the same. And it was further declared that the appointment contained in the will of Samuel Heywood, as to the two thirds of the real estate of Ballygrubane, to the trustees for the separate use of *Anne Eliot, was invalid; but that the appointment of the same two thirds by that will to Anne Eliot in tail was a valid appointment; and that under the covenants contained in her marriage settlement, she was bound to settle the same to the several uses in the settlement expressed concerning the one third of the hereditaments and premises thereby granted and released; and that Anne Eliot should convey the same to the trustees of her marriage settlement, and settle the same accordingly; and that the trustees of Serjeant Heywood's will should pay to William Granville Eliot, as being entitled thereto under the settlement, a moiety of the rents received by them, and which became due after the decease of Samuel Heywood, and prior to the decease of Phœbe Augusta Heywood, in respect of the two undivided thirds of the said real

[*240]

estate, and also the entirety of the rents of the same two undivided thirds which had accrued due, and had been received by them since the death of Phœbe Augusta Heywood.

The defendant Mrs. Eliot appealed against so much of the VICE-CHANCELLOR's decree, as declared the appointment of two thirds of the estate of Ballygrubane to be void, and against the consequential directions.

The *Solicitor-General* and *Mr. Lovat*, in support of the appeal.

Mr. Jacob and *Mr. Norton*, in support of the decree. [242]

Mr. Stevens and *Mr. Gresley* appeared for other parties. [245]

The *Solicitor-General*, in reply.

[The arguments of counsel and the cases cited by them sufficiently appear from the following judgment.]

THE LORD CHANCELLOR [after stating the facts and documents, and the substance of the decree, said :]

The effect of this decree is to declare that the testator had no power to direct the payment of the rents to his daughter Anne for her separate use, and to treat the appointment as creating a valid estate tail, inasmuch as it directs her to convey the two thirds to the trustees of her own settlement under the covenant, although the estate tail was given only in the event of Anne surviving her husband, who is still alive, and although the covenant in her settlement was by the husband only, and was to operate only in the event of the instrument under *which she might become entitled to the property not directing otherwise. The effect of the decree is to give to the husband an estate for life in his own right, contrary to the express directions of Serjeant Heywood's will, and unless she should survive her husband, to deprive the wife of all benefit from the property, and if she should survive him, to give her only a life estate, although, in that event, the testator gave her an estate tail.

The first question to be considered is whether Serjeant Heywood was authorised by his own settlement to appoint the rents of

THORNTON
v.
BRIGHT.

Dec. 16.

[247]

[*248]

the two thirds of the estate to the separate use of his daughter Anne ; because, if he was, the question whether such interest as she took under his will was, or was not, subject to the covenant in her own settlement, will not arise. Now, his power is to appoint in favour of children for such estate and estates, charged with such annual or gross sums, and in such manner and form as he should think fit. As to so much of and such interest in the estate as Serjeant Heywood should not effectually appoint, Mrs. Eliot, in the events which have happened, would, by the provisions of the settlement of 1780, be entitled in tail. It is said that what Serjeant Heywood has attempted to do, by way of appointment, in the event of Mrs. Eliot dying in the lifetime of her husband and sister, namely, to give her a power of appointing amongst her children, and, in default of her so appointing, to give the estate to the heirs of her body, is not within the power, and therefore void. But he has also appointed the rents of the estate, during the joint lives of herself and her husband, to trustees for her separate use, and the estate itself to her in tail, if she should survive her husband ; and the decree declares that his appointment to her in tail is valid; but that the appointment of the rents for her separate use is invalid ;

[*249]   and the decree directs Mrs. *Eliot so to deal with this estate tail as to settle it according to the covenant in her own settlement. Now it is to be observed, that if the appointment of the rents to her separate use, and of the estate, in the event of her dying in her husband's lifetime, be invalid, Mrs. Eliot is entitled to an immediate estate tail under the settlement of 1780; but the estate tail, under the appointment in the will of Serjeant Heywood, is made to depend upon her surviving her husband, who is still alive; and, therefore, it does not appear how such an estate can be made subject to the covenant in her settlement, even supposing the object of that settlement to be to give interests to the husband, and not to protect the wife against the exercise of his marital rights.

It has not been disputed at the Bar, and the decree affirms, that the appointment of the estate tail is good ; but if it be good, it must prevail according to the terms and conditions of the appointment, namely, to take effect after the termination of the joint lives of Mr. and Mrs. Eliot, and in the event only of Mrs. Eliot surviving her husband.

Serjeant Heywood, in exercising this power, has given to his daughter the rents for her separate use, during the joint lives of herself and her husband, and, if she survive him, then the estate, in tail; the obvious object being to protect his daughter against the marital power of her husband, and to exclude the husband from any participation in the benefit of that property. The decree, however, wholly defeats this object in two ways. It declares the gift of the rents for the separate use of Mrs. Eliot to be invalid; and it treats the estate tail, under the appointment, which it declares to be good, as a present interest; and it gives to the husband the same benefits in the two thirds of the estate as he had *under his own settlement in the one third. [*250] The terms of the power are as large as they can well be: " for such estate and estates, and in such parts, shares, and proportions, and with such limitations over, and charged with such annual or gross sums, such limitations over and charges to be to or for the benefit of the same children, and in such manner and form," as Serjeant Heywood should, at any time or times, direct, limit, or appoint. What is there to prevent the donee of such a power from directing the rents of the estate, the subject of the power, to be paid to a married daughter, during the joint lives of her and her husband, and, if she survive her husband, the estate itself to her in tail ?

In support of the decree it was first contended that the words " in such manner and form " applied only to the charges to be created, and the limitations over to be made, under the power; but this is clearly contrary to the meaning of the clause; the copulatives run through the whole of it, and every limb of it is part of the whole body,—" for such estates, *and* in such parts, *and* with such limitations, *and* charged with such sums, *and* in such manner and form."

It was contended, secondly, that under such a power the donee could only appoint so as to create legal estates. Could he then, in executing the power to charge, create only a legal rent charge? and what do the words " in such manner and form " imply? The argument assumes that under such a power the donee could

THORNTON
v.
BRIGHT.

not, for any purpose, create a trust. It was said, indeed, that a court of equity would not interfere to carry such intention into effect. But the Court interposes only as it does to enforce the execution of all other trusts; the appointment creating a legal estate in trustees during Mrs. Eliot's life; and the argument

[*251]

was *necessarily confined to appointments of which the subject is a legal estate in land; this very decree giving effect to a precisely similar appointment over a sum of stock. The objection, therefore, is not that the appointment is not within the terms of the power, but that such a power, to be exercised over land, including the legal estate as well as the beneficial interest, must be confined to creating a legal estate and cannot create a trust. This must depend upon the terms of the power, and the intention by those terms expressed; for, undoubtedly, every mode of dealing with an estate may be effected through the means of a power which could be exercised by the original authors of the power.

All this reasoning, however, must yield to the weight of authority, if the point has been established by authority. *Alexander* v. *Alexander* (1) was cited for the appellant; and that case establishes that, under a power to appoint a personal fund in such proportion as the donee should direct, an appointment to one of the objects for life, to her separate use, was good. So far it is a strong authority for the appellant; but the respondent contended that another part of that case was in his favour, that is to say, the part which related to the share of Francis. Now, as to Francis's share, the case was this: the donee having power to appoint amongst children, gave, contingently, a part of the fund to two of the children, to apply it at their discretion for the benefit of another child, namely, Francis, his wife, and children. This was clearly bad on two grounds. It was a delegation of the power, and was to be exercised in favour of the wife and children, who were not objects of the power. The decision upon this point cannot possibly aid the argument of the respondent.

[252]

The respondent's counsel also attempted to draw an argument from *Herrey* v. *Herrey* (2), which, they contended, established

(1) 2 Ves. Sen. 640.   (2) 1 Atk. 561.

the proposition, that a power to appoint in favour of a particular person cannot be executed by an appointment to trustees for such person.   In that case there was in a settlement a power to a father to make a jointure to the amount of 600*l.*, interposed between his own legal estate for life and a legal remainder to his son ; and he attempted to execute the power by appointing the estate to trustees, upon trust, to pay 600*l.* a year to his wife. Lord HARDWICKE held that a power to jointure was a power to create a legal estate, and was not well executed by creating a trust ; but he, nevertheless, considered the wife as entitled to her jointure, and decreed accordingly.   That is no authority to show that such a power as is found in this case cannot be executed by creating a trust ; but it does prove, that where there was at law a failure in the execution of the power, this Court gave to the object of it, being a wife, the full benefit of it.   The report of *Churchman* v. *Harvey* (1) establishes the same principle. No other cases were relied upon for the respondent.   Several were cited for the appellant, in which, under such a power of appointment as in the present case, over a fund of personalty, an appointment for the separate use of a married daughter had been held good.   To that class belong cases like *Alexander* v. *Alexander* and *Maddison* v. *Andrew* (2), upon which it is not however, necessary to observe particularly ; the decree in this very case establishing the proposition as to the one third of the Long Annuities.

It was contended, however, that the rule does not apply to lands, at least when the subject of the power *is a legal estate in lands.   No case, as I have already stated, was cited in support of this proposition.   Against it there are several.   The first of these is *Pitt* v. *Jackson* (3), where a sum of money was covenanted to be laid out in land, to be settled upon the husband for life, remainder to the wife for life, remainder to the children in such shares, for such estates, and subject to such powers, limitations, and provisoes as the husband should appoint.   Real estates were purchased with the trust fund : but the husband, by his will, directed that 10,000*l.*, which he considered to be part of the

[*253]

---

(1) Amb. 335.   (3) 2 Br. C. C. 51.
(2) 1 Ves. Sen. 58.

trust fund, should be laid out in land, to be conveyed to a
daughter of the marriage for life, for her separate use, with
remainder to her children in tail. The cause was first heard by
Lord KENYON, then Master of the Rolls, sitting for the Lord
Chancellor, when it was decreed that as to this sum of 10,000*l*.,
it should be laid out in land, to be settled to the use of trustees
for the daughter and the heirs of her body ; but that the profits
should be pai l for her separate use. The cause was afterwards
reheard by Lord ROSSLYN upon a bill of review, under the name
of *Smith* v. *Lord Camelford* (1), when his Lordship decided that
the appointment did not operate upon the land purchased, the
husband having intended to appoint the fund ; nor upon the
fund, because it had ceased to exist, being invested in the land.
The judgment of the MASTER OF THE ROLLS, however, with
respect to the effect of the appointment of the 10,000*l*., if there
had been a proper subject-matter upon which the appointment
could operate, is not affected by the decision of Lord ROSSLYN.
On the contrary, Lord ROSSLYN (2) expresses an opinion in favour
of Lord KENYON's judgment upon this point.

[254]   The case of *Pitt* v. *Jackson* is admitted to be an authority for
the appellant ; but its weight is attempted to be lessened by a
statement, that the same counsel appeared for the husband and
the wife. In *Crompe* v. *Barrow* (3), the subject of the power was
leasehold property in trust. It is, however, an authority, that
an appointment to the separate use of a married woman is a
good appointment under a less extensive power than this. In
Kenworthy v. *Bate* (4), the power was over a legal estate in land ;
the settlement being to the use of the husband for life, remainder
to the wife for life, remainder to such children of the marriage
as their father should by will direct and appoint. The father,
by his will, directed that the estate should be sold and the
proceeds divided among the children ; and this appointment was
supported, upon the authority of *Long* v. *Long* (5), *Thwaytes* v.
Dye (6), and *Roberts* v. *Dixall* (7). How then can it be contended,

(1) 3 R. R. 36 (2 Ves. Jr. 698).
(2) 3 R. R. 42 (2 Ves. Jr. pp. 711,
712).
(3) 4 R. R. 318 (4 Ves. 681).
(4) 6 R. R. 46 (6 Ves. 793).

(5) 5 R. R. 101 (5 Ves. 445).
(6) 2 Vern. 80.
(7) 2 Eq. Ca. Ab. 668, pl. 19 ; and
1 Atk. 607.

that such a power as this over a legal estate in lands can only be executed by creating legal estates? If the contrary be the law, where then is the difference between such appointments over personalty and over land; and what is the ground of the difference which this decree establishes? The cases of *Bennet* v. *Davis* (1) and *Doe* v. *Martin* (2) were cited for the appellant, to prove, that if there were any objection in the appointment to trustees, the wife's right would be the same in equity; but in my view of the case, it is not necessary to resort to that ground.

It was lastly contended for the respondent, that supposing the appointment for the separate use of Mrs. Eliot to be good, she was bound by the covenant to devest *herself of it, and to settle the estate according to the terms of her own settlement, which would have the effect of giving to her husband an estate for life, and so defeat the object of the appointment. To this argument, however, there are three answers: 1st, That the covenant is the husband's only, and applies only to that over which he might have dominion; 2ndly, That it does not apply to property, as to which any express order or direction was given inconsistent with the purposes of the settlement; and, 3rdly, That the decree in this cause concludes this argument, because the one third of the Long Annuities would be as much within the terms of the covenant as the two thirds of the real estate.

[*255]

Upon the whole, therefore, after paying every attention to the argument in favour of the decree, and with the utmost respect for the authority from whence it proceeded, I cannot come to the opinion that this appointment for the separate use of Mrs. Eliot is void.

The result is, that I must reverse so much of the decree as declares the appointment to be invalid, and directs the conveyance to the uses of Mrs. Eliot's settlement, and as directs payment of the rents according to the declaration; and in lieu of that part of the decree, I must declare this appointment to be good, and direct the trustees to pay the rents to the separate

(1) 2 P. Wms. 316.   (2) 2 R. R. 324 (4 T. R. 39).

4—2

use of Mrs. Eliot during the joint lives of herself and her husband.

There being no conveyance at present to be executed, it does not seem proper to make any further declaration as to the ulterior interests in the property.

1837.
March 18.
——
Lord
COTTENHAM,
L.C.

[275]

IN THE MATTER OF THE NORWICH CHARITIES.

(2 My. & Cr. 275—308.)

When a reference has been made to the Master to appoint trustees of a charity, it is the rule of the Court to adopt the Master's appointments, unless the persons appointed can be shown to be objectionable; and the Court will not enter into the question of the fitness of other persons whom the Master has refused to appoint.

Where, however, under the Municipal Corporations Regulation Act, a reference had been made to the Master, to appoint new trustees of charity property, in the stead of the old corporation, who had been the former trustees, and the Master had received evidence which tended to show that there was a suspicion of the old trustees having exercised their trust for political purposes, and had declined to re-appoint any of the old trustees, and had written a memorandum, stating that he had come to that determination "in consequence of the case made against the old trustees;" the Court entered into the consideration of the propriety of the Master's conduct in rejecting all the old trustees; and held, that the existence of a general suspicion of impropriety on the part of the old trustees in the exercise of their trust, whether that suspicion were well or ill founded, justified the Master in declining to re-appoint any of the old trustees.

An institution for the maintenance and education of poor children, founded in 1617, and chartered in 4 Car. I. (1628), was held, under the circumstances, to be not exclusively a Church of England charity, so as to make it proper to place it under the superintendence of a body of trustees consisting entirely of members of the Church of England.

THIS case came before the Lord Chancellor upon a petition to confirm the Master's report of his having appointed certain trustees of the Norwich charities, under the Act for the regulation of municipal *corporations (1), and upon a cross-petition, presented by Samuel Bignold and William Rackham, which prayed that the report might not be confirmed.

[*276]

By an order made by the LORD CHANCELLOR, on the 20th of August, 1836, it was referred to the Master to appoint proper persons to be trustees of the charity estates and property, then

(1) 5 & 6 Will. IV. c. 76. Repealed; see now 45 & 46 Vict. c. 50, s. 131.

late vested in or under the administration of the corporation of Norwich, or any of the members thereof in that character, which were affected by the seventy-first section of the Act; with liberty to the Master to state special circumstances.

Among the charities of which it was necessary to appoint new trustees, were the Great Hospital, Doughty's Hospital, the Boys' Hospital, and the Girls' Hospital.

The petitioners, who now prayed the confirmation of the Master's report, carried in before the Master a list of names of persons to be appointed trustees; and the petitioners in the cross-petition also carried in a like list on their part. In the latter list were inserted the names of certain persons who had been trustees of the charities, in their capacity of members of the old corporation, including the cross-petitioners themselves.

Upon the prosecution of the order of reference, there was produced before the Master a printed copy of a report with respect to the city of Norwich, made in the year 1835, by the Commissioners appointed, by his Majesty's commission, to inquire into the state of municipal corporations in England and Wales. This report stated, that the voters at the local elections at Norwich *had long been divided into two parties; the one [*277] called the purple and orange party, and the other the blue and white party; and that it had been clearly proved that bribery had been very frequently and extensively practised by both parties at the local elections. The report then particularised various instances of bribery; and it is also stated, that a mode of bribing which had been frequently practised, consisted in giving notes, promising to get freemen into the hospitals, and to make them allowances until they could be admitted. * *
The Commissioners' report declared, that in the instances therein [278] mentioned, and in others, the property and patronage entrusted to the corporation for purposes of charity had been rendered subservient to the purposes of a party.

[A great deal of evidence was adduced before the Master both in support of and in contradiction to the conclusions of the Commissioners' report. The latter evidence included affidavits by Mr. Bignold, who was mayor of the city at the time when the Commissioners' inquiry took place, and also affidavits by several

aldermen denying that the patronage had been employed for
political purposes.]

The Master * * came to the conclusion, that it would be
improper to select any person as one of the new trustees who
had been a member of the old corporation; and he wrote a
memorandum to this effect; viz., that, " after careful consideration of the case made against the old trustees," he was of
opinion that he should not be justified in re-appointing any
of them.

The Master then proceeded to nominate two sets of trustees
one of which sets consisted entirely of members of the Church
of England; under whose superintendence the Master placed
all those charities which he considered to be essentially of the
character of Church of England charities: and the other set
of trustees, consisting of twenty-one individuals, comprised
seventeen *members of the Church of England, and four
Dissenters ; under whose superintendence the Master placed all
the remaining charities.

The charities called the Boys' Hospital and the Girls' Hospital
were two of those which were placed under the superintendence
of the mixed body of trustees.   The following particulars with
respect to the history of those charities, except such as are
expressly cited from the affidavits filed in support of the cross-
petition, are taken from the report of the Commissioners of
Charities, dated the 10th of July, 1833, and printed by order of
Parliament in the year 1834, and which, by the consent of both
parties, was received in evidence before the Master, and also
afterwards before the Lord Chancellor.

The Boys' and Girls' Hospitals, though they are now in every
respect distinct, derive their origin from the same founder, were
established under the same charter, and were originally one
establishment, called The Children's Hospital.

Thomas Anguish, by his will, bearing date the 22nd of June,
1617, devised to the mayor, sheriffs, citizens, and commonalty
of the city of Norwich and their successors, the east part of his
houses, yards, and grounds, with the appurtenances, in the
parish of St. Edmund of Fishergate ; to hold the same for ten
years after his decease, to the uses thereinafter mentioned ; and

he desired, that when the said mayor, sheriffs, &c. should have
possessed the same for ten years after his decease, the said
premises should be from thenceforth let for terms of seven or
ten years at the most; that they should be kept in repair out of
the rents and profits, until, by some godly-minded man, or by
the general charge of the city, a hospital or convenient place for
*the keeping, bringing up, and teaching of young and very poor   [*286]
children, born and brought up in the city of Norwich, should be
erected :   *   *   and if neither the premises given by him should
be found convenient, nor any other place be given for the purpose,
he directed that the *overplus of the rent, after paying for the   [*287]
repairs, should be applied by the mayor for the time being, and
four of the ancientest aldermen of the wards of East Wymer,
Coslany, Fybrigge, and North Conisford, for the helping and
curing of poor distressed men, women, and children that should
be hurt by falls or otherwise, or should be diseased and likely to
be cured, as also for and towards the clothing of poor children,
and especially towards helping and curing poor children that
should not have friends to help them, and that should be cut
for the stone or ruptured, as many had been, and for placing
persons that should be diseased and thought incurable, in the
lazar-houses near the gates of the said city; and this course to
be continued till a hospital should be founded for the bringing
up and keeping poor diseased children.

The premises devised by Thomas Anguish, in the parish of
St. Edmund, are now used for the Boys' Hospital.

[Other bequests were afterwards made by various testators for
the same purposes.]

By letters patent, bearing date the 28th of November, 4   [288]
Charles I.,   *   *   the King granted to the mayor, sheriffs,
&c. and their successors, licence to take and enjoy the said
devised premises for the purpose aforesaid, and that the said
houses devised by the said Thomas Anguish, and the yard and
grounds thereto belonging, should continue for ever a hospital
and place of sustentation, relief, and maintenance of poor children, in such sort as in the will of the said Thomas Anguish was
mentioned, to *be called The Children's Hospital, of the Founda-   [*289]
tion of King Charles; and licence was granted to the said mayor,

sheriffs, &c. to take lands, tenements, and hereditaments to the
yearly value of 300*l.* ; and it was declared that it should be
lawful for the mayor and aldermen, or the greater number of
them, as often as it should seem expedient to them, to make
constitutions and rules for the right governing of the said poor
children in the said hospital, so as the same should not be
repugnant to the law, or to the provision of any of the donors
to the charitable uses aforesaid ; and also to create such and
so many officers, ministers, or governors of the said house, to
provide for and govern the said children, as to them should seem
meet, and to receive into the said hospital any children whatsoever born in the said city, suburbs or hamlets thereof, being
under the age of ten years, and to maintain, educate, teach and
instruct in learning, set on work, and otherwise dispose of, as
many such children as the revenues would extend to, as to them
should seem convenient, and to discharge the said children and
all the officers of the said hospital from year to year or day to
day, at their will and pleasure.

After the date of the charter of King Charles the First, various
benefactions were made to the Children's Hospital, and also to
the Boys' Hospital and the Girls' Hospital respectively.   One of
these was a devise of lands in 1666, by John Vaughan, who
directed the rents to be applied to the support of six boys in the
hospital ; such boys being presented, alternately, by the corporation of Norwich, and the vicar, churchwardens, and overseers of
the parish of Saxthorpe.   The premises in St. Edmund's parish,
devised by Thomas Anguish, to be converted into a hospital,
consist of a dwelling-house, in which the master of the Boys'
[*290]   Hospital resides with his mother, who is the mistress *of the
Girls' Hospital, and of a yard, with a school-room for each
establishment.   The clear income of the Boys' Hospital is
applied in the educating, maintaining, clothing and apprenticing
sixty-one boys.   One of these is recommended by the minister
and churchwardens of the parish of Saxthorpe, in respect of
Vaughan's gift, and others are appointed upon the recommen-
dation of the parish officers of different parishes in Norwich,
in respect of various other benefactions.   The rest are nominated by the aldermen in rotation, as vacancies happen.   All

the boys are admitted at a court of mayoralty. Up to the
year 1798, the boys were lodged and maintained in the hospital,
and there were at that period twenty-one boys thus provided
for: it was, however, thought expedient to alter this system,
and in 1798 the number was increased to thirty, and the
yearly sum of 10*l.* was allowed to the parents or friends of
each boy, who were to provide him with lodging and maintenance, and also to pay the master of the hospital for his education. The same sum is still paid for each boy, but the number
has been gradually increased from thirty to sixty-one.

The master of the hospital, who, by this new arrangement,
has no other duty but that of schoolmaster, is appointed by
the mayor and aldermen. Out of the yearly allowance of 10*l.*
are paid the charges of the master for stationery, and a certain
quarterage of 5*s.*, 7*s.*, or 8*s.*, according to what the children
learn ; and the residue remains as a fund for maintaining them.
Each boy receives annually, at Lady Day, a blue cloth jacket, a
pair of trowsers, a stuff waistcoat, and a red cap.

By one of the rules established by the mayor and aldermen,
the boys are required to meet at the school every Sunday, and
to go thence, with the master, to the *cathedral. They are   [*291]
examined once a year by the committee, and are catechised,
annually, by the minister of St. Edmund's.

UP to about the year 1650, boys and girls were maintained,
lodged, and educated together in the hospital, in the parish of
St. Edmund's, now called the Boys' Hospital. The foundation
of a separate hospital for girls is attributed to Robert Baron, who
died in the year 1649, and who, by will, bequeathed to the city of
Norwich 250*l.*, which it was his desire should be employed for
the training up of women children, from the age of seven till
fifteen, in spinning, knitting, and dressing wool, under the
tuition of an aged, discreet, religious woman, appointed thereto,
at some public place, by the magistrates' appointment; hoping
that some other would add to the same, that it might become a
means of great benefit to the city and comfort to the poor: and
he desired that the same should be paid within one year after his
decease, in case some place should be appointed thereto by the
city, and an overseer thereof as aforesaid.

To this bequest several other benefactions were subsequently added.

The management of the property, and of the whole establishment, is under the same committees, and the accounts are kept by the same treasurer as those of the Boys' Hospital.

Up to the year 1802 the girls were supported in a particular building. In that year an alteration in the system was adopted, similar to that made in the Boys' Hospital. The number of girls was increased from twenty-two to twenty-four, and it was agreed to allow the sum of 8l. to the parents or friends of each girl, who [*292] were *therewith to maintain and educate her, paying to the schoolmistress or master appointed for the purpose by the mayor and aldermen, 7s. 6d. per quarter, and the charges for stationery and books usual in other schools. The number of girls was increased in 1807, to thirty-two, and in 1824, to forty-four. The girls are taught needlework in a schoolroom appropriated to their use, (part of the Boys' Hospital in St. Edmund's parish) by the schoolmistress, on three days in the week; and on the other three days of the week they are taught reading, writing, and accounts by the master of the Boys' Hospital in the same schoolroom with the boys. The girls are appointed by the aldermen in rotation, except such as are appointed from different parishes in respect of particular donations; and they are all admitted at a court of mayoralty.

The same school hours and the same holidays are prescribed for the girls as for the boys, and the girls are examined and catechised in the same manner, and also required to attend at the school every Sunday, and to go from thence with the master to the cathedral.   *   *   *

[293]   The petitioners in the cross-petition submitted that it would be an entire departure from the principle of the foundation of these charities, to place them under the administration of any trustees not being members of the Church of England, at least so long as competent members of the Church of England were to be found, and that they ought to be placed under the administration of the first mentioned set of trustees.

The cross-petition prayed that the Master's report, as to the appointment of trustees, might not be confirmed; and that it might be referred back to him to review his report in that behalf, with such declarations or directions as might be necessary to prevent all objection to the appointment of the petitioners and the other persons therein mentioned, or any other persons, on the ground of their having been formerly, and previously to the 1st of August, 1836, members of the late corporation of Norwich: and further, that the report might not be confirmed, so far as the mixed set of trustees were appointed to be trustees of the Boys' Hospital and the Girls' Hospital respectively; and that those charities might be comprised in the number of Church of England charities, and placed under the administration of the set of trustees consisting exclusively of members of the Church of England.

In re NORWICH CHARITIES.

Affidavits were filed in support of the cross-petition, in addition to those before mentioned.

Mr. *Wigram* and Mr. *O. Anderdon*, in support of the cross-petition.

[298]

The *Solicitor-General* and Mr. *Blunt*, for the Master's report.

[299]

Mr. *Wigram*, in reply.

[302]

THE LORD CHANCELLOR:

[303]

Upon the first part of the case, if it had not been for the memorandum made by the Master, the question is one which the Court would not have allowed even to be stated; for it is the well established rule, that the Court gives credit to the Master's report of the appointment of trustees, unless the parties complaining can show some objection to the persons who have been selected. Now, against the individuals appointed in this case, no allegation of any sort or kind is made; and the only case of the petitioners is, that the Master, in the memorandum which he has made of the grounds upon which he proceeded, uses this expression, viz., "After careful consideration of the case made against the old trustees, I am of opinion that I should not be justified in re-appointing any of them." It becomes, therefore, incumbent on me to consider whether there was sufficient ground for excluding from the number of the new trustees the individuals who formed the body of the old trustees.

It is obvious that the Master only meant, that those who had
been the old trustees had been acting under such circumstances,
and in such a manner, as had (whether rightly or not) given rise
to the suspicion of their exercising their trust for party purposes;
and he thought it expedient, in selecting a body of new trustees,
[*304] *to appoint others who were not liable to suspicion, or to discussion, or invidious remark.   What is stated with respect to the
foundation for such a suspicion, I have on the best possible
evidence, that of Mr. Bignold's own affidavit, explaining another
which had been made on the other side.   I do not think that
there are any material discrepancies between the two affidavits.
It is stated, that the corporation, being the trustees of these
charities, divided the patronage among themselves, and that the
patronage was used, in fact, for the purposes of political party
and influence in Norwich; that the decision, or balance, was
always turned in favour of the person who happened to be of
the political party of the alderman whose turn it was to make
the appointment.   Anything more inconsistent with the objects
of the charities could not well be thought of.   Can any body say
that that is a proper administration of the charities?

Nothing could be more injurious, nothing more to be avoided,
than to stir again all the feelings of suspicion which had before
existed.

There the feeling exists: it may be, quite independently of
any really improper conduct on the part of the old trustees;
but if the Master were again to plunge the charities into all the
suspicion and contest which have heretofore prevailed, he would
very ill execute the duty he had to perform.   Seeing this to be
the case, I think the Master has done very wisely in endeavouring,
if possible, to deliver these charity funds from this party feeling
which has unhappily so much prevailed.   Against the individuals
appointed by the Master no case is made.   I think the Master
was not only perfectly justified in the course which he has
[*305] adopted, but that he would have acted extremely improperly, *if
he had not endeavoured to rescue the charity funds from this
liability to suspicion.

As to the other point raised by the cross-petition, I am asked
to vary the Master's report, by placing the Boys' and Girls'

Hospital under the care of a different set of trustees, from that under the care of which the Master has placed them.

The Master, in selecting new trustees, has, with my entire concurrence, whenever the charity was for church purposes, selected, as trustees, persons who were members of the Church of England. It has been thought proper, that when the object of the trust has been exclusively connected with one particular religious party, the trustees who were to have the control over it should be of the same religious party.

The question is, what are to be considered church purposes. When I look to this foundation, I can find nothing alluding to a church purpose; and I cannot hold, because I may have reason to suppose that Thomas Anguish, when he made his will in the year 1617, was a member of the Church of England, that, therefore, he intended that the only objects of his charities should be persons who belonged to the Church of England. He could easily have declared such an intention, if he entertained it.

His object was to found a hospital "for the keeping, bringing up, and teaching of young and very poor children that should not have friends to help them."

Mr. Blunt has very properly observed, that members of the corporation might then have been Dissenters.

The founder declared that he gave the premises to the intent, that if it should be thought convenient, the same, being large, spacious, and well built, and having many rooms therein, might, after the ten years, be employed for the placing a master and dame, or other teachers, to bring up children that should be very poor, and should not have friends to help them, from the age of five, six, or seven years, to fourteen or fifteen, to be taught in the meantime according to their disposition, as that they might be fitting for service, or able to maintain themselves by their work.

Then, having so established the school, he directs, that if neither the premises given by him should be found convenient, nor any other place be given for the purpose, the overplus of the rent, after paying for the repairs, should be applied for the helping and curing of poor distressed men, women, and children that should be hurt by falls or otherwise, or should be diseased and likely to be cured, as also for and towards the clothing of

[306]

poor children, and especially towards the helping and curing of
poor children that should not have friends to help them, and
that should be cut for the stone, or ruptured, as many had been,
and for placing persons that should be diseased and thought
incurable in the lazar-houses near the gates of the said city; and
this course to be continued, till a hospital should be founded for
the bringing up and keeping poor diseased children.

Now I am told that these charities have been confined exclusively to persons belonging to the Church of England. In order
to justify such an administration of the charities as this, it must
be found in the terms of the foundation. The royal charter,
which refers to the purposes for which the institution was

[*307] established by Mr. *Anguish, provides that the charity of the
Children's Hospital shall continue " in such sort as in the will of
the said Thomas Anguish was mentioned."

According to the terms of the charter, the mayor, sheriffs, &c.,
were " to maintain, educate, teach, and instruct in learning, set
on work, and otherwise dispose of as many such children as the
revenues would extend to, as to them should seem convenient."

There is nothing, then, in the charter, at all alluding to any
exclusive description of parties who were to share the benefits
of the charities; and all that can be said is, that there is a
subsequent gift or settlement of 13s. 4d. to be paid to a clergyman of the Church of England for catechising the children; and
that is, no doubt, highly beneficial; whatever the object of the
charity may be, as to confining it or not to a particular class;
for, if members of the Church of England send their children to
the school, it is very fit that they should be catechised by a
clergyman of their own church. That, however, is no reason
why I should infer that the original institution was intended to
be confined to the children of members of the Church of England.
It is quite impossible that any superadded gift can alter the
original purpose of the foundation. I am not called upon now
to lay down any rules for the future support and regulation of
the school. My principle has been, to confine the trustees to
members of the Church of England, where I found that the
foundation was exclusively confined to the purposes of the
Church of England. I do not find that here.

If I thought that there was any danger that the rules, which have for the time past been observed with respect *to this charity, were likely to be departed from, it might require more consideration; but when I find that out of twenty-one trustees who have been now selected, only four are not members of the Church of England, it is impossible to suppose that there is any real danger of altering the course of management and education which has heretofore prevailed.

If, on the other hand, I should say that the Master was wrong in appointing the four trustees who are not members of the Church of England, I could only come to that decision, upon the ground that I found something in the charter, or in the constitution of the charity, which would lead me to conclude that it was meant to be exclusively confined to the children of members of the Church of England; and I should then be, in fact, excluding all others from it.

For this there are no grounds; and as I am quite sure that, in confirming the Master's report, I incur no risk of altering the management of the charity, the petition must be

Dismissed with costs.

PHILLIPO v. MUNNINGS (1).
(2 My. & Cr. 309—315.)

1837.
March 16.

Lord
COTTENHAM
L.C.

[309]

A suit to make an executor account for a sum of money which had been bequeathed to him by his testator upon certain trusts, and which had been severed by the executor from the testator's personal estate, and the interest of which had, for a time, been applied upon the trusts of the will, is not a suit to recover a legacy, within the meaning of the Limitation Act (3 & 4 Will. IV. c. 27).

MATTHEW BUSCALL, of Fakenham, by his will, dated the 19th of October, 1785, amongst other bequests, gave the sum of 400l. to Edmund Buscall, upon trust to place the same out at interest upon real or Government securities, and to pay the interest and dividends to the testator's sister, Sarah Buscall, for her life; and after her decease, to pay and apply the interest and dividends, or so much thereof as should be necessary, for and towards the maintenance and education of John Buscall, son

(1) *In re Smith, Henderson-Roe* v. *Hitchins* (1889) 42 Ch. D. 302, 304, 58 L. J. Ch. 860, 61 L. T. 363.

of Matthew Buscall, of Fransham, until he should attain his age of twenty-four years; and then in trust, in case the testator's sister should then be dead, and if not, then, on her decease, to assign, transfer, and pay the legacy of 400*l.* and all interest then due and unapplied as aforesaid, and the securities on which the same should be invested, to John Buscall, to and for his own use. The testator bequeathed certain legacies in trust for Philip Buscall and James Buscall, and the plaintiffs, by their names of Sarah Buscall, Martha Buscall, and Ann Buscall, therein also described as the children of Matthew Buscall of Fransham. And the testator declared that if any of them, Philip Buscall, John Buscall, and James Buscall, Sarah Buscall, Martha Buscall, and Ann Buscall, should happen to die before his, her, or their legacy or legacies should become payable, then the legacy or legacies of him, her, or them so dying, and all interest, if any, then due thereon, and unapplied *for maintenance as aforesaid, should be equally divided and paid to and amongst the survivors and survivor of them, share and share alike, at such time and times as his, her, or their original legacy should become payable. And the testator appointed Edmund Buscall his executor.

[*310]

Sarah Buscall died in the testator's lifetime.

The testator died on the 31st of January, 1787, leaving Philip Buscall, John Buscall, James Buscall, and the plaintiffs, and Edmund Buscall surviving; and Edmund Buscall, shortly after the testator's decease, proved the will, and possessed the testator's personal estate, and paid all the debts and legacies, other than the legacy of 400*l.*, and set apart the sum of 400*l.* to answer that legacy. In the year 1799, Edmund Buscall died, having appointed the defendant, James Munnings, his executor, who proved his will.

The bill, which was filed on the 18th of August, 1834, stated that Philip Buscall died in the year 1797, and that John Buscall died in the year 1800, under the age of twenty-four years, leaving the plaintiffs, and James Buscall surviving him; and that James Buscall died in the year 1814, intestate, and without having been married, leaving the plaintiffs his only next of kin, and that they had commenced proceedings, and intended

forthwith to procure letters of administration to his effects. It
alleged, that the defendant had possessed himself of the 400*l.*,
or of the securities upon which that sum had been invested, and
that he had refused to pay it to the plaintiffs, but intended to
convert it to his own use : and it charged that he had received
the interest or dividends, and had converted them to his own
use. The bill prayed that it might be declared that the plaintiffs,
in their own right, and as the next of kin of James Buscall,
in the events which had happened, were beneficially *interested
in, or entitled to, the whole of the principal sum of 400*l.*, or the
stocks or funds or other the securities, if any, upon which the
same had been invested, and also the interest and dividends
accrued upon or in respect of the same ; and that the same
might be paid or transferred or accounted for by the defendant
to the plaintiffs ; and that the necessary accounts might be
taken ; that the defendant might be restrained, by injunction,
from parting with the 400*l.* or the securities upon which the
same had been invested ; and that that sum, or such securities,
and the arrears of interest and dividends received by the
defendant, might be paid or transferred into the name of the
Accountant-General, in trust in the cause.

The defendant, by his answer, stated and admitted that
Edmund Buscall, out of the personal estate of the testator
Matthew Buscall, paid all his debts and funeral and testamentary expenses, and all the legacies given by his will, except
the legacy of 400*l.*, and thereout set apart the sum of 400*l.*
given, in trust, for the purposes before mentioned, and invested
the same on mortgage, at 5 per cent. The defendant then
stated, that the sum of 400*l.*, so invested, remained upon that
security until about two years after the decease of Edmund
Buscall, when the mortgage was paid off ; and that the defendant
then invested the mortgage-money, in his own name, in the
purchase of the sum of 410*l.* Navy five per cent. Annuities : and
that in the year 1813 or 1814, the defendant sold out that stock,
and did not afterwards invest the produce, but retained it in his
own hands. The defendant admitted that he received the interest
on the mortgage, and the dividends on the sum of stock ; he
stated that certain payments had been made, by Edmund

Buscall and by himself, to a brother of John Buscall, on his
behalf, on account of the interest of the 400*l.*, the last of which
payments was made on the *1st of March, 1801, and of which
16*l.* had been paid by Edmund Buscall and 40*l.* by himself;
and that the dividends or interest received by him, (the defendant,) amounted to 246*l.*; or thereabouts, and that, under the
circumstances before mentioned, he had converted and applied
only such part of such dividends or interest to his own use, as
had not been paid over by him as therein-before stated.   The
defendant also stated that he believed it was a fact, that John
Buscall had never been heard of since the year 1800, except as
having died at or about that time ; and the defendant admitted
that he had never heard of him since that time.   The defendant
stated that he had not been able to ascertain whether John
Buscall attained the age of twenty-four years; but that he had
been informed and believed that Philip Buscall died in the lifetime of John Buscall, and about the year 1797, and that John
Buscall left James Buscall and the plaintiffs surviving him.
The defendant, by his answer, also claimed, in bar of the suit,
the same benefit of the Statute of Limitations, and of the *laches*
of the plaintiffs, in putting their claim in suit, as if he had
pleaded the same in bar to the bill.

The plaintiffs, after the filing of the original bill, procured
letters of administration to John Buscall and to James Buscall ;
and, by supplemental bill, they stated these administrations, and
insisted that all difficulty as to the time of the death of John
Buscall was removed by their obtaining administration to him.

Affidavits were subsequently made, which tended to prove
that John Buscall died in the month of January, 1800, under
the age of twenty-four ; and which showed that dividends to
the amount of 392*l.* 3*s.* 2*d.*, would have accrued, between the
year 1814 and the present time, upon the stock which had been
sold out and upon *the other stocks into which, if not so sold,
it would have been converted.

The VICE-CHANCELLOR, upon motion, supported by these
affidavits, ordered that the defendant should transfer into the
name of the Accountant-General, in trust in the cause, 430*l.* 10*s.*
New 3½ per cent. Annuities, being the amount which the sum

of 410*l.* Navy 5 per cent. Annuities, admitted by the defendant's
answer to have been sold out by him in the year 1818 or 1814,
would have produced if the same had not been sold out by him,
and had been standing in his name in the books of the Bank on
the conversion of Navy 5 per cent. Annuities into 4 per cent.
Annuities, and the subsequent conversion of the last mentioned
annuities into New 3½ per cent. Annuities; and that the defendant should pay into the Bank, with the privity of the
Accountant-General, to the credit of the cause, the sum of
598*l.* 3*s.* 2*d.* cash (1), subject to the further order of the Court.

The defendant now moved that the VICE-CHANCELLOR's order
might be discharged.

Mr. *Wigram* and Mr. *Rogers*, in support of the motion:

The fortieth section of the recent Statute of Limitations (2)
is a complete bar to the plaintiffs' demand in *this suit. * * *   [*314]

THE LORD CHANCELLOR (without calling on Mr. *Wakefield* and
      Mr. *Goodere*, who were counsel on the other side:)

A man, who, being in possession of a fund which he knows to
be not his own, thinks proper to sell it and apply the produce to
his own use, certainly does not come before the Court under
circumstances which entitle him to much indulgence; and the
only question is, whether, by the statute which has been referred
to, I am prohibited from entertaining this suit to make him
responsible for that breach of trust. The whole fallacy *of the   [*315]
defendant's argument consists in treating this suit as a suit for
a legacy. Now, the fund ceased to bear the character of a
legacy, as soon as it assumed the character of a trust fund.
Suppose the fund had been given by the will to any body else,
as a trustee, and not to the executor; it would then be clearly
the case of a breach of trust. In this case, the executor, when
he severed the legacy from the general personal estate, could

---

(1) This amount was produced by
adding the before-mentioned sum of
392*l.* 3*s.* 2*d.* to the sum of 206*l.*, which
last was the amount admitted to have
been received by the defendant for
dividends or interest, after deducting

therefrom the sums which he alleged
that he had paid on account of John
Buscall.

(2) 3 & 4 Will. IV. c. 27 [s. 40
rep. by 37 & 38 Vict. c. 57, s. 9.].

not pay it over to any other person; he was bound by the direction of the testator to hold it upon certain trusts until the legatee attained twenty-four. What he would have done by paying it to a trustee, he has done, by severing it from the testator's property, and appropriating it to the particular purpose pointed out by the will.

It is impossible to consider that the executor, so acting, is acting as an executor: he has all this while been acting as a trustee.

This suit must be considered, not as a suit for a legacy, but as a suit to compel a party to account for a breach of trust; and it is clear, therefore, that it is not within the terms of the Act in question.

Motion refused with costs.

1836.
Nov. 7, 12, 14.
15, 22, 25.

1837.
Feb. 17, 18, 24.

Lord
COTTENHAM,
L.C.

[316]

IN THE MATTER OF THE LUDLOW CHARITIES.
MR. LECHMERE CHARLTON'S CASE.
(2 My. & Cr. 316—361 (1).)

A barrister, who was also a Member of Parliament, appeared before a Master, as counsel in support of a petition presented by himself and others; and he afterwards addressed a letter to the Master, which was expressed in threatening terms, and the tendency of which was to induce the Master to alter the opinion he was supposed to have formed upon the case; and he subsequently wrote a letter to the Lord Chancellor, in which he avowed the authorship of the letter to the Master. The Lord Chancellor committed him to the Fleet, during pleasure.

IN this case, two petitions had been presented to the Lord Chancellor, under the seventy-first section of the Act 5 & 6 Will. IV. c. 76, for the regulation of municipal corporations, praying that proper persons might be appointed trustees of certain charities at Ludlow: and by an order made by the LORD CHANCELLOR upon both petitions, and bearing date the 20th of August, 1836, it was referred to the Master in attendance during the vacation, to appoint proper persons to be trustees of the charity estates and property, late vested in or under the administration of the corporation of Ludlow, or any of the members thereof in that character, which were affected by the seventy-first section of the Act of Parliament.

(1) *R.* v. *Castro* (1873) L. R. 9   [1900] 2 Q. B. 36, 69 L. J. Q. B.
Q. B. 219, 28 L. T. 222; *R.* v. *Gray,*   502.

Edmund Lechmere Charlton, Esquire, one of the Members of
Parliament for the borough of Ludlow, and a barrister, was one
of the petitioners by whom one of the petitions was presented;
and in the prosecution of the order, he attended as counsel, on
behalf of his co-petitioners and himself, before Master Brougham,
who sat for the vacation Master. After some proceedings had
been taken, both Master Brougham and Mr. Charlton left town,
and Mr. Charlton subsequently addressed to Master Brougham
the following letter:

"LUDFORD, 24th October, 1836.

" SIR,—I am informed by my solicitor, that the inclosed
memoranda appear on the statement of facts *submitted to you   [*317]
in the case of the Ludlow charities, which induced your clerk to
say, that he believed that the trustees were appointed. Permit
me to say, this is exceedingly unfair; nay more, it is practising
a deception on me that is unwarrantable, and which entitles me
to call on you for an explanation; in doing which, I hope I shall
not exceed the limits that are allowed to a gentleman who feels
himself to have been undeservedly aggrieved. As a mere barrister, advocating the cause of my clients, I question if I have
any right to dispute, in this stage of the business, your authority,
your law, or your decision, in a private communication, as there
is another tribunal open to me for appeal; but, in the present
case, I maintain that I am justified in adopting this mode of
proceeding, because you have in these notes that are ascribed to
you, either stated what is not true, or you have drawn conclusions
from my statements and affidavits, which are at variance with
the facts, and which, directly or indirectly, cast an imputation
on my character as an advocate, or as a gentleman. First, with
respect to the word 'settled,' I assert that the matter was not
settled, and I have your authority for saying it was not settled.
You told me, and I dare you to deny it, that if my reply would
take up a long time, you must defer it; and you must recollect
that it was only on this express understanding, that I refused
to depart without having your permission to take out another
warrant, which you allowed. With what propriety then, I ask,
did you write the word 'settled?' But let me remind you of
another circumstance. *Mr. Romilly* made a long speech to prove
that the estate derived from Edward the Sixth was for 'corporate'

MR. LECH-
MERE CHARL-
TON'S CASE.
as well as for 'charitable' purposes. Mr. Downes swore

[*318]

(* * * * * *) (1) that it was given for corporate purposes; but
not a proof, or the semblance of proof, was in evidence in support
of this *assertion, save and except a single sentence in the report
of the charity commissioners, which, so far from bearing out the
assertion of Mr. Downes and the logic of *Mr. Romilly*, proves, if
it proves anything, directly the reverse of what they would infer.
Well, when *Mr. Romilly* had done, and proposed his pure disinterested squad for trustees, did you not say 'Let us first go into
the question of the merits of the respective trustees proposed by
each side; after which you' (addressing yourself to me) 'will
have the opportunity of replying as to the proper disposal of
the estate in question?' That reply I have never had; it was
deferred at your own request, because you said you had no time
to hear it, if it would take up much time. With what propriety
or justice, then, do you say that the question at issue is 'settled?'
And now to your other memoranda. You assign two reasons for
not appointing any members of the old corporation, which, if
they are intelligible, (and it is really with some difficulty that I
make them out) are untrue. You say that the deeds, &c. were
deposited in the Ludlow bank, under the advice of *Mr. Serjeant
Merewether*, and that I admitted it to be true. I say I did no
such thing. Read the report in the *Times* newspaper, the reporter
of which was happily present to confirm the accuracy of my statements. *Mr. Serjeant Merewether* merely advised that the books and
deeds which related to the charity property should not be given to
the new council. It was the old corporation, in their capacity of
trustees, that deposited the property confided to their care in that
place that was most secure from any lawless violence that the
rabble may attempt. You next refer to my affidavit as the ground
on which you refuse to make any of the old corporators trustees,
which is unfair and unjust towards me. My affidavit goes to prove

[*319]

that the old corporators, as trustees of the charity *estate under the
Municipal Act, did no more than fulfil the trust reposed in them
without fear or favour; and I defy you to point out a passage
that impugns their past conduct or their eligibility for the future.
I now come to your 'addition.' You assert that the old corporation are 'in contempt.' This is not true; and I need only recal

(1) *Sic* in original report.

to your recollection what passed, to satisfy you that it is not true.　I stated that I was prepared in the first instance, to maintain, among other reasons to which I should advert, that they were not in contempt, because Mr. Downes, by adding what he had to your order without your permission, had weakened, if he had not destroyed, its effect.　I stated that I had in my possession affidavits from the parties concerned, which they had left to my discretion to produce or not to produce as I thought fit: and I was proceeding in my argument, when *Mr. Romilly* interrupted me, and remarked he would pass the subject over for the present; in reply to which I said, I would not agree to such an arrangement; that is, that he should pass it over altogether, or he should then proceed with the charge.　You then interposed and said, that it appeared better to pass it over altogether, as you understood that the business could proceed without the papers in question; and it was on this understanding, namely, that it should be passed over altogether, that the matter proceeded.　With what propriety then, I ask, do you assert that the old corporation are ' in contempt'?　It is, however, on these grounds that you say you have named none of the old corporators as the new trustees, when there is not a shadow of blame imputed to them in the affidavits; and in the inferences that you have drawn, you are wholly unsupported by facts.　And who is it that you propose to appoint in their places?　Every one of the persons recommended by the new council, to the number of ten, every one of *the persons supported by ' the well-beloved' hack of　[*320] * * * * (1) the *Attorney-General*, for party purposes; the majority of whom deny that the funds were given for charitable uses; the majority of whom have adopted every means that ingenuity could devise to prevent the rents from the charity estates being paid to the trustees; the majority of whom have used threats and menaces to procure the charity funds for their own benefit; the majority of whom have publicly declared that they only want these charity funds to pay off their own debts; the majority of whom, you yourself have in an authenticated paper declared, ' ought not to be appointed.'　Yes!　These are the persons that you have selected, together with seven others, (a palpable minority)

(1) *Sic* in original report.

to administer honestly and conscientiously the charity funds of this borough. These are the persons that you, as a wise and incorruptible Judge, presume to recommend for that important trust, giving the depredators (for so they are if they attempt to purloin the charity funds for their own benefit) a majority of ten to seven, when you will remember, and I dare you to deny it, that after I had urged the same argument against the council having any thing to do with these funds that I have now, that you yourself admitted that they were improper persons, and you asked me if I would be satisfied if you gave to the petitioners a majority over the council, in order to prevent such misapplication of the charity money that I anticipated. Such conduct, Sir, may be becoming enough in Master Brummagem, but in Master Brougham it is as unexpected as it is inexcusable. In order to make out something like a case to justify you, you have, if I am to understand that this decision of yours is conclusive, and is to be reported to the Chancellor, thrown all the blame on me, to which I will not submit. Far be it, however, from me to throw out, in this stage of the business, a threat to you in your capacity of a Judge. I *have too much respect for that high office, when it is held, as it ought to be, for the protection of its suitors, to be unmindful of my duty. All I ask is, that there should be a rehearing, and that you should set yourself right where you have been led into error. All I ask, in short, is, even-handed justice, in which case this letter shall never be made public, nor shall your serenity be again disturbed by any further remonstrance from
" Your obedient and very humble servant,
"E. L. CHARLTON.

[*321]

" P.S.—I shall be in London on the first day of Term, and shall wait for your answer at ' Fendall's Hotel,' Palace Yard.

" To WM. BROUGHAM, Esq."

The following are the inclosures to which the foregoing letter refers.

" Copy of notes written on the state of facts :

' Settled.

' Stated and admitted to be true, that the corporation being in debt to the Ludlow Bank, and feeling doubtful whether they ought to hand over the deeds and securities belonging to the corporation to the new council, deposited, under the advice of *Serjeant Merewether*, with the bank, who now claim a lien upon them; and also that there were important questions pending between the old trustees and the present town council. See also affidavit of Mr. Charlton respecting money borrowed by the late trustees from the same bankers, with whom deeds deposited : I think this makes it improper to appoint them new trustees. In addition to the objection to appoint any of the old trustees arising out of the above admission of Mr. Charlton, who appeared before me as counsel for the petitioners, Sankey and others, and also from what appears in the affidavit *of Mr. Charlton, [*322] it is to be observed, that the said petitioners are in contempt, inasmuch as they have refused to comply with my order to produce before me the deeds, books, papers, and writings relating to the estates and property of the charity in question ; I am therefore of opinion that in this case none of the old trustees ought to be appointed, and have accordingly selected some other names from the list proposed by the said petitioners, Sankey and others.

'30th Sept. 1836.   (Signed)   'W. BROUGHAM.'

' W. Edwards.	Wm. Felton.
J. Hutchens.	Wm. Jennings.
J. Smith.	H. Salway.
Wm. Tinson.	Sir E. Thomason.
Geo. Hooper.	J. G. Clay.
Joseph Sawyer.	Geo. Wellings.
Richard Marshall.	Jos. Cooper.
Richard Jones.	Thomas Childe.
Rd. Baugh.	

' The above seventeen names approved, subject to consent.

'30th Sept. 1836.   (Signed)   'W. B.'

'LUDLOW.—Stated that the estates under Edward the Sixth's Charity are solely for charitable purposes. *Query* whether, the corporation contending that this is corporate property, it is safe to appoint them ? Assuming that the whole is

MR. LECH-
MERE CHARL-
TON'S CASE.

applicable to charity, the present corporation ought not to be appointed.

'Richard Marston.   Sir E. Thomason.
Richard Jones.   J. G. Clay.
Geo. Wellings.   Jos. Cooper.'
Thomas Childe.

[*323]

"The above is not written on the state of facts, but on a separate sheet of paper ; but to it there is neither the *name nor the initials of Mr. Brougham, so that it stands for nothing."

Nov. 7.

At the sitting of the Court, on Monday the 7th of November, the LORD CHANCELLOR said :

I feel it my duty to state an occurrence in the office of one of the Masters of the Court, to which I have seen no parallel in the course of above thirty years' experience.

Master Brougham has put into my hands a letter received from a gentleman, who describes himself as a barrister, and as having attended the Master upon a reference made by an order of this Court.   I abstain, at present, from mentioning the name of the gentleman to whom I have alluded ; but I think it right to say it is not the name of any gentleman whom I am accustomed to see practising in this Court.   The letter states the proceedings in the Master's Office ; and, after complaining of an opinion which the Master is supposed to have formed—not stating any report, but, on the contrary, that the case is still pending—and after using expressions in the letter which no gentleman could permit to be used towards himself, and pro-ceeding in terms which I at present abstain from characterising, and throwing out insinuations of the most calumnious nature, concludes with a direct threat, the object of which is to induce the Master to alter the opinion he was supposed to have formed, and to come to a conclusion favourable to the case advocated by the writer of the letter ; and the writer then adds, that he shall be in London on the first day of Term, and shall wait for the Master's answer at the place which he mentions.

[324]

It is quite obvious what course the Master should have pursued.   He should have referred the letter at once to the Court.   It appears, however, that the Master adopted a course which I cannot approve. He put the letter into the hands of a friend. That friend doubted whether he could permit the matter to proceed in a hostile manner, and consulted with another gentleman of high rank and character. They both agreed that it was impossible the matter should proceed in that course, and that the Master could not treat it as a personal quarrel ; but that it being a letter, addressed to him in the exercise of his judicial functions, it should be referred to me. It is impossible not to disapprove of the course the Master took in the first instance : for it is quite obvious, that if the Masters are to take up such matters as personal quarrels, not only do they put themselves at the mercy of those who might wish to attain their ends by any means, but there may arise an influence of a private or personal nature, which cannot but interfere materially with the due administration of the law ; and I, therefore, entirely approve of the advice which the Master has received, to place the case before the Court.

It remains for me to consider what course I ought to adopt. It is obvious, that if the Masters are not to consider matters of this kind in the light of personal quarrels, it is the duty of the Court to throw its protection round them. What I have said, however, has been necessarily said in the absence of the party whose name was subscribed to the letter ; and, indeed, I have no judicial knowledge that it was written by him.

A case of this nature has never occurred within my knowledge. It has often occurred that letters have been improperly addressed to Judges, sometimes from *ignorance, and sometimes from [*325] improper motives, with reference to matters pending before them ; but never before, that I have known, in such insulting language, and in absolute threats. In all those cases, the practice has been adopted, of handing over the letter to the opposite side. I propose, therefore, in this instance, to direct, that as many copies should be made of this letter as there were parties before the Master upon the inquiry in question, and that each party should be furnished with a copy. The course which the parties may take, may render it unnecessary for me to adopt any further measures. Let the further consideration of this matter be adjourned to Saturday next.

MR. LECH-
MERE CHARL-
TON'S CASE.
On the 9th of November, 1836, Mr. Lechmere Charlton addressed the following letter to the Lord Chancellor:

" FENDALL'S HOTEL, Palace Yard,

9th November, 1836.

" MY LORD,

" By the report in the *Times* newspaper of yesterday, of the proceedings in Chancery on the preceding day, I am given to understand that your Lordship says that you have 'no legal knowledge' that a certain letter of the 24th of October, signed with my name, and dated from my residence, to Master Brougham, respecting his conduct in the matter of the charity trusts of Ludlow, was written by me. I am uncertain, therefore, whether this letter will throw any additional light on the subject; but the motive I have in writing it is, to avow the authorship, and to say, with all becoming respect, that I shall not shrink from the responsibility."

[The letter then recapitulated at length the opinions which the writer had expressed in his letter to Master Brougham, and concluded as follows:]

[331]
" Towards Master Brougham I freely declare that I harbour no sort of ill-will; it is of his judicial conduct alone that I complained, and which I hope would have been corrected. If I had been in any way misinformed respecting the accuracy of his notes, or if, in my zeal for the object that I had at heart, I had done anything unbecoming a man of honour, or lowered, in the slightest degree, the high functions of the judicial character, which it has been the object of my life to venerate and uphold, I should have been willing to make any atonement that a gentleman can; but if, on the contrary, I have, by my conduct, attempted to preserve the dignity and sanctity of the office, by resisting, as became me, the abuse of power, I glory in what I
[*332]
have done, and will willingly brave your Lordship's *authority before I will retract or apologise for a syllable that I have written.

" I have, &c.

" E. L. CHARLTON.

" The Lord High Chancellor,
    &c. &c. &c."

[An order was made by the LORD CHANCELLOR on the 15th day of November, 1836, requiring Mr. Charlton to show cause why he should not be committed for contempt and] ·

At the sitting of the Court on Friday, the 25th of November, the Registrar having, by the LORD CHANCELLOR'S order, called on "the Matter of the Ludlow Charities" three successive times, and no person appearing,

THE LORD CHANCELLOR [after stating the circumstances of the case and reading the letters, said :]

It is quite unnecessary to advert to the letters themselves. Every gentleman, at all acquainted with the proceedings in this Court, must obviously see that they contain a most gross and aggravated contempt of Court ; a gross contempt in the first instance, and very much aggravated by the letter to myself, which is not only itself a contempt of Court, but it shows that after the *writer's attention had been called to the expressions used in his letter to the Master, and after he had had time for reflection, he had deliberately determined to adhere to the terms of that letter : and he added, in his letter to me, expressions which were, in themselves, a serious contempt of this Court.

The power of committal is given to courts of justice, for the purpose of securing the better and more secure administration of justice. Every writing, letter, or publication which has for its object to divert the course of justice is a contempt of the Court. It is for that reason that publications of proceedings which have already taken place, when made with a view of influencing the ultimate result of the cause, have been deemed contempts. It would be strange, indeed, if the Judges of the Court were the only persons not protected from libels, writings, and proceedings, the direct object of which is to pervert the course of justice. Every insult offered to a Judge, in the exercise of the duties of his office, is a contempt ; but when the writing or publication proceeds farther, and when, not by inference, but by plain and direct language, a threat is used, the object of which is to induce a judicial officer to depart from the course of his judicial duty, and to adopt a course he would not otherwise pursue, it is a contempt of the very highest order. The writer of these letters supposes Master Brougham to have finally made his report, and that from that report there was no appeal ; and the avowed object of the letter to the Master, is to induce him to alter his decision in the absence of the opposite party, by holding out threats, and concluding by saying, that if the Master would depart from the decision to which he was supposed to have come, and come to one directly opposite, then that letter should never be made public, and the Master should not be disturbed by

[*340] any further *remonstrance from the writer. This is intelligible language, which no one can misunderstand.

[After referring to *Pool* v. *Sacheverel* (1), an *Anonymous* case before Lord Hardwicke (2), and other cases, his Lordship said :]

[342] All these authorities tend to the same point ; they show that it is immaterial what measures are adopted, if the object is to taint the source of justice, and to obtain a result of legal proceedings different from that which would follow in the ordinary course. It is a contempt of the highest order : and although such a foolish attempt as this cannot be supposed to have any effect, it is obvious that if such cases were not punished, the most serious consequences might follow. If I consulted my own personal feelings upon the subject, I should pass by these letters as a foolish attempt at undue influence ; but if I were to adopt that course, I should consider myself guilty of a very great dereliction of my high duty. The order must therefore be made absolute for the committal of Mr. Lechmere Charlton to the Fleet.

[It is not considered necessary to reprint the form of the committal order which is given in the original report.]

Nov. 26.   The LORD CHANCELLOR, on the 26th of November, issued a
[344]   warrant, addressed to the Warden of the Fleet prison, or his deputy attending the Court of Chancery, which, after reciting the order of the 25th of November, required him to search for and apprehend Mr. Charlton, and carry him to the Fleet prison, there to remain until the LORD CHANCELLOR's further order.

1837.   Mr. Lechmere Charlton evaded the execution of the warrant, until the 3rd of February, 1837, when he was taken, and

(1) 1 P. Wms. 675.   (2) 2 Ves. Sen. 520.

conveyed to the Fleet. In the meantime, however, Parliament
met on the 31st of January, and the LORD CHANCELLOR, on that
day, addressed the following letter to the Speaker :

" 31st January, 1837.

" MR. SPEAKER,

" I have the honour of making known to you, for the information of the House of Commons, that I issued my warrant on
the 26th of November last, for the commitment *of Edmund   [.*315]
Lechmere Charlton, Esq., one of the Members for the borough
of Ludlow, for a contempt of the High Court of Chancery, in
writing and sending a certain letter, dated the 24th of October
last, to William Brougham, Esq., one of the Masters of the
Court ; which was followed by a certain other letter, dated
the 9th of November last, addressed to myself. I have thought
it right to make this communication, for the purpose of
accounting for the probable absence of the Honourable Member,
and of testifying my profound respect for the Honourable House.

" I have the honour to be, Sir,

" Your most obedient servant,

" COTTENHAM."

On the same day Mr. Charlton wrote to the Speaker, as
follows :
" FENDALL'S HOTEL, Palace Yard,
" 31st January, 1837.

" SIR,

" I have just reason to believe that Mr. William Pell (who
is a messenger in the Court of Chancery) and others employed
by him, are determined, under the directions of the Lord
Chancellor, to interrupt me in my progress to the House of
Commons this day, and I humbly request, therefore, as I am
thereby deterred from attending, that you will vouchsafe to
extend to me your protection.

" I seek not to withdraw myself from the criminal jurisdiction
of the realm, well knowing that privilege of Parliament, which
is allowed in cases of public service for the commonwealth, must
not be used to the danger of the commonwealth.

" To be protected, however, from ' any violence of the Crown   [346]
or its ministers,' is, I apprehend, the established and undoubted

privilege of a Member of Parliament.   To this hour, I know not
of what I am accused, except from public report; but, nevertheless, I ask for no more than to be allowed, without molestation,
to take my seat, that I may state what I do know of the matter
to the House, and then bow, with respect, to their decision, be it
what it may.

> " I have the honour to be, Sir,
>> " Your obedient humble servant,
>>> " E. L. CHARLTON.

" To the Right Honourable
  The Speaker."

On the 1st of February, a Committee of Privileges was
appointed by the House of Commons, by whom the letters to
the Speaker from the Lord Chancellor and Mr. Lechmere
Charlton were referred to the Committee.

On the 3rd of February, Mr. Charlton, having been apprehended, sent the following letter to the Speaker :

" SIR,

"I have the honour to inform you, that persons stating that
they have a warrant from the Lord Chancellor, have forced their
way into the house in which I am staying, and have compelled
me to go to the Fleet prison with them.

"I had flattered myself that while the matter was under
the consideration of a Committee of Privileges, such violent
proceedings as these would have been avoided ; but I am sorry
to say I am mistaken.

[347]   "I have only to add that I hope you will be so good as to read
this letter to the House, and that they will extend to me the
privilege that under similar cases has been given to Members of
Parliament.

> " I have, &c.
>> " E. L. CHARLTON.

" Friday evening, half past five o'clock.
" To the Right Honourable the Speaker."

On the 16th of February, the Committee, after having
examined Mr. Lechmere Charlton, and several witnesses, made
the following report to the House :

"In reporting upon the question which has been referred

to your Committee, they propose to follow the course which usually has been adopted upon such occasions, of first stating the circumstances of the particular case, and afterwards the law and usages of Parliament as it appears to apply to them.

" The warrant for Mr. Charlton's commitment to the Fleet, and the order of Court on which it was founded, were produced to the Committee, and it appeared that he was committed by the LORD CHANCELLOR for writing a letter, addressed to William Brougham, Esquire, one of the Masters of the High Court of Chancery, containing matter scandalous with respect to the said Master, and an attempt improperly to influence his conduct in the matter pending before him, ' which the said Lord Chancellor deemed to be a contempt of the Court of Chancery.' The order not proceeding to set forth the letter in question, or to specify the parts of it on which these charges were grounded, your Committee therefore directed the letter to be produced, inasmuch as they considered, that although the LORD CHANCELLOR had the power to declare what he deemed *to be a contempt of the High Court of Chancery, it was [*348] necessary that the House of Commons, as the sole and exclusive judge of its own privileges, should be informed of the particulars of the contempt, before they could decide whether the contempt was of such a character as would justify the imprisonment of a Member. They also summoned Mr. Charlton before them, and afforded him an opportunity of fully stating his case.

" Upon the whole examination, the letter appears to your Committee to be expressed in an intemperate and improper manner. The letter, however, was occasioned by information derived from the solicitor in the cause, the correctness of which Mr. Charlton had no reason to doubt; but they are of opinion that it is offensive to the Master, and thereby to the authority of the Court under which he acted, and was an attempt improperly to influence his conduct in the matter pending before him, with a view to obtain a further hearing, to which, if applied for in a proper manner, Mr. Charlton would have been entitled.

" It was found, in the course of the investigation, that Mr. Joseph Parkes, the solicitor for the parties who appeared before the Master in opposition to Mr. Charlton's clients, had, during the interval which occurred between the issue of the warrant and its execution, written a letter, at the request of a third person, containing the following assurance, 'Mr. Charlton may take my honour, and I have never yet violated it, that he is perfectly secure in coming to my house to see if we can adjust the Ludlow matters,' and that Mr. Charlton did afterwards, in consequence, attend a meeting at the house of Mr. Parkes, without any interruption, or attempt to execute the

[*349] warrant by the *officers who held it. Your Committee therefore felt it necessary to ascertain whether the execution of a process issued on the ground of punishing a contempt of the Court of Chancery, had in any manner been allowed to be enforced or suspended at the discretion of one of the litigant parties, or to be rendered subservient to his objects. This inquiry has tended considerably to lengthen their proceedings, but the result has satisfied them that no power had ever been given by any person, or exercised by the solicitor for that purpose.

"Upon the law and usage of Parliament, as affecting this case, your Committee beg leave to refer to the statement contained in the report of the Committee of Privileges on the case of the Honourable William Long Wellesley, presented to the House on the 26th of July, 1831, the precedents cited in which they will not here repeat.

"The Committee are deeply impressed with the difficulty and importance of the question referred to them, in the absence of authorities to which they can refer as clearly in point and directly bearing on this particular case. It will be seen, from the early cases, that the ancient definition of privilege of Parliament, is, that it belongs to every Member of the House, except in cases of treason, felony, or refusing to give surety of the peace. These exceptions, by the statement of the Commons in 1641, are further extended to all indictable offences; by their resolution in 1697, to forcible entries and detainers; and, in 1763, in conformity with the principle of the declaration of 1641, and of a subsequent resolution in 1675, to printing and publishing seditious libels; to which may be added the resolution of the Lords in 1757, that privilege shall not protect Peers against process to enforce the *habeas corpus*.

" The ordinary process for contempts against persons having privilege of Parliament or of peerage, has not been that of attachment of the person, but that of sequestration of the whole property, which has been found sufficient to vindicate the authority of the Courts, even in cases of some aggravation.

" It is stated by Blackstone, that 'contempts committed even by Peers, when enormous and accompanied with violence, such as forcible rescous and the like, or when they import disobedience to the King's writs of prohibition, *habeas corpus*, and the rest, are punishable by attachment;' and the same doctrine has, on different occasions, been expressed by other writers, and by Judges of high authority.

" The only cases, however, in which attachments have been found by the Committee to have been actually issued against privileged persons, are that of Earl Ferrers, by the King's Bench, and that of Mr. Long Wellesley, by the Court of Chancery, already referred to. The former was a case of disobedience to a writ of *habeas corpus*, to which, while the discussion was pending, it had been declared, by the House of Lords, privilege of Parliament did not extend; the other was that of the forcible removal of a ward of the Court of Chancery, and placing her out of the jurisdiction of the Court, which obviously could only be checked by the most prompt and efficacious remedy.

" Since the sitting of the last Committee of Privileges, the Act of 2 & 3 Will. IV. c. 93, intituled, 'An Act for enforcing the Process upon Contempts in the Courts Ecclesiastical of England and Ireland,' has passed, by which contempts of the Ecclesiastical Courts, 'in face of the Court, or any other contempt towards such Court, or *the process thereof, are directed to be signified to the Lord Chancellor, who is to issue a writ *de contumace capiendo*, for taking into custody persons charged with such contempt,' in case such person 'shall not be a Peer, Lord of Parliament, or Member of the House of Commons.'

[*351]

" Under all the circumstances of the case, your Committee are of opinion that Mr. Charlton's claim to be discharged from imprisonment, by reason of privilege of Parliament, ought not to be admitted.

" 16th February, 1837."

On the 17th of February, *Sir Charles Wetherell*, on behalf of
Mr. Charlton, informed the Lord Chancellor of the decision of
the Committee of Privileges, and applied to his Lordship for an
order for Mr. Charlton's appearance at the rising of the Court.
The LORD CHANCELLOR said, that the matter must be brought
before him by petition in the usual way.

On Saturday, the 18th of February, 1837, Mr. Charlton presented a petition to the Lord Chancellor, stating that neither
the order of the 25th of November, nor the orders of the 15th
and 22nd of November were ever personally served upon him,
and that he was induced to abstain from appearing in Court, in
pursuance of those orders, from the consideration that it was
his duty, as a Member of the Legislature, so to do, and that he
should otherwise compromise the privileges of the Members of
the House of Commons, and not from any feeling of disrespect
entertained by him towards the Court, and that he was actuated
by the same motives in avoiding the execution of the warrant
until the meeting of Parliament. The petition then stated the
[*352]   report *of the Committee of Privileges, and went on to state,
that the petitioner's object, in addressing the letter to the
Master, was solely with the view of obtaining from him a further
hearing of the matter, and that he had no intention of expressing
himself offensively towards the Master, or of endeavouring to
influence his conduct in the matter pending before him, or
of bringing into contempt the authority of the Court; and
that, although he was betrayed into intemperate and improper
expressions towards the Master, they arose entirely from an
anxiety on his part to protect the interests of the persons on
whose behalf he appeared before the Master, and which, from
the information he had received, he had every reason to believe
had not been properly attended to; and that the petitioner
regretted, and was sorry for having made use of any expressions
which could be considered as offensive to the Master or disrespectful towards the Court. The petition prayed that the
petitioner might be forthwith discharged out of custody.

Sir Charles Wetherell, who appeared in support of the petition,
took occasion to say, that if he had been consulted by Mr. Charlton

at the proper time, he should have advised him to dispute
the validity of the order, by raising the question, whether the
LORD CHANCELLOR had power to delegate to the Master the
appointment of new trustees under the Municipal Corporations
Regulation Act; and whether, consequently, the letter written
to the Master was a contempt of the Court.

THE LORD CHANCELLOR [after referring to the circumstances of
   the case, and after pointing out that the petition contained no
   expression of regret by the petitioner for his conduct, said :]

I say nothing as to the time which may be considered as the   [357]
proper period for the expiation of the offence which has been
committed.   Bound as I am to protect the administration of
justice in this Court, and bound, therefore, to hold out to all
parties who have any transactions in this Court, that they
cannot with impunity be guilty of that offence for which, by my
order, this gentleman has been committed to prison, I should
feel I was not doing my duty, if, on such a petition, I should
order his discharge. If he came before me with a petition
differently expressed, and treating the matter in a mode very
different from that in which he has treated it in this petition,
I say nothing as to the time when I might feel myself justified
in ordering his discharge; but I am bound to vindicate the
authority of the Court; and, therefore, to take care that a party
who offends against its jurisdiction and its dignity, is not to be
discharged on the mere asking for it, without even having the
grace to acknowledge the offence of which he has been adjudged
to be convicted; but yet, without calling in question the propriety
of the order, or disputing the judgment so passed upon him.

I wish it be understood that I say nothing as to the time.
If the time had been much longer than it is at present, the
language of this petition, and the submission found in it, are
not such as this Court has a right to expect.

Another petition was afterwards presented by Mr. Charlton,   *Feb.* 24.
which was couched in precisely the same terms as his former   [358]
petition, down to and including the statements of the report of
the Committee of Privileges; but in which the petitioner added,
that his object in addressing the letter to the Master, was solely

with the view of obtaining from him a further hearing of the matter; and that this motive arose entirely from an anxiety on his part to protect the interests of the persons on whose behalf he appeared before the Master, and which, from the information he had received, he had every reason to believe, had not been properly attended to; and that he regretted and was sorry that under such feelings, and without any intention to commit a contempt of the Court, he should have written and sent a letter to the Master which had been adjudged by the Lord Chancellor to contain matter scandalous with respect to the Master, and an attempt improperly to influence his conduct or judgment in the matter pending before him; or which, in its tenor or language, might be considered as offensive to the Master, or disrespectful to the Court; and that the regret so expressed by the present petition was intended, by the petitioner, to be the import of the expressions set forth in the petition lately presented by him.   The petitioner concluded by praying that he might be forthwith discharged.

Sir C. Wetherell, in support of the petition.

THE LORD CHANCELLOR:

The ground of the order for commitment has been questioned, neither by any application to show cause against the order, which, in the first place, was an order *nisi*, nor by any application to discharge it by reason of its having proceeded on a mistaken or unfounded ground; and Mr. Charlton states that
[*359]
another tribunal, *with which this Court has no connexion, but before which he states that his case has been investigated, has also come to the same conclusion as to the nature and character of that letter.   Mr. Charlton, in the petition which he presented last week, confined his contrition to that which constitutes the smallest part of the offence, namely, having used expressions offensive to the Master and disrespectful to the Court; thus challenging, in his petition, the main ground on which the order for his commitment proceeded, namely, his having attempted, by writing the letter, to influence the conduct of the Master.   This Court will never permit the propriety of its orders to be in that way questioned.   If a party chooses to come before the Court for the purpose of drawing in question

the propriety of an order, he must do it in the regular form;
but while he is a prisoner, for having violated his duty towards
the Court, and committed a contempt, the Court will not permit
him to challenge the authority of the Court or dispute the
grounds of the commitment: that is not the mode in which
the Court will permit a complaint to be made of its proceedings.
Mr. Charlton has now been in prison nearly a week beyond the
time when that petition was before me, and he has now varied
the grounds on which he asks for his discharge.   He says that
his object in addressing the letter to the Master was solely with
a view of obtaining from him a further hearing of the matter,
and that that motive arose entirely from an anxiety on his part
to protect the interests of the persons on whose behalf he
appeared before the Master, and which, from the information
he had received, he had every reason to believe had not been
properly attended to.   Now, it is not inconsistent with these
terms, that the object was to obtain a rehearing, and that the
object of the rehearing was to induce the Master to come to a
decision directly the reverse of *that to which, as appears by   [*360]
that letter, the writer of it supposed the Master to have come.   The
petition then states that the petitioner regrets, and is sorry that,
under such feelings—and, not without any intention to induce the
Master to alter his opinion—but without an intention to commit
a contempt of the Court, he should have written and sent a letter
to the Master which has been adjudged by the Court to contain
matter scandalous with respect to the Master, and an attempt
improperly to influence his conduct or judgment in the matter
pending before him, or which, in its tenor or language, might be
considered as offensive to the Master, or disrespectful to the Court.

Now I do not find in the language of this petition any thing
which, directly, at least, challenges the authority of the Court,
or the propriety of the order which the Court issued.   The
petitioner says that his object was to obtain a rehearing; but it
is quite clear that his object, in obtaining that rehearing, was to
induce the Master to come to a decision contrary to that to which
the writer supposed he had come.   He says the act was done
without an intention to commit a contempt of the Court; but it
is not denied that it was done with an intention to induce

MR. LECH-
MERE CHARL-
TON'S CASE.

the Master, by threats and intimidation, to come to a decision contrary to that which the petitioner supposed he had expressed.

I do not find that this petition contains that challenge of the authority of the Court, or of the propriety of the order, which is found in the former petition; and although the Court might have had reason to expect a more ample submission than that which is found in this petition, yet I do not think it inconsistent with my duty to receive this petition as an expression of contrition for the offence which the petitioner has committed.

[361]

I, therefore, now order the discharge of Mr. Charlton. He has been in prison three weeks; and I feel satisfied that what has taken place will convince all persons that no station, no rank in life, no position in which the party may stand before this Court, will justify or enable any person to commit a similar offence with impunity.

I now make the order for Mr. Charlton's discharge in the usual way.

1837.
April 6, 7, 8.

Lord
COTTENHAM,
L.C.
[361]

REED *v.* NORRIS.

(2 My. & Cr. 361—376; S. C. 6 L. J. (N. S.) Ch. 197; 1 Jur. 233.)

A surety who compounds a debt for which his principal and himself have become jointly liable, and takes an assignment of that debt to a trustee for himself, can only claim, against his principal, the amount which he has actually paid.

* * RICHARD BEVAN the elder, being indebted to Lord Vernon, in the sum of 500*l.*, prevailed upon his son, Richard Bevan the younger, to join him, as his surety, in a bond to Lord Vernon in the penal sum of 1,000*l.*, dated *the 24th of August, 1801, and conditioned to be void upon payment of 500*l.* and interest. * * *

[*362]

Richard Bevan the younger, by his will, dated the 13th of March, 1806, [appointed his wife his executrix. He died, without issue, on the 1st of January, 1815, and his wife proved his will. She died on the 23rd of December, 1828, having appointed the defendant John Norris her executor, who subsequently proved her will, and thus became the personal representative of Richard Bevan the younger. After the death of Elizabeth Bevan, Elizabeth Drayton Smith entered into possession of the real

estates devised by Richard Bevan the younger as residuary
devisee under his will.]

In the meantime, Richard Bevan the elder died on the 8th of
February, 1818; having, by his will, appointed John Bevan
and Thomas Davies his executors. Thomas Davies died in his
lifetime, and John Bevan renounced probate; and letters of
administration, with the will annexed, were subsequently granted
to the plaintiff, Richard Bevan Reed. * * *

On the 19th of January, 1828, the personal representatives of
Lord Vernon filed a bill in Chancery against R. B. Reed and
Elizabeth Bevan, as the personal representatives of R. Bevan the
elder and R. Bevan the younger, respectively, stating the bond for
500l., and praying the usual accounts of the personal estate of
R. Bevan the elder and R. Bevan the younger, and praying payment of what was due to Lord Vernon's estate for principal and
interest upon that bond. This last-mentioned suit, having become
abated by Elizabeth Bevan's death, was afterwards revived
against John Norris as her personal representative, and subsequently came on to be heard, on the 22nd of June, 1830, before
the Master of the Rolls, when a decree was made, declaring that
the plaintiffs, as executors of Lord Vernon, were creditors, by
the bond of 1801, of R. Bevan the elder and R. Bevan the
younger, for the sum of 500l. and interest from the 24th of
August, 1813; and directing that the usual accounts should be
taken of the personal estate of R. Bevan the elder and R. Bevan
the younger; and that their personal estates should be applied
in payment of their debts and funeral expenses, and that the
residue should be paid into the Bank, in trust in the cause.
John Norris, who did not appear to have himself received any
part of the personal estate of R. Bevan the younger, nevertheless,
passed his accounts under this decree, and paid into Court the
balance reported to be due from him, being the amount which
Elizabeth Bevan had received in her life time. R. B. Reed also
passed *his accounts, but he did not pay in the balance reported
to be due from him; and part of that balance was afterwards
levied by means of a sequestration against him. * * The whole
of the personal estate paid into Court under the last-mentioned
decree, was absorbed in payment of costs; and Lord Vernon's

executors then filed a supplemental bill, for the purpose of
making the real estates of R. Bevan the elder and R. Bevan the
younger answerable for the amount due upon the bond for 500*l.*

[By an indenture, dated the 5th of September, 1835, made
between the surviving executors of Lord Vernon of the first part,
the representative of a deceased executor of the second part,
John Norris and Elizabeth D. Smith of the third part, and

[366]   Henry Jeremy of the fourth part;] after reciting that the sum
of 949*l.* 6*s.* 1*d.* was due for principal and interest upon the bond
for 500*l.*; and that the sum of 198*l.* 6*s.* 6*d.*, or thereabouts, was
claimed by the executors of Lord Vernon for costs incurred in
their suit, beyond the costs already paid; and reciting that
Lord Vernon's executors had contracted and agreed with John
Norris and Elizabeth D. Smith for the absolute sale to them of
the bond debt of 500*l.*, and of all interest then due or thereafter
to become due in respect thereof, and of all benefit and advantage which might thenceforth be derived from the suit instituted
by them, for enforcing payment of the principal sum of 500*l.*
and interest, and the further costs so incurred as before mentioned, and all further costs of the suit, with full power to
prosecute such suit, at the price or sum of 600*l.*, which had been
agreed to be advanced in the following proportions, viz., 400*l.*
by John Norris, and 200*l.* by Elizabeth D. Smith; it was
witnessed, that in consideration of the sum of 600*l.* paid by
John Norris and Elizabeth D. Smith in the proportions before
mentioned, Lord Vernon's executors bargained, sold, and
assigned to Henry Jeremy, the bond debt or principal sum of
500*l.*, so due as before mentioned, and also certain sums therein
mentioned to be due for interest, amounting to 449*l.* 6*s.* 1*d.*, and
all other interest then due and thereafter to grow due; and all
costs then due to the assignors, or which they might claim in
respect of their suit, and all benefit of that suit; to hold the
same in trust for John Norris and Elizabeth D. Smith as tenants
in common, in the same proportions as those in which the
purchase money of 600*l.* had been contributed by them as before
mentioned; and Lord Vernon's executors constituted H. Jeremy,
John Norris and Elizabeth D. Smith, jointly and severally, their
attornies and attorney, for the recovery of the sums assigned.

The plaintiff, R. B. Reed, then filed a bill against Norris, Elizabeth D. Smith, and Jeremy, stating this assignment, [and praying] that it might be declared that the defendants were not entitled, as against the plaintiff, or as against the estate either of R. Bevan the elder, or of R. Bevan the younger, to be allowed, in respect of the bond for 500*l*., more than they had so paid to Lord Vernon's executors.   *   *   *

The answers of the defendants Norris and Smith to this bill, submitted that they were entitled to stand in the place of Lord Vernon's executors, and to have, against the estate of R. Bevan the elder, the same right to be paid or allowed the whole principal and interest due on the bond for 500*l*., and all costs of suit, as Lord Vernon's executors would have had, in case the assignment had not been made; and further, that the estate of R. Bevan the elder ought to make good to the estate of R. Bevan the younger, all costs which had been incurred by that estate, in the suit of Lord Vernon's executors, and all costs which might be incurred by that estate or by the defendants Norris and Smith in respect of the bond for 500*l*. and interest.

The [cause] now came on to be heard.

Mr. Wigram and *Mr. Teed*, for the plaintiff, [cited *Ex parte Rushforth* (1) and *Butcher* v. *Churchill* (2).

Mr. Wakefield and *Mr. Lovat*, for the defendant John Norris:

*   *   The defendants Norris and Miss Smith purchased the debt due to Lord Vernon's executors on the bond for 500*l*., with their own proper monies. They did not make that purchase as sureties. Norris never stood in any fiduciary relation to Richard Bevan the younger. *He merely became, by operation of law, his legal personal representative, because he was the executor of Elizabeth Bevan. No personal estate of R. Bevan the younger ever came to his hands, and all that which came to the hands of Elizabeth Bevan, and was unapplied by her in her lifetime, has been paid into Court by Norris, as her executor.   *   *   *

(1) 8 R. R. 10, see p. 15 (10 Ves. 409. 420).

(2) 14 Ves. 567, where a surety for a bond who had paid the debt was allowed to claim both debt and subsequent interest to the extent of the penalty of the bond as against the estate of the principal bond debtor.

[371]

Mr. Richards and *Mr. Puller*, for the defendant Elizabeth
Drayton Smith:

* * If an incumbrancer pays off a prior incumbrance at
less than the full amount, and takes an assignment of that prior
incumbrance, he has the same title to claim the full amount
against the estate, as the person whose charge he has paid off;
and what difference is there between such a case, and the
purchase, by a surety, of the debt of his principal? There are
cases, certainly, in which a person standing in a fiduciary character cannot purchase; but it is impossible to say that the
surety in the present case stands in a fiduciary character as
regards the debtor. Miss Smith does not represent the debtor,
except as she takes his real estate, subject to the debt. *Ex parte
Rushforth* was a case in bankruptcy; but it does not follow from
that case, that, as against the bankrupt himself, the surety
would not be entitled to the full amount. In *Butcher* v. *Churchill*
the question was not raised.

Mr. Wigram, in reply:

The contract between principal and surety is a contract for
indemnity merely; and a surety cannot act also as a stranger,
for the purpose of acquiring an additional right against his
principal. The defendants Norris and Smith made use of their
position as executor and devisee to induce Lord Vernon's
executors to compound the debt, by telling them that the estate
of the surety was insufficient to pay it.

April 8.

THE LORD CHANCELLOR [after deciding a question which is not
material for the purpose of this report, said:]

[374]

The other question is, how far the representatives of the son,
the surety, having come to an arrangement with Lord Vernon's
executors, by which the bond for 500*l*. has been got rid of and
discharged, are entitled, as against the father's estate, to demand
more than they have actually paid to Lord Vernon's executors
in exoneration of the liability of the son's estate upon the bond
for 500*l*.

Now, if there had been no authority upon this subject, I
should have found very little difficulty in making a precedent

for deciding that, under these circumstances, the surety is not entitled to demand more than he has actually paid. I take the case of an agent. Why is an agent precluded from taking the benefit of purchasing a debt which his principal was liable to discharge? Because it is his duty, on behalf of his employer, to settle the debt upon the best terms he can obtain; and if he is employed for that purpose, and is enabled to procure a settlement of the debt for any thing less than the whole amount, it would be a violation of his duty to his employer, or, at least, would hold out a temptation to violate that duty, if he might take an assignment of the debt, and so make himself a creditor of his employer to the full amount of the debt which he was employed to settle. Does not the same duty devolve *on a surety? He enters into an obligation and becomes subject to a liability, upon a contract of indemnity. The contract between him and his principal is, that the principal shall indemnify him from whatever loss he may sustain by reason of incurring an obligation together with the principal. It is on a contract for indemnity that the surety becomes liable for the debt. It is by virtue of that situation, and, because he is under an obligation as between himself and the creditor of his principal, that he is enabled to make the arrangement with that creditor. It is his duty to make the best terms he can for the person in whose behalf he is acting. His contract with the principal is indemnity. Can the surety, then, settle with the obligee, and instead of treating that settlement as payment of the debt, treat it as an assignment of the whole debt to himself, and claim the benefit of it, as such, to the full amount; thus relieving himself from the situation in which he stands with his principal, and keeping alive the whole debt?

[*375]

As I have said, I would make a precedent if there were none; but it is very satisfactory to me to find that the question came before Lord Eldon, and that he decided it in the cases which have been cited, viz. *Ex parte Rushforth* (1), and *Butcher* v. *Churchill* (2). Lord ELDON did not decide those cases upon particular grounds of equity between the parties; but he lays it down as what he considers to be the rule of this Court, that

(1) 8 R. R. 10 (10 Ves. 420).   (2) 14 Ves. 567.

REED
v.
NORRIS.

[*376]

where a surety gets rid of and discharges an obligation at a less sum than its full amount, he cannot, as against his principal, make himself a creditor for the whole amount; but can only claim, as against his principal, what he has actually paid in discharge of the common *obligation. I am clearly of opinion, therefore, that the representatives of Richard Bevan the younger can in this case claim only the amount which was actually paid in satisfaction of the bond given to Lord Vernon.

1836.
June 8, 9.
1837.
Jan. 20.
——
Lord
COTTENHAM,
L.C.

[376]

CHAMBERS *v.* TAYLOR.

(2 My. & Cr. 376—389 ; S. C. 6 L. J. (N. S.) Ch. 193.)

Lands were limited by deed to the use of the settlor for life ; remainder to the use of his wife for life ; remainder to the use of the heir female of the body of the settlor, on the body of his wife already begotten and now living, or which may be begotten hereafter ; and in default of such issue, to the use of the heir male of the body of the settlor on the body of his wife to be begotten ; remainder to the right heirs of the settlor. At the time when this deed was executed, the settlor and his wife had issue four daughters, and no issue male ; but at his death the same four daughters and also several sons of the marriage survived him : Held, that under the limitation to the heir female, the daughters took a life estate in the lands as purchasers.

By an indenture made the 2nd of February, 1758, between Joseph Chambers of the one part, and the Reverend John Chambers and George Messenger of the other part, reciting that for and in consideration that Martha, the wife of Joseph Chambers, had agreed to sell part of her estate for the discharge of her said husband's debts, and also for the settling, conveying, and assuring the several closes of land thereinafter mentioned, on the issue of Joseph Chambers and Martha his wife, and for divers other good causes and considerations him thereunto especially moving, he, Joseph Chambers, did thereby grant, bargain, and sell, alien, release, and confirm, unto John Chambers and George Messenger all those his several closes of arable, meadow, or pasture ground therein particularly described, to hold the same with their appurtenances unto the said John Chambers and George Messenger, their heirs and assigns, to the use of Joseph Chambers for the term of his natural life ; and from and after the determination of that estate, to the use of the said John Chambers and *George Messenger, their heirs and assigns, for the life of Joseph Chambers, upon trust for pre-serving contingent remainders ; and from and after the death of Joseph Chambers, to the use of his wife Martha, for the term of her natural life, in part of her jointure or dower, but not in full, in case she survived her said husband ; and from and after the decease of his said wife, as for and concerning all and singular the premises (except the dwelling-house in which Joseph Chambers then lived), " to the use and behoof of the heir female of the body of the said Joseph Chambers, on the body of his said wife Martha already lawfully begotten and now living, or which may be begotten hereafter ; and in default of such issue, to the use and behoof of the heir male of the body of the said Joseph Chambers on the body of his said wife Martha to be begotten ; and in default of such issue, to the use and behoof of the right heirs of the said Joseph Chambers for ever ; upon condition that they pay the sum of 100l. of lawful money of Great Britain to the right heirs of the said Martha Chambers within twelve months next after they come into possession of the above granted premises."

At the time when this deed was executed, Joseph Chambers had issue, by his wife Martha, four daughters only ; but at the time of his death, which happened a few years afterwards, he left, besides those daughters, several *sons, by his wife Martha, surviving him, of whom John, the eldest, was his heir-at-law. John Chambers, the eldest son, some time afterwards died without issue, leaving William Chambers, his next brother and heir-at-law, who thereupon became the heir-at-law of Joseph Chambers, the settlor, and who also subsequently died, leaving the present plaintiff, John Chambers the younger, his only son and heir-at-law, and also the heir-at-law and heir male of Joseph Chambers, the settlor.

Martha Chambers, the widow, upon the death of her husband, entered into possession of the settled premises, and continued to receive the rents and profits thereof until her death, which took place in the year 1800.   Her four daughters survived her. Martha, one of the daughters, married a person named Taylor, who, in right of his wife, entered into possession, or enjoyed the

CHAMBERS rents and profits of the premises, on behalf of his wife and her
v.
TAYLOR. three sisters.   Martha Taylor survived her husband and her
three sisters ; and, having taken possession of the premises
immediately after her husband's death, she continued in such
possession until the year 1832, when she died, leaving several
children, of whom her son John was her heir-at-law.   On the
death of Martha Taylor, John Chambers the younger claimed
to be entitled to an estate in fee simple in the property comprised in the settlement ; and a person who had occupied the
premises as a tenant under Martha Taylor was induced to attorn
to him as tenant.   An action of ejectment was thereupon commenced by the children of Mrs. Taylor, against John Chambers
the younger, to recover possession of the premises, to which they
claimed title under their mother's will ; and Chambers, the
defendant in that action, then filed the present bill, praying a
discovery and production of the settlement of 1758, and an
injunction in the meantime.

[379]   The case came before the Court, in the first instance, upon
a motion that the defendants might produce the settlement,
which was admitted by their answer to be in their possession ;
but, in order to save unnecessary litigation, it was ultimately
agreed that the judgment of the LORD CHANCELLOR should be
taken upon the construction of the settlement, and that all
parties in the cause and in the action of ejectment should be
concluded by his Lordship's decision.   This arrangement was
made in the time and with the assent of Lord Chancellor
BROUGHAM.   The matter stood over for a considerable period in
consequence of accidental circumstances, and the question now
came on to be argued before Lord Cottenham.

> *Mr. Wigram, Mr. Wray,* and *Mr. Wightman,* for the
> plaintiff :

Under the limitation to the heir female of the settlor on the
body of his wife already begotten and now living, or which may
be begotten hereafter, the daughters of the settlor took a life
estate in the settled property as purchasers ; and upon the death
of Mrs. Taylor, the last survivor of those daughters, in the year
1832, the title of the plaintiff accrued.   *   *   *

The *Solicitor-General* and *Mr. Purris*, for the defendants. * * *

Mr. Wigram, in reply.

[The arguments of counsel and the authorities cited in support of those arguments sufficiently appear from the following judgment.]

THE LORD CHANCELLOR :

By deed, after marriage, the property in question was settled to the use of the husband for life, with remainder to the use of the wife for life ; and after her decease, to the use of the heir female of the bodies of the two, lawfully begotten, and now living, or which may be begotten hereafter ; and in default of such issue, to the use of the heir male of the bodies of the two, to be begotten ; and, in default of such issue, to the use of the right heirs of the husband, who was the settlor. There were issue of the marriage several sons and daughters. The plaintiff is the son of the second son, the eldest being dead without issue. The defendants are the son and daughters of Martha, the surviving daughter. The plaintiff alleges that the daughters took an estate for life only, and that the plaintiff, as heir male or heir-at-law of the settlor, became entitled upon the death of Martha the surviving daughter. The defendants contend, that the *limitation to the settlor's heir female, gave to the daughters an estate tail ; or that the remainder to the heir female was void ; and that the plaintiff's title having accrued upon the death of the widow of the settlor, thirty-six years ago, it is now barred by time.

There are, therefore, two questions : 1st, whether the remainder to the heir female was void ; 2ndly, if not, what estate did the daughters take.

Of the real intention there can be no doubt. When a man speaks of his heir female, he means such person as would be heir, if females only were capable of being heirs. But the defendants contend that, as there were sons, the daughters were not heirs-at-law, and that the remainder is therefore void.

The law upon this subject has undergone a considerable change ; but there never was a time, I apprehend, in which

CHAMBERS
v.
TAYLOR,
[381]
[384]

1837.
Jan. 20.

[*385]

these remainders would have been held void. The words of the limitation are, " to the heir female of the body now living, or which may be begotten hereafter."

The older cases upon the subject are collected and ably discussed by Mr. Hargrave in a note to the First Institute (1), in which he strongly supports Lord Coke's doctrine, that the party to take must be very heir, as well as female, but admits that it might be otherwise if there were additional words showing that the word " heir " is used in a special sense ; as where land is devised to the heir male " now living," the very words to be found in this deed. At the conclusion of that note, in laying down what he then conceived to be the rule, Mr. Hargrave

[*386]
confines it to cases in which the words stand unexplained *by any other words or circumstances ; and, in another note to the same book (2), he considers the rule in all cases as having been greatly shaken, if not altogether destroyed, by the subsequent decisions there referred to. In *Goodtitle* d. *Bailey* v. *Pugh* (3), Lord MANSFIELD says, " Since *Newcomen* v. *Barkham*, the doubts about the necessity of being very heir have been at an end."

It is not, however, necessary to consider the merits of this contest ; because, according to the most strict construction of the rule, the words " heir female " might at all times have been good words of description of a purchaser, although the party was not heir-at-law, if there were other words to explain the sense in which the words were used ; and the words used in this case are, I think, quite sufficient for that purpose.

What estate then did the heir female, that is, the daughter, take ; for it was not argued that the parent took more than an estate for life? In *Lewis Bowles's* case (4), an estate was settled by deed to the use of the husband for life, remainder to the wife for life ; and after their decease, to the use of their joint issue male, and the heirs male of such issue ; and it was held, that there being issue male, the parents were tenants for life ; remainder to the issue male in tail. In *Bayley* v. *Morris* (4 Ves. 788), a limitation by deed, after life estates to the husband

(1) Co. Litt. 24 b, note 3.   573.
(2) Co. Litt. 164 a, note 2.   (4) 11 Rep. 79.
(3) App. to Butler's Fearne, C. R.

and wife, to the heir male of their bodies, and to his heirs, and for want of such issue, to the daughters; and if there should be no issue of the marriage, to the right heirs of the husband, was held to be a contingent remainder in fee to the person who should be the heir male at the determination of the life estates.

Here is a gift to the heir female of the body, in a deed, without any words of inheritance; for the words " in default of such issue" mean only, in default of an heir female of the body now living, or hereafter to be begotten, and do not carry the interest beyond the original gift.

A passage in Co. Litt. 22 a, was cited for the defendants, where Lord Coke refers to a decision that a limitation to a man and his wife and one heir of their bodies, and one heir of the body of such heir was an estate tail. He does not express any approbation of this; but says that a limitation *hæredi*, in the singular number, would not give a fee simple at common law. The case so put, however, differs essentially from the present, because, in that case, there were words of inheritance and succession. The same observation applies to *Richards* v. *Lady Bergavenny* (1), which was a case arising upon a will: there, the limitation, which was to a mother, and such heir of her body as should be living at her death, was held to be an estate tail in the mother.

In *Dubber* v. *Trollope* (2), which was the case of a will, Ch. J. EYRE guards himself against being supposed to give any opinion as to what would be the effect of the words if used in a deed. *White* v. *Collins* (3) was also the case of a will, and only proves, what many other cases establish, that a limitation by will to A. for life, with remainder to the heir of his body, without words of inheritance superadded, creates an estate tail in the first taker, when nothing explains the testator's intention to the contrary; otherwise not. And *Archer's* case is to the like effect (4).

These cases, indeed, prove that the word "heir," in the singular number, has sometimes the same effect as the word

(1) 2 Vern. 324. (3) 1 Com. Rep. 289.
(2) Amb. 453. (4) 1 Co. 66.

" heirs " in the plural ; but if words of limitation are superadded to the word " heir," it is considered as conclusively
showing that the word is used as a word of purchase. When
that is not the case, it is considered, in construing wills, as
nomen collectivum, for the purpose of creating an estate tail in
the first taker, and not as creating an estate tail in the person
answering the description of heir. If the word " heir " would,
per se, give an estate of inheritance to the party answering the
description, there would be no reason for any distinction, whether
words of limitation or inheritance were or were not superadded.
These cases, therefore, prove that the daughters would not have
taken estates of inheritance as purchasers under a will ; and
it is not pretended that their parents took more than estates
for life.

It was argued that the statute *De Donis* provides that the will
of the donor shall be observed, and that cases upon wills are,
therefore, authorities upon the present question. Lord Coke,
however, says (1), that such will must agree with the rules
of law. Therefore a gift to a man *et exitibus de corpore suo
legitime procreatis*, or *semini suo*, gives only an estate for life ;
and the word " issue " is not allowed in a deed to operate as a
word of limitation. Accordingly in *Makepiece* v. *Fletcher* (2)
a limitation, in a deed, to the settlor's daughter and the issue
of her body, and in default of such issue, over, was held not to
give an estate tail to the daughter.

I am, therefore, of opinion that the daughters of Joseph
Chambers took, by purchase, but for life only, and that the
title of the plaintiff accrued upon the death *of Martha, the
survivor of the daughters, and that he is now entitled.

[*389]

In so holding, I am following the more modern authorities,
and am not violating any rule to be found in the older cases ;
and I have no doubt that this construction carries into effect the
real intention of the parties.

(1) Co. Litt. 20 b.   (2) 2 Com. Rep. 457.

JOMBART v. WOOLLETT.

(2 My. & Cr. 389—404; 6 L. J. (N. S.) Ch. 211.)

1837.
Jan. 31.
March 18.

Lord
COTTENHAM,
L.C.

[389]

A merchant abroad sent drafts from time to time to his London correspondent for acceptance, under an authority for that purpose, and upon
an understanding that the liabilities of the latter in respect of all such
acceptances, should be covered by means of bills payable in London to
be remitted to him from time to time.   Under such an arrangement, the
presumption is, until an agreement to the contrary is shown, that the
London correspondent was not intended or entitled to treat the bills, so
remitted, as cash, or to discount them before maturity; and, therefore,
it was held that two of such bills, which were existing in specie in his
hands at the time of his bankruptcy, and were not then due, did not
pass to his assignees, but were the property of the party who had
remitted them.

THE plaintiffs were the partners in a mercantile house established at Lille in Flanders, and carrying on business under
the firm of Jombart & Co.   In the months of July and August,
1836, Jombart & Co. employed the defendant Joseph Woollett,
who was a merchant in London trading under the firm of
Woollett and Son, as their banker or commission agent for
the purpose of accepting and taking up bills of exchange on
their behalf.   The transactions between Jombart & Co. and
Woollett and Son, did not extend to any other commercial
dealings, but were entirely confined to such banking or commission agency, in which it was agreed that Jombart & Co.
should draw bills of exchange upon Woollett and Son, which
Woollett was to accept in the name of his firm; and that in
order to provide *funds for the payment of such bills when at   [*390]
maturity, Jombart & Co. should transmit to Woollett cash or
bills of exchange payable in London.

In the months of July and August, 1836, Jombart accordingly
drew upon Woollett, in the name of Woollett and Son, the
following bills of exchange: A bill for 588*l.* 5*s.* 8*d.* dated
July 21, 1836, in favour of Osborn and Son, which became due
on the 24th of October following; a bill for 478*l.* 6*s.* 5*d.* in
favour of Moens and Dauncey, dated July 29, 1836, and which
became due on the 27th of October; a bill for 340*l.* in favour of
Schaezler and Brentanos, dated July 27, 1836, and which
became due on the 28th of October; a bill for 500*l.* in favour
of Charles Fea, dated August 2, 1836, and which became due on

the 31st of October ; a bill for 58*l.* 11*s.* 3*d.* in favour of Hives
and Atkinson, dated August 5, 1836, and which became due on
the 28th of August; and a bill for 644*l.* 19*s.* 9*d.* in favour of
Charles Fea, dated August 9, 1836, and which became due on
the 9th of November following.   All these bills were duly
accepted by Joseph Woollett in the name of the firm of Woollett
and Son.

In order to enable Woollett and Son to take up these acceptances, as they became severally due, Jombart & Co. from time
to time remitted to Woollett and Son, by whom they were duly
received and acknowledged, the following bills of exchange,
which Jombart & Co. had purchased, and which were duly
accepted and made payable in London ; namely, a bill for 300*l.*
on Esdaile & Co., which became due on the 16th of September,
1836 ; another bill for 300*l.* on Esdaile & Co. which became due
on the 25th of October ; a bill for 500*l.* on Gower & Co., which
became due on the 3rd of November; a bill for 50*l.* on Guillaume
[*391] & Co. which became *due on the 18th of November ; a bill for
1,000*l.* on Messrs. Trye and Lightfoot, which became due on the
20th of November ; and a bill for 440*l.* on Messrs. Trye and
Lightfoot, which became due on the 23rd of November ; together
with a Bank of England note for 10*l.*, which was received by
Woollett on the 18th of October.

The nature of the arrangement and the course of dealing
between the parties were chiefly to be collected from the
language of the correspondence which passed between them,
while these transactions were going on.

In the month of July, Jombart & Co. sent the following letter
to Woollett and Son : " LILLE, 26th July, 1836.   On our particular account you have accepted our draft in favour of Osborn
and Son, for 588*l.* 5*s.* 8*d.* under date 21st current, at ninety
days' date, for which your account is credited.   We have this
day drawn upon you a bill for 478*l.* 6*s.* 5*d.* at ninety days' date
in favour of Moens, Dauncey & Co.   And we have also the
pleasure to inform you that Messrs. Schaezler & Co. of Liverpool
will draw on our account a sum of about 380*l.*"

On the 28th of July, Jombart & Co. again wrote to Woollett and Son as follows : " Be so good to take note that we

have authorised Mr. C. Fea of Canterbury to draw upon you
on our account, for the sum of 500*l*., which we beg you will duly
honour.''

Immediately afterwards, Woollett and Son wrote and sent the
ollowing letter to Jombart & Co.: "LONDON, 29th of July, 1836.
We have to observe that we have accepted, on your account, your
bills upon us, 588*l*. 5*s*. 8*d*., due the 21st of October, in favour
of Osborn and Son, and 478*l*. 6*s*. 5*d*. due 24th of October, in
*favour of Moens & Co., which we have carried to your debit,   [*392]
relying upon you to cover us in due time. According to your
authorisation, your friends Messrs. Schaezler & Co. have drawn
upon us on your account 340*l*., 27th current, at ninety days
date.''

In the month of August, Jombart & Co. wrote to Woollett and
Son as follows: "LILLE, 2nd August, 1836. We have your letter
of the 29th ult. You have now under acceptance for our account
the sum of   -   -   -   -   -   - £1,906 12 1
and moreover we have drawn upon you   -   -   644 13 9
                                                    ——————
which will make together   -   -   -   - 2,551 5 10.
We shall not draw upon you beyond this sum without having
your authorisation, considering it as if you had limited our
credit with you by acceptance less in amount. You must tell us
frankly, and we will cover you immediately.''

On the 4th of the same month Woollett and Son wrote to
Jombart & Co. as follows: "We are favoured with yours of the
2nd, by which we observe that you intend drawing upon us for
644*l*. 13*s*. 9*d*., which we shall accept to your debit. You are
already informed of our principle of credit which we afford to our
friends. Above all in banking affairs, as you desire us to speak
frankly, for the future you will consider this facility established
between us for the amount of 2,000*l*.''

On the 9th of August, Woollett and Son wrote to Jombart
& Co. as follows: "We have received your letter of the 6th,
advising your bill of 644*l*. 13*s*. 9*d*. in favour of C. Fea, which we
have accepted to your debit.''

On the 8th of the same month, Jombart & Co. wrote to   [393]
Woollett and Son as follows : "We confirm our letter of the 6th,

advising our bill of 644*l.* 13*s.* 9*d.* in favour of C. Fea, at three months' date. Enclosed we remit you 300*l.*, due the 13th of September, which we beg you to carry to the credit of your account."

On the 11th of August, Woollett and Son wrote to Jombart & Co. as follows : " We confirm our letter of the 9th current, which was crossed by yours of the 8th, by which we have received 300*l.*, due 13th (16th) of September, which shall be carried to your credit."

On the 23rd of the same month, Jombart & Co. wrote to Woollett and Son as follows : " We have your letter of the 11th which requires no answer. Enclosed we remit 300*l.*, due 25th of October, which we request you to get accepted, and carry the same to the credit of our account. We recall to your recollection a bill for 53*l.* 11*s.* 3*d.* payable 25th current. Be pleased to pay it, and pass it to our credit."

On the 26th of August, Woollett and Son wrote to Jombart & Co. as follows : " You remit us, by your favour of the 23rd current, 300*l.* due 22nd (25th) October, upon Esdaile & Co., upon which we will do the needful, and pass it to your credit as soon as received."

On the 15th of October, Jombart & Co. wrote to Woollett and Son as follows : " Enclosed we remit 500*l.* due 31st October, 50*l.* due 15th November, 10*l.* at sight, making 560*l.*, of which please to give credit and acknowledge receipt."

[*394] On the 17th of the same month, Woollett and Son wrote to Jombart & Co. as follows : " We have received *your favour of the 15th current, covering 10*l.* at sight, 500*l.* due the 31st October (3rd November), 50*l.* due 15th (18th) November, amounting to 560*l.*, to your credit when due."

On the 19th of October, Jombart & Co. wrote to Woollett and Son as follows : " By your letter of the 17th current, you acknowledge the receipt of remittances which you have carried to the credit of our account. You have herewith a bill for 1,000*l.* upon Trye and Lightfoot of your city, to your debit. Please to acknowledge the receipt."

On the 21st of the same month, Woollett and Son wrote to Jombart & Co. as follows : " We have received your favour of the

19th, covering 1,000*l*., due the 17th (20th) of November, upon Trye and Lightfoot of this city, to your credit."

On the 24th of October, Jombart & Co. wrote to Woollett and Son as follows: "By your favour of the 21st current you acknowledge our remittance of 1,000*l*. Enclosed you have a bill for 440*l*. due 20th November, upon Trye and Lightfoot, which we beg you to place to our credit."

Several other letters passed between the parties, in the course of these transactions, but the foregoing are the most material.

On Saturday the 22nd of October, 1836, Joseph Woollett became insolvent, and early on the following Monday he stopped payment. He gave immediate notice of the fact to Jombart & Co.; and by a letter, dated the 26th of October, after acknowledging the receipt of the bill for 440*l*., he informed them that he had sent it for *acceptance, and would hold it at their disposal; and by another letter dated the following day, he returned that bill to them.

[*395]

With the exception of the bill for 58*l*. 11*s*. 3*d*. drawn on Woollett and Son, in favour of Hives and Atkinson, all the bills accepted by Woollett on the plaintiffs' account were dishonoured, and remained unpaid at the time of his insolvency, and were all subsequently taken up and paid by the plaintiffs. Of the bills remitted by the plaintiffs to Woollett for the purpose of meeting his acceptances, the whole had been discounted or sold, and the proceeds received by him prior to his insolvency, with the exception of the two bills for 50*l*. and 1,000*l*. which then remained in his hands. It appeared that, at the date of Woollett's insolvency, he was indebted to the plaintiffs in upwards of 1,000*l*. beyond the amount of these bills. Under an arrangement with the creditors of Woollett, the two bills were afterwards sold, and the proceeds carried to the account of the other defendants (who were three of the principal creditors), upon trust to abide the result of any legal proceedings that might be taken.

The bill prayed that the right of the plaintiffs to the property in the two bills of exchange might be declared, and the proceeds paid to the plaintiffs, and that, in the meantime, the defendants might be restrained from distributing such proceeds among the insolvent's general creditors.

Woollett afterwards became a bankrupt, and his assignees were brought before the Court by supplemental bill.

[*396] The VICE-CHANCELLOR having granted the injunction, the defendants appealed against his Honour's order; *and it was arranged between the parties, that the LORD CHANCELLOR's judgment on the appeal-motion should be taken as concluding the question in the cause.

The motion was supported by an affidavit, which detailed the facts and set forth the letters as they have been already stated.

Mr. Wigram and *Mr. Richards*, in support of the appeal-motion :

[*397] * * The accidental circumstance that these two bills happened *to remain in specie in the hands of the London agent, cannot affect the question.   If they were his to deal with as his own, it signified nothing whether they were actually converted into cash, or continued in the form of paper at the time of his insolvency. [Unless he was to be at liberty to treat the bills as cash, he must have been out of pocket by large sums.]

[398] In *Bent* v. *Puller* (1), a case which in its circumstances strongly
[*399] resembled this case, Mr. *Justice BULLER said, that " in order to make it a specific appropriation of bills, there must be a lodging of a bill for a bill, or at least several deposited at once as one entire transaction to answer some particular purpose; whereas here the bills were paid in on a general running account, and the amount of the bills claimed as a deposit not even corresponding with the amount of those for which they were supposed to be deposited.

The *Solicitor-General* and *Mr. Bligh, contrà :*

[400] * * The bills were remitted for the purpose of "covering," that is, being security to Woollett for, the amount of the liabilities which he was from time to time undertaking on the plaintiffs' behalf by accepting their drafts.   For the amount of those liabilities he had a lien on the bills remitted; and as those

(1) 2 R. R. 654 (5 T. R. 494); and see *Ex parte Sargeant*, 1 Rose, 153.

bills became due and were paid, he was entitled to reimburse himself out of the proceeds. * * *

It formed an essential part of the arrangement, as stated in Woollett's letter of the 4th of August, that the extent of credit to be afforded by him should not exceed 2,000l. Upon inspecting the account, however, it will be found that, if Woollett was to be at liberty to discount the remittances as he received them, instead of affording any credit to the plaintiffs, he would never be in advance a single shilling on their account; a consequence *utterly irreconcileable with the nature of the transaction and the whole tenor of the correspondence. * * As the bills were fixed in the hands of Woollett with a trust which he has failed to perform, the plaintiffs, upon the ordinary principle applicable to trust property, are now entitled to recover them from the hands of Woollett's assignees. *In *Bent* v. *Puller* (1) there was this broad distinction, that the bills did not remain in specie, but had actually been negotiated; but the authority of the case itself is extremely doubtful, it having been determined before the law on this subject had been much considered, or well settled. * * *

[*401]

[*402]

Mr. Wigram, in reply.

THE LORD CHANCELLOR :

March 18.

In the transactions between the foreign merchants and the London house, it appears that two bills, viz. one for 1,000l., and another for 50l., were remitted to the London house by the foreign merchants; and the question is, whether these two bills belong to the assignees of the London agent, or to the foreign merchants.

The law on this subject is laid down with sufficient clearness in the cases of *Thompson* v. *Giles* (2), *Ex parte Pease* (3), *Ex parte Smith* in the matter of *Power* (4), and *Ex parte Frere* in the matter of *Sikes* (5), the result of which is, that unless there be a contract to the contrary, if a person, having an agent elsewhere,

(1) 2 R. R. 654 (5 T. R. 494).
(2) 26 R. R. 392 (2 B. & C. 422).
(3) 1 Rose, 232.

(4) Buck, 355.
(5) 1 Mont. & Mac. 263.

remits to him, for a particular purpose, bills not due, and that purpose is not answered, and then the agent carries them to account, and becomes a bankrupt, the property in the bills is not altered, but remains in the party making the remittance.

[403]   That of course may be regulated by usage, but *primâ facie*, without special contract, the presumption is, that the bills are received by the agent for the purpose of indemnifying him against any eventual loss, and are not to be dealt with as his own, and immediately converted into cash.

In *Ex parte Smith* in the matter of *Power* (1) a bill of exchange was remitted with a direction " to do the needful," which was construed not to give the house to which it was remitted a right to sell the bill, but only a right to keep it until the time arrived, when it was properly payable.   Unless, therefore, there is to be found, in the correspondence in this case, a special contract authorising the London agent to deal otherwise with the bills, viz. to make them immediately his own, he would be bound to keep them until they became due.

In the course of these transactions a number of letters passed between the parties, some few of which I shall refer to for the purpose of showing what really was the contract between them. Among others I find a letter dated the 29th of July, 1836, from the London house to the foreign merchants. [His Lordship read the letter.]   Now the expression " to cover us in due time," can only mean that funds should be sent in due time to meet the obligation into which the writers had entered by accepting the bill referred to in the letter.

There is another letter from the foreign merchants to the London house, dated the 8th of August, 1836.   [His Lordship read this letter also.]   Here the remitters, Jombart & Co., request the London agent to carry the 300*l*., due on the 18th of

[*404]   September, " to the credit *of*" his account.   That expression is ambiguous.   It might mean either that the bill or that the money should be carried to the credit of the account ; but it is obvious that if the bill had been discounted, there would not be 300*l*. to be carried to the credit of the account, because the amount would be diminished by the sum paid for discount.

(1) Buck, 355.

[The LORD CHANCELLOR then read the letters of the 11th, 23rd, and 26th of August, and proceeded :]

In the letter I have last read we have the identical expression, "do the needful," which occurred in *Ex parte Smith*, but explained, as it was not in *Ex parte Smith*, by the clause which follows : there, without any such explanation, it was held that as the bills were remitted for a particular purpose which affected them with a trust, they did not pass to the assignees ; whereas here, the writer explains what he means by " doing the needful," that is to say, passing the bill to the credit of the remitters as soon as received.

There is then another letter from Woollett and Son, dated the 17th October, in these words, &c. [His Lordship read this letter.]

In order to make good the title of the assignees, and to displace the title of the remitters of the bills, it would be necessary to establish, from the correspondence, a contract entitling the London house to make the bills their own. The cases show, that unless there was such a contract, the London house were agents only for receiving the amount of the bills when due. Instead of containing any authority to the London agent to deal with the bills as his own, the correspondence proves the very reverse to have been the understanding of both *parties. The only obligation of the foreign house, was to keep the London agent in cash to meet the bills when due. It was not intended to establish a cash balance in his hands.

[*405]

Another question might have arisen which it is not necessary for me to decide, because there are facts enough to enable me to dispose of the case independently of it. It is obvious that these remittances were made for the purpose of meeting certain obligations ; those obligations were not met ; so that the condition upon which the bills were remitted has not been performed ; and the London agent, therefore, it may be said, has not done that which was requisite to complete his title. This, however, is a consideration into which I am not now called upon to enter.

Here are the bills not disposed of, not discounted, and the obligation not performed. I think, therefore, that the foreign house have clearly established their title. The motion to discharge the VICE-CHANCELLOR's order must be refused with costs.

1837.
May 6, 27, 31.
ATTORNEY-GENERAL *v.* MAYOR AND CORPORA-TION OF NORWICH.

(2 My. & Cr. 406—431; S. C. 1 Jur. 398.)

[A NOTE of this appeal, affirming the decision of the MASTER OF THE ROLLS, will be found at the end of the report below. (See 44 R. R. 143, taken from 1 Keen, 700.)]

———•———

1837.
Feb. 22.
———
Lord
COTTENHAM,
L.C.
[441]

IN THE MATTER OF WEAVER (1).

(2 My. & Cr. 441—442.)

Order made to restrain an action brought by an auctioneer, against the solicitor in a lunacy, for the amount of his bill for appraising and selling property belonging to the lunatic, the sale having been made under the authority of the Court, and the auctioneer having acted on the instructions of the solicitor, and with the sanction of the Master, before whom he had at first carried in his claim; and a reference directed for the purpose of ascertaining what would be a proper sum to be allowed him on that account.

THIS was a petition by the committees of a lunatic's estate. It prayed that a person of the name of Overton, who had been employed to appraise and make an inventory of the goods, stock in trade, and implements of husbandry, and farming utensils, live and dead stock, and crops, belonging to the lunatic, with a view to their being sold, and who had also acted as the auctioneer at the sale, might be restrained from prosecuting any action at law against the petitioners or their solicitor, for the costs and charges which he claimed in respect of his services in that behalf; and that the Master might be directed to inquire and certify what would be a proper sum to be allowed him on that account.

[442]   It appeared, from the affidavits filed in support of the petition, that the sale had taken place under the authority of the Court; that Overton had been employed by the solicitor of the petitioners, with the sanction of the Master in whose office the proceedings in the lunacy were prosecuted; and that he had originally carried in his claim before the Master; but that having found the claim disputed, on the ground that many of the items charged were exorbitant and unnecessary, he subsequently commenced an

(1) *In re Clarke* [1898] 1 Ch. 336, 67 L. J. Ch. 234, 78 L. T. 275, C. A.

action against the solicitor, for the sum of 230*l.*, being the full amount of his bill.

Mr. Sharpe, for the petition.

Mr. Koe, for Overton, opposed the application.

The LORD CHANCELLOR said that the affidavit did not show any special contract between Overton and the solicitor, the action being founded merely on a *quantum meruit*. A claim arising in the course of an employment under a lunacy, and for the purpose of carrying into effect the directions of the Court in that lunacy, unless there was some special agreement to the contrary, would be properly the subject of inquiry before the Master. He should therefore make the order as prayed by the petition, reserving the question of costs.

————•————

MASON *v.* BOGG (1).

(2 My. & Cr. 443—452; S. C. 1 Jur. 330.)

Discussion of the principles upon which a specialty creditor whose debt is also secured by a mortgage or lien should prove his debt under a decree in a creditor's suit.

1837.
April 12.
May 4.

———
Lord
COTTENHAM,
L.C.

[443]

THIS was a creditor's suit, for the administration of the estate of an intestate named Thomas Bogg.

The intestate, in his lifetime, purchased of one Joseph Wilson a freehold estate, subject to a mortgage for 900*l.*, which the intestate, by the deed of conveyance, dated the 13th of October, 1829, covenanted to pay, but which he had not paid at the time of his decease. After his death, William Morton and Jane his wife, in right of the wife as executrix of Joseph Wilson, brought an action at law, upon this covenant, against the defendant John Bogg, as the administrator of Thomas Bogg. On the 29th of

(1) In bankruptcy the secured creditor can only prove for the balance after giving credit for the value of his security, but the rule in equity as established in *Mason* v. *Bogg* applies in the winding up of companies (*Kellock's* case (1868) L. R. 3 Ch. 769, 39 L. J. Ch. 112) as in administration of deceased person's estates, unless the estate is insolvent, in which case s. 10 of the Judicature Act, 1875, directs the substitution of the rule applied in bankruptcy.— O. A. S.

MASON
r.
BOGG.

April, 1836, a decree was made in the present suit, for an account of the intestate's debts, and the due administration of his estate; and the defendant thereupon moved that Morton and wife might be restrained from proceeding in their action. Upon that motion, the VICE-CHANCELLOR ordered that Morton and wife should be at liberty to proceed to judgment in their action, but that the judgment should be dealt with as the Court should direct.

The VICE-CHANCELLOR, subsequently, on the application of Morton and wife, made an order, dated the 19th of December, 1836, by which it was directed that William Morton and Jane his wife, in right of the said Jane as executrix of Joseph Wilson, deceased, should have a lien on the hereditaments described in the indenture of the 13th of October, 1829, for the sum of 900*l.*, being the amount of the purchase money for the hereditaments

[*444]

sold by Joseph Wilson to the intestate Thomas *Bogg, and then remaining unpaid, together with interest at 5 per cent.; and that William Morton and Jane his wife, in right of his wife as such executrix, should be considered as specialty creditors for 900*l.* and interest, and that the costs of that application should be paid by the defendant.

The defendant now moved to discharge the last-mentioned order.

  Mr. Koe, in support of the motion [relied on *Greenwood* v. *Taylor* (1).]

   Mr. Sidebottom, contrà :

[445]

  *   *   A mortgagee may prove for the full amount of his debt as a specialty creditor, and may keep the security in his pocket, until required to convey the land to a purchaser; which he can only be compelled to do upon receiving full payment.   *   *   *

[447]

  It is to be observed, that no case was cited in *Greenwood* v. *Taylor*, and the decision has not been acted on in the Masters' offices.

  Mr. Koe, in reply.   *   *   *

    (1) 1 Russ. & My. 185.

(THE LORD CHANCELLOR : I cannot distinguish this case from *Greenwood* v. *Taylor* ; but, with respect to the principle of that case, it is to be observed, that a mortgagee has a double security : he has a right to proceed against both, and to make the best he can of both. Why he should be deprived of this right because the debtor dies, and dies insolvent, it is not very easy to see. The question can only arise when there is a deficient security and an insolvent estate. So that the worse the creditor's case, the harder the course of the Court against him. What you contend is that the creditor shall not proceed to enforce his legal rights unless he gives up his security.)

The decree of this Court is in the nature of a judgment for all creditors.

(THE LORD CHANCELLOR : Not for the purpose of altering the securities of the creditors. It is a judgment according to their legal rights.)

    *   *   *   *   *

I am contending for what is expressly decided by *Greenwood* v. *Taylor*.

(THE LORD CHANCELLOR : I take it for granted you can find no other case. It is an extremely important case, and should not be disposed of hastily. I am desirous of having it thoroughly investigated before I act upon it.)

  The counsel on both sides admitted that they had been unable to find any other case : but they differed upon the question whether the rule laid down in *Greenwood* v. *Taylor* had been acted upon ; and the motion stood over in order that the counsel might make further searches, and that the Registrar might search for precedents upon the subject, which he was directed by the LORD CHANCELLOR to do.

  Mr. Koe, on a subsequent day, renewed his application for the discharge of the VICE-CHANCELLOR's order, and mentioned the case of *Perry* v. *Barker* (1). *Mr. Sidebottom* opposed the

  (1) 9 R. R. 171 (8 Ves. 527; 13 Ves. 198).

MASON
v.
BOGG.

application ; but neither of them produced any authority upon the point decided in *Greenwood* v. *Taylor.*

The LORD CHANCELLOR said it appeared to him that the VICE-CHANCELLOR'S order asserted that about which there could be no doubt, namely, that Joseph Wilson, the deceased vendor, had a lien, and that he was a specialty creditor, and that it left the question quite open as to how his rights were to be dealt with. The effect of discharging the order would be to leave the injunction which had been granted in force, and to deprive the creditor of the means of enforcing his rights. His Lordship thought that the matter was not in such a state as to call for an opinion upon the question which arose in *Greenwood* v. *Taylor,* and which had been before discussed ; and he refused the motion with costs.

[451]

It appeared by the affidavit of a clerk of the agents for Morton and wife, sworn on the 26th of April, that * * he had shown the report of the case of *Greenwood* v. *Taylor* to the Master and nine chief clerks, and that they all informed the deponent that they had not been previously aware that the case had been decided.

1837.
April 6, 8.

Lord
COTTENHAM,
L.C.

[459]

FLOWER *v.* MARTEN.

(2 My. & Cr. 459—475; S. C. 1 Jur. 233.)

A bond for a sum of money ordered to be delivered up to be cancelled ; the LORD CHANCELLOR being of opinion, upon the evidence, first, that the bond was not intended to operate as a security for money at all events, but was given for a collateral purpose, which had been fully satisfied ; and, secondly, if that were doubtful, that the obligee's subsequent conduct and mode of dealing with the bond during the whole of his life amounted, in equity, to a release of the debt.

THE plaintiff was the only son and heir-at-law of the late Sir Charles Flower, Bart. Some time prior to the year 1822, his expensive habits and mode of life had occasioned much dissatisfaction to his father, and had led to differences, which terminated in a total estrangement and suspension of intercourse between them. In the course of that year, however, the plaintiff, who was then married, having got into further pecuniary difficulties, was induced to apply to his father, and to request him to advance a sum of money to relieve his immediate necessities. The application was referred by Sir Charles Flower to the defendants Robert Humphrey Marten and John Petty Muspratt, two of Sir Charles's old and confidential friends, with a request that they would take into consideration all matters in difference between the plaintiff and himself, more especially as regarded the plaintiff's debts and the expenses of his mode of living, and that they would give him their impartial advice as to the course he ought to adopt towards his son, by which advice he professed himself willing to be governed. Those gentlemen undertook the reference, and entered into communication with the plaintiff, who likewise consented to abide by the determination to which they should come with respect to his future course: and, after having fully investigated and considered the state of the plaintiff's affairs, they communicated the result of their deliberations in the form of a letter, addressed to Sir Charles Flower, and containing a number of distinct propositions, which were intended and understood by all parties as the basis of the proposed arrangement between the father and the son.

This letter, after stating that the amount of the plaintiff's debts and liabilities, as ascertained by a written statement made out and signed by the plaintiff, did not exceed 4,000*l.*, exclusive of some tradesmen's bills and other demands not then liquidated, proceeded as follows: "Having now for several weeks given our anxious attention to this interesting subject, and trusting that our decision will lead to a sincere and lasting reunion between you and your son, we recommend and determine,—

1st. That over and above the large sums already paid and advanced for your son, you relieve him from all the debts and liabilities referred to in the statement so signed by him; it being understood that you are, against the payments made and to be made for him, to retain the balance received, or to be received for him from the Brewery, and the produce of the Indian Stock lately sold, and of the lease and furniture in Bedford Square, and to have such security from Mr. L. as you may be enabled to obtain, for 1,100*l.*, or whatever sum may appear to be due from him in any way to your son; and

FLOWER
v.
MARTEN.

[460]

8—2

for obtaining which, you are to have all requisite legal authority from your son.   You are likewise to have the advantage of any securities, bonds, judgments, agreements, abatements, compromises, &c., from any parties, whereby the nominal amount of your son's debts may be diminished.

2ndly. That your son shall give you his bond, bearing date from the last payment of any sum in the aforesaid statement, for 4,500*l*., in satisfaction of all pecuniary claims upon him, including the payments in the said statement to be yet made, such bond to be payable on demand, with interest at 4 per cent. per annum.   But the bond is to remain in our hands, and not

[*461] to be acted *upon for the recovery of principal or interest within six years from the date of the bond, without the consent in writing of us, or of the survivor of us ; and moreover, that in case we or the survivor of us shall, at any time within six years, by a memorandum in writing direct the bond to be delivered up and cancelled, such cancellation, or an order from us or the survivor of us for that purpose, shall operate as a total extinguishment of the debt, both as to principal and interest."

The 3rd and 4th propositions were, for the present purpose, immaterial.   The 5th and 6th were as follows :

" 5thly. As your son must again have a house to reside in, and as he is content to have one suited to his income, we further recommend and determine that you present your daughter-in-law with 500*l*., to be laid out in furnishing the house in which they may intend to reside, on their having fixed upon such house and declaring their want of furniture for it.   Their linen, plate, &c., now in their possession, to remain their own.

6thly. Should any misunderstanding arise on this our determination, we reserve to ourselves, in order to fulfil our undertaking for both parties, the power to decide on such matters as may be the subject of doubt."

The letter then informed Sir Charles, that his son, so far as he was concerned, was perfectly ready to accede to these propositions, and that he was anxious to be allowed to renew his intercourse with his father, and to testify his deep sense of the obligations which he owed to him.   It concluded by expressing the anxious hope of the writers, that the arrangements which they had proposed might be carried into effect, and might lead to a cordial and lasting reconciliation between the parties.

The terms recommended in the foregoing letter were accepted and acted upon by both parties; and the plaintiff, in compliance with the second proposition stated in the letter, executed and delivered to the referees, Messrs. Marten and Muspratt, his bond to Sir Charles Flower, dated the 2nd of October, 1822, in the penal sum of 9,000*l.*

The condition annexed to the bond was as follows : "Whereas the said Sir Charles Flower has agreed to accept from the said James Flower his son, the above written bond or obligation, with a condition for payment of 4,500*l.* and interest, as hereinafter mentioned, in full satisfaction of all claims and demands upon him; and the said James Flower has agreed to enter into and execute such bond accordingly; but under the special understanding and agreement of both parties, and particularly of the said Sir Charles Flower, that the said bond shall remain in the hands of Robert Humphrey Marten and John Petty Muspratt of the city of London, merchants, and shall not be acted upon for the recovery of principal or interest, within six years from the date thereof, without the consent in writing of them, or of the survivor of them : and, moreover, that in case they or the survivor of them shall, at any time within six years, by a memorandum in writing, direct the said bond to be delivered up and cancelled, such memorandum or cancellation shall operate as a total extinguishment of the debt both as to principal and interest : now the condition of the above written obligation is, that if the said James Flower, his heirs, executors, or administrators, do and shall well and truly pay or cause to be paid to the above named Sir Charles Flower, his executors, administrators, or assigns, the full sum of 4,500*l.* on the 2nd day of October, 1823, with interest for the same in the mean time, by half yearly payments, at the rate of 4*l.* per cent. *per annum, or if the said Robert H. Marten and John P. Muspratt or the survivor shall, in manner aforesaid, direct the above written bond or obligation to be cancelled, then the same is to void ; or else to remain in full force and virtue."

Sir Charles Flower advanced the money that was necessary to

discharge the amount of the plaintiff's debts ; the other parts of the arrangement were at the same time carried into effect, and the plaintiff renewed his intercourse with his father. No further misunderstanding or disagreement arose between them.   The subsequent conduct of the plaintiff was in the highest degree satisfactory to his father, and from the time of their reconciliation to the period of his father's death, they continued to live upon terms of intimacy and affection. No demand was made against the plaintiff, during the life time of Sir Charles Flower, in respect of any part of the principal or interest secured by the bond.   The bond itself was suffered to remain in the custody of Messrs. Marten and Muspratt ; but no memorandum in writing, directing it to be delivered up and cancelled was ever made by those gentlemen or either of them ; and at the time of Sir Charles Flower's death, it was lying in their hands uncancelled.

Sir Charles Flower died in the month of September, 1834, leaving a will, by which he bequeathed his residuary personal estate to trustees, upon trust for the plaintiff for life, with remainder to his children, and in default of such issue, upon certain trusts for the benefit of his (the testator's) five daughters and their respective issue.

[*464]
When the executors of Sir Charles Flower were informed of the existence of the bond, a question arose *whether, under the circumstances stated, it ought to be considered as a subsisting instrument and be put in force against the obligor ; and the present suit was instituted in order to have that question determined.

The bill, which was filed against Messrs. Marten and Muspratt, and against the executors of Sir Charles Flower's will, charged, among other things, that the bond was never intended as a security for the repayment of the sum of 4,500l. ; but was executed under the circumstances, and for the considerations stated in the letter ; and that the purposes for which it was given having been fully satisfied, it ought now to be delivered up to be cancelled.

The plaintiff had no issue living. The daughters of Sir Charles Flower and their respective children, who had an interest in the residuary estate, expectant on the plaintiff's death without children, were not made parties to the suit.

The defendants, Messrs. Marten and Muspratt, by their answer stated, that their intention in procuring the plaintiff to execute the bond, was to enable Sir Charles Flower to hold the same as a security for the prudent conduct of the plaintiff for the future; and that they on that account reserved to themselves the right of cancelling the bond, in case the plaintiff's conduct should be satisfactory to his father; and that they further intended that the monies advanced by Sir Charles Flower to the plaintiff might be treated, either as a gift to, or as a debt due from, the plaintiff, according as his future conduct should be prudent and satisfactory to his father, or otherwise; and they stated their belief that Sir Charles Flower fully understood such to be their intention, and acquiesced in the propriety thereof.

The depositions of the same defendants (who were examined as witnesses in the cause) among other things stated, that they distinctly understood, at the time when the bond was executed, that it was taken by Sir Charles Flower as a sort of security for the future good conduct and economy of his son, and that it was not to be acted upon or enforced, if the plaintiff's mode of living and behaviour were satisfactory to his father. These were the views with which they recommended the bond to be taken and deposited with them; and they were convinced, that it was the intention of Sir Charles Flower, when he took the bond, not to interfere, or to require payment of any part of the sum secured by it, if the plaintiff conducted himself to his satisfaction. The deponents further stated, that they considered themselves to hold the bond upon trust to act respecting it, according to the intention and meaning of their letter, and to be perfectly at liberty to cancel it, if they saw fit, within six years from its date, without any reference to Sir Charles Flower.

The defendants, the executors, by their answer stated that, although Sir Charles Flower was remarkably accurate in keeping the accounts of his pecuniary transactions, and was in the habit of regularly making out a yearly statement or balance sheet in

[465]

which he entered every item of the assets and securities of which his property consisted, no entry relative to the bond in question, or to the principal or interest which it purported to secure, was to be found in any of the papers or account books which had come into their possession as his executors.

It was also deposed by a person who had lived for many years with Sir Charles Flower in the capacity of a confidential clerk, that no part of the principal or interest due upon the [*466] bond was ever demanded of the *plaintiff by his father, although if any such demand had been made, the deponent must have been acquainted with the fact, as all Sir Charles's pecuniary transactions passed through his hands. The witness further deposed, that he knew from communications with Sir Charles Flower at the time when the bond was given, that it was not Sir Charles's intention to enforce it, or to require the payment of any part of the sum secured by it, if the plaintiff's conduct was satisfactory to him.

That the reconciliation between the parties had been complete and permanent, and that the subsequent conduct of the plaintiff had been entirely satisfactory to his father, was proved by the evidence of all the witnesses.

Mr. Wigram and *Mr. Fisher*, for the plaintiff :

[467]   * * The intention and understanding of all parties were, that if the plaintiff's conduct during the [six years] proved satisfactory, the instrument should l e no longer a valid and subsisting obligation. [The power of cancelling the bond vested in the trustees was a power coupled with a trust,] and the trustees having omitted, through carelessness, to perform the trust, the Court ought now to supply the omission : *Harding* v. *Glyn* (1), *Brown* v. *Higgs* (2). [They also cited *Aston* v. *Pye* (3), *Eden* v. *Smyth* (4), *Byrn* v. *Godfrey* (5), *Wekett* v. *Raby* (6), *Gilbert* v. *Wetherell* (7), and *Leche* v. *Lord Kilmorey* (8).]

(1) 4 R. R. 334, 338 (1 Atk. 469).   (5) 4 R. R. 155 (4 Ves. 6).
(2) 4 R. R. 323 (4 Ves. 708 ; 5 Ves.   (6) 2 Br. P. C. 386, Toml. ed.
495 ; 8 Ves. 561).   (7) 25 R. R. 203 (2 Sim. & St. 254).
(3) 5 R. R. 66, 67 (5 Ves. 350, n.).   (8) 24 R. R. 19 (T. & R. 207).
(4) 5 R. R. 60 (5 Ves. 341).

Sir W. Horne and *Mr. James*, for the executors of Sir Charles Flower's will :

* * The Court has no right to look at parol evidence, to aid the construction of a deed. Here the instrument must speak for itself, and there is nothing in its frame or language, which, if fairly construed, favours the supposition that its operation was to cease at the end of the six years. [The right of cancellation was simply a power which vested in the trustees a discretion ; the power is altogether gone, and the defect cannot now be supplied. *Brown* v. *Higgs* and cases of that description have no application.] In *Aston* v. *Pye* and all the other cases that have been cited, the Court has inferred an intention, on the part of the obligee, to release or cancel the debt, from some positive act done or express declaration made : here there is an entire absence of acts and declarations ; and the Court is called upon, first to imply from that absence, the existence of a purpose, and then to give effect to the purpose so implied.

Mr. Geldart, for Messrs. Marten and Muspratt.

Mr. Wigram, in reply, said that the residuary legatees over had not been made parties to the suit, because they were extremely numerous, and their interest was uncertain and remote. Besides, they were sufficiently represented by the executors. The facts of the case were fully before the Court upon the cause as it stood, and no additional light was to be hoped for from further inquiry before the Master.

The LORD CHANCELLOR said he entertained no doubt as to the jurisdiction : the only difficulty he felt arose from the absence of the other residuary legatees.

THE LORD CHANCELLOR :

April 8.

It was not from any difficulty which I felt as to the law of the case, that I took time to consider my judgment ; but because I was called upon to deal with a large sum of money, in the absence of persons who had an interest in the fund, and when, in strictness, there were no parties before the Court to litigate the question adversely. For that reason it occurred to me, that the *safest course might be to direct a preliminary inquiry into the facts. On looking into the papers, however, I think it is clear that the question must depend solely upon the evidence of these two gentlemen, Messrs. Marten and Muspratt, from whose testimony the intention of the father is necessarily to be collected, and that nothing would be gained by sending the cause into the Master's office.

Of the jurisdiction of the Court I entertain no doubt whatever.

In this case a large sum of money was advanced by the plaintiff's father, for the purpose of paying off the debts of his son.   That advance may either have been made by way of gift, or as a loan to the son.   The taking a security for the amount is, *primâ facie,* evidence that the father meant originally to treat the sum as a debt: but that presumption is capable of being explained away and rebutted; and even if the sum constituted a debt in the first instance, the debtor, according to the authorities, is at liberty to show that the creditor subsequently altered his intention and treated it as a gift.

In the present case both circumstances concur.   Upon the evidence of the gentlemen with whom the bond was deposited, I cannot suppose that the father intended to treat the money, which he advanced on his son's behalf, as being, at all events, a debt.   He plainly meant to keep alive the security for a time, as a means of controlling and influencing the conduct of his son; and that was the main object of the instrument, to which the securing of the sum advanced was only collateral and subsidiary; but it does not appear from the testimony of the referees, that

the father ever actually dealt with *the bond as creating a debt, or as forming a part of his assets.

With respect to the six years during which the referees had the power of entirely discharging the obligation by executing a memorandum to that effect, the father had delegated that discretion to them as two of his confidential friends; and the discretion was wholly inconsistent with the notion that the bond was given merely, or principally, to secure the repayment of a sum of money.   Within that period, events had taken place which, as the referees themselves state, induced them to think that the claim was no longer available: the father and son were completely reconciled and united; and the conduct of the son throughout had been highly satisfactory to the father. Now, if the events took place which would render it the duty of the referees to exercise the trust reposed in them by indorsing upon the bond the proposed memorandum, of which the effect would be to avoid the security and discharge the debt at law, the situation of the plaintiff cannot, in a court of equity, be affected by their omission to do that which they ought, under the circumstances, to have done.

That of itself would be a sufficient ground on which to rest the plaintiff's title to relief. But there is also another ground, to be deduced from the principles which were distinctly laid down in the cases of *Wckett* v. *Raby* (1) and *Eden* v. *Smyth* (2), namely, that whether this obligation constituted a debt or not, either originally or during the continuance of the prescribed period, the father subsequently did not intend that it should be treated as a debt due from his son to his own *estate, and be put in force accordingly. Nearly six years elapsed after these two gentlemen ceased, according to the letter of the condition, to have any authority or control; nevertheless, throughout the whole of that period, the father left the bond in their hands, and treated his son in a manner expressive of his entire reconciliation and satisfaction with him, and showing that the object of the transaction having been attained, he understood and considered the instrument as no longer subsisting and in force.

[*475]

Both points seem to me to concur in the present case. Upon the evidence, I think that the bond was not in the first instance intended to operate as a debt at all events: at any rate, the father, by his subsequent conduct and his mode of dealing, showed that he did not mean it should now so operate; but that in fact he abandoned any claim in respect of it.

Under such circumstances the authority of the cases referred to sufficiently establishes the jurisdiction of the Court to deal with the instrument in question. There must, therefore, be a decree that the bond be delivered up to be cancelled.

(1) 2 Br. P. C. 386, Toml. ed. (2) 5. R. R. 60 (5 Ves. 341).

1837.
June 16, 17,
24.

HOWELL *v.* HOWELL.

(2 My. & Cr. 478—486; S. C. 1 Jur. 492.)

Lord
COTTENHAM,
L.C.

[478]

The account of rents given against a purchaser for value, who, after being in possession, is evicted by a party having a better title, ought not to extend to such rents as, without his default or neglect, might have been received, if no special case of fraud is made against him.

The decree for such an account ought to contain a direction for just allowances.

[Upon the point stated in the above head-note,]

June 24.

The Lord Chancellor said:

[485]

This was a case of adverse possession, the defendant who is sought to be charged, having an apparent title, which, however, was defeated by an equitable settlement, under which the plaintiff took an estate tail in the property in question. The result has been, that though the defendant purchased and paid for the estate, a jury has found that he took it with notice of the settlement; and he has consequently lost the benefit of his purchase. There are no special circumstances in the case, beyond the fact of the defendant having purchased with notice.

The question then is, whether it is consistent with the practice, that the decree should charge the defendant with the rents and profits which might have been received without his default or neglect. The introduction of these words at once struck me as

[*486]

unusual; *and I have ascertained on inquiry that no precedent for it can be found, this being neither the case of a mortgagee in possession, nor of a trustee against whom a special breach of trust is charged. With this view, I was desirous of ascertaining the terms of the decree in *Pultney* v. *Warren* (1), and I directed a search to be made in the Registrar's book; but, on inquiry, it appears that the decree in that case was never drawn up.

Under these circumstances, no case being cited in support of such a decree, and all the precedents and the practice being against it, I cannot permit the decree to stand.

I am further of opinion that a clause should be inserted empowering the Master to make just allowances: in short the decree must be such a decree, and in such a form, as is usual in a case where there are no special circumstances.

(1) 5 R. R. 226 (6 Ves. 73).

It is clear that, in point of form, I can make no order upon the exception, the decree on which the report was founded having been so materially varied that it can no longer be considered as the same decree upon which the Master has proceeded ; but it may save future discussion and exception that the matter has been now brought before me, and that I have expressed an opinion upon it.

HORLOCK *v.* SMITH (1).

(2 My. & Cr. 495—526 ; S. C. 6 L. J. (N. S.) Ch. 236 ; 1 Jur. 302.)

1837.
April 20, 21.
May 4.

Lord
COTTENHAM,
L.C.

[495]

If a client, having paid his solicitor's bill of costs, without pressure or undue influence, wishes afterwards to have it taxed, he must state in his petition, and prove by evidence, that the bill contains such grossly improper charges, as furnish evidence of fraud ; and the petition must point out the particular items to which that description applies, and those items must be proved by evidence to answer the description.

An allegation that a solicitor has received monies on account of his client, for which credit has not been given in the settlement of a bill of costs, is not sufficient, although supported by evidence, to warrant an order for the taxation of the bill.

Principles of the Court with respect to the taxation of a solicitor's bill after payment.

[THIS was an appeal from an order made by the MASTER OF THE ROLLS for taxation of a bill of costs more than twelve months after payment. The facts of the case are sufficiently stated for the purposes of this report in the following judgment of the LORD CHANCELLOR, who said :]

The Court will always be anxious, in every possible way, to protect the client against any improper dealing on the part of the solicitor ; but it is absolutely necessary that some rule should be laid down, by which professional gentlemen shall know when they may consider their bills of costs as finally settled, and whether the money which they have received in respect of those bills is their own, or whether those bills are subject *to investigation or review upon the application of the client.

It requires, therefore, and all the cases show that it requires, a strong case to be made against the solicitor, when the client applies for a taxation of the bill after payment ; and when, after

(1) *Watson* v. *Rodwell* (1878—9) affirmed 11 Ch. Div. 150, 48 L. J. Ch.
7 Ch. D. 625, 631, 47 L. J. Ch. 418, 209, 39 L. T. 614.

HORLOCK
v.
SMITH.

proper time and opportunity for investigating the items which the bill contained, he has thought proper to pay it. The Court will, no doubt, give relief after any length of time, if a case of fraud or improper conduct is made out against the solicitor; but it is quite necessary that it should be understood that the client is not, after payment, to have a taxation merely for asking for it.

The facts of this case appear to be these: Messrs. Goode were employed by the late Mr. William Yems, from the year 1818, in certain suits in which he was a defendant, and they so continued to be employed until September, 1833, when he died. The representatives of Mr. Yems did not think fit to employ Messrs. Goode; but Messrs. Harris and Rye were employed by them; and from that period, of course, Messrs. Goode ceased to be employed as the solicitors in those affairs. These gentlemen, Messrs. Harris and Rye, applied to Messrs. Goode for their bill against the late Mr. Yems' estate; and on the 4th of April, 1835, a bill was delivered to the amount of 790*l.* On the 23rd of May following another bill to the amount of 23*l.* was delivered; and accompanying this bill there was a statement of account, giving credit for certain sums as received; the balance of the account being 510*l.* due to the solicitors. On the 25th of May, being about six weeks after the principal bill was delivered, but only two days after the second bill for 23*l.* together with the cash account was delivered, the petitioners, that is to say the repre-

[*511]

sentatives *of the client, applied to have a meeting with Messrs. Goode, for the purpose of settling their account. It was investigated by them, as they thought proper to investigate it, and the balance of 510*l.* was paid, and Messrs. Goode were required to deliver up the papers belonging to the estate of Mr. Yems. Of course, some little time was required before they could be looked out and ascertained; and in October, 1835, some of the papers were delivered to the representatives of Mr. Yems; but it appears that others were not then delivered.

The petition states, that the petitioners were unable to examine the items in the bill, until the papers were delivered out, that is, until October, 1835.

If it had been intended to support the case upon that allegation, it should have been distinctly proved; but no evidence was

given upon the point: the statement is made in the affidavit in
general terms ; but no reason is stated to show why the papers
were necessary ; and I must observe, that if that was the case,
Messrs. Goode ought to have been informed of it, when the
petitioners professed to settle the bill.   A case, to which I shall
presently have occasion to refer, will show that that circumstance
struck Lord ELDON as being matter of very serious observation.
If the petitioners obtained the papers from Messrs. Goode, upon
the supposition that the bill was finally settled, intending, however, to apply afterwards for a taxation, upon the ground of
Messrs. Goode's possession of the papers, but concealing that
intention from Messrs. Goode, I think they ought not very easily
to be allowed to take advantage of that circumstance at a future
time.   It was competent for them, if the papers were necessary
to enable them to tax the bill, to inform Messrs. Goode of that
necessity: that would have led to some settlement of the bill.
The petitioners, however, obtain possession of the papers *from
Messrs. Goode, without any notice, leaving them under the idea
that they had finally settled the account of their client ; and then,
after Messrs. Goode have parted with the papers which they were
entitled to retain until the bill should have been taxed, the
petitioners come here and apply for a taxation.

[*512]

The petition contains a general allegation of improper charges,
but specifies none, except the expenses of two alleged journeys
to Northampton ; and then, afterwards, it says that William
Yems ought to have received credit for sums for which he did not
receive credit ; but no particular sum is specified in the petition.
That is the whole of the petition.   I conceive, and so it was considered by Lord ELDON, in several cases which came before him,
that if an application is made to open a bill upon the ground
of improper charge, the respondent is as much entitled to have
the particular items stated in the petition, as a defendant to a
bill, filed for the purpose of opening a settled account, is entitled
to have the particular items on which the plaintiff intends to rely
stated in the bill.   The Court must not only have something
amounting, in the language of the cases upon this subject, to
fraud, but also a distinct statement of particular items which
shall enable the respondent to meet the charge made by the

HORLOCK
v.
SMITH.

petition: otherwise the greatest possible injustice may be done. If the Court gives credit to the statements in such a petition, it leads to an order for taxation; and then a large part of the bill may be taken off, upon strict taxation, which the solicitor might well be entitled to charge the client; at all events, if the client was aware of the amount of charge, and did not think proper to object to it. It is, therefore, absolutely necessary, in order to justice being done between the parties, that a client, applying to have his solicitor's bill taxed, should allege and prove specific errors, amounting to what the cases mean, when

[*513]

they speak of gross errors *amounting to evidence of fraud. I am speaking, of course, of cases in which the client, without pressure or improper influence, with every means of examining the bill, thinks proper to pay it, and then afterwards applies for a taxation.

[After referring to the affidavits filed in support of the petition, and to a number of earlier authorities to which any further reference is now unnecessary, his Lordship continued his judgment as follows:]

[520]

Here is a bill delivered, and subsequently paid; the relation of solicitor and client has ceased; another solicitor has been employed by the client. There is no evidence of pressure, no necessity for the papers stated or proved, or suggested to Messrs. Goode when they were applied for.

The utmost that the cases establish is, that under such circumstances, the Court will open a bill and have it taxed, upon proof of specific errors so gross as to amount to evidence of fraud; and, if specific errors had been alleged and proved, I might not have been justified in refusing taxation, notwithstanding all that has passed.

[After further comment on the items of taxation as appearing in the evidence, the LORD CHANCELLOR continued:]

[522]

In this case, as in a bill to open an account, *primâ facie* errors are not enough; the error must be alleged and proved. For if, because there is a *primâ facie* error, the account were to be opened, that *primâ facie* error might afterwards be explained; and the very ground upon which the order is to stand may be taken from under the party obtaining it; and yet the effect

of the order remains.   I apprehend that it is absolutely
necessary, that, when an application for taxation is made upon
the ground of errors, it should be distinctly stated in the petition,
and proved, that such errors exist.

[Some further remarks on the details of the case are omitted
as no longer useful to the profession.]

WATERS *v.* TAYLOR.

(2 My. & Cr. 526—558; S. C. 6 L. J. (N. S.) Ch. 245; 1 Jur. 375.)

1837.
Feb. 23.
March 3.
May 24.

Lord
COTTENHAM,
L.C.

[526]

Refusal to order the taxation of a solicitor's bill of costs, the amount
of which had been secured by a deed in the year 1819, although the suit
was then pending ; the client's affairs having, since the year 1822, (when
that solicitor died) been in the hands of another solicitor, and there being
no proof of such dealings between the solicitor and client, or of such
errors or improper charges in the bill, as could amount to evidence
of fraud.

THIS was an appeal from an order made by the VICE-
CHANCELLOR on the 21st day of November, 1836, directing the
taxation of certain bills of costs delivered previously to the
20th of July, 1819, the payment of which costs had been secured
by a deed of that date.

The original report sets forth the various transactions and
documents at great length, but the following judgment of the
LORD CHANCELLOR sufficiently states the facts and the result of
the evidence filed in support of the application for taxation and
the grounds upon which the application was based.]

THE LORD CHANCELLOR :

Having very recently, in the case of *Horlock* v. *Smith* (1), had
occasion to state my view of the cases relating to taxing bills of
solicitors, which had been settled and paid, it will only be
necessary in this case for me to state the facts as they appear
in evidence, and to apply the doctrine to be deduced from those
cases to such facts.

That part of the VICE-CHANCELLOR's order which has given
rise to the discussion in this case directs the taxation of all bills
of costs of the late Mr. Mills, and of his firm of Mills, Robinson,

(1) See the preceding case.

and Young, delivered before the 20th of July, 1819, in respect
of business done for Mr. Waters, and of the receipts on his
account, and declares that the sum so found due shall be treated
as the sum secured by the deed of the 20th of July, 1819.

There is but little dispute as to the facts. It appears that in
1814 and 1815 Mr. Mills became assignee, in trust for Waters,
of two annuities, supposed to be charges upon the Opera House;
and it appears, from a recital in the deed of 1817, that Waters
was, before that time, indebted to Mills in a certain sum due on
a mortgage made by Mr. Goold, to whom Waters was executor;
but, whatever may have been the nature of that security, by the
deed of 4th of February, 1817, that sum, recited to be so secured,
and another sum stated to have been that day ascertained to be
due to Mills & Co., upon an account stated, are charged upon
the two annuities, and the arrears due. The deed of the 20th
of July, 1819, recites that there was then due to Mills upon that
security 2,018l., and to Mills & Co. 4,078l., and that it was
[*552] desirable, to enable Waters to settle his purchase *money,
that their lien upon the annuities should be released: they
accordingly released such charge; and Waters, with the concurrence of Chambers and Mayhew, who appear to have had
themselves a charge upon the property, assigns all his interest
in the theatre, and in the monies arising therefrom, to secure
the debt so secured by the deed of 1817, and subsequent
additions to it, making, together, due to Mills 2,979l., and to
Mills & Co. 5,087l.

In 1822 Mr. Mills died, and Dr. Sutherland is his
representative. From that time, Mr. Leake acted as solicitor
for Waters.

From Mr. Young's affidavit it appears, that in 1811, the first
bill of costs was delivered; that in 1815, Waters gave a bill
of exchange for the balance due at that time; that in 1816,
other bills were delivered, and the amount secured by the deed
of 1817: that upon the dissolution of partnership between Mr.
Mills and Messrs. Young and Robinson, the latter were desirous
of having Waters's debt paid; that a meeting took place, at
which Mr. Waters and Mr. Mayhew were present: that Waters
stated his inability to pay at that time; and that, thereupon,

Mills undertook to satisfy his partners their shares, and take the debt to himself, which he afterwards did, and so became solely entitled to receive what is due : that the sums were then filled in, Mr. Mills asking Waters if he had looked through the bills, and Waters answering that they came to much less than he expected, and that he would not examine them further. I mention the fact that Mr. Mayhew was present, not because I find any proof of his acting for Waters, but because if there had been any inaccuracy in Mr. Young's statement of what took place, Mr. Mayhew might have been called upon to explain it.

[553]

Founded upon these securities, and there being a large sum in Court subject to this charge, Dr. Sutherland, as representative of Mr. Mills, in July last, presented a petition for payment of what was due to his estate; but that petition having been adjourned to November, Mr. Winchester, as assignee of Mr. Waters, presented a cross petition, praying, in substance, what the order has directed. In support of this application to have the bills taxed, prior to the security of 1817 and 1819, this petition alleged, that the bills had not been investigated by any person on behalf of Waters ; that 747*l.* 4*s.* 4*d.*, part of the sum secured by the deed of 1819, was for Waters's costs in *Taylor* v. *Waters;* that that suit was dismissed with costs in 1821, and that his taxed costs amounted only to 229*l.* 19*s.* 4*d.* ; that, in 1830, the costs of all parties in *Waters* v. *Taylor* were or lered to be taxed and paid, and that Waters's costs, comprised in the bills secured by the deed of 1819, were claimed at 5,855*l.* 9*s.* 10*d.*, but were reduced to 3,971*l.* 5*s.* 3*d.*—1,884*l.* 4*s.* 7*d.* having been taken off ; and the petition infers, though it does not in terms state, that this taxation was attended by Messrs. Young & Co. as solicitors for the representative of Mr. Mills ; and Mr. Bury's affidavit is calculated to lead to the same conclusion: but Mr. Elliott positively denies that the attendance was on behalf of Mr. Mills's estate ; and states, that it was given at the request of Mr. Leake, for the protection of Mr. Waters's estate : and the charges for such attendance, mentioned in Mr. Bury's affidavit, leave no doubt in my mind that such was the fact. These taxations, therefore, of *Taylor* v. *Waters* in 1821, and of *Waters* v. *Taylor* in 1830, were not between Mr. Mills's estate and the

[*554]

clients, but between the parties in the causes, and cannot, therefore, be used as evidence against Mr. Mills's representatives;
besides which, it does not appear what portion of the costs
claimed and *taxed off in *Taylor* v. *Waters*, related to the period
between the years 1819 and 1821; and Mr. Young states, that
of 10,000*l.* of costs, only 4,500*l.* related to this suit; and Mr.
Elliott states that many of the items struck out upon taxation,
were so struck out, only because they did not belong to the suit,
the costs of which were then in question, and I do not find that
denied in any subsequent affidavit.

Now, if the results of these taxations do not establish the right
to have the bills before the year 1819 taxed, I look in vain for any
other ground; because, though some other objections are made
to the bills, in the petition, I do not find any of them supported
by evidence.   The petition alleges, that Mr. Mills appeared for
Mr. Palmer, a defendant in *Waters* v. *Taylor*, and that he has
charged attendance for him against Mr. Waters, although Mr.
Palmer, by his answer, declined acting as trustee.   It is not
disputed that Waters was properly charged with Mr. Palmer's
costs, but it is intended to be inferred that the costs subsequent
to the answer might have been spared.   I find nothing in any
affidavit to prove this to have been so; and if there had been
any such evidence, it would amount only to this,—that the cause
in this respect might have been more economically conducted,—
a position which, if established, would not avail for the present
purpose.   The only other allegation of error in the petition is,
that the bills contained various charges for sequestration fees,
which appeared, upon taxation, not to have been paid: but what
those charges were, or in what bills they are to be found, is not
stated; and I find no evidence to support the charge.   It may,
indeed, well be supposed, that after so many years, and with the
admitted fact of the loss and destruction of papers, and the
unrestricted access to all other papers afforded to the solicitors

[*555]

of Mr. Waters, and the delivery *to them of all they required,
the evidence of many payments cannot now be produced by the
representative of Mr. Mills; which affords the strongest possible
reason against a taxation at this time.

The result of all this evidence comes to this: that the business

to which the bills apply commenced twenty-eight years ago, and
was concluded eighteen years ago; that some of the bills were
delivered so early as 1811, twenty-six years ago; that, in 1817,
the amount then claimed to be due was secured upon certain
property : that in 1819, for the convenience of the client, the
solicitor gave up this security, and, with the concurrence of
prior incumbrancers, took a new charge upon other property;
that, upon that occasion, the sum being ascertained, the solicitor,
Mr. Mills, with the knowledge of the client, Mr. Waters, and for
his accommodation, bought and paid for his partners' shares
of the debt; that from 1822, now fifteen years ago, Mr. Waters's
affairs have been under the care of another solicitor; but that
no attempt was ever made to open the account so closed in
1819, until last November, and that the attempt then made was
not supported by that which alone could give it any title to
success, namely, allegations and proof of such dealing between
the solicitor and client, or of such errors and improper charges
in the bills, as could amount to evidence of fraud.   It is made
to rest entirely upon the alleged reduction of the bills, upon
a taxation to which neither the solicitor nor his representative
was a party, and under the circumstances upon which I have
before observed. The client has not only permitted eighteen
years to elapse since the date of the security, without objection,
but has had the use and possession of all the papers he required;
and he has had the benefit of the long forbearance of his creditors,
*to obtain which, Mr. Mills, with his privity, purchased the   [*556]
shares of his partners in this debt.

It would require a very strong case indeed, to induce me to
open the account, if there had been nothing else in answer to
this attempt; but not only are there these strong grounds of
resistance to the application for a taxation, but there is an absence
of all that is required to support it.

The case indeed differs from that of *Horlock* v. *Smith* (1), in
this,—that the security was taken whilst the suits were depending:
and whilst the relation of solicitor and client continued, but so it
was in *Cooke* v. *Setree* (2); and in *Plenderleath* v. *Fraser* (3), and

(1) P. 125, *supra*.   (3) 3 V. & B. 174.
(2) 1 V. & B. 126.

Gretton v. *Leyburne* (1), the relation of attorney and client continued at the time of the settlement. No doubt, the settlement or payment of a solicitor's bills, pending a suit, and whilst the relation continues, affords grounds upon which the account will be much more easily opened, and the bills referred for taxation, than in other cases ; but, if these circumstances alone were in all cases to be held sufficient ground for a taxation, no solicitor who continues to act for a client would be secure of any settlement during the life of his client ; and the continuance of one of those suits which not unfrequently occur in this Court would prevent the possibility of any settlement between the solicitor and the client. It is, however, unnecessary to consider this point further, because, in this case, I find acquiescence, for from twenty-six to eighteen years, and the enjoyment of the forbearance during that time, and the consequent destruction of vouchers and delivering up of papers, and the important fact of the purchase

[*557]

by *the solicitor, with the privity of the client, and for his benefit, of part of the debt so secured, and the absence of any proof of improper dealing on the part of the solicitor, or of any such errors in the bills settled as the decided cases require for the purpose of opening an account settled and sending a solicitor's bill, so long settled and secured, to a taxation.

Having, in this case and in that of *Horlock* v. *Smith*, had the misfortune to differ from the MASTER OF THE ROLLS and the VICE-CHANCELLOR, I have endeavoured, by a careful examination of the cases, to ascertain the limits of the rule as laid down in them. To that rule, as I find it laid down, I am anxious to adhere, being persuaded that, whilst it affords ample protection to the client against any improper dealing and extravagant charges on the part of the solicitor, it does not deny to the solicitor that justice to which all men are entitled, or the means of settling their accounts, and of winding up their affairs, which, if the rule were to be further relaxed, it would be in most cases impossible for them to accomplish.

I am bound to act upon the opinion I have formed, that the settlement and security of 1819 has not been successfully impeached. The subsequent bills must be taxed, and the account

(1) T. & R. 407.

founded upon the security of 1819 must be taken. All this
would have been ordered upon the petition of Dr. Sutherland.
The petition of Mr. Winchester was unnecessary, except for the
purpose of obtaining a taxation of the bills prior to 1819 : and,
as it has failed in that object, it ought, I think, to be dismissed
with costs.

It was objected, upon the authority of some of the cases cited,
that Mr. Winchester, not being the client, *could not have the
bills taxed ; but this is not a case for taxation simply under the
statute ; but Dr. Sutherland seeks to enforce payment out of a
fund in Court ; and, when necessary and proper, in order to
ascertain the amount of the charge, the Court will direct a
taxation as between the party claiming the charge and the party
representing the fund, who in this case is Mr. Winchester.

WATERS
r.
TAYLOR.

[*558]

BEHRENS v. SIEVEKING.

(2 My. & Cr. 602—603 ; S. C. nom. *Sieveking* v. *Behrens*, 1 Jur. 329.)

A plea of proceedings in another Court of competent jurisdiction must
show not only that the same issue was joined as in the suit in this Court,
but that the subject-matter was the same, and that the proceedings in
the other Court were taken for the same purpose.

THE LORD CHANCELLOR [giving leave to amend a plea of proceedings in another Court of competent jurisdiction] said, that
in order to support the plea, it was necessary to show that the
proceedings in which the plaintiffs were alleged to have failed,
were taken for the same purpose as the present suit ; for, the
issue might have been the same, while the object was different ;
and the circumstance that the matter had been tried, as a matter
of evidence, could not be conclusive. The defendant had to show
that the subject-matter was the same ; that the right came in
question before a Court of competent jurisdiction ; and that the
result was conclusive, so as to bind the judgment of every other
Court. [His Lordship then pointed out that the particular plea
before him did not satisfy these conditions.]

1837.
May 4.

Lord
COTTENHAM,
L.C.
[602]

[603]

1836.
April 26.
___
Rolls Court.
On Appeal.
1836.
Nov. 21, 23.
___
Lord
COTTENHAM,
L.C.

[606]

[1 Keen,
817]

COOKSON *v.* HANCOCK.

(1 Keen, 817—825 ; S. C. 5 L. J. (N. S.) Ch. 245 ; affirmed, 2 My. & Cr.
606—610 ; 6 L. J. (N. S.) Ch. 56.)

A testator by his will gave 3,000*l.* to his brother B. for life, with
remainder, as to 1,000*l.*, to his wife for life; remainder, as to the whole,
to his children ; he then gave 6,000*l.* to his sister S. for life, with
remainder to her husband for life, remainder to her children ; and, after
bequeathing 10*l.* a year to each of his two maid servants for their lives,
he gave all his real estate, and the residue of his personal estate to his
sister H. absolutely. By a testamentary paper described as a codicil
to his will, he left his brother B. an equal share of his effects with his
sisters, to have the interest for his life, with remainder to his children,
subject to a life interest in 1,000*l.* to his wife, if living at his death ; and
his sister S. was to have an equal share with his sister H. By a subsequent testamentary paper, also described as a codicil, he left his two maid
servants 10*l.* a year each for their lives, and nominated a person to act
as trustees with the executors named in the will:

Held, upon the effect of all the testamentary papers taken together,
that the will, though modified, was not wholly revoked by the first
codicil ; and that, in lieu of the 6,000*l.* legacy given them by the will,
S. and her children were entitled to one third share of the personal
estate, in the same manner and subject to the same limitations as had
been expressed by the will with respect to that legacy.

THE will and other testamentary papers, upon the construction
of which the question in this cause turned, are stated in Mr.
Keen's report of the case on the hearing at the Rolls [as follows
(1 Keen, 817)].

Thomas Baker, by his will, dated the 26th of January, 1826,
gave and bequeathed to his brother, the defendant, George Baker,
the interest of 3,000*l.* for his life, and after the decease of George
Baker, he directed that the principal sum of 3,000*l.* should be on
trust for the said George Baker's children, share and share alike,
provided George Baker's wife should not be then living ; but in
case she should be then living, he directed that 2,000*l.*, part of
said sum of 3,000*l.* should only be in trust for the said children at
the death of his, the testator's, brother ; and that the interest of
the remaining 1,000*l.* should be paid to the wife of his said
brother for her life ; and that at her decease, the said sum of
1,000*l.* should be in trust for the said children, share and share
alike. And the testator gave and bequeathed the interest of
6,000*l.* to his sister Catharine Smith for her life ; and in case
her husband Thomas Smith should survive her, he gave and

bequeathed the interest of the said sum of 6,000*l.* to him for his life, and from and after the decease of the survivor of them, his said sister and her husband, he directed that the said principal sum of 6,000*l.* should be in trust for their children, share and share alike; and he gave and bequeathed to his two maid servants, the sum of 10*l.* a year a piece for their *respective natural lives, and as to all his real estates whatsoever and wheresoever, and all the rest, residue, and remainder of his personal estate and effects whatsoever, not therein before disposed of, he gave, devised, and bequeathed the same, and every part thereof to his sister the defendant Jane Hancock, her heirs, executors, administrators, and assigns, according to the several natures and tenures thereof; and he appointed John Philipson and Thomas Smith executors of his will.

The testator afterwards made two codicils to his will, which were unattested. The first of these codicils was dated the 3rd of January, 1827, and was in the following words: "Codicil to my will. I hereby leave my brother George Baker an equal share of my effects with my sisters, to have the interest during his life, and after his decease the principal to be divided amongst his children, share and share alike, provided his wife should not be then living; but in case she shall be then living, in such case she shall have the interest of 1,000*l.* during her life, and at her decease the said sum of 1,000*l.* shall be in trust for the said children, share and share alike: my sister Catharine Smith to have an equal share with my sister Jane Hancock."

The second codicil, dated the 29th of November, 1828, was as follows: "Codicil to my will. I leave to my two maid servants each 10*l.* a year during their natural lives; and I appoint Mr. John Hunter to act with Mr. Thomas Smith and Mr. John Philipson as trustees."

The testator died in the month of April, 1829, leaving his brother George Baker and Elizabeth his wife, and their six children, his sister Catharine Smith, and Thomas Smith her husband, and his sister Jane Hancock surviving him; and his will and codicils were proved by *John Smith alone, who died on the 15th of May in the same year; and the other executors, named in the will, having renounced probate thereof, administration

COOKSON
r.
HANCOCK.

with the will and codicils annexed, was granted to the defendant
Jane Hancock.

Catharine Smith survived her husband, Thomas Smith, and
died on the 10th of August, 1833, leaving two children, the
defendant Edward Smith, and Elizabeth Smith, who intermarried with the plaintiff Charles Cookson. Elizabeth Cookson
died in the month of April, 1833, and the plaintiff thereupon
took out administration to her personal estate.

The bill was filed by the plaintiff against Jane Hancock,
George Baker, and his wife and their children ; and the plaintiff,
as administrator of his deceased wife, claimed to be entitled to
one moiety of the legacy of 6,000*l.* and one sixth part of the
residuary personal estate of the testator.

[2 My. & Cr.
606]

By the decree of the MASTER OF THE ROLLS it was (among other
things) declared that, according to the true construction of the
codicils to the will, the residue of the testator's personal estate,
subject to annuities of 10*l.* to each of his two maid servants, but
not subject to the 3,000*l.* and 6,000*l.* given by his will, was
divisible into three equal shares, and that one of such shares
belonged to the defendants George Baker and his wife, and their
children, in the same manner as was by the will directed with
respect to the 3,000*l.*, and that one other of such shares belonged
to the children of Thomas Smith and Catherine his wife (both
deceased), in the same manner as was by the will directed as to
the 6,000*l.*, and that the remaining third share belonged to Jane
Hancock. The defendant Edward Smith, as executor of his
mother Catherine Smith, and in that character claiming the
whole of her third, appealed against this part of the decree.

[607]

Mr. Temple, Mr. Wigram, and *Mr. Bagshawe,* in support
of the appeal, contended that the operation of the first codicil
was wholly to revoke the legacy of 6,000*l.* bequeathed to
Catherine Smith and her children, and to give to her, in lieu of
a life interest in that sum, an absolute interest in one third
share of the testator's personal estate.

Sir C. Wetherell, Mr. Swanston, and *Mr. Purvis,* for the
plaintiff, submitted that the first codicil was to be confined in
its effect to the testator's residuary personal estate only, and

that it did not revoke or at all affect the legacy of 6,000*l*. If that construction, however, should be rejected as inadmissible, they then contended, in support of the decree, that the share of the residue given by the first codicil must be considered as substituted for the legacy given by the will, and subject, by implication, to the same limitation in favour of the children of Catherine Smith, after their mother's death, as that legacy had been.

THE LORD CHANCELLOR, [after stating the substance of the will and codicils (1) :]

It was observed at the Bar that there are only three constructions which can possibly be put upon the first codicil. The first is, that the pecuniary legacies given by the will are not revoked by that codicil, but that the codicil operates only upon the residue by the will bequeathed to Jane Hancock; and that the object of the codicil, therefore, was to leave the sums of 8,000*l*. and 6,000*l*. exactly as they stood upon the will; and to declare the brother and the other sister should participate equally with her in the residue. The second is the construction contended for by the appellant; namely, that the codicil has the effect of revoking the whole of the *provisions of the will, not by any express declaration, but by operating upon the whole of the property of which the will purported to dispose, and so superseding its provisions. The third is the construction which the MASTER OF THE ROLLS has adopted, that the codicil was only intended to affect the proportions of the estate to be taken by those legatees respectively, and to make that equal which was, by the will, unequal.

The first of these constructions was not insisted upon by the appellant. The MASTER OF THE ROLLS decided against it; and it is quite clear that it cannot for a moment be maintained. The expression "effects," used in the codicil, is quite conclusive against holding that the testator was there intending to deal only with that which he had described in the will as the residue of his personal estate. Such a construction, besides, would wholly

(1) The will was duly attested to pass freehold estate, but it did not appear whether the testator left any real property.

defeat the object of the codicil, which is manifestly equality—
equality, not in reference to any particular portion of the assets,
but in reference to the effects generally, that is, the entire
personal estate. The consequence of preserving the bequests
contained in the will would be to produce gross inequality
among the legatees ; George would not be placed on an equality
with his sisters, or Catherine with Jane ; but they would each
take the property in very different proportions, and Jane would
be entitled to much the smallest share. As this construction,
however, has not been insisted upon, it is needless to consider
it further.

Upon the second construction proposed, the MASTER OF THE
ROLLS said he had no right to look at the amount of the estate
otherwise than as it appeared in the testamentary papers. If,
however, it appears from those papers, that the testator knew
or believed the estate to be of a certain amount, that knowledge,
so expressed, may very properly be called in aid of the construction. *Now, it is clear from the codicil, that the testator
considered the residue to be greater than the 6,000*l.* bequeathed
to his sister Catherine ; for he says that Catherine shall have
an equal share with Jane ; an expression which he would hardly
have employed, unless he had conceived that the residue
previously given to Jane exceeded the amount of the legacy to
Catherine. So, again, there is no direct gift in terms to Jane at
all ; the testator assumes Jane to be already in possession of
something ; and the object of the codicil is to take a portion of
that from her, for the purpose of raising Jane's sister to an
equality with Jane.

[*609]

If the codicil has the effect contended for by the appellant,
it entirely revokes the will. But it revokes the will, not by any
declared intention as to the legacies of 6,000*l.* and 3,000*l.*,
but by dealing with the property which is the subject-matter of
the dispositions ; and, if the appellant's construction be correct,
it must have operated as much on the annuities given to the two
maid servants as on those money legacies. According to that
view, the testator, when he executed the first codicil, intended to
make an entirely new disposition, which should embrace the
whole of his property. If that were the case, he has certainly

taken a very singular way of accomplishing his object. Why should he not rather have at once proceeded to make a new will? Instead of that, however, he describes each of these testamentary papers as a codicil to his will; assuming, therefore, that the will was a subsisting instrument; and in neither of them is there any gift of his estate, in terms. And yet, according to the appellant's argument, the will was virtually revoked for every purpose except the appointment of executors.

It was argued that the repetition, in the second codicil, of the bequest for the benefit of the two maid servants, *showed an impression in the testator's mind, that he had, by the previous codicil, revoked all the legacies given by the will, and, among others, the annuities given to the maid servants. That circumstance may indeed prove, that in November, 1828, he was afraid he might have done so; but it rather tends to show that in January, 1827, he had not intended so to do: and the reference to the two executors named in his will and the addition of a third prove that he then considered the will to be a subsisting instrument. If he had intended to revoke the whole of his will, he would have given his estate in equal shares, and not have brought Catherine up to Jane, and George up to them both. But, if his object was not to alter the disposition by his will, otherwise than by making the division equal, the expressions used in his first codicil are all explained. They are imperfect expressions for either purpose; but they are consistent with the third construction, and inconsistent with the second.

It was further said that the settlement of George's share shows that Catherine was to take her share absolutely. Had the settlement of the 6,000l. and of the 3,000l. been the same, the observation would have had weight; but, as the case is, the fact favours the third construction, because it proves that the testator had in his mind, and intended to a certain extent to maintain the provisions of the will, even as to quantity and proportion; namely, by giving to George's widow the interest of 1,000l. only. Had he devoted to George's family one third of the residue simply, his widow might have claimed one third of the income of the substituted provision, as she had one third of the income of the 3,000l. As to her, therefore, the testator says she shall not participate in the increase ; a circumstance leading to the construction that increase of the shares of George and Catherine, and not a new disposition, was the object of the codicil.

[611]

Upon these grounds I am of opinion that the third construction, which has been adopted by the MASTER OF THE ROLLS, is the true construction of these testamentary papers. The decree must therefore be affirmed, but as the question is one of difficulty, and created by the testator himself, it shows that the appeal is not censurable, and that the costs of it should be added to the costs of the cause.

1837.
Jan. 16, 17.
Aug. 15.

Lord
COTTENHAM,
L.C.

[611]

SAWYER *v.* BIRCHMORE.

(2 My. & Cr. 611—612.)

[A NOTE of this appeal, varying the decision of the MASTER OF THE ROLLS as reported in 1 Keen, 391, will be found at the end of the report in the Rolls Court. See 44 R. R. 93, at p. 100.— O. A. S.]

1836.
May 25, 27,
30.
July 4.

Rolls Court.
Lord
LANGDALE,
M.R.

On Appeal.
1837.
Jan. 9, 10.
Nov. 11.

———
Lord
COTTENHAM,
L.C.

[613]

THE ATTORNEY-GENERAL *v.* ASPINALL.

(1 Keen, 513—544 ; reversed on appeal, 2 My. & Cr. 613—634 ; S. C. 7 L. J. (N. S.) Ch. 51 ; 1 Jur. 812.)

The funds belonging to the municipal corporations of boroughs named in schedules A. and B. of the 5 & 6 Will. IV. c. 76 (the Municipal Corporation Act)(1) became, upon the passing of that Act, subject to certain public trusts, to be exercised by the new council, only in the manner and for the purposes prescribed by the Act.

An appropriation of such funds, made by the old corporation, after the passing of the Act, but before the election of the new council, and having for its object to endow the churches and chapels of the established church within the borough with fixed stipends, for their several ministers, is not an appropriation warranted by the Act, and is therefore a breach of trust.

The ordinary jurisdiction of the Court over such a transaction, by means of an information seeking to have the funds recalled, and the appropriation rescinded, as being a breach of trust, is not ousted by the special remedies provided in certain cases by the 97th section of the Municipal Corporation Act.

Where property is devoted to trusts which are to arise at a future time, and be exercised by trustees who are not yet in *esse*, any intermediate act done by the holders of such property, inconsistent with the

(1) Repealed by the Municipal Corporations Act, 1882 (45 & 46 Vict. c. 50), s. 5.

security of the property, or the performance of the trusts when they A.-G.
shall arise, will be set aside; and if the trusts are of a public nature, *r.*
the Court will entertain this jurisdiction upon an information by the ASPINALL.
Attorney-General, notwithstanding that the trustees, after they have
come into *esse,* themselves decline to interfere.

THE substance of the supplemental information in this suit
[is sufficiently stated in the LORD CHANCELLOR's judgment].

The MASTER OF THE ROLLS having made an order allowing
a demurrer, the *Attorney-General* appealed from his Lordship's order.

*   *   *   *   *

The *Attorney-General,* the *Solicitor-General, Mr. Kindersley,*
and *Mr. Booth,* in support of the appeal.

Mr. Pemberton, Mr. Wigram, and *Mr. Turner,* in support of [614]
the demurrer.

*   *   The most important of the topics urged in behalf of the
respondents, are stated and considered in the judgment. *   *   *

THE LORD CHANCELLOR: 1837.
Nov. 11.
The demurrer in this case is to a supplemental information,
filed against parties who were not parties to the original information, but who derive title through the defendants to the original
information, by deeds executed subsequently to the institution
of the suit.

The original information, filed after the passing of the
Municipal Corporation Act, sought to restrain the corporation
of Liverpool, as it existed before that Act came into operation,
from appropriating certain property *of the corporation to [*615]
purposes alleged to be foreign to the objects of the Act.

The demurring defendants claim under deeds executed by the
corporation after the institution of the suit, and immediately
before the provisions of that Act came into operation. These
defendants, therefore, though not parties to the original information, claim under those who were such parties, and derive from
them a title created *pendente lite.* I observe this state of the
record, because I find observations made upon the omission, in
the supplemental information, of certain allegations· contained
in the original information. I do not, however, pursue the

question further, but proceed to consider what is alleged in the supplemental information.

The supplemental information states, in the usual way, the filing of the original information, and proceeds to recite some, if not all, of its allegations; and, as to the greater part of them, it recites them with this addition, "as the fact was and is,"— words which are usually introduced for the purpose of putting in issue facts alleged in the recited proceeding, and the introduction of which makes the recital itself as much an allegation of the facts stated in it, as if those facts had been substantively alleged. I proceed, therefore, to consider the allegations of the supplemental information, considering every fact so alleged as forming part of it, and, therefore, admitted by the demurrer to be true.

The information commences by stating the possession, by the corporation, of a large real and personal estate, and that the corporation was indebted in divers sums of money, to divers persons, to a very considerable amount in the whole.

[616] It then states that the corporation were patrons of certain churches in Liverpool, the ministers of which had theretofore received stipends or allowances, amounting in the whole to 5,695*l.* per annum; that is to say,

1,080*l.* under endowments by certain Acts of Parliament,

510*l.* out of pew rents,

100*l.* payable out of the funds of the corporation,

450*l.* by rates leviable under Acts of Parliament,

1,040*l.* gratuitously paid out of parish rates, and

2,515*l.* which had been gratuitously paid out of the funds of the corporation.

Of this last-mentioned sum of 2,515*l.*, the sum of 1,865*l.* had been so paid for more than seven years before the 5th of June, 1835, and was therefore protected by the 68th section of the Act; and the remaining 650*l.* had been paid for less than seven years. The information then states that the corporation were about to raise a sum of 105,000*l.* upon the security of their corporation property, and to vest the same in trustees, upon trust to pay 3,665*l.* of the interest to the incumbents of the churches in the town; and that, for this purpose, they proposed to charge certain property not before liable to such payments.

The supplemental information then recites certain charges contained in the original information, but without the allegation "as the fact was and is;" and, among others, that the debt due by the corporation amounted to the sum of 792,000*l*., and that there was reason to expect that the income of the corporation would not be sufficient to defray the charges imposed upon it by the Act, and that a rate would therefore be necessary.

It is unnecessary to decide, whether these charges ought to be considered as part of the supplemental information, because there is a statement clearly forming part of it, which is, I think, equivalent, for the purpose of the demurrer; namely, the allegation that the corporation was indebted before the execution of the deeds in question, to a considerable amount.

[617]

The supplemental information then states, as supplemental matter, that the corporation had borrowed 63,440*l*. upon mortgage of part of their property, under a deed of the 21st of December, 1835, and had paid that sum, together with 41,560*l*., making in all 105,000*l*., to certain of the new defendants, as trustees, upon trust, out of the interest, to pay to sixteen clergymen certain stipends, amounting together to 4,000*l*., per annum, which provision, it was stipulated, should be accepted by the ministers in lieu of the rates payable under the Acts of Parliament, and of the allowances made to them for the preceding seven years; and the surplus income, and any portion forfeited by the ministers not complying with the condition, were to be paid to the treasurer of the borough fund. It then states, that the trustees had notice of the facts stated, and had undertaken to restore the fund, if the appropriation could not be supported: that the members of the corporation, under the Municipal Corporation Act, and the treasurer, came into office on the 26th of December, 1835; and that the council had applied for the repayment of the money, but refused to take any further step to procure such repayment, without the direction and sanction of the Court.

The ministers are made defendants, and the information prays that the appropriation may be declared to be unlawful and invalid, and the 105,000*l*. restored, and the income paid to the Treasurer.

To this information the trustees and the ministers demurred,

[618]

generally, and the demurrer was allowed by the MASTER OF
THE ROLLS.

If the property in question be subject to any public trust, and
if the appropriation complained of be not consistent with such
trust, but for purposes foreign to it, and if there be not, in the
Municipal Corporation Act, any provision taking from the Court
its ordinary jurisdiction in such cases, then it will follow that
the *Attorney-General* has, under the circumstances stated, a
right to file the information, and to pray that the fund may be
recalled, secured, and applied for the public, or in other words,
charitable purposes, to which it is by the Act devoted.

I will consider these three questions in their order.

1. First, then, is the property in question, according to the
statement in the information, subject to any trust?

It is immaterial to consider what was the power of the corporation over this and their other property, before the passing
of the Municipal Corporation Act. That Act passed on the 9th
of September, 1835, and the new officers were to come into
office on the 9th of November in that year; but, by an Order
in Council, that time was enlarged to the 26th of December
following.

By the 1st section of the Act, all laws, statutes, and usages,
charters, grants, and letters patent inconsistent with, or contrary
to the provisions of the Act, are repealed and annulled. The
power of the corporation, as it existed prior to the passing of
the Act, depended upon the law and usage then in force. So
far, therefore, as such law and usage authorised an exercise of
[*619]   such *power inconsistent with, or contrary to the provisions
of the Act, it was, from the time of passing that Act, annulled.

The 92nd section directs, that after the election of a treasurer,
which was to take place on the 9th of November, though afterwards postponed by Order in Council till the 26th of December,
all the income of all the property belonging or payable to any
of the corporations named in schedules A and B, that is, so
belonging or payable when the Act passed, was to be paid to
the treasurer; and the fund so created, subject to the payment
of the debts owing by the corporation at the time when the Act
passed, or of so much as the council, that is, the new council,

should think it expedient to redeem, and to the interest of such debt, was to be applied in payment of the salaries of certain officers, expenses of borough elections, expenses of borough sessions and prosecutions, gaols, and corporate buildings, police, and all other expenses incident to carrying the Act into effect: and in case the borough fund should be more than sufficient for those purposes, then the surplus was to be applied, under the direction of the council, that is, of the new council, for the public benefit of the inhabitants and improvement of the borough. The reduction or remission of any tolls or dues charged with, or subject to the payment of any debts, is then prohibited, so long as such debt remains unpaid, unless a majority of the creditors shall consent; and in case the borough fund shall not be sufficient for all the purposes enumerated, a power is given to the council to raise the deficiency by a borough rate, in the nature of a county rate.

It is to be observed upon this section, that no power is given to touch the principal of any part of the corporate property. The income alone constitutes the *borough fund. The whole of the income is, in the first place, subjected to the payment of the corporation debts, and afterwards to other purposes, all of them of a public nature, and in which the inhabitants at large have a direct interest, not only as entitled to participate in the benefit to arise from the execution of such purposes, but because the deficiency is to be raised upon them by a rate.

[*620]

The 94th section restrains the new council from selling, mortgaging, or alienating any lands, tenements, or hereditaments of the corporation, except in cases of contracts made before the 5th of June, and from leasing the same, except upon certain prescribed terms, without the consent of the Lords of the Treasury.

This clause not only regulated, for the future, the power of the corporation over its lands, tenements, and hereditaments, but invalidated any contracts inconsistent with such regulations, made after the 5th of June: and this could only be done by a distinct enactment; for, whatever might be the effect in equity of the provisions of the Act upon any contracts of the corporation, entered into after the Act passed, and before the election of the new officers, nothing but a distinct enactment could affect the power exercised by the corporation prior to the passing of the Act.

This, and the 95th and 96th sections are confined to lands, tenements, and hereditaments ; and there does not appear to be any provision respecting any appropriation of any other property of the corporation, made prior to the passing of the Act, except those contained in the ninety-seventh section. That section is most important to be considered, upon two grounds ; first, with reference to the evidence which it affords of the intention *of the Legislature, as to such appropriations of other property, besides lands, tenements, and hereditaments ; and secondly, with reference to the question raised for the defendants, that the jurisdiction of this Court is ousted, by reason of that clause having provided another remedy for the cause of complaint raised by this information. I propose at present to consider only the first of these points.

[*621]

As it was thought right that the new council should have a power of calling in question acts relative to the corporate property, carried into effect before the period of their election, it was absolutely necessary to give them a distinct legislative authority for this purpose ; because, in the first place, there would otherwise be no means of impeaching any acts of the corporation done prior to the passing of the Act of Parliament, however improper ; and secondly, because, the identity of the corporation continuing, notwithstanding the alterations effected by the Act, any such attempt, on the part of the new council, would be an attempt by the corporation to impeach its own act. Some such provision was therefore absolutely necessary ; and the obvious intention of that clause was to subject to revision all acts of the corporation after the 5th of June, effecting any disposition of the corporate property ; and for that purpose (confining myself to the words which can alone be thought applicable to the present case) the 97th section makes it lawful for the council to call in question all divisions and appropriations of the monies, goods, and valuable securities, or any part of the real or personal estate, of which, on or before the 5th of June, the body corporate was possessed, made between the 5th of June and the declaration of the election ; and for that purpose, if it should appear to the council that such division or appropriation was collusively made, *for no consideration, or for an inadequate consideration, to institute the proceedings prescribed.

The duty imposed upon the jury is to ascertain the value of the " premises," and the " consideration" given for the appropriation thereof ; and it is enacted that if the jury shall find that no consideration, or a consideration less than that which they shall find to be the value which ought therefore to have been given, had been collusively given, or contracted to be given, by the terms of the appropriation, the party to such appropriation was to have the option of restoring the premises and receiving back his consideration, or of making up the consideration to what the jury might find ought of right to have been given.   There is some obscurity in part of this clause : the expressions used in the directions as to summoning the jury, are, it was contended, to be confined to lands, tenements, and hereditaments.   Upon that I give no opinion ; but supposing them to apply to appropriations of the personal, as well as of the real property of the corporation, the intention to be inferred from the whole clause obviously is to secure the corporations, and therefore the public, from all appropriations of property, after the 5th of June, made collusively for less than the full value ; the word " collusively " not being used in a bad sense, but certainly including the case of persons taking part of the corporation property for their own benefit, with a knowledge of the circumstances of the property, and of the question which would arise as to the right of the corporation to make such alienation.

In my opinion, the 92nd section did not require the aid of the others, and particularly of the 97th section ; but, taking them all together, I cannot doubt that a clear trust was created, by this Act, for public, *and therefore, in the legal sense of the term, charitable purposes, of all the property belonging to the corporation at the time of the passing of the Act ; and that the corporation in its former state, holding, as it did, the corporate property until the election of the new council and treasurer, were in the situation of trustees for these purposes, subject to the restrictions specifically imposed by the Act, and subject to the general obligations and duties of persons in whom such property is vested.

That the application of the income of the property to the
particular purposes specified in the Act was not to commence till
a future time, namely, the election of the council and the
appointment of a treasurer, cannot affect the question. If the
income of a fund be devoted to a trust from a particular day not yet
arrived, the party in whom such fund is vested is bound to hold
and manage it so as to have the fund applicable to such purposes
at that time, whatever may become of the intermediate profits.

Upon the first point, therefore, I am clearly of opinion that
from the time when the Municipal Corporation Act passed, the
corporate property was trust property : and, upon this point, I
have the satisfaction of thinking that no material difference
exists between my opinion and that of the MASTER OF THE ROLLS ;
for in the notes of his judgment, I find it stated that he expressed
such to be his view of this part of the case.

2. Assuming, therefore, that the corporation property was,
on the 21st of December, 1835, trust property, vested for the
time in the corporation as it then existed, by reason of the post-
ponement of the time for the election of the council and the
appointment of a treasurer, but awaiting the arrival of that time
[*624]   in order to *be applicable to the several public purposes
prescribed by the Act,—the second question is, whether the
transaction relative to the 105,000l., as stated in the supplemental information, was consistent with the existence of such a
trust, or conformable to the provisions of the Act.

In the first place, it consisted, in part, of a mortgage of the
property of the corporation, which the new council are by the
94th section prohibited from making ; but, principally, it was an
appropriation of a portion of the income of the corporate property
for purposes, which, however laudable in themselves and beneficial to the interests of the inhabitants, cannot, according to the
statements in the information, be said to be consistent with the
trust to which the property was by the Act devoted, or conformable to the provisions of the Act. Of the amount of the income
of the corporate property, or of the debt due by the corporation,
or of the amount of the several payments by the Act directed to
be paid out of the income, the information does not state any
thing : but the debt is stated to be large ; and, by the Act, the

whole of the income is made primarily liable to pay the interest of the debt, and, at the discretion of the new council, to the payment of the principal, and, next, in making the several other payments directed. Whether there will be any surplus of such income, is not stated; and that, probably, must depend upon the discretion to be exercised by the new council as to the payment of the principal of the debt out of the income of the property—a discretion which, by the appropriation in question, is taken away to the extent of the interest of the 105,000l.

Again, although there is no statement that there will not be any surplus income, after payment of the prescribed expenses, yet there is no statement that there *will be any such surplus; and the whole income being primarily liable to those payments, the inhabitants, and the *Attorney-General* on their behalf, may justly complain of a diversion of any part of the income, whilst those objects remain unprovided for. A trustee cannot justify an application of part of a trust fund to other purposes, by suggesting that enough will remain of the fund to answer the purposes of the trust.

The appropriation in question has not been defended upon the ground of its being an appropriation for a full consideration, under the 97th section. The appropriations referred to by that section seem to be dispositions for which an equivalent in money or other property was, or was pretended, to be received by the corporation, and not appropriations the consideration for which were services or benefits to the public. But, even if that were so, the services or benefits reserved by the arrangement with the clergy could not be supported upon this ground, as the new provisions exceed what they could claim without it; and although the individual ministers give up the right to receive certain stipends raiseable by rates, the sums so given up are not of equal amount to the sums secured by the arrangement; and the amount of rates so given up is not receivable by the corporation in lieu of the interest of the 105,000l. appropriated in exchange for them; nor are they, it is alleged, payable by the same persons who will have to pay the borough rate, in case of a deficiency of the borough fund.

A case may certainly be supposed of the income of the

[*625]

[*626]

corporate property being so large, that after providing for the
payment of the interest of the debt due by the corporation, and
so much, if any, of the principal as the council may think it
advisable to pay, and after *supplying means of defraying the
expenses of all the other services directed by the 92nd section to
be provided for, a surplus would remain, applicable, under the
provisions of that section, for the public benefit of the inhabitants, and improvement of the borough ; and, under such
circumstances, the appropriation in question might be the most
proper. But at whose discretion, and under whose direction, was
this application of the surplus to be so made? Not of the corporation, as it existed before the election of the council, and before
such surplus could be ascertained ; but of the new council, and
after the existence of a surplus should have been proved by all
the prior objects having been previously provided for.

It must also be observed, that the only payments to be made,
out of the income of the borough fund, to the ministers of any
church or chapel are, by the 68th section, such as shall have
been paid for seven years before the 5th of June, 1835. Such is
the limit of the trust for this purpose, declared by the Act. It
cannot be consistent with such declaration of trust to appropriate for the ministers, not only what they had received for
seven years before the 5th of June, 1835, but also the amount of
income which had commenced within that period.

So, by the 139th section, all advowsons and church property
belonging to the corporation are directed to be sold, and the
proceeds invested, and the income paid to the treasurer, as part
of the borough fund. How inconsistent with the object and
spirit of that clause is the appropriation of corporate property,
not in the purchase of advowsons, which might therefore be
received back upon the sale as directed, but in adding to the
provision for the ministers of the churches, when the money so
expended, though the value of the advowsons might be in *some
degree increased, could not, upon the sale, be in any considerable
degree received back. And yet this was one of the grounds upon
which the transaction was defended at the Bar : it was stated
to be merely an application of one part of the property in
augmentation of another part.

[*627]

Upon the second head, therefore, I am also of opinion that the facts stated upon the information constitute a case which entitles the *Attorney-General*, on behalf of the inhabitants, to demand the interference of this Court, unless its jurisdiction be taken away by the Act of Parliament.

3. Upon this third point, I am happy to find the MASTER OF THE ROLLS concurring in the opinion I have formed, and stating that the jurisdiction of this Court is not excluded by the 97th section, if a proper case for relief be made. The argument in support of the proposition, that the jurisdiction of this Court is taken away, rests entirely upon the 97th section, which, in the cases there specified, authorises and enables the new council to institute certain proceedings, and to submit the matter in dispute to a jury. It is argued, that this clause gives a new right, and prescribes the remedy; that the right exists only in the remedy; and that no other course of proceeding but that prescribed can be resorted to. This may be true, as to transactions between the 5th of June and the 9th of September, the day when the Act passed; because, at that time, there was no trust. But, if it be true, as seems to be universally admitted, that from the passing of the Act, a trust existed, such trust had all its legal consequences, and the cestuis que trust were entitled to all their legal remedies.

[His Lordship, after dealing at some length with this question, concluded his judgment by saying:]

I have considered this case with the greatest care and attention. This, the amount of the property at stake, and the opinion expressed by the MASTER OF THE ROLLS upon those parts of the case which led to his decision, though he agrees with me in the most important points, demanded of me. I purposely avoid giving any opinion upon the transaction, beyond the statement upon the supplemental information. But upon that statement, and with reference to the provisions of the Municipal Corporation Act, I cannot come to the conclusion that the case is one in which this Court ought to refuse to entertain its admitted jurisdiction.

I am, therefore, of opinion that the demurrer ought to have been over-ruled.

[634]

Judgment reversed.

1837.
June 22.
Nov. 6.
———

LOCKE *v.* COLMAN.

(2 My. & Cr. 635—639.)

[SEE 43 R. R. 229.]

———•———

1837.
March 22.
April 5.
Aug. 11.
———
Lord
COTTENHAM,
L.C.

[642]

[661]

IN THE MATTER OF DOWNING COLLEGE.

(2 My. & Cr. 642—683.)

Effect of long and undisturbed possession in influencing the decision
of a visitor, in a case where the right may be doubtful.

THE petition in this case was presented by Alfred Power, Esq.,
barrister-at-law, late one of the lay fellows in Downing College
in the University of Cambridge ; and it was addressed to the
King's most Excellent Majesty in his High Court of Chancery, as
visitor of the college [and stated] that Robert M. Rolfe [a lay
fellow of the college], having resigned his fellowship in May, 1824,
it was agreed at a meeting of the resident members of the college
that it was expedient to elect a clerical fellow ; and accordingly,
Thomas Worsley, B.A., of Trinity College, was, on the 8th of
May, 1824, elected a clerical fellow, and thereupon subscribed
his name as such in the college books.

The petition further stated that the election [of Thomas
Worsley] was made without any notice of vacancy and without
any previous examination.   That on the 8th of May, 1824,
Worsley was upwards of twenty-four years of age, and that
within four months afterwards he entered into holy orders.
That on the 25th of May, 1836, William Frere, the then Master
of the college, died, and that on the 23rd of June following the
Rev. Thomas Worsley, who had been so elected a clerical fellow
in the room of Robert M. Rolfe, was chosen his successor by a
majority of the electors appointed by the Charter for that purpose;
although at the time [the petitioner and other lay fellows] were
laymen eligible to the office.

[662]   The petition [after setting forth the Charter] submitted that,
according to the provisions of the Charter, no vacancy in a
fellowship, created and constituted as a lay fellowship, could be
duly filled up by a clerical fellow ; but that, according to the
Charter, a vacancy in a lay fellowship ought to be filled up by a

layman ; and further, that under the provisions of the Charter, a clerical fellow was not, under any circumstances, eligible to the office of Master. Upon these grounds the petitioner submitted that the election of the Rev. Thomas Worsley to be Master of the college was void.

The petition prayed that his Majesty, as visitor, would make a declaration accordingly; and would direct the electors to proceed to make choice of some other person to be the Master, from amongst the professors and lay fellows, qualified to be Master according to the provisions of the Charter; or if, under the circumstances, the nomination to the mastership devolved on the Crown, then that his Majesty would forthwith nominate to the office.

The matter was referred, in the usual course, to the Lord Chancellor, who was assisted, on the hearing of the petition, by the Master of the Rolls and the Vice-Chancellor.

The *Attorney-General, Mr. Pemberton, Mr. Knight, Mr. Loftus Lowndes*, and *Mr. Romilly*, in support of the petition.

The *Solicitor-General, Sir W. W. Follett*, and *Mr. Jacob*, *contrà*.   [663]

[The question whether the original election of Mr. Worsley as a fellow of the college was valid depended upon the construction of the Charter, and the validity of his election as Master depended upon his qualification as a fellow of the college.

The argument upon this point consisted principally of a minute and critical commentary on the effect of the different clauses and provisions contained in the Charter and Statutes of the college. It is unnecessary to set forth this part of the case, since this report is merely intended to preserve a passage from the judgment of the LORD CHANCELLOR bearing upon the effect of lapse of time in curing the supposed defect in Mr. Worsley's title as fellow, and in inducing courts of justice and visitors to abstain from exercising a discretionary jurisdiction in such a manner as would disturb a state of things which had been long acquiesced in. Upon this point *Rex* v. *Dickin* (1), *Rex* v. *Clarke* (2),

(1) See 5 R. R. 509 *n*. (4 T. R. 282).   (2) 5 R. R. 505 (1 East, 38).

Rex v. *Trevenen* (1), *The Attorney-General* v. *Hartley* (2), and other cases were cited, and the LORD CHANCELLOR said:]

[688]

I cannot hold that Mr. Worsley is not Master, without holding that he has never been a fellow, although he has enjoyed his fellowship since the year 1824 ; and I cannot hold his election to be void, without holding that the rules and regulations in the Charter and Statutes, as to the election of fellows, apply to elections taking place before the completion of the College, which I am not prepared to do.

The cases which have been referred to, as to the period within which the validity of elections to offices in municipal corporations can be questioned, though not binding in the present case, afford a strong analogy to regulate the discretion of a visitor. In the exercise of that discretion, and in conformity with the opinion I have expressed upon the points on which Mr. Worsley's title to the Mastership of Downing College has been impeached, I am bound to declare his election good. The case, however, is one of considerable doubt, upon the instruments which constitute the title. [His Lordship then disposed of the costs.]

WOOD v. COX (3).

1837.
March 9.
Aug. 30.

(2 My. & Cr. 684—694; S. C. 6 L. J. (N. S.) Ch. 366; 1 Jur. 720; reversing
1 Keen, 317; 5 L. J. (N. S.) Ch. 301.)

Lord
COTTENHAM,
L.C.
[684]

A testatrix, by her will, bequeathed all her personal estate to C., whom she appointed one of her executors, for his own use and benefit for ever, trusting and wholly confiding in his honour, that he would act in strict conformity with her wishes. Afterwards, on the same day, she executed a testamentary paper, which contained a list of a number of persons by name, and among others, the name of the person who was her sole next of kin, with the several sums to be given to them respectively, and concluded with a declaration that such was the testatrix's wish:

Held, upon appeal, that C. took the personal estate for his own use, absolutely, subject only to the payment of the legacies specified in the testamentary paper, and three other sums, which, by his answer, C. admitted that the testatrix had directed him, and which he submitted, to pay.

THE will of Sarah Crompton, dated the 25th of April, 1833, so far as is material, was in the following words: " I hereby

(1) 20 R. R. 461 (2 B. & Ald. 339).   (3) *McCormick* v. *Grogan* (1869)
(2) 22 R. R. 167 (2 Jac. & W. 353).   L. R. 4 H. L. 82.

devise, give, and bequeath all my house in Bryanstone Square, and all the furniture, jewels, plate, and effects therein, and also all my monies whatsoever, and all my estate, property, and effects whatsoever and wheresoever, both real and personal, and of whatsoever nature or kind the same may be, unto Sir George Matthias Cox, Bart. [and Thomas Wilson their] his heirs, executors, administrators, and assigns, for his and their own use and benefit for ever, trusting and wholly confiding in his honour, that he will act in strict conformity with my wishes. I hereby appoint the said Sir George Cox, and Thomas Wilson, solicitor, the executors of this will, and hereby revoke all former wills."

On the same day the testatrix dictated another testamentary paper, which was as follows :

"Miss Mary and Miss Betsey Trussell, for life, 100l. a year to be equally divided between them. Mr. James Jones, 50l. per annum for life.

"Miss Clements, 100l., as a present.

"My cousins, the children of James Heald of Chelmsford, a Quaker, 20l. to each of his children.

"Old Mrs. Sarah Jones, 10l. per annum for life ; and *after her death, to her daughter, and after her death, to her (the daughter's) daughter.

"Elizabeth and Lydia Wood, daughters of Joseph Wood, 50l. a piece.

"Hannah Wood, widow, 100l.

"Daniel Wood, her father, 100l.

"Mr. Curtis, 50l. per annum for life.

"Miss Cordelia Jane Clode, 20l.

"My coachman, 100l.

"Mary Kite, 100l.

"Jones, 20l. and his mourning to the late Mr. Clifton

"Fanny Eales, 20l.

"The cook, 20l.

"My wardrobe to Lady Cox and Miss Trussell.

"Mr. Thomas Wilson, 200l.

"To the poor of St. Mary's, 25l.

"The Clergyman. 25l.

"Such is the wish of Sarah Crompton.

Of this paper the last clause only, " Such is the wish of Sarah Crompton," was in the testatrix's own handwriting.

The words in the will printed within brackets, " and Thomas Wilson their," were directed by the testatrix to be struck out, and a line was accordingly drawn through them in the original; and they formed no part of the will, as proved. The death of the testatrix took place three days after the execution of her will; and probate of the will and testamentary paper was thereupon granted to the executors.

Daniel Wood, the person to whose name, in the testamentary paper, the sum of 100*l.* appeared annexed, was the testatrix's uncle, and sole next of kin; and, in the latter character, he filed the bill against the executors, *claiming the residuary personal estate, as being undisposed of.

[*686]

The defendant, Sir George Cox, by his answer, stated his belief that the testatrix intended the testamentary paper solely for his private information and guidance, in the disposal of the property she had bequeathed to him, and not by way of codicil, or instructions for a codicil. His answer further stated that the testamentary paper was drawn up, in consequence of the testatrix having previously expressed her wishes to him verbally, and of his having requested that the particulars thereof might, for greater certainty, be reduced to writing: that in the evening of the 25th of April, after the testatrix had dictated and signed the testamentary paper, she stated to him, that she had forgotten to include Mr. Thorn in the list, and she then verbally directed the defendant to give 500*l.* to Samuel Thorn of Chelmsford, after her death, and the sum of 100*l.* to Dr. Sayer, her medical attendant, and the like sum of 100*l.* to John Varley. The defendant then, by his answer, after saying that he was ready and willing to pay these three several sums, according to the testatrix's direction, if he could do so with safety, went on to state that, after the testatrix had made her will, she spoke to the defendant respecting the probable amount of the proceeds of the sale of the house in which she then resided, which she estimated, upon that occasion, at 11,000*l.*, adding that, after payment of her debts, legacies, and expenses, there would be something handsome left for the defendant—at least 3,000*l.* And the defendant, by his answer, insisted, that the residuary personal estate of the testatrix belonged to him, for his own absolute use and benefit, as her residuary legatee, and that there was no resulting trust in favour of her next of kin.

The facts stated in the answer, relative to the three sums of 500*l*., 100*l*., and 100*l*., were subsequently found, upon a reference, and an order was made for payment of them to the persons entitled to them respectively.

The cause afterwards came on at the Rolls, for further directions; and the sole question then made was, whether the plaintiff, as the testatrix's next of kin, was beneficially entitled to the residuary personal estate, after paying the debts, funeral expenses and legacies, and the three sums mentioned in the defendant's answer; or whether the residue, subject to those charges, belonged to the defendant Sir George Cox, for his own use, absolutely.

The MASTER OF THE ROLLS decided that Sir George Cox was a trustee of the residue for the plaintiff [1 Keen, 317]; and an appeal was now brought from his Lordship's decision.

Mr. Knight, *Mr. James Russell*, and *Mr. Williamson*, for the appeal.

Mr. Wigram, *Mr. Richards*, and *Mr. Bigg*, in support of the decree.

[The principal cases cited by counsel are referred to in the following judgment:]

THE LORD CHANCELLOR:

The testatrix, by her will, dated the 25th of April, 1833, devised, gave, and bequeathed all her house in Bryanstone Square, and all the furniture, jewels, plate, and effects therein, and also all her monies whatsoever, and all her estate, property, and effects whatsoever and wheresoever, both real and personal, and of whatsoever nature or kind the same might be, unto Sir George Matthias Cox, his heirs, executors, administrators, and assigns, for his and their own use and benefit for ever, trusting and wholly confiding in his honour, that he would act in strict conformity with her wishes; and she thereby appointed the said

WOOD
v.
COX.

[*689]

[*690]

Sir George Cox and Thomas Wilson, solicitor, the executors of her will, and thereby revoked all former wills.

Another paper, of which probate was granted, is without date ; but the bill states, and the answer admits, that it was written on the same 25th of April, 1833 ; and the *particular language of this paper seems to me to be material, especially as one important word of it appears to have been misapprehended in the discussion at the Rolls.

This paper was as follows: (His Lordship read the whole of the paper, ending with the words, "such is the wish of Sarah Crompton," and then continued :)

The word " wish," in the sentence just read, appears to have been mistaken at the Rolls, and to have been supposed to be " will ;" a difference which is so far important as the word "wish " corresponds with the same word used in the prior testamentary paper. In the first, the testatrix expresses her confidence that Sir George Cox will act in conformity with her wishes; and in the latter, she expresses what her wishes are. It is also to be observed, that there are no words of gift throughout this testamentary paper; a circumstance which, coupled with the repetition of the word " wish," affords an inference, deducible from the documents themselves, that the latter was merely an enumeration, in writing, of those wishes which the former assumes to have been previously communicated to Sir George Cox, as is stated in his answer to have been the case.

Taking then these two papers together, they amount to this : The testatrix gives all her property to Sir George Cox, for his own use and benefit, trusting that he will execute her wishes ; such wishes being, that the several persons named in the second paper should have the several provisions therein specified. How does this differ from a gift of her property to Sir George Cox, subject to the payment of such several provisions ? If the word " wish" in the second paper is to be considered as in connection with the same word in the first paper, *the construction must be the same as if she had commenced the second paper in these words : " The wishes referred to in the preceding writing, are that Miss Mary and Miss Betsey Trussell should have 100l. a year for life ;" and so on, through the several other gifts ; and if such had been the form of the second paper, no doubt could, I conceive, have been entertained of the construction. The construction must have been the same as if the expression of the wishes had been contained in the first paper, which would have been a gift of the property to Sir George Cox, for his own use and benefit, subject to the several payments to the several persons enumerated. There would have been no inconsistency in any of these dispositions, no repugnancy in any of the clauses, no forced construction to be adopted, and no words to be omitted; whereas, before any construction can be adopted, making Sir George Cox a trustee of the whole property, the words "for his own use and benefit" must be expunged from the will, or, by reason of some irresistible evidence, derived from other parts of the testamentary disposition, treated as if they had never been inserted; a construction which nothing but absolute necessity would justify.

It was argued that the original of the first paper proved that Mr. Wilson was at first intended to be associated with Sir George Cox in the gift of the property, Mr. Wilson's name having been inserted after that of Sir George Cox, and the word "their" for "his" heirs; and his name being afterwards erased, and the word "his" substituted for "their;" and that such intended gift to the two was inconsistent with the intention of giving a benefit to the one. Assuming that these erased words may be looked at, for the purpose of construing those of which probate has been granted, it appears to me that the consideration *of them would lead to an opposite conclusion. In the first [*691] place, the erasure of Mr. Wilson's name appears to have taken place before the sentence was concluded; the latter part of it "trusting to *his* honour" must have been written after the erasure of Mr. Wilson's name, which, clearly, therefore, must have been inserted by mistake. But if Sir George Cox was to be only a trustee for others, why was Mr. Wilson, who is a co-executor, not to be associated with him in the trust? There could be no reason for this, if the trust was to apply to the whole property; but it was necessary, if the gift was intended to confer a benefit upon Sir George Cox, subject only to a trust to the extent of the specified provisions for others. If, in the language

of some of the cases to which I shall presently refer, it was a
gift upon trust, why exclude one of the executors from the trust?
If, however, it was a gift subject to a charge, the reason is obvious.
The testatrix, having communicated her wishes to Sir George Cox,
probably considered that the performance of them was as effectually secured as if she had expressed them in her will ; and the
question, as to what precatory words amount to a trust, would not
probably have been thought by her material to be considered, if
she had been aware of the decisions upon that subject.

It was said that the testatrix need not have trusted to the
honour of Sir George Cox, if she had intended to give to him
the beneficial interest, subject to the payment of the legacies
enumerated.   But neither need she so have trusted, if she
intended that he should be a trustee of the whole.   The fact
seems to be, that she considered her confidence in the honour
of Sir George Cox just as well founded, and the interest of the
[*692]   legatees as secure, as if she had, in the first instance, *done
what she afterwards did, namely, specify the legacies.

It was argued that the words "trusting and wholly confiding
in his honour, that he will act in strict conformity with my
wishes," prove that the testatrix did not use the words " for his
own use and benefit " in an absolute and unrestricted sense.
Certainly she did not use these words in their absolute and
unrestricted sense, as to the whole of her property, namely, as
to that part which would be required to pay the legacies given
to others, or, in other words, to execute her wishes.   But is there
any thing unusual or inaccurate in a gift of property to an
individual, for his own use and benefit, subject to the payment
of an annuity, or other provision for another; and yet the
observation would apply with equal force to such a gift?
Assuming, however, that these words are inapplicable to so
much of the property as would be required to provide for the
execution of the testatrix's wishes, as expressed, can that be a
sufficient reason for rejecting them altogether, when they are
strictly and correctly applicable to so much of the property as
was not required for those purposes ?

It was then asked, if these words cannot be applied to the
whole of the property, by what rule can it be ascertained to

what part they do, and to what part they do not apply? The
answer seems obvious : they must apply to all the property as to
which the testatrix did not express any other wish.   Every gift
of a residue, for the benefit of the residuary legatee, is subject to
the payment of other legacies and prior charges, which frequently
exhaust the whole.

It was said further, that the second paper only expresses the
testatrix's wishes *pro tanto*, it appearing *from the answer of   [*693]
Sir George Cox, that she had afterwards mentioned other
legacies which she wished to have paid.   If the answer be to
be looked at for this purpose, the whole statement must be taken
together ; and the statement there made is, that she, in the
evening of the same day, mentioned to him that she had forgotten
to include in the list certain legacies she wished to have paid,
and that after payment of her debts and legacies there would
be something handsome for Sir George Cox.   In my consideration of the claims of the parties in this case, I wholly reject this
statement in the answer ; but then I do not think that it can
properly be relied upon for the purpose of showing, that the
testatrix intended to treat the whole of the property given to Sir
George Cox as a trust, because subject to the future expression
of her wishes.   It was undoubtedly subject to any other disposition she might make of it, as every residuary gift is ; but the
question is, to whom was that portion of it to belong, which was
not otherwise disposed of.

I have in this case, as I do in every case in which I have the
misfortune to differ from the Master of the Rolls, felt every
disposition to doubt the correctness of the several steps of
reasoning by which I have come to a different conclusion.   But
when I find one construction which makes every part of the
testamentary disposition consistent, and which is consistent
with every circumstance connected with it, I cannot feel justified
in adopting another, which creates an intestacy as to the residue,
which requires striking out of the will certain expressions of
ordinary use, and of well known meaning, and which would
leave unexplained several other provisions appearing upon the
face of the testamentary papers.

In cases of this kind little assistance is to be derived from   [694]

Wood
r.
Cox.

former decisions; but what is said by Lord Hardwicke, in *Hill v. The Bishop of London* (1), and by Sir William Grant, in *Walton* v. *Walton* (12 Ves. 318), and Lord Eldon's decision in *Dawson* v. *Clarke* (2) (proceeding, as it appears to have done, upon the terms of the gift, and not upon the claim of the executor as such) and in *King* v. *Denison* (3), which was a stronger case in favour of a resulting trust than the present, would have confirmed me in the opinion I have formed, had I felt more doubt upon the particular circumstances of this case.

Adopting the distinction expressed by Lord Eldon, in the cases referred to, I am of opinion that this is not a gift upon trust, but a gift subject to a charge, and that Sir George Cox is therefore entitled to the property, subject to the legacies given by the testatrix, including those verbally given, as found by the Master's report.

Judgment reversed.

1837.
June 26.
July 4.
Nov. 25.

Lord
Cottenham,
L.C.

[695]

MIREHOUSE *v.* SCAIFE.

(2 My. & Cr. 695—709; S. C. 7 L. J. (N. S.) Ch. 22; affirming 1 Jur. 134.)

A testator, after bequeathing a number of pecuniary legacies to different persons, and giving a certain field to his godson, directed that all his debts and the above legacies, should be paid and discharged within six months after his decease; and all the rest and residue of his estate, both real and personal, he gave to N. The personal estate proving insufficient to pay the debts and legacies, it was held, upon demurrer to a bill by some of the legatees, seeking to charge their legacies on the real estate which passed under the residuary devise to N.,

First, that there was no equity, in favour of pecuniary legatees, to have the assets marshalled, so as to throw the debts upon the real estate devised to N.; but,

Secondly, that both the debts and legacies were, by the words of the will, effectually charged upon that estate.

The will of John Brockbank, yeoman, which bore date the 21st of October, 1833, and was duly executed and attested to pass freehold estates by devise, was, so far as is material, in the following words: " First, I give and bequeath unto my cousin William Perry, the sum of 100*l.* ; unto my cousin Nancy Carter, 50*l.* ; unto my cousin Mary Cape, widow of the late John

(1) 1 Atk. 618.   (3) 12 R. R. 227 (1 V. & B. 260).
(2) 11 R. R. 188 (18 Ves. 247).

Cape, 50*l.*; unto my cousins Robert Scaife, Isabella Scaife, and
Mrs. Jane Mirehouse, the sum of 200*l.*, share and share alike,
or the whole to the survivors at my decease.   Also I give unto
Robert Scaife all my interest in the brig *Solon;* unto Hannah
Lewthwaite, my servant woman, 10*l.*; unto James Brockbank,
my godson, the son of John Brockbank of Chapples, I give and
bequeath one field, known by the name of Gillfoot, as a memorandum, to be by him enjoyed at my decease.   It is my will that
all my debts, and all the above legacies, be paid and discharged
within six months after my decease; and all the rest and residue
of my estate, both real and personal, lands, messuages, and
tenements, I give unto Mary Newton, the wife of George Newton
of Green, by her freely to be possessed at my decease; and I do
hereby constitute and appoint John Brockbank of Chapples, and
Robert Scaife of Maryport, to be the executors of and to this my
last will and testament."

The testator died in the month of February, 1836, and the
executors proved his will.   The bill was filed by Jane Mirehouse,
and Mary Cape, two of the legatees named in the will, against
Scaife and Brockbank, the executors, against Mary Newton, the
residuary devisee, and her husband, and against William Perry,
who was the testator's heir-at-law.   James Brockbank, the
devisee of Gillfoot, was not made a defendant.

The bill alleged that the testator's personal estate was insufficient to pay his debts and funeral and testamentary expenses
and legacies; but that the real estates devised to Mary Newton
were more than sufficient for those purposes.   The bill prayed a
declaration that, according to the true construction of the will,
the testator's debts and legacies were a charge upon his real
estates thereby devised to Mary Newton; and, in case, on taking
the accounts, his personal estate should prove insufficient to pay
such debts and legacies, then that the deficiency might be raised
by sale or mortgage of such real estates; or, if the Court should
be of opinion that the testator's real estates were not charged
with the legacies, then that his assets might be marshalled, and
that the amount of the personal estate which should have been
applied in payment of his debts, or so much thereof as should be
sufficient for payment of the legacies, might be raised by sale or

mortgage of the said real estates, and applied in payment of the legacies.

To this bill, George Newton and Mary his wife filed a general demurrer, which the VICE-CHANCELLOR, upon argument, over-ruled, and the present appeal was then brought from his Honour's decision.

[*697] *Mr. Jacob* and *Mr. Booth*, for the appellants, made two points; first, that equity would not marshal the assets, in favour of pecuniary legatees, against a devisee *of a real estate, whether given specifically, or in the form of residue, every devise of land being in fact specific : and secondly, that the words to be found in this will were not strong enough to charge the testator's legacies upon the lands devised to Mary Newton. * * *

Mr. Wigram, and *Mr. Walker*, *contrà*. * * *

[The principal cases cited by counsel were referred to in the following judgment.]

Nov. 25.   THE LORD CHANCELLOR :

[698]   This was an appeal from an order of the VICE-CHANCELLOR, overruling a demurrer. The question is, therefore, whether the bill states a case which entitles the plaintiffs to any relief against the party demurring. The plaintiffs are legatees of general pecuniary legacies. The defendant who demurs is the devisee of the residue of the testator's real estate. (His Lordship read the material parts of the will, and proceeded :)

[*699]   The plaintiffs, who are the two legatees, Jane Mirehouse, and Mary Cape, contend—first, that by this will *the residue of the testator's freehold estate, that is, the whole of his freehold estate except James Brockbank's interest in Gillfoot, is charged with the payment of his legacies ; and secondly, if not, that they and the other legatees are entitled to have the assets marshalled, so as to throw the debts upon these devised estates, so far as may be necessary to leave enough of the personalty to pay the legacies.

The VICE-CHANCELLOR was of opinion against the plaintiffs upon the first point, but in their favour on the second, and

therefore overruled the demurrer. I concur with the VICE-
CHANCELLOR in thinking that the demurrer cannot be maintained; but as the two points raised are of much importance,
and are not unlikely to arise in other cases, I think it right to
make some observations upon both.

I will begin with the second point. The proposition contended
for by the plaintiffs is, that the rule, that pecuniary legatees are
not entitled to have the assets marshalled against a devisee, is
confined to specific devises of land, and that pecuniary legatees
are so entitled against lands which pass under a residuary
devise.

I will first consider the authorities, and then the reason of the
rule, as I understand it.

[His Lordship then referred at length to a number of early
cases to which it is no longer necessary to refer, including the
case of *Hanby* v. *Roberts* (1), and coming to the later authorities
he said :]

The case of *Keeling* v. *Brown* (2), before Lord Alvanley, is
directly in point against the claim to marshal, *and is in every
respect very like the present. There was in that case no charge
of legacies upon the lands: there were specific devises of particular lands; and there were also lands which passed under a
residuary clause of " all the rest, residue, and remainder of the
testator's estates and effects whatsoever, whether real or personal." The legatees claimed to have the assets marshalled,
not against the land specifically devised, but against that which
passed under the residuary clause, so that the attention of the
Court was expressly drawn to the distinction. Another point,
however, was raised, namely, whether the legacies were by the
will charged upon the lands. Lord ALVANLEY decided that they
were not; and then, adverting to the point of marshalling, says,
" I cannot marshal the assets for the payment of the legacies;"
and then, adds his Lordship, " I have formerly fully expressed
my opinion upon this point, as to the difference between debts
and legacies. I understand the LORD CHANCELLOR expressed some
doubt about it in the case of *Williams* v. *Chitty* (3), but upon

[702]
[*703]

(1) Amb. 127; *S. C.* 1 Dick. 104,   (2) 5 R. R. 70 (5 Ves. 359).
nom. *Hamly* v. *Fisher*.   (3) 3 R. R. 71 (3 Ves. 551).

reflection I still remain of the same opinion." This passage "I have formerly fully expressed," &c. has been supposed to refer to the question of marshalling; and from its position it would at first appear to do so. The error is, probably, in the report; but it is, I think, clear that it refers to the other question, before disposed of, namely, whether the will charged the legacies upon the land. Neither of the cases referred to have any thing to do with marshalling; and it is well known that Lord ALVANLEY and Lord ROSSLYN differed as to what words would be sufficient to charge legacies upon land.

[704]   The case of *Aldrich* v. *Cooper* (1) was between creditors only and a devisee of copyhold, and does not appear to me to bear upon the present question.

It has been supposed, however, that the point has been set at rest by the decree in *Spong* v. *Spong* (2). The case itself does not very closely apply to the present, as there was no question about marshalling; the only question being, between devisees, upon the construction of the will, as to whether part of the estate was not primarily liable, the whole being by the will made subject to the payment of the legacies. The testator, after devising some particular lands to one person, and giving certain legacies, charged and made liable all his real and personal estate, with the payment of his aforesaid legacies, and then gave to his son the residue of his real and personal estate, and appointed him executor. It had been held, in the Court of Exchequer, that the lands specifically devised, and those which passed under the residuary clause, were equally liable to the payment of the legacies, upon the principle that, as all devises of freehold were specific, there was no ground for any distinction. In the House of Lords, this was otherwise decided; and, so far, Lord ELDON and Lord REDESDALE, who appear to have been consulted, would seem to have concurred: but it does not follow, that they concurred in all the reasons assigned by another peer in moving the judgment. The decision certainly proceeded upon a distinction between lands specifically devised and a residuary devise of lands, as to which should be primarily liable to a general charge created

(1) 7 R. R. 86 (8 Ves. 382).   (2) 32 R. R. 16 (1 Y. & J. 300, and
                                            3 Bligh (N. S.) 84).

by the will, to which both were subject ; and it is precisely the
case put by Lord HARDWICKE in *Hanby* v. *Roberts*, except *that
the case put by Lord HARDWICKE is between a residuary devisee
and a specific legatee ; whereas *Spong* v. *Spong* is between a
residuary devisee and a specific devisee.   In neither was there
any question of marshalling, but of priority of liability to the
charge. Lord MANNERS, indeed, is made to say, " by the general
rule, a specific devisee or specific legatee shall not contribute to
make good a pecuniary legacy ; but there can be no such rule
applicable to a residue."   It does not appear how this observation could apply to the case before the House, inasmuch as the
will charged all the real estate with the legacy ; and it does not
appear, that it had any reference to a case of marshalling,
although it might in its terms embrace that case.   At most,
it is only a *dictum*, which, if it was intended to apply to the case
of marshalling, was not referable to any matter in judgment at
the time.

Such, as I understand them, is the state of the authorities.   It
is to be considered whether there be reason for the proposition,
so often laid down, that in the sense in which the term must be
understood for the purpose under consideration, every devise of
land is to be considered as specific.   The case put by Lord
HARDWICKE in *Hanby* v. *Roberts*, and the decision of the House of
Lords in *Spong* v. *Spong*, do not determine that the devise of
lands, as a residue, is not, in this sense, a specific devise ; but
that, upon the construction of the wills, and, according to the
intention of the testators, in those cases, such devises were to be
subject to the charges, in priority to the other property specifically given.   If the distinction between specific and residuary
devises is to be maintained, and the same terms are to be held
to constitute a residuary devise of land, which amount to a
residuary gift of personalty, it will be found that the right to
marshal, by legatees, will arise in a very *large proportion of
cases, as, for example, in devises of " all my real estate," "all
my lands in A. B., and elsewhere," &c.   It cannot be necessary
that the terms " rest and residue " should be used in the one
case more than in the other.

When a testator gives the residue of his personal estate, he

MIREHOUSE
v.
SCAIFE.

[*705]

[*706]

knows that it will be uncertain, till his death, what will be comprised in that gift. But it is certain that the gift will operate upon part only of what he may be possessed of at his death, all debts, funeral expenses, and other charges being to be paid out of it; and the expression necessarily imports what will remain, after all charges are defrayed. On the other hand, the testator knows precisely upon what real estate such a gift will operate, unless there be charges affecting the land beyond what the personal estate can satisfy.

If the term "residue" was used by this testator, with reference to what remained, after deducting Gillfoot, before given, the meaning and the construction must be the same as if he had first enumerated all his lands, and then had given Gillfoot, and then had devised all the rest of his enumerated lands. Beyond all doubt, that would have been as specific a devise of the rest, as of Gillfoot, or as if he had enumerated all the other parts. It would, indeed, have been so in the case of personalty. Upon this supposition, therefore, the land which passed under the residuary clause was strictly a specific devise; and, if so, it is admitted, that no case of marshalling can arise. The words " rest and residue of my real estate, lands, messuages, and tenements," must mean what the testator had at the time of making his will, deducting Gillfoot, or deducting some other matter or thing which would diminish the amount or value [*707]   of the lands so possessed by him. The only *matters or things referred to in the will, which could cause such diminution, are the debts and legacies which he had before directed to be paid. But if the terms " rest and residue " were used in that sense, they would, according to the authority of many cases, coupled with the direction to pay his debts and legacies, amount to a charge of such debts and legacies upon the land ; and as the plaintiffs would, in that case, have, in their own right, a title to be paid out of the real estate, after exhausting the personalty, the question of marshalling would be effectually excluded.

This view of the case opens the way to another consideration, namely, whether the terms of the will do not, according to the authorities, create a charge of debts and legacies upon the land. The testator gives several pecuniary legacies, and one specific

MIREHOUSE
r.
SCAIFF.

legacy, and one field—whether of inheritance or leasehold does not appear, except that no words of inheritance are used—and then he says, " It is my will that all my debts and all the above legacies be paid and discharged within six months after my decease ; and all the rest and residue of my estate, both real and personal, lands, messuages, and tenements, I give unto Mary Newton, by her freely to be possessed at my decease." There is a direction that all his debts and legacies shall be paid, and then a devise of his real estate. This, in many cases, from *Stanger* v. *Tryon* (1), and *Kay* v. *Townsend* (2), down to *Clifford* v. *Lewis* (3), has been held sufficient to charge the lands; but there is also a devise of the rest and residue of the real estate, following a direction to pay debts and legacies, as *in *Hassel* v. *Hassel* (4), and in the cases put by Lord HARDWICKE in *Brudenell* v. *Boughton* (5). There is, moreover, a blending of the real and personal estate, and a gift of the residue of both, as in *Hassel* v. *Hassel, Bench* v. *Byles* (6), *Cole* v. *Turner* (4 Russ. 876), circumstances which relieve this case from the question discussed by Lord ALVANLEY and Lord ROSSLYN in *Chitty* v. *Williams* (7), and *Keeling* v. *Brown* (8), as to whether words, admitted to be sufficient to charge lands with debts, ought to be held sufficient to charge them with legacies.

[*708]

If, indeed, this charge were to be confined to debts, a new ground of marshalling would be opened, though not the ground upon which the VICE-CHANCELLOR is said to have decided. To attribute different meanings to the same words in the same sentence, may sometimes be necessary ; but nothing but necessity can justify it. When the testator spoke of "the rest and residue" of his personal estate, he certainly meant what would remain after payment of his debts and legacies. Is it not natural to suppose that he used those words in the same sense when applied to his real estate ?

I cannot feel justified in departing from the rules established in the cases which preceded the 3 & 4 Will. IV. c. 104, on account

(1) 2 Vern. 709, Raithby's note.
(2) *Ibid*. in the note.
(3) 22 R. R. 228 (6 Madd. 33).
(4) 2 Dick. 327.

(5) 2 Atk. 268.
(6) 20 R. R. 292 (4 Madd. 187).
(7) 3 R. R. 71 (3 Ves. 545).
(8) 5 R. R. 70 (5 Ves. 359).

MIREHOUSE
r.
SCAIFE.

of the very beneficial provisions of that Act. To do so would create great confusion and much uncertainty and litigation; and the provisions of that Act can have no bearing upon the construction of a charge of legacies; and indeed, as to debts, a charge by the will is not (1) inoperative, in consequence of that Act.

[709]

It is said that the direction to pay the debts and legacies was only intended to fix a time for the payment of them. That, no doubt, was part of the object: but that it was not the whole object, may be inferred from the gift, which follows, of the rest and residue of the real and personal estate, which the observation leaves untouched.

If I were to allow the demurrer, I should be deciding that under this will Mary Newton was to enjoy all the testator's real estates, except James Brockbank's interest in Gillfoot, leaving all the legacies unpaid. This I am not prepared to do. I agree with the VICE-CHANCELLOR in thinking that the demurrer must be overruled; but, not concurring in all the observations made by his Honour as to the two points upon which that question depends, I have thought it right to state, so far, the view I entertain upon the principles and authorities which have been brought under my consideration.

The appeal must be dismissed, but without costs (2).

1836.
Dec. 6, 7, 8.
1837.
July 22.

Lord
COTTENHAM,
L.C.

[711]

THE MARQUESS OF BREADALBANE *v.* THE MARQUESS OF CHANDOS.

(2 My. & Cr. 711—742; S. C. 7 L. J. (N. S.) Ch. 28.)

An antenuptial settlement made in England must be construed by the law of England, and an alleged omission which might have been implied by Scots law, if the settlement had been made there, cannot be inserted in the settlement on the ground that some of the parties to the settlement

(1) By a clerical error in the original report the word " now " was printed here instead of the word " not; " see 4 My. & Cr. 269.—O. A. S.

(2) The effect of a charge of debts or legacies upon a general or residuary devise of real estate, is not materially altered by the Wills Act (1 Vict. c. 26); see *Hensman* v. *Fryer* (1867) L. R. 3 Ch. 420, 37 L. J. Ch. 97, 17 L. T. 394, as explained in *Lancefield* v. *Iggulden* (1874) L. R. 10 Ch. 136, 44 L. J. Ch. 203.—O. A. S.

THE
MARQUESS OF
BREADAL-
BANE
v.
THE
MARQUESS OF
CHANDOS.

who were domiciled in Scotland believed that the English law in this respect resembled Scotch law.

The Court will not reform an antenuptial settlement, on the ground of mistake, unless the evidence, as to the mistake, and as to the real intention of the parties, is perfectly clear and satisfactory. The fact that there is a variance between the settlement and the previous proposals for a settlement is not sufficient reason for reforming the settlement.

ON a treaty of marriage in the year 1819, carried on in London, between the only son of the Marquess of Buckingham and the daughter of a Scotch Earl (the late Earl of Breadalbane) the terms of a marriage settlement were embodied in a paper called "Proposals;" which paper was approved by the respective fathers, on behalf of their children. The Proposals stipulated that the Earl should pay or advance, as the portion of his daughter, certain sums of money, at the times, and in the manner therein specified; and that, in consideration of those sums and of the marriage, the Marquess and his son should concur in charging large estates in England, Ireland, and the West Indies, with certain provisions for the husband, during his father's life, and for the wife and the younger children of the marriage; and subject thereto, should settle the same estates upon the Marquess and his son, successively, for life, with remainders to the issue of the marriage, according to the series of limitations therein specified. The Proposals concluded with a proviso, that the settlement should contain the usual powers of appointing new trustees, the usual clause of indemnity to trustees, and all other usual and necessary clauses. A settlement was then prepared and executed in London, to which the intended husband and wife, with their respective fathers, and certain other persons, as trustees, were parties, and of which the provisions, though different in several particulars, were similar in their general character to the terms contained in the Proposals; and the marriage took effect. [In the year 1834] the Earl, who was a domiciled Scotchman, died, leaving a large personal estate; and a suit having been thereupon instituted in Scotland, in which all persons, who were competent to contest the question, intervened, it was adjudged by the Court of Session, and also, on appeal, by the House of Lords, that according to the law of Scotland, the daughter of the deceased

THE
MARQUESS OF
BREADAL-
BANE
v.
THE
MARQUESS OF
CHANDOS. Earl was entitled to a proportionate share of her father's personal estate, called, in that law, her legitim, inasmuch as she had not renounced that right by her marriage settlement, or otherwise. Very shortly before this decision of the Court of Session, the Proposals, which had been mislaid, were discovered; and the present bill was then filed against the husband and wife [Lord and Lady Chandos], alleging that the settlement had been prepared in pursuance, and on the basis, of the Proposals; that in Scotland, a clause barring legitim was a usual and necessary clause in the marriage settlement of a child for whom the father thereby advanced a portion; that the proviso in the Proposals was understood, by all the contracting parties, as applying to and comprising such a clause; that as no such clause was to be found in the settlement, as executed, the settlement did not effectuate the intention of the contract, as expressed in the Proposals; and that it was in this respect erroneous, and ought to be reformed. The bill prayed a declaration accordingly, and that, in the meantime, the defendants might be restrained by injunction from proceeding to enforce the decree obtained in the Scotch Court for payment of the sum found due to the defendants on account of the legitim.

The VICE-CHANCELLOR granted an injunction.

[In order to explain the judgment of the Lord Chancellor on this appeal it is necessary to state here more fully some of the details of the Proposals and Settlement above referred to.]

[713]   The Proposals began by stating that three sums of 10,000*l*., each, were to be advanced or secured by Lord Breadalbane, by way of portion for his daughter, on her marriage, and declaring the manner in which, and the times when, they were to be so advanced or secured respectively: they next stated the several terms of years which it was proposed to create out of the Duke of Buckingham's estates in the counties of Bucks, Oxon, Warwick, and Hants, and in Ireland and the West Indies, (the yearly income of which estates was stated to be 44,500*l*.,) for the purpose of providing an annuity of 5,000*l*. for Lord Chandos, during the life of his father, and pin-money and a jointure for the intended wife, and certain allowances and

portions for the younger children of the marriage, in the different events which might arise. They then proceeded to provide for the settlement of the same estates, subject to those trust terms, upon the Duke of Buckingham and Lord Chandos, successively, for their respective lives, with remainders to the first and other sons of the marriage, successively, in tail male, with divers remainders over. The Proposals then went on to specify, in detail, the particular trusts upon which the several terms of years were to be held by the respective trustees, with a view to the *various contingencies therein expressed and provided for ; and, for that purpose, they reserved to the intended husband and wife certain powers of appointment, in different events, over the sums which were to be secured upon, or raised by means of the trust terms. The Proposals concluded in these words : " the settlement to contain the usual powers of appointing new trustees, the usual clause of indemnity to trustees, and all other usual and necessary clauses."

These Proposals, having been submitted to the Duke of Buckingham and Lord Breadalbane, and approved of by them, subject to some variations, the precise nature of which did not appear, were subsequently returned to Mr. Vizard ; under whose instructions a settlement was soon afterwards prepared by an eminent conveyancing counsel in London.

The settlement was dated the 11th of May, 1819, and was made between the Duke of Buckingham of the first part, the Marquess of Chandos of the second part, the late Marquess of Breadalbane of the third part, the Lady Mary Campbell, now the Marchioness of Chandos, of the fourth part, and the different trustees, of the fifth, sixth, and seventh parts, respectively ; and it was duly executed by all parties. It recited, among other things, that, upon the treaty for the intended marriage, it was agreed that Lord Breadalbane should pay or secure the sum of 30,000*l*. as the portion or fortune of Lady Mary Campbell ; of which the sum of 10,000*l*. was to be paid on or before the solemnization of the marriage, the further sum of 10,000*l*. at the expiration of eighteen calendar months after the marriage, with interest at 5 per cent. in the meantime, and the remaining 10,000*l*. within six calendar months after the death of Lord Breadalbane,

THE
MARQUESS OF
BREADAL-
BANE
v.
THE
MARQUESS OF
CHANDOS.

[*714]

THE
MARQUESS OF
BREADAL-
BANE
r.
THE
MARQUESS OF
CHANDOS.

[*715]

with interest from the *day of his decease: that it was further
agreed that the Duke of Buckingham should receive from
Lord Breadalbane the two first-mentioned sums of 10,000*l.* and
10,000*l.*, with the interest upon the latter sum from the day of
the solemnization of the marriage; and in consideration thereof
should enter into the covenant thereinafter contained, for the
payment of the sum of 20,000*l.* within two years after the
solemnization of the marriage, with interest for the same in the
meantime; and that such sum of 20,000*l.*, and the interest
thereof should be further secured in the manner thereinafter
expressed: and that it was agreed that the said sum of 20,000*l.*,
so to be covenanted to be paid by the Duke of Buckingham,
and the said sum of 10,000*l.*, the residue of the portion of
30,000*l.*, to be secured by the bond of Lord Breadalbane, and
to be payable after his decease, and the several securities for
the same, should be vested in the trustees therein named (parties
thereto of the fifth part), upon the trusts thereinafter declared:
and that in further consideration of the intended marriage, and
also of the portion or fortune of Lady Mary Campbell, the Duke
of Buckingham and the Marquess of Chandos had proposed and
agreed to settle and assure the several manors and estates, in
the counties of Buckingham, Oxford, Warwick, and Northampton, in England, and in the counties of Westmeath, Longford,
Clare, and Queen's County in Ireland, and in the island of
Jamaica, respectively, thereinafter particularly described, to
the several uses, and upon and for the several trusts, intents,
and purposes, and with, under, and subject to the several
powers, provisoes, limitations, declarations, and agreements
thereinafter expressed.

After these recitals, the settlement proceeded to create, out of
the estates enumerated in the recitals, various terms of years,

[*716]

which were vested in trustees, in *order to secure an annuity
of 5,000*l.* to Lord Chandos, during his father's lifetime, as also
pin-money and a jointure for his wife, and certain allowances
and portions for the younger children of the marriage: it then
went on to specify and declare particularly the trusts of the
several terms, and to give to the trustees the powers necessary
for the purposes contemplated, with reference to the different

THE
MARQUESS OF
BREADAL-
BANE
v.
THE
MARQUESS OF
CHANDOS.

contingencies which were provided for ; and, subject to those trusts, it limited the same estates to the Duke of Buckingham, and the Marquess of Chandos, successively, for life, with remainders to the first and other sons of the marriage, succes- sively, in tail male, with divers remainders over.

The various trusts, provisions, and limitations contained in this settlement, differed in several particulars from those which had been specified in the Proposals ; but in their general character and objects they were substantially the same. The estates in Hampshire, which, according to the Sketch and Proposals, had been proposed to be comprised in the settle- ment, were omitted ; and the Northamptonshire estates were substituted in their place. No explanation was given of the reason for this alteration, or of the circumstances under which it was made.

On the 11th of May, 1819, the day on which the settlement was executed, Lord Breadalbane also executed two bonds, one of which was to secure the payment, to the Duke of Buckingham, of the sum of 10,000l., within eighteen months from the day of the marriage, and the other was to secure the payment, to the trustees named in the settlement, of a like sum of 10,000l., at the expiration of six months from the day of his own decease, with interest from that day. The marriage took effect shortly after the execution of the settlement ; and Lord *Breadalbane   [*717] paid the two sums of 10,000l. each, which he had agreed to advance to the Duke of Buckingham, as part of his daughter's portion, at the respective times appointed by the settlement for that purpose.

By certain trust dispositions, executed in the years 1823 and 1828, in the Scotch form, and which were in the nature of a will, Lord Breadalbane conveyed all his real estates in Scotland, of which he was seised in fee, and all his personal estate, after his own death, to Viscount Maitland, and certain other persons therein named, as trustees and executors, upon the trusts, and for the purposes declared in those dispositions, and in certain testamentary papers.

In the month of October, 1831, the Lady Elizabeth Campbell, the other daughter of Lord Breadalbane, intermarried with Sir

THE
MARQUESS OF
BREADAL-
BANE
v.
THE
MARQUESS OF
CHANDOS.

John Pringle. Upon her marriage, her father advanced a sum
of 20,000l. by way of portion, and in the contract of marriage,
executed on that occasion, a clause was inserted, declaring
that the sum so advanced was to be in full satisfaction of all
her claim to the provision known, in the law of Scotland, by
the name of legitim. According to that law, the younger
children of a father domiciled in Scotland, living at his death,
are entitled, in equal shares, to one third of his personal estate,
called the children's legitim, unless their right has been barred,
either by a distinct provision to that effect in the marriage
settlement of the father, or by a renunciation or release executed
by the children.

The late Lord Breadalbane who was a domiciled Scotchman
at the time of Lady Chandos's marriage, had himself married
without any settlement being made upon his marriage. On the

[*718]

29th of March, 1834, he died, being *entitled, at the time,
to large real estates in Scotland, and also to personal property,
to the amount of 400,000l. and upwards, which was chiefly
situate in England. His widow, now the Dowager Marchioness
of Breadalbane, survived him; and the present Marquess of
Breadalbane, who was his only son and heir-at-law, and Lady
Elizabeth Pringle and the Marchioness of Chandos were his
only children and next of kin. Probate of his trust dispositions and testamentary papers was granted by the Prerogative
Court of Canterbury, to Viscount Maitland. The debts, and
funeral and testamentary expenses were paid by the trustees
and executors; and one third of the clear surplus of the
personal estate was invested by them, in their own names, in
the English funds.

Shortly after the death of Lord Breadalbane, who had continued to be a domiciled Scotchman from the time of Lady
Chandos's marriage, down to the period of his decease,
various claims were made, by different parties, upon his trust
estates, and, among others, a claim was made by Lord and
Lady Chandos, in right of Lady Chandos, to a share of the
personal estate, in respect of her legitim. On the 12th of
November, 1834, the acting trustees and executors under the
trust dispositions, commenced an action of multiplepoinding

THE
MARQUESS OF
BREADAL-
BANE
v.
THE
MARQUESS OF
CHANDOS.

in the Court of Session in Scotland (a proceeding analogous to an interpleading suit in this Court), to which the Dowager Marchioness, and the present Marquess of Breadalbane, the Marquess and Marchioness of Chandos, and all other necessary parties were made defendants, and of which one object was to obtain the decision of that Court upon the validity of the claim set up by Lord and Lady Chandos. On the 26th of January, 1836, the Court of Session gave judgment in that suit (1), and thereby, among other things, found, *that the Marchioness of Chandos had not, by her contract of marriage, or otherwise, renounced her legitim ; and that she was, therefore, entitled to make her claim for the same; and that, inasmuch as she was the only younger child of the late Lord Breadalbane, who had not renounced the right of legitim, her claim extended over one third part of her father's personal estate. An appeal against the judgment of the Court of Session was afterwards presented to the House of Lords.

Pending that appeal, the Marquess of Breadalbane, who was the party prosecuting the appeal, filed the present bill against the Marquess and Marchioness of Chandos, and against the trustees and executors under his late father's testamentary dispositions.

The bill, after stating the transactions already mentioned with respect to the treaty of marriage between Lord and Lady Chandos, and the circumstances under which the settlement of May, 1819, was prepared and executed, as well as the legal proceedings which had taken place in Scotland, after the death of the late Lord Breadalbane, relative to the question of Lady Chandos's title to legitim, went on to allege that the Sketch and Proposals before mentioned had come to the hands of the plaintiff on the 5th of January, 1836, only a few weeks before the decision of the Court of Session (2), having been discovered in consequence of a recent and diligent search among some old papers in the possession of Mr. Vizard. It charged that the

---

1. 14 Shaw & Dunlop, 309 ; and 15 Shaw & Dunlop, 48.

(2) The cause was at that time waiting for judgment, the LORD ORDINARY having reported it to the second division of the Court, and the Judges having taken time to consider their decision.

THE
MARQUESS OF
BREADAL-
BANE
v.
THE
MARQUESS OF
CHANDOS.

[*720]

Proposals were duly considered by the late Lord Breadalbane
and by the Duke of Buckingham, and also by Lord and Lady
Chandos, and were approved of by them; and that all those
*parties, when they gave such approval, expected and intended
that, in the settlement about to be executed in pursuance of the
Proposals, all clauses would be inserted which were usually
inserted upon the marriage of a daughter whose father had
property affected by the laws of Scotland: that in the settlement made upon the marriage of such a daughter, a clause by
which the daughter renounced her right to legitim, or declared
that she accepted the provision, thereby made for her, in lieu
and satisfaction of legitim, was a clause usually inserted : that
when the Duke of Buckingham and Lord and Lady Chandos
approved of the Proposals, they knew that the late Lord Breadalbane was a domiciled Scotchman, and was possessed of large
property both real and personal, which was affected by the laws
of Scotland; and that they, as well as the late Lord Breadalbane
himself, who must be presumed to have been well acquainted
with those laws, fully expected and intended, or understood,
that the settlement to be executed in pursuance of the Proposals
would contain such a clause.

The bill further charged, that any person conversant with the
laws of Scotland, and knowing that the late Lord Breadalbane
was a domiciled Scotchman, would, upon reading the proviso,
in the Proposals, for the insertion in the settlement of all other
usual and necessary clauses, have known that a clause by which
Lady Chandos should renounce her legitim, or accept the portion
given her by her father in lieu of that right, was a usual and
necessary clause : that the preparation of the settlement was
left by all parties entirely to Mr. Vizard, on the supposition that
all proper and necessary clauses, according to the Proposals,
would be inserted therein ; but that Mr. Vizard, who was an
English solicitor, and not conversant with the law of Scotland,
[*721] was not aware of *the right of a child to legitim, according to
that law: that Mr. Vizard, having received from Mr. Robson
the Proposals so approved, immediately caused the settlement
of the 11th of May, 1819, to be prepared, upon the basis and
in execution of the Proposals; but that, owing to mistake or

THE
MARQUESS OF
BREADAL-
BANE
v.
THE
MARQUESS OF
CHANDOS.

misapprehension, such settlement was not prepared in conformity with them.

The bill further charged, by way of evidence of the late Lord Breadalbane's intention and understanding that the provision, made by him for Lady Chandos, should be in lieu of legitim, that in all the instruments executed by his Lordship, both prior and subsequently to the marriage of his younger children, in which he made provision for such younger children, he declared that the provision so made was in satisfaction of their right to legitim; and, in particular, that in three several bonds which he executed for that purpose, in the years 1794, 1798, and 1812, respectively, a declaration was inserted to that effect; and further, that in a bond executed by his Lordship in the year 1824, by which the sum of 10,000*l*., payable, according to the settlement, six months after his death, was secured upon his Scotch property, a declaration was contained that such provision was in full of all legitim, which Lady Chandos could claim against his estate upon his decease.

The bill further charged, that in the before-mentioned proceedings carried on in the Court of Session in Scotland, that Court, according to its own practice, and according to the laws of Scotland, was not competent to take into consideration the matters herein-before stated.

The bill prayed, in substance, a declaration that according to the true construction of the settlement of the *11th of May, 1819, the sum of 30,000*l*. advanced by the late Lord Breadalbane on the marriage of Lady Chandos, was a satisfaction of her claim to legitim, and was accepted by Lord and Lady Chandos as such; and that Lord and Lady Chandos, by being parties to that settlement, had duly renounced or released all their right thereto: but if the Court should not be of that opinion, it then prayed, in the alternative, that the settlement might be reformed and amended, by inserted therein a proper clause, whereby Lord and Lady Chandos should renounce and release the right to legitim, or declare that the sum of 30,000*l*. was given to, and accepted by them, in lieu of that right; and that Lord and Lady Chandos might be restrained from availing themselves of the judgment in their favour, obtained in the Court of Session

[*722]

THE
MARQUESS OF
BREADAL-
BANE
v.
THE
MARQUESS OF
CHANDOS.
against the other defendants, the trustees of the late Lord
Breadalbane, and from doing any act to compel such trustees
to pay over to them the amount of the legitim, or the funds in
which the same was invested ; and that the trustees might, in
like manner, be restrained from paying over or transferring such
funds to Lord and Lady Chandos.

The defendants, the Marquess and Marchioness of Chandos,
by their answer, among other things, said that they did not
know or believe that it was usual in Scotland, upon the marriage
of a child, for the father to give such child a marriage portion
in lieu of the right to legitim ; for, they said they had been
informed and believed that, in most cases, it was a matter
of special contract and arrangement among the various contracting parties, what should and what should not be done in
that behalf ; and that it was only where there was a special and
express purpose and intention to exclude the claim of legitim,
that it was usual in Scotland, upon the marriage of a child, for

[*723]   the father to give such child a marriage *portion in bar or
satisfaction of legitim ; and that where it was intended to exclude
such claim, a clause accepting such marriage portion, and
acknowledging it to be in lieu thereof, and expressly releasing
the claim, was usually introduced into the marriage settlement
of such child ; but they stated that they did not know or believe
that the late Lord Breadalbane ever expressed any intention,
that the provision made by him for his daughter Lady Chandos,
on her marriage, should be in satisfaction of her claim to
legitim, and that they did not believe that he ever entertained
such intention.

The defendants, by their answer, further stated that the
terms of the marriage settlement were arranged with the assistance, and under the advice, of the Earl of Lauderdale, who was
educated for the Scotch Bar, and was a member of the faculty
of advocates, and was well acquainted with the law of Scotland,
and particularly with the law of legitim, and was also well aware
of the fact that the father and mother of Lady Chandos had
married without any settlement ; and they further stated that
the portion or fortune of Lady Chandos was a subject which
was left by the defendants to their respective parents.   The

THE
MARQUESS OF
BREADAL-
BANE
v.
THE
MARQUESS OF
CHANDOS.

defendants, by their answer, positively denied that they expected
or intended, or that they believed that the other persons who were
parties to the treaty of marriage, and approved of the Proposals,
or any of them, expected or intended that there should be a clause
in the settlement by which Lady Chandos would be made to
release or renounce her right to legitim, or by which it would
be declared that the provisions contained in the settlement were
given to, and accepted by her in lieu of that right.   They said
they believed that the Proposals and settlement were made
without any reference whatsoever, on the part of any of the
persons who were parties thereto, or who took part in the *treaty,
to the right of Lady Chandos to legitim ; and that they did not
know or believe that it was the intention of the late Lord
Breadalbane, and they positively denied that it was the intention
of the defendants, that the settlement should contain a clause
barring or releasing that right.   They further denied, that it was
owing to mistake or misapprehension, or for any other reason,
that the settlement was not prepared by Mr. Vizard in conformity
with the Proposals; for, they said that, to the best of their
knowledge and belief, such settlement was prepared, as to
the matters in question in the cause, entirely in conformity
with the Proposals, although it varied therefrom in several
particulars as to other matters, not relevant to the questions
in the cause.

They further stated that the preparation of the settlement was
left by the parties entirely to Mr. Vizard, who was the solicitor
of the late Lord Breadalbane ; and that they believed that the
settlement did, in fact, contain all the clauses which were introduced
to be introduced therein.   They denied that, according to the
true construction of the settlement, the sum of 30,000*l.*, advanced
by the late Lord Breadalbane, was in full satisfaction of any
right which Lady Chandos had, or might thereafter have, to
legitim, or that the defendants, by being parties to and executing
the settlement, had renounced or released such right.   They
stated, that in the action of multiplepoinding in the Court of
Session it was competent to the parties to such action to bring
forward any defence, whether legal or equitable, to the claim to
legitim set up by the defendants, in right of Lady Chandos ;

THE
MARQUESS OF
BREADAL-
BANE
r.
THE
MARQUESS OF
CHANDOS.

[725]

and that it was competent to the plaintiff to insist, in that action, that, if the marriage settlement did not expressly or effectually exclude such claim, the settlement ought to be corrected or reformed accordingly. * * The defendants, Lord and Lady Chandos, now moved that the injunction might be dissolved.

Mr. Tinney, Mr. Pemberton, Mr. Burge, Mr. Wigram, and *Mr. Stuart*, for the motion.

Mr. Knight, Mr. Jacob, and *Mr. Richards, contrà*.

The case was very fully and elaborately argued ; first, upon the preliminary question how far this Court had, under the circumstances, a right, or if it had the right, would, in the exercise of its discretion, be inclined, to adjudicate upon a matter which had already been entertained and disposed of by a foreign tribunal of competent jurisdiction ; especially when that tribunal was legally, though not actually, in possession of the fund, and the trustees were properly amenable to its jurisdiction ; and, secondly, upon the merits, as appearing from the admissions contained in the defendants' answer. * * *

[727]

The points mainly insisted upon by the plaintiff, in support of the injunction, are stated and considered in the judgment.

[Numerous cases were cited by counsel, but the decision of the LORD CHANCELLOR makes any reference to those cases unnecessary for the purpose of this report.]

[728]

The *Solicitor-General* and *Mr. T. J. Phillips* appeared for the defendants, the trustees.

1837.
July 22.
———

THE LORD CHANCELLOR :

This was a motion to discharge an order of the VICE-CHANCELLOR for an injunction restraining Lord and Lady Chandos from taking advantage of a judgment of the Court of Session in Scotland. The case was argued before me some considerable time ago. The magnitude of the sum in question between the parties, and the order which has been pronounced by the VICE-CHANCELLOR, made me desirous to postpone my judgment, until I should have had time to go through the whole of the papers, and to consider the

THE
MARQUESS OF
BREADAL-
BANE
v.
THE
MARQUESS OF
CHANDOS.

various points which had been argued at the Bar.   I have now had an opportunity of doing so ; and I hope the parties have not experienced any material inconvenience from the delay which has taken place.

The bill raises three propositions.   It first prays the Court to declare, that by the construction of the settlement of 1819, the claim to legitim is barred.   It then alleges, that if that should not be found to be so, it was a matter of contract and agreement between the parties at the time of the marriage settlement of Lord and Lady Chandos, in the year 1819, that the legitim should be barred ; and lastly, it alleges that a paper has lately been discovered, being the Proposals which preceded the settlement, and that those Proposals furnish evidence of the intention of the parties, or at least contain words amounting to a contract, that the settlement should contain a provision barring Lady Chandos's title to legitim ; and on these three grounds—the *construction of the settlement of 1819, the alleged contract between the parties, and the effect of words found in the Proposals, though not introduced into the settlement,—it prays that the Court will grant an injunction to restrain Lord and Lady Chandos from taking advantage of the judgment of the Court of Session, by which Lady Chandos has been decreed entitled to her legitim.

[*729]

The sum in question is of great magnitude ; for it is one third part of the whole personal estate of the late Lord Breadalbane, which personal estate is said to amount to 400,000*l.*

Now, as to the first of the propositions raised by the bill, that is finally disposed of by the judgment of the House of Lords. The construction of the settlement of 1819 has been the subject of a judgment of the Court of Session, and that judgment has been affirmed by the House of Lords, by which it has been decided that the settlement does not bar the title to legitim in this case.

The next proposition in the bill, namely, that it was a matter of contract, that the legitim should be barred, and that the settlement therefore did not carry into effect that which was agreed upon between the parties, is positively denied by the answer ; and this being a motion upon the answer, it must, for the present purpose, be assumed, and indeed, looking at all the

THE
MARQUESS OF
BREADAL-
BANE
v.
THE
MARQUESS OF
CHANDOS.

[*730]

transactions between the parties, I have not the slightest doubt, that there was no such contract between them.

The only remaining point, therefore, is that which has been put forward, as the principal equity in support of the plaintiff's claim to this injunction, namely, that the Proposals, which were not in evidence before the Court *of Session, and which, it is alleged, have been since discovered, contain within themselves that which amounted to a contract, whether the parties had it in contemplation or not, that the legitim should be barred.

The Proposals were prepared in London by Mr. Vizard. It is stated that they were approved of by the Duke of Buckingham, acting for his son Lord Chandos, and by Lord Breadalbane, acting for his daughter Lady Chandos. The Proposals were, in substance, that Lord Breadalbane should pay 20,000*l*.—10,000*l*. down, and 10,000*l*. within eighteen months after the marriage— and further, that he should enter into a security for the payment of 10,000*l*. more after his own death. In consideration of these three sums, making, in all, 30,000*l*., the Duke of Buckingham agreed to settle very large estates on the issue of the marriage, and out of those estates to provide a jointure for Lady Chandos, and portions for younger children ; and then, after enumerating the various trusts of the sums of money to be thus raised, the Proposals went on to provide for the different purposes which the parties had in view, with regard to the settlement of the real estates and the application of the 30,000*l*. for the benefit of the younger children. The Proposals then contained these words. " the settlement to contain the usual clause of indemnity to trustees, and all other usual and necessary clauses."

It is contended, that inasmuch as it is usual in Scotland, when a father provides a portion for a child, that he should require the child to enter into a renunciation of the claim to legitim, these words in the Proposals amounted to a contract between the parties, whether they had it in contemplation or not, that the settlement should contain that which is alleged to be a usual provision in Scotch settlements.

[731]

Now, the settlement itself was entirely of English manufacture : it was prepared by Mr. Vizard, who was an English solicitor ; and, in point of fact, it contains no such clause ; but it recites that Lord Breadalbane was to pay and secure 30,000*l.* as the portion or fortune of Lady Chandos. That has been adjudged not to amount to a renunciation of legitim; it being clearly established, that, in the Scotch law, legitim cannot be renounced by inference, but that express contract and distinct renunciation are required, for the purpose of depriving a child of legitim.

Lord Breadalbane afterwards executed two bonds; one, to secure the 10,000*l.*, payable eighteen months after the marriage; and the other, to secure the 10,000*l.* payable after his own death.

It appears that in the year 1831 the other daughter of Lord Breadalbane, now Lady Elizabeth Pringle, married; and in her marriage settlement there is an express renunciation of her title to legitim.

It appears also that, in the year 1824, Lord Chandos's marriage having taken place in the year 1819, Lord Breadalbane was desirous, under a power given him by an Act of Parliament, of charging upon his estates the 10,000*l.* which he had contracted to pay within six months after his decease; and in the bond, which he then executed for that purpose, he expressly declared, that the 10,000*l.* so charged, was to be in bar of Lady Chandos's title to legitim. That circumstance, however, can only be material in so far as it may evidence the impression upon Lord Breadalbane's mind: it cannot affect the rights of the parties, which are to be determined, not by any thing which Lord Breadalbane did *after the marriage, but by that which took place between the parties at the time of the marriage.

It appears, moreover, that anterior to the marriage, that is to say, in the years 1794, 1798, and 1812, Lord Breadalbane executed certain instruments, making provision for his younger children; and that in all those instruments it is declared, that the provision so secured was to be in bar of the children's title to legitim. These instruments, of course, are immaterial to the present purpose; they are important only as showing Lord Breadalbane's knowledge of what was necessary in order to bar a child's claim to legitim.

The Court of Session in Scotland is, unquestionably, a court of equity as well as a court of law; and I apprehend there can

THE
MARQUESS OF
BREADAL-
BANE
v.
THE
MARQUESS OF
CHANDOS.

[*732]

THE
MARQUESS OF
BREADAL-
BANE
v.
THE
MARQUESS OF
CHANDOS.
be no doubt, that it was within the jurisdiction of the Court of
Session to entertain the question which the plaintiff has thought
proper to raise upon this record. The suit in Scotland was a
suit of multiplepoinding, in which all parties, having any claim,
were called before the Court, for the purpose of asserting their
title to the personal property of Lord Breadalbane. The question, whether Lady Chandos's title to legitim was barred by the
settlement, was distinctly raised in that suit; but no question,
with respect to that title, founded on the supposed effect of the
terms of the Proposals, was then brought forward. It certainly
is contrary to the practice of this Court to assume jurisdiction
in favour of parties who, having had an opportunity of asserting
their title in another Court, where the matter has been properly
the subject of adjudication, have either missed that opportunity,
or have not thought proper to bring their title forward.

[733]   In the view I have taken of this case, however, it is not
necessary to pursue that topic further. I have adverted to it
only that I may not be misunderstood; that it may not be
thought to be clear that this Court would entertain or enforce a
claim to an equity, after the case had been the subject of adjudication by another Court, of competent jurisdiction, and in which
the matter of equity was equally cognizable, upon the ground of
the party not having thought proper, or having from accident,
or for any other reason, taken no steps, to bring the claim before
that Court.

Such being the case made by the bill, the defendants, by their
answer, positively deny all contract or understanding on the
subject. They say that the whole negociation was left to the
Duke of Buckingham, on the one side, and to Lord Breadalbane,
on the other: they admit that it is usual in Scotland to insert
clauses barring legitim; but they state, that which was established to be the law of Scotland by the decision of the House of
Lords in this very case, that although it is usual to insert a
clause barring legitim, yet legitim cannot be barred except by
distinct contract. They also admit that, on Lady Elizabeth
Pringle's marriage, her legitim was barred; but they allege that
it was barred by express contract, introduced into her marriage
settlement.

Now, by what is stated in the answer, and by what was decided in the Court of Session, and confirmed by the House of Lords, two points are clearly established; first, that the mere giving a portion is no bar to legitim, but that in order to bar legitim it is necessary there should be express renunciation; and secondly, that the settlement in this case did not operate as a bar to the right claimed by Lady Chandos.

THE MARQUESS OF BREADALBANE *c.* THE MARQUESS OF CHANDOS.

The sole consideration, therefore, is whether the provision in the Proposals, for the insertion of "the usual and necessary clauses" entitles the plaintiff to have the settlement reformed by the insertion of such a clause.

[734]

The first question is, was that the intention of the parties? First of all, was it the intention of Lord and Lady Chandos, the parties from whom this very valuable right is supposed to have been taken away by what took place in the year 1819? By their answer they positively deny, not only that there was any such intention, or any such contract, on their parts, but that the subject-matter was present to their minds at all. In short, they state that they knew nothing about legitim; and there is no reason to suppose that the case is at all misrepresented by the answer.

The next question is, was it the intention of the Duke of Buckingham to surrender the claim to legitim? It is equally clear that he thought nothing about it: it is probable that he knew nothing about it; and there is an absence of all evidence that he ever had present to his mind the claim of legitim, to which his son, in right of his wife, would become entitled, or that he ever intended to consent to the barring of any such claim.

It is then said, though that may be true, yet Lord Breadalbane, living in Scotland, and being acquainted more or less with Scotch law, and having the assistance of a very experienced Scotch lawyer, Lord Lauderdale, whom he appears to have consulted on all the arrangements with regard to the settlement, must have known the law of Scotland with reference to the child's title to legitim, and have known that it was usual to insert clauses barring legitim, in settlements made by a father on his children; and that he must therefore have understood

[*735]

THE
MARQUESS OF
BREADAL-
BANE
v.
THE
MARQUESS OF
CHANDOS.

the words "usual and necessary clauses" as intending to provide that the settlement to be prepared in pursuance of the Proposals should contain a clause barring Lady Chandos's title to legitim.

The first observation that arises upon that proposition is this, that Lord Breadalbane was afterwards a party to the settlement itself, which contains no such clause. It also appears that subsequently, namely, in the year 1824, he executed a deed of that date, by which he charged the sum of 10,000l., payable within six months after his decease, upon his Scotch estates, and declared that it should be in bar of legitim. Now, if he had supposed that legitim had been already barred by the settlement, it would have been perfectly unnecessary, in a deed which was meant to carry into effect the provisions of the settlement, to specify that the sum thus secured should be in bar of legitim.

But, supposing that Lord Breadalbane had any such intention, —supposing that, as he resided in Scotland, he was more or less cognizant of Scotch law, and that the right of the child to legitim, and the means by which that right might be barred, had been present to his mind—it is quite clear that he never even communicated his intention to the other parties. The renunciation of legitim by his daughter was a proceeding which would enure to his own benefit : he was authorised to treat, on her behalf, with the father of her intended husband, with respect to such rights as he conferred upon her by the provision of 30,000l. which he then made in her favour ; but he had no authority, nor was it ever supposed that he was invested with any authority, to treat, not as with the father of the husband, but as between himself and his daughter on the subject of her claim to *legitim ; the daughter and her intended husband being entirely ignorant of the existence of any such claim, or of any such effect being given, or intended to be given, to the transaction then in progress.

[*736]

Now, if Lord Breadalbane put that construction upon those words—of which, however, there is not only no evidence, but as to which I am perfectly satisfied that the subject-matter, strange as it may appear, was as absent from his mind and from the mind of Lord Lauderdale, who was acting for him, as it was from the minds of Lord and Lady Chandos, or of the solicitor who was acting for them, or of the Duke of Buckingham, who was acting for Lord Chandos—but if that was the impression upon his own mind, and it was not communicated to the other parties, or present to their minds, it would be extremely difficult, from that impression, to contend that the title of Lady Chandos to legitim out of his personal estate was to be barred.

THE
MARQUESS OF
BREADAL-
BANE
v.
THE
MARQUESS OF
CHANDOS.

If Lord Breadalbane did so understand the words in the Proposals, it must have been because he was acquainted with the Scotch law, and knew that such provisions were usually inserted in Scotch settlements : and yet it is most extraordinary, that, with that knowledge, and with the supposed construction put by himself upon the words, he should have afterwards executed a settlement which contained no such provision ; although the proposition assumes that he, being conversant with Scotch law, knew that by that law an express renunciation of legitim was necessary, in order to carry his intention into effect.   It is positively denied that the parties, sought to be affected by this injunction, knew anything about the claim to legitim ; and the result of the whole leaves no doubt upon my mind that the matter was not present to the minds of any of the parties.

Still, however, though the parties had not the subject-matter present to their minds, they may have used words which would operate upon rights of which they were not cognizant.   If a person thinks proper to bar all the rights which he has, it is not necessary to prove that he knew all his rights, or that he had ascertained what his rights were.

[737]

That brings the case to the question—the only arguable question,—what is the effect of these words in the Proposals. Now it must always be kept in view that, by the law of Scotland, nothing but an express renunciation will have the effect of barring the title to legitim ; and it would be a strange conclusion, indeed, if the Court were to decide, that the introduction of these words into the Proposals had the effect of depriving one of the contracting parties of a title to property of so enormous an amount, although none of the parties to the arrangement intended that the words should have any such operation.

Nevertheless, it is possible that the words may have had that effect.   Now the Proposals relate entirely to English subject-

THE
MARQUESS OF
BREADAL-
BANE
v.
THE
MARQUESS OF
CHANDOS.

[*738]

matter.   They are made between parties resident in England : they were made with reference to the marriage settlement of the son of an English nobleman marrying the daughter of a Scotch nobleman : they were prepared in England : the subject-matter was English, and all the parties were English; and, after providing for all the purposes usual in a settlement of that description,— pin-money and a jointure for the wife, portions for the younger children, and then for the settlement of the estate,—the Proposals conclude in these words, " the settlement to contain the usual clause of indemnity to trustees, and all other usual and necessary clauses."   Now, I apprehend, taking these Proposals *according to their ordinary sense, that, when parties, after stating what they profess to do, and the provisions which they intend to make, provide that " all usual and necessary clauses " shall be inserted, they must be understood to mean all clauses usual and necessary for the purpose of carrying into effect the provisions before expressed; and of these the right to legitim formed no part.

In *Anstruther* v. *Adair* (1) the case arose out of a settlement which was executed in Scotland, between parties domiciled in that country, and the question was with respect to the equity of the wife according to the English law.   It was decided, and most properly decided, by Lord BROUGHAM, that the settlement being executed in Scotland between Scotch parties, it must be dealt with according to the law of Scotland; and that you cannot apply the equities of the English law between parties living in Scotland, and who never had those equities in their contemplation.   So, here, in the case of a settlement to be executed in England, between English parties, relating to English subject-matter, and providing for its objects by the usual clauses, and not with reference to anything *dehors* the settlement, or to any right which might arise by the law of a foreign country,—Scotland being for this purpose a foreign country, and under the administration of different laws,—the obvious meaning of these words in the proviso would be, that there should be all such clauses as were usual and necessary for the purpose of carrying into effect the contract between the parties.

(1) 39 R. R. 263 (2 My. & K. 515).

There were cited, not, I believe, in the argument here, but in the course of the argument in the House of *Lords, a variety of cases with respect to that part of our law which bears the nearest analogy to the law of legitim in Scotland ; I mean the law with respect to the right of children, under the customs of London and York, to a share of their deceased parents' estate ; and several instances were referred to, in which the title of the child had been barred by the provision given by the father to the child. Cases were cited in which the father had advanced a portion to his child, and had stipulated that such advancement should bar the orphanage part ; but no case was produced, and I presume no case exists, in which the title of the child has been held to be barred by that which has taken place here, namely, by simply advancing the portion of the child, in terms such as those which are contained in this settlement ; the only words, in the settlement, on which the argument was founded, being, that the 30,000l. were there expressed to be given " as the portion or fortune " of Lady Chandos.

The ground upon which this motion is rested, is, that there is evidence which would justify the Court in correcting the settlement. The Proposals having been afterwards matured into a settlement, it is the settlement which binds the rights of the parties, unless there be something bringing the case within the authority of other cases, in which the Court has felt itself authorised to correct a settlement, upon the ground of mistake or misapprehension, and to introduce into the instrument something which appears to have been the intention of the parties, as evidenced by other means than the settlement itself.

Now, in order to justify the Court in taking such a course, it is obvious that a clear intention must be proved ; it must be shown that the settlement does not *carry into effect the intention of the parties. If there be merely evidence of doubtful or ambiguous words having been used, the settlement itself is the construction which the parties have put upon those doubtful or ambiguous words. They have themselves removed any doubt, which might have existed, upon that which forms the foundation of the settlement. But, in this case, although it is unnecessary for me to pursue that subject farther, there is, in fact, an absence

THE
MARQUESS OF
BREADAL-
BANE
v.
THE
MARQUESS OF
CHANDOS.

[*739]

[*740]

of proof that the settlement did grow out of these Proposals.   It differs from the Proposals in some most important parts.   No doubt those were the Proposals originally suggested : what passed between the time when the Proposals were prepared, and the execution of the settlement—what gave rise to any change of intention, or why it was that the settlement was not in conformity with the Proposals in other matters,—does not at all appear ; but there is evidence of a manifest departure, in the settlement, in some important points, from the arrangement as contained in the Proposals.   In order to justify the Court in correcting the settlement, it must be proved, not only that the contract was different from that which the settlement carried into effect, but that there was no change of intention, by which the circumstance that the settlement did not follow the terms of the original contract might be explained.

If Lord Breadalbane had the knowledge which is the foundation of the whole argument—if, seeing these words in the Proposals, he imagined that the settlement would contain terms barring Lady Chandos's title to legitim out of his estate, he would of course have expected that the settlement should be so framed as to effect that purpose ; and, as the benefit of her renunciation would enure to him, he would naturally look to see that his

[*741]   object had been accomplished.   Lord *Breadalbane, however, is made a party to that settlement, not for the purpose of taking the benefit of Lady Chandos's renunciation, but because he was a party contracting to make further provision for Lady Chandos by paying 20,000l. at a future period to the trustees ; and there is nothing in the settlement, which could induce him to suppose, that the intention which he is assumed to have had in his mind, of protecting his personal estate from the claim of Lady Chandos to legitim, had been carried into effect.

In the course of the argument here, many books were referred to, for the purpose of showing, that, in Scotch settlements, it is usual to insert clauses barring legitim.   That only proves, however, that it is usual so to contract ; for it is decided that, without special contract for that purpose, legitim cannot be barred ; and the question is, not whether it is usual in Scotch settlements, but whether it is usual in English settlements, in

THE
MARQUESS OF
BREADAL-
BANE
v.
THE
MARQUESS OF
CHANDOS.

which no reference is made to legitim, or to any rights dependent upon the Scotch law, to insert such a clause.

It is sworn by the answer, by which I am, on this motion, bound, that Lord and Lady Chandos never intended to give up their claim to legitim; and I am satisfied, from all the facts of the case, as they are now before the Court, that the question never once occurred to the minds of any of the parties. If it had, that claim might have been barred: but, looking to the settlement, I am equally clear that it provided " all the usual and necessary clauses " which the parties intended; and I must construe the Proposals to mean, all clauses usual and necessary for the purpose of carrying into effect the arrangement before detailed, of which the renunciation of legitim formed no part.

I am also of opinion that if this were doubtful, the settlement afterwards executed removes the doubt, and proves what the parties meant; and that there is not any such evidence to show a mistake in the settlement, as would justify a court of equity in interfering to reform the settlement upon that ground.

[742]

Upon these grounds, I am bound to dissolve the injunction which the VICE-CHANCELLOR has granted.

MOTLEY v. DOWNMAN.

(3 My. & Cr. 1—17; S. C. 6 L. J. (N. S.) Ch. 308.)

Principles and rules upon which the Court interferes, by injunction, to prevent a defendant from using a trade mark where the claim of the plaintiff to have the exclusive use of the trade mark has not been legally established, and is open to question.

[UPON the point stated in the head-note, the LORD CHANCELLOR said:]

The Court, when it interferes in cases of this sort, is exercising a jurisdiction over legal rights; and, although, sometimes, in a very strong case, it interferes, in the first instance, by injunction, yet, in a general way, it puts the party upon asserting his right by trying it in an action at law. If it does not do that, it permits the plaintiff, notwithstanding the suit in equity, to bring an action. In both cases, the Court is only acting in aid of, and is only ancillary to, the legal right.

[14]

MOTLEY
v.
DOWNMAN.

I can hardly conceive a case in which the Court will at once interfere by injunction, and prevent a defendant from disputing the plaintiff's legal title. The present order interposes the injunction, and does not put the parties in a situation to try the question at law.

[The remaining portion of the judgment is occupied with the special facts which in his Lordship's opinion made it a question of considerable nicety whether the plaintiff's claim was valid, and the injunction was accordingly dissolved.]

1887.
July 20.
Aug. 3.
——
Lord
COTTENHAM,
L.C.
[31]

MARCH *v.* RUSSELL.

(3 My. & Cr. 31—44; S. C. 6 L. J. (N. S.) Ch. 303; 1 Jur. 588.)

In the year 1810 a sum of stock was transferred into the names of A. and B., in trust for a father and mother, in certain proportions, for their respective lives, with remainder to their children. Shortly afterwards, the stock was transferred by A. and B. into the name of B. only, who appropriated it to his own use. In the year 1818, the father and mother filed a bill against A. and B., to have the stock replaced; and the children (two in number) were co-plaintiffs, and, being infants, sued by their father, as their next friend; but that suit was soon afterwards compromised, upon B. giving security for the payment of interest for the time past and for the time to come. A. subsequently died, and his personal estate was distributed among his legatees; and two of those legatees then died, having received their legacies; and the residuary personal estate of one of them was paid over to her residuary legatee. These distributions were made in ignorance of any demand arising out of the breach of trust in which A. had concurred. The eldest of the two children attained twenty-one in 1821, and the other in 1823. In 1833 they filed a bill alone against B. and the personal representative of A. and his surviving legatees, and the personal representatives of his deceased legatees, and the residuary legatee of one of those deceased legatees, and against the father and mother of the plaintiffs, praying to have the fund replaced:

Held, that the plaintiffs were entitled to call upon the surviving legatees of A., and the personal representatives and legatees of his deceased legatees to refund; and that, without any previous inquiry, as to whether the plaintiffs had known of or acquiesced in the breach of trust, or the compromise of the suit of 1818.

BY a deed, dated the 18th of November, 1807, and made between Thomas March and Prudence his wife of the one part, and George Russell and George Hodgson of the other part, it was declared that Russell and Hodgson should stand possessed of a sum of 1,000*l.* Navy 5 per cent. Bank Annuities, which had been transferred into their joint names by Thomas March,

upon trust to permit Thomas March to receive one third of the
dividends for his life, and to pay the remaining two thirds to
Prudence March during the joint lives of her husband and
herself, for her separate use; and, after the death *of Thomas
March, and in the event of his wife surviving him, to pay the
whole of the dividends to Prudence March, for her life; and,
after the death of Prudence March, whether in the lifetime or
after the decease of Thomas March, to stand possessed of the
Bank Annuities (subject to the trust for payment of the
dividends of one-third to Thomas March during his life), in
trust for George March and John March, children of Thomas
and Prudence March, and all and every other child and
children of Thomas March by Prudence his wife, thereafter
to be born, who should be living at the time of the decease of
Prudence March, and the issue of such of them as should be
then dead, leaving issue, in equal shares, such issue taking the
shares to which their parents would have been entitled, to be
vested interests when they should attain twenty-one, with benefit
of survivorship. The deed contained a power, enabling Prudence
March to appoint a new trustee, in the stead of any trustee who
should die, or be desirous of being discharged, or refuse to act.

[*32]

In the month of March, 1810, Thomas Grant was appointed a
trustee of the above-mentioned deed of settlement in the stead
of George Hodgson, who retired from the trust; and the Navy
5 per cent. stock was thereupon transferred into the joint names
of George Russell and Thomas Grant.

Soon after Grant's appointment as trustee, Russell and Grant
transferred the stock into the name of Russell only, who
subsequently sold it out, and applied the produce to his own use.

Thomas and Prudence March had no children besides those
already mentioned, of whom George was born in *or about the
year 1800, and John, in or about the year 1802.

[*33]

*   *   *   *   *

In the year 1818, Thomas and Prudence March, and George
and John March, their sons, then infants, by Thomas March,
their father and next friend, filed a bill in Chancery, against
Russell and Grant, for the purpose of compelling them to replace
the stock; but that suit was compromised, soon after its institution,

[34]

upon Russell giving additional security for the payment of
interest for the time past, and for the punctual payment of
interest for the future. Grant, however, had put in his answer
to the bill, and had set forth in it a written document, purporting to be signed by Thomas and Prudence March, expressly
authorising him to transfer the stock to his co-trustee, Russell.

Grant died in the year 1820 ; having, by his will, given all his
personal estate, not specifically bequeathed, to his sister Sarah
Matson, widow, and to John Perkins and William Wise, upon
trust to convert it into money ; and, after payment of his debts,
to pay one third to Sarah Matson, and one other third to Mary
Smith ; and, as to the remaining third, to pay one third part of it
to Alicia Eliza Arrowsmith, wife of Thomas Arrowsmith ; and,
as to the remaining two thirds of the last-mentioned third,
to invest it upon Government or real securities, and pay the
interest to Alicia Eliza Arrowsmith for life, for her separate use ;
and after her death to divide the capital equally amongst all her
children, the shares of daughters being vested at the age of

[*35]   twenty-one, or at marriage, *and the shares of sons at the age
of twenty-one, with benefit of survivorship. Sarah Matson,
John Perkins, and William Wise, were appointed executors of
this will ; and the will was proved, together with a codicil, by
Sarah Matson and John Perkins, on the 18th of July, 1820.

Sarah Matson died in the year 1830 ; having, by her will,
given all the residue of her personal estate to Sarah Prudence
Arrowsmith, spinster, and appointed John Perkins her sole
executor, who afterwards proved her will.

Mary Smith also died, having appointed George Ray and John
Grant Smith her executors, both of whom proved her will.

The present bill was filed, in the year 1833, by George March
and John March, as the only children of Thomas and Prudence
March, against Russell, Perkins, Thomas Arrowsmith, and Alicia
Eliza his wife, Sarah Prudence Arrowsmith, who was one of the
children of Alicia Eliza Arrowsmith, and also against her other
children, against Thomas and Prudence March, against Ray, and
against John Grant Smith, who was out of the jurisdiction of the
Court ; and it prayed that Russell, and Perkins, as executor of
Grant, might be decreed to lay out the amount produced by the

sale of the 1,000*l.* 5 per cent. Navy Bank Annuities, or the value of that stock, in the purchase of stock, in the name of the Accountant-General, upon the trusts of the settlement; and that the rights and interests of the plaintiffs, and of the defendants, Thomas and Prudence March, in the stock so to be purchased, might be ascertained and declared ; and that Perkins might either admit assets of Grant, or that the usual accounts of Grant's personal estate might be *taken ; and that, in case it should appear, in taking such accounts, that any part of Grant's personal estate had been received by Sarah Matson, Mary Smith, or the Arrowsmiths, as residuary legatees of Grant, then that the personal estate of Sarah Matson and Mary Smith might be charged with, and the Arrowsmiths might be ordered to refund a sufficient part of the personal estate so received, to answer the plaintiffs' demands ; and that Perkins, as executor of Sarah Matson, and Ray and J. G. Smith, as executors of Mary Smith, might admit assets of their respective testatrixes, or that the usual accounts of the personal estates of those testatrixes might be taken ; and if it should appear that any part of the personal estate of Sarah Matson had been received by Sarah Prudence Arrowsmith, as her residuary legatee, then that she might refund the whole or a sufficient part of what she should so have received.

[*36]

Perkins, by his answer, stated that in the year 1823 Grant's affairs were finally wound up by Sarah Matson, by whom alone his personal estate had been possessed, and that the net residue of 2,036*l.* 11*s.* 4*d.* was appropriated by her, according to the directions of Grant's will ; the two thirds of a third, set apart for Alicia Eliza Arrowsmith and her children, being invested in the funds, in the joint names of Sarah Matson and Perkins ; and that Grant's personal estate was thus applied and administered, without his (Perkins's) having any notice of the claim now made by the plaintiffs in this suit. He admitted, also, that he had paid to Sarah Prudence Arrowsmith the clear surplus of Sarah Matson's estate, being 129*l.* 15*s.* 11*d.*, or thereabouts, but without any notice or knowledge of the plaintiffs' claim, or of the circumstances under which it was now made ; and that, in January, 1833, he changed the security of that part of Grant's estate, which had been set apart for the *Arrowsmiths, from the funds to a

[*37]

mortgage. The statements of Thomas Arrowsmith and his wife, and such of her children as were of age, were to the same effect.

The defendant Ray, by his answer, stated that he had possessed the personal estate of Mary Smith to a very small amount, and not sufficient to pay her funeral and testamentary expenses and debts, exclusive of the sum which the bill alleged that she had received as one of Grant's residuary legatees; as to which he was unable to state whether it had been received by Mary Smith or not.

By the decree made in this cause by the present MASTER OF THE ROLLS, it was declared that Russell and the assets of Grant were liable to make good the 1,000*l.* Navy Bank Annuities, and to pay the plaintiffs' costs of this suit; and an account of Grant's assets was directed; and it was declared that his residuary legatees, to the extent of the sums received by them, were liable to make good the plaintiffs' demand; and an account was directed of what had been paid to each of the legatees; and an account of Sarah Matson's assets was directed; and it was declared that Sarah Prudence Arrowsmith, as her residuary legatee, to the extent of the sum received by her, not exceeding the sum which should be found to have been received by Sarah Matson in respect of Grant's residuary estate, was liable to make good the plaintiffs' demand; and an account was directed of what had been received by Sarah Prudence Arrowsmith in respect of the residuary estate of Sarah Matson: and it was declared, that Thomas Arrowsmith was liable for the one third of a third of the residuary personal estate of Thomas Grant, which had been received by his wife Alicia Eliza Arrowsmith; and the remaining two thirds of such third, invested in the name of Perkins, were *declared to be also liable to the plaintiffs' demand; and an inquiry was directed, whether Mary Smith had received any thing, and what, in respect of Grant's residuary personal estate; and it was ordered, that what should appear to have been received by her, should be answered by Ray out of her assets. It was also ordered that, out of the funds so declared to be liable, the 1,000*l.* Bank Navy 5 per cent. Annuities, now reduced to 3½ per cent. Annuities, should be replaced. It was referred to the Master to tax

[*38]

the plaintiffs' costs, and it was ordered that such costs should
be paid by Russell, and by the other defendants, out of the
funds so declared to be liable ; and that, when the stock should
have been replaced, any of the parties should be at liberty
to apply with respect to the dividends.

All the defendants, with the exception of Russell and Thomas
March and Prudence March, appealed from the whole of this
decree, except so far as it affected Russell.

Mr. Barber, Mr. Koe, and *Mr. Loftus Lowndes,* in support
of the appeal, * * urged that the present plaintiffs, as well as
the defendants March and wife, must be deemed to have had
full notice, not only of the breach of trust, but of what was
done in the suit of 1818, and to have acquiesced *in the abandon-   [*39 ;
ment of that suit, and the consequent undisturbed distribution
of Grant's assets; for one of the plaintiffs attained twenty-one
in the year 1821, and the other, two years afterwards. * * *

Mr. Wakefield and *Mr. W. T. S. Daniel, contrà,* cited
Bennett v. *Colley* (1).

Mr. Barber, in reply.

THE LORD CHANCELLOR [after stating the facts of the case, and   *Aug.* 3.
the substance of the decree :]

The appeal is not by Russell, but by the personal representative and legatees of Grant; and although the representative
of Grant joined in the appeal, yet, in the result, the case, as far
as Grant was concerned, was not pressed in argument. It
seemed to be admitted that the decree could not be impugned,
so far as Grant's assets were concerned; but, in opposition to
the plaintiffs' *right to call on the legatees of Grant to refund,   [*40]
two questions were made: first, that the assets of Grant, having
been administered in ignorance of this demand, ought not to be
followed; and secondly, that the Court ought not to have made
the decree which it has made, without a previous inquiry, whether
the plaintiffs knew of, or acquiesced in, the breach of trust, or in
the arrangement stated to have been made in the year 1818.

(1) 35 R. R. 135 (5 Sim. 181 ; 2 My. & K. 225).

Now, as to the first point, which raises the proposition that assets cannot be followed in the hands of legatees, to whom they have been handed over by the personal representative, in ignorance of the demands of creditors which existed at the time, it is to be observed, that almost all, I may say all, the cases in which legatees have been compelled to refund, have been cases in which the assets have been distributed in ignorance of the claim. It can hardly be supposed that the personal representative would take upon himself the responsibility of handing over the assets to the legatees, if he was aware that any creditors of the deceased were still unpaid. Upon this branch of the argument, several cases were cited which, in my opinion, have no application whatever to the present question. They were cases in which an executor or administrator has been held protected for payments which, though not regular, were payments made in ignorance of the superior claims of other parties. They were cases in which the executor or administrator had honestly and faithfully discharged his duty, to the best of his knowledge; and he was held to be protected. But the question here is, whether the creditor shall not be entitled to follow the assets, which are his fund, (the debts not having been paid,) in the hands of persons who have not purchased them, but to whom they have been delivered in mistake.

[41] That a creditor may follow assets in the hands of legatees to whom they have been delivered in ignorance of the creditor's demand, has been an established principle of this Court from the earliest period, of the decisions in which we have any traces. In *Hodges* v. *Waddington* (1), the rule was laid down; and in *Noel* v. *Robinson* (2), it was said to be the constant practice to allow a creditor to compel a legatee to refund: From that period to the decision of Lord ELDON in *Gillespie* v. *Alexander* (3), there is no instance of any doubt being entertained as to the right of the creditor to follow assets in the hands of a legatee to whom they have been delivered upon the supposition of there being assets to pay that legatee: and what Lord ELDON says in *Gillespie* v. *Alexander* is applicable to more than one of the points in this case; for he says, that where a decree has directed an

(1) 2 Vent. 360.   2 Vent. 358.
(2) 1 Vern. 90; and see *S. C.*   (3) 27 R. R. 35 (3 Russ. 130).

account of debts, a creditor is permitted to prove his debt, as long as there happens to be a residuary fund in Court, or in the hands of the executor ; and that if he has not come in till after the executor has paid away the residue, he is not without remedy, though he is barred the benefit of that decree ; for, if he has a mind to sue the legatees, and bring back the fund, he may do so. Now, that is a case in which the assets have been administered in ignorance of the claim, because they have been administered by the Court, after means have been taken for the purpose of bringing forward all those who have claims upon the fund ; but that proceeding shall not protect a legatee from the liability to refund.

Formerly, when legacies were paid, it seems to have been the practice to oblige the legatee to give *security to refund, in case any other debts were discovered. That practice has been discontinued, but the legatee's liability to refund remains. The creditor has not the same security for the refunding as when the legatee was obliged to give security for that purpose, but he has the personal liability of the legatee.

[.*42]

The first proposition, therefore, cannot be maintained in point of law ; but is contrary to the established rule of the Court from the earliest period to which it can be traced.

The second point made by the appellants is, that there ought to be an inquiry whether the plaintiffs knew of or acquiesced in the breach of trust, or the arrangement said to have been made in the year 1818.

Now, in order to make it proper to direct that inquiry, it would be necessary to show that such knowledge and acquiescence would afford a defence, and also that sufficient matters are put in issue by the pleadings to entitle the party to ask for that inquiry. It cannot be meant that the plaintiffs acquiesced in the breach of trust at the time at which it was committed ; because it was committed in or soon after the year 1810, when one of the plaintiffs was only ten years of age, and the other was only eight. What is meant, therefore, must be, knowledge and acquiescence after the two plaintiffs attained twenty-one, which as to one of them, was in the year 1821, and as to the other, in the year 1823.

The knowledge or acquiescence would not be knowledge of or acquiescence in the breach of trust, but it would be knowledge in 1821 of a title to the property (supposing they became informed of their title then), and abstaining to sue, from that

[*43]

time until the year 1833 : *but it was admitted that, as against Russell and the estate of Grant, the plaintiffs were not barred by the time that had elapsed. It was admitted (and indeed it could not have been disputed) that the time was not such as to prevent the plaintiffs from instituting this suit against one of the trustees and the representatives of the other. There appears, therefore, to be nothing to prevent them from suing Grant's legatees, unless there have been acquiescence, and knowledge, and concurrence, on the part of the plaintiffs.

Not only has no knowledge, on the part of the plaintiffs, of the breach of trust been proved, but there is no allegation in the bill from which their knowledge would appear, nor is any such defence put in issue.

It was said, that in the year 1818 another bill was filed, and that the plaintiffs may have known of the compromise of that suit.

The only evidence of that is, that one of the witnesses deposes to the fact of a bill having been filed, in which the children were joined as co-plaintiffs, but of the proceedings having been stopped, by Russell having offered to give security for the payment of the arrears of interest, and for due payment of the interest for the future. This would be an agreement wholly for the benefit of the tenants for life, and affording no security, indemnity, or remedy to the children, who are the present plaintiffs. It is not to be supposed that, if they did know of this agreement, many years afterwards, when they came of age, they would acquiesce in an arrangement which gave them no sort of benefit, but on the other hand, would deprive them of their remedy for the recovery of the

[*44]

property ; nor are there any allegations, *in the pleadings, of their having known of it, or of their having adopted it, so as to make it an act of their own.

Then I was referred to the decree made in *Smith* v. *Birch* (1), which directed an inquiry, whether the plaintiffs had assented to or acquiesced in the funds remaining in wrong hands, by means

(1) An unreported case before Sir John Leach in 1831.

of which they were lost : but, without knowing all the circumstances of that case, it is impossible to know whether the facts justified that decree.   If any breach of trust had there been committed, by the funds being allowed to be in improper hands, and if the parties to whom the funds belonged chose to acquiesce in that state of circumstances, they could not very well complain of an act to which they were themselves parties.   That decree, therefore, affords no ingredient for coming to a conclusion in the present case.

When the plaintiffs first became informed, either of the breach of trust or of the abandonment of the suit of 1818, does not appear; and whatever may have taken place before the year 1821 is immaterial, inasmuch as, up to that period, they were both under age.   There is no allegation with respect to the time at which they became aware of any of the circumstances, except that they came of age in the years already mentioned, and that the bill was not filed until the year 1833.   It is not contended that the lapse of time will bar their right to the remedy to which, according to the practice of this Court, they are entitled.   I see nothing to interfere with that right so vested in them, and the appeal must therefore be dismissed with costs.

Decree affirmed.

MOORE v. FROWD (1).

(3 My. & Cr. 45—51 ; S. C. 6 L. J. (N. S.) Ch. 372 ; 1 Jur. 653.)

A trustee, who is a solicitor, is entitled to be repaid such costs, charges, and expenses only as he has properly paid out of pocket ; and it makes no difference in this respect, that the instrument creating the trust may have directed that the trust monies should be applied in payment of all expenses, disbursements, and charges, to be incurred, sustained or borne by the trustee, in professional business, journeys or otherwise ; and that the trustee might retain all reasonable costs, charges, and expenses which he might sustain or be put unto ; such costs, charges, and expenses to be reckoned, stated, and paid as between attorney and client.

THIS cause was heard before the Lord Chancellor, when Master of the Rolls, and the parties consented to receive his Lordship's judgment after he had become Lord Chancellor.

One of the questions discussed at the hearing was, whether

(1) *In re Fish* [1893] 2 Ch. 413, 62   *In re Webb* [1894] 1 Ch. 73, 63 L. J.
L. J. Ch. 977, 69 L. T. 233, C. A. ;   Ch. 145, 70 L. T. 318, C. A.

1835.
Dec. 18, 19, 21.
1836.
Jan. 13.
1837.
Aug. 15.
Lord
COTTENHAM.
L.C.
[45]

four trustees, who were all attorneys and solicitors, were entitled
to any costs or charges beyond those which they might have paid
out of pocket.

By indentures of lease and release, of the 6th and 7th of April,
1827, certain property was conveyed by the plaintiff (Charlotte
Moore) and others, to Edward Frowd, Robert Bond, William
Palmer, and William Elkington, who were all attorneys and
solicitors, in fee, upon trust to sell, in lots for building, and to
apply the produce of the sale, and the rents and profits to accrue
in the mean time, in payment of the costs, charges, and expenses
of preparing the indenture of release, and all the expenses, disbursements, and charges, already or thereafter to be incurred or
sustained or borne by the trustees, or the trustees or trustee for
the time being, either in professional business, journeys, or otherwise, for the purpose of negotiating or performing the agreements,
trusts, and purposes thereinbefore mentioned or directed to be
carried into execution ; and also all the costs, charges, and expenses
of the persons who had been, or should or might be employed by
the trustees for the time being, as surveyors, auctioneers, bailiffs,
[*46]   agents, or servants, in *preparing and making maps, plans,
surveys, estimates, particulars and conditions of sale, roads,
bridges, sewers, or other improvements upon the property, or
in managing the same, and receiving the rents and profits thereof,
or of selling clay and brick earth thereon, or otherwise letting
or selling the same premises, or any part thereof ; and also all
sums of money which the trustees might deem expedient and
proper, for the purchase of any estate or interest of any person
in the property, to enable them to make a good and marketable
title or titles to any purchaser or purchasers ; and also of all the
expenses of abstracts of title, and copies of deeds and other documents for perfecting the same; and all other the expenses of carrying
the trusts, powers, and authorities therein mentioned into execution, and then to make such payments as were therein mentioned.

It was further provided that the trustees should, out of the trust
monies, deduct, retain to, and reimburse themselves all such
reasonable costs, charges, and expenses as they or any of them
should or might sustain, expend, or be put unto, in or about the
execution of all or any of the trusts thereby in them reposed ;

such costs, charges, and expenses to be reckoned, stated, and paid as between attorney and client.

Mr. Pemberton and *Mr. Heathfield*, for the plaintiff, contended that the trustees were only entitled to their costs out of pocket; they cited *Robinson* v. *Pett* (1), and *New* v. *Jones*, in the Exchequer, before Lord Lyndhurst, on the 9th of August, 1833 (2).

Mr. Willcock, for the defendant Frowd, contended that the trustees were entitled to have their professional *charges allowed. * * *

[*47]

Mr. Bickersteth and *Mr. Wright*, for Bond.

Mr. Tinney and *Mr. Bird*, for Palmer.

Mr. Bethell, for the assignee of Elkington, who had become bankrupt.

Mr. Pemberton, in reply.

THE LORD CHANCELLOR (after disposing of other questions in the cause) said:

1837.
Aug. 15.

The next and the most important point is, as to the claim by the plaintiff, to have disallowed all the defendants' bills of costs, except money out of pocket.

It appears that the four trustees were all solicitors, and the bill alleges that Mr. Frowd's two bills amounted to 790*l.* 5*s.* 2*d.*, the joint bill of Elkington and Palmer to 680*l.* 15*s.* 3*d.*, and Bond's bill to 238*l.* 1*s.* 7*d.*, making, altogether, 1,709*l.* 2*s.* That all these bills are to be examined and taxed is not disputed; but the question is, whether such taxation is to be a taxation of a solicitor's bill, in the usual course, between solicitor and client, or *whether the Master is to be directed to allow only costs out of pocket, properly expended.

[*48]

The first question is, whether the deed of trust disposes of this question; because the parties may, by contract, make a rule for themselves, and agree that a trustee, being a solicitor, shall have some benefit beyond that which, without such contract, the law

(1) 3 P. Wms. 249.

(2) An unreported case; see Lewin on Trusts.

would have allowed; but, in such a case, the agreement must be
distinct, and in its terms explain to the client the effect of the
arrangement; and the more particularly, when the solicitor for
the client, becoming himself a trustee, has an interest, personal
to himself, adverse to that of the client.   It is not easy, in such
a case, to conceive how, consistently with the established rules
respecting contracts between solicitors and their clients, a solicitor
could maintain such a contract, made with his client, for his own
benefit, the client having no other professional adviser, and in
the absence of all evidence, and of any probability, of the client
(a woman, too) having been aware of her rights, or of the rule of
law, or of the effect of the contract: but the necessity for following
up these considerations does not arise in this case, unless the deed
contains a distinct agreement for this purpose.

There are two parts of the deed applicable to this point; first,
that part in which the trusts are declared, wherein it is provided
that all costs, charges, and expenses of the deed, and all expenses,
disbursements, and charges already or hereafter to be incurred,
sustained, or borne by the trustees, or any of them, either in
professional business, journeys or otherwise, for the purpose of
negotiating or performing the agreements, trusts, and purposes
before mentioned, and all costs, charges, and expenses of persons
to be employed by them as surveyors, &c., and all other expenses
[*49]   of carrying the *trusts into execution, shall be paid, in the first
place, out of the produce of the intended sales.

Now the costs in question being the ordinary remunerations
of a solicitor, as distinguished from the costs out of pocket, cannot
be considered as charges and expenses incurred, sustained, or
borne by the trustees; but such expressions in terms apply to
payments made or liabilities incurred.

The next provision is more specific; it provides that each
trustee is to be at liberty to retain and reimburse himself all
such reasonable costs, charges, and expenses as he may sustain
or be put unto, such costs, charges, and expenses, to be reckoned,
stated, and paid as between attorney and client; but this
provision does no more than the rule of law would have done,
a trustee's costs being taxed as between attorney and client.
And what are the costs so to be taxed?   Costs which the

trustee may sustain or be put unto; terms wholly inapplicable to sums claimed as remuneration.

There is nothing in either of these provisions which is peculiarly applicable to the case of the solicitor being also trustee. It cannot, therefore, be assumed that the intention was to provide for some other mode of dealing with that union of characters, than what the law would have enforced; and still less that, under such provision, a solicitor dealing with his client can be permitted to claim that which, without, at least, a specific contract with the client, and proof that the client was fully cognizant of her legal rights independently of such contract, and of the effect and legal consequences of the act upon such legal rights, he would not be entitled to claim.

It remains, therefore, to be seen what is the rule of law in cases in which no specific contract regulates the rights of the parties. It is clear that if an attorney be allowed to make profit, by means of professional business, of his office of trustee, it will constitute an exception to a rule well known and established in all other cases: *Robinson* v. *Pett* (1). A factor acting as executor is not so entitled: *Scattergood* v. *Harrison* (2); nor a commission agent: *Sheriff* v. *Axe* (3). Why is the case of a solicitor to constitute an exception to the rule? What is the reason given for the rule? It is, I think, well stated in *Robinson* v. *Pett*, "The reason seems to be, for that on these pretences, if allowed, the trust estate might be loaded, and rendered of little value." It is not because the trust estate is in any particular case charged with more than it might otherwise have to bear; but that the principle, if allowed, would lead to such consequences in general. In the case of the factor or agent, if the executors had employed other persons in those capacities, they would probably have been allowed the expenses; but if they are to perform those duties themselves, and to charge a profit upon such employments, what protection can the plaintiff have against extravagant charges? Do not these reasons apply to the case of solicitors? Does not this very case strongly exemplify the danger, and illustrate the merit of the rule which would avert

[50]

(1) 3 P. Wms. 249.
(2) Moseley, 128.

(3) 4 Russ. 33.

MOORE
v.
FROWD.

it? If, therefore, it had been necessary for me to come to a conclusion upon this point, without the aid of previous decisions directly applicable, I should not have felt much difficulty in the performance of that duty; but still, I am glad to be relieved from that necessity, and to find my own opinion confirmed by that of Lord LYNDHURST, in the case of *New* v. *Jones* (1), in which that question was deliberately considered, and decided conformably to the opinion I have expressed.

[*51]

It was, indeed, said that a contrary decision had taken place in the case of *Daniel* v. *Goldson* (2), but I do not find that the point was there raised or decided. The Master, indeed, may have allowed such costs; but I do not find any judgment of the Court upon it.

In Lord LYNDHURST's judgment I entirely concur, and must, therefore, in this case, direct that, in taking the accounts against the trustees, they should be allowed only the costs out of pocket.

The Master, in taking the accounts of the trustees, is not to allow to them any professional charges, or charges for loss of time, or other emoluments, but to allow only such charges and expenses actually paid by them out of pocket as he shall find to have been properly incurred and paid by them.

1836.
Nov.
1837.
Nov. 15.

Lord
COTTENHAM,
L.C.
[52]

[58]

MALCOLM *v.* O'CALLAGHAN (3).

(3 My. & Cr. 52—63; S. C. 1 Jur. 838.)

Principles and practice of the Court with respect to allowances made to receivers for extraordinary services.

Unauthorized and unprofitable expenditure disallowed.

[IN this case the LORD CHANCELLOR (in reference to the point mentioned in the head-note) said:]

What are the ordinary duties of a receiver authorized to sue for a particular part of the estate supposed to be outstanding, when he exercises his own discretion without any other specific authority or direction from the Court? It has not, and cannot

(1) See *ante*, p. 207.
(2) Before the Vice-Chancellor in 1833. No reference is given to any

report of this case.
(3) *Harris* v. *Sleep* [1897] 2 Ch. 80, 66 L. J. Ch. 596, 76 L. T. 670, C. A.

be contended that his ordinary duty would justify him in incurring the expenses of journeys to, and of residence in, a foreign country, whilst prosecuting in that country a suit which he had been authorized to commence. [His Lordship here referred to the proceedings to show that certain special orders which had been made authorizing the receiver to attend certain proceedings in Paris did not include the particular visits here in question.] A country solicitor is not, in general, allowed his costs of attending a suit in London, although his client may have requested him so to do. If, indeed, success had attended the exertions of the receiver, and he could have shown that such success had arisen from his presence in Paris, it might have been thought inequitable for the parties to take the benefit of such exertions without defraying the expenses which had attended them, although no previous authority for incurring them had been given. But the present is the case of an unauthorized and unprofitable expenditure. In the case of *In re Montgomery* (1), which was cited in the *course of the argument, the receiver of a lunatic's estate instituted proceedings which, being wrong in form, he abandoned, and having afterwards taken other proper proceedings, he was successful for the estate. The COURT there refused to allow him the costs of the abandoned proceedings, although the Master reported that the receiver acted *bonâ fide*, and ought to be allowed the costs. It is not easy to conceive a case in which such a claim, not founded upon the general practice of the Court, or upon any special order, and not sanctioned by success, could be maintained against the estate.

[*39]

[The remainder of the judgment is occupied with an investigation of the special facts, showing that the expenditure was unprofitable as well as unauthorized.]

(1) 1 Molloy, 419.

1837.
Jan. 17, 18.
Nov. 18.
———
Lord
COTTENHAM,
L.C.
[63]

TASKER *v.* SMALL (1).

(3 My. & Cr. 63—71 ; on appeal from 6 Sim. 625—633; S. C. 5 L. J. (N. S.)
Ch. 321.)

As a general rule only the parties to a contract or their representatives can be properly made parties to a suit for specific performance of the contract.

Strangers to a contract, even though necessary parties to the consequent conveyance, cannot be properly made parties to the suit for specific performance.

[THIS was an appeal from a decree for specific performance of a contract for the sale of certain lands to the plaintiff.

Certain persons who were not parties to the contract, but who disputed the vendors' power to sell the property, in which they claimed to be interested, were made defendants to the suit for specific performance.

[64]   One of the defendants,] Mrs. Small, by her next friend, presented a petition of rehearing; and submitted, first, that the VICE-CHANCELLOR'S decree was erroneous upon the merits; and, secondly, that the record was wrong in point of form, and that she ought not to have been made a party to the suit. The arguments urged by the respondents on the second point are stated and considered in the judgment, in which the material facts of the case are also shortly recapitulated.

Mr. Knight and *Mr. Spence*, for the purchaser, in support of the decree.

Mr. Cooper, for the defendants Baker and Mann [who were the vendors, selling by the direction of the defendant Arthur George Small.]

Mr. Jacob and *Mr. Willcock*, for the appeal.

Nov. 18.   THE LORD CHANCELLOR :

[65   * * The facts of the case, as stated in the bill, are shortly these: Mr. Small, previously to his marriage, was entitled to the estate in question, in tail male, subject to the life estate of Mrs. Lucas; and by his marriage articles, dated the 3rd of

(1) But where an action properly seeks other relief arising out of a contract, it may be proper to make other persons parties to the action. *Bishop of Winchester* v. *Mid Hants Ry. Co.*, (1867) L. R. 5 Eq. 17.—O. A. S.

December, 1830, his intended wife, the present appellant, Mrs.
Small, being then an infant, he contracted with her uncle, Mr.
Ashford, that subject to the life estate of Mrs. Lucas, and to the
raising, by mortgage or otherwise, of any sum or sums of money,
not exceeding in the whole 15,000*l.*, by himself, the estate should
be conveyed and assured upon the trusts of a settlement; and
for that purpose he covenanted that, as soon as conveniently
might be after the marriage, subject and without prejudice to
the raising by any ways or means, and at any time or times he
should think proper, of any sum or sums of money, not exceeding
in the whole 15,000*l.*, by mortgage, annuity, or otherwise, for
his own use and benefit, and to any deed or deeds and assurances which he might thereafter make or execute for securing
the repayment of such sum or sums of money and the interest
thereof, he would make and execute all necessary and proper
acts and deeds for the purpose of settling the estate to the use
of Mr. Ashford, during the life of the wife, in trust to pay the
rents to her, for her separate use, with remainder to himself for
life, remainder amongst the children of the marriage, remainder
to the survivor of the husband and wife, with various powers of
management and application of the rents for the benefit of the
children—all applicable to the real estate—and a provision that
there should be inserted in the settlement all such powers,
provisoes, covenants, clauses, and agreements as might be
considered essential for the parties interested therein, or as
might be proper for effecting the several purposes, and as were
usually contained in settlements of the like kind.

By indentures of the 2nd and 3rd of March, 1831, Mr. Small, [66]
having borrowed 5,000*l.* of Thomas Phillips, conveyed the estate
comprised in the articles to Phillips, subject to the usual proviso
for redemption, and covenanted to levy a fine for that purpose.
Phillips had a power of sale given to him by the mortgage deed,
and it contained an assignment of a policy of insurance for
5,000*l.* upon the life of Mrs. Lucas.

A fine was accordingly levied in Easter Term, 1831.

By indentures of the 26th and 27th of October, 1832, Mr.
Small, having borrowed another sum of 5,000*l.* of the defendant
Wakeford, secured the repayment of it in a similar manner; but

for this loan the defendants, Benjamin R. Baker and Thomas
Mann, joined as sureties in the covenant for payment.

By indentures of the 28th and 29th of October, 1832, to which
Mr. Small and Mr. Ashford, Phillips and Wakeford, two of the
mortgagees, and Benjamin R. Baker and Thomas Mann were
expressed to be parties, Mr. Small conveyed the estate to Baker
and Mann, subject to the life estate of Mrs. Lucas, and subject
also to the mortgages, upon trust, if Small made default in
paying the interest upon the mortgages or the premiums upon
the policies, to sell the estate, at their discretion, and to apply
the proceeds in reimbursing themselves, repaying the premiums
paid, paying the mortgage debts due to Phillips and Wakeford,
and to pay the surplus to Mr. Small, or to the persons entitled
thereto under the articles of the 3rd of December, 1830.

Mr. Small subsequently raised two other sums, one of 2,500*l.*
by mortgage to the defendant Hawkins, and the other of 1,000*l.*,

[*67]   by sale of an annuity now vested in the *defendant Sarah
Baker; so that of the whole 15,000*l.* the sum of 1,500*l.* only
remained to be raised.

The defendants, Baker and Mann, are the vendors under the
deed of the 29th of October, 1832; and they, by an agreement,
dated the 21st of December, 1833, (to which they were parties of
the first part, Mr. Small, of the second part, and the plaintiff,
of the third part,) agreed, in consideration of 19,250*l.*, to sell the
fee-simple of the estate to the plaintiff, expectant upon the death
of Mrs. Lucas, so far as such estate had been acquired under the
fine, or as Small could acquire it during her life with her concurrence.   It appears that, by deeds executed in pursuance of the
statute (1), Mr. and Mrs. Lucas having consented, the effect of a
recovery was obtained, and the legal estate vested in Phillips the
mortgagee.   There is no allegation in the bill respecting Mrs.
Small's interest, except in the statement of the marriage articles.

To this bill Mr. Ashford and Mrs. Small put in a general
demurrer, upon the discussion of which, or at the hearing, two
questions were made; first, whether the marriage articles authorised Mr. Small to sell the estate to raise the 15,000*l.*, and, if so,
whether, under the circumstances, such power was duly exercised;
and, secondly, whether Mrs. Small was a proper party to the suit.

(1) 3 & 4 Will. IV. c. 74.

From the report of the case in the Court below upon the
demurrer (1), it appears that the counsel for Mrs. Small, being
desirous of obtaining a decision upon the other points, waived
the objection of Mrs. Small being a party to the suit, and the
Vice-Chancellor, being of *opinion that the articles authorised   [*68]
the sale, over-ruled the demurrer; but his Honour expressed
some doubt whether Mrs. Small ought to have been made a
party to the suit. Upon the argument at the hearing, reported
in the same book, both points were again raised; but his Honour
made a decree declaring that Small was entitled to sell the fee-
simple and inheritance in remainder of the whole estate, for the
purpose of raising the 15,000l., and referred it to the Master to
inquire whether that sum, or any and what part thereof, had been
raised, and whether the contract of the 21st of December, 1833,
was, at the time, a fit and proper contract.

The decree adjudicates nothing as to the propriety of the
contract, and cannot, therefore, be objected to, if the declaration
be correct, that, under the articles, Small was entitled to sell the
fee-simple in remainder of the whole estate, for the purpose of
raising the 15,000l.; all questions as to the manner in which
that power was exercised being reserved : but I understand the
declaration to decide, that such power existed from the moment
of the execution of the articles.

The second question is to be considered first, because, if Mrs.
Small be not a proper party to the suit, it will not only be unnecessary, but improper, to give any opinion as to any point in the cause.

It is not disputed, that, generally, to a bill for a specific performance of a contract of sale, the parties to the contract only
are the proper parties; and, when the ground of the jurisdiction
of courts of equity in suits of that kind is considered, it could not
properly be otherwise. The Court assumes jurisdiction in such
cases, because a court of law, giving damages only for the non-
performance of the contract, in many *cases does not afford an   [69]
adequate remedy. But, in equity, as well as at law, the contract
constitutes the right, and regulates the liabilities of the parties;
and the object of both proceedings is to place the party complaining as nearly as possible in the same situation as the
defendant had agreed that he should be placed in. It is obvious

(1) 6 Sim. 625,

TASKER
v.
SMALL.

that persons, strangers to the contract, and, therefore, neither entitled to the right, nor subject to the liabilities which arise out of it, are as much strangers to a proceeding to enforce the execution of it as they are to a proceeding to recover damages for the breach of it. And so is the admitted practice of the Court; but it is said that this case ought to be an exception to the rule, because Phillips, in whom, as first mortgagee, the legal estate is vested, is not willing to convey it to the plaintiff, the purchaser, without having competent authority for so doing, and that, the question being raised whether the legal estate can be so conveyed, Mrs. Small is of necessity made a party to the suit.

This proposition assumes two points; first, that Phillips is himself a proper party to the suit; and, secondly, that, being so, it is competent for him to require that Mrs. Small should be made a party to it.

Phillips is merely a mortgagee, against whom no bill can properly be filed, except for the purpose of redeeming his mortgage, and that by a party entitled to redeem. This bill does not pray any redemption of Phillips's mortgage, and, if it had, the plaintiff would not be entitled to file such a bill. He is only connected with the property by having contracted to purchase the equity of redemption, and until that purchase is completed he cannot redeem the mortgage. Phillips has no interest in the specific performance of the contract; he is no party to it; and the performance of it cannot affect his security

[*70] *or interfere with his remedies. Supposing, however, that it was competent for the plaintiff to redeem Phillips's mortgage, he can only be so entitled as standing in the place of the mortgagor; but a mortgagee can never refuse to restore to his mortgagor, or those who claim under him, upon repayment of what is due upon the mortgage, the estate which became vested in him as mortgagee. To him it is immaterial, upon repayment of the money, whether the mortgagor's title was good or bad. He is not at liberty to dispute it, any more than a tenant is at liberty to dispute his landlord's title. Phillips, therefore, is bound, upon payment, to restore the legal estate to his mortgagor or to those who claim under him. By Phillips's mortgage deed the equity of redemption was reserved to Small. If the plaintiff could show such equity of redemption

to be vested in him, he would be entitled, upon paying the
mortgage debt, to demand a re-conveyance of the estate, without
regard to any other question affecting the title to the property.

I am, therefore, of opinion that Phillips himself is not a
proper party to this suit, and that he cannot, by not himself
insisting upon the objection, make Mrs. Small a proper party;
and that, even if he were himself properly made a defendant, the
objection raised by him at the Bar, though not by his answer—
for by his answer he offers to re-convey upon being paid his
mortgage debt—would not make Mrs. Small a proper party.

But it was argued at the Bar that the plaintiff was, in equity,
invested with all the rights of Mrs. Small, upon the principle
that, by a contract of purchase, the purchaser becomes in equity
the owner of the property. This rule applies only as between the
parties to the contract, and cannot be extended so as to affect the
interests of others. If it could, a contract for the purchase of an
*equitable estate would be equivalent to a conveyance of it. Before   [*71]
the contract is carried into effect, the purchaser cannot, against a
stranger to the contract, enforce equities attaching to the property.

In *Mole* v. *Smith* (1), Lord ELDON says, that when a bill is filed
for a specific performance, it should not be mixed up with a prayer
for relief against other persons claiming an interest in the estate.
Such was his opinion in a case in which the vendor was plaintiff,
and the defendants were persons whom the vendor sought to compel
to join in completing the title. How much stronger is the objection where the purchaser is the plaintiff, and the only connection
between him and the defendants is the incomplete disputed contract.

I am, therefore, of opinion that Mrs. Small is not a proper
party to this suit; and that the bill ought to have been dismissed
with costs as against her.

It is to be regretted that this opinion will prevent the parties
from having the question between them so effectively decided as
it might otherwise have been; but I cannot, to avoid an inconvenience in a particular case, sanction a proceeding which I
consider to be inconsistent with the rules of pleading, and which,
if recognised, might lead to much difficulty and confusion in the
proceedings of the Court.

(1) Jac, 490; see p, 494,

1837.
Jan. 25, 26,
27.
Nov. 17.

Lord
COTTENHAM,
L.C.

[72]

MILLIGAN *v.* MITCHELL.

(3 My. & Cr. 72—84 ; S. C. 7 L. J. (N. S.) Ch. 37 ; 1 Jur. 888.)

Upon a bill filed by two persons, pew-holders in a chapel, and members of the congregation, and, in virtue of certain offices which they held, entitled to be trustees of the chapel, on behalf of themselves, and all other persons interested as such pew-holders and members, except the defendants, against the other persons entitled to be such trustees, and against the person in whom the legal interest in the lease was vested, alleging that the lease of the chapel was held upon an exclusive trust for religious service according to the doctrines and discipline of the Church of Scotland, charging the defendants with introducing preachers into the pulpit who were not ministers of the Church of Scotland, and with other acts in violation of the trust, and praying that the defendants might be compelled to perform the trust, the Court granted the relief prayed ; holding, first, that, upon the evidence in the cause, the alleged trust was sufficiently made out ; secondly, that the acts complained of amounted to a breach of trust ; and, thirdly, that the record was properly framed with a view to the object of the suit.

An amendment making the plaintiffs in the original bill sue on behalf of themselves and all other persons having the same interest, does not so alter the parties or the frame of the record that depositions taken in the original suit cannot be used in the amended suit.

[THE facts of this case, the result of the evidence, the object of the suit and other matters material to this report, are sufficiently stated in the judgment.]

[74]   Mr. *Wigram* and Mr. *James Russell*, for the plaintiffs.   *   *   *

[75]   Mr. *Agar*, Mr. *Daniell*, and Mr. *Chandless*, for the defendants.   *   *   *

[76]   Mr. *Miller*, for the personal representative of the surviving trustee of the lease.

Nov. 17   THE LORD CHANCELLOR :

[*77]   This is a bill by Charles Milligan and Cornelius Sharp, on behalf of themselves and all persons, except the defendants, *who, at the time of the alleged breach of trust, were holders of, or are now entitled to be holders of, seats or pews in the church or chapel comprised in a lease of the 14th of July, 1800, or entitled to vote in the election of a minister of the said church or chapel ; and the object of the bill is to have it declared that such lease, and church, or chapel, are held in trust for religious

worship according to the institutions and observances of the
Church of Scotland, with the necessary directions for the purpose
of restoring and confining the form of worship and service in such
church or chapel accordingly.

The only questions I have to consider, are, first, whether the
property in question was held upon the trust alleged by the bill;
secondly, whether there has been a breach of such trust; and,
thirdly, if there has, whether the plaintiffs are entitled to be relieved
against such breach of trust, in a suit constituted as this is.

1. As to the first point, the case being before me only as it
affects property, and the title to the property commencing with
the lease in the year 1800, I have nothing to do with the history
of the congregation at an earlier period, except in so far as it
throws light upon the purposes of the trust so originating in
that lease. It appears, however, that by an entry in the books
of the congregation, dated the 18th of June, 1798, recording the
proceedings at a meeting had for the purpose of making arrangements for building a new church, the meeting call themselves
the " Scots Presbyterian Church," and direct that the case
should be laid before the " Scots Presbytery in London," with
a request that they would give it their sanction and support:
that, in a statement prepared for circulation at the time, the
object is stated to be " to accommodate the members of the
Established *Church of Scotland:" that the project of building   [*78]
the new church was carried into effect by a committee of the
congregation, assisted by a committee of the Scotch Presbytery
in London : that the record of these meetings is headed " Scots
church; " and that, in an entry dated the 21st of May, 1799,
they call themselves the " Scotch Presbyterian Congregation,"
and state their object to be to erect a new " Scots Presbyterian
Church." It is also proved, that, on the 8th of July, 1799, it
was resolved that a stone containing the arms and motto of the
Established Church of Scotland should be placed in the front of
the new place of public worship. At a meeting of the 10th of
June, 1800, it was resolved that the lease should be in the names
of the minister and elders, and the trustees for managing Mrs.
Drake's donation, and their successors in office. The chapel
was opened, and two sermons were, on that occasion, preached

in it by the ministers of two other Scotch Presbyterian churches; and at a meeting of the 20th of July, 1800, the chapel being now called the " New Scots Church," it was resolved, " that the treasurer be requested to write to each of the ministers, who was a member of the Scottish Presbytery in London, to solicit a collection from their congregations towards defraying the expenses of the building."

By the will of Mrs. Drake, dated the 9th of January, 1730, a sum of 30l. per annum was given " to the Protestant dissenting minister of the congregation of Protestant dissenters at Woolwich,"—an expression which concludes nothing upon the present question : but it appears that the 30l. per annum had been received by the minister of this congregation at a time when it was clearly a congregation of Scotch Presbyterians. The chapel having been erected, a lease of it, dated the 14th of July, 1800, for sixty-one years, was granted, expressed *to be in consideration of the expenses of erecting the Scots church or kirk; and it was declared to be held in trust to be assigned and disposed of as the elders and trustees of the said Scots church or kirk at Woolwich should direct ; and, in default of such direction, " upon trust to permit and suffer the same to be used as and for a place of religious worship, and for such other purposes as by the custom of the Church or Kirk of Scotland the same ought to be used ; " and the trustees were " not to permit the same to be had or used for any other purpose than religious worship, and such other meetings and assemblies as by the custom of the Kirk of Scotland ought to be there holden," without the written consent of the lessors, their executors, administrators, or assigns.

[*79]

This is the most important part of the evidence upon the first point, as it shows the purpose for which the ground was obtained and the building erected ; and it establishes beyond all doubt the affirmative of the first proposition, that the property in question was held upon trust to be used as a chapel for the Scotch Presbyterian form of worship. What followed the opening of the chapel is in conformity with this view of the case, and is strongly confirmatory of it. On the 29th of March, 1803, it was resolved " that no minister receive a call, nor be appointed a pastor, of the congregation, who hath not been licensed to preach the Gospel, according to the regulations observed in the Established Church of Scotland." There is also in the minute-book an entry, of the 24th of April, 1807, in which it is stated that the church was built for the purpose of worship according to the forms and ceremonies of the Church of Scotland, as by law established. On the 25th of February, 1811, a question was made whether there should be singing before and after the service, as being a practice *contrary to the discipline of the Church of Scotland; and it was determined that there should not.

[*80]

In answer to this, the evidence on behalf of the defendants of some practices said to be contrary to the practice of the Established Church of Scotland, but not meeting these facts, can be of no weight. In the year 1829, Dr. Blythe, who had been regularly ordained pastor by the Scotch Presbytery of London, died. Mr. Scott, having been elected by the congregation, according to the regulations, application was made to the Scotch Presbytery of London, in the usual course, to moderate his call; and, upon his examination for that purpose, it was found that his tenets were not in conformity with the doctrines of the Church of Scotland: he declined to sign the confession of faith of the Church of Scotland, and he accordingly withdrew and resigned his claim to be pastor of the church.

No opposition appears to have been made to this decision of the Scotch Presbytery of London; but, on the contrary, measures were taken to procure another minister, and accordingly several licentiates of the Church of Scotland were invited to preach as probationers; and a party in the congregation having requested Mr. Scott again to become a candidate, he was, on the 22nd of January, 1831, again elected, notwithstanding the remonstrances of the Scotch Presbytery of London.

The consequence of this was that the Presbytery of Paisley withdrew their licence from Mr. Scott, which sentence was, upon appeal to the General Assembly of the Church of Scotland, affirmed; and all ministers were prohibited from employing him to preach in their pulpits. Mr. Scott, notwithstanding, continued to *officiate as minister until the month of December, 1832, when he finally withdrew.

[*81]

MILLIGAN
v.
MITCHELL.

Upon the whole, it appears to me to be clear that the chapel was originally built and the lease obtained for the purpose of worship according to the doctrine and discipline of the Scotch Presbyterian Church; that the chapel continued to be so used, for upwards of thirty years; and that it was, therefore, held upon trust for that purpose: *Craigdallie* v. *Aikman* (1), *Attorney-General* v. *Pearson* (2), *Foley* v. *Wontner* (3).

2. The next point is, I think, equally clear; and in fact little, if any, question is made about it. The second election of Mr. Scott, unless made in the hope that he might conform to the confession of faith of the Church of Scotland and be accepted by the Presbytery, was of itself a breach of trust; and undoubtedly the continuing to receive and employ him as minister, after his licence had been withdrawn by the sentence of the Presbytery of Paisley, and that sentence affirmed by the General Assembly, was a direct departure from the trusts of the lease, and an open violation of the laws and regulations of the 29th of March, 1803. The subsequent mode of providing for the service of the church, and, above all, the attempt to get rid of the laws and regulations of the 29th of March, 1803, by the resolution of the 4th of November, 1833, were further violations of the same trusts; and the issue joined by the defendants is, not whether the present be or be not a departure from the system of the Scotch Presbyterian Church, but whether the majority of the congre-

[*82]

gation have not a right *to depart from it, and whether they have not effectually done so by the resolution of the 4th of November, 1833.

I must assume the church to be vacant; and, in this state of circumstances, I have to consider according to what rule the election or appointment of a minister ought to take place. For this purpose, it is necessary to examine, not only the original trust upon which the lease of the building was held, but how far the parties to the resolutions of the 4th of November, 1833, were competent to alter such trusts, and devote the lease and the building to other purposes.

This question may be solved without precisely defining the

(1) 21 R. R. 107 (2 Bligh, 529).   (3) 22 R. R. 110 (2 Jac. & W. 245).
(2) 17 R. R. 100 (3 Mer. 353).

extent of the power of altering the laws and regulations of the
29th of March, 1803, as defined and restricted by the ninth of
those regulations. The resolution of the 4th of November, 1833,
was not an attempt to alter the laws, by the congregation existing
as contemplated by the laws and regulations, (in respect of which,
all pewholders of six months standing, and being, therefore,
members of the congregation, as constituted by those laws and
regulations, would have a vote, and in respect of which, no
person taking a seat after the church had become vacant—a
period which would probably be dated from the death of Dr.
Blythe, in September, 1829—would have been entitled to vote) ;
but it was the resolution of a meeting of persons, calling themselves the congregation, who, from the course pursued after
Mr. Scott's re-election in the year 1831, must have compelled
many of the congregation, members of the Church of Scotland,
to withdraw, and comprising probably many individuals who
were not entitled to vote according to the laws and regulations
which they assumed the power of rescinding.

If, however, it were necessary to come to any conclusion as   [83]
to the extent of the power of altering the laws, possessed by
persons entitled to vote, it might safely be assumed that such
power did not extend to altering the fundamental principles upon
which the association was formed, and destroying the trusts
upon which the property was held, but only to altering the laws
or making new laws, so far as might be consistent with such
principles and trusts. It will be observed that the object of
making the laws and regulations is, upon the proceedings stated
to be "for preventing feuds and controversies, and preserving
order and unanimity in the Scots' Presbyterian Church or Kirk
at Woolwich." I am, therefore, of opinion that the course
adopted by the defendants amounts to a breach of trust.

3. It still remains to be considered, whether the plaintiffs are
entitled to be relieved against such a breach of trust, in a suit
constituted as this is.

It is proved that the plaintiffs are trustees of Mrs. Drake's
charity; and that one of them, Mr. Milligan, was an elder;
and that they are, therefore, trustees, though the lease is not
legally vested in them. It is also proved that both of them

MILLIGAN
v.
MITCHELL.

were pewholders at the time when the wrong was committed, and had done what was requisite to entitle them to vote; that they were entitled to all the privileges of members of the congregation; and that they were, therefore, cestuis que trust of the property in question, and entitled to the assistance of this Court, to enforce the due execution of trusts, in which they had the same species of interest as *the plaintiffs had in the cases of *Davis* v. *Jenkins* (1), and *Foley* v. *Wontner* (2). Of their title to sue, therefore, I have no doubt.

[*84]

What then are the objections to the form of the bill? The other cestuis que trust are those members of the congregation, who at the time of the wrong committed were, by the laws and regulations, to be considered as entitled to the benefit of being members, and who are, I think, accurately described, in this bill, as persons on whose behalf the plaintiffs profess to sue. The object of the bill is for the common benefit of all such persons, according to the purpose for which they were associated, and, therefore, within the rules which in such cases permit bills to be filed by some, on behalf of themselves and others. It is obvious, besides, that in no other way could justice be obtained for the injury complained of. The defendants allege that the plaintiffs, not having paid their rents, are not now pewholders, and, therefore, have no interest. That they were entitled, however, at the time when the wrong was committed is proved; and the defendants cannot, by altering the form of worship used in the chapel, first deprive the plaintiffs and others, in part, of their rights, and then allege such deprivation as a legal objection to their title to sue.

Upon these grounds I am of opinion that the plaintiffs are entitled to the decree which they ask.

I think the plaintiffs ought to have their costs out of the fund. The acts which have rendered this suit necessary being the acts of a large majority of the congregation, I cannot throw those costs upon the defendants; but as the defendants have all concurred in the breach of trust, I do not think them entitled to their costs out of the fund.

(1) 13 R. R. 168 (3 V. & B. 151).   (2) 22 R. R. 110 (2 Jac. & W. 245).

SIMPSON v. LORD HOWDEN (1).

(3 My. & Cr. 97—109; S. C. 6 L. J. (N. S.) Ch. 315; 1 Jur. 703.)

There is no jurisdiction in equity to order a legal instrument to be
delivered up, on the ground of illegality which appears upon the face of
the instrument itself (2).

1837.
June 17, 23.
Aug. 30.

Lord
COTTENHAM,
L.C.

[97]

THE MASTER OF THE ROLLS having overruled a general
demurrer to the bill (1 Keen, 585), the defendant (Lord Howden)
now appealed.

*   *   *   *   *

The prayer of the bill was, that it might be declared that [a
certain] agreement was against public policy, and void in law;
and that it might be delivered up to be cancelled; and that the
defendant might, in the meantime, be restrained from further
proceeding at law, to enforce payment of the sum of 5,000*l.*
[thereby agreed to be paid]. It was contended, in support of the
demurrer, that there was no jurisdiction in equity to order an
instrument to be delivered up upon the ground of its illegality,
if such illegality appeared on the face of the instrument itself.

[98]

[99]

The *Solicitor-General*, *Mr. Koe*, and *Mr. Bethell*, in support
of the demurrer.

Sir C. Wetherell, *Mr. Wigram*, and *Mr. Wilbraham*, in
support of the bill.

THE LORD CHANCELLOR [after stating certain matters recited
in the agreement, which were supposed to show that the
agreement was against public policy, and illegal (2), said:]

Aug. 30.

To this bill a general demurrer was put in; and in support of
it the argument was, first, that the contract was not void, as being
illegal or against public policy, and that there was therefore no
ground for interfering with the obligations imposed by it; or,

[100]

(1) *Brooking* v. *Maudslay, Son* and
Field (1888) 38 Ch. D. 636, 57 L. J.
Ch. 1001, 58 L. T. 852.

(2) It was ultimately decided by
the House of Lords in *Simpson* v.
Lord Howden (1842) 9 Cl. & Fin. 61
on appeal from a decision of the
Exchequer Chamber, 10 Ad. & El.

793) that the instrument in question
in these proceedings in Chancery
was not illegal. It is, therefore,
unnecessary to retain those portions
of this report which state and discuss the question whether or not the
instrument was illegal.—O. A. S.

secondly, if it be impeachable, yet, as the grounds of objection to it
appear upon the face of the contract itself, and might *therefore
be taken advantage of at law, equity ought not to interfere.

The MASTER OF THE ROLLS, as I am informed, decided the
case, and overruled the demurrer, upon the first point, not
particularly alluding to the second. [The LORD CHANCELLOR did
not think it necessary to determine the first point, and continued
as follows :]

[102]   The second objection to the bill is, that the illegality, if any,
appearing upon the face of the contract, is cognisable at law,
and that equity, therefore, ought not to interfere. This must
depend upon authority ; it being alleged, for the defendant, that
there was no instance of a court of equity having entertained
jurisdiction to order an instrument to be delivered up and cancelled, upon the ground of illegality, which appeared upon the
face of it ; and in which case, therefore, there was no danger
that the lapse of time might deprive the party to be charged
upon it of the means of defence.

[103]   In *Colman* v. *Sarrel* (1), a case is referred to, in the argument,
as having been then recently decided by Lord THURLOW, in
which he is stated to have held, that, where an instrument
cannot be proceeded upon at law, there is no ground to come
into equity for relief ; and in the case of *Colman* v. *Sarrel* itself,
his Lordship dismissed the original bill, seeking to have a deed
delivered up, although, upon a cross bill seeking a performance
of its provisions, he gave the parties an opportunity of trying the
question of illegal consideration at law.   In *Franco* v. *Bolton* (2),
Lord THURLOW allowed a demurrer to a bill to set aside a bond,
alleged to have been given *pro turpi causâ*, after a verdict for
the obligee, although the illegality of the consideration did not
appear upon the face of the bond. In *Gray* v. *Mathias* (3), a
bill was filed to set aside a bond which appeared, upon the face
of it, to have been given *pro turpi causâ*. The question of
jurisdiction upon that ground was argued ; and Chief Baron
MACDONALD, with the assent of the three other Barons, dismissed
the bill with costs, not professing to decide upon the question

(1) 1 R. R. 83 (1 Ves. Jr. 50).   (3) 5 R. R. 48 (5 Ves. 286).
(2) 6 R. R. 71, *n*. (3 Ves. 368).

of jurisdiction, but, what amounts to the same thing, that in such
a case a court of equity ought not to interfere; stating that the
plaintiff himself alleged that the instrument was a piece of
waste paper, and was good for nothing, upon the face of it;
that, whenever it was produced, it would appear to be good for
nothing, the plaintiff himself alleging that he had an irrefragable
defence against it.   This is a very distinct authority against the
jurisdiction contended for by the plaintiffs.   The cases upon the
Annuity Acts, *Byne* v. *Vivian* (1), *Byne* v. *Potter* (2), and *Bromley*
v. *Holland* (3), all in the fifth volume of Vesey, and *the latter
case reported, upon appeal, in the seventh volume of Vesey, do
not appear to me to be applicable to the present case; for in
none of them did the circumstance which created the invalidity
of the transaction appear upon the face of the deeds, and in
none of them were the objections confined to defects in the
memorial, but depended upon evidence *dehors*, such as the mode
of paying the consideration, of which the evidence might, at
a future time, be lost.   In the latter of these cases, *Bromley* v.
Holland, Lord ALVANLEY expressed great doubts as to the jurisdiction, but thought himself bound by the prior decision of
Byne v. *Vivian*.   When the same case came before Lord ELDON (4),
he expressed a similar opinion as to the jurisdiction, but supported it, in that case. upon the preceding authorities, and by
suggesting (5) that, by destroying the deed and giving evidence
of its contents, the variance between the deed and the memorial
might no longer appear.   He also refers the jurisdiction to
deliver up bills and notes to a similar ground, viz. that the
evidence might be lost; and observes (6), " There is considerable
difference between the case of a bill of exchange upon which, on
the face of it, there can be no demand, and an instrument which,
upon the face of it, purports to affect real property; and that
is to be applied in some measure to the case of a bill without a
stamp;" and he again says, " I do not go the length that, if it
is clear that no use can be made of the instrument, that is
ground enough for the equitable jurisdiction to take it out of

[*104]

SIMPSON
v.
LORD
HOWDEN.

(1) 5 R. R. 126 (5 Ves. 604).   (4) See 6 R. R. 61 (7 Ves. 16).
(2) See 5 R. R. 130, n. (5 Ves. 609).   (5) See 6 R. R. 64 (7 Ves. 20).
(3) 6 R. R. 58 (5 Ves. 610; 7 Ves. 3). (6) 6 R. R. 65.

the possession of the party who can make no use of it beneficial to himself."

[His Lordship then distinguished several reported cases in which instruments had been successfully impeached in equity on the ground of gross fraud or illegality not appearing on the face of the instrument, and continued as follows :]

[106]

It is to be observed, as to one class of cases generally referred to upon this subject, viz., bills to set aside annuities, that they not only depend upon facts not appearing upon the face of the instrument, but that, except in those cases in which the statute gives authority to set aside the instrument, law affords a very inadequate remedy ; for, first, the annuitant may repeat his action as often as the annuity becomes payable, and if the invalidity of the annuity be fully established, still the consideration money would remain in hands which ought not to retain it; and by the mode in which courts of equity deal with the payments on account of the annuity as against the consideration paid for it, an account is raised which a court of equity alone can properly take. It is not a mere declaration of the illegality of the instrument, but it involves the duty of restoring the parties, as nearly as possible, to their original situation, which a court of equity alone can effect.   So, the cases upon policies of insurance always represent transactions, which, if true, would afford a defence to an action, yet, as proceeding from misrepresentation or fraudulent suppression, clearly give jurisdiction to courts of equity ; and, in these cases also, the return of the premium would be to be arranged, if such cases were ever brought to a hearing, of which, however, there are very few precedents. In *Jackman* v. *Mitchell* (1), Sir S. ROMILLY stated that there was no case of a decree for delivering up a bond appearing upon the face of it to be void, and referred to the case of *Ryan* v. *Mackmath* (2).   Lord ELDON did not controvert that proposition, but said, that the proposition

[*107]

did not *arise, the instrument not being bad upon the face of it, but bad only as it might be proved to be so *aliunde*.   In *Harrington* v. *Du Chastel*, referred to by Lord ELDON in *Bromley* · v. *Holland* (3), and reported in a note in the second volume of

(1) 9 R. R. 229, p. 232 (13 Ves.   (2) 3 Br. C. C. 15.
581, p. 585).   (3) 6 R. R. 63 (7 Ves. 19).

Mr. Swanston's Reports (p. 158), the illegality did not appear upon the face of the bond, and the corrupt contract was not between the obligor and obligee; and, upon the motion for the injunction, the LORD CHANCELLOR expressed doubts whether a court of law could relieve. In *Law* v. *Law* (1), the LORD CHANCELLOR says, "It is agreed on all hands that this bond is good at law; wherefore the representative of the obligor is obliged to come hither for relief."

If, then, there be no case in which this jurisdiction has been exercised, and if I find Lord THURLOW, in the case referred to in *Colman* v. *Sarrel*, and the Court of Exchequer in *Gray* v. *Mathias*, deciding against it; Lord ALVANLEY, in *Bromley* v. *Holland*, regretting that the jurisdiction had been assumed in the cases of annuities; and Lord ELDON, in the same case, directly, and in *Ware* v. *Horwood* inferentially (14 Ves. 28), disclaiming the jurisdiction contended for; it only remains to be considered, whether any such cogent reason exists in the present case, as to make it my duty to assume the jurisdiction, and so, for the first time, to establish a precedent for it.

Now, I find no fact stated in this bill impeaching the legality of the instrument, beyond what appears upon the face of the instrument. If there should be a decree for the plaintiffs, it would be merely to deliver it up—no consequential relief, no account to be taken, no provision for restoring the parties to their original position. *Whether the defendant proceed in the action he has brought, [*108] or bring another, the same questions must be raised and decided at law as are raised in the bill. Why should a court of equity, in this case, assume to itself the decision of a mere legal question, contrary to its usual practice? Would it do so if a bill were filed to have a note or bill delivered up drawn upon unstamped paper, or upon a wrong stamp? But what would be the consequence of retaining such a bill? Unless an injunction were granted, the action would proceed. If the plaintiff at law were to recover, it can hardly be supposed that this Court would restrain execution, upon its own opinion of a point of law, after a court of law had decided it in favour of the demand. That a party has not effectually availed himself of a defence at law, or that a court of law

(1) Cas. temp. Talb. 140.

has erroneously decided a point of pure law, is no ground for
equitable interference; and if the defendants at law obtain a
verdict, and the illegality of the instrument be thereby established,
the whole object of the plaintiffs in equity will be obtained. Is
it, then, a case in which a court of equity will, by injunction,
restrain further proceedings in the action, and take to itself the
exclusive jurisdiction over this legal question? I apprehend not;
for not only will the Court wish, in some way, to obtain the
opinion of a court of law upon a purely legal question, but, by
permitting the action to proceed, it will afford to the parties the
most speedy, cheap, and satisfactory means of deciding the
question between them.

As to the points raised by the bill, whether, in the events which
have happened, the plaintiffs in equity are liable to pay the
5,000*l.*, it is purely a question of construction, which may be
dealt with at law quite as well as in equity, and which, therefore,
cannot affect the question of jurisdiction.

[109]   In the absence, therefore, of any decision in favour of the jurisdiction contended for by the plaintiffs, and with the authorities
against it to which I have referred, and seeing no benefit which
can arise, in this or any other such case, from this Court
assuming the jurisdiction, I am of opinion that the

Demurrer ought to be allowed.

SKEELES *v.* SHEARLY.

(3 My. & Cr. 112—121; S. C. 7 L. J. (N. S.) Ch. 3; 1 Jur. 888.)

[FOR a note of this appeal at the end of the report of the case
before the Vice-Chancellor (8 Sim. 153), see 42 R. R. at p. 144.]

1837.
Aug. 9, 10, 11.

KNATCHBULL *v.* FEARNHEAD (1).

(3 My. & Cr. 122—126; S. C. 1 Jur. 687.)

Lord
COTTENHAM,
L.C.
[122]
The executors of a deceased trustee, having admitted the receipt of
assets which would have been sufficient to answer a particular breach
of trust committed by their testator, besides his other debts, held chargeable with the loss occasioned by such breach of trust, although they had

(1) *Brittlebank* v. *Godwin* (1868)   but Statutes of Limitation may now
L. R. 5 Eq. 545, 37 L. J. Ch. 377;   be pleaded in cases like this, where

paid all his debts of which they had any knowledge out of the assets, and had distributed the whole surplus among his residuary legatees many years before, and at a time when they had no notice of the breach of trust, or of any claim in respect of it.

THIS suit was instituted in the year 1833, by persons interested in a sum of 5,000*l.*, which, in the year 1801, had been vested in John Bradshaw and George Sayer, upon certain trusts for the benefit of the children of the late Sir Edward Knatchbull by Dame Mary Knatchbull his wife. The object of the suit was to charge the personal representatives of the trustees, both of whom were dead, with the loss consequent on a breach of trust which they were alleged to have committed in paying over the trust fund to the late Sir Edward Knatchbull, who was entitled to a life interest in the fund, and by whom it had never been replaced.

The acts complained of as constituting the breach of trust took place in the years 1801 and 1804 respectively. The late Sir Edward Knatchbull died in the month of September, 1819, leaving ten children by Dame Mary, his wife. Two of those children afterwards died under age : of the surviving eight, all of whom were parties to the suit, some as plaintiffs and others as defendants, several were still infants. Sayer, one of the trustees, died in the month of May, 1814, leaving the defendants Catherine Sayer, Nicholas R. Toke, and Edward Cage his executrix and executors, who duly proved his will. Bradshaw, the other trustee, died in the year 1823, and his will was proved by the defendants Fearnhead and Tipler (1).

The answer of the defendants, the personal representatives of Sayer, among other things, stated that their testator died in the year 1814; and that they had received assets of his estate sufficient to pay all his debts which had come to their knowledge, and also to answer the 5,000*l.* in question, in case the Court should be of opinion that their testator's estate was liable for the same. It further stated that the will of their testator, after

[123]

the claim of the beneficiaries would have been barred if there had not been any trust; see Trustee Act, 1888, s. K.—O A. S.

(1) From the pleadings it appeared that Bradshaw died in the lifetime of Sayer; but this was admitted at the Bar to be a mistake, and it was stated that Bradshaw died in the year above mentioned.

giving divers specific and pecuniary legacies, bequeathed the residue of his personal estate to the defendants, his executrix and executors, upon trust, to be divided among all his children, except his eldest son ; and that they had paid all the legacies, and, many years ago (1), paid and divided the residue of the personal estate among the residuary legatees ; and that they had not any fund out of which to answer any demand which might be established by the plaintiffs against his estate. The same defendants by their answer also stated, that they were wholly ignorant of the existence of any such trust as in the bill alleged until the year 1830.

. By the Master's report, made in pursuance of the decree pronounced at the hearing of the cause, it was, among other things, found that a sum of 1,612*l.* 16*s.*, (being part of the trust fund,) which in the year 1802 had been invested in the purchase of 2,393*l.* 15*s.* 4*d.* 3 per cent. Consols, in the joint names of Sayer and Bradshaw, had been afterwards sold out, under a power of attorney from them, on the 11th of February, 1804; and that the produce of the sale, amounting to the sum of 1,328*l.* 11*s.*, had

[*124]

been, by their authority, paid over on *the same day to the account of Sir Edward Knatchbull, by whom it had been applied to his own use.

Certain exceptions taken to the Master's report by the defendants, the representatives of Sayer, having been overruled, the cause came on to be heard at the Rolls, for further directions, on the 5th of July, 1836; when an order was made, declaring, among other things, that the respective estates of Sayer and Bradshaw were liable to make good the sum of 2,393*l.* 15*s.* 4*d.* 3 per cent. Consols, together with the dividends which would have accrued thereon since the death of the late Sir Edward Knatchbull; and the Master was directed to ascertain what, at the market price on the 5th of July, 1836, (being the day of the date of the order,) would be sufficient to have purchased the same amount of such stock, and to take an account of the dividends which

---

(1) This was the expression used in the answer; but it was admitted, on all hands, that the period referred to was anterior to the time at which the defendants had notice of the breach of trust, or even of the existence of the trust itself.

would have accrued thereupon from the day of Sir Edward
Knatchbull's death ; and it was declared that the defendants, the
personal representatives of Sayer, having admitted assets, were
liable to make good such sum of stock, and the dividends in
respect thereof ; without prejudice however to any right which
they might have, upon satisfying the claims of the plaintiffs and
of the defendants in the same interest, to call upon the other
defendants, the executors of Bradshaw, for contribution.

A petition of appeal, presented by the personal representatives
of Sayer against the original decree, and also against the order
made on the exceptions and on further directions, having come on
to be heard,

The LORD CHANCELLOR, after argument, dismissed so much of
the appeal as related to the original decree, and to the order
overruling the appellants' exceptions.   That part of the petition
which appealed against the *order on further directions was then
brought on for discussion, when several points were raised and
debated, which it is not material to report, as they referred
exclusively to other sums, being portions of the trust fund which
had never been invested in stock, and for the loss of which also
the appellants had been declared answerable.   With respect to
those sums, the LORD CHANCELLOR varied the order by directing
a number of preliminary inquiries.

[*125]

Sir William Horne, Mr. Monro, and *Mr. Purvis*, for the
appellants, then submitted that, with respect to the sum of
stock which the Master's report found to have been sold out by
the trustees, and paid over, by their authority, to the late Sir
Edward Knatchbull, it would be extremely hard and unjust that
the representatives of Sayer should be made personally responsible for the act of their testator, when it appeared from their
answer, and was not disputed, that they had been in total
ignorance of the breach of trust complained of, and indeed of the
existence of the trust itself, until after the lapse of sixteen years
from the death of their testator, and of eleven years from the
death of Sir Edward Knatchbull ; and when, moreover, as they
had sworn by that answer, they had, many years ago, in the

regular discharge of their duty as executors, paid off all their
testator's debts of which they had any knowledge, and distributed
the surplus of his personal estate among his residuary legatees,
and had not now a single shilling of his assets in their hands to
answer the claim set up against them. If, under such circumstances, they were held personally liable, an executor could
never safely administer his testator's estate, except under the
indemnity afforded by a decree of the Court; and yet, if he
insisted upon having recourse to that indemnity in a case where
[*126]
he had no notice of any *doubtful or contingent claim to justify
such a proceeding, he would do so at the risk of being saddled
with the costs.   For these reasons it was impossible to hold that
the appellants had been guilty of any *devastavit* with which they
ought to be charged in a court of equity: *Hawkins* v. *Day* (1),
The Governor and Company of Chelsea Waterworks v. *Cowper* (2),
Davis v. *Blackwell* (3).

The LORD CHANCELLOR said, that, where an executor passes his
accounts in this Court, he is discharged from further liability,
and the creditor is left to his remedy against the legatees; but,
if he pays away the residue without passing his accounts in
Court, he does it at his own risk.

The *Solicitor-General* and *Mr. Lovat, contrà,* were not
called upon to argue the point.

———————

1837.
Aug. 3, 4.
Nov. 4.
———
Lord
COTTENHAM,
L.C.
[127]

ELLICOMBE *v.* GOMPERTZ.

(3 My. & Cr. 127—154.)

Bequest of a residue upon trust for the testator's grandson, B., the son
of Isaac, at twenty-five, for life; and, after the death of B., in case he
shall have a son who shall attain twenty-one, then for such son of B.,
who shall first attain twenty-one, absolutely; and in default of such
son of B., and after B.'s death, then upon trust for the testator's grandson, J., the son of Isaac, at twenty-five, for life; and after the death of
J., in case he shall have a son who shall attain twenty-one, then to such
son of J. who shall first attain twenty-one, absolutely; with the like

———————

(1) Amb. 160; and see App. 803,   (2) 1 Esp. 275.
Blunt's ed.   (3) 35 R. R. 503 (9 Bing. 5).

ELLICOMBE
v.
GOMPERTZ.

limitations successively in favour of any other grandsons, sons of Isaac, born in the testator's lifetime, and their respective sons first attaining twenty-one ; and in default of a son of any such grandson attaining twenty-one, then upon trust for any son of Isaac, born after the testator's decease, who shall first attain twenty-one, absolutely ; and in case no son of any son of the testator's son Isaac, then born, or thereafter to be born in the testator's lifetime, nor any son of his son Isaac, born after his decease, shall live to attain twenty-one, then from and immediately after the decease of all the sons and grandsons of his son Isaac, upon trust for the testator's nephew, G., for life ; and upon the decease of his nephew, G., in case he shall have a son who shall live to the age of twenty-one, then upon trust for such son who shall first attain twenty-one, absolutely :

Held, upon the whole context of the will, that the words "after the decease of all the sons and grandsons," must be read as if they had been "after the decease of all the aforesaid," or "all such sons and grandsons ; " and that the limitation over in favour of the first son of G. attaining twenty-one, was therefore not too remote.

THE will upon the construction of which this case depended, was very special, and is set out at great length in the original report, but the statement of the will contained in the judgment of the LORD CHANCELLOR is sufficient for the purposes of the report. The judgment also indicates the arguments of counsel, and refers to the principal cases cited by them.

The plaintiff contended that the ulterior limitations of the will were void for remoteness.

The defendant demurred.

Mr. Wigram and *Mr. Richards,* for the defendant in support   [137]
of the demurrer.

Mr. Jacob, Mr. Hodgson, and *Mr. James Russell,* for the   [140]
plaintiff.

Mr. Wigram, in reply.]   [143]

THE LORD CHANCELLOR :   *Nov.* 4.

The question raised by this demurrer is, whether the gift of the residue in the will of Henry Isaac be void, as too remote.

It appears that at the time of making the will the testator had two sons, Hyam Isaac and Isaac Isaac; and *that this Isaac   [*144]
Isaac had two sons, Benjamin and Joseph Isaac; and that the testator had also a nephew, Joseph Gompertz, the son of a sister

ELLICOMBE
v.
GOMPERTZ.

and the father of the defendant. Hyam, the testator's eldest
son, appears from the will to have been guilty, in the opinion of
the testator, of extravagance.   The testator, by his will, devised
all his freehold and copyhold estate, except some premises in
London, and an estate at Walthamstow, to the use of Isaac
Isaac, his son, for life ; remainder to his first and other sons in
tail male : remainder to his nephew, Joseph Gompertz, in fee,—
passing over all children of Hyam and all issue female of Isaac
Isaac.   The premises in London, with the furniture and effects
therein, he devised and bequeathed to trustees, in trust for
Isaac Isaac, for life ; remainder to Hyam, for life ; remainder to
his nephew, Joseph Gompertz, absolutely—thus preferring him
to any issue of either of his sons.

The estate at Walthamstow he directed should be sold, and
the proceeds applied as the residue of his personal estate.

The residue of his personal estate he gave to trustees, upon
trust to pay his debts and legacies, in which were included a
legacy of 300*l.* to Hyam; and to Isaac Isaac a legacy of 500*l.*,
and 2,000*l.* in payment of Hyam's debts, and to Hyam himself
400*l.* per annum, in monthly payments, for his subsistence; to
Isaac Isaac the yearly sum of 1,100*l.*, and to his wife surviving
500*l.* per annum, for the support of herself and his children till
twenty-five; to the sons of Isaac Isaac, living at the testator's
death, 2,000*l.* each at twenty-five; and to his daughters 2,000*l.*
each at twenty-one, or marriage.   He also gave other annuities
for life, and directed that the residue of his personal estate should
be invested in the public funds ; and that the dividends should

[*145]

be laid out *to accumulate until his grandson, Benjamin Isaac,
the eldest son of his son Isaac Isaac, should have attained twenty-
five ; and after that time, that his trustees should pay the interest
of his residuary estate and of the accumulations to his said
grandson for life ; and, after his death, to pay the principal to
such son of his said grandson Benjamin as should first attain
twenty-one, with maintenance in the meantime for such expectant
son of his grandson.

If his grandson Benjamin should have no son who should
attain twenty-one, then there was a similar direction to pay the
dividends to his grandson Joseph Isaac, from his age of twenty-

five, for life ; and after his death, to pay the principal to such
son of his said grandson Joseph, as should first attain twenty-
one, with maintenance for such expectant son of Joseph. And if
Joseph should have no son who should attain twenty-one, then
a precisely similar provision was made for any other son of the
testator's son Isaac Isaac, who might be born in the testator's
lifetime, who should, for the time, be the eldest son of Isaac
Isaac, for life, from twenty-five, with remainder to such eldest
son of such other son of Isaac Isaac as should first attain
twenty-one. And in case no son of such other son of Isaac Isaac,
so born in the testator's lifetime, should attain twenty-one, then
the trustees were to pay and transfer the residue to such son of the
testator's son Isaac Isaac, born after the testator's death, as should
first attain twenty-one, with maintenance in the meantime for
such expectant son of Isaac Isaac, born after the testator's death.

Then follow the words upon which the question turns : " And
in case no son of any son of my said son Isaac Isaac, now born,
or hereafter to be born in my lifetime, nor any son of my said
son Isaac Isaac, born after *my decease, shall live to attain the   [*146]
age of twenty-one years, then, from and immediately after the
decease of all the sons and grandsons of my said son Isaac
Isaac, I do hereby will, order, and direct, that my said trustees
shall and do," &c. He then directs the income to be paid to
his nephew Joseph Gompertz, for his life, and after his death,
the principal to be paid to such son of the said Joseph Gompertz
as should first attain twenty-one. And in case Joseph Gompertz
should have no son who should live to attain twenty-one, he
directed the principal of the residue and the accumulations to be
paid to his (the testator's) next of kin. And he directed that all
the dividends and interest which should arise from such residue,
and the accumulations thereof, " during the time or times that
any of the sons of my said son Isaac Isaac, now born, or hereafter to be born, during my lifetime, and entitled to take under
this my will, shall be under the age of twenty-five years, or
during the time or times that any son of my said son Isaac
Isaac, to be born after my decease, or any grandson of my said
son Isaac Isaac, or any son of my said nephew Joseph Gompertz,
entitled to take under this my will, shall be under the age of

twenty-one years, over and above what shall be, from time to
time, advanced by my said trustees for the maintenance and
education of any grandson or son of my said son Isaac Isaac, or
any son of my said nephew, as aforesaid, shall be from time to
time laid out and accumulate and be deemed and taken as part
of the residuum," &c.

The testator's son, Hyam, having died, he by a codicil revoked
the provision made for him, and made other alterations in the
legacies and annuities given by his will; but nothing in this or
the other codicil seems to bear upon the question made upon the
gift of the residue by the will.

[147]   It is obvious, from the provisions of the will, that the author
of the will knew well to what extent the law would permit the
vesting of the residue to be postponed, and intended to keep
within those limits.

For this purpose the testator, having a son, Isaac Isaac, and
two grandsons, sons of that son, after providing for the subsistence of the father, Isaac Isaac, gives to the sons life estates,
to commence at twenty-five years of age, and gives the principal
to such of those sons' sons as shall first attain twenty-one.
Considering, also, that this Isaac Isaac might have other sons
born in the testator's lifetime, for whom and for whose sons he
might by law make similar provisions, he provides for sons, who
might be born in his own lifetime, and for their sons, in the
same manner : but he also contemplated the possibility that
Isaac Isaac might have sons born after his (the testator's) death,
and knowing that he could not make a similar provision for such
sons, he directs that, upon failure of the prior gifts, the property
should vest in such of such sons as should first attain twenty-one.

The object in this arrangement appears to have been, first, to
keep the property together ; there being no provision for any
younger sons, or for any daughters of Benjamin or Joseph, or
of any other sons of Isaac Isaac, born in his own lifetime, or
for any children of Isaac Isaac, born after the testator's death,
except such son as should first attain twenty-one ; and secondly,
to postpone the vesting as long as the rules of law would admit,
but carefully to keep within them.

It is said, however, that the gift over, under which the

defendant claims, is only to take effect after the decease of all
the sons and grandsons of Isaac Isaac ; *and that such limitation is too remote, and therefore void.   Undoubtedly, if these
words are to be construed literally, it would be too remote.   But
the first consideration is, can they, consistently with the prior
gift, be construed literally ?   Of all the grandsons of Isaac, who
might come into *esse*, the testator provided only for one, who, to
become entitled, must have attained twenty-one, and be born
of a father himself born in the testator's lifetime.   But the
testator's son, Isaac Isaac, might have had sons, born after the
testator's death, who might have died under twenty-one, leaving
sons; and as Isaac Isaac had three daughters, there was every
probability that he might have grandsons, the sons of such
daughters.   For such grandchildren, however, no provision is,
in any event, made ; and yet, if the words are to be construed
literally, the provision for Joseph Gompertz and his son is not to
take place until after the death of all such grandchildren of Isaac
Isaac, although all the objects of the testator's care had failed.

To account for this, it was suggested, that this might have
been purposely done, by permitting the property to pass to such
grandchildren as next of kin.   If the testator had had any such
object in contemplation, he might have provided for it.   Why
could he not provide for the children of a son of Isaac Isaac,
born after his own death, in the event of such son himself dying
under twenty-one ; and why could he not provide for the children
of daughters of Isaac Isaac, as he did provide for sons of his
sons?   Such an intention would, in fact, be inconsistent with
the whole scheme of his testamentary dispositions, and with the
intention manifest from all its provisions.

That the author of the will knew the rule of law is manifest.
To construe these words literally would imply *an intention
to violate it, and thereby to defeat the declared intention of
benefiting Joseph Gompertz and his son.

It is said, however, that the testator did intend the gift to
Joseph Gompertz to take place, but that the vesting of it was
purposely postponed until after the death of all the grandsons of
Isaac Isaac.

This of course assumes an intention, that the gift should take

effect, and that it should be so postponed ; but the accumulation
clause is entirely inconsistent with this supposition.   He would
in that case have directed an accumulation during this suspension
of the vesting, as he has in the other specified case of suspension :
whereas he has in terms confined it to the times during which a
son of a son of Isaac Isaac, born in his (the testator's) lifetime
should be under twenty-five, or any son of Isaac Isaac, born after
his own death, or any grandson of Isaac Isaac, entitled to take
under his will, should be under twenty-one.   It is also obvious that
the provision, so supposed to have been intentionally made, would
not in all probability have effected the supposed intended object.
The income of the property, between the time of the failure of
all the persons designated to take and the deaths of all the sons
and grandsons, being, according to the supposition, undisposed
of, would have become the property of the next of kin at the time
of the testator's death ; and the next of kin might have been some
of those designated persons, not intended to be benefited, unless
they attained a certain age, or might have been the discarded
son Hyam, for whom it is clear that the testator intended to
provide a mere subsistence.   It was also well observed that the
gift to the Gompertz family is made subject to the annuities and
[*150]   charges given and created by the will ; *whereas, according to
the construction contended for, it was also to be subject to a
different application of the income during the lives of all sons
and of all grandsons of Isaac Isaac.

If, therefore, these words are to receive their literal construction, I cannot doubt but that the testator's intention will be
wholly defeated.

It was indeed contended, for the defendant Lyon Gompertz,
that the literal construction of the particular words was not such
as is contended for by the plaintiffs.   I cannot assent to that
proposition.   It appears to me that in order to reconcile the
different parts of the will, the words must be read as if they
stood thus,—after the decease of " all the said," or " all such
sons and grandsons," &c.   It was said that the words " from
and immediately after," &c., would be useless repetition according
to the construction of the defendant.   But that is not so ; for
although it is true that the contingencies upon which the gift

over was to take effect are before specified, the word "then,"
if the subsequent words had been omitted, would not have been
an adverb of time, but would have meant "in those events;"
and the testator's object, as afterwards expressed, was, in those
events, to give the property to Joseph Gompertz, but not until
after the deaths of such sons and grandsons of Isaac Isaac, so
contingently entitled, during whose lives the accumulation is
afterwards directed: and the words "from and immediately
after the decease," were probably introduced with a view to the
accumulation afterwards directed, and, if so, they must be confined to periods during which the accumulations are directed,
namely, the lives of grandsons of Isaac Isaac, who would have
taken had they lived, and not the lives of grandsons who in no
event could have been entitled.

These other parts of the case appear to me to leave no doubt   [151]
of the testator's intention. But suppose the case had stood
simply thus: Provision is made for certain members of a class
answering a particular description, and then a gift over is made
upon the failure of the class. If it be clear that the whole of
the class were not to take, the gift over, though made to depend
upon the failure of the whole class, will be construed to take
place upon the failure of that description of the class, who were
to take; and, on the other hand, if it appears that all the class
were intended to take, although some only are enumerated, and
the gift over be upon the failure of the whole class, the Court
will adopt such a construction as will extend the benefit, in the
best way the law will admit, to the whole class. Of both these
propositions the authorities present many examples.

In *Trickey* v. *Trickey* (1), the testator had provided for the
children of his daughter at twenty-one, with a proviso that the
children of any child of his daughter dying in the mother's
lifetime should stand in the place of the parent; and then made
a gift over, upon the death of all children of his daughter under
twenty-one, or not leaving issue who should live to attain that
age. This limitation over was held not too remote, the generality
of the expression being confined by the prior provisions.

In *Bristow* v. *Boothby* (2), decided by Sir JOHN LEACH, and

(1) 41 R. R. 125 (3 My. & K. 560).   (2) 25 R. R. 248 (2 Sim. & St. 465).

[*152]

affirmed by Lord LYNDHURST on appeal (1), the decision was the other way, upon the circumstances of the case; but the principle is recognised, Lord LYNDHURST, in his judgment, observing that the question was, whether *the term "issue" was to be taken generally, or to be restricted so as to denote issue before mentioned, and concluding by saying that it did not appear to him that there were any circumstances to lead to the conclusion that the term ought to be taken in the restricted sense with respect to the previous limitation (2). In *Ginger* d. *White* v. *White* (3), and *Goodright* d. *Docking* v. *Dunham* (4), there were gifts to children of a person named, and gifts over if that person should die without issue, an expression which was held to mean such issue as before mentioned, that is, children.

The cases in which a gift over, upon a tenant for life under the will dying without issue, has been held to enlarge the estate for life into an estate tail, where some children only of such tenant for life have been before provided for, in order to let in others, proceed upon the supposed intention; and the rule is not applied where such intention to provide for all appears to be negatived, as in *Blackborn* v. *Edgley* (5), in which a gift over in case the tenant for life should die without issue, was construed as if it had been, "should die without such issue." In *Morse* v. *Lord Ormonde*, affirmed by Lord ELDON on appeal (6), estates in tail male were given to sons of the testatrix's daughter, with remainder to the daughters of such daughter in tail, and then various sums charged on the estates were bequeathed after the decease and failure of issue of the daughter; and, upon a question with respect to the validity of those charges, it was held that the

[*153]

words "failure of issue" must be construed *"failure of issue aforesaid;" that is, failure of the objects of the prior limitations.

In *Malcolm* v. *Taylor* (7), the words "dying without issue" were construed to mean "without such issue as would take under the prior limitation;" Sir JOHN LEACH, Master of the

(1) 30th June, 1829.
(2) The LORD CHANCELLOR here referred to a note of Lord LYND-HURST's judgment, with which he had been furnished by Mr. Russell.
(3) Willes, 348.

(4) Doug. 264.·
(5) 1 P. Wms. 600.
(6) 25 R. R. 85 (1 Russ. 382).
(7) 34 R. R. 117 (2 Russ. & My. 416).

Rolls, saying, that it is a reasonable intendment that a subsequent limitation is meant to take effect upon failure of the prior gift, and as a substitution in that event.

The cases of this kind, referred to for the plaintiffs, of *Langley* v. *Baldwin* (1), and *Attorney-General* v. *Sutton* (2), do not decide that a general devise upon which a gift over is expressed to depend cannot be confined by the intention apparent upon other parts of the case; but they are cases in which it was thought necessary to give to such words their full ordinary meaning, in order to effectuate the apparent intention, and to let in children, to exclude whom there did not appear to be any intention, but with respect to whom it simply appeared that the former enumeration would not include them. In all the cases of limitation over of personal property upon a dying without issue, or upon a failure of issue, after a prior gift to issue of a particular description, that is, children, collected by Mr. Jarman, in his edition of Powell on Devises (3), the words "such issue," or "issue aforesaid," are important.

There is, in the present case, a peculiarity which distinguishes it from most others. There is no ambiguity as to the contingency or event upon which the gift *over is to take effect; but the only question is, whether, such contingency or event having happened, the gift over is to be suspended in enjoyment until after the deaths of certain persons, who are not, in any construction, to be objects of the gift.

[*154]

The result of all the authorities is that in such cases as the present, if it be necessary to put a restricted sense upon the words used in the gift over, in order to effectuate the intentions of the testator, as evidenced by other parts of the will, it is competent for the Court to do so; and being satisfied, for the reasons I have before given, that the intention of this testator was, that the gift over should take effect upon the failure of the objects particularly described as the objects of his prior gift, I am of opinion that I must hold Lyon Gompertz to be entitled, and consequently that the

Demurrer must be allowed.

(1) 1 Eq. Ab. 185 ; and 1 Ves.   (2) 1 P. Wms. 754.
Sen. 26.   (3) Vol. ii. p. 530.

1837.
May 31.
Aug. 30.

Lord
C OTTENHAM,
L.C.
[157]

PRICE *v.* CARVER (1).

(3 My. & Cr. 157—164.)

A decree of foreclosure against an infant in the case of an equitable mortgage by deposit must give the infant a day to show cause against the decree, after he attains twenty-one, notwithstanding the provisions of the Act 11 Geo. IV. & 1 Will IV. c. 47, ss. 10, 11.

IN this case the bill was filed by an equitable mortgagee of copyhold property, by deposit of copies of court roll, praying a foreclosure. Some of the parties interested in the equity of redemption were infants. At the hearing, before the Lord Chancellor, on the 8th of April, 1837, his Lordship made the usual decree for a foreclosure ; but, in drawing up the decree, a question arose whether the infant defendants were to have a day to show cause against the decree when they should attain twenty-one.

[The arguments turned upon the question whether the Act 11 Geo. IV. & 1 Will. IV. c. 47, ss. 10, 11 (2), which abolished demurrer of the parol at law, thereby also indirectly overruled the analogous practice in equity of giving an infant a day to show cause against a decree directing him to convey property on

(1) See the cases upon this point collected in a note to *Williamson* v. *Gordon* (1812) 12 R. R. 149. The question is also discussed at length in Fisher on Mortgage, 5th ed., pp. 554 —556.—O. A. S.

(2) The tenth and eleventh sections of this Act are in the following words :

Sect. 10. And be it further enacted, that from and after the passing of this Act, where any action, suit, or other proceeding for the payment of debts, or any other purpose, shall be commenced or prosecuted by or against any infant under the age of twenty-one years, either alone or together with any other person or persons, the parol shall not demur, but such action, suit, or other proceeding shall be prosecuted and carried on in the same manner and as effectually as any action or suit could before the passing of this Act be carried on or prosecuted by or against any infant, where, according to law, the parol

did not demur. [Rep. 46 & 47 Vict. c. 49, s. 4 ; S. L. R. (No. 2) 1888.]

Sect. 11. And be it further enacted, that where any suit hath been or shall be instituted in any court of equity for the payment of any debts of any person or persons deceased, to which their heir or heirs, devisee or devisees, may be subject or liable, and such court of equity shall decree the estates liable to such debts, or any of them, to be sold for satisfaction of such debt or debts ; and by reason of the infancy of any such heir or heirs, devisee or devisees, an immediate conveyance thereof cannot, as the law at present stands, be compelled, in every such case such Court shall direct, and, if necessary, compel such infant or infants to convey such estates so to be sold, (by all proper assurances in the law), to the purchaser or purchasers thereof, and in such manner as the said Court shall think proper and direct ; and every such infant shall

attaining twenty-one.   This question and many authorities
bearing upon the point are fully stated and considered in the
judgment of the LORD CHANCELLOR.]

Mr. Turner, for the plaintiff [cited *Sheffield* v. *The Duchess
of Buckingham* (1), *Blatch* v. *Wilder* (2), and other cases].   The   [159]
proper form of the decree in this case will be to direct an
account of what is due for principal, interest, and costs; to
declare that, in default of payment, all parties shall be foreclosed;
and that the adult defendants shall convey immediately, and the
infant defendants shall convey when they come of age, unless,
being served with a *subpœna*, they shall show cause against
the decree.   *   *   *

Mr. Heberden, for the infant defendants :

The Legislature can only be considered as having abolished   [160]
the strict technical demurrer of the parol.   *   *   Where a
conveyance is directed, it follows, of necessity, that a day must
be given to show cause.

The Act of Parliament was passed for the particular object
of facilitating the payment of debts out of real estate.   Its terms,
however, are general enough to apply to all cases ; but that they
were not intended to be understood in their largest extent, appears
from the circumstance that the case of an infant heir of a vendor
is provided for by a subsequent statute.

This case is precisely similar to *Spencer* v. *Boyes* (3).

Mr. Turner, in reply.   *   *   *   [161]

THE LORD CHANCELLOR :   *Aug.* 30.

The question argued in this case upon the minutes was,
whether the infant defendants were to have a day to show
cause after attaining twenty-one.   I have not seen the pleadings,

---

make such conveyance accordingly ;
and every such conveyance shall be
as valid and effectual, to all intents
and purposes, as if such person or
persons, being an infant or infants,
was or were at the time of executing

the same, of the full age of twenty-one
years.
  (1) West's Rep. temp. Hard. 682 ;
see p. 684.
  (2) *Ibid.* 322 ; see p. 324.
  (3) 4 R. R. 215 (4 Ves. 370).

but, from the form of the decree, I presume that the
plaintiff is an equitable mortgagee, and that the legal estate
is in the infants. The decree, in the event of the mortgage
not being redeemed, after directing a foreclosure, directs a
surrender or conveyance of the legal estate to the plaintiff.
Whether this be the proper form of decree, has not been
argued before me; but the parties may probably be advised
to consider whether a sale would not be the proper course.
I proceed, however, to consider the only question argued
before me, namely, whether, supposing the decree to be in
other respects correct, the infant defendants ought to have
a day to show cause, after attaining twenty-one. That they
would have had a day to show cause, according to the course
hitherto pursued, is quite clear, the decree being both to fore-
close and to procure a conveyance from the infants. But it is
said that the stat. 11 Geo. IV. & 1 Will. IV. c. 47, s. 10, has
altered the course of proceeding. That statute only enacts that
the parol shall not in future demur. If the parol demurring
and the giving a day to an infant be synonymous terms, then
this statute has prohibited the giving a day in future; but if the

[*162] terms be not synonymous, then the statute does *not affect the
practice in question in this case. I have always conceived that
the parol demurred in equity in those cases only in which it
would have demurred at law. The origin and limits of this
course at law are well explained in *Plasket* v. *Beeby* (1); and
the cases there put, of the parol demurring, have no reference
to the cases in equity in which a day is given to an infant to
show cause; indeed, the shape of the decree in the two cases is
perfectly different. When the parol demurs in equity, nothing
is done to affect the infant; but when a day is given, the decree
is complete; but the infant has a day given to show cause
against it, and if he do not show good cause within the time
specified, he is bound. In some cases, indeed, the distinction is
most apparent, the Court deciding that the parol did not demur,
and therefore making the decree, but giving the infant a day to
show cause. In *Uvedale* v. *Uvedale* (2), Lord HARDWICKE puts a
case in which the parol could not have demurred, but the infant

(1) 4 East, 485.   (2) 3 Atk. 117.

would have had a day given. So in *Chaplin* v. *Chaplin* (1), it was
held that the parol did not demur; but the legal estate, being in
the son, could not have been got from him till twenty-one, and
the decree must have given him a day to show cause. In
Fountain v. *Caine* (2), there was a trust to pay debts, and the
parol did not demur, but a day was given to the infant. *Powell*
v. *Robins* (3) was a case in which the parol demurred, and no sale
was directed till the heir attained twenty-one. In *Pope* v. *Gwyn* (4)
the assets were held to be equitable; and the parol did not demur,
but a day was given to the infant heir. *Spencer* v. *Boyes* (5) was
not a case of the parol demurring, but a day to show cause was
given to the infant heir. All *cases of foreclosure and partition,   [*163]
and all others in which a conveyance is required from an heir,
except those in which the parol would demur at law, are cases in
which a day is given, but the parol does not demur. Of all such
cases the statute takes no notice, and affords no remedy for them,
except that by the eleventh section it enables the Court to take
from the infant the legal estate of property decreed to be sold for
the payment of debts, but for that purpose only. In all other
cases in which a conveyance is required from an infant, the law
remains as before, and the practice, therefore, must remain
the same. There must be a decree for the infant to convey
at twenty-one, and he must have a day to show cause, as
before (6).

The present is precisely such a case; and I think, therefore,
that the decree, if taken in its present form, must be according
to the former practice, which I apprehend to be as the minutes
stood altered by the plaintiff.

The form of the decree is here set out in the original report.]

(1) 3 P. Wms. 365 ; see p. 368.   (4) 8 Ves. 28, *n.* ; 2 Dick. 683.
(2) 1 P. Wms. 504.   (5) 4 R. R. 215 (4 Ves. 370).
(3) 7 Ves. 209 (legal estate in   (6) See *Scholefield* v. *Heafield*, 40
infant).   R. R. 215 (7 Sim. 669).

1837.
Aug. 9, 11.
———
Lord
COTTENHAM,
L.C.
[171]

FRANK *v.* FRANK.

(3 My. & Cr. 171—179.)

A feme covert is not competent, during the coverture, to elect between a jointure made to her after marriage and her dower at common law.

[UPON the point mentioned in the head-note, the LORD CHANCELLOR said :]

[179]

The statute which regulates this question, the 27 Hen. VIII. c. 10, provides, in the ninth section, that in case of a jointure made after marriage, the wife, if she outlive her husband, shall be at liberty, after the death of her husband, to refuse to accept the lands given to her in jointure. There is, therefore, an express provision that her election shall be made at the time when the right is claimed, that is to say, after her husband's death ; and a case in the 19 Eliz. reported in Dyer (1), proceeds upon the authority, or rather is a judicial exposition, of that clause in the statute, and decides that the period of election shall not be until after the right has accrued.

———————

HESLOP *v.* METCALFE.

1837.
Dec. 20, 22.
———
Lord
COTTENHAM,
L.C.
[183]

(3 My. & Cr. 183—190 ; S. C. 7 L. J. (N. S.) Ch. 49 ; 1 Jur. 816.)

Order made on a solicitor, who withdrew from the conduct of the plaintiff's cause, that he should deliver up to the plaintiff's new solicitor the briefs of the pleadings, counsel's opinions thereon, office copies of the several answers, and all such other papers and documents, connected with the cause, as, upon inspection, the new solicitor might deem necessary for the hearing : without prejudice to any right of lien for costs, and upon an undertaking to return them undefaced within ten days after the hearing.

RICHARD TILLYER BLUNT was employed as the plaintiff's solicitor in the conduct of this suit, from the period of its institution, in the month of September, 1834. On the 12th of January, 1836, he delivered his bill of costs, from which it appeared that, after giving credit for certain sums advanced by the plaintiff, there was due to him, on account of his charges in this cause, independently of other charges, a balance of 97*l.* On the 12th of February, 1836, Mr. Blunt sent a letter to the

(1) *Anon.* 358 b.

plaintiff, in which he stated that he had no funds in his hands available to the prosecution of the suit, and that he must, therefore, request payment of the balance of 215*l.* 1*s.* 4*d.*, due on his general bill of costs delivered, and the subsequent costs; otherwise, the plaintiff must abide the consequences. On the 9th of the same month, Mr. Blunt had sued out a writ against the plaintiff for the amount of the alleged balance; and upon that writ the plaintiff was, on the 15th of February, arrested and held to bail. A second bill of costs, amounting to 36*l.* 19*s.*, and including the charges for business done in this cause from the 12th of November, 1835, to the 15th of February, 1836, was subsequently delivered; and, on the 26th of May, 1836, the plaintiff received a letter from Mr. Blunt, in which, referring to an application made to him by the clerk in Court in the cause of *Heslop* v. *Metcalfe*, the petitioner stated that he (Blunt) should proceed no further in that cause, unless the request contained in his letter of the 12th of February were complied with before one o'clock on the following day. On receiving this communication, the plaintiff instructed another solicitor, of the name of Green, to take the *necessary steps for proceeding with the cause. Those steps were accordingly taken, and the cause was afterwards set down for hearing before his Honour the Vice-Chancellor. On the 18th of October, 1836, Blunt commenced an action to recover the amount of his second bill of costs. To this action the plaintiff put in a plea, on the 13th of December, and since that time no further proceedings had been taken in the action.

[*184]

Pending the proceedings at law, the cause in this Court being likely to be soon in the paper for hearing, the plaintiff's solicitor, Mr. Green, applied by letter to Mr. Blunt, requesting him to give up the papers in the suit, upon his (Green's) undertaking to hold them subject to any lien which Blunt might have upon them. In reply to that application, Mr. Blunt declined to part with any of the papers, alleging that he had a lien upon them for costs of proceedings both in equity and at law; but he offered to allow the plaintiff or his solicitor to inspect, peruse, and take copies of them at all reasonable times, and offered to undertake to produce them at the hearing. Some further negotiations were afterwards had to induce Mr. Blunt to give up the papers in his hands, with a view to their being used at the approaching hearing, but without success; Mr. Blunt declining to part with them unless his costs were paid.

The VICE-CHANCELLOR then made an order, upon the petition of the plaintiff, that the briefs of the pleadings in the cause, counsel's opinion thereon, office copies of the answers of the several defendants, and all such other deeds and papers, documents and proceedings, in or connected with the cause, as, upon inspection, his solicitor might deem to be necessary on the plaintiff's behalf, on the hearing of the cause, should be delivered over by Mr. Blunt to Mr. Green, on the latter giving

[*185]

*his undertaking that they should be received without prejudice to any right of lien, and also that they should be returned, undefaced, to Mr. Blunt within ten days after the hearing of the cause.

An appeal-petition, presented by Mr. Blunt against his Honour's order, now came on to be heard.

Mr. Jacob and *Mr. Addis*, in support of the appeal:

No case has occurred in which an order, at all similar to the present, has been made, with the exception of *Colegrave* v. *Manley* (1), which occurred in the year 1823, and which is at variance with the whole current of authorities both before and since. There, the solicitor had discharged himself by selling his business to another solicitor; and the main question in the cause had reference to the legality of that transaction. The order for the delivery of the papers was, apparently, not much discussed, the question of lien being only a subordinate point. In *Ross* v. *Laughton* (2), which occurred in the year 1813, and is the earliest reported case upon the subject, it was not the client, but his assignees, who discharged the solicitor. Lord ELDON thought that circumstance made no difference, and held that a solicitor, who was discharged, was bound to produce, but not to deliver up, the papers of his client. The papers there in question were vouchers, that is, original documents, and not, as in the present instance, papers

(1) 24 R. R. 83 (T. & R. 400).   (2) 12 R. R. 232 (1 V. & B. 349).

prepared by the solicitor, or copied and made out at his expense.
The next case was *Commerell* v. *Poynton* (1), where the solicitor
had himself declined to proceed, and the order made was of the
same kind, for production and inspection only.

[They also cited *Lord* v. *Wormleighton* (2), *Clutton* v. *Pardon* (3),
and other cases.]

THE LORD CHANCELLOR (without calling upon *Mr. Wigram*, who   [187]
was on the other side) :

Since this question was first brought on, I have taken the
opportunity of looking at all the cases; and I have now to
consider whether I will act on *Colegrave* v. *Manley* (4), or will
undo what Lord ELDON did in that case.   The point was there
directly raised, whether, if the Court is of opinion that there
should be a production, the order ought to go beyond giving
liberty to inspect and take copies. Lord ELDON, in his judgment,
first considered the question arising upon the sale of his business,
by the solicitor ; an act which he held to amount to a discharge
by the solicitor of himself. His Lordship says, " I look upon
Mr. Raphael as having dissolved the connection of solicitor and
client; for it is not enough that he was willing to superintend
the plaintiff's business. Now, where the solicitor discharges
himself, the rule is quite different from what it is where the
solicitor is discharged by the client; " and afterwards he adds,
" so far as the use of papers is concerned, the suitor, when his
solicitor discharges himself, must have his business conducted
with as much ease and celerity, and as little expense, as if the
connection of solicitor and client had not been dissolved."

Accordingly, the order in *Colegrave* v. *Manley* was almost in
the very terms of the present order.

It is true that in several preceding cases, where the solicitor
had discharged himself, orders were made, giving to the client
the right of inspection only : but it cannot be supposed that
Lord ELDON, who, with all his experience, had decided *Colegrave*
v. *Manley*, in the year 1823, was not acquainted with the prior

(1) 18 R. R. 1 (1 Swanst. 1).   see p. 304).
(2) 23 R. R. 146 (Jac. 580).   (4) 24 R. R. 83 (T. & R. 400).
(3) 24 R. R. 68 (T. & R. 301;

authorities. In *Cresswell* *v. *Byron* (1), his Lordship intimates, in the form of a doubt, his opinion that a solicitor discharging himself cannot claim a lien; an expression which must be understood as meaning, not that the solicitor loses the lien altogether, but that he cannot set it up so as to prevent the client from proceeding in the cause. And his Lordship's language in *Lord* v. *Wormleighton* (2) is to the same effect.   •

Undoubtedly, that doctrine may expose a solicitor to very great inconvenience and hardship, if, after embarking in a cause, he finds that he cannot get the necessary funds wherewith to carry it on. But, on the other hand, extreme hardship might arise to the client, if,—to take the case which is not uncommon in the smaller practice in the country,—a solicitor, who finds a poor man having a good claim, and having but a small sum of money at his command, may go on until that fund is exhausted, and then, refusing to proceed further, may hang up the cause by withholding the papers in his hands. That would be a great grievance and means of oppression to a poor client, who, with the clearest right in the world, might still be without the means of employing another solicitor. . The rule of the Court must be adapted to every case that may occur, and be calculated to protect suitors against such conduct. Now, a solicitor, if he knows that he must trust to the result of the cause for his remuneration, will, of course, be disposed to proceed with it in such a way as, while it promotes the interest of his client, is most likely to render his lien available. I have no doubt, therefore, that the existence of the lien, while it is a great protection to the solicitor against his client, is *also a great benefit to the client; but the benefit would be entirely lost, if the solicitor might stop short in the middle of the suit, and insist upon retaining the papers, because then no other solicitor could take up and carry on the cause.

[*189]

It is admitted that, when the solicitor discharges himself, the client and his new solicitor shall, at all events, have free access to inspect and copy the papers at the office of the former solicitor. The mere giving of access, however, is, nine times out of ten, of no practical value; for if the papers are to remain,

(1) 9 R. R. 275 (14 Ves. 271).   (2) 23 R. R. 146 (Jac. 580).

notwithstanding, in the custody of the solicitor who has discharged
himself, it is obvious that they cannot be made use of in the
further progress of the suit.   The result would be, that the client
is to be put to the expense of fresh copies; that fresh briefs must
be prepared for counsel; in short, that all the costs arising from
making copies of the papers and documents to be used in the
cause must be incurred over again, and so the client is to be
greatly damnified.   That is entirely inconsistent with the *dictum*
of Lord ELDON, that the suitor must have his business conducted
with as much ease and celerity, and as little expense, as if the
connection had not been dissolved.

On the other hand, if all that expense be, in fact, incurred by
the client, what is the use of the solicitor's lien?   There may,
indeed, be original papers; but supposing them, as here, to be
papers in the cause, the effect of the rule would only be to
impose a very great hardship on the client, without any benefit
to the solicitor.   But if the expense is to operate so as to compel
him rather to pay the solicitor's bill than to go to the expense of
fresh copies, the admission of access and inspection would be
nugatory, and of no value.   Now, that a suitor, whose solicitor
withdraws himself from the *further conduct of a cause, shall be   [*190]
permitted to have the free use of the papers held by that solicitor,
so far as they may be required in the prosecution of the cause,
is quite consistent with the observations of Lord ELDON in
Commerell v. *Poynton* (1), and *Lord* v. *Wormleighton*.   Those
observations, coupled with the express decision to that effect in
Colegrave v. *Manley*, leave no doubt in my mind as to what Lord
ELDON considered to be the rule in such cases, and I entirely
concur in the propriety of that rule.

It remains only to be considered, whether Mr. Blunt must be
held to have retired from the performance of his duty as solicitor
in this cause.   (The LORD CHANCELLOR entered into an examination of the particular facts of the case, as stated in the affidavits,
and then continued:)   I cannot but consider that the result of
these transactions amounted, on the part of Mr. Blunt, to a
withdrawing of himself from the office of solicitor for the plaintiff.
I then take the law as laid down by Lord ELDON, and, adopting

(1) 18 R. R. 1 (1 Swanst. 1).

that law, must hold that Mr. Blunt is not to be permitted to impose upon the plaintiff the necessity of carrying on his cause in an expensive, inconvenient, and disadvantageous manner.

I think the principle should be, that the solicitor claiming the lien should have every security not inconsistent with the progress of the cause. But it is clear that there will neither be, to use the expression of Lord ELDON, the same ease and celerity, nor as little expense, in the conduct of it, if the new solicitor is merely to have access to the papers, as where they are placed in his hands, upon his undertaking to restore them after the immediate purposes of the production have been served.

Appeal dismissed with costs.

1838.
March 10, 28,
30.

Lord
COTTENHAM,
L.C.

[197]

WILSON *v.* BATES (1).

(3 My. & Cr. 197—204 ; S. C. 7 L. J. (N. S.) Ch. 131.)

A plaintiff is entitled to sue out an attachment against a defendant for want of answer, although he is himself in custody for a contempt in non-payment of costs.

THE bill was filed on the 12th of April, 1887. On the 17th of April a motion, made by the plaintiff, was refused, with costs, which were afterwards taxed at 11*l.* 18*s.* 6*d.* The plaintiff having refused to pay those costs, an attachment, dated the 22nd of June, 1837, issued against him. On the 17th of July the attachment was lodged with the sheriff of Leicestershire, in whose custody the plaintiff then was. On the 27th of June, 1837, the time allowed to the defendants, under the new orders, for answering the plaintiff's bill, expired. On the 28th of August, the plaintiff gave the defendants notice that he should sue out an attachment against them for want of an answer: and, on the 20th of September, an attachment was sued out accordingly, under which the defendants were arrested, and thereupon entered into bail bonds. The plaintiff was then, and still continued to be, detained in the custody of the sheriff of Leicestershire at the suit of the defendants, for non-payment of 11*l.*18*s.* 6*d.*, the costs of the motion.

---

(1) *In re Wickham* (1887) 35 Ch. D.   *Sutton*, (1897) 2 Ch. 367, 66 L. J. Ch.
272, 56 L. J. Ch. 748; *Graham* v.   666, 77 L. T. 35, C. A.

The VICE-CHANCELLOR having refused a motion, on behalf of the defendants, that the attachments against them might be set aside for irregularity, and that the bail-bonds might be ordered to be cancelled, the motion was renewed before the Lord Chancellor, by way of appeal.

Mr. Wakefield and *Mr. G. L. Russell*, in support of the motion :

By the seventy-eighth ordinance of Lord Bacon (1) it *is declared that, " they that are in contempt, especially so far as proclamation of rebellion, are not to be here, neither in that suit, nor any other, except the Court of special grace suspend the contempt" (1). Whether this is to be read that a party in contempt shall not be here, that is, in Court, or shall not be heard, as suggested by Mr. Beames, it equally precludes a person in the situation of the plaintiff from suing out an attachment against defendants in default for want of answer. * * Reference has been made for the purposes of the present case to the Clerks-in-Court and to the Registrars. Of the former, thirteen have signed a certificate stating that, according to what they conceive to be the universal practice, a *plaintiff in contempt cannot sue out an attachment for want of an answer ; and the Registrars, with one exception, entertain the same opinion. * * *

[*198]

[*199]

Mr. Bethell, contrà :

 * * Lord Bacon's ordinance, if construed literally, is not the rule at the present day ; for it is perfectly settled that a party in contempt in one cause may, notwithstanding, be heard in another ; and that, even in the same cause, he may be heard to defend himself against any proceeding by which his adversary brings him into Court, or in which even the latter has been guilty of irregularity. *Lord Bacon's ordinance was intended to have reference exclusively to defendants who were in contempt, and not to plaintiffs. At all events it has never been construed as applicable, in practice, to attachments sued out for want of answer, which, at no period in our legal history, were proceedings in Court,

[*200]

(1) Beames' Orders, 35.

WILSON
v.
BATES.

but were always obtained, without motion, on the mere application of the party at the proper office. * * *

March 30.   THE LORD CHANCELLOR:

The question raised on this application was, whether the plaintiff, being himself in contempt for non-payment of a sum of money for costs, was entitled to sue out an attachment against the defendants for not answering the bill : and this, in effect, involved another question, viz. whether, under such circumstances, he could take any step in the cause ; for, if he could not compel an answer, of course the cause would be entirely stopped.

No case upon the point was produced ; and the argument was mainly grounded upon the seventy-eighth ordinance of Lord Bacon. That ordinance, although the foundation of the practice,

[*201]

can only be construed *now by the practice which has since prevailed with reference to it. It is quite obvious that its terms, if strictly acted upon, would produce a very different state of practice from that which is recognised in modern times. If I had to decide upon that in the first instance, and were called upon to settle a rule for future guidance, I certainly never should lay down any such rule. It would seem extraordinary that a party, who may not be able to pay the costs of a refused motion, should be therefore absolutely stopped from asserting his rights. At the same time, if the practice be established, it would not be for me to alter it.

Now, although it may be generally true that a party in contempt cannot be heard to make a motion, he is nevertheless permitted to be heard upon a motion to get rid of that contempt, a case for which, so far as I can see, Lord Bacon's ordinance makes no provision. It is also well settled, that if a party in contempt is brought into Court by any proceedings taken against him, he has a right to be heard in his defence, and in opposition to those proceedings ; another case which is inconsistent with Lord Bacon's ordinance, if construed strictly.

The real question, therefore, comes after all to be, what is the present practice. Decision, it is admitted, there is none. A certificate, signed by a number of the Clerks-in-Court, has been produced, not alleged to be founded on any authority, but stating the opinion of the individuals who sign it, that a party in contempt cannot do that which the plaintiff has done in the present instance. The certificate is valuable, no doubt, from the experience of those individuals, speaking to what they consider the universal practice; but no case is referred to in support of the opinion; and if I find *that the practice is not and cannot be as they have supposed, its value entirely fails. According to them, if a plaintiff gets into contempt, the cause is absolutely stopped. If that were so, of course a plaintiff in contempt could never bring his cause to a hearing without clearing his contempt. On this point there is not an absence of authority; for in the case of *Wild* v. *Hobson* (1) the very question must have arisen. The plaintiff, in the course of that cause, had made two motions to enlarge publication, in both of which, having failed, he was ordered to pay the costs of them, and attachments had issued against him for non-payment. This took place on the 2nd and 28th of November, 1818. Now, according to what the certificate states to be the practice, the first suing out of the attachment put a stop to the plaintiff's further proceedings; there was an end of his power to advance a single step with his cause. Nevertheless, it appears that the cause actually came on for hearing on the 29th of January, 1819, the plaintiff being then in contempt; and that the costs of his contempt were made matter of arrangement, and were provided for in the decree. That at once brings to the test the accuracy of the certificate that a plaintiff in contempt cannot go on. I also find that in the case of *Ricketts* v. *Mornington* (2), before the present Vice-Chancellor, the same question arose. There, the plaintiff in contempt brought on his cause to a hearing. According to the certificate, how could he have done it? The Six-clerk who had the management of that cause could not have been aware that the practice was as stated in the certificate. The plaintiff could not have *taken a single step, according to the terms of Lord Bacon's ordinance, whether it be read "here" or "heard;" and yet when the cause came on for hearing, although a party in

[*202]

[*203]

(1) The proceedings in the cause of *Wild* v. *Hobson* appeared from entries in the Registrar's book for the year 1818, B. fols. 20, 201, and 490, with extracts from which the Lord Chancellor was furnished by Mr. Colville, one of the Registrars.

(2) 40 R. R. 107 (7 Sim. 201).

contempt, and therefore not to be heard, here he was, asking
a decree.   It was objected that he could not do so because he was
in contempt; but the VICE-CHANCELLOR over-ruled the objection,
and he *was* heard; and that decision has been acquiesced in.
So much for what is said to be the universal practice of not permitting a plaintiff to go on under such circumstances. Universal,
certainly it is not; for here are two reported cases in which the
particular facts stated show a course of proceeding adopted,
incompatible with the practice alleged by the certificate to prevail.

The question has also been raised indirectly in other cases,—
in those cases, I mean, in which, the plaintiff being in contempt,
the defendant has applied to the Court to stay further proceedings
until the costs of the contempt shall have been paid. If the
circumstance of a plaintiff being in contempt of itself puts an end
to his power of proceeding, that would be an unnecessary and
useless step on the defendant's part. Instead of that, the defendant would be content to remain passive and quiescent. Such,
however, is not the course taken by parties litigant, or sanctioned
by the practice of the Court: the course is, for the Court, upon
a motion for that purpose, and not before, to make an order staying
the proceedings until the plaintiff has paid the prior costs; that
is to say, it makes a special order.   In *Eddowes* v. *Neville*, before
Lord Hardwicke, according to the note with which I have been
furnished by the Registrar (1), the defendant moved that all pro-
[*204]   ceedings under a writ *of execution of the decree might be
suspended until the plaintiff should have paid certain costs, for
non-payment of which she was in prison; and the *Attorney-
General*, on behalf of the plaintiff, thereupon applied that an
attachment might issue against the defendant: and the Court
made a special order, adjudicating upon the whole matter. So,
in another case of *Price* v. *Dalton* (2), before the same Judge, upon
a motion by the defendant that all proceedings for want of answer
might be stayed until the plaintiff had paid certain costs, the Court
gave the defendant three weeks' time to answer, after the costs
should have been paid. These cases clearly recognise the propriety of the application to stay proceedings; and they tend to
show, moreover, that though a plaintiff may be in contempt to an

(1) Mr. Colville.   (2) July, 1745.

attachment, he has still a right to the process of the Court to compel an answer, or to prosecute his suit, if the defendant does not apply specially that proceedings may be stayed.

In the absence of all authority to support the proposition contended for, and with the cases I have referred to, which, though not expressly in point, are in direct contradiction to the statement in the certificate, and having no disposition whatever to extend the practice of the Court in the construction of Lord Bacon's ordinance beyond what I find to be established, I am of opinion that the VICE-CHANCELLOR was right in what he has done, and the

Motion must therefore be refused.

WILSON
v.
BATES

IN THE MATTER OF THE OXFORD CHARITIES.

(3 My. & Cr. 239—244; S. C. 1 Jur. 620.)

Property appropriated by a municipal corporation, to the maintenance of lecturers to preach before the corporation, is not property held by the corporation upon a charitable trust, within the meaning of the seventy-first section of the Act 5 & 6 Will. IV. c. 76.

[PREVIOUSLY to the Act 5 & 6 Will. IV. c. 76 regulating Municipal Corporations (repealed by the Municipal Corporations Act, 1882, s. 5), certain funds belonging to the corporation of Oxford had been invested by the corporation in the names of the mayor, recorder, and aldermen, and by deed dated the 28th January, 1778, to which they were parties, it was declared that the said investments were held by them] in trust for the maintenance of four lecturers, to preach before the mayor and corporation of Oxford, at such times and place as they should from time to time appoint, a sermon in the forenoon, and another in the afternoon, upon every Sunday throughout the year; and to pay unto, [or permit the said four lecturers to receive the income thereof equally, share and share alike. And it was thereby provided] that the said lecturers should, from time to time, be nominated and chosen by the mayor, recorder, aldermen, and assistants, *of the city of Oxford, for the time being, or the major part of them, by ballot; and should be masters of arts, or bachelors of law, or superior graduates of the University of Oxford, who should be generally resident there, and in holy orders].

1837.
Aug. 1, 2.

Lord
COTTENHAM,
L.C.

[239]

[241]

[*242]

17—2

It was also provided, that every person so elected to be a lecturer should continue such until his death, resignation, or removal; and that, so often as three fourths of the number of electors for the time being should, in their discretion, think proper to remove any such lecturer, they should have power so to do, in a particular manner. * * *

[243] Ever since the date of this indenture, four lecturers have been from time to time chosen in pursuance of its provisions.

[By s. 71 of 5 & 6 Will. IV. c. 76, special provision was made for the future administration of property held by any corporation upon any charitable trust.]

Sir C. Wetherell, for certain petitioners, contended that these lectureships came within the operation of the seventy-first section of the Act of Parliament. * * *

Mr. Blunt, contrà, for the corporation of Oxford.

Mr. Goodere [for other persons].

THE LORD CHANCELLOR:

It appears that this was a sum of money given to the corporation of Oxford, in terms which gave them a right to dispose of it as they pleased, and that they thought proper to appropriate it to the endowment of four lectureships, and to apply the income to the payment of the four lecturers. The question now is, whether that be or be not a charitable trust, within the meaning of the seventy-first section of the Municipal Corporation Regulation Act. It may be so far for the benefit of the corporation, that every member of the corporation may have a right to insist, that it shall not be appropriated to any purposes beyond the limits of the corporation. I do not apprehend that the seventy-first section of the Act of Parliament meant to take away any funds exclusively appropriated for a corporate purpose. I consider the appropriation of this property in the same light as if the corporation had appropriated it to the maintenance of any other officer for the corporation, and for the corporation exclusively. If the property be now carried to trustees, the
[*244] trustees who *will be the persons to pay will also be the persons

to appoint, and the appointment may then be for the benefit of the inhabitants of Oxford, but no longer for the benefit of the corporation exclusively.

If this be not a charitable trust, for purposes *dehors* the corporation, it is not within the seventy-first section, and never was in the hands of the corporation, subject to be dealt with, by the members of the corporation, as a charitable trust. If this be a charitable trust at all, it is a charitable trust within the limits of the corporation. The corporation may say, the sermons shall be preached to themselves with closed doors; for there is no provision that they shall be preached in any particular church. The whole trust is exclusively for the corporation; the congregation of no one church can claim it.

There is no middle course; the property must either be left in the corporation, or it must be handed over to trustees, who will then have the power of appointing the lecturers. I find the property subject to no trust, except for the benefit of the corporation; and I therefore think, that it is not within the seventy-first section of the Act of Parliament.

BACON *v.* CLARK.

(3 My. & Cr. 294—301.)

A trustee for sale of property in India duly converted the property, but allowed the proceeds to remain in the Indian house of business in which he was a partner. By the terms of the trust the proceeds were to be remitted to England at the request in writing of the settlor and his wife first made. No such request was made until after the death of the trustee, who had retired from the business, leaving the proceeds in the hands of his partners, by whom the proceeds were subsequently invested by the direction of the settlor. The trust fund was subsequently lost by the bankruptcy of the Indian house of business: Held, that the estate of the deceased trustee must make good the loss.

1836.
Nov. 29.

1837.
Nov. 15.

——

Lord
COTTENHAM,
L.C.

[294]

THIS was an appeal from a decree of the VICE-CHANCELLOR. The facts of the case are sufficiently stated in the LORD CHANCELLOR's judgment.

THE LORD CHANCELLOR:

The decree of the VICE-CHANCELLOR declares that the estate of William Fairlie is liable to make good a sum of 10,000*l.*, and

1837.
Nov. 15.

[295]

BACON
v.
CLARK.

gives the usual directions to enforce the payment of it. The question upon the appeal is, whether W. Fairlie's estate is liable to the payment of this sum.

W. Fairlie was a trustee under a deed of settlement of the 12th of August, 1806. It appears, from the recitals in that deed, that John Fergusson Bacon, who was then at Calcutta, and had certain property there, which he was desirous of selling, discharged of his wife's dower, procured her to levy a fine for that purpose; and, as a compensation to her, agreed with W. Fairlie as her trustee, that he would forthwith, or as soon as conveniently might be, raise a sum of 10,000*l.*, and settle the same upon her and the issue of the marriage, and that, in order to raise that sum, he had agreed to appoint the property of which the fine had been so levied, to W. Fairlie, in trust to sell, as after directed, and to execute a bond to him in 160,000 sicca rupees, for making good any deficiency, and to secure to Mrs. Bacon and the issue of the marriage the net and clear sum of 10,000*l.* The deed then proceeded to appoint and convey the premises to W. Fairlie in fee, upon trust to sell the same as soon as conveniently might be, for the purpose of raising the said sum of 10,000*l.*, or so much as the premises would produce, with the usual powers to give receipts for the purchase money: and it was provided that as soon as W. Fairlie, his heirs, executors, administrators, or assigns, should have realised the net and clear sum of 10,000*l.* by means of the sale of the premises or by means of the bond, and should, at the request

[*296]

and direction of Mr. and Mrs. Bacon, in *writing under their hands or the hand of the survivor for that purpose being to him first made, have remitted the same to England to Henry Slade, John Davis, and John Slade, or the survivor of them, or the executors or administrators of such survivor, in the best, and, as to him, his heirs, executors, administrators, and assigns should seem the most eligible manner, then and immediately after, he, W. Fairlie, his heirs, executors, and administrators should stand discharged of the trusts, and should not be answerable for the payment of the bill or bills in or on which the same should be remitted, or for any loss or misapplication or non-application of the said sum of 10,000*l.* further than for his or their wilful default or neglect.   And it was declared that Henry Slade, John Davis, and John Slade, when they should have received the 10,000*l.*, should, with all convenient speed, invest the same in Government or real security, upon trust for Mrs. Bacon for life, with remainder upon trust for their children, equally, at twenty-one, or marriage of daughters.   And it was declared that W. Fairlie should, until the sale be seised of the premises, and after the sale, and until the money to arise from the sale should be remitted as aforesaid, should stand interested in the proceeds upon the same trusts, and for the same intents and purposes as before expressed and declared of and concerning the 10,000*l.* so to be remitted to the trustees.

In execution of these trusts, W. Fairlie sold the property in the year 1811, though the purchase of the whole was not completed until the year 1813, and the proceeds amounted to above 145,000 sicca rupees, which much exceeded the value of the 10,000*l.*, the rate of exchange being admitted to have been at that time at 2*s.* 6*d.* the sicca rupee.   In 1825 W. Fairlie died, and the defendants, David Clark, John Innes, and James Fairlie, are *his executors.   In the year 1827 John Fergusson Bacon, the settlor and tenant for life, died.   The plaintiffs are the only children of the marriage.   The 10,000*l.* never was remitted to Henry Slade, John Davis, and John Slade, and the plaintiffs therefore call upon the executors of William Fairlie to pay the 10,000*l.*

[*297]

Such is the *primâ facie* case of the plaintiffs, which, if the defendants cannot show good ground for the discharge of the estate of William Fairlie from this liability, undoubtedly entitles them to the decree which has been pronounced.

The circumstances upon which the defence is founded are the following: That W. Fairlie was a partner in the house of Fairlie, Fergusson, & Co., of Calcutta, which firm were the agents at Calcutta of Mr. Bacon: that W. Fairlie was himself in England at the time of the sale; and that, upon the completion of the sale, in the year 1813, a sum of 80,000 sicca rupees, being then of the value of 10,000*l.*, was, by the direction of W. Fairlie, set apart by Fairlie, Fergusson, & Co., out of the proceeds of the sale received by them, and carried to an account

of W. Fairlie and Hugh Reid, trustees of the settlement : that
the 80,000 sicca rupees continued on that account in 1818, when
W. Fairlie retired from the firm, and until 1826, when, at the
request of Mr. Bacon, Messrs. Fergusson & Co. invested it in a
note of the East India Company, of 80,000 sicca rupees, in the
names of the partners in the house of Fergusson & Co., and not
of the trustees of the 10,000*l.* : that, in 1832, Mrs. Bacon having
called upon the executors of W. Fairlie to procure a remittance
to this country of the 10,000*l.*, they directed the house of
Fergusson & Co. to do so, in bills payable to Henry Slade and
John Slade, the surviving trustees : that the house of Fergusson

[*298] & *Co. thereupon sold the note of the East India Company, and
drew a bill (1) upon the firm, in London, of Fairlie, Clark,
Innes, & Co., payable to the executors of W. Fairlie ; but, before
the bill arrived, the drawees, Fairlie, Clark, Innes, & Co., had
stopped payment, and Fergusson & Co., the drawers, also
failed (2), so that nothing has been received from that bill.
These facts are all stated in parts of the answer read by the
plaintiffs ; and there was also read a letter from W. Fairlie, to
Fairlie, Fergusson, & Co., dated the 20th of May, 1812, directing
them to transfer a sum equal to 10,000*l.* into the name of the
trustee of the settlement, being himself (3), and to hold the
residue to answer Mr. Bacon's drafts.

Upon this state of facts, three points were made for the
defendants : 1. That no breach of trust had been committed by
W. Fairlie.   2. If there had, that it was cured by the purchase
of the East India Company's note.   3. That the rights of the
plaintiffs were limited to such an amount of pounds sterling as
the 80,000 sicca rupees, set apart in 1813, are now equal to, and
that they are not entitled to demand the whole 10,000*l.*

The first point does not appear to me to be very important,
because, whether a breach of trust was committed or not, as
W. Fairlie received the proceeds of the property out of which the

---

(1) This bill was for 7,979*l.* 1*s.* 9*d.*
being the value of 80,000 sicca rupees,
according to the then rate of exchange
(1*s.* 11*d.*), and certain interest.

(2) Before the bill became due.

(3) The expression in the letter
was, "Let the transfer of the 10,000*l.*
be made in the name of the trustees
for the settlement ; I believe Captain
Reid and myself."

10,000l. was to be paid, his estate must remain liable to pay
what is due in respect of that sum, unless payment or a
sufficient *excuse for non-payment can be shown; but I have
not any doubt of a breach of trust having been committed.
W. Fairlie, who was solely entitled to receive the proceeds of the
sale, and out of them to appropriate the 10,000l., permits, in
the year 1813, the house in which he was a partner to receive
the money, and to hold it till his death in 1825, and even after
he quitted the firm in 1818.   Either this was his possession, in
which case what happened to that firm is immaterial; or it was
a lending the trust money to this company, without security,
which would clearly be a breach of trust.   It was said that he
could not remit the trust money without the direction of Mr.
and Mrs. Bacon; but it is to be observed that, by the deed, he
had no right to appropriate the 10,000l., and to separate it from
the rest of the proceeds of the sale, except for the purpose
of remitting it to the trustees; for until that was done, he
was to hold the proceeds subject to the same trusts as were
declared of the 10,000l.; that is, the whole proceeds were to be
liable to the payment of the 10,000l. until it was actually
remitted.   This, if acted upon, would have insured the direction
to remit from Mr. Bacon.   The payment to Fairlie, Fergusson,
& Co., or permitting them to receive and retain the proceeds
of the sale; the appropriation of the 10,000l. by them under the
direction of W. Fairlie; the payment of the interest to Mr.
Bacon, and the payment to him of the residue of the proceeds,
were all in direct violation of W. Fairlie's duty as trustee, and
each constituted a breach of trust; and this view of the trusts
of the deed at once disposes of the point that the plaintiffs'
title is not to 10,000l., but to the proceeds of 80,000 sicca
rupees so appropriated.   It is quite clear to me that the whole
proceeds of the estate were to be liable to realise the 10,000l.
when it should be remitted, and, consequently, that the plaintiffs are entitled to have that sum realised in this country at
this time.

But then it is said that the purchase of the note of the East
India Company cured all former omissions or breaches of trust,
because, when that took place, the fund was in a proper state

BACON
v.
CLARK.

of investment.   Whether such a mode of investment would, under any circumstances, be a discharge, need not be considered; because if W. Fairlie was, at the time of his death, personally liable to realise the 10,000*l.* in this country, as I think he certainly was, his estate must remain liable to that debt, unless his representatives can show payment or something equivalent to it.   How then can an act of the house of Fergusson & Co., acting under the direction of Mr. Bacon after W. Fairlie's death, which did not lead to any payment of this debt, operate as a discharge of his estate from this debt?   The security was taken by Fergusson & Co., who were strangers to the trust, in their own names; and they sold the security, and received the proceeds.   Similar observations apply to the bill drawn by Fergusson & Co. upon Fairlie, Clark, Innes, & Co., in London.

The deed undoubtedly intended to protect the trustee, W. Fairlie, if, acting to the best of his judgment, he had purchased a bill of good credit upon England for the purpose of remitting the 10,000*l.*; but the bill in question was not drawn by him or by his representatives, and could not, at the time, have been a bill entitled to any credit, and it was not a bill purchased with the trust fund, but a mode adopted by the debtor for payment, which failed, and which therefore left the debt as before.   W. Fairlie, in violation of his duty as trustee, and in breach of his trust, permitted the trust fund to remain in the hands of private traders, Messrs. Fergusson & Co., and in their hands it has been lost; their buying and afterwards selling the East India Company's bill, and their bill [*301] drawn upon the London house, which was never paid, *are transactions from which the estate of W. Fairlie can derive no protection.   Had those transactions operated to reproduce the trust fund, they would, *pro tanto*, have released his estate, by satisfying the demand upon it; but, as they were wholly unprofitable for that purpose, that liability remains unaffected by them.

I have, therefore, no hesitation in

Affirming the Vice-Chancellor's decree with costs.

Mr. *Treslove*, Mr. *Koe*, and Mr. *Hallett*, for the plaintiffs.

The *Solicitor-General* and Mr. *Blunt*, for the defendants, the executors of Fairlie.

Mr. *Wakefield*, and Mr. *Purvis*, for Mrs. Bacon the widow.

Mr. *W. Robertson*, for the trustees, Henry Slade and John Slade (now Sir John Slade).

BACON
v.
CLARK.

THE MARQUESS OF EXETER *v.* THE MARCHIONESS OF EXETER AND OTHERS (1).

(3 My. & Cr. 321—326; S. C. 7 L. J. (N. S.) Ch. 240; 2 Jur. 335.)

The Court being satisfied, upon the evidence, that a general description of property had been inserted inadvertently in a settlement, and not for the purpose of passing an estate, which the general description would in terms comprise, made a declaration that the general description had been inserted by mistake, so far as regarded the estate in question, and gave the parties liberty to apply as they might be advised.

1837.
Dec. 22.
1838.
Jan. 31.
June 22.

Lord
COTTENHAM,
L.C.
[321]

UPON the treaty of marriage between the plaintiff and the defendant, the Marchioness of Exeter, then Isabella Poyntz, daughter of W. S. Poyntz, Esq., written proposals for a settlement were, by the plaintiff's directions, drawn up by his solicitors, Messrs. Foulkes, Langford, and Walford, and by them submitted to the solicitors employed on behalf of Miss Poyntz, Messrs. Forster, Frere, and Cook, by whom, after some alterations, they were finally agreed to and adopted.

The proposals stated that Lord Exeter would convey a portion of his estates, to be thereafter agreed on, to trustees, in the first place, for securing an annual sum of 350*l.*, for pin money for Miss Poyntz, during the joint lives of herself and Lord Exeter, and subject thereto, to the use of his Lordship for life; and after his decease, for securing a jointure of 4,000*l.* a year to Miss Poyntz, if she survived him, to be reduced however to 3,000*l.* a year in the event of her becoming entitled in possession to one third of her mother's estates; and, subject to this jointure, to trustees, in the usual manner, for raising sums, not exceeding 20,000*l.* in the whole, as portions for younger children; with

[322]

(1) *White* v. *White* (1872) L. R. 15 Eq. 247, 42 L. J. Ch. 288, 27 L. T. 752.

THE
MARQUESS OF
EXETER
v.
THE MAR-
CHIONESS OF
EXETER.

remainders to the use of the first and other sons of the marriage,
and their issue male, and on failure of such issue, to the use
of Lord Exeter, his heirs and assigns.

A list of the names and rentals of the several estates intended
to be comprised in the settlement, and the total rental of which
was stated at the sum of 20,934*l.*, was subsequently laid before
Messrs. Forster, Frere, and Cook, on behalf of Miss Poyntz, for
their approbation; and, after some slight variations, was finally
agreed to.   In this list the estates were arranged alphabetically
under the counties in which they were respectively situate: the
only Lincolnshire estates specified in it were Bourne, Bourne
Fen Lands. and Morton, of which the rentals were stated at
1,528*l.* 12*s.*, 279*l.* 4*s.*, and 275*l.* 13*s.* respectively.

Shortly afterwards, an indenture of settlement was executed,
dated the 8th of May, 1824, by which the estates therein specified
and described were conveyed by Lord Exeter to uses and upon
trusts similar to those stated in the proposals.   In the deed,
after a particular enumeration and description, by their parcels
and occupying tenants, of the several estates therein comprised,
situate in the counties of Northampton, Bedford, Buckingham,
[*323] *and Lincoln, which estates corresponded exactly with those
enumerated in the list before mentioned, came these words,
"and all other the manors, messuages, lands, tenements,
hereditaments, and premises of the said Marquess of Exeter,
within the said counties of Northampton, Bedford, Buckingham,
and Lincoln."

The marriage of the plaintiff and Miss Poyntz was solemnised
a few days after the execution of the settlement, and there were
issue of the marriage four children.

Besides, the Lincolnshire estates enumerated in the list, and
specifically mentioned and described in the settlement, the
plaintiff, at the time when he executed it, was also seised in fee
simple of another estate in the county of Lincoln, within the
borough of Stamford, commonly called the Stamford estate,
extending over several parishes within the borough of Stamford,
and yielding a rental of nearly 5,000*l.* a year.

Doubts having arisen, whether, by force of the general words
before stated, the Stamford estate was not, by legal construction,

comprised in the indenture, so as to pass by the conveyance and be subject to the uses of the settlement, the present bill was filed to have it declared that the estate in question was not intended to be so comprised, and ought to be released from the trusts thereof, and that the general words had been inserted by mistake; and to have the mistake rectified.

THE
MARQUESS OF
EXETER
v.
THE MAR-
CHIONESS OF
EXETER.

Samuel Forster (one of the partners in the house of Forster, Frere, and Cook) identified a paper writing, marked B, as being the list of the estates which were proposed and intended to be settled by the plaintiff, and which were agreed to by all parties as the estates to be comprised in the settlement. He further deposed that it was his firm conviction and belief, that the plaintiff did *not intend that any other estate besides those enumerated in the list should be included in the parcels contained in the settlement; and that it was never proposed, either by or to him (the deponent) as the acting solicitor of the lady, that any other estates besides those named in the produced list should be settled by the plaintiff on the occasion of his marriage: that no instructions were ever given by the plaintiff to the deponent, or, to the best of his knowledge, to any other person, that the general words in question should be inserted in the settlement; and that he could only, therefore, account for their insertion by supposing that they had been introduced inadvertently, or merely for the purpose of including any of the lands specified in the list, which might possibly have been omitted in the description given of them in the parcels.

[*324]

It appeared upon an inspection of the document marked B, that the estates specified in it were the same as those described in the settlement, exclusive of the general words which were used in the settlement, and, of course, exclusive of the Stamford estate.

It was proved, by the evidence of Mr. Walford the younger, a partner in the house of Walford & Sons, who were the successors in business of Messrs. Foulkes, Langford, and Walford, that he had found, tied up with the proposals and the other papers relating to the settlement, a list of the estates proposed to be settled, and that on comparing the parcels contained in the settlement, they fully and accurately described the parishes and townships within which the estates named in the list were situate, together with

THE
MARQUESS OF
EXETER
c.
THE MAR-
CHIONESS OF
EXETER.

[*325]
the names of the occupying tenants, and that they did not
mention or include any other lands beyond those specified in
such list, except by the general words. The same witness farther
deposed that the Stamford estate *was, in point of rental, double
the value of any of the estates mentioned and enumerated in the
settlement, and that the number of tenants upon it amounted to
380 ; that it was not in any manner comprised or included in
the list; and that neither the estate nor any of the townships or
parishes within which it was situate, nor any of the occupying
tenants thereof, were mentioned by name in the settlement.

Sir C. Wetherell and *Mr. Jemmett*, in support of the bill,
submitted first, that from the instruments on which the settlement was based, namely, the proposals and list, it was obvious
that the Stamford estate was never meant to be included in it ;
secondly, that the evidence with respect to the object and intention of the parties was such as to be clearly admissible ; and
thirdly, that that evidence, if admitted, placed beyond a doubt
the existence and nature of the mistake, which the Court, as it
had the means, so it had also the jurisdiction to rectify.   They
referred to *Rogers* v. *Earl* (1), *Thomas* v. *Davis* (2), *Young* v.
Young (3), *Alexander* v. *Crosbie* (4), *The Duke of Bedford* v. *The
Marquess of Abercorn* (5).   *   *   *

Mr. Sidebottom, for some of the parties, did not deny the
jurisdiction of the Court; but he observed that the list which was
proved in the cause, came out of the hands of the Marchioness's
solicitor, and the evidence did not distinctly connect it either
with the proposal, or with any thing in the way of contract
between the parties.

[326]   *Mr. Barber* and *Mr. F. Walford* appeared for other parties.

The LORD CHANCELLOR, after remarking that there could be
no question as to the jurisdiction, said that although he saw
no difficulty in the case, he should look into the documentary
evidence and the depositions before making a decree.

(1) 1 Dick. 294.   (4) 1 Ll. & G. 145.
(2) 1 Dick. 301.   (5) 43 R. R. 200 (1 My. & Cr. 312).
(3) Cited in 1 Dick. 295 and 303.

THE LORD CHANCELLOR:

THE
MARQUESS OF
EXETER
v.
THE MAR-
CHIONESS OF
EXETER.

1838.
June 22.

I have looked through the pleadings in this cause, and the papers and the three exhibits, 1st, the proposal for a settlement, 2ndly, the list or particular of the estates proposed to be settled, and 3rdly, the settlement itself; and I am of opinion that the evidence (the two former documents being distinctly identified), brings the case within the principle upon which this Court exercises its jurisdiction of correcting mistakes in settlements.

It is, I think, clear that what is called the Stamford estate in Lincolnshire, no part of which is specified in the list, or described in the settlement, except under the words, "all other the manors, lands," &c. of Lord Exeter "within the counties of Northampton, Bedford, Buckingham, and Lincoln," was not intended to be included in the settlement; and that it formed no part of the proposal or of the contract, but was so included by mistake. I think, therefore, that the decree ought to declare that to be so, and direct a reconveyance of that estate (1).

The decree, as drawn up, merely declared that the general words had been inserted by mistake, so far as regarded the Stamford estate, and gave the parties liberty to apply, as they might be advised.

MILLINGTON *v.* FOX (2).

(3 My. & Cr. 338—355.)

1838.
March 16, 17,
23, 24.

Lord
COTTENHAM,
L.C.

[338]

The Court will grant a perpetual injunction against the use, by one tradesman, of the trade marks of another, although such marks have been so used in ignorance of their being any person's property, and under the belief that they were merely technical terms.

As a general rule, the costs of the cause should follow the result of the cause; but an exception will be made where a party has established his object by means of an unnecessary degree of litigation.

THE bill, which was filed on the 7th of August, 1834, stated that the plaintiffs, Crowley Millington and Thomas Isaac Millington, carried on, and had for many years carried on,

(1) But whether a reconveyance was necessary, qu.?—O. A. S.

(2) Approved in H. L., *Singer Machine Manufacturers* v. *Wilson* (1877) 3 App. Cas. 376, 391, 396, 47 L. J. Ch. 481; *Cellular Clothing Co.* v. *Maxton & Murray* [1899] A. C. 326, 334, 335, 341, 68 L. J. P. C. 72, 80 L. T. 809.

the business of manufacturing steel for sale, at Swalwell, Winlaton Mill, and Team, all in the county of Durham, near Newcastle, and at Greenwich, in Kent, and in Thames Street, London; and that the plaintiffs' works at Swalwell were known as " The Crowley Works : " that the business carried on by the plaintiffs was originally founded at the end of the seventeenth century, or in the early part of the eighteenth century, by a person of the name of Crowley, who invented or introduced a particular mode of manufacturing steel, which has ever since been followed by the plaintiffs and those whom they succeeded in business: that some descriptions of steel so manufactured were known as Crowley's German, or shear steel, and the same and other descriptions, by the name of Crowley steel: that about the year 1782, the plaintiffs' grandfather, Isaiah Millington, became a partner in the business, and that it has ever since been carried on by him or his descendants, either alone or with
[*339]   partners; and that, from the time at which *he entered the business, the firm has been known by the name of Crowley, Millington, & Co., and the steel manufactured by them has been known in the market by the name of Crowley steel, or Crowley Millington steel: that the steel manufactured by the plaintiffs and their predecessors has always been distinguished by certain marks upon the bars or pieces of steel so manufactured : that the principal of these marks was originally " Crowley," and afterwards " Crowley, Millington," or one of those names; and that such marks have been stamped on shear steel, faggot steel, cast steel, blistered steel, and coach-spring steel: that the letters " I. H." were, upwards of fifty years ago, introduced into the marks stamped on double shear steel made by the plaintiffs' firm, being the initials of the name of John Heppel, their principal workman in that steel.

The bill went on to state that the defendants, James Fox and Samuel Fox, had, for more than six years before the filing of the bill, carried on, at Sheffield, the business of manufacturers of steel, under the name of " Fox Brothers," or " Fox, Brothers, & Co. ; " and that they had manufactured considerable quantities of steel, which they had marked with the plaintiffs' before-mentioned marks ; and that they had so marked steel manufactured

by them, in order that it might be sold in the market as steel   MILLINGTON
manufactured by the plaintiffs; and further, that other persons   v.
besides the defendants had marked steel with the plaintiffs'   FOX.
marks; and that the defendants had bought the steel so marked
and sold it again. The bill charged that the defendants were
still in the habit of selling, or sending for exportation, great
quantities of steel stamped with the plaintiffs' marks.

The prayer of the bill was, that the defendants might account
to the plaintiffs for the profits made by them *by the sale of   [*310]
steel stamped with the plaintiffs' before-mentioned names or
marks, and might deliver up to be destroyed all steel not manufactured by the plaintiffs, but stamped with their names or
marks, and all instruments used or intended to be used in
making such marks; and that the defendants might be
restrained by injunction from stamping steel with the before-
mentioned names or marks, and from manufacturing or selling
steel so stamped.

The defendants' case was that the terms "Crowley" and
"Crowley Millington" were descriptive, not of the maker, but
of a particular quality of steel, and that these marks had been
used by them to a very limited extent, and in total ignorance of
the existence of the plaintiffs' business, and without any intention to defraud, and that as soon as the defendants were aware
of the plaintiffs' claim their solicitor wrote a letter on the 2nd of
August, 1834, to the defendants, explaining the circumstances,
disclaiming all future intention of using the marks, and offering
compensation for any injury or loss sustained by the plaintiffs
in consequence of such user. That letter was not received by
the plaintiffs until the 9th of August, 1834, two days after the
filing of the bill. On that same day] the plaintiffs obtained an   [350]
injunction against the use of the marks in question by the
defendants. This injunction was obtained *ex parte*, upon the
affidavits of one of the plaintiffs and of Mr. Milner, and the
defendants never attempted to dissolve it.

The cause now came on to be heard. [The result of the
evidence is sufficiently stated in the judgment for the purpose
of this report. The plaintiffs' solicitor stated that he had
applied to one of the defendants on the 28th of July, 1834, to

MILLINGTON ascertain whether they had used the marks, and that the
v.
Fox.   defendant declined to make any admission that his firm had
used the marks.]

> *Mr. Wigram* and *Mr. James Russell* argued the case for the
> plaintiffs.

> The *Solicitor-General* and *Mr. Stuart*, on behalf of the
> defendants.   *   *   *

[351]   *Mr. Wigram*, in the course of his reply, upon being asked
by the LORD CHANCELLOR whether he persisted in asking for the
account, said that he did not think it worth while to do so.

The LORD CHANCELLOR expressed an opinion that the plaintiffs
had made out a case which entitled them to an injunction,
but said that he doubted whether they were entitled to costs
as against the defendants, and should wish to hear the
plaintiffs' counsel further on that point, and to look into the
pleadings.

Mr. Wigram then contended that the plaintiffs were entitled
to the costs of the suit; and stated that the letter of the 2nd of
August, 1835, was directed to the plaintiffs' works near Newcastle; and that, the plaintiffs being then in London, the letter
did not reach them in London until the 9th of August, the day
on which the injunction was obtained.

1838.   THE LORD CHANCELLOR :
March 24.
——   The sole object I had in looking into the pleadings in this
[*352]   cause was to satisfy myself as to what ought to be *done with
respect to the question of costs; having previously come to the
conclusion that there was sufficient in the case to show that
the plaintiffs had a title to the marks in question; and they
undoubtedly had a right to the assistance of a court of equity
to enforce that title.   At the same time, the case is very different
from the cases of this kind which usually occur, where there has
been a fraudulent use, by one person, of the trade marks or
names used by another trader.

I see no reason to believe that there has, in this case, been a fraudulent use of the plaintiffs' marks.   It is positively denied by the answer; and there is no evidence to show that the defendants were even aware of the existence of the plaintiffs, as a company manufacturing steel; for although there is no evidence to show that the terms " Crowley," and " Crowley Millington," were merely technical terms, yet there is sufficient to show that they were very generally used, in conversation at least, as descriptive of particular qualities of steel.   In short, it does not appear to me that there was any fraudulent intention in the use of the marks.   That circumstance, however, does not deprive the plaintiffs of their right to the exclusive use of those names; and therefore I stated, that the case is so made out as to entitle the plaintiffs to have the injunction made perpetual.

With regard to the other part of the case, namely the account, it is of so infinitely minute importance that the plaintiffs have (very discreetly, in my opinion,) abandoned it.

The question remains, what is to be done as to the costs? Now, the question of costs in Chancery is left to the discretion of the Court.   That discretion ought to *be exercised, as far as possible, according to some principle; and I am very much disposed, as a general rule, to make the costs follow the result; because, however doubtful the title may be, or however proper it may be to dispute it, it is but fair that the party who really has the right should be reimbursed, as far as giving him the costs of the suit can reimburse him.   But then there is another object which the Court must keep in view, namely, to repress unnecessary litigation, and to keep litigation within those bounds which are essential to enable the parties to vindicate and establish their rights.   I find no fault with the filing the bill, provided the parties had not then had the letter of the 2nd of August, which has been referred to; for it appears that there was, on the 28th of July, an application by the plaintiffs, which was met by the defendants in a manner which justified the plaintiffs in filing the bill.   If that circumstance had been stated in the bill, it might have given the defendants some means of explaining it; but, at all events, it is in evidence.   On the

[*353]

MILLINGTON
v.
Fox.

2nd of August, however, the defendants took a very different
view of the case, and, on that day, they wrote a letter to the
plaintiffs, first of all attempting, as it is stated in the letter,
to find the person who acted as agent of the plaintiffs at
Sheffield ; and not being able to find him, they wrote a letter
to Newcastle, the place where the plaintiffs' manufactory was
carried on. By some accident, or in consequence of the neglect
of those who carried on the business of the plaintiffs at Newcastle, the letter did not reach London, where the plaintiffs then
were, until the 9th of August, two days after the bill was filed,
and the very day upon which the injunction was applied for,
and obtained. That was not the fault of the defendants. They
did, as early as the 2nd of August, all that it was in their power
to do to remedy the fault they had committed on the 28th

[*354]

of July. If the letter had been received *in London before
the bill was filed, the bill ought not to have been filed. That
letter gives the plaintiffs every thing they could be entitled to.
It states—what the answer also states—that from the time
at which an injunction had been obtained against another
party (with whom the defendants had no connection) they
ceased to use the marks, and had never since used them, and
did not intend to use them.

The letter, therefore, was an entire abandonment of that
which constituted the plaintiffs' demand ; and it also states
that, as to what had passed—ignorantly as they say—they
were willing to make compensation for any injury which the
plaintiffs might have sustained through the use of the marks
in question by the defendants. It therefore gave the plaintiffs
every thing which they did or could ask for by the suit which
they had instituted when the letter was received, but which they
had not instituted when the letter was sent. I am told that
some subsequent communication took place, which, if before me,
would take off the effect of that letter : but no such communications are in evidence ; and, seeing that letter in the answer,
it was quite competent for the plaintiffs so to deal with this
cause as to bring those facts before the Court. I can, however,
only deal with the case as it comes judicially before me.

Now I say, that having received that letter, it was not proper for the plaintiffs to apply, *ex parte*, for the injunction; or, if they had obtained an order for it, they should not have drawn up the order. That letter made it, as to costs at least, incumbent upon the plaintiffs to put to the test whether the defendants were sincere in their offer, and not to go on with the suit unless they found that they were insincere. The injunction was obtained, and has not been displaced. No attempt has *been made by the defendants to displace it. That is quite consistent with what is stated in their answer, and in the letter to which I have referred. For what purpose, then, was the suit prosecuted? Why simply, and only, for the sake of the account; which is so small that the plaintiffs abandon it at the hearing. Here, then, has been a very expensive suit, with no possible object but the account; which, when the cause comes on for hearing, the plaintiffs' counsel very properly abandons. Now, under these circumstances, I think that a great deal of very useless litigation has been carried on, and that a great deal of very improper expense has been incurred. It strikes me, therefore, that this is exactly a case in which the Court is repressing useless litigation by refusing the plaintiffs the costs of the cause. They waive the account. They must have a perpetual injunction against the use of the marks in question, but without the costs of the cause.

MILLINGTON
v.
FOX.

[*355]

POWYS *v.* MANSFIELD.

6 Simons, 528—565; reversed on appeal, 3 My. & Cr. 359—379; 7 L. J. (N. S.) Ch. 9; 1 Jur. 861.)

The proper definition of a person in *loco parentis* to a child is a person who means to put himself in the situation of the lawful father of the child, with reference to the father's office and duty of making a provision for the child.

A person may stand in *loco parentis* to a child, although the child lives with and is maintained by its father.

Parol evidence is admissible to prove that a person did mean to put himself in *loco parentis* towards a child, so far as relates to the child's future provision; and evidence of the declarations, as well as the acts of such a person, are admissible for that purpose.

If the presumption of law against double portions provided by a person in *loco parentis*, be attempted to be rebutted by parol evidence, it may be supported by evidence of the same kind.

Declarations of a person in *loco parentis* are admissible in evidence upon

1835.
Nov. 20, 21,
23, 24.
Dec. 4.

1836.
Feb. 23.
———
SHADWELL,
V.-C.

On Appeal.
1836.
Dec. 14, 16,
17, 19, 20.

1837.
Nov. 17.

Lord
COTTENHAM,
L.C.

[359]

POWYS
v.
MANSFIELD.

the question of his intention as to providing a double portion for a child to whom he stands in that relation.

A codicil republishing a will, makes the will speak as from the date of the codicil, for the purpose of passing after purchased lands; but not for the purpose of reviving a legacy revoked, adeemed, or satisfied.

[THE following statement of this case is taken from the report in 6 Simons.]

[6 Sim. 528]   Sir John Barrington was tenant for life with remainders to his first and other sons in tail-male, with remainder to his brother Fitzwilliam Barrington for life, with remainder to his first and other sons in tail-male, with remainder to himself in fee of an estate in the Isle of Wight, called the Swainston estate. Sir John was a bachelor, his brother Fitzwilliam was married, and [529]   had issue six daughters. In 1813 the eldest daughter married Sir Richard Simeon ; and, on that occasion, Sir J. Barrington, by a deed (1) to which his brother was not a party, charged his reversion in fee in the Swainston estate with the payment of 10,000*l.* to the trustees of the settlement, in trust for Sir Richard and Lady Simeon, for their lives successively, and, after the death of the survivor, for their children : and, on the same occasion, Sir John made a will, by which he gave his reversion in fee, to trustees, for 1,000 years, in trust to raise 50,000*l.*, which he gave to the five younger daughters of his brother, equally, on their attaining 21, or marrying ; and, subject thereto, he devised the reversion to Lady Simeon and her sisters for their lives successively, with remainders to their first and other sons in tail-male.

Sir John subsequently obtained a lease from Trinity College, Cambridge, of the rectory and tithes of Hadfield (2) Broad Oak, in Essex.

In the beginning of the year 1817, the plaintiff, Henry Philip Powys, with the knowledge and sanction of Sir John and of Fitzwilliam Barrington, paid his addresses to Julia, the third daughter of Fitwilliam Barrington, and a marriage was, afterwards, agreed upon between them.

Sir John, by his will dated the 28th of March, 1817, gave to his sister-in-law, Edith Mary Barrington, the wife of his brother, Fitzwilliam (after the death of the survivor of himself and brother)

(1) Prepared by his own solicitors   (2) *Sic.* Should be Hatfield.
see 3 My. & Cr. 360.

an annuity of 800*l*. for life, charged upon his reversion in fee
in the Swainston estate; and, subject thereto, he devised the
reversion to William Browne and the Rev. John *Mansfield for
the term of 1,000 years, upon the trusts thereinafter mentioned;
and, subject thereto, he gave his said reversion, and also all
his other real estates, except his lease of the rectory and tithes
of Hadfield Broad Oak, to his daughters successively in tail-male,
with remainder to his niece Louisa, wife of Sir Richard Simeon,
and eldest daughter of his brother, Fitzwilliam Barrington, for
her life, with remainder to her first and other sons successively
in tail-male, with remainders, in like manner, to his other nieces,
the younger daughters of his brother, for their lives, and to their
sons in tail-male successively.

And he gave the rectory and tithes to Browne and Mansfield,
in trust to accumulate the rents during the life of his brother,
Fitzwilliam; and, after the decease of the survivor of himself
and his brother, to sell the rectory and tithes, and invest the
proceeds in the usual securities, and to stand possessed thereof,
and of the monies which should arise and be accumulated from
the rents of the rectory and tithes during the life of his brother,
upon the trusts after mentioned.

And he gave all the 5*l*. per cent. stock which he might have
at his decease, or, in case those stocks should be paid off during
his lifetime, then all the new 4*l*. per cent. stock which he might
have at his decease, to the same trustees, upon trust to accumulate the dividends during the life of his brother, and, after the
decease of the survivor of himself and his brother, to stand
possessed of the stock and accumulations upon the trusts
thereinafter mentioned.

And he declared that the term of 1,000 years was limited to
Browne and Mansfield in trust, after the *decease of the survivor
of himself and his brother, in case they should both die without
leaving any issue male of their respective bodies, or in case either
of them should leave any such issue male and all such issue male
should die under the age of 21 years, then, immediately after the
death of such issue male under the age of 21 years, to levy and
raise, by sale or mortgage of the hereditaments comprised in the
term, such sum of money as would, with the monies to arise from

the rents of the rectory and tithes and from the accumulations
thereof, and from the sale of the rectory and tithes, and with
the 5*l.* per cent. or 4*l.* per cent. stock and the accumulations
thereof, make up the clear sum of 50,000*l.*, it being his will that
that sum should be raised by the means aforesaid, and that the
rents of the rectory and tithes and the accumulations thereof,
and the monies to arise from the sale thereof, and the 5*l.*
per cent. or 4*l.* per cent. stock and the accumulations thereof
should be first applied towards the raising of the 50,000*l.*; and
that the hereditaments comprised in the term should be liable to
raise the deficiency only.

And he directed the trustees to invest the 50,000*l.* in the usual
securities and to stand possessed thereof upon the trusts thereinafter mentioned : and, after directing one-fifth part of the 50,000*l.*
to be held upon trusts, for the benefit of his niece Jane Elizabeth
Barrington, the second daughter of his brother Fitzwilliam, and
her husband and issue (if any) and with limitations over corresponding with the trusts and limitations hereinafter mentioned
with respect to the share of his niece Julia, he directed the
trustees to pay the further sum of 10,000*l.*, being one other fifth
[*532]   part of *the 50,000*l.*, unto his niece, Julia Barrington, the third
daughter of his brother Fitzwilliam, for her life, and, after her
decease, in case she should leave any husband her surviving,
then to pay the dividends thereof to such surviving husband of
his niece Julia, for his life, and, after the decease of such surviving husband of his niece Julia, or, in case she should leave no
husband, then, after her decease, to stand possessed of the last-
mentioned sum of 10,000*l.* in trust for all and every the children
and child of his niece Julia who should be then living, and the
issue of any of them who should be then dead leaving issue,
such issue to take equally amongst them the shares of their
respective parents, equally to be divided between and amongst
such child and children and their issue as aforesaid, share and
share alike, and to be vested and transmissible interests in such
child and children at the usual periods, with benefit of survivorship
amongst such children and their issue respectively, in case of the
death of any of them before their respective shares should become
vested : and in case no child of his niece Julia, nor the issue of

any such child should obtain a vested interest in the said last-
mentioned sum of 10,000*l.*, then he directed his trustees to stand
possessed of that sum in trust for the person and persons who,
for the time being, should be entitled to his manors, messuages,
&c., thereinbefore devised, under the limitations thereinbefore
contained, and for such estate and interest, estates or interests,
as the same person or persons should be entitled to therein, or
as near thereto as the rules of law and equity would permit; it
being his will that, in the event of no child or children, nor the
issue of any child or children of his niece Julia obtaining a vested
interest in the last-mentioned sum of 10,000*l.*, *then that the
same should sink into and become incorporated with his said
manors, messuages, &c., thereinbefore devised, for the benefit of
the person and persons entitled thereto.

[*533]

And he directed that the remaining three fifth parts of the
50,000*l.* should be held upon trusts for the benefit of his nieces,
Ann Emma, Ellen Flack, and Mary, their husbands and issue
(if any), and with limitations over corresponding with the
trusts and limitations of the two other fifth parts: and he
directed that no part of the hereditaments comprised in the
term of 1,000 years, should be sold until some or one of the sums
of 10,000*l.* thereinbefore provided for his said five nieces and
their children, or some part thereof, should have become vested
in and payable to their children, nor until the other funds
out of which he had directed the 50,000*l.* to be raised, should
have been applied in payment of those sums of 10,000*l.*: and
he gave, to Edith Mary Barrington and her daughters, 100*l.*
each to buy mourning, and the residue of his personal estate
to his brother Fitzwilliam, and appointed him sole executor of
his will.

On the 20th of April, 1817, the proposals for the settlement
on the marriage of the plaintiff with Julia Barrington, were
forwarded, by Sir John or his solicitor, to the plaintiff.

The terms of the settlement having been arranged between Sir
John Barrington and the plaintiff, without any interference on
the part of Fitzwilliam Barrington, by an indenture dated the
2nd day of June, 1817, and made between the plaintiff and his
father and mother, Sir John Barrington, Julia Barrington, who

was described as the niece of Sir John Barrington and one *of
the daughters of Fitzwilliam Barrington, (who was not a party to
the deed,) and certain other persons, after reciting, (amongst
other things) the intended marriage, and that, in consideration
of the natural love and affection which Sir John Barrington had
and bore to his niece Julia Barrington, and for her advancement
in life, and to provide a maintenance for her, in addition to the
provision thereinafter made for her by the plaintiff's father and
mother and by the plaintiff, and for enabling the said Julia
Barrington to carry into effect the contract and agreement for a
settlement as thereinafter expressed, Sir John Barrington had
agreed to charge his reversion in fee in the Swainston estate with
the payment of the annual sums and sum in gross thereinafter
mentioned, in the event, and to be applied to the uses and upon
the trusts thereinafter expressed : and that it had been agreed,
between the plaintiff's father and mother, Sir John Barrington,
the plaintiff and Julia Barrington, that such provision and
settlement should be made for the plaintiff and Julia Barrington,
in the event of her surviving her intended husband, and also
for the issue of the intended marriage, and other settlements,
benefits, powers, provisoes and limitations as were thereinafter
expressed and contained : it was (amongst other things) witnessed
that, in performance of the recited agreement on the part of
Sir John Barrington, and for the considerations therein mentioned, and, particularly, in consideration of the natural love and
affection which Sir J. Barrington had and bore to Julia Barrington
his niece, Sir John Barrington covenanted with the plaintiff and
Julia Barrington that his reversion in fee in the Swainston
estate, and all other manors, messuages, &c., whereof Sir John
Barrington then received the rents for his life, should, after the
decease of the survivor of himself and his brother Fitzwilliam

*Barrington without issue male, but not before, or, in case there
should be any issue male of Sir John or of his brother living at
the death of such survivor, and all such issue male should afterwards die under 21, then after the death of such issue male,
stand charged with the payment, to the plaintiff for his life, of
an annual sum equal to the interest of a sum of 10,000_l._ at the
rate of 5_l._ per cent., and, after his decease, of the payment of the

like sum to Julia Barrington, for her life, and, after the decease
of the survivor, in case there should be any issue of the marriage,
and until some or one child, being a son, should attain 21, or,
being a daughter, should attain that age or be married, with the
payment, to the trustees of the settlement, of a like annual sum,
to be applied by them for the maintenance, education, and support of all the children of the marriage except an eldest or only
son, but in case there should be only one child, then for the
maintenance &c. of such child, or, otherwise, to suffer the same,
or such part or parts thereof as the trustees should think proper,
to accumulate for the benefit of any such children or child as the
case might be ; and, immediately after any such child, being a
son, should attain 21, or, being a daughter, should attain that
age or be married, or in case any child or children, being a son
or sons, should have attained 21, or, being a daughter or
daughters, should have attained that age or be or have been
married at the decease of the survivor of the plaintiff and Julia
Barrington, then, after the decease of the survivor of them, with
the payment of the gross sum of 10,000l. to the trustees, to be
held by them upon the trusts thereinafter declared : and Sir John
Barrington further covenanted that the annual sums should be
issuing and payable and raised and paid out of the rents of the
said hereditaments, *and that the plaintiff and Julia Barrington   [*536]
and the trustees should have, and they were thereby invested
with a power of distress, entry and sale for the levying thereof
on the premises ; and also that the annual sums, in case the
rents should, at any time, be insufficient, should be raised by
sale or mortgage of a competent part of the premises, and that
the 10,000l. when the same should become raisable, should be
raised by sale or mortgage of a competent part thereof : and Sir
John Barrington charged all the hereditaments then vested in or
belonging to him, and of which he then received the rents for his
life, and of which the reversion in fee was then vested in him,
with the payment of the same annual sums and the said sum of
10,000l. accordingly : and Sir John Barrington, for himself and
his heirs, covenanted with the trustees, to stand seised of the
reversion and fee-simple of the Swainston estate, to the use of
the trustees, their heirs and assigns, for enabling them to raise

the said sums in manner aforesaid, and, subject thereto, to the use of himself in fee : and it was thereby agreed between all the parties thereto, and Sir John directed that the trustees should stand possessed of the 10,000*l.* when raised, upon the following trusts, that is to say, in case there should be issue of the marriage an eldest or only son and one or more or other child or children who, being a son or sons, should attain 21, or, being a daughter or daughters, should attain that age or be married, then in trust for such child or children other than and except an eldest or only son, and if but one, then for such one child, his or her executors, &c., and, if more than one, equally to be divided amongst them, and to be vested and transmissible interests in them respectively at the ages and times aforesaid, and to be then paid to them if the 10,000*l.* should have become

[*537]   *raisable, but if not, then as soon as the same should become raisable. "And the same sum, and every part thereof shall be, and the same is hereby made, limited and settled so as to admit of and with benefit of survivorship between and amongst such children and their issue respectively, in case of the death of any one or more of them leaving issue respectively, before he, she or they shall have obtained a vested interest or vested interests in the said sum of 10,000*l.* under the trusts aforesaid : " and, in case there should be issue of the marriage an eldest or only son or only daughter and no other child or children, or, being such other child or children, in case no such child or children, or issue of such child or children should obtain a vested interest in the 10,000*l.*, then in trust for such eldest or only son or only daughter, as the case should be, and to vest in and be paid to him or her, at the respective times aforesaid : and, in case of the death of such eldest or only son or sons so becoming an only child, as the case should be, without having obtained a vested interest in the 10,000*l.* under the trusts aforesaid, leaving issue, then in trust for such issue, if more than one, share and share alike, and, if but one, then for such one absolutely, and to vest in and be paid to such issue at the like ages and times aforesaid, and in like manner as thereinbefore directed and declared concerning the said sum of 10,000*l.* in case and in the event of the same becoming vested and payable to any children or child of

the marriage (1) : and the trustees were directed, after the 10,000*l*.
should have become raisable, to invest the shares thereof which
should not be actually payable, in the usual securities, and to
apply a sufficient part of the interest for the maintenance,
*education and support of the persons presumptively entitled to
the principal, and to accumulate the residue of the interest for
the benefit of the same persons: and the trustees were empowered to apply one-fourth of the shares for the advancement
of the persons presumptively entitled thereto : provided that in
case Sir John Barrington, his heirs, devisees, or assigns, or other
the person or persons for the time being entitled to the hereditaments the reversion whereof was so charged as aforesaid, should,
either before or as soon as the 10,000*l*. should become raisable,
pay the sum of 10,000*l*. to the trustees, then the aforesaid
charges of the annual sums and of the gross sum of 10,000*l*.,
should cease : and, if such payment should be made in the lifetime of the plaintiff and Julia Barrington, the trustees were
directed to invest the same sum in the usual securities and pay
the interest to the plaintiff and to Julia Barrington for their
lives successively, in lieu of the annual sums made payable to
them as aforesaid, and, after the decease of the survivor of them,
the trustees were to stand possessed of the 10,000*l*., so to be paid
to them, upon the trusts thereinbefore declared concerning the
10,000*l*. charged on the reversion of the said hereditaments, and
in exoneration thereof (2).

The marriage was solemnized shortly after the execution of
the settlement.

On the 23rd of June, 1818, Sir John Barrington made a codicil
to his will, which was duly executed and attested, and was as
follows : " Whereas I have lately *conveyed, to the Vicar for the
time being of the parish of Hadfield Broad Oak in the county of
Essex, a messuage in the town of Hadfield Broad Oak called
Chalks, to be, for ever thereafter, held and enjoyed as a vicarage
house, but have reserved to myself, my heirs and assigns, the
pond or orchard on the east of the same premises, and which I
have since laid to the premises adjoining now in the occupation

---

(1) So in copy settlement.   settlement was correctly taken from
(2) The above statement of the   a copy of it.

of Thomas Cocks : now it is my will that such pond and orchard
shall, for ever hereafter, be attached to the same premises : and
I give and devise the same to the owners and proprietors of the
said premises, to be held and enjoyed by them in succession,
upon the same trusts and for the same uses, estates, &c. as the
said messuage shall be, from time to time, held and enjoyed :
also I give and dispose of the pew in the parish church of
Hadfield Broad Oak aforesaid, which also lately belonged to the
said premises called Chalks, and reserved by me as aforesaid,
unto and to the use of the proprietors and owners for the time
being of the Barrington estate in Essex, for ever hereafter : and
in all other respects I confirm my said will."

On the 7th of July, 1818, Sir John made another codicil,
which also was duly executed and attested ; but he did not
thereby alter any of the devises or bequests in his will or
former codicil.

On the 11th of July, 1818, Sir John wrote a letter to his
brother, from Barrington Hall, his seat in Essex, which was
as follows :

"MY DEAR BROTHER :

[*540]   "I should quit life with the greatest dissatisfaction, if I *did
not leave, in your hands, a written testimony of my full conviction of your unceasing affection and attention to me at all times :
and, beyond that, I have greatly to admire your never-failing
forbearance for so many years past, so as never to have been
induced, in any single instance, during that long period, to
deviate from it ; I mean with respect to the slightest intimation
that an advance of money might be desirable, if not necessary
to you : founding this, and with great truth, on a confidence in
me that I was always preparing to supply you with cash *en masse,*
not always readily attainable.   Whenever it has chanced to pass
over my imagination, at any time for years past, that I might
possibly survive you, I have always turned from it as the greatest
affliction that could possibly befall me.   I thank God it will now
happen otherwise in the natural course of succession.   I trust I
shall be found, on the whole, to have been more of a just than
an unjust steward.   When Louisa married, I was induced to

make a disposal of the Isle of Wight property for the benefit of your
family. On the marriage of Julia, I found occasion to make
another will, improved upon, I hope, by the destination of my
tithe property in Essex, in trust to form a consolidated fund,
eventually to aid the very heavy demands that will be found to
press upon the Isle of Wight estate. This will become a sum
of no inconsiderable amount. In the formation of these wills
I have acted, altogether, free from any personal consideration
whatsoever, following the order of priority of birth as the rule
for it. God bless you, my dear brother, my sister, and all your
six children. I remain, &c."

The testator died on the 5th of August, 1818, without issue,
leaving his brother Fitzwilliam, who thereupon *became Sir   [*541]
Fitzwilliam Barrington, his only brother and heir-at-law.

Julia, the plaintiff's wife, died in September, 1821, leaving
issue a son, her only child.

Jane Elizabeth Barrington remained unmarried. Ann Emma
Barrington died unmarried shortly after the testator. In May,
1824, Ellen Flack Barrington married I. G. Campbell, and died
in May, 1832, leaving two children, Walter and Charlotte.
I. G. Campbell died in 1830. In 1827 Mary Barrington married
T. Vandeleur, and died in 1829 without issue. Lady Barrington,
Sir Fitzwilliam's wife, died in 1829. Sir Fitzwilliam died on
the 26th September, 1832, having, by his will, given one moiety
of his personal estate to Jane Elizabeth Barrington, and the
other moiety to Walter and Charlotte Campbell, subject to the
payment of a legacy of 200l. to the plaintiff's son by his late
wife, and of a legacy of 100l. to each of the younger children
of his daughter, Lady Simeon, and of a legacy of 400l. to
T. Vandeleur, the husband of his late daughter Mary.

On Sir Fitzwilliam's death, Lady Simeon, Jane Elizabeth
Barrington, Philip Lybbe Powys, the infant child of the plaintiff
by Julia his late wife, and Walter Campbell, became the co-heirs
of Sir John Barrington, and Lady Simeon became tenant for
life in possession, with remainder to her eldest son in tail-male,
of the Swainston estate.

After Sir Fitzwilliam's death, a document in his own

Powys
v.
Mansfield.

[*542]

hand-writing, was found amongst his papers, containing *an account of the sums from time to time advanced to him by his brother, with the following words written under it. "Fifth August, 1818. My most revered, worthy and beloved brother departed this life at his seat Barrington Hall, Hadfield Broad Oak, Essex; and, in an interval of 38 years, as the above account shows, gave me, out of his private purse, 41,380*l.*, besides lots of money to my family not in this statement."

The bill was filed, in May, 1833, by Henry Philip Powys against the trustees of the will, Sir Richard and Lady Simeon and their eldest son, the trustees of the settlement, Philip Lybbe Powys, the infant child of the plaintiff by Julia his late wife, T. Vandeleur, Jane Elizabeth Barrington, and the two infant children of the late Ellen Flack Campbell. It alleged that, on the decease of Sir Fitzwilliam Barrington, the plaintiff became entitled, under the settlement, to receive the yearly sum of 500*l.* out of the Swainston estate, during his life, and under the will of Sir John Barrington, to receive the interest of 10,000*l.*, during his life: that the provision made by the settlement, was in addition to, and not in satisfaction of the provision made, by the will, for Julia Barrington, her husband and issue, inasmuch as Sir John did not (as Sir R. and Lady Simeon pretended) stand *in loco parentis* to Julia Barrington. The bill prayed that the annual sum of 500*l.* might be paid to the plaintiff, out of the rents of the Swainston estate; that Sir John's will might be established, and the trusts thereof performed; and that the 50,000*l.* might be raised, and the interest of one-fifth part thereof be paid to the plaintiff, during his life.

[543]

Sir Richard and Lady Simeon, by their answer, admitted that Mrs. Powys, before her marriage, lived with her parents, and was maintained and educated by her father, partly at his own expense: that Sir John Barrington always entertained the warmest affection for Sir Fitzwilliam and his family, and treated and considered them as the successors to his title and estates, and was anxious that they should maintain themselves in their proper rank of life; but that Sir Fitzwilliam's fortune was comparatively small, and insufficient to maintain him and his family according to Sir John's wishes; for which reasons Sir

John, invariably and at all times, took upon himself the relation
and duty of a parent towards Sir Fitzwilliam's children, and
constantly acted as such, and that he, in a great measure,
superintended their education, was invariably consulted in all
matters of importance relative to their welfare, and, particularly,
upon the marriages of such of them as were married; and that
he gave, to Sir Fitzwilliam, from time to time, sums amounting
to 40,000l. and upwards, for the purpose of maintaining himself
and family: that Sir John expressed, to divers members of his
family and other persons, his intention to dispose of his Isle of
Wight estates, in the event of failure of issue of himself and
of issue male of Sir Fitzwilliam, for the benefit of all Sir Fitzwilliam's daughters and the children of such daughters in tail,
successively, according to priority of birth, and to provide, for
each of the younger daughters and their husbands and children,
a sum of 10,000l. and no more: that Sir John, when he made his
will and long before, had taken upon himself the relation and duty
of a parent to Mrs. Powys and to all the other children of Sir
Fitzwilliam, and that he made the provision for her *by his will,
in discharge of such duty; that the plaintiff, on his marriage,
treated and negotiated with Sir John solely and exclusively;
and that, at the time of making the settlements and frequently
afterwards, Sir John declared his intention to be that the
provision made by him, by the settlement, for the benefit of the
plaintiff and his wife and their issue, should be in satisfaction
of the provision made, for Mrs. Powys, her husband and children,
by his will.

A music-master and a drawing-master, who had given lessons
to the young ladies, and a dress-maker who had been employed
by them, were examined as witnesses for the plaintiff. They
deposed that their bills were paid by Sir Fitzwilliam and Lady
Barrington.

Evidence was given, on the part of Sir Richard and Lady
Simeon and their son, for the purpose of proving, first, that
Sir John Barrington stood in loco parentis to his nieces; and,
secondly, to prove declarations, made by Sir John, that he
intended the settlement to be in lieu of the provision made by
his will for his niece Julia, her husband and issue.

Powys
v.
Mansfield.

[*544]

The witnesses deposed, as to the first point, as follows: That
Sir Fitzwilliam, in compliance with the wishes of Sir John,
resided near Sir John in the Isle of Wight, and maintained a
more expensive establishment than his income (which did not
exceed 400l. a year) would allow of: that Sir John and his
brother lived on the most affectionate terms with each other:
that, for several years, Sir John gave Sir Fitzwilliam 1,000l.
a year: that he took the greatest interest in his nieces, behaved

[*545]   to them as a father, and always acted towards them as *the
kindest of parents, not showing more partiality to one than to
another: that he frequently gave them pocket-money and
made them other presents, and, occasionally, advanced money
to defray the expense of their clothing and education: hat he
allowed them to use his horses and carriages, and had them
frequently to dine with him, and that one or other of them was
almost always staying in his house: that he was consulted as to
the appointment of their masters and governesses, and as to the
marriages of such of them as were married, and that, on the
plaintiff's marriage, the terms of the settlement were negotiated
between the plaintiff and Sir John, and their respective solicitors,
without any interference on the part of Sir Fitzwilliam: that
Sir John, who gave the instructions for the settlement on the
20th of April, 1817, proposed that the 10,000l. should be settled
on *all* the children of the marriage, but, afterwards, on the
suggestion of the plaintiff, it was agreed that the 10,000l. should
be settled on the younger children only, as the eldest son would
be entitled to a considerable estate on his father's side.

The witnesses who were examined as to the declarations made
by Sir John Barrington, were his confidential solicitors and some
of his relations and intimate friends. The substance of their
evidence was that they had heard Sir John say that he did
not intend to give his younger nieces more than 10,000l. a-piece,
and that he meant to limit the Swainston estate to his eldest
niece, Lady Simeon, and her issue male, so as to place her in
the situation of an eldest son, and that his object in purchasing
the tithes of Hadfield Broad Oak, and directing the rents to be
accumulated, was to form a fund to relieve his Swainston estate

[*546]   from the *burthen of providing the 50,000l.: that, both before

and after the execution of the settlement, Sir John uniformly
spoke of the fortune of Julia, as well as of the other younger
daughters of his brother, as being 10,000*l.* and no more: and
two of the witnesses said that they believed and had always
understood, from declarations made by Sir John, that he considered the provision made, by the settlement, for his niece Julia,
was in lieu and satisfaction of that which he had provided for
her by his will (1).

Mr. Knight, Mr. Jacob, Mr. Walker, Mr. Chandless and
Mr. Pole, for the plaintiff and the defendant his infant son, contended that a person could not stand *in loco parentis* to a child
whose father and mother were living and who resided with them ;
* * that the provision by the settlement was charged only on
the reversion of the Swainston estate, * * whereas the provision by the will was to be raised out of the rectory and tithes
and the stock, as well as the reversion of the Swainston estate ;
* * that the provision by the will extended to every husband
that Mrs. Powys might marry, and to *all* the children she might
have by them ; but the provision by the settlement was confined
to the husband and younger children of the then intended
marriage : * * that, if the provision by the will was satisfied   [547]
or adeemed by the settlement, the first codicil, by confirming the
will, restored or revived it : that evidence was not admissible to
raise the presumption, especially as Sir John Barrington did not
stand *in loco parentis* to Mrs. Powys. * * *

   Sir C. Wetherell, Mr. Kindersley, Mr. Wray, and *Mr. Bethell,*   [548]
      for the defendants, Sir Richard and Lady Simeon and their
      infant son:

   * * In deciding on questions of satisfaction, the Court does   [549]
not regard slight differences ; it only looks to see whether the
principal object of both the provisions is the same person. Here
Mrs. Powys was the principal object of both provisions, and the
intention of both of them was the same, namely, to limit the

---

(1) The evidence upon this point is
set out at some length in the report
of the appeal in 3 My. & Cr.; see
pp. 361—365 ; but the summary here
given of the evidence appears to be
sufficient for the purpose of this
report.—O. A. S.

10,000*l.* in the manner most beneficial to her, under the existing
circumstances. The will and the settlement are, in many
respects, identical : the discrepancies between them are owing
to the marriage being uncertain when the will was made ; and,
on that account, provision was made for every husband that Mrs.
Powys might marry, and for the issue of every marriage she
[550]   might contract. * * The discrepancies between the two provisions are not sufficient to prevent ademption : in both instances
the testator had in view the giving of a portion of 10,000*l.* to
his niece. * * *

[551]   Next, with respect to the admissibility of the evidence to raise
the presumption. Most of the cases in which the evidence has
been rejected, are cases in which the settlement was made first,
and the will afterwards. There, of course, evidence is not admissible ; for evidence cannot be given to explain or contradict a
written instrument. Our object is not to show what Sir John
Barrington meant by his will, but what was his intention in doing
a subsequent, independent act. The authorities are uniform,
that evidence may be produced to show the intention with which
the testator made the advance in his lifetime. * * *

The codicil, though it confirmed the will, could not have the
effect of restoring the adeemed legacy ; for the rule of law is that
an adeemed legacy forms no part of the will : *Rider* v. *Wager* (1).

[552]   *Mr. Jemmett, Mr. Sewell,* and *Mr. Short* appeared for the
other defendants.

[The principal cases cited by counsel are referred to in the
judgment of the LORD CHANCELLOR on the appeal.

The VICE-CHANCELLOR held that Sir John Barrington had not
assumed the parental obligation of making provision for his
nieces, and that no presumption of satisfaction was established.

Sir Richard and Lady Simeon and their son appealed from this
decree, as reported in 3 My. & Cr. 359. The case was re-argued
on the appeal by the same counsel as before, except that *Mr.
Wigram* took the place of *Mr. Kindersley.*

The report of the appeal does not state any further
arguments.]

(1) 2 P. Wms. 328.

THE LORD CHANCELLOR :

The facts of this case being already in print in the sixth volume of Mr. Simons' Reports, it is not *necessary for me to detail them further than may be necessary to explain the observations I shall have to make upon some of the points which arise.

The case is one of much importance, not so much on account of the property in question, which, however, is considerable, as because it raises questions as to which the rules and principles of this Court are not very easily to be laid down or defined, and as to which the authorities are, unfortunately, not very consistent. Not finding myself able to concur in the judgment of the VICE-CHANCELLOR, I have most carefully examined the grounds upon which it is founded, and have anxiously considered the authorities applicable to the subject.

Some points have been properly assumed, and may be considered as settled points, upon which the argument on each side must proceed. It is not to be disputed, that if Miss Julia Barrington had been a daughter, instead of being a niece of Sir John Barrington, the provision made for her by him upon her marriage would have been an ademption of the legacy given to her by his will of 1817. I do not understand the VICE-CHANCELLOR to doubt this, in the observations which are to be found at the 563rd page of the report. If that be so, it is, I apprehend, equally clear, and so I understand the VICE-CHANCELLOR to assume, that the same consequence would follow, if Sir John Barrington ought to be considered as having placed himself *in loco parentis;* but the VICE-CHANCELLOR rests his judgment principally upon this, that Sir John Barrington ought not to be considered as placed *in loco parentis.* The first point, therefore, to be considered is, whether that be correctly so assumed; and, no doubt, the authorities leave, in some obscurity, the question as to what is to be considered as meant by the expression, universally adopted, of one *in loco parentis.* Lord ELDON, *however, in *Ex parte Pye* (1) has given to it a definition which I readily adopt, not only because it proceeds from his high authority, but, because it seems to me to embrace all that is necessary to work out and carry into effect

POWYS
v.
MANSFIELD.

1837.
Nov. 17.

[3 My. & Cr.
365]
[*366]

[*367]

(1) 11 R. R. 173; see p. 180 (18 Ves. 140, 154).

the object and meaning of the rule. Lord ELDON says, it is a
person "meaning to put himself *in loco parentis*; in the situation of the person described as the lawful father of the
child;" but this definition must, I conceive, be considered as
applicable to those parental offices and duties to which the subject in question has reference, namely, to the office and duty of
the parent to make provision for the child. The offices and
duties of a parent are infinitely various, some having no connection whatever with making a provision for a child; and it
would be most illogical, from the mere exercise of any of such
offices or duties by one not the father, to infer an intention in
such person to assume also the duty of providing for the child.
The relative situation of the friend and of the father may make
this unnecessary, and the other benefits most essential.

Sir WILLIAM GRANT's definition is, "A person assuming the
parental character, or discharging parental duties" (1), which
may seem not to differ much from Lord ELDON's, but it wants
that which, to my mind, constitutes the principal value of Lord
ELDON's definition, namely, the referring to the intention, rather
than to the act of the party. The VICE-CHANCELLOR says, it
must be a person who has so acted towards the child as that he
has thereby imposed upon himself a moral obligation to provide
for it; and that the designation will not hold, where the child
has a father with whom it resides, and by whom it is maintained. This seems to infer that *the *locus parentis* assumed by
the stranger must have reference to the pecuniary wants of the
child; and that Lord ELDON's definition is to be so understood;
and so far I agree with it; but I think the other circumstances
required are not necessary to work out the principle of the rule,
or to effectuate its object. The rule, both as applied to a father
and to one *in loco parentis*, is founded upon the presumed intention. A father is supposed to intend to do what he is in duty
bound to do, namely, to provide for his child according to his
means. So, one who has assumed that part of the office of a
father is supposed to intend to do what he has assumed to
himself the office of doing. If the assumption of the character
be established, the same inference and presumption must follow.

[*368]

(1) See 13 R. R. 230 (19 Ves. 412).

The having so acted towards a child as to raise a moral obligation to provide for it, affords a strong inference in favour of the
fact of the assumption of the character ; and the child having a
father with whom it resides, and by whom it is maintained,
affords some inference against it ; but neither are conclusive.

If, indeed, the VICE-CHANCELLOR's definition were to be adopted,
it would still be to be considered whether, in this case, Sir John
Barrington had not subjected himself to a moral obligation to
provide for his brother's children, and whether such children
can be said to have been maintained by their father. A rich
unmarried uncle, taking under his protection the family of a
brother, who has not the means of adequately providing for them,
and furnishing, through their father, to the children, the means
of their maintenance and education, may surely be said to intend
to put himself, for the purpose in question, *in loco parentis* to
the children, although they never leave their father's roof. An
uncle so taking such a family under his care, will have all the
feelings, intentions, and objects, as to providing *for the chil-   [*369]
dren, which would influence him if they were orphans. For the
purpose in question, namely, providing for them, the existence
of the father can make no difference. If, then, it shall appear,
from an examination of the evidence, that Sir John Barrington
did afford to his brother the means of maintaining, educating,
and bringing up his children according to their condition of life ;
and that the father had no means of his own, at all adequate to
that purpose ; that this assistance was regular and systematic,
and not confined to casual presents, the repetition of which could
not be relied upon ; that he held out to his brother and his
family, that they were to look to him for their future provision, it
will surely follow, if that were material, that Sir John Barrington
had so acted towards the children as to impose upon himself a
moral obligation to provide for them, and that the children were,
in fact, maintained by him, and not by their father. But it has
been said, that Sir John Barrington would not have been guilty
of any breach of moral duty, if he had permitted the property
to descend to his brother. Undoubtedly, he would not, because
that would have been a very rational mode of providing for the
children ; but if he had reason to suppose that his brother would

act so unnaturally as to leave the property away from his children, Sir John Barrington would have been guilty of a breach of moral duty towards the children, in leaving the property absolutely to their father. I should, therefore, feel great difficulty in coming to a conclusion, that Sir John Barrington had not placed himself *in loco parentis* to these children, even if I thought every thing necessary for that purpose, which the VICE-CHANCELLOR has thought to be so.

Adopting, however, as I do, the definition of Lord ELDON, I proceed to consider whether Sir John Barrington did mean to
[*370] put himself *in loco parentis* to the *children, so far as related to their future provision. Parol evidence has been offered upon two points; first, to prove the affirmative of this proposition; secondly, to prove, by declarations and acts of Sir John Barrington, that he intended the provision made by the settlement should be in substitution of that made by the will. That such evidence is admissible, for the first of these purposes, appears to me necessarily to flow from the rule of presumption. If the acts of a party standing *in loco parentis* raise, in equity, a presumption which could not arise from the same acts of another person not standing in that situation, evidence must be admissible to prove or disprove the facts upon which the presumption is to depend, namely, whether, in the language of Lord ELDON, he had meant to put himself *in loco parentis ;* and, as the fact to be tried is the intention of the party, his declarations, as well as his acts, must be admissible for that purpose; and if the evidence establish the fact, that Sir John Barrington did mean to place himself *in loco parentis*, it will not be material to consider, whether his declarations of intention as to the particular provision in question be admissible *per se*, because the presumption against the double portions, which, in that case, will arise, being attempted to be rebutted by parol testimony, may be supported by evidence of the same kind.

I, at present, look to the evidence, for the purpose of seeing how far it supports the proposition that Sir John Barrington meant, for the purpose of making provision for the family in general, and particularly for Miss Julia Barrington, to place himself *in loco parentis,* In the first place, it appears that Sir

John Barrington allowed his brother 400*l.* per annum, which he, in the year 1797, voluntarily bound himself to pay during his life. I take no notice of Sir Fitzwilliam Barrington's diary, as I do not consider that it can be evidence between these parties of the facts it contains, there being no proof that it was *known to Sir John Barrington. Sir John Barrington's banker's books prove the payment to his brother of large sums in addition to this annuity ; but his letter of the 11th of July, 1818, referred to by the VICE-CHANCELLOR, is the most important document, showing that he had taken his brother's family under his protection, and that his principal object in the application of his property was to provide for them ; that he had been always preparing to supply his brother with cash *en masse ;* that, upon Lady Simeon's marriage, he had made a disposal of the Isle of Wight property for the benefit of his brother's family ; and that upon Mrs. Powys's marriage, he had made another will, improved upon, as he hoped, by the destination of the tithe property in Essex, in trust to form a fund to aid the very heavy demands that would press upon the Isle of Wight estate : that in the forming of those wills, he had acted altogether free from any personal consideration, following the order by priority of birth, as the rule for it. Part of these demands upon the Isle of Wight estate was the provision for Mrs. Powys ; and it is to be observed that he speaks of the object of the arrangement in 1817 as being to provide an additional fund to answer the pre-existing demands, and not as intended to increase them. The testimony of the witnesses carry this part of the case somewhat further, and prove that the brother's family were, in fact, maintained by Sir John Barrington ; the income of the brother not exceeding 400*l.* or 500*l.* per annum, and Sir John making up the deficiency of the income to discharge the expenses of the family, which were considerable. It cannot be material whether the music-master, the drawing-master, and the dress-maker, received what was due to them by the hands of the father, as it was the uncle who furnished the means. The arrangements upon Lady Simeon's marriage in 1813 are important, as showing that, at that time, Sir John Barrington treated his brother's family as his own, in the disposition of his *property, and destined 10,000*l.* as the

POWYS
v.
MANSFIELD.

[*371]

[*372]

portion of each of his younger nieces. The letter of the 11th of
July, 1818, shows that, at the time of making the will of the
28th of March, 1817, Sir John Barrington knew of the intended
marriage of his niece Julia, and that such will was made, as he
says, upon the occasion of such marriage. At that time, therefore, this will proves, that he intended that 10,000*l.* and no more,
should be the portion of Mrs. Powys. Nothing can more completely show the assumption of the office of parent towards the
children, so far as relates to the disposition of property, than
this circumstance. Had his nieces been his own children, the
disposition and arrangement would probably have been the same,
so far as they affect them. If Sir John Barrington had died
between the 28th of March and the 2nd of June, 1817, Miss
Julia Barrington's fortune would have been but 10,000*l.*; but
that 10,000*l.* would have been so settled by the will as to have
precluded the necessity of any other settlement of this 10,000*l.*
But although this object was so attained, and the chances of
life guarded against by this will, the negociation proceeded with
the intended husband. To this negociation the uncle was the
sole party on behalf of the intended wife, the father not interfering. On the 2nd of June the settlement is executed : the
father is no party to it, but the uncle is, and he puts in settlement a sum of 10,000*l.*, charged upon the reversion of the
Swainston estate, which was, by the will, to go in succession to
the nieces, for the advancement in life, and to provide for the
maintenance, of the niece who was about to marry. Did not
Sir John Barrington, by this settlement, exercise the office or
duty of advancing his niece in life, and of providing for her
maintenance, and that by a sum charged upon an estate settled
upon her eldest sister and herself in succession? Was not this
a portion? and if so, was not the 10,000*l.* appropriated to the
same purpose, and ultimately charged upon the same property,
[*373]   by *the will, also intended as a portion? But, if these were
given as portions, and are so to be considered, the giving them
affords the strongest evidence of an intention in the giver to
place himself for that purpose *in loco parentis ;* and on the other
hand, if the assumption of that character be proved by other
means, then the sums so given must be considered and treated

as portions. I consider both points established by the evidence, POWYS
and the proof of either is sufficient proof of the other, and so to MANSFIELD.
raise the presumption in equity that both gifts were not intended
to take effect; a presumption not only not rebutted by the evidence for the plaintiff, but, in my opinion, established beyond
all doubt by the evidence of the defendants; for, independently
of the presumptions in equity against double portions, and of
the positive testimony of several witnesses that Sir John Barrington intended that his nieces should have only one sum of
10,000*l.*, there is the strongest ground for presuming, from the
documents, that such must have been his intention. That such
was his intention in 1813 is quite clear; that he continued to
entertain the same intention from that time up to and at the
time of making his will in 1817, is also clear, as he not only
does not give his niece Julia any more, but disposes of all his
property, appropriating 10,000*l*. and no more, for her. What
ground is there for supposing that he had altered his intention
by the 20th of April, after making his will?   No stipulation for
that purpose appears on the part of the intended husband. Ten
thousand pounds was the whole he stipulated for, and the whole
he had any reason to expect. Had Sir John Barrington, at the
time he executed the settlement, an intention that his niece
should have another 10,000*l*. under his will, would he not have
made such additional sum the subject of the negotiation, instead
of leaving it as it stands upon the will, which gives to the
intended husband the uncontrolled life interest in that sum?

But upon what ground is the direct evidence of Sir John   [374]
Barrington's intention with respect to those two sums to be
rejected? The whole question is one of intention; and upon such
an issue the declarations of the party are, I conceive, admissible;
and so the cases have decided. It has been said that the trusts
of the 10,000*l*. by the settlement differ from those prescribed by
the will; and that the will charges the Hadfield Broad Oak tithes,
and other property, with the payment; whereas, by the settlement, the reversion of the Swainston estates alone is charged.

After the decision of the House of Lords in *Wharton* v. *Lord
Durham* (1), the variation in the trusts cannot be relied upon.

(1) 39 R. R. 13 (3 Cl. & Fin. 146).

That case having been argued before I had the honour of a seat
in the House of Lords, I abstained from taking any part in the
judgment, and I was glad to be enabled to do so, because I had
been counsel in the cause; but I fully concur in that judgment.

As to the observation that the 10,000*l.* was, by the settlement,
only charged upon the reversion of the Swainston estate, and
might, therefore, have failed altogether, or have been postponed
for a long period, it is to be observed that, although the charge
upon the reversion was, by possibility in law, liable to fail by
Sir John Barrington or his brother having issue male who
should attain twenty-one, and bar the reversion, yet the 10,000*l.*
portion could not, in that event, have failed, it being, in that
event, charged upon the post office annuity : so that the charge,
either by itself, or by being the means of purchasing the charge
upon the post-office annuity, did, in fact, secure the 10,000*l.*
But where was the probability, in fact, of the charge upon the
reversion being defeated ? I am not aware that the age of the
parties is *distinctly in evidence; but Fitzwilliam Barrington
had been married twenty-eight years, and had no son, and Sir
John Barrington, the best judge of the probability of his marrying
and having issue male, evidently considered that event as one
not to be taken into consideration, so that the reversion of the
Swainston estate, although, in law, contingent, was, in fact, equal
in value to an absolute estate, and must have been so considered
by the parties : nor was the omission of the other property in the
settlement necessarily any departure, in fact, from the intention
declared by the will of making the other property primarily
liable to the 50,000*l.* ; for, if such other property was not thought
equal to raising the whole 50,000*l.*, it was immaterial that the
10,000*l.*, part of it, was to be raised out of the reversion.

It has been supposed that the evidence of Mrs. Williams and
of Miss Barrington to the twentieth interrogatory, and of Mr.
Cocks to the ninth, show that Sir John Barrington intended
that both sums of 10,000*l.* should be paid. What Mr. Cocks
says, " he thinks he understood," is not sufficiently certain or
specific to be relied upon. Miss Barrington does not give
any date to the conversation referred to. It may have taken
place before her sister Julia's marriage. The deposition of

[*375]

Mrs. Williams referred to, that is, her answer to the ninth interrogatory, explained by her answer to the twentieth, speaks of the 10,000*l.* secured by the settlement made on the marriage being to be paid out of the tithes, which is clearly a mistake; but she is positive that there was to be only one sum of 10,000*l.*

It has been argued that the codicil of the 23rd of June, 1818, confirming the will, makes the will speak as of the date of the codicil, and therefore revives the legacy, if it had been adeemed by the settlement; and, *at all events, is evidence of an intention that the legacy should take effect.   It is very true that a codicil republishing a will makes the will speak as from its own date for the purpose of passing after-purchased lands, but not for the purpose of reviving a legacy revoked, adeemed, or satisfied. The codicil can only act upon the will as it existed at the time; and, at the time, the legacy revoked, adeemed, or satisfied formed no part of it.   Any other rule would make a codicil, merely republishing a will, operate as a new bequest, and so revoke any codicil by which a legacy given by the will had been revoked, and undo every act by which it may have been adeemed or satisfied.   The cases are consistent with this rule, as *Drinkwater* v. *Falconer* (1), *Monck* v. *Lord Monck* (2), *Booker* v. *Allen* (3); and the case of *Roome* v. *Roome* (4) is not an authority against these decisions, because the codicil was not considered in that case as reviving an adeemed legacy, it having been decided that there was no ademption; but the codicil was referred to as an additional proof that no ademption was intended.   And as to the argument that the codicil must, at any rate, be evidence of an intention that both sums should be paid, the same answer may be given which has been given to a similar argument in other cases; namely, that the testator, if he knew the rule of law, must have known that the codicil would not revive the adeemed legacy, and, therefore, it was unnecessary for him to mention it: the probability, however, is, that his attention being directed to the only object of the codicil, the words of confirmation

[*376]

(1) 2 Ves. Sen. 623.
(2) 12 R. R. 33 (1 Ball & B. 298).

(3) 34 R. R. 91 (2 Russ. & My. 270).
(4) 3 Atk. 181.

[377]

of the will were introduced as words of course, without any reference to the legacy is question.

I have not said any thing as to the identity of purpose in the two gifts, namely, making a provision for the niece, in contemplation of her marriage ; but there are some strong observations of Lord ELDON upon that subject, in the case of *Trimmer* v. *Bayne* (1). Indeed, the facts of that case, in almost every particular, strongly resemble the present. It was the case of a natural child, the father of which is, for this purpose, considered as a stranger. The trusts of the provision by the will and the marriage settlement materially varied. Verbal declarations were received in evidence of the father's intention ; and the provision by the will, though not settling the property upon the parties to the marriage, and the issue, as in this case, had reference to the child's marriage ; upon which Lord ELDON observes, that if there had been no general rule as to the ademption of the legacy by the settlement, it would be well worthy of discussion, whether it ought not to prevail in that particular case, the legacy being given with express and peculiar reference to the marriage of the daughter. Unless, therefore, it be adopted as a positive rule, that no one can, for these purposes, put himself *in loco parentis* to a child who is living with its father, this case of *Trimmer* v. *Bayne*, cannot in substance be distinguished from the present.

There is then the case which I before mentioned, of *Monck* v. *Lord Monck* (2), which bears a strong resemblance to the present, in many points. In that case a testator had by will given 5,000*l.* to his brother, and contemplating his marriage, directed that in that event it should be applied as a provision for the family. He afterwards advanced 1,000*l.* for his brother, and, upon his brother's marriage settled 4,000*l.* upon him and his family.

[*378]

*Lord MANNERS held, that he had placed himself *in loco parentis*, and that the legacy was adeemed by the settlement, although in that case the evidence to show the assumption of the office of parent was only to be found in the instruments themselves. In that case it was also decided that parol evidence was admissible in such a case, to show the intention, and that a codicil ratifying

(1) 6 R. R. 173 (7 Ves. 508).   (2) 12 R. R. 33 (1 Ball & B. 298).

and confirming a will did not set up an adeemed legacy. Lord Manners also relied upon the identity of purpose of the two provisions, though that was certainly not stronger than in the present case. *Booker* v. *Allen* (1), also embraces many of the points in question in this cause, and except that the legatee had no father, was a case much less strong than the present, against the double portions: but Sir J. Leach, M.R. held that the testator had placed himself *in loco parentis*, that the presumption therefore was raised against double portions, that evidence of intention was admissible, and that the codicil did not set up an adeemed legacy.

Upon these authorities, and for these reasons, I am of opinion that the evidence adduced to prove that Sir John Barrington had placed himself *in loco parentis* to his niece, for the purpose of providing for her, is admissible for that purpose, and establishes that point, although the niece was living with her father: that the presumption against double portions, therefore arises, and is not repelled by the evidence adduced by the plaintiff; but on the contrary, that the result of the whole of the evidence is very strong to show that Sir John Barrington intended that his niece should have only one sum of 10,000*l.*, and that the legacy given by the will, therefore, should not take effect. I am also of opinion, that the legacy so adeemed by the settlement, was not set up again by the codicil.

The result therefore is, that the plaintiff has failed in so [379] much of his suit as sought payment of the 10,000*l.* legacy, and that so much of the decree as provided for payment of the legacy must be reversed without costs, and so much of the bill as prayed payment of the legacy be

Dismissed with costs.

(1) 34 R. R. 91 (2 Russ. & My. 270).

1888.
Jan. 16, 17,
20.

Lord
COTTENHAM,
L.C.
[407]

NEATE v. THE DUKE OF MARLBOROUGH (1).

(3 My. & Cr. 407—421 ; S. C. 2 Jur. 76.)

Consideration of the origin and nature of the remedies afforded by
courts of equity to judgment creditors against the lands of their debtors
where the remedy by *elegit* was impracticable in consequence of some
legal impediment.

[REFERRING to the jurisdiction of courts of equity in the case
mentioned in the head-note, the LORD CHANCELLOR said :]

[416]   That jurisdiction is not for the purpose of giving effect to a
lien which is supposed to be created by the judgment. It is
true that, for certain purposes, the Court recognises a title by
the judgment,—as for the purpose of redeeming, or, after the
death of the debtor, of having his assets administered ;—but the
jurisdiction there is grounded simply upon this, that inasmuch
as the Court finds the creditor in a condition to acquire a power
over the estate, by suing out the writ, it does what it does in
all similar cases ; it gives to the party the right to come in and
redeem other incumbrancers upon the property. So again, after
the debtor is dead, if, under any circumstances, the estate is to
be sold, the Court pays off the judgment creditor, because it
cannot otherwise make a title to the estate ; and the Court never
sells the interest of a debtor subject to an *elegit* creditor. That
was very much discussed in the case of *Tunstall* v. *Trapps* (2).
But there was there a necessity for a sale ; and the question was
not as to the right of the judgment creditor against his debtor,
he being willing ; but where, from other circumstances, a sale
having become indispensable, it was necessary to clear the estate
from the claims of parties who had charges upon it.

[417]   It is, therefore, not correct to say that, according to the usual
acceptation of the term, the creditor obtains a lien by virtue of
his judgment. If he had an equitable lien, he would have a
right to come here to have the estate sold ; but he has no such
right. What gives a judgment creditor a right against the estate
is only the Act of Parliament (3) ; for independently of that, he

(1) *Anglo-Italian Bank* v. *Davies*   L. J. Ch. 775, 71 L. T. 8, C. A.
(1878) 9 Ch. Div. 275, 47 L. J. Ch.   (2) 3 Sim. 286.
833, 39 L. T. 244 ; *Cadogan* v. *Lyric*   (3) 13 Edw. I. c. 18.
Theatre, Limd. [1894] 3 Ch. 338, 63

has none ?   The Act of Parliament gives him, if he pleases, an option by the writ of *elegit*—the very name implying that it is an option—which, if he exercises, he is entitled to have a writ directed to the sheriff to put him in possession of a moiety of the lands.   The effect of the proceeding under the writ is to give to the creditor a legal title, which, if no impediment prevent him, he may enforce at law by ejectment.   If there be a legal impediment, he then comes into this Court, not to obtain a greater benefit than the law, that is, the Act of Parliament, has given him, but to have the same benefit, by the process of this Court, which he would have had at law, if no legal impediment had intervened.   How then can there be a better right ; or how can the judgment, which, *per se*, gives the creditor no title against the land, be considered as giving him a title here ?   Suppose he never sues out the writ, and never, therefore, exercises his option, is this Court to give him the benefit of a lien to which he has never chosen to assert his right ?   The reasoning would seem very strong, that as this Court is lending its aid to the legal right (and Lord REDESDALE expressly puts it under that head, namely, the right to recover in ejectment), the party must have previously armed himself with that which constitutes his legal right; and that which constitutes the legal right is the writ (1).   This Court, in fact, is doing neither more nor less than giving him what the Act of Parliament and an *ejectment would, under other circumstances, have given him   [*418] at law.   *   *   *

The sole reason for coming into this Court being founded on a right which the writ of *elegit* confers, the creditor cannot come, without having obtained that right.   [His Lordship then referred to some alleged decisions to the contrary reported in Dicken's reports, and showed that they were not consistent with the original records which the Registrar had extracted and supplied for comparison].

(1) Since the Judicature Act it is no longer necessary to issue a writ of *elegit* before applying for the appoint- ment of a receiver : *Ex parte Evans* (1879) 13 Ch. Div. at p. 260.— O. A. S.

1838.
July 11, 23,
24, 25.

Lord
COTTENHAM,
L.C.

[439]

SALMON v. RANDALL.

(3 My. & Cr. 439—451.)

A person whose property is required by Commissioners under the powers and for the purposes of an Act of Parliament is not entitled to restrain them, by injunction, from taking the steps prescribed by the Act for obtaining possession of the property, until they shall have shown a sufficient fund in hand to satisfy the price which may be awarded to him, or until they shall have shown the means by which they propose to procure it.

THE question in this case principally turned upon the construction of two local Acts of Parliament, the 28 Geo. III. c. lxiv., intituled " An Act for the better paving, cleansing, and lighting the town of Cambridge; for removing and preventing obstructions and annoyances; and for widening the streets, lanes, and other passages within the said town;" and the 34 Geo. III. c. civ., intituled "An Act to enlarge the powers" of the last-mentioned Act. As the LORD CHANCELLOR, however, in dealing with that question and disposing of the injunction granted by the VICE-CHANCELLOR, found it necessary to consider a general principle of some importance with reference to the control of courts of equity over persons invested with powers by local Acts of Parliament, it has been deemed expedient to report his Lordship's judgment, in which all the material facts are shortly summed up.

Mr. Jacob and Mr. Geldart, for the plaintiffs.

Mr. Knight Bruce and Mr. Girdlestone, for the defendants, the Commissioners, and Randall, their clerk.

Mr. Greene, for the defendants, Trinity Hall and Corpus Christi College, Cambridge, who were the owners of the houses in question.

July 25.   THE LORD CHANCELLOR:

[*440]   In this case an application had been made to the Vice-Chancellor by the plaintiffs, who were interested *as lessees, in certain houses in Cambridge, for an injunction to restrain the Commissioners, acting under two local Acts of Parliament, from proceeding to enforce the compulsory purchase of the houses,

under the powers supposed to be conferred on them by
those Acts.

It appears that notice had been given to the plaintiffs, by the
Commissioners, of their intention to take the houses in question,
and that they were proceeding to have the value of the premises
ascertained by a jury; and the application made to the Vice-
Chancellor was to stop all proceedings. The VICE-CHANCELLOR'S
order was confined to their proceeding to summon, and lay the
case before a jury, his Honour declining to carry the injunction
any further.

The present application, on the part of the Commissioners,
is to dissolve that injunction; and, on the other hand, the
plaintiffs have given a notice of motion for the purpose of
extending the injunction to the other objects which the Commissioners had in view, and particularly of restraining the
defendants from taking possession of the premises in question.

Two grounds were laid in support of the application. The
first was, that, under the Acts of Parliament, the Commissioners
had no authority to take the premises in question: the second
was, that, assuming they had such authority, still, inasmuch as,
according to the plaintiffs' statement, it appeared they had not
funds applicable to the purpose, they ought to be restrained by
this Court from exercising the legal right, supposing them to
have such right.

[Upon the first point his Lordship agreed with the VICE-
CHANCELLOR that the Commissioners had the power   they
assumed. The judgment then proceeded as follows:]

It was argued, however, that, although they have the legal   [442]
power, and although they are within the provisions of the Acts,
and although the time has not gone by within *which they are   [*443]
to exercise the power, still they ought to be prevented from
doing so, because there do not appear to be funds in their hands,
that is to say, now in their hands, immediately applicable to this
purpose, so as to enable them to carry their proposed compulsory
purchase into effect. The VICE-CHANCELLOR clearly does not
understand the object and effect of his order to be to prevent
the Commissioners from proceeding at all times, but merely
to prohibit this at the present time; because he contemplates

some other mode of proceeding, some other means of procuring
money, and suggests the propriety of their making a rate before
they complete the purchase, in order partly to have the question
raised upon the legality of the rate, and partly to put themselves in possession of funds by means of which they may be
enabled to carry the purchase into effect.   His Honour granted
an injunction to restrain the Commissioners from proceeding to
have the value of the premises assessed before a jury.

In support of his view, the VICE-CHANCELLOR referred to two
cases before Lord Eldon, *The Mayor of King's Lynn* v. *Pemberton* (1), and *Agar* v. *The Regent's Canal Company*, which is
mentioned in the note to that case (2).   In the judgment of Lord
ELDON in *The Mayor of King's Lynn* v. *Pemberton*, we have a
statement by Lord ELDON himself of the ground on which he
proceeded in the case of *Agar* v. *The Regent's Canal Company*.
Lord ELDON there (3) said, " In the case of *Agar* v. *The Regent's
Canal Company*, I acted on the principle that, where persons
assume to satisfy the Legislature that a certain sum is sufficient
for the completion of a proposed undertaking, as a canal, and
the event is that that sum is not nearly sufficient, if the owner

[*444]   of an estate through which the *Legislature has given to the
speculators a right to carry the canal, can show that the persons
so authorised are unable to complete their work, and is prompt
in his application for relief, grounded on that fact, this Court
will not permit the further prosecution of the undertaking."
His Lordship then refers to another case which does not appear
to me to have any application to the present.   His words are,
" So, in another case, a Mr. Taylor filed his bill, stating that,
at the time of subscribing, he expected that, when he had paid
the whole of his instalments, he should find the canal complete ;
but that, with the present fund, it would not pass to the east of
Hampstead ; and the Court thought him entitled to relief."
That must have been upon the ground of misrepresentation or
fraud practised on the party purchasing a share in the canal,
and does not appear to me to be applicable.

The case of *Agar* v. *The Regent's Canal Company*, however,

(1) 18 R. R. 62 (1 Swanst. 244).   (3) 18 R. R. 68 (1 Swanst. 250).
(2) See also 14 R. R. 217.

undoubtedly lays down a principle which may be extremely important in its application; and I apprehend Lord ELDON must have gone upon this ground, that where Acts of Parliament impose certain severe burthens on individuals, by interfering with their private rights and private property, for the purpose of obtaining some great public good, if the Court sees that the undertaking cannot be completed, and therefore that the public cannot derive that benefit which was to be the equivalent for the sacrifice made by the individual, the Court will protect the individual from being compelled to make that sacrifice, under the circumstances, and until it appears that the public will derive the proposed benefit from it. It is impossible to suppose Lord ELDON could have meant that, after an Act of *Parliament has been passed giving certain powers, and authorising a body of persons to carry on certain works, those against whose rights such works are to be carried into effect are to come into this Court and say, " We will undertake to prove that you cannot, with the money which you have in hand, carry those works into effect;" and that therefore, and immediately, in that state of circumstances, the Court is to interfere. If that were so, it is quite obvious that, not a single bill passes the Legislature, authorising the formation of a railway or a canal, but would be brought immediately into this Court; thus making it the duty of the Court to investigate the probable expense of the speculation; and if it appeared that the money which the parties had at the time would not enable them—as in those cases, generally, it would not enable them—to carry their speculation into effect, the Court would be called upon to say they should be prohibited from going on with it altogether.

[*445]

The consequence would be, that this Court would be assuming to itself a power which would be neither more nor less than the repealing of an Act of Parliament. Lord ELDON, it is clear, could never have meant that; and he must, therefore, be supposed to have put his decision on the ground I have referred to. In the case of *The Mayor of King's Lynn* v. *Pemberton*, it appears that the defendants were not working on any land belonging to the plaintiffs; and Lord ELDON refused the injunction. One reason stated in answer to the application was, that, although there appeared to be a deficiency of funds to enable the Company to complete their work, they were applying to Parliament to get further powers—not that they had obtained further powers, but that they were applying for them.   Lord ELDON upon that observed, " A peculiarity in this case is the pending application

[*446] to Parliament."   I do not perceive *how that could make any difference, because it is open to all companies, and to all parties, to apply to Parliament.   If they got a new Act, that might alter the case; but how the circumstance of the parties applying to Parliament was to give them a right which they would not have if they had not been making that application, I confess I do not understand.   I cannot but think that, on further consideration, Lord ELDON was disposed to limit, and felt the necessity of limiting, the proposition which he is supposed to have laid down in *Agar* v. *The Regent's Canal Company*.

The question then is, assuming the rule to be as Lord ELDON is supposed to have laid it down in the case of *Agar* v. *The Regent's Canal Company*, what application it has to the present. The principle of that case, taking it in the way assumed, was, not that the Company had no power to purchase the land they proposed to purchase, but that they did not appear to have the means of carrying into effect the whole of the plan they had projected ; and that, therefore, the ground on which they acted in taking from the individual the right of dominion over his own property, could not be supported ; and the consideration failed. Now what analogy has that to the present case ?   There is no one individual object to be accomplished here : the powers of this Act are for a variety of objects, all tending to the same effect.   There is no one defined purpose to be carried into effect ; but the Commissioners are, from time to time, to be at liberty to exercise their powers for the purpose of widening and improving the streets of Cambridge.   Every purchase they make, every house they take down, is a distinct work in itself, and to that extent accomplishes the object.   The principle, therefore, of Lord ELDON'S observations does not, as it strikes me, apply in the

[*447] slightest degree to the present case.   *If Lord ELDON had laid it down that, wherever a public body of this description, wherever commissioners or an incorporated company propose to purchase

or take any particular property, the Court will see beforehand, before the contract is complete, before the sum to be paid is ascertained, not only that they have the means of paying for the property so proposed to be purchased or taken, but that the money which they have, and mean to apply for the purpose, is raised according to a particular mode prescribed by the Act of Parliament, then such a proposition would come up to the present case. But no such proposition is laid down by his Lordship; and it would be quite a new principle to contend that a party who is under an obligation to sell his property, either under the provisions of an Act of Parliament or otherwise, has a right to ask the purchaser—where do you get the money from, with which you are to pay for the property you are purchasing of me?

The clauses which enable the Commissioners to complete the purchase provide that, upon payment of the sum awarded by the jury, they are to have a conveyance; that, upon the conveyance being made, they are to have a right of entry after a certain notice; and the means of payment would naturally flow from those powers which they are, by force of the Acts of Parliament, authorised to put in execution for the purpose of raising the money. But no authority is to be found, either in those Acts of Parliament or in any decision, for holding that a party, being compelled to sell his property, has a right to put to the purchaser any such question as I have just mentioned. It is not pretended that the seller has any interest in the source from which the money comes; but the argument is, that, being an owner of premises which the Commissioners wish to buy, he has a right to say—"You *shall not purchase my premises except with money raised in a particular way under the Act of Parliament;" and that is the very ground on which the plaintiff, Mr. Salmon, has resisted this purchase.   [*448]

No doubt the power to raise the money is extremely important, in determining the extent to which the right to purchase goes. The argument may be very sound, that if the power to raise money is limited, the right to purchase ought not to be carried beyond the power given to raise the money for the purchases by means of which the objects of the Acts of Parliament are to be

effected. But that is not the question here : the question is,
assuming the power of purchasing to be within the provisions
of the Acts, has the vendor a right to say, "Let me know
exactly where the money comes from, and how it was got,
which you mean to apply in completing this purchase?" The
cases cited have a reference to no such right, and proceed on
totally different principles.

Now, although there is, on the affidavits, very great difficulty
in ascertaining how the Commissioners are, within a reasonable
period, to raise the money for completing this purchase, yet I do
find that there is a power to raise money. I know not what
the value of the property may be : that is a matter of total
uncertainty. The affidavits on the different sides differ
extremely, as one might expect, with respect to the supposed
value of the premises. I cannot tell what the jury may assess
as their value ; and I am equally unable to ascertain how much
money the Commissioners may be able to raise by the 1$s.$ rate,
or by the 1$s.$ rate and the 3$d.$ rate, which they are authorised to
raise, or by the tolls ; all of which are within their power by the
terms of the Acts of Parliament ; and, according to the construction I put *upon the Acts of Parliament, whatever moneys may
be raised in that way, and which they are authorised to raise,
may be applied to the purposes of the Acts. I entirely abstain
from going into the question, how far the Corporation or the
University may be liable to contribute ; but I find a power,
beyond all doubt, vested in the Commissioners under the Acts
of Parliament, by which they are enabled to raise money for
these purposes, and I am left entirely in the dark as to what
amount of money is required.

[*449]

What ground, then, is there for the interposition of this Court,
to prevent the Commissioners from exercising their legal right ?
Assuming that the VICE-CHANCELLOR and myself are correct in
our construction, there is no doubt that they have the power,
and no question as to their legal right to purchase. They have
given a notice ; the Act of Parliament is imperative, that the
jury shall assess the value ; and the Commissioners must tender
the value so assessed. The owner is to hold, until the value has
been assessed by the jury, and the tender made : then, upon

the tender, certain acts are to be done, which will vest the premises in the Commissioners; but till then the property remains in the owner, untouched. The order of the VICE-CHANCELLOR prevents them, therefore, from having the property vested in them, or acquiring the dominion over the premises; but it still leaves the parties in the situation of vendor and purchaser, inasmuch as the Commissioners have given the notice; and the VICE-CHANCELLOR'S order cannot disturb the position of the parties.

I find no authority in the cases referred to which distinguishes this case from any other in which parties are exercising a legal right. The parties, I conceive, are put into the situation of vendor and purchaser by the *notice (1); and like every other vendor and purchaser, they must of course complete their purchase, according to the provisions, not of the contract, but of those arrangements which the Act of Parliament has substituted in lieu of the contract, in a case where no contract can take place.

[*450]

It would, as it seems to me, be most inconvenient for both parties if the Court were to leave them in their present position; a position in which neither of them can interfere with the property, the notice effectually preventing them. It is vain for the owner of the property to suppose that he is at liberty to go on dealing with this land, and expending money upon it, as if it were his; because if the Commissioners complete their purchase, he is building not on his own land, but on the land of the Commissioners. It is impossible to say what view the jury may take of the matter; but I apprehend, that if they take a correct view, they will look at the situation of the property, and fix the value as it stood at the time when the notice was given; from which time it was the property of the Commissioners, and ceased to be the property of the vendor (1). While, therefore, it would be most inconvenient for the owner to be left in his present situation, it would be also most inconvenient for the Commissioners; because the only thing they could do would be to make a rate to enable them to complete the purchase of the property; which property they are, by the injunction of this Court, restrained from purchasing.

(1) *I.e.*, for certain purposes, but the *quasi* contractual relation is not complete until the purchase-money has been fixed.—O. A. S.

SALMON
v.
RANDALL.

If any case arises after the jury has assessed the value; if payment is not made; or if any other difficulty occurs, that will form the subject of a new and distinct case. I am only considering now how far the Court ought to interfere by injunction between the parties, to prevent the jury from assessing the value.

[451]

I am of opinion that it is not only consistent with the rights under the Acts of Parliament, but the most convenient course for all parties, that the jury should go on to assess the sum at which the Commissioners may purchase these premises; and whether they can, or whether they cannot, purchase them, still it is necessary that the jury should tell them what the sum is which they will have to pay.

Upon these grounds, I am of opinion that the order of the VICE-CHANCELLOR, for the injunction, should be discharged; and as the motion on the part of the plaintiffs for extending the injunction of course necessarily fails also, that motion must be

Refused with costs.

1838.
Feb. 8, 9.
Nov. 13.
———
Lord
COTTENHAM,
L.C.

BOOTH *v.* LEYCESTER.

(3 My. & Cr. 459—470.)

[SEE the report of this case before the Master of the Rolls, 44 R. R. 75, 77 (1 Keen, 247) where a note of the judgment upon this appeal will be found.]

1838.
Nov. 14.
———
Lord
COTTENHAM,
L.C.

ATTORNEY-GENERAL *v.* CORPORATION OF EAST RETFORD.

(3 My. & Cr. 484—490.)

[SEE a note of this appeal in 39 R. R. at p. 128, *n.* (2 My. & K. 39).]

1837.
Nov. 24, 25.
1838.
Nov. 17.
———
Lord
COTTENHAM,
L.C.

[490]

CLOUGH *v.* BOND.

(3 My. & Cr. 490—499; S. C. 8 L. J. (N. S.) Ch. 51; 2 Jur. 958.)

On the death of an intestate, administration to her estate was granted to her son and daughter. The daughter being then under coverture, the assets were, in May, 1831, paid into a banking house, to the joint account of her husband and her brother, the administrator; and the whole of the fund, with the exception of the share of one of the next

of kin, who was abroad, was soon afterwards paid away among the
several parties entitled, by means of cheques signed by the two persons
in whose names the account stood.   The husband of the administratrix
died in December, 1831, and, ten months afterwards, her brother and
co-administrator drew out the balance, and, having applied it to his own
use, absconded : Held, that the estate of the husband of the administratrix
was answerable for the loss.

ANN DIXON died in the month of November, 1829, leaving
certain testamentary papers, but intestate as to the bulk of her
personal estate, which, therefore, became distributable among
her next of kin, who were very numerous.   Letters of administration, with the testamentary papers annexed, were granted to
her two surviving children, Emily Bond, then the wife of John
Bond, and Thomas Reup Dixon.   The residuary estate consisted
chiefly of Government stock.   This stock *was sold in the month   [*491]
of May, 1831, and, with a view to distribution among the several
persons entitled, the proceeds, to the amount of about 18,000l.
were paid into the banking house of Child & Co., and there
placed to an account in the joint names of John Bond and
Thomas Reup Dixon.   At the same time it was arranged that all
cheques drawn on Child & Co. upon that account should be
signed by both the parties in whose names the fund stood.   In
the course of a few months afterwards, the whole of the respective
shares of the next of kin were duly paid or provided for, by
means of cheques drawn in that form, except the share of Louisa
Revell Clough, the wife of John Clough, who, with her husband,
was then expected very shortly to return from India.   The value
of Mrs. Clough's share being one eighteenth of the clear fund,
amounted, after deducting the duty and costs, to 988l. 6s. 8d.;
and this sum, together with a further sum reserved to answer
the expenses of administration, and making a total of 1,848l.,
remained in the hands of Child & Co., upon the joint account,
down to the death of John Bond, which happened on the 15th of
December, 1831.   In the months of October and November in
the following year, Thomas Reup Dixon drew out, by cheques,
the balance of the account at Child's, and applied the money to
his own use ; and shortly afterwards he absconded and left
the kingdom.

Mr. and Mrs. Clough did not arrive in this country from India

CLOUGH   until the end of the year 1834.   Soon after their return they filed
v.   the present bill, praying for an account of Ann Dixon's personal
BOND.   estate, and for payment of Mrs. Clough's share of the undisposed
            of residue; and praying also that the defendant Emily Bond,
            and the other defendants, the personal representatives of John
            Bond, might be declared liable for any loss sustained through
[*492]   the default or misconduct of Thomas *Reup Dixon, who was also
            a nominal defendant, though out of the jurisdiction.

            The decree of the VICE-CHANCELLOR, made at the hearing of
the cause, after directing a general account of the estate, and an
account of Mrs. Clough's share, went on to declare that the
defendants, the personal representatives of John Bond, were
personally chargeable with the sum of 1,348*l.*, admitted by their
answer to have been drawn out of Child's Bank by Thomas Reup
Dixon, together with interest at 4*l.* per cent. upon that sum from
the time when the same was so drawn out.   And it reserved the
consideration of the question, how far the defendant Emily Bond
was answerable for the said sum, until the Master should have
made his report.

The defendants, Emily Bond and the personal representatives
of John Bond, appealed against this part of the decree.

Mr. Jacob, Mr. Whitmarsh, and *Mr. Whitmarsh,* junior, for
the appeal.   * * *

[494]   *Mr. Wigram,* and *Mr. Walker,* in support of the
decree.   * * *

Mr. Jacob, in reply.

[The principal cases cited by counsel are referred to in
the judgment.]

1838.   THE LORD CHANCELLOR :
Nov. 17.
——   The facts of this case are short and simple.   The question
raised upon them is important in principle, but, in my opinion,
not difficult of solution.

[495]   The plaintiffs are, under the will of Ann Dixon, or, rather, as
her next of kin, entitled to an interest in her personal estate.
Letters of administration of the estate of Ann Dixon, with her

will annexed, were, in the year 1829, granted to Thomas Reup
Dixon and Emily Bond, then the wife of John Bond.

In the month of December, 1831, John Bond died, and the
appellants are his widow and personal representatives.

In October, 1832, and in the following month, Thomas Reup
Dixon drew out from Messrs. Child & Co. a sum of money, part
of Ann Dixon's estate, which has not been recovered from him,
and is lost to the estate; and the question is, whether the estate
of John Bond is liable to make good the loss by replacing that
sum. His personal representatives, by their answer, admit the
joint possession of the property by Thomas Reup Dixon and
John Bond, with the consent of Emily Bond, and that the
balance was paid into Child's, in the joint names of Thomas
Reup Dixon and John Bond; and that it was agreed between
them that all drafts should be signed by them both.

Some attempt was made in the answer and by the evidence to
set up a settlement with Dixon; but the attempt did not succeed
in showing any settlement of the demand in question.

The ground upon which the plaintiffs support the claim against
the estate of Mr. Bond leaves his character for integrity unimpeached; and, if successful, will certainly prove a hard case
against those interested in his estate. It is this; that the
payment of the money into Child's, in the names of himself
and of Mr. Dixon, *was not a correct discharge of the duty which
he owed to the estate; and that, as the effect of such payment
has been to give Mr. Dixon the control over the fund by which
the loss has arisen, his estate is responsible.

It will be found to be the result of all the best authorities
upon the subject, that, although a personal representative, acting
strictly within the line of his duty, and exercising reasonable
care and diligence, will not be responsible for the failure or
depreciation of the fund in which any part of the estate may be
invested, or for the insolvency or misconduct of any person who
may have possessed it, yet, if that line of duty be not strictly
pursued, and any part of the property be invested by such personal
representative in funds or upon securities not authorised, or be
put within the control of persons who ought not to be intrusted
with it, and a loss be thereby eventually sustained, such personal

CLOUGH
v.
BOND.

[*496]

CLOUGH
v.
BOND.

representative will be liable to make it good, however unexpected
the result, however little likely to arise from the course adopted,
and however free such conduct may have been from any improper
motive. Thus, if he omit to sell property when it ought to be
sold, and it be afterwards lost without any fault of his, he is
liable: *Phillips* v. *Phillips* (1); or if he leave money due upon
personal security, which, though good at the time, afterwards
fails: *Powell* v. *Evans* (2), *Tebbs* v. *Carpenter* (3). And the case is
stronger if he be himself the author of the improper investment,
as upon personal security, or an unauthorised fund. Thus, he is
not liable, upon a proper investment in the 3 per cents., for loss
occasioned by the fluctuations of that fund: *Peat* v. *Crane* (4);

[*497]

but he is for the fluctuations of any unauthorised *fund: *Hancom*
v. *Allen* (5), *Howe* v. *Earl of Dartmouth* (6). So, when the loss
arises from the dishonesty or failure of any one to whom the
possession of part of the estate has been entrusted. Necessity,
which includes the regular course of business in administering
the property, will, in equity, exonerate the personal representative. But if, without such necessity, he be instrumental
in giving to the person failing possession of any part of the
property, he will be liable, although the person possessing it
be a co-executor or co-administrator: *Langford* v. *Gascoyne* (7),
Lord Shipbrook v. *Lord Hinchinbrook* (8), *Underwood* v. *Stevens*
(1 Mer. 712) (9).

Applying these principles to the present case, the inquiry is
necessarily confined to two points; first, was the payment into
Child's of the money in question, in the joint names of Mr. Bond
and Mr. Dixon, a proper mode of deposit; and, if not, secondly,
was the loss occasioned by such mode of deposit?

Bond had nothing to do with the estate, except as husband of
the administratrix. During the coverture he was entitled to
interfere in her right; but that authority was determinable with
the determination of the coverture. In the event, therefore,

(1) Freem. Ch. Ca. 11.
(2) See 14 R. R., pref., p. ix.
(5 Ves. 839).
(3) 16 R. R. 224 (1 Madd. 290).
(4) 2 Dick. 499, *n*.
(5) 2 Dick. 498.

(6) 6 R. R. 96 (7 Ves. 137).
(7) 8 R. R. 170 (11 Ves. 333).
(8) 8 R. R. 138 (11 Ves. 252; 16
Ves. 477).
(9) And see *Hanbury* v. *Kirkland*,
30 R. R. 165 (3 Sim. 265).

which happened, of his death before his wife, her authority would remain to be exercised by herself alone, and so she would be enabled to control her co-administrator—a security to the estate of which he had no right to deprive it. By depositing the money in his own name and that of the co-administrator Dixon, he did exclude the administratrix from ever possessing this control, so far as affects *the funds in question, and in the event [*498] of Dixon's death before him, gave to himself the absolute power over it; and in the event, which has happened, of his dying first, enabled Dixon to appropriate it to himself without the control of his co-administratrix. This mode of deposit, therefore, was an act by which, without necessity, one of the personal representatives was excluded, who had at one time possession, and by which exclusive possession was likely to vest in a person not entitled to it; and that event having happened, and such person having, by virtue of such possession, appropriated the fund to himself, there can be no doubt that the deposit was improper, and that it has been the cause of the loss. The principle, therefore, of the cases referred to subjects Bond's estate to the liability of making good this fund; for although the wife was the personal representative, and she survives, yet the *devastavit* consisted in the improper deposit, which took place during the coverture; the money lost was part of the estate which came to the hands of the husband, and from which nothing has taken place that can discharge him. He was himself the author of the *devastavit*, and his estate is liable, as is fully illustrated by Lord REDESDALE in *Adair* v. *Shaw* (1 Sch. & Lef. 243) (1).

I have therefore no difficulty in dismissing the petition of appeal, with costs.

I find that the decree adopts the statement of the sums as set out in the answer, with which I presume all parties are satisfied, as none have complained of that part of the decree. I cannot, however, but observe, upon the apparent inconsistency of adopting these sums, and particularly of declaring that the 988*l*. 6*s*. 8*d*. *formed the share or part of the share of the plaintiff in the [*499] residue of the estate, and at the same time directing the general accounts, and declaring that what shall be found due, including

(1) See *Soady* v. *Turnbull* (1866) L. R. 1 Ch. 494.

CLOUGH
v.
BOND.

the sums in question, shall be applied in a due course of administration. But as that part of the case has not been brought before me, I only mention it for the purpose of excluding the supposition that, in dismissing the petition of appeal, I intend to express any opinion upon this part of the case.

───────●───────

1838.
Jan. 24, 31.

Lord
COTTENHAM,
L.C.

STUBBS *v.* SARGON.

(3 My. & Cr. 507—514; S. C. 7 L. J. (N. S.) Ch. 95; 2 Jur. 150.)

[A NOTE of this appeal will be found at the end of the report before the Master of the Rolls (2 Keen, 255). See 44 R. R. at p. 250].

───────●───────

1838.
Feb. 8, 10.
─────
Lord
COTTENHAM,
L.C.

[515]

DESBOROUGH *v.* RAWLINS (1).

(3 My. & Cr. 515—525; S. C. 7 L. J. (N. S.) Ch. 171; 2 Jur. 125.)

Confidential communications are made by A. to B. in the presence of B.'s solicitor. The solicitor cannot afterwards refuse to disclose these communications on the ground that his information was acquired as professional adviser of B.

THE bill was filed by the plaintiff, as representing the Atlas Insurance Company, against the defendants Sir W. Rawlins and John Richards, as two of the directors of the Eagle Insurance Company, and against the defendant Smith as the actuary, and the defendants the Beethams, as the solicitors, of that company; and prayed that a policy of insurance, effected by the Eagle Company in the names of the defendants, Sir W. Rawlins and Richards, with the Atlas Company, upon the life of one John Cochrane, might be declared fraudulent and void, and be delivered up to be cancelled; and that the Eagle Company, and the defendants Smith and the Beethams, might be ordered to pay the costs of the suit, and that, in the meantime, proceedings on the policy might be restrained.

[516]

The bill stated, amongst other things, that in the month of September, 1834, and before the time at which the policy in question was effected, a proposal was made by the defendant Smith, on behalf of the Eagle Company, to the Economic

(1) *Kennedy* v. *Lyell* (1883) 23 Ch. Div. 387, 48 L. T. 455; aff. 9 App. Cas. 81.

Insurance Company, for an insurance by them upon Cochrane's
life, for the sum of 4,000*l.*, and that, after some negotiation, Mr.
Travers, the medical officer of the Economic Company, was
desired by them to see Cochrane; which he accordingly did, on
the 20th of September, 1834; and that he also had an interview
with one Mr. Bennett respecting Cochrane's health and habits;
and that, on the same day (viz. the 20th of September, 1834) he
wrote and sent to Mr. Knowles, the managing director of the
Economic Company, a letter, which was set out in the bill, and
which contained a report upon Cochrane which was, in some
respects, unfavourable.

The bill then alleged that, on Monday, the 22nd of September,
1834, Mr. Downes, the actuary of the Economic Company, called
at the office of the Eagle Company, taking with him Mr. Travers's
letter, and that he then had an interview with the defendant
Smith, and told him that the Economic Company had had an
unfavourable report of Cochrane, and would refuse the proposed
insurance on his life, and that he (Mr. Downes) thought it right
to apprize the Eagle Company of it immediately, and in candour
to show them Mr. Travers's letter, which was the reason of the
refusal; and that Mr. Downes then handed Mr. Travers's letter
to the defendant Smith, by whom it was perused, and returned
to Mr. Downes, who thereupon went back to the Economic office,
and wrote and sent to the Eagle Company a formal letter,
rejecting the proposed insurance on Cochrane's life.

The answer of the defendants, the Beethams, stated that,
although when the transactions mentioned in the bill took place,
they were the solicitors and attorneys of the Eagle Company,
yet that they had since ceased to be such solicitors and attorneys,
and that they had delivered up to the present solicitors and
attorneys of that company all books and papers which they had
formerly in their possession, containing entries relating to the
matters mentioned in the bill, and had taken a receipt containing a list of the books and papers given up; and it submitted
that, even if they could set forth a list of all such books and
papers as was required, or could set forth the purport of the
entries inquired after, they ought not so to do, inasmuch as the
books and papers in question had been in their possession as the

[517]

DESBOROUGH solicitors and attorneys of the Eagle Company; and it stated
v.
RAWLINS. that some one or two days before the 24th of September, 1884,
an interview took place between Downes and Smith, at the office
of the Eagle Company where Downes called : and then it contained the following passage : " But they, these defendants,
refuse to answer or to discover, and set forth, whether at such
time as last mentioned, when the said Mr. Downes did call at
the office of the said Eagle Company, he did, at such time, take
with him the aforesaid letter of the said Mr. Travers ; and
whether the said Mr. Downes did, at the interview with the
said Mr. Downes and the said Henry Porter Smith, make such
statements and give such information to the said Henry Porter
Smith as thereinbefore in that behalf in the said bill particularly
alleged, and did then make any other and what statements
relative to the matters in the said bill mentioned, to the like
or to any other or what purport or effect ; and whether the said
Mr. Downes did then, after any statement, hand over to the
said Henry Porter Smith the aforesaid letter of the said Mr.
Travers ; and whether the said Henry Porter Smith did take
[*518] and peruse the aforesaid letter ; but this defendant, *Francis
Beetham, for himself saith, and this other defendant saith he
believes the same to be true, that this defendant, Francis
Beetham, was the only person present at the said interview
between the said Mr. Downes and the said Henry Porter Smith.
And these defendants do so refuse to answer and set forth,
because they say that, long before and on the said 22nd day of
September, 1834, they, these defendants, were the solicitors and
attorneys, and the professional and confidential advisers, of the
said Eagle Company, and that this defendant, Francis Beetham,
was present at the aforesaid interview as the solicitor and attorney
and professional adviser of the said Eagle Company, and acquired
his information touching all and singular the matters and things
which these defendants have as aforesaid refused to answer and
discover and set forth, solely and only from the fact of his being
present at the time in his capacity of such solicitor and attorney
and professional and confidential adviser ; and these defendants
humbly submit that they are not bound therefore to answer all or
any of such matters and things."

The plaintiff having excepted to this answer for insufficiency, the Master allowed the exceptions, so far as they related to the parts of the answer above referred to; but, upon exceptions to the Master's report being taken, and argued before the Master of the Rolls, his Lordship allowed them; and thus, in effect, overruled the plaintiff's exceptions to the answer.

The plaintiff now appealed from the order of the MASTER OF THE ROLLS.

Mr. Wigram and *Mr. James Russell*, in support of the appeal, cited *Parkhurst* v. *Lowten* (1), *Williams* v. *Mundie* (2), *Greenough* v. *Gaskell* (3), *Bramwell* v. *Lucas* (4), *Sawyer* v. *Birchmore* (5).

[*519]

Mr. Wakefield and *Mr. W. Hislop Clarke*, contrà, cited *Purcell* v. *Macnamara* (6), *Robson* v. *Kemp* (7), *Paxton* v. *Douglas* (8), [and other cases].

Mr. Wigram, in reply.

THE LORD CHANCELLOR:

Since this case was before me the other day, I have looked not only at all the cases which were then cited in the argument, but also at several which were not cited.

I do not think that it is necessary that I should now lay down any rule as to the length to which the privilege should extend. It would not be very easy to do so, consistently with the cases; but I am to consider whether the defendant clearly brings himself within the privilege; for a defendant who relies upon the privilege, is undoubtedly bound to bring himself clearly and distinctly within it. Now, the situation of the parties is very material to be considered with reference to the doctrine on this subject, which is laid down in all the cases.

This was a transaction between two companies, in which the two companies were so far in opposition to each other, that the

[520]

(1) 19 R. R. 63 (2 Swanst. 194).
(2) Ry. & Moo. 34.
(3) 36 R. R. 258 (1 My. & K. 98).
(4) 2 B. & C. 745.
(5) 41 R. R. 133 (3 My. & K. 572).
(6) 9 R. R. 78 (9 East, 157).
(7) 8 R. R. 831 (5 Esp. 52).
(8) 12 R. R. 175 (19 Ves. 225).

Eagle Company were desirous of insuring a particular life in the
Economic, and the Economic Company were desirous to obtain
information with respect to that life; and the meeting in question
was a meeting of an officer of the Economic, with an officer of
the Eagle. The communication was the result of that inquiry.
Now, it is very difficult to suppose how that could be the subject
of professional communication between the officer of the Eagle
Company, and the solicitor of the same company. It was a
communication from an adverse party. If it had been made
directly to the solicitor, for the purpose of being communicated
to the company, it would not be very easy to consider it as a
privileged communication. That was the exact case in *Spenceley*
v. *Schulenburgh* (1), where a communication took place undoubtedly
(in the terms of this answer) with a solicitor, in the character of
solicitor ; but it was a communication which, first, the Judge at
Nisi Prius, and, afterwards, the Court of King's Bench thought
that the solicitor was not privileged to withhold. The Court
there said, in substance, "This is no privileged communication.
The object of the rule as to privileged communications is to secure
to parties, who have confidential communications with their
professional advisers, the benefit of secrecy as to those communications. This case is not within the mischief which that rule
is intended to guard against; and, therefore, not within the rule."

Whether the case of *Bramwell* v. *Lucas* (2) was rightly decided
or not, is not very material for the present purpose; and the
[*521]   observations made upon it by Lord *BROUGHAM, in *Greenough* v.
Gaskell (3), are not made with reference to the principle of the
case, but with reference to the question, whether the principle
was properly applicable to the facts. Undoubtedly, looking at
the facts of that case (I mean of *Bramwell* v. *Lucas*), it is not
very easy to come to the conclusion to which the Court there
came in point of fact. The question was, whether the client
had committed an act of bankruptcy on a particular day. On
that day, the client inquired of his solicitor, whether he could
safely attend a particular meeting of his creditors, without being
arrested for debt. The solicitor advised him to stay in his office;

(1) 7 East, 357.   (3) 36 R. R. 258 (1 My. & K. 98).
(2) 2 B. & C. 745.

and he accordingly did stay there for upwards of two hours, to
avoid being arrested.   The question was whether what passed
between the solicitor and his client was receivable in evidence.
That looks undoubtedly very like a professional communication
for the purpose of obtaining advice ; and the Court said, if it
was a professional communication, it was privileged.   If, therefore, the client asked the solicitor his advice in point of law,
whether he could with safety attend the meeting of his creditors,
the communication would be privileged, but the Court said that,
in its nature, it could not be privileged, but that it was merely
an inquiry of fact, whether the client's creditors, because they
had clearly all their legal rights, would arrest him ; and that the
only question was, whether they had agreed not to do so : and
the Court held that the question was one of fact, and not of law.
There was no question, therefore, as to the principle upon which
the Court intended to act : the only question was whether the
facts justified the application of the principle.   But both *Bramwell* v. *Lucas* and *Greenough* v. *Gaskell* show that the privilege
only applies to cases in which the client makes a communication
to his solicitor *with a view to obtaining his legal advice.   That
is undoubtedly the same ground upon which I held, in *Sawyer* v.
Birchmore (1), that a solicitor, when examined as a witness, was
bound to produce letters communicated to him from collateral
quarters, and to answer questions seeking information as to
matters of fact, as distinguished from confidential communications : and I so decided, not on the authority of *Bramwell* v.
Lucas only, but I distinctly referred to *Spenceley* v. *Schulenburgh.*
In *Sawyer* v. *Birchmore* the question arose as to a solicitor being
bound to disclose the circumstances of certain transactions in
which he had been concerned as solicitor.   I was of opinion that
the facts were not sufficiently brought before me to show that
they were privileged ; and finding it laid down by the Court of
King's Bench, that communications are not privileged, if coming
from any other quarter, but that they would be, if they came
from the client, I found that a case might exist in which many
papers in a solicitor's hands would not be privileged.   It was
precisely the same in *Spenceley* v. *Schulenburgh ;* I thought,

(1) 41 R. R. 133 (3 My. & K. 572).

DESBOROUGH
v.
RAWLINS.

[*522]

DESBOROUGH
v.
RAWLINS.

therefore, that the facts did not bring the case within the privilege applicable to confidential communications.

There is nothing in the doctrine laid down by Lord BROUGHAM in *Greenough* v. *Gaskell* inconsistent with this; and the only observation is, not that the doctrine laid down was wrong, but that there might be a question how far the facts were sufficient to entitle the Court to apply the doctrine to the facts. There, Gaskell was employed as solicitor by a person named Darwell. He had advanced money for his principal upon the security of a promissory note given on behalf of his principal

[*523]

by the plaintiffs ; and the question was, whether Gaskell *had not induced the makers of the note to give it, and whether he had not fraudulently concealed from them the fact that his principal was insolvent. He put in an answer, in which he denied that the note had been given by the plaintiffs at his instance ; but he admitted that he had been aware of his client's circumstances at the time in question, and he also admitted the possession of books, papers, and letters relating to the matters mentioned in the bill : and he set forth a list of them in a schedule ; stating, however, that the entries in the books were made, and the papers and letters written and received by him in his capacity of confidential solicitor for his client. Lord BROUGHAM refused to order the books, papers, and letters to be produced.

As to many of those papers, undoubtedly the privilege would apply. It did not appear to me at the time (1), nor does it now appear to me, that there might not be papers to which that privilege would not apply. The defendant, the solicitor, stating what he did, I should doubt whether the Court would not call on him to set out the papers in particular, and to give them in more detail. It is, however, not at all essential to go further into the examination of the particular circumstances of that case, for it is quite clear that Lord BROUGHAM intended to lay down the rule as he found it laid down in all the cases ; and his only observations upon *Bramwell* v. *Lucas* had reference to the facts of that case.

Such being the rule, the only question is, whether the defendant in the present case has used such words in his answer as clearly and distinctly to bring himself within it.

(1) The Lord Chancellor was counsel in the case.

Now the very first question is one which I should think it very difficult for him to protect himself from answering, for he says Downes came to the office, but he objects to state whether he came with a particular letter in his hand; and then, upon reading the terms in which the defendant has put his refusal to answer, the first observation which suggests itself is, that if the reasons which he gives for that refusal be good, it is quite clear that the decision in *Spenceley* v. *Schulenburgh* (1) was wrong; for the party for whom the witness in that case was solicitor, and the party with whom he was dealing, were opposed to each other. On one side a person comes on the part of the plaintiff, and brings to the defendant's solicitor a certain paper, the contents of which the defendant's solicitor is called upon to prove; and the Court of King's Bench said that the privilege was restricted to communications, whether oral or written, from the client to his attorney, and could not extend to adverse proceedings communicated to him, as attorney in the cause, from the opposite party, in the disclosure of which there could be no breach of confidence.

Suppose that it had been to or from Beetham personally that the letter had been communicated, the case would be exactly within *Spenceley* v. *Schulenburgh*; and the question would be, whether the solicitor, to whom, as solicitor, the communication was made, would be entitled to withhold it. The Court of King's Bench said he would not, because it was not confidential between himself and the party for whom he was solicitor.

As to all the rest, I dare say this gentleman intended it to be supposed that the words were used in their *ordinary sense. He has not pledged his oath to the circumstances under which he obtained the information, in such a manner as to show that it is to be considered privileged.

It may be that the defendant (Francis Beetham) was present accidentally, and so heard what passed; but at all events those who claim the privilege are bound to bring their case within it. I cannot say, till I have learned how the defendant came to be present, who sent for him, and so forth, whether the communication was privileged.

(1) 7 East, 357,

DESBOROUGH
v.
RAWLINS.
[524]

[*525]

DESBOROUGH   I say nothing as to what the result will be when the circum-
RAWLINS.   stances shall be more distinctly stated. The question I have to
decide is, whether the defendants have on their answer protected
themselves from the discovery: and I think that they have not.

As to whether they were properly made defendants, I cannot enter
into that question, because I find them defendants; and the only
question before me is, whether being defendants, they have put
in a sufficient answer: but I trust that nothing I say in this or
in any other case will tend to promote the practice of making
witnesses defendants to a suit.

Exceptions to the Master's report over-ruled.

1838.
June 15.

Lord
COTTENHAM,
L.C.

[526]

ADAMS *v.* FISHER (1).

(3 My. & Cr. 526–549; S. C. 7 L. J. (N. S.) Ch. 289; 2 Jur. 508.)

The production of documents scheduled to the defendant's answer is
not enforced where they do not support the equity asserted by the bill.

[THE facts of the case are concisely but sufficiently set out in
the following judgment:

Mr. O. Anderdon, in support of a motion for the production
of documents by the defendant, on appeal from a refusal of the
motion by the MASTER OF THE ROLLS.]

[546]   THE LORD CHANCELLOR:

As I understand the facts of the case, Fisher the solicitor was
employed by Pinckard, he knowing, as he must have known, that
in the transaction which was the subject of the suit, Pinckard was
acting under a power of attorney from Adams: but still the
retainer was entirely between Pinckard and Fisher. Pinckard
settles the account with him. Then Adams says, I certainly have
a right to an account against my trustee, and if he has improperly
paid sums on account of the costs, they must, as a matter of course,
be disallowed. The bill is then filed, and a claim made against
the trustee, alleging that he has retained, on account of costs,
more than he ought. Mr. Fisher, by his answer, denying all
connection with the plaintiff, and all privity between them, the

(1) Questioned in *Swinborne* v. *Nelson* (1853) 16 Beav. 416, 22 L. J. Ch. 331.

question is, whether, in such a state of the pleadings, Adams is entitled to enforce the production of the documents mentioned in Fisher's answer.

Now I took leave to ask *Mr. Anderdon* how far he carried the principle ; and he very properly limits it within its due bounds; that is, he admits, as to every document not necessary to make out the plaintiff's equity, that the plaintiff is not entitled to see it. Whatever may make out the plaintiff's title he may have a right to see. The documents in question, however, are not to make out Adams's title to have the bills taxed, and the production of them could not possibly aid the assertion of the equity which Adams has asserted by his bill.

[His Lordship then referred to and distinguished some cases which had been cited, but which had no real application to the case, and continued as follows :]

As to *Hardman* v. *Ellames* (1), it is not very pertinent to the present case. It was certainly no new decision, and I was very much surprised to hear any one treat it as such; and when I came to look into the doctrines laid down in the books, I felt no doubt upon the subject. *Where a party has thought proper to put his defence upon a particular document, he himself having introduced it and put it forward, he cannot be permitted to make any representation of it, however unfounded, which he pleases ; but the plaintiff is entitled to see whether the defendant has rightly stated it. It is because the defendant chooses to make it part of his answer that the plaintiff is entitled to see it ; not because the plaintiff has an interest in it. The principle is, that a defendant shall not avail himself of that mode of concealing his defence. But, whether that decision be right or wrong, it is quite distinct from the present case. I apprehend it is a mistake to say that the documents scheduled are part of the answer : the schedule itself is part of the answer. All that the plaintiff asks is, that the defendant may set forth a schedule of the documents. Can you except, because he has set out the documents in the schedule instead of in the [answer] (2) ? You did not ask that they should

[548]

[*549]

---

(1) 39 R. R. 344 (2 My. & K. 732).
(2) By a clerical error in the original report the word " bill " was
inserted here in two places instead of "answer."—O. A. S.

ADAMS
v.
FISHER.

be set out in the [answer]. If that had been asked, the defendant must have defended himself in the regular way, and shown that he was not obliged to comply with your demand. But if the defendant sets them out in the schedule to his answer, the question is, upon the whole record, whether the plaintiff has such an interest in them as entitles him to call for their production ? Here the defendant has denied the plaintiff's interest ; he has, on the record, stated that which, as it stands, in my opinion excludes the plaintiff from instituting this suit against him. As long as that stands, I think the plaintiff is not entitled to see the documents.

Sir W. Horne and *Mr. Bagshawe* appeared for the defendant Fisher, but were not called upon.

1888.
Feb. 21, 28.
——
Lord
COTTENHAM,
L.C.
[559]

BERNAL *v.* BERNAL.

(3 My. & Cr. 559—583; S. C. C. P. Coop. 55; 7 L. J. (N. S.) Ch. 115;
2 Jur. 273.)

" Male children " in a Dutch will, held to mean " male descendants " : and " male descendants " held to mean, according to English law [and *semble* according to Dutch law also] descendants claiming through males only.

[IN this case a question arose upon a foreign will whether the expression " male descendants," denoting a class taking by inheritance, was to be confined to descendants claiming through males only.

The case, so far as it turned upon the special context of the will, is of no practical utility ; but the judgment of the LORD CHANCELLOR contains some general observations upon the meaning of the expression " male descendants," independently of the context, and the following passages from the judgment containing these observations are retained accordingly :

THE LORD CHANCELLOR said :]

[581]

It must be considered, for the purpose of ascertaining who are to take, in the nature of an inheritance ; the qualification to take being derived from the parties' descent ; and that qualification is being *male descendants*. The general class is, descendants : the qualification of the class is, being male. To entitle any one

to claim, he must show that he is one of the favoured class ; that
is, one of the class of male descendants.   A male, descended from
a female of the family, would undoubtedly answer the description,
as he would be a descendant and a male ; but he would not be
one of the class of male descendants.

Such would be the ordinary acceptation of the terms.   In
speaking of a man and his male descendants, as a class, no one
would conceive the son of a female descendant as included ; and such
is the construction which our law has put upon the words ; as "issue
male," which is, in fact, the same thing as male descendants.

The case of *Oddie* v. *Woodford* (1) appears to me to be a strong
authority for the same purpose ; for although the word "lineal"
was much relied upon, the force of that word was to mark the
class to which the party was to belong, in contradistinction to the
particular description of the individual.   In no other sense could
the term "lineal" be of any importance, as the party must have
been lineally descended, whether descended through a male or a
female ; but, considering the word "lineal" as indicating the
class, and therefore as meaning a descendant of the male line
rather than a male descendant, the House of Lords held the
grandson of the testator's second son (2) not to be entitled.   In
this case, it is clear that the testator is speaking of and describing
a class ; which brings it directly within the principle of *Oddie* v.
Woodford. [His Lordship concluded his judgment by saying
that he thought there was enough upon the face of the will to
lead to the conclusion that the parties for claims were to be
descendants in the male line.]

ODDIE *v.* WOODFORD (3).

(3 My. & Cr. 584—631 ; S. C. 7 L. J. (N. S.) Ch. 117.)

The designation of "eldest male lineal descendant," held to be
inapplicable to a male person claiming in part through a female.

[IN this case the question was whether the expression "eldest
male lineal descendant" was confined to a descendant claiming

1821.
Feb. 8, *et seq*
April 7.

1822.
Nov. 9, 10.

1825.
June 23.
—
[584]

(1) See next case.
(2) Being the son of a daughter of
the testator's second son.

(3) *Lord   Rendlesham*   v.   *Roberts*
(1856) 23 Beav. 321.

through males only. The question, however, turned upon the special context of the will, which strongly supported that construction. It seems hopeless to attempt to extract any general principle from Lord ELDON's judgment, which deals minutely and at great length with the interpretation and construction of the whole will, but some passages of the will have already been printed in the Revised Reports (see 8 R. R. 106) which will illustrate the way in which the expression was used by the testator.

Upon appeal to the House of Lords, an opinion was delivered in the House of Lords by Lord Chief Baron ALEXANDER, on behalf of the Judges, in answer to certain questions which had been proposed to them by the House.

That opinion contained the following passage:]

[628]   (1.) We are of opinion that in the case put in the first question, the grandson of the testator's second son, being a male descendant through a male, would be entitled to nominate or present to the vacant living.

We are of this opinion, because we think the words "eldest male lineal descendant" of his three sons respectively, according to the true construction of the testator's will, designate male persons descended from such sons in the male line only. The other construction contended for is, that the testator meant to confer the power of nomination on the eldest male who was a descendant of his sons respectively, without regard to his being descended through males. If he had intended this, he would have pointed out in terms the eldest male descendant. That is the obvious and natural mode of expressing such intention. The word "lineal" would not have been introduced. On that construction it is totally useless. It was introduced, as it appears to us, in order to intimate the testator's desire that the person to nominate should be a male descendant of a son in the male line. No sense or operation can, in phrase, be given to the word "lineal," but by connecting it with "male," and giving it the sense just stated.

1825.
June 23.   [This opinion was adopted by the House of Lords, and Lord ELDON's decision was affirmed.]

BOWES v. FERNIE.

(3 My. & Cr. 632—638.)

1838.
March 10.
———
Lord
COTTENHAM,
L.C.
[632]

Upon a motion for discovery and inspection of documents, grounded on a defendant's answer, the Court is not at liberty to disregard the statements in the answer, as to parts of the documents which are not disclosed, however suspicious those statements may be; but if they are inconsistent with each other, the Court will adopt the statement which is most favourable to the plaintiff; and if such parts of the documents as are disclosed contradict the answer as to the other parts, the Court will order an inspection of such other parts.

THE bill was filed for an account of certain pecuniary dealings and transactions, in which the defendants had been concerned with the late Lord Glamis. The defendant Fernie was an accountant, who had acted for a number of years in the capacity of receiver of Lord Glamis's estates, and generally in the management of his affairs. By his answer he admitted that he had in his possession certain deeds, documents, books, and accounts, which related exclusively to the matters in question in the cause, and which he particularized in a schedule; and that he had also, in his possession, divers other books and ledgers (specified in the same schedule) which contained some entries relating to those matters, but which likewise contained many entries relating to other and distinct matters, and to which he had daily occasion to refer in the course of his ordinary business; and he submitted that no inspection of such books and ledgers ought to be given.

With respect to the deeds, documents, books, and papers, to the inspection of which no objection was suggested by the answer, the VICE-CHANCELLOR, on the 8th of June, 1837, made the common order for their production; and he further ordered that the plaintiff's clerk-in-court, or solicitor, should be allowed to inspect and take extracts from the other books and ledgers at the defendant's office, upon giving a day's notice of his intention; with liberty to the defendant to seal up, upon oath, all such parts of them as did not relate to any of the matters in question in the cause.

Accordingly, the plaintiff's solicitor, in the months of August and September, 1837, inspected the last-mentioned books and ledgers in the defendant's office; the defendant having previously

[633]

Bowes
v.
Fernie.

fastened up certain parts of them, and made an affidavit that he had fastened up such parts only as did not relate to any matters in question in the cause.

The plaintiff afterwards moved that a more extensive inspection of those books and ledgers might be granted.

The affidavit of the plaintiff's solicitor, filed in support of the motion, stated, amongst other things, that the ledgers which were produced to the deponent, under the order of the 8th of June, 1837, had certain parts of them sewed up or fastened up, and that each of them contained an index to the contents, which index was one of the parts so fastened up, so that the deponent was unable to see by the index what accounts relating to the affairs of Lord Glamis were entered in such ledger; although the deponent believed that such indexes, if open to inspection, would be found to contain references to those accounts. The affidavit further stated, that all the items in the cash book marked E., as well receipts as disbursements, appeared, as in the customary method of book-keeping, to have been posted into certain pages in the defendant's ledgers, the numbers of those pages being entered opposite to the items in the cash book; and that on reference to the corresponding pages in the ledgers it appeared that many of such items were so posted accordingly; but that others of them appeared to be posted into pages of the ledgers which were fastened up and not open to inspection; and that several of such last-mentioned items (which the affidavit specified) were entries relating to the accounts of Lord Glamis.

[634]

The defendant Fernie, by an affidavit in reply, stated that the indexes of the ledgers contained nothing relating to any of the matters in question in the cause, except the numbers of the pages in the ledgers, and that those pages themselves were left open. He further deposed, that the entries in the cash book marked E. were not entered or posted in any ledgers or books in his possession, except in a ledger marked K., which had been left entirely open to the inspection of the plaintiff's solicitor, and which was kept by the deponent expressly for the accounts between himself and Lord Glamis; and that the deponent kept such part of the accounts as related to Lord Glamis's estates at

Redburn, and to various other receipts and payments made
on his account, in another book, which was taken away by
Lord Glamis in 1833, and retained. He further deposed that
such entries in the cash book E. as were not to be found posted
in ledger K., referred to the book so retained.

In a second affidavit the defendant specified the particular
pages which he had sewed up in his several account books
and ledgers. In the ledger marked H., he stated that he had,
among other pages, sewed up from page 1 to page 45, and in
the ledger marked I. from page 1 to page 68, both inclusive,
and that in none of the pages of the said several books so
sewed up was contained any entry relating to the matters
in question in the cause. In accordance with this affidavit,
the indexes, and also several pages, which had on former
inspections been fastened up in the body of the ledgers, were
now left open.

By a subsequent affidavit of the plaintiff's solicitor it appeared
that upon an inspection had by him in *August, 1837, pages 35,
36, and 37 of ledger H. and page 48 of ledger I. (which were
now fastened up), were open on that occasion, and that they
then contained entries relative to the matters in question
in the cause. The defendant, by an affidavit in answer,
admitted the fact, but stated that the pages specified had been
afterwards accidentally closed, in consequence of the leaves
having been inadvertently fastened up to a wrong page, and
that immediately on discovering the mistake he had proceeded
to rectify it.

Upon these affidavits, the VICE-CHANCELLOR made an order,
referring it to the Master to open and inspect the several books
and ledgers last mentioned, and report what parts of them
(if any) ought not to be inspected by the plaintiff, and to seal
up such parts only; and further, that the defendant should
produce and leave the same books and ledgers in the Master's
office as the Master should direct: but the plaintiff and her
solicitor were not to inspect them without the Master's
permission.

The defendant Fernie now moved that this order might be
discharged.

BOWES
v.
FERNIE.

[*635]

Mr. Simpkinson, for the motion :

The VICE-CHANCELLOR proceeded upon the ground that the
four pages which are now sealed up were open in August, 1837,
and are sworn by the plaintiff's solicitor, and not denied by the
defendant, to have then contained entries relating to matters
in question in the cause, a circumstance which raised such a
degree of suspicion as, in his Honour's opinion, warranted
[*636]   the reference to the Master. Suspicion, however, is no *sufficient ground, in a case of this description, for inducing the
Court to subject the whole of a tradesman's books and ledgers
to the inquisitorial scrutiny of a Master.   *   *   *

Sir W. Horne and *Mr. Lovat, contrà :*

The VICE-CHANCELLOR's order was grounded upon this, that a
defendant shall not be permitted to contradict himself. If he
does, the Court refers it to the Master to inquire into and state
how the fact stands. If, therefore, he falsifies his own answer
or his own affidavit, an inspection will be directed to be had,
qualified in the manner which has been directed here. The
principle of the cases referred to is, that you shall not be
permitted to contradict, by extrinsic evidence, the statement
of the party himself : but that principle does not apply where,
to use the gentlest expression, the defendant has convicted
himself of gross incorrectness and inconsistency.

[637]   THE LORD CHANCELLOR :

If the practice of the Court, or any precedent, had been found
to authorise such an order as the present, I should feel no dis-
inclination to support it, for certainly the circumstances are
most suspicious, and the defendant's statements any thing but
satisfactory. On the face of them, it was clear that the indexes
must have related to the matters in question in the cause, and
that fact is not now denied ; and I should therefore, have no
hesitation in giving as much discovery as, consistently with the
practice, I could give.

So far as the defendant's affidavits contain statements at
variance with each other, or so far as the document itself shows
a discrepancy in his statements, it would be quite consistent

with the rules of the Court to get at the truth by compelling the party to give discovery : and if there be now any matters which are open to that observation, either from contradiction in the affidavits, or from the character of the entries themselves, I am ready to make the order for inspection to that extent; but it is quite new to me, and no authority has been produced for holding, that an order of this sort may be directed upon an answer. It is not because you *suspect* that a defendant has stated facts incorrectly or untruly in his answer, that you are at liberty to disregard those statements. If, with respect to a particular matter, a defendant has made inconsistent and contradictory statements, the plaintiff may adopt and act upon that which is most in his own favour. But his answer may be open to every possible suspicion, and yet, according to the practice, the Court cannot reject it.

I do not think that the order can be maintained in its present shape ; but as it was open to the VICE-CHANCELLOR, upon the motion before him, to order the production *and inspection of any books or accounts, as to which the defendant had made contradictory statements, or as to which the documents themselves showed a discrepancy, let any such be pointed out to me now, and I will order them to be inspected. It seems to me, however, now that access has been given to the indexes and to the four pages formerly open in ledgers H. and I., the plaintiff has got all she can require.

[*638]

BOYS *v.* MORGAN.

(3 My. & Cr. 661—669; S. C. 7 L. J. (N. S.) Ch. 247 ; 2 Jur. 608.)

1838.
July 7.
—
Lord
COTTENHAM,
L.C.
[661]

The following passage at the end of a will, " I guess there will be found sufficient in my banker's hands to defray and discharge my debts, which I hereby desire E. M. to do, and keep the residue for her own use and pleasure," was held, under the circumstances and upon the whole context of the will, to amount to a gift of the general residuary personal estate to E. M.

It is irregular to comprise in one petition of appeal an appeal against orders made in distinct suits.

THE original bill, which was filed in September, 1835, stated, in substance, that in the year 1825, John Boys formed a connection with Eliza Morgan, who shortly afterwards went to reside

with him, and who continued to live under his protection from
that time until his death : that she gradually acquired great
influence *over him : that having become acquainted with the
nature and extent of his property, she formed a plan for securing
the possession of it to herself; and that in furtherance of that
plan, having by various fraudulent artifices established a complete
ascendancy over his mind, she prevailed upon him, in the
months of October and November, 1831, to transfer two several
sums of 6,000*l.* each, in the 3½ per cents., and afterwards, in the
month of October, 1834, two further sums of 6,817*l.* 4*s.* 8*d.*
3 per cent. Consols, and 5,200*l.* 3 per cent. Reduced Bank
Annuities, from his own name into hers in the books of the
Company of the Bank of England. The bill charged that at
the time when such last-mentioned transfers were made, Boys
was of the age of eighty-two years, and from his great age,
childish imbecility, and unsoundness of mind, was wholly
incapable of managing his affairs : that he died in August, 1835,
intestate; and that letters of administration were thereupon
granted to the plaintiff as one of his next of kin. The bill
prayed that the transfers of the several sums of stock might be
declared fraudulent and void, and that Eliza Morgan might be
ordered to transfer them to the plaintiff, for the purpose of being
applied in a due course of administration.

On the 9th of May, 1838, the plaintiff filed what was termed
a supplemental bill, whereby after setting forth the substance of
the former bill, he stated that Eliza Morgan alleged that John
Boys had left a will which was in the following words:
"London, No. 11, Gower Street North, 28th June, 1835. To
my friends and relations who may be curious to inquire, be it
known that a few years back of my own free will, I gave to
Eliza Morgan commonly called Eliza Castillo, all my furniture,
table, and bed linen, and apparel, plate, watches, and trinkets

[*663]   of any kind then in my possession, a pianoforte, all my *library,
manuscripts, papers, &c., whatever have been added and may
hereafter be added previous to my decease, without any exception
whatever, to her sole use and disposal, under promise from her
that she will take care that I shall never be in want of any
articles as long as I live. Having attained to the eighty-second

year of my existence, and finding the infirmities of age increasing, I choose to give her this voucher of the truth, that none may question or trouble her to make declaration of it.   She knows that thirty years ago, I agreed with Dr. Hector Campbell that he should have my carcase for chemical and anatomical experiments to be by him performed upon it, if he could prevail on her to give it to him; doubting her compliance, I will trouble my head no more about it.   The world may think this to be from a spirit of singularity or whim in me.   Be that as it may, I have always had a mortal aversion to funeral pomp and expense; and, therefore, trust she will avoid it; and had rather be given away with the sum a funeral would cost, for the purpose of dissection and chemical experiments.   I guess there will be found sufficient in my banker's hands to defray and discharge my debts, which I hereby desire Mrs. Eliza Morgan to do, and keep the residue for her own use and pleasure.   JOHN BOYS.''

The supplemental bill then stated that, in November, 1835, a suit was instituted by Eliza Morgan in the Prerogative Court, for the purpose of establishing the validity of the before mentioned will: that, after various proceedings in that suit, judgment was finally pronounced in March, 1838, declaring the instrument to be a valid will, revoking the letters of administration previously granted to the plaintiff, and granting probate of the will to Eliza Morgan, as executrix according to the tenor. The bill then charged that Eliza Morgan was *a stranger in   [*664] blood to the testator: that the before-mentioned sums were transferred into her name by the testator without any consideration whatever, and that she continued to hold them as a trustee for the testator : that, at the date of the will, the testator had at his banker's more than sufficient to pay all the debts which he then owed.   The bill prayed a declaration that the general residue of the testator's estate did not pass by the will, and that Eliza Morgan was a trustee of the aforesaid several sums of stock for the benefit of the plaintiff and the rest of the testator's next of kin; and that those sums might be transferred into Court and secured, until distribution should be made among the parties beneficially interested.

The defendants to both these bills were Eliza Morgan and

22—2

BOYS
v.
MORGAN.

the several persons who, together with the plaintiff, were the next of kin of the testator.

On the 24th of May, 1838, the defendant Morgan put in a plea to the first bill, pleading the judgment of the Prerogative Court and the grant of probate of the will to her; and she, on the same day, filed a demurrer to the second bill, for want of equity. The plea and demurrer came on to be heard together, when the VICE-CHANCELLOR made two separate orders, allowing them both, without costs (1).

The plaintiff presented a petition of appeal against both orders. The petition was presented in one of the causes only; and as the parties to the two were precisely the same, it did not clearly appear in which it was presented.

[*665]

The *Solicitor-General* took a preliminary objection to the petition, on the ground that it included, as the *subject of appeal, two several orders made in distinct suits.

The LORD CHANCELLOR considered the objection valid; but on the appellant's counsel electing to treat the appeal as an appeal against the order on the demurrer only, and undertaking to amend his petition by restricting it accordingly, he allowed the argument to proceed.

Mr. Wigram and *Mr. Richards*, for the appeal.

The *Solicitor-General, Mr. Jacob,* and *Mr. J. Russell,* for the defendant Morgan, in support of the demurrer.

[*Legge* v. *Asgill* (2), *Ommanney* v. *Butcher* (3), *Hastings* v. *Hane* (4), and other cases were cited.]

THE LORD CHANCELLOR:

The question turns upon the meaning which the testator attached to the term "residue"—whether he meant the residue of whatever balance there might be in his banker's hands, or whether he meant the residue of the property which he had to

(1) See 9 Sim. 289.   (3) 24 R. R. 42 (T. & R. 260).
(2) 24 R. R. 51 (T. & R. 265. *n*.).   (4) 38 R. R. 79 (6 Sim. 67).

dispose of. Now, it is to be assumed as a fact, upon the present consideration, that he had transferred certain funded property into the name of the person to whom probate of this will has been *granted, and to whom the residue, whatever it may be, is given. On the face of his will he desires that his friends and relations, that is, those persons who are interested in his estate, may be apprised that he had given furniture, and a variety of other articles which he enumerates, to the same person. It is quite clear he considered that he had divested himself of the whole of his property, and that this person was the depositary of that property: for when he states that he had done so under a promise from her that she would take care he should never be in want of any thing as long as he lived, it is impossible not to suppose that he conceived her to be the donee of the property, without the use of which he would not be able to continue enjoying the comforts of life, and that he had done so in consequence of her promise that he should not want for anything as long as he lived.

[*666]

In considering what he meant by the word " residue," it is extremely important to see what, on the face of his will, he shows to have been his view of the interest which this person was to take in his property. He supposed she had got the whole or nearly the whole of it. He had actually transferred to her his funded property ; or at least a great portion of it, for it is not alleged to have been the whole. He states that he had made over to her a variety of other articles ; and accompanies that statement with the expression I have already referred to.

The next passage which is at all material, is that in which, after disposing of his body for the purpose of dissection, the testator speaks of his funeral. He says he has a great aversion to funeral expense, and therefore trusts she will avoid it. How is she to avoid it? What had she to do with it? If he had named her *executrix, no doubt, as incident to the office, whatever might be the ultimate disposition of the property, he might consider her as having the disposal of it, as far as the funeral expenses were concerned ; but there is no nomination of an executrix in terms. She obtains the appointment of executrix, not because he has in terms nominated her, but because she is

[*667]

considered by the Ecclesiastical Court as having been so treated, with reference to the property to be administered, as to come within the rule of that Court by which it grants probate to a person as executor, though not named as such. It is quite clear she was to have the control of what would be the amount of the funeral expenses. Thus far, no property had been given to her over which she could have any control for funeral expenses. Of course it is not to be supposed that, after having made her a present of the stock by transferring it to her—after having also given her all his other articles of property, on condition that she should not let him want for any thing as long as he lived,—he could have meant that his funeral expenses should be defrayed out of those funds. It is quite clear he considered that Eliza Morgan would, after his death, be in possession and have the discretion over, and the control and administration of, the funds out of which the funeral expenses were to be defrayed.

It is also to be observed, with regard to the funeral expenses, that the testator not merely limits the amount of money to be spent, but seems rather to have had a more extensive object in view. His words are, " I had rather be given away with the sum a funeral would cost; " not directing it to be done, but expressing a preference that the money, which would be otherwise expended on a funeral, should be given away, and not spent in that manner.

[668] Then comes the last and most material clause : " I guess there will be found sufficient in my banker's hands to defray and discharge my debts, which I hereby desire Mrs. Eliza Morgan to do, and keep the residue for her own use and pleasure." The appellant's argument is that the operation of this clause must be confined to such balance only as might be in the banker's hands. But what is it that he has desired to be done, for there can be no ambiguity about that? It is not contended that the direction to pay the debts is to be confined to the sum in the banker's hands: that might or might not be enough—it is a mere guess ; and although it may be said that this particular direction is unnecessary, inasmuch as the law would itself give effect to the purpose, still it is material as throwing light on the testator's meaning. Undoubtedly he expresses a desire that his debts shall be paid at all events ; be paid by whom ? By the individual whom, from

the beginning of the will to the end, he has considered to be the person who had the control over his property, part of which he had given her in his lifetime, and who, as he conceived, would have the control over the whole of it at his death. Immediately after the passage as to discharging his debts comes the clause desiring that she shall keep the residue for her own use and pleasure. There is undoubtedly no expression showing that he contemplated a surplus beyond what would be required to satisfy the debts: it is quite uncertain—a mere conjecture—"I guess there will be found sufficient in my banker's hands to defray and discharge my debts." But I cannot confine the operation of the last clause to the balance in the banker's hands, without at the same time confining the direction as to the payment of the debts to the same balance; and if I were to do so, I should be doing violence to the words, and supposing what it is quite absurd to suppose, viz., that he intended *to direct that the debts should be paid out of the particular balance, which might or might not be sufficient for the purpose. The legatee could not control the payment of the debts, and the creditors would have a right to payment out of any property they could find, whether in the banker's hands or not. The question is, did the testator mean that the debts should be paid only in the event of there being a balance in the banker's hands sufficient for the purpose? No such intention is imputed to him: on the contrary, the contention imputed is that the person to whom he gives the residue of his property is to pay the debts out of that property; that is to say, out of the property claimed under his residuary gift: and what is found in the will relative to the balance at the banker's is merely an expression of his conjecture with respect to the amount of that portion of the residue.

It appears to me that the cases that have been referred to are not cases which exactly govern the present: the expressions are not precisely the same; but the principles on which Lord ELDON proceeded in *Crooke* v. *De Vandes* (1), and *Legge* v. *Asgill*, go the full length which is required in the present case.

I therefore
Dismiss the appeal, but without costs.

BOYS
v.
MORGAN.

[*669]

(1) *Crooke* v. *De Vandes* (9 Ves. 197) turned upon the special context of the will. *Legge* v. *Asgill* will be found in 24 R. R. 51.—O. A. S.

1837.
Nov. 8, 15.

1838.
Nov. 17.

———

Lord
COTTENHAM,
L.C.

[670]

DRYDEN *v.* FROST.

(3 My. & Cr. 670—676; S. C. 8 L. J. (N. S.) Ch. 235; 2 Jur. 1030.)

If the same person is agent both for the vendor and purchaser, or is himself vendor and agent for the purchaser, whatever notice he may have will affect the purchaser; and a purchaser taking a conveyance from a vendor, who has not possession of the title-deeds, will take it with notice of any claim which the party in possession of the title deeds may have.

The benefit of the vendor's lien for purchase money unpaid may be assigned by parol to a third party; *semble.*

An equitable mortgagee is not entitled to have out of the estate his costs of an unsuccessful attempt to defend an action at law for recovery of the mortgaged premises.

THIS was the appeal of two of the defendants, the personal representatives of John Frost deceased, against a decree of his Honour the VICE-CHANCELLOR.

The *Solicitor-General* and *Mr. J. J. Jervis,* for the appeal.

Mr. Wigram and *Mr. Duckworth,* in support of the decree.

The material facts of the case, and the points raised by the appeal, are fully stated and considered in the judgment.

1838.
Nov. 17.

———

THE LORD CHANCELLOR:

The decree in this case gives to the plaintiff the ordinary relief as an equitable mortgagee for the sum of 66*l.* 13*s.* 4*d.*, as to which there is no dispute: but the questions raised by the appeal are, whether the decree is right in also giving to the plaintiff the benefit of a lien for another sum of 50*l.*, and in directing that the costs at law which the plaintiff has been compelled to pay to the defendants should be repaid by them personally to the plaintiff; and in giving to the plaintiff payment of his own costs at law out of the estate.

The facts, as admitted or proved, appear to be that James Kelsey, the original owner of the property, created several mortgages by demises for terms of years, prior to the mortgage claimed by the plaintiff; and on the *16th of May, 1821, demised part of the property to Thomas Sharpe for nineteen years, to secure 66*l.* 13*s.* 4*d.* and interest, which mortgage term has become vested in the plaintiff by assignment of the executrix of Thomas Sharpe, dated the 20th of October, 1831.

[*671]

On the 12th of June, 1829, Kelsey, the owner of the inheritance, conveyed the property, subject to the mortgages, to one Atkinson, upon trust to sell; and on the 2nd of June, 1830, Atkinson, Kelsey, and all the mortgagees except the executrix of Sharpe, who, though named as a party, did not execute the deed, joined in conveying the inheritance and assigning the terms to one Edward John Marr. The consideration money, as stated in the deed, was sufficient to pay what was stated to be due to the several incumbrancers, including the mortgage to Sharpe, and 100*l.* more; which sum, therefore, was agreed to be paid to Atkinson, the trustee for sale.

The plaintiff acted in this transaction as agent and attorney for Atkinson, the trustee for sale, and for the executrix of Sharpe, she not having at that time assigned the mortgage to him; and in one, or other, or both those characters, he had in his possession the title-deeds of the property mortgaged to Sharpe. It also appears that Marr was clerk to Charles Frost, an attorney; and the answer admits that this deed was prepared by Marr, and perused on his behalf by Charles Frost. It further appears that Marr subsequently borrowed 1,340*l.* of John Frost, and by lease and release, of the 24th and 25th of August, 1830, conveyed this property to him, by way of mortgage, to secure that sum. The answer of the appellants admits that Marr prepared this deed also, as solicitor or agent for himself and the said John Frost, and that Charles Frost looked over the draft *of it as a friend, after it was prepared. Atkinson was examined as a witness in the cause; and he states that the plaintiff had a lien for costs on account of the sale of the property, and that it was agreed that he should receive the 100*l.* due from Marr as part of the purchase-money, and agreed to be paid to him (Atkinson) on account of such claim; that 50*l.* were accordingly paid by Marr to the plaintiff, and a promissory note given for the other 50*l.*, which, not being paid, is the sum of 50*l.* in question.

[*672]

Upon these facts the questions are, first, had the plaintiff a lien for this 50*l.*? and, if he had, secondly, are the defendants, as representing the mortgagee under Marr, affected by such lien; that is, had the mortgagee actual or constructive notice of it at the time when his mortgage-money was advanced?

That Atkinson had a lien for 50l., being part of the purchase-money unpaid, cannot be disputed: and he states himself that he agreed that the plaintiff should receive that sum from the purchaser Marr, and that Marr agreed to pay it to him; that is, he (Marr) gave the plaintiff his promissory note for the amount; and this transaction took place whilst the title-deeds were in the plaintiff's possession, which he would be clearly entitled to hold till the amount of Sharpe's mortgage was paid, and which, after such payment, he would have been entitled to retain as against his client Atkinson until his bill was discharged; and Atkinson's interest in these title-deeds would in that case have been to retain them till Marr had paid the whole of his purchase-money, that is, the remaining 50l.

[*673]

Under these circumstances, could Marr, without paying the 50l. to the plaintiff, have demanded these deeds *from him? I think clearly not, and that the plaintiff had an equitable lien upon them for the 50l.; and, if so, I think it clear that the mortgagee was affected with notice of this lien. It is admitted that Marr acted as the attorney of John Frost, the mortgagee; and Marr of course knew that 50l. of the purchase-money remained unpaid, and that the plaintiff was to receive that sum. Now Marr was vendor and attorney or agent for the purchaser, John Frost, as in *Sheldon* v. *Cox* (1), or concerned both for vendor and purchaser, as in *Le Neve* v. *Le Neve* (2). Independently, however, of the knowledge of Marr, John Frost the mortgagee was in this case taking the title from a purchaser (Marr) who was not in possession of the title-deeds. They were in the possession of the plaintiff, a circumstance which, according to the authority of *Hiern* v. *Mill* (3), was of itself sufficient notice of the title of the party in possession of them.

I think, therefore, that upon both these grounds, John Frost, and the defendants, who represent his interest, cannot support the defence of his having been a purchaser without notice.

It was contended, on the part of the appellants, that to give to the plaintiff the benefit of the vendor's lien for purchase-money unpaid would be contrary to the Statute of Frauds; as

(1) Amb. 624.   (3) 9 R. R. 149 (13 Ves. 112).
(2) 3 Atk. 646.

he could only claim it by parol assignment from Atkinson, the vendor. It is to be observed, however, that the lien for the benefit of the vendor himself, as well as the lien by the possession of title-deeds, are not reconcilable with the principle of that statute, but that nevertheless equity gives effect to them; and that the plaintiff's title rests upon the latter as well as upon the *former; for here we have the vendor and the purchaser, to one or other of whom the title-deeds must, after satisfying the mortgages, belong, concurring in an arrangement for the payment to the plaintiff, being in possession of the title-deeds, of what remained unpaid of the purchase-money.

DRYDEN
v.
FROST.

[*674]

I am, for these reasons, of opinion that the decree of the VICE-CHANCELLOR is right, so far as it gives to the plaintiff the benefit of the lien to secure the 50l.

The appeal, however, embraces another point; namely, that direction in the decree by which the defendants are directed personally to repay to the plaintiff the costs which he has been compelled to pay to them in the action of trover to be presently adverted to, and which gives to the plaintiff payment out of the estate of his own costs at law.

The facts of this part of the case must be taken wholly from the bill, so far as they are admitted by the answer, there being no evidence applicable to it; and from them it appears that one William Mortimer—who, from the statement in the bill, " that the plaintiff at the time, and for some time afterwards, believed him to be a tenant of part of the premises," must be assumed to be a stranger—called at the plaintiff's office, and left a key of the premises; whereupon John Frost, in whom the legal estate was vested, brought an action of trover for the key, against the plaintiff and Mortimer, which the plaintiff took upon himself to defend; and a verdict, subject to a case, was found for John Frost. Afterwards, Frost having died, his executors had the case argued, and judgment was entered up for the plaintiff in the action; and the defendant, the plaintiff in this suit, thereupon paid the costs and delivered up the key. The bill appears to *have been filed after the argument of the case and judgment of the court of law, but before execution thereupon; as it states the judgment and prays an injunction against the execution.

[*675]

But, from the statement in the answer, that injunction, if ever applied for, must have been refused, as the costs were paid, and the key delivered up.

The VICE-CHANCELLOR's decree directs the defendants personally to repay to the plaintiff the costs at law which under the judgment he had paid to them, and that the plaintiff should have his own costs at law raised and paid out of the mortgaged premises.

This Court, in settling the account between a mortgagor and mortgagee, will give to the latter all that his contract, or the legal or equitable consequences of it, entitle him to receive, and all the costs properly incurred in ascertaining or defending such rights, whether at law or in equity.   But even as to the costs in equity this Court exercises a discretion, and refuses to him his costs if his conduct has been improper; and, in some cases, orders him to pay them.   In *Detillin* v. *Gale* (1) Lord ELDON says he ought to be indemnified to the extent that he acts reasonably as mortgagee; which must mean reasonably with respect to such rights as his mortgage title gives him : *England* v. *Codrington* (2), *Morony* v. *O'Dea* (3), *Anonymous* v. *Trecothick* (4).

In this case the plaintiff's title was in equity only; but, without applying to a court of equity, he assumes to himself the right of taking possession, and adversely retains the key, the symbol of possession, to the extent *of defending the action of trover.   In all this he was wrong, as the judgment at law proves.   The costs he has incurred, and been compelled to pay in that useless and ill-advised contest, were not in furtherance of any rights to which he was entitled as mortgagee, but in asserting a supposed right which did not belong to him.   Did he in so doing act *reasonably* as an equitable mortgagee?   Were those costs necessarily or properly incurred in asserting or defending the right which his mortgage gave him?   Certainly not.   Those costs arose from a mistake as to his rights, from an attempt to obtain that to which he was not entitled, and cannot, therefore, be brought within any rule or principle under which a mortgagee is entitled to costs.

[*676]

(1) 6 R. R. 192 (7 Ves. 583; see p. 585).

(2) 1 Ed. 169.

(3) 1 Ba. & Be. 109.

(4) 13 R. R. 57 (2 V. & B. 181).

I am therefore of opinion that the costs of this unprofitable
contest about the key must be borne as the judgment prescribes;
and that there is no equity for relieving the plaintiff from them at
the expense of the defendant, or of the estate.

I regret that there exists this ground for the appeal, as I
should have been much better satisfied if I had found myself
justified in dismissing it with costs, and thereby indemnifying
the mortgagee; but, as the case stands, the decree must be
varied by striking out so much of it as relates to the costs of
the action of trover; and there can be no costs of the appeal.

BARBER v. BARBER (1).

(3 My. & Cr. 688—702; S. C. 8 L. J. (N. S.) Ch. 36; 2 Jur. 1029.)

1838
July
Nov. 12
—
Lord
COTTENHAM,
L.C.
[688]

A residuary bequest of real and personal estate to four persons as
tenants in common, who, with two others, were appointed executors.
One of the four having renounced probate: Held, that his fourth share
lapsed.

The intermediate income of a gift of residue which is liable to be divested
on a future contingency belongs to the original donee absolutely.

JOHN MACKINTOSH, by his will, which was duly executed and
attested to pass freehold estate by devise, after directing that
his real and personal estate and effects should be sold, and his
debts paid, and that an investment should be made to answer
a certain annuity therein mentioned, and giving the capital of
the fund so to be invested, after the death of the annuitant, to
his son John, and his daughter Eliza Jane, gave and bequeathed
unto his son John Mackintosh, his daughter Eliza Jane Mackintosh, Mary Ann Shears, and Martha Shears, the whole residue
of his property of every description, to be divided among them
in separate and equal proportions. And, after giving special
directions with respect to the investment and application of the
respective shares of Mary Ann Shears and Martha Shears, his
will continued as follows:

"After the sale of my estate and property as before directed,   [689]

(1) But see Griffiths v. Pruen (1840)
11 Sim. 202, where an executor who
died before probate was held not
to have forfeited his title under a
residuary bequest in the will.—
O. A. S.

I desire that the property I have bequeathed to my son John Mackintosh and my daughter Eliza Jane Mackintosh may be invested in the public funds of Great Britain, in separate accounts, in the names of trustees appointed by my executors, and also in the names of my son and daughter, and for the sole use and benefit of my son and daughter. And it is also my will and desire that the interest or dividends, arising from the said funded property for my son John, be applied for his maintenance, education, &c., until he arrives at the age of twenty-one years; and after that period he shall have the power of receiving such interest or dividends himself, and dispose of it as he may think proper, until he arrives at the age of twenty-five years : then the whole of the property I have bequeathed to him shall be at his own disposal without control.

" It is my will and desire that half the property which I last bequeathed to my daughter Eliza Jane may be invested in the public funds of Great Britain, in the name of herself and trustees appointed by my executors for that purpose, for her maintenance, education, use, and benefit during her life; and for her child or children, if any, living at the time of her decease. But if there is no issue living at the time of her decease, that the said property shall devolve to my son John Mackintosh; and in case he is dead also, and has left no issue, the said property shall devolve to my executors herein named : but if there is issue of my son John living, then it shall devolve to that issue. And the other half of the property bequeathed to her shall be invested in the public funds for her sole use and benefit until she arrives at the age of twenty-one years; then the said property shall be at her own disposal without control.

[690]   " It is my will and intention that my son John Mackintosh may dispose of his property by will after he has attained the age of twenty-one years; but should he die before he arrives at that age, then the said property shall devolve to my daughter Eliza Jane, if she is living; and should Eliza Jane die before she is twenty-one years of age, then the property bequeathed to her shall devolve to my son John; but should both die before they arrive at twenty-one years of age, then the property

bequeathed to them shall devolve to and become the property **BARBER**
of Mr. Joseph Barber, America Square, Mr. John Stapp, of   *v.*
Snowhill, Mr. Frederick Grigg, of the Old South Sea House, **BARBER.**
and Mr. George Capper, of Crosby Square, in London, to be
divided betwixt them in equal proportions, and to their heirs
for ever; which last mentioned four persons I also appoint as
my executors, to see that every thing is duly executed and
performed according to my will and desire herein.   I also
appoint Mr. Francis Garratt and Mr. John Garratt as executors,
in addition to the above persons; for which I request these
two friends will accept of 50*l.* each, as a testimony of my
regard.   I also request that Messrs. Francis and John Garratt
will act as guardians in conjunction with Mr. Capper, Mr.
Barber, Mr. Grigg, and Mr. Stapp, for the care of the persons
and property of my son John, and Eliza Jane, and Mary Ann,
and Martha Shears."

The testator, by an unattested codicil (1), stated his will to be,
that if any of his executors should refuse to accept the trust
and act as executor according to the directions in his will,
then he annulled totally his bequest of his property to every
such person who should so refuse.

The testator died in the year 1818, leaving his son and
daughter, John Mackintosh and Eliza Jane Mackintosh, *his   [*691]
sole next of kin; and a bill was soon afterwards filed to have
the rights of the different parties interested under the will
ascertained, and the property administered and secured for
their benefit, under the direction of the Court.   George
Capper, Francis Garratt, and John Garratt renounced probate
of the will, which was proved by the three other persons named
as executors, who alone acted in the execution of the trusts.

John Mackintosh, the son, died in November, 1834, an infant
of the age of nineteen years, and without issue; having, by his
will, bequeathed all his personal estate to Eliza Jane Mackintosh,
his sister, and appointed the said Joseph Barber his sole executor.
Eliza Jane Mackintosh died a few months afterwards, also under

(1) As to the admissibility of ex-   to the office, see *In re Appleton* (1885)
trinsic evidence in connection with   29 Ch. D. 893, 54 L. J. Ch. 954, 52
the ordinary presumption that a   L. T. 906.—O. A. S.
bequest to an executor is annexed

age and unmarried, and leaving a will: and upon her death a bill of revivor and supplement was filed by her personal representatives against the six persons named as executors in the will of the original testator, and against the other persons interested in his residuary estate, praying that the rights of the plaintiffs, as representing Eliza Jane Mackintosh, might be declared.

The decree of the MASTER OF THE ROLLS, made at the hearing of this supplemental cause, contained, amongst other things, the two following declarations: first, that so much of the income of the several shares of John Mackintosh and Eliza Jane Mackintosh, in the residue of the original testator's estate, as accrued during their respective lifetimes, and was not applied in their maintenance or education, belonged absolutely to them, respectively, and passed by their respective wills; and, secondly, that the share which George Capper would, under the original testator's will, have taken in the two several moieties of the one fourth share of the residuary estate thereby bequeathed [*692] to Eliza Jane Mackintosh, and to her *and her children, and also in the one fourth share of such residuary estate, thereby bequeathed to John Mackintosh, had, in consequence of Capper having renounced probate, devolved upon the defendants Barber, Stapp, and Grigg, as tenants in common; and that those three persons were entitled, in equal thirds, to the said two one fourth shares accordingly.

The plaintiffs and the defendants, the acting executors of the original testator, presented cross-petitions of appeal against the decree of the MASTER OF THE ROLLS (1), which came on to be heard together.

The plaintiffs, by their appeal, submitted that the contingent bequest over of the shares of residuary estate, previously bequeathed to the testator's son and daughter, was not a gift to the persons, as a class, who should take upon themselves the office of executors, but was a gift to the four individuals named, as tenants in common; and that the one fourth, therefore, of that residue, which Capper had lost in consequence of his declining to act, was a lapsed legacy, and went to the testator's next of kin.

The defendants' petition of appeal submitted that, upon the

(1) See 7 L. J. (N. S.) Ch. 70, 1 Jur. 915.

true construction of the will, such portion of the income as had
accumulated upon the respective shares of residue, bequeathed
to the testator's son and daughter respectively during their
minorities, did not vest in the son and daughter absolutely,
so as to form part of their estate, and pass to their respective
personal representatives; but that in the event, which had
happened, of their both dying under age, it had passed, under
the ulterior limitation, to the persons who, upon that event,
were appointed to take in remainder the shares of capital out
of which such accumulation of income had arisen.

The petitions of appeal also raised two other questions; but   [693]
as these turned merely upon the construction of particular
clauses and expressions in the will, and involved no general
principle, it has not been considered expedient to report the
case as to them, or to set out those parts of the will upon which
they arose.

Mr. Wigram, Mr. Humphry, Mr. Elderton, and *Mr. Loftus
Wigram,* for the plaintiffs.

Mr. Tinney, Mr. Knight Bruce, Mr. Richards, and *Mr.
Romilly,* for the defendants, the executors.

The cases referred to upon the question raised by the plaintiffs
appeal are stated and considered in the judgment.

Upon the question raised by the defendants' appeal, *Nicholls* v.
Osborn (1), *Chaworth* v. *Hooper* (2), *Skey* v. *Barnes* (3) were cited.

THE LORD CHANCELLOR [after affirming the judgment of the   *Nov.* 12.
    MASTER OF THE ROLLS upon another question, raised by
    the defendants' appeal :]

The remaining question upon the appeal of the defendants is,
as to the interest upon the shares of the residue bequeathed to
John and Eliza Jane, they having both died under twenty-one,
and thereby lost the benefit of the capital of such shares.

The gift is to the four residuary legatees absolutely, subject   [*694]
to the following directions : The investment *is to be for the
sole use and benefit of John and Eliza Jane. The interest and

(1) 2 P. Wms. 419.   (3) 17 R. R. 91 (3 Mer. 335).
(2) 2 Br. C. C. 82.

dividends of John's share are to be applied for his maintenance
and education till twenty-one: from that age till twenty-five he
is himself to receive and to have power to dispose of such
interest and dividends; and at twenty-five the whole property
is to be at his disposal. Half the property last bequeathed to
Eliza Jane is to be invested for her maintenance, education,
use, and benefit, for her life, with remainder to her children:
and if there should be none, the said property is to devolve to
John: and if he should also die without issue, the said property
is to devolve to the executors. The other half of the property
bequeathed to Eliza Jane is to be invested for her sole use and
benefit till twenty-one, when the same is to be at her sole
disposal. If both John and Eliza Jane die before twenty-one,
the property bequeathed to them is to devolve and become the
property of the four executors.

The gifts are absolute, except in the event of death under
twenty-one; and the interest of Eliza Jane's share is, in the
mean time, to be applied for her use and benefit as to one half,
and her sole use and benefit as to the other half. The interest
and dividends of John's share are directed to be applied for his
maintenance, education, &c. till he attains twenty-one. As to
both, the investments are to be for the sole use and benefit of
the legatee; and the gift over is of " the property bequeathed,"
the expression throughout used in describing the capital.

As to the whole of John's share, and as to one half of Eliza
Jane's share, the gift is absolute; but the power of disposition
is postponed till a certain age; and of the other one half of
Eliza Jane's share she is tenant for life; and as to all, there is

[*695]

a gift over, upon the happening *of certain events; but till such
events happen, the property belongs to the legatees John and
Eliza Jane, and they are entitled to the interest of it. It is
vested, subject to be devested. The ordinary result of such
vesting is to give to the legatee a right to the intermediate
interest; and he cannot be less entitled to it because the testator
has directed the interest to be applied for his maintenance,
education, &c., for his use and benefit, or for his sole use and
benefit. And who is it who contest this claim of the legatees?
Why, the legatees over. Do the terms of the gift over give it?

The terms used are " the property bequeathed " to the first legatee—the very terms used in describing the capital, and terms by no means applicable to the interest upon the property bequeathed, which might arise after the bequest had taken effect. If they cannot claim under the terms of the gift over, that is, if the interest accrued be not, in terms, given over with the capital, they, as legatees of that capital upon a contingency, can have no title to the interest which arose prior to the contingency. I think, therefore, the judgment of the MASTER OF THE ROLLS entirely right upon this point also; and, as this exhausts the grounds of the appeal of the defendants, I think that such appeal must be dismissed with costs.

[The LORD CHANCELLOR then stated the two questions which had been raised on the appeal of the plaintiffs, and after disposing of the first, as to which he concurred in the judgment of the MASTER OF THE ROLLS, continued as follows:]

The last question is one of much more difficulty. The plaintiffs claim the share of George Capper as undisposed of, the gift to him having failed by his refusing to act as executor. The three other executors named with him as residuary legatees, on the other hand, contend *that they are entitled to the residue   [*696]
in thirds, including, therefore, the share destined for George Capper. The direction in the will is that, in the event of the death of John and Eliza Jane under twenty-one, the property bequeathed to them shall devolve to, and become the property of the four persons, each particularly named and described, to be divided betwixt them in equal proportions, and to their heirs for ever; which last mentioned four persons he appoints executors; and he afterwards appoints two other executors. It is not now in dispute that this bequest was made to these four persons as executors; that is, upon condition that they took upon themselves that office, and consequently that Mr. Capper, having renounced, cannot claim his share; but that being so does not appear to me to assist in the solution of the present question. That would have been so, just as much as if Capper had been the only executor, and the only legatee over. That question depends entirely upon whether the gift be conditional or not.

The question to be decided is, who are the legatees? It is quite

BARBER
v.
BARBER.

clear that, if the legatees had not been appointed executors, the gift to them would have created a tenancy in common, and therefore that, upon the failure of the gift to any one, his share would have been undisposed of, and that the three others could not have claimed. And it is equally clear that, if any other condition had been imposed upon these four tenants in common, upon which their title to the legacy was to depend, and one had refused to perform the condition, his share would have been undisposed of, and that the other three could not have claimed it. The ground upon which the title of the executors who proved is rested leaves these propositions untouched; for it stands upon this ground, that *the gift is to a class, and that the three executors who proved constitute the class; and it was contended that there was no distinction between a gift to executors as tenants in common, and a gift to certain persons as tenants in common who are afterwards appointed executors.

[*697]

This, as all other questions of construction, must depend upon the intention. A gift to a class implies an intention to benefit those who constitute the class, and to exclude all others; but a gift to individuals described by their several names and descriptions, though they may together constitute a class, implies an intention to benefit the individuals named. In a gift to a class you look to the description, and inquire what individuals answer to it; and those who do answer to it are the legatees described. But if the parties to whom the legacy is given be not described as a class, but by their individual names and additions, though together constituting a class, those who may constitute the class at any particular time may not, in any respect, correspond with the description of the individuals named as legatees. If a testator give a legacy to be divided amongst the children of A. at a particular time, those who constitute the class at the time will take; but if the legacy be given to B., C., and D., children of A., as tenants in common, and one dies before the testator, the survivors will not take the share of the deceased child. The question must be, was the intention to bequeath to those who might, at the time, constitute the class, or to certain individuals who, it was supposed, would constitute it? Such would appear to be the question to be asked, and the point to be ascertained;

but the more important inquiry is, whether the authorities justify and support this view of the case.

In *Page* v. *Page* (1), decided by Lord KING in 1728, and approved by Lord TALBOT in 1734, there was the gift of a residue to six persons, to each one sixth ; and they were appointed executors.   It was held that the one sixth of one who died in the lifetime of the testator lapsed for the next of kin.   In this case there is a gift to four equally, to be divided betwixt them, i.e. to each one fourth.   In *Owen* v. *Owen* (2) the testator gave the residue of his estate to his two nieces, to be equally divided between them, and appointed them executrixes.   One died in the testator's lifetime ; and Lord HARDWICKE said that he had followed *Page* v. *Page* in *Holderness* v. *Reyner* (3) ; and that the reasoning of Sir J. JEKYLL, in *Hunt* v. *Berkley*, could not be supported ; and held that the share intended for the deceased niece lapsed for the benefit of the next of kin, and did not go to the surviving niece.

In *Knight* v. *Gould* (4) the gift was of the residue " to my executors hereinafter named, to pay my debts, legacies, &c., and also to recompense them for their trouble, equally between them ; " and three persons were then named executors, one of whom died in the testator's lifetime ; and Sir JOHN LEACH first, and Lord BROUGHAM, upon appeal, held that the two survivors were entitled to the whole.   The latter relied upon two grounds principally, first, that the persons to take were those who were to perform the duties, and the survivors were such persons ; secondly, that the gift was to the executors as a class in terms : for the words " hereinafter named " were mere surplusage, inasmuch as the result would have been the same if they had been omitted, it being absolutely necessary to name them in order to appoint them.   In *that case the gift was to executors described as such ; in this, it is to individuals particularly named and described.   In that, the fund given was what should remain after part had been administered.   Those who were to take and those who were to administer were considered as identical.

The result, therefore, of the authorities, supposing them

(1) 2 P. Wms. 489.   (3) Mos. 47.
(2) 1 Atk. 491.   (4) 39 R. R. 212 (2 My. & K. 295).

BARBER
v.
BARBER.

strictly to apply, is in favour of the claim of the next of kin.
There is the case of *Page* v. *Page*, decided by Lord KING and
approved by Lord TALBOT, and in two cases approved and acted
upon by Lord HARDWICKE ; whereas, in support of the claim of
the acting executors, there is only the case of *Hunt* v. *Berkley*,
decided, indeed, by a high authority, Sir JOSEPH JEKYLL, but
disapproved by Lord HARDWICKE, and over-ruled by every subsequent case in which the point has arisen. It is also to be
observed that the case of *Hunt* v. *Berkley* would not, if it were
clearly a right decision, necessarily govern the present case ;
because, in that case, the residuary legatees and the executors
were the same, and the decision must have proceeded upon this,
that the testator did, in fact, intend to give the residue to whomsoever of the parties named might be his executors. But it is
clear that, if *Page* v. *Page*, *Holderness* v. *Reyner*, and *Owen* v.
Owen, be right, they necessarily include the present case ; the
claims of the next of kin being much stronger in this case than
in any of those ; inasmuch as, in all those cases, those named
residuary legatees and executors were the same ; so that the
question might arise, whether the intention was to give the
residue to the individuals, or to the class which they composed ;
whereas, in the present case, the residuary legatees do not
constitute any class to which a name can be given, without
including the description of residuary legatees. If the three

[*700]

surviving executors to *whom the share of the residue was given
are entitled, they must be so entitled as constituting the class
intended to be benefited ; but what is the class which they so
constitute? Not the executors ; because there were two other
executors named besides the persons intended to be so benefited ;
and although the two others also declined to prove, so that the
three, in fact, are the only acting executors, yet the class of
executors, as contemplated by the testator, consisted of six ; and
there was clearly no intention to give the benefit to such of the
six as might act as executors, for that might have given the
benefit to the two. This case, therefore, has nothing in common
with *Knight* v. *Gould*, or any other case in which the gift has
been construed to be in favour of such as might act as executors.
If, then, the class intended to take be not such as might, at the

time, be the executors, it must be such of the executors named as might, at the time, be also of the number of the residuary legatees named ; but that is only another mode of describing the residuary legatees ; and, if their situation as residuary legatees be considered, they are only tenants in common of the residue, between whom there can be no survivorship.

There seems also to be some confusion in terms in considering legatees as constituting, as such, a class for the purpose in question.   They have no existence as a class, except under the description in the will.   To such persons a testator may undoubtedly give a right of survivorship *inter se*, by expressly directing it, or by creating a joint tenancy.   The first the testator in this case has not done, and the second he has, in terms, excluded, by creating a tenancy in common ; and he could not have intended that those who proved should take the whole in the event of some not proving, and not in the event of their dying before him.   To effectuate a gift to those of the class he has himself constituted, *who may be in a condition to take at a particular time, he must have used expressions from which that intention may be fairly deduced.   Such an intention cannot be deduced from a gift to four persons by name, between whom the share of the residue is to be divided.

[*701]

It was contended that, at all events, the three survivors of the four residuary legatees must be entitled to the half of Eliza Jane's share, which is directed to devolve to "my executors herein named."   But I think that direction clearly superseded, or, rather, qualified and explained, by the subsequent gift of all he had bequeathed to John and Eliza Jane, to the four executors. The words first used would, indeed, unless so qualified and explained, carry that half, not to the four, but to all the six executors.

The MASTER OF THE ROLLS considered this question as attended with very considerable difficulty, a circumstance which relieves me from much of the embarrassment I always feel when I have the misfortune to differ in opinion from him ; but, after taking all the means in my power to come to a right conclusion, I should not be doing justice to the parties if I did not declare that I have come to a conclusion, quite satisfactory to my own

BARBER
v.
BARBER.

mind, that the three survivors of the four executors, named as residuary legatees of the part of the residue, cannot take the share destined by the will for Mr. Capper; but that he having given up his title to it, such share became undisposed of, and, as such, belongs to the plaintiffs.

In this respect, therefore, I am of opinion that the decree of the MASTER OF THE ROLLS must be varied, but affirmed upon all the other points. Of course there can be no costs of this appeal.

[702]

There was also a question of costs raised by the defendants' appeal, to which I omitted to advert. The decree directs the costs to be paid out of the share of the residue destined for John and Eliza Jane, as to which alone the question arose; and this I think was clearly the right direction.

1838.
June 4, 5, 9.
———
Lord
COTTENHAM,
L.C.
[702]

URCH *v.* WALKER.

(3 My. & Cr. 702—710; S. C. 7 L. J. (N. S.) Ch. 292; 2 Jur. 487.)

The acceptance of the trusteeship of a leasehold house specifically bequeathed by a will may be evidence of the acceptance of the trusteeship of a legacy bequeathed to the same trustees upon different trusts by the same will.

JOHN FRANKLING, by his will, gave and bequeathed unto Robert Blackburrow and Edward Wood (since deceased) the sum of 1,100*l*., upon trust to invest the same, and to pay the interest thereof to his daughter Mary, then the wife of John Urch, for her separate use, for life; and after her decease, or in case she should incumber the same, to apply the interest in the maintenance of such of her children as should be then living, (except John Frankling Hewlett and Joseph Hewlett, her children by a former marriage,) until the youngest should attain the age of twenty-one, when he directed the capital to be equally divided among them. The testator then made certain other devises and

[*703]

bequests; *and in particular he devised the dwelling-house in which he then lived, with the garden, orchard. and close of ground thereunto belonging, situate at Banwell, and held under the Bishop of Bath and Wells, upon a lease for three lives, unto the same trustees, Blackburrow and Wood, to hold the same, upon trust, to permit and suffer his wife, Ann Frankling, and her assigns, to receive the rents and profits of the premises during her life ; and, after her decease, to apply the same in the maintenance and education of his grandson, John Frankling Hewlett, until he should attain the age of twenty-one years, when he directed his said trustees, or the survivor, &c., to convey the premises to his said grandson, his heirs and assigns, and also to pay over to him the unapplied rents and profits, accrued during his minority.   The testator gave the residue of his estate and effects to his wife, Ann Frankling, whom he appointed his sole executrix.

The testator died in the year 1818 ; and his will was shortly afterwards proved by his widow.

The bill was filed by the parties interested in the legacy of 1,100l.: it prayed an account of the testator's estate and effects received by the widow, who was now dead, and the defendant Walker as her personal representative, and it further prayed that the defendant Blackburrow might be declared personally liable to make good the legacy in question with interest, on the ground that he had accepted and acted in the trusts of the testator's will.

To support the case made against Blackburrow, the bill alleged various acts done, and conversations had by him, with reference to the property given and bequeathed upon the trusts of the will, and which it was submitted *amounted to or evidenced   [*704] an acceptance of the trusts of the legacy in question.   It also alleged that Blackburrow took upon himself to act, and acted, as a trustee, in the paying or assigning over to other legatees named in the will, and, amongst the rest, to the testator's grandson, John Frankling Hewlett, property specifically bequeathed in trust for such other legatees.

The defendant Blackburrow, by his answer, positively denied that he had ever accepted or acted in the trusts of the will, or in any way intermeddled with any of the property which was the subject of the trusts, otherwise than by executing, on the 18th of May, 1822, the indenture after mentioned. His answer then stated that, at the earnest solicitation and request of John Frankling Hewlett, he, Blackburrow, and Wood executed to Hewlett an indenture of release, dated the 18th of May, 1822,

and expressed to be made between them, Blackburrow and Wood,
of the one part, and Hewlett of the other part, whereby, after
reciting an indenture of lease between the Bishop of Bath and
Wells and the testator, and by which the Bishop demised to the
testator a messuage, lands, and premises therein described,
within the manor of Banwell, to hold the same to the testator
and his heirs during the lives of three persons therein named,
and the longest liver of them ; and further reciting that the
testator, by his said will, had given and devised unto him, the
defendant Blackburrow, and Wood, the dwelling-house in which
he then lived, with the garden, orchard, and close of ground
thereunto belonging, situate at Banwell aforesaid, and held
under the Bishop of Bath and Wells, upon trust to permit and
suffer Ann Frankling, the testator's wife, to receive the rents
and profits of the premises during her life, and, after her decease,
to apply the same in the maintenance and education of his

[*705] grandson John Frankling *Hewlett, until he should attain the
age of twenty-one years, when he directed his said trustees, or
the survivor &c., to convey the said premises to his grandson,
his heirs and assigns, and also to pay over to him the unapplied
rents and profits thereof, accrued during his minority ; and
reciting that Ann Frankling survived the testator, but was then
also deceased, and that in her lifetime, John Frankling Hewlett
attained the age of twenty-one years, whereby it became
unnecessary for the defendant and Wood to act in the trust
declared by the will, and in fact they never intermeddled therein ;
but, inasmuch as the legal estate in the said messuage and lands
was still outstanding in them by virtue of the said recited will,
they had consented, at the request of John Frankling Hewlett,
to convey such estate to him in manner thereinafter mentioned ;
it was witnessed that, in pursuance and performance of the said
agreement, and of the trusts so reposed in them, and for conveying the said messuage or dwelling-house, garden, orchard, and
premises, unto him, John Frankling Hewlett, and his heirs, as
aforesaid, they, the defendant Blackburrow and Wood, and each
of them, thereby granted and released unto John Frankling
Hewlett all .that the said messuage, &c., granted by the said
indenture of lease unto the said testator, and by him given and

devised unto Blackburrow and Wood, upon trust as aforesaid, to hold the same unto John Frankling Hewlett, his heirs and assigns, &c.

The depositions on behalf of the plaintiffs did not succeed in proving any of the acts or conversations which the bill alleged as evidence that Blackburrow had accepted the trusts.

The defendant Blackburrow proved, by the evidence of his solicitor, that, before the execution of the deed of *May, 1822, a case, together with the draft of the proposed deed, had been laid, on his behalf, before counsel, for his opinion upon the question, whether it would be safe for him and Wood to execute such a deed, and that counsel thereupon advised that they might safely execute it.

[*706]

The decree of the VICE-CHANCELLOR declared, among other things, that Blackburrow had accepted the trusts of the will; and directed an inquiry whether, but for his wilful default, he might have received the 1,100l. or any part thereof.

An appeal by Blackburrow against that part of the decree now came on to be heard.

Mr. Temple and *Mr. Purvis*, for the appeal :

The only act which furnishes the least pretence for saying that the appellant ever accepted the trusts of the will is the execution of the deed of May, 1822, conveying the leasehold property to Hewlett. It is obvious, however, that, in becoming a party to that deed, he never intended to make himself liable as a trustee. On the contrary, his declared object in so doing was to repudiate or get rid of any liability in that character : and, although the deed may have been inartificially and improperly framed for that purpose, the Court will look to the expressed object and intent, rather than to the form of the instrument ; according to the principles laid down by LORD ELDON in the analogous case of *Nicloson* v. *Wordsworth* (1). The deed of May, 1822, is substantially a disclaimer of the trusts, and it distinctly states, in the recital, that the parties of the first part *never interfered therein. It is also to be observed that the appellant, in executing that deed, acted under the advice of counsel, and at

[*707]

(1) 19 R. R. 86 (2 Swanst. 365).

the earnest request of Hewlett, for the sole purpose of perfecting the title of the latter to the property, the legal estate in which was supposed to have become vested in Blackburrow and Wood under the will. The recitals in the deed, even supposing them to be binding as between the parties to the instrument, cannot be used as evidence upon any question between those parties and strangers, such as the plaintiffs must for the present purpose be considered to be. Even if it were fully established, however, that the appellant had accepted and acted in the trusts of the property devised for the benefit of Hewlett, it by no means follows, as a necessary consequence, that he must also be held to have accepted and acted in the trusts of the legacy with which the bill seeks to charge him, or generally in the trusts reposed in him by the will.

Mr. Jacob and *Mr. Girdlestone*, in support of the decree.

June 9. THE LORD CHANCELLOR (after stating the question):

In this case evidence was gone into for the purpose of showing that the appellant had, in certain conversations, admitted himself to be a trustee. Upon carefully looking into the depositions, however, I do not find that this fact is satisfactorily proved; and, although they might have been sufficient to ground an inquiry, I should not have thought that they justified the Court in making a decree against the appellant.

[*708] There was, however, another piece of evidence upon which the plaintiffs mainly relied; and that was a deed *which the appellant had executed with respect to certain leasehold property of which also he was appointed a trustee by the will. That leasehold property was bequeathed to him and an individual of the name of Wood, upon trust for a person upon his attaining the age of twenty-one; and the deed in question was a conveyance of that leasehold to the person so entitled, and to which the appellant and his co-trustee were executing parties. This deed contained the following recitals:

[His Lordship here read the recitals, and stated the effect of the deed, and then continued:]

The question is, whether the execution of this deed was not of itself an acceptance of the trusts of the will? I think it would be sanctioning a gross deceit on the part of the appellant, if it were to be construed otherwise, because it was for the purpose of giving effect to the devise of the property. If the trustees never did accept the property, then they had no legal estate in them, and they had no means of doing that which they professed to do, and which, by this deed, they held out that they were doing.

In the case of *Nicloson* v. *Wordsworth* (1), which was referred to in support of the appellant's argument, one of three trustees, being desirous of throwing off the obligations of the trust, and disclaiming, executed a release to the other trustees. Now it had been previously decided by Lord ROSSLYN, in *Crewe* v. *Dicken* (2), that that act, of itself, amounted to an acceptance of the trust, upon the ground that it was at once an assumption of the interest and an attempt to get rid of it,—his Lordship thus taking a distinction between a mere disclaimer and a *release. Lord ELDON, in *Nicloson* v. *Wordsworth*, comments upon that case, and questions the soundness of that distinction; but the ground on which Lord ELDON rests his objection leaves the present case quite untouched. His Lordship there said, " If the essence of the act is disclaimer, and if the point were *res integra*, I should be inclined to say that, if the mere fact of disclaimer is to remove all difficulties and vest the estate in the other trustees, a party who releases, and thereby declares that he will not take as trustee, gives the best evidence that he will not take as trustee. The answer, that the release amounts to more than a disclaimer, is much more technical than any reasoning that deserves to prevail in a court of equity." His Lordship subsequently observed, " My opinion is, that if a person, who is appointed co-trustee by any instrument, executes no other act than a conveyance to his co-trustees, when the meaning and intent of that conveyance is disclaimer, the distinction is not sufficiently broad for the Court to act upon. I can find no case which has decided, nor can I see any reasons for deciding, that, where the intent of the release is disclaimer, the inference that the releasor has accepted the estate shall prevent the effect of it."

This reasoning has no application to the case of a person who

[*709]

(1) 19 R. R. 86 (2 Swanst. 365).   (2) See 19 R. R. 86 (4 Ves. 97).

is not repudiating, but acting upon the interests which the will
purports to give.   Is there any thing on the face of this instrument to show that the appellant repudiated the trust ?   He
recites that the property vested in him, and that, in execution
and pursuance of the trust, he executes the deed in question.   It
was said, there is a recital that he had not intermeddled.   But
there is no recital that he never intended to intermeddle, or that
he executed the deed because he disclaimed the trust.   On the

[*710]   contrary, the *reason assigned is, that the party having attained
twenty-one, " it became unnecessary for the defendant and Wood
to act in the trust declared by the said will, and, in fact, they
never intermeddled therein."   So far, therefore, from this instrument showing any intention on his part to repudiate the trust,
the appellant there expressly says that he executes it in pursuance of and acting upon the trust, and is dealing with the
property as the testator intended he should deal with it.

It is also to be remarked that, in *Nicloson* v. *Wordsworth*,
although the observations of Lord ELDON are entitled to the
greatest possible weight, there was no adjudication upon the
point raised by the case.   The bill was filed by a purchaser,
stating that the vendor could not make a title, because one of the
trustees had refused to join in the conveyance ; and the object
of the suit was to obtain a declaration from the Court which
should clear the title.   Lord ELDON said that he could not come
to any decision ; and the declaration was taken by consent, as
appears from the terms of the order stated in Mr. Swanston's
report (1).   It cannot, therefore, be considered as the judicial
decision of the Court.   How far the reasoning of Lord ELDON in
that case is correct, I am not called upon to express any opinion.
At all events, I am clear that it has no bearing in the appellant's
favour ; but, on the contrary, that it is quite consistent with the
declaration under appeal.

So far, therefore, as his Honour's decree has declared that the
defendant Blackburrow has accepted the trusts of the will, I
think it is impossible to impeach it.

(1) See 19 R. R. 87 (2 Swanst. p. 372).

SAUNDERS AND BENNING v. SMITH AND MAXWELL.

1838.
June 16, 20, 22, 23.

Lord
COTTENHAM,
L.C.

[711]

(3 My. & Cr. 711—737 ; S. C. 7 L. J. (N. S.) Ch. 227 ; 2 Jur. 491—536.)

Injunction refused to restrain alleged infringement of copyright, before trial at law, where the conduct of the plaintiffs had been such as, in the opinion of the Court, was calculated to induce the defendants to believe that the course taken by them would not be objected to by the plaintiffs.

[THE plaintiffs in this case, by their bill, filed in May, 1838, claimed to be entitled to the copyright of certain series of law reports (1), and to have the sole and exclusive right of printing and reprinting those several books ; and they alleged] that no consent in writing or otherwise had been given by them or either of them, authorising the defendants to print or reprint, or cause to be printed or reprinted, the before-mentioned several books, or any part or parts of them, or of any of them :

[714]

[The bill further stated]

That John William Smith, of the Inner Temple, barrister-at-law, and Alexander Maxwell, of Bell Yard, in the county of Middlesex, bookseller, [had lately printed, published and sold,] divers copies of a certain book, intituled " A Selection of Leading Cases on various Branches of the Law, with Notes, vol. ii. part 1, by John William Smith, Esq., of the Inner Temple, Barrister-at-Law : "

That the greater part of the last-mentioned book had been copied and pirated by the defendants, without the consent of the plaintiffs, from the several books before mentioned, the copyright of which was vested in the plaintiffs :

That the book so printed and published by the defendants consisted, in the whole, of 305 pages, out of which 182 pages were copied *verbatim*, except a very few trifling and minute verbal alterations in six of the cases, from parts of the plaintiffs' said several books ; and that the book contained twenty-seven cases, all of which, except three, were copied *verbatim*, except as before mentioned, from the plaintiffs' said several books :

(1) The Term Reports, East's Reports, Barnewall & Cresswell's Reports, Taunton's Reports, and Bingham's Reports, comprising in all 52 volumes, and containing, as stated in argument, 15,340 reported cases, of which 24 cases had been copied by the defendant.—O. A. S.

[The bill further stated] that in the year 1837 the defendants published the first volume of their work, and that the reports of the cases contained in that first volume were taken and copied from various books, the copyright of some of which belonged to the plaintiffs :

[717] That they did not take any means to prevent the sale of that first volume, because, out of forty-two cases contained in the said first volume, only the case of *Master* v. *Miller*, and part of the cases of *Mills* v. *Auriol* and *Lickbarrow* v. *Mason*, were copied from books of which the plaintiffs have the copyright, and the plaintiffs did not consider such infringement of their rights to be carried to such an extent as to render it worth their while to take any proceedings in respect of the same ; however, the plaintiffs never gave the defendants any reason to believe or expect that the plaintiffs assented or would assent to or acquiesce in the infringement of their copyright :

That the defendant, John William Smith, previously to the publication of the said first volume, proposed to the plaintiffs to publish the said work, and to be interested with him in the profits thereof, which proposal the plaintiffs declined : and that Smith stated, as a reason why he should prefer having the work published by the plaintiffs, that he should otherwise be unable to make use of the cases contained in reports published subsequently to the Term Reports : and that the plaintiff, Benning, thereupon observed to Smith, that he, Smith, certainly could not take any cases the copyright of which belonged to the plaintiffs :

That for some time after the first publication of the first part of the second volume, and until on or about the 19th of May, 1838, the plaintiffs were not aware of the nature of the contents of the second volume, but presumed that it was similar to the first part, and did not interfere with any of the plaintiffs' copyrights, or only in a very small and trivial degree : and that as soon as they were aware that a great part of the second volume was copied from books, the copyright of which belonged to the plaintiffs, they immediately complained of the piracy :   *   *   *

[718] That on the 19th of May they gave instructions for proceedings to be taken in this Court for relief :   *   *   *

The bill prayed an account of the defendants' receipts in respect

of the first part of the second volume of the " Leading Cases,"   SAUNDERS
and an injunction to restrain its further sale ; and the delivery   *v.*
up of all copies in the defendants' hands ; the plaintiffs waiving   SMITH.
all penalties.

The defendant Smith, by his affidavit, stated that he was the
author of the work mentioned in the plaintiffs' affidavit. * * *

That before the publication of the first volume, the deponent   [719]
sent for the plaintiff Benning, who waited on the deponent at his
chambers, and the deponent then proposed to Benning that he
and his partner should become the publishers of the work, and
should pay the deponent a certain sum of money for the first
edition, and account to him for half the profits of every subsequent edition : That the deponent on that occasion told Benning
that he made him the first offer of the work, and that his reason
for doing so was that, in order to complete his plan, it would be
necessary to take cases from modern reports, the copyright of most
of which was, as he believed, vested in the plaintiffs: That
Benning requested time to consider the deponent's offer and
consult his partner on it, and, on a subsequent occasion, came
again to the deponent and declined it, but offered that he and
his partner would publish the work at half profits, which the
deponent declined :

That he never offered the work to the plaintiffs on any other
occasion, and that he is sure that he did not express an opinion
that he should be unable to make use of the cases contained in
the reports published subsequently to the Term Reports, in case
of his not publishing the said work with the plaintiffs, although
he would have preferred that the work should have been published by the plaintiffs, on account of the necessity of inserting
such modern reports.

The plaintiffs having, on the 9th of June, moved, before the   [722]
Vice-Chancellor, for an injunction to restrain the publication of
the first part of the second volume, his Honour refused the application, but gave the plaintiffs leave to bring an action, and liberty
to all parties to apply to the Court as they might be advised.

The motion was now renewed before the Lord Chancellor.

Mr. Jacob and *Mr. James Russell*, in support of the motion :
* * It will be said that the plaintiffs have, by neglecting
to take steps to restrain the publication and sale of the first
volume, induced the defendants to persevere in their undertaking and to publish the second ; but neither of the defendants
swears that he was induced to go on by any thing the plaintiffs
did or omitted to do ; nor does either of the defendants swear
even to his belief of the legality of what they have been doing.
Besides, the quantity taken from the plaintiffs' books for the
first volume was too small to be worth complaint, and the
plaintiffs could not know what the contents of the second volume
would be.

[725]

Mr. Wigram, Mr. Willcock, and *Mr. Warren, contrà :*

* * The principle upon which the Court grants injunctions
in cases of this sort is the same as that upon which it decrees
specific performance of contracts ; viz., because it cannot give
the plaintiff compensation in damages ; but the objection to the
injunction in this case is, that the Court, by granting it, would

[*726]

be giving the plaintiffs the largest *possible damages to which
they can be entitled, and yet the damage may be so minute that
it is impossible to appreciate it, and that, too, in a case, like the
present, in which the defendant has been led into enormous
expense with the connivance of the plaintiff; for, in Messrs.
Saunders and Benning's Catalogue of Law Books sold by them,
which was issued at the beginning of this year, appears the first
volume of Smith's Leading Cases, with a notice that a second
volume is in the press.

The work in question is, substantially, any thing but a piracy :
for the substantial part of it consists of the treatises on the law
which are contained in the notes. * * *

The whole amount borrowed extends over 128 of the plaintiffs'
pages, and 190 of the defendants', and, of the 15,340 cases, the
defendants have published twenty-four. * * *

[727]

Mr. Jacob, in reply. * * *

[For the reasons given in the judgment it is unnecessary to
refer to the numerous cases cited by counsel.]

THE LORD CHANCELLOR:

SAUNDERS
v.
SMITH.
June 23.

[728]

I have looked through the affidavits, and the authorities which have been referred to, and I am clearly of opinion that the VICE-CHANCELLOR came to the right conclusion, and that his order ought to be supported ; and I have formed that opinion upon grounds which make it quite unnecessary for me to go into the question of law, which has been discussed at the Bar.

This Court exercises its jurisdiction, not for the purpose of acting upon legal rights, but for the purpose of better enforcing legal rights, or preventing mischief until they have been ascertained. In all cases of injunctions in aid of legal rights—whether it be copyright, patent right, or some other description of legal right which comes before the Court—the office of the Court is consequent upon the legal right; and it generally happens that the only question the Court has to consider is, whether the case is so clear and so free from objection upon the grounds of equitable consideration, that the Court ought to interfere by injunction, without a previous trial at law, or whether it ought to wait till the legal title has been established. That distinction depends upon a great variety of circumstances, and it is utterly impossible to lay down any general rule upon the subject, by which the discretion of the Court ought in all cases to be regulated.

In this case, I find the publication complained of to be of a character which, whether it be or be not an infringement of the copyright of the plaintiffs, is a course of proceeding which has been pretty largely admitted, and pretty generally adopted. Several cases occurred to me, and several were mentioned to me at the Bar, in which a gentleman at the Bar, desirous of *publishing a work upon a particular subject, has collected the cases upon that subject, and has taken those cases, generally speaking, *verbatim*, from reports which are covered by copyright. No instance has been represented to me in which those entitled to the copyright have interfered ; no judgment, therefore, has been pronounced upon that subject. I am not stating whether the owner of the copyright is entitled to interfere in such a case, or whether that use of published reports is or is not to be permitted. That is a question of legal right, upon which I

[*729]

24—2

SAUNDERS
v.
SMITH.

find, at present, no reason for coming to an adjudication. But, in considering whether I am to exercise an equitable jurisdiction in such a case, before the legal right has been established, it is very important to observe, that, for many years, such a course as I have stated has been pretty generally adopted; more particularly, when I find that these plaintiffs have themselves acquiesced in a similar course of proceeding. In a book which was mentioned in the course of the argument, I mean Chitty on Bills, I don't know whether all the cases are printed *verbatim*, but certainly many cases are printed, *verbatim*, from the published reports, of which the plaintiffs have the copyright. Whether that was a matter of indulgence or not, it could not have been a matter of arrangement; for I put that to the learned counsel at the time, who had the opportunity of satisfying themselves whether it was or was not so. I repeat, that I state this case, not for the purpose of showing that the proceeding I have stated interfered with the legal right, but for the purpose of considering whether I ought to exercise jurisdiction by injunction before that legal right is established.

The case, however, may be carried very much farther; for I find, in the dealings of the plaintiffs in this case, what amounts to that species of conduct which *prevents, in this stage of the cause at least, the interposition of this Court.

[*730]

Before I observe upon these facts, I will refer to what Lord ELDON said in *Rundell* v. *Murray* (1), a case certainly very much stronger than the present, but in which Lord ELDON lays down the rule which ought to regulate the discretion of the Court in cases of this sort. The owner, or the party who asserted the copyright, had permitted Mr. Murray to publish the work, which, after a certain time, turned out to be productive; and, fourteen years having elapsed since the transaction took place, the plaintiff was desirous of reasserting her title to the copyright, and gave notice to Mr. Murray, not to publish after that time, as she herself was desirous of publishing. Lord ELDON refused the injunction for which she applied, and, after commenting upon the case, said, "There has often been great difficulty about granting injunctions where the plaintiff has previously, by

(1) 23 R. R. 75 (Jac. 311).

acquiescing, permitted many others to publish the work; where
ten have been allowed to publish, the Court will not restrain
the eleventh.   A court of equity frequently refuses an injunction
where it acknowledges a right, when the conduct of the party
complaining has led to the state of things that occasions the
application; and, therefore, without saying with whom the right
is, whether it is in this lady, or whether it is concurrently in
both. I think it is a case in which strict law only ought to
govern" (1).   Lord ELDON there lays it down, that not only
conduct with the party with whom the contest exists, but conduct with others may influence the Court in the exercise of its
equitable jurisdiction by injunction.   Now, here, I find permission,
whether express or implied, given to others.

I now proceed to advert to the particular facts appearing   [731]
in this case; and here, unfortunately, there is some discrepancy
in the statements made in the affidavits; but there are some
facts unquestionably clear from all doubt.   What is stated in
the preface to the first volume appears to me to afford me a very
safe guide as to what parts of the affidavits to follow.   It is to be
understood that I assume that the plaintiffs are entitled to the
copyright which they assert.

(His Lordship then proceeded to read the statement contained
in the plaintiffs' affidavit, as to what passed between Mr. Benning
and Mr. Smith before the publication of the first volume.)

From the number of the modern reports, of which the plaintiffs
have the copyright, it was natural to suppose that Mr. Smith
could not publish his book without using some of the reports
of which the plaintiffs had the copyright.   The plaintiffs say,
that Mr. Smith stated reasons why he should prefer that they
should publish his book; but they do not represent him as
asking a permission, without which he could not carry on his
undertaking.

Now, the fact is, that the first volume was published in
March, 1837: and in the preface I find this announcement:
"The period over which this collection extends, commences
in the 44 Elizabeth, and terminates in the 34 Geo. III., *Twyne's*
case being the earliest, and *Waugh* v. *Carver* the latest case

(1) 23 R. R. at p. 79 (Jac. 316).

SAUNDERS
v.
SMITH.

[*732]

in the volume. The oldest reports made use of are Lord Coke's;
the most modern Henry Blackstone's. It would have been
impossible to carry the work down to the present day, without
the addition of another volume: this addition will hereafter
be made, should that which is now published be *found adapted
for the purposes to which it is intended to be subservient."
Here is, therefore, a statement by Mr. Smith, in March, 1837,
that if the first volume succeeds, there is an intention of carrying
it down by the addition of another volume. That is made after
a supposed conversation between one of the plaintiffs and the
defendant Mr. Smith, in which the latter was informed that
he could not take any cases, the copyright of which belonged
to the plaintiffs. This preface, however, was a notice not only
to the plaintiffs, but also to those by whom this application
is made, that he intended to do it.

Then Mr. Smith, by his affidavit, makes a statement of what
passed between him and the plaintiff Mr. Benning. (His
Lordship read the affidavit.) This statement is quite consistent
with one passage in the plaintiffs' affidavit, in which Mr. Smith
is stated to have said that he should prefer dealing with the
plaintiffs; and it was very natural, that, as he was using
the plaintiffs' property—whether he had a right to use it or not
—he should prefer dealing with them. Mr. Smith positively
denies that which the plaintiffs impute to him, namely, that he
expressed an opinion that he should be unable to make use
of the cases contained in the reports published subsequently
to the Term Reports, in case of his not publishing his work with
the plaintiffs; but he leaves untouched the passage in the
plaintiffs' affidavit, which states that Mr. Benning observed
to him, "that he certainly could not take any cases, the copyright of which belonged to the plaintiffs." I can come to no
conclusion as to that which is said to have been so stated to him ;
but I have the concurrence of both affidavits as to the proposal
made by Mr. Smith. Then I have the preface to the defendant's
book, and I have no doubt, upon the result of these two affidavits,

[*733]

that it *was known to the plaintiffs, before the first volume was
published—and, indeed, they acknowledge that they knew—
that the first volume did contain some cases taken from their

books, and that it was intended to carry on the work to a more
recent time; and when the work is published, they have a distinct
statement, on Mr. Smith's part, that he intends to do so.

I do not find, in either affidavit, any statement of an intention,
on the part of the plaintiffs, to apply for an injunction to restrain
the publication or sale of the first volume.   The reason which
has been stated at the Bar, namely, that the injury was too
small to make it worth while to interfere, may be an explanation
of that circumstance; but yet that is not exactly the view the
plaintiffs must have taken of the case; for, according to what
was stated in the preface to the first volume, and according
to what was communicated to them by Mr. Smith, they knew
that the first volume was merely the commencement of the plan,
and that it was intended to bring it down to more modern times,
in the reports of which the plaintiffs were more immediately
interested.   They do not complain, however; and there is
nothing before me to show that they interfered, after the publication of the first volume, to caution Mr. Smith against interfering
with their rights.   On the contrary, I find, by an affidavit made
by Mr. Maxwell, a statement of a communication between himself and one of the plaintiffs, after the publication of the first
volume, and which is not met by any affidavit of the plaintiffs
in reply.   Mr. Maxwell, in his affidavit, which was sworn on
the 31st of May, says that "two or three months ago" he
"mentioned to the said plaintiff, William Benning, that he
understood that the plaintiffs were desirous of having a share
in 'Smith's Leading Cases,' and that the deponent was willing
to grant the same, provided that they *would give him a pro-   [*734]
portionate share in 'Smith's Commercial Law' in exchange;
and though the said plaintiff, William Benning, stated that
his partner would not accede to such a proposition, he made
no complaint or observation to the deponent as to the publication of 'Smith's Leading Cases' in any way interfering with
any copyright of the said plaintiffs."

Now this communication took place when the first volume had
been published eleven months, and after the first part of the
second volume had not only been announced, but had been
included in a catalogue published by the plaintiffs themselves.

Can it be supposed that their attention was not drawn to the fact, not only of what had been done, but of what Mr. Smith had announced his intention of doing?

Now, when I look at this book—I am not sufficiently acquainted with it to give an opinion upon its merits—but I have no doubt that the opinions expressed by others who have had more opportunities of examining it, are deserved—when I look at this book, I see that it is a work of very great labour, and I find the principle is to take, first, the marginal note, sometimes with some alteration, and then to take the leading case, as a principle, and then, by very voluminous and obviously laborious notes, to work out the principle. It is clear, therefore, that the work is one of great labour, and that this was evident from the first volume; and I find that the plaintiffs were informed, in March, 1837, of an intention to deal with the existing reports in the manner now complained of. I find the first volume published, announcing the intention of going on with the same plan, which necessarily would run over the period to which the copyrights of the plaintiffs relate, and that no remonstrance is made to Mr. Smith upon the nature *of the work, but he is permitted to go on with this laborious undertaking until the period at which the first part of the second volume is published. In the mean time, there was a communication between the plaintiffs and Mr. Maxwell, who was interested in the publication of the work, and who has as much right to the protection of the Court as Mr. Smith; and, in the proposal which he makes to the plaintiffs, he deals with the work as property he is entitled to deal with, wishing to make it the subject of arrangement between himself and the plaintiffs; and I do not find that this leads to any caution or interference on the part of the plaintiffs as to that course which Mr. Smith had pursued in part, and which the plaintiffs must have been fully aware that he intended to pursue farther.

I do not give any opinion upon the legal question. I am only to decide whether the plaintiffs are entitled, under the circumstances, to the interposition of the Court to protect their legal right, when that legal right has not yet been established. But I assume the existence of the legal right, and I say, that

[*785]

SAUNDERS
v.
SMITH.

whatever legal right the plaintiffs may have, the circumstances
are such as to make it the duty of a court of equity to withhold
its hand, and to abstain from exercising its equitable jurisdiction,
at all events until the plaintiffs shall come here with the legal
title established.

In doing this, I am only doing what Lord ELDON did in
Rundell v. *Murray* (1), and what is very generally done upon
questions of patent right. The Court always exercises its
discretion as to whether it shall interfere by injunction before
the establishment of the legal right.

I am quite clear that the VICE-CHANCELLOR was right, and   [736]
that it is not the duty of the Court to interfere by injunction
in this case—at all events in the present stage of the cause—
and therefore I must refuse this motion with costs.

Before I dismiss the subject, however, I wish to say a few
words with respect to a case which appears to have been relied
upon by the VICE-CHANCELLOR in his judgment, and which has
not been reported (2). It is quite clear that his Honour had not
any accurate information with respect to the result of that case ;
for he supposed, from the representations made to him, that
I had decided it upon a calculation of the quantity of the
plaintiff's book which had been taken by the defendant. In
the first place, I never decided that case at all ; for it went off
upon an arrangement between the parties. Mr. Halcomb pressed
that the injunction should be dissolved, and that a particular
inquiry, which could only be directed by the consent of the
parties, should be ordered ; and, upon that, the injunction was
dissolved. Then it appeared that there had been an assignment
of the copyright, which brought other parties into the field,
and, of course, nothing could be done finally to dispose of the
case, and it stood over, and was never brought on again. I
understand that it fell to the ground in consequence of the death
of Mr. Bramwell in the mean time.

So far, however, from considering that the question turned
upon a mere measure of quantity, I find, from a note with
which Mr. Craig has furnished me, that I said, in the course
of the argument, " When it comes to a question of quantity

(1) 23 R. R. 75 (Jac. 311).   (2) See next page.

it must be very vague. One *writer might take all the vital part of another's book, though it might be but a small proportion of the book in quantity. It is not only quantity, but value that is always looked to. It is useless to refer to any particular cases as to quantity." Now there could hardly be anything less likely to lay down a rule as to quantity. Indeed, quite the reverse; and yet that is all which appears to have been said by me upon the question of quantity. There was no judgment at all, however, upon the general question of law; and the course I adopted in that case is exactly the course which I adopt now, and proceeded upon the same principle; namely, that the injunction would be an extreme hardship upon the defendant, as compared with the hardship the plaintiff would sustain, by being put, in the first instance, at all events, to establish his title at law.

Motion refused, with costs.

1836.
July 6, 7.

Lord
COTTENHAM,
L.C.
[737]

BRAMWELL *v.* HALCOMB.

(3 My. & Cr. 737—741.)

The question whether one author has made a piratical use of another's work, does not necessarily depend upon the quantity of that work which he has quoted or introduced in his own book.

THE plaintiff was the author of a Treatise upon the Manner of Proceeding on Bills in the House of Commons, and the defendant Halcomb was the author of a Practical Treatise on passing Private Bills through both Houses of Parliament. The bill was filed for an injunction to restrain the publication of the defendant's book, upon the alleged ground that it contained very numerous passages copied from the plaintiff's work.

The *Solicitor-General* and *Mr. Halcomb*, for the defendant, moved to dissolve the injunction which had been granted by the VICE-CHANCELLOR.

Mr. Stuart supported the injunction :

*   *   *Mr. Stuart* contended, amongst other things, that the quantity of Mr. Bramwell's book, which had been quoted by

Mr. Halcomb, would be an unfair quantity, even if Mr. Halcomb had avowed that he took it from Mr. Bramwell; and he referred to *Mawman* v. *Tegg* (1).

BRAMWELL
v.
HALCOMB.

THE LORD CHANCELLOR:

When it comes to a question of quantity, it must be very vague. One writer might take all the vital part of another's book, though it might be but a small proportion of the book in quantity. It is not only quantity but value that is always looked to. It is useless to refer to any particular cases as to quantity.

In my view of the law, Lord ELDON, in *Wilkins* v. *Aikin* (2), put the question on a most proper footing. He says, "The question upon the whole is, whether this is a legitimate use of the plaintiff's publication, in the fair exercise of a mental operation, deserving the character of an original work."

At the conclusion of the *Solicitor-General's* reply, [739]

THE LORD CHANCELLOR said:

I am clearly of opinion that this is a case in which I ought not to exercise the jurisdiction of this Court, without giving the parties an opportunity of trying their rights at law; for, where any doubt exists as to the right of the parties, if the Court were to exercise jurisdiction without giving an opportunity of trial at law, there would be different law in this Court and in the courts of law upon the subject. The proceeding here is merely for the purpose of making effectual the legal right, as Lord ELDON says in *Wilkins* v. *Aikin* (2). Where any doubt exists as to the legal right, it is very proper to be tried. The only question is, whether, in the meantime, the injunction is to be continued, or whether it is to be dissolved, on the undertaking, which the defendant has offered, of keeping an account. It is obvious that it is the interest of both parties that the injunction should be dissolved, for if, in consequence of piracy, the defendant is, in fact, selling the plaintiff's work, the plaintiff will have the profits of the publication; but if, on the contrary, no piracy has been committed, a very great hardship is inflicted

(1) 26 R. R. 112 (2 Russ 385).   (2) 11 R. R. 118 (17 Ves. 422).

BRAMWELL
v.
HALCOMB.

upon the defendant; and, on that supposition, he has already experienced a severe hardship, because the injunction has prevented the sale of his book during the season. If *Mr. Stuart* thinks it proper to press for the continuance of the injunction, I must look through the passages in the respective books.

Mr. Stuart:

[*740]

We should not merely have the profits of the sale in the meantime, but we should be indemnified for the *loss which we may sustain by reason of the sale of the defendant's book preventing the sale of our book in the meantime. If the Master would estimate what loss we had sustained, I have no objection. * * *

Mr. Stuart then stated that Mr. Halcomb had sold his copyright to some other persons who were also made defendants on the record.

*   *   *   *   *

[741]

It was then arranged that the injunction should be simply dissolved, as against Mr. Halcomb, and that the costs of his application should be costs in the cause: and that the other defendants should give notice for Wednesday next, for a motion to dissolve the injunction as against themselves.

The reporters believe that the case was never mentioned again. The plaintiff soon afterwards died.

1838.
April 23, 24.
——
Lord
COTTENHAM,
L.C.
[763]

BICKHAM *v.* CRUTTWELL (1).

(3 My. & Cr. 763—772 ; S. C. 7 L. J. (N. S.) Ch. 198; 2 Jur. 342.)

A testator, who was possessed of considerable real estate, comprising, among other property, three houses in N., upon which he owed a sum of 2,900*l.* secured by mortgage, devised his three houses in N., together with several other houses therein described, "the whole subject to the payment of the mortgage debt of 2,900*l.* borrowed on mortgage of the houses in N.," to C. and H. in fee. He then devised and bequeathed

(1) Although Locke King's Act, 17 & 18 Vict. c. 113 (and the amending Acts passed in 1867 and 1877) have relieved the personal estate of its primary liability for mortgage debts, yet this decision contains some obser-vations of general interest, especially the reference to *Hancox* v. *Abbey*. 8 R. R. 124 (11 Ves. 179), which justify, if they do not require, the retention of the case in the Revised Reports.—O. A. S.

the residue of his real estates and all his personal estate and effects whatsoever, subject nevertheless, as to his personal estate, to the payment of his debts, except such debts as were therein excepted therefrom, to trustees, in trust as to the particular estates therein specified ; and, among others, as to certain messuages therein specifically described, subject to the mortgages made on the same, and from the payment of which he thereby exempted his personal estate ; and as to all the residue and remainder of his said real and personal estates, in trust for the persons therein mentioned :

Held, that the testator's personal estate was the primary fund for the payment of the mortgage debt of 2,900l.

THE will of Richard Bowsher, late of the city of Bath, solicitor, which bore date the 4th of July, 1834, and was duly executed and attested to pass freehold estate by devise, was in part as follows: "I give, devise, and bequeath * * my three houses in Norfolk Crescent, called Norfolk House, and Nos. 1 and 3, my house, No. 17, Great Stanhope Street, and my two houses Nos. 11 and 12, Kensington Place ; the whole subject to the payment of the mortgage debt of 2,900l. (borrowed on mortgage of the houses in Norfolk Crescent by Richard Orchard, of whom I purchased the same), to the representatives of the late Archdeacon Willes, or such part thereof as shall remain undischarged at my decease, and subject likewise to the annual ground rents reserved and made issuing and payable to me out of the said several messuages, unto Charles Currie Bickham *and Harriet his sister, and their heirs, as tenants in common. And as to all the rest, residue, and remainder of my real estates, and as to all my personal estate and effects whatsoever, I give, devise, and bequeath the same, subject nevertheless, as to my personal estate, to the payment of my just debts, funeral and and testamentary expenses, except such debts as are herein excepted therefrom, and the expenses attending the trusts hereof, unto John Routh the elder, Thomas Macauley Cruttwell, and the said Charles Currie Bickham, their heirs, executors, administrators, and assigns, upon the trusts, and to and for the intents and purposes hereinafter declared concerning the same." The testator then proceeded to enumerate and describe the several messuages and parcels of which the residue of his real estate consisted, one portion of which he mentioned as follows : "And also my four messuages Nos. 3, 4, 5 and 6, in Nelson Place

[*764]

BICKHAM
v.
CRUTTWELL.

aforesaid, subject to the mortgages made on the said last-mentioned messuages, or such part or parts thereof as may remain unpaid at my decease, and from the payment of which said mortgages I hereby exempt my personal estate, and also subject to the payment of the several yearly fee-farm rents, made issuing and payable thereout, in trust as therein mentioned." And all the rest, residue, and remainder of his said real and personal estates, subject as aforesaid, the testator gave in trust for Ann Routh, wife of the said John Routh the elder, for her separate use for life; and, after her decease, in trust for the said John Routh the elder, for his life, with remainder among their children as therein mentioned.

[*765]

The bill was filed by Charles C. Bickham, to whom the moiety of the houses in Kensington Place, Norfolk Crescent, and Great Stanhope Street, specifically *devised to his sister Harriet, had been previously conveyed by her, against his co-executors and co-trustees, and also against the persons beneficially interested in the testator's residuary estate. It prayed a declaration that the testator's personal estate, not specifically bequeathed, was liable to pay the mortgage debt of 2,900l. in exoneration of the three houses in Norfolk Crescent.

The answer of the defendants, the executors, admitted that the testator's personal estate not specifically bequeathed was more than sufficient to satisfy the amount of his funeral and testamentary expenses and all his debts.

The evidence in the cause proved that the [2,900l. said to have been borrowed by Richard Orchard on the mortgage of the houses in Norfolk Crescent, was really borrowed on behalf of the testator as to 900l. on one house and as to 2,000l. on the two other houses, and that Orchard was really a trustee for the testator at the dates of those mortgages].

[766]

The cause now came on to be heard.

[767]

The *Solicitor-General, Mr. Willcock*, and *Mr. T. Platt*, for the plaintiff, contended that although the whole property comprised in the devise to the plaintiff and his sister was charged with the mortgage debt, the personal estate, which was the natural and primary fund, was not exonerated from the

obligation to discharge the burthen; and [they cited *Tait* v.
Lord Northwick (1), and other cases to the same effect].

Mr. Tinney and *Mr. Piggott*, for John Routh, the elder, and
the other parties beneficially interested in the residuary estate,
insisted that the testator, by extending the security so as to
include the additional property comprised in the devise to the
plaintiff and his sister, had shown a clear intention to exonerate
the personal estate altogether; and they relied strongly upon
Hancox v. *Abbey*, which was, they contended, the case of a
specific devise, subject, like the devise in the present case,
to the payment of a particular debt, such payment being the
condition of the gift (2). They also referred to *Burton* v.
Knowlton (3), *Tower* v. *Lord Rous* (4), *Bootle* v. *Blundell* (5),
Greene v. *Greene* (6), *Clutterbuck* v. *Clutterbuck* (7). * * *

Mr. Barlow, for Cruttwell, the other executor.   [768]

The LORD CHANCELLOR entered into an elaborate and minute   *April* 24.
examination of the history of the transactions between Orchard
and Bowsher, and then continued as follows:

The result of this examination is to leave no doubt in my
mind, that the whole of this debt was really the debt of Bowsher;
that he was the person who owed the money, although, as
between himself and the mortgagee, he did not appear as the
party who contracted the debt. It comes, however, to much
the same thing; for if a man borrows money in the name
of a trustee, the debt is, in one way or other, his from the
commencement, either to the person who advances the money,
or to the trustee in whose name it is borrowed.

If then, the fact has been clearly made out in evidence,
as I think it has, that this debt of 2,900*l.* was the debt of the
testator, the question of law is a matter of little or no difficulty.
The testator, in connection with these three houses in Norfolk
Crescent, gives certain *other property, and he devises the   [*769]

(1) 4 R. R. 358 (4 Ves. 816).   (5) 15 R. R. 93 (19 Ves. 494).
(2) 8 R. R. 124 (11 Ves. 179).   (6) 13 R. R. 277 (4 Madd. 148).
(3) 3 R. R. 62 (3 Ves. 107).   (7) 36 R. R. 242 (1 My. & K. 15).
(4) 11 R. R. 169 (18 Ves. 132).

whole to the plaintiff and his sister, subject to the payment
of the mortgage debt of 2,900*l.* to the representatives of Archdeacon Willes. He then gives the residue of his real estates,
and all his personal estate and effects whatsoever, subject
nevertheless, as to his personal estate, to the payment of his
just debts, funeral and testamentary expenses, except such debts
as are therein excepted therefrom, to his trustees, upon the
trusts therein declared; and, in another part of his will, he
gives his four messuages in Nelson Place, described as subject
to certain mortgages thereon, from the payment of which
mortgages he thereby exempts his personal estate. So that the
testator, in effect, gives certain specified premises, subject to
one mortgage, without any direction that they shall bear the
mortgage, and he gives other mortgaged premises, with an
express direction that the personal estate shall not be called
upon to pay them. The gift of the residue of his personal
estate, subject to the payment of his debts, except such debts as
are therein excepted, amounts to a declaration that the personal
estate shall bear all such debts as are not specifically excepted.
His attention, too, was particularly called to mortgage debts.

Now what is there to be found on the face of this will referable
to the particular houses in question? The gift is of the houses,
subject to the payment of the mortgage. That expression
however, it is clear, will not exonerate the personal estate;
it is merely a description of the state of the property, and it
has often been decided that such a form of expression does not
amount to an exoneration of the personal estate. It is true,
the devise subject to the charge also includes other property;
that is to say, it charges other property which was not before
subject to the mortgage debt. But that circumstance will not,
[*770]   *of itself, exonerate the personal estate; it is merely an
additional charge, giving a further security beyond what the
mortgagee previously had. Why the testator should have so
done does not appear. Very possibly he may have conceived,
if we are to speculate on his motives, that by making the devise
in this way he was exonerating the personal estate; but it is
decided that the throwing in an additional security, where
nothing but a mere charge is created, has no such effect.

It was supposed, indeed, that *Hancox* v. *Abbey* (1) was an authority to the contrary. The circumstances of that case, however, were extremely different, and whether rightly decided or not, it does not touch the present question. That was not a devise of property subject to a mortgage ; it was a devise of property upon trust to sell and pay a mortgage ; and there was no gift of the estate until after the debt was paid off. Who, in that case, could take the estate, if it was not sold ? Surely the devisee could not take it, and have the mortgage debt paid out of the personal estate. Sir WILLIAM GRANT, undoubtedly, in his judgment, makes a distinction between a general and a particular charge ; but his observations must be understood with reference to the facts of the case before him, and not to any general principle.

Certainly, when that passage in this will was first called to my attention, I felt, as I still feel, a difficulty in discovering the motive which actuated the testator in charging these additional houses in aid of the original security. We know that the three houses had become of much less value. It may have been that the testator was desirous of protecting the lender from the consequences of the depreciation ; or it may have arisen from a notion floating in his mind, that his personal *estate would not be liable to the payment of the mortgage money. But this is mere speculation ; and although certainly the rule has been much relaxed, the burthen of showing from the will itself that the ordinary administration of the assets is intended to be altered, still remains upon the party who seeks to relax it. The Court must be clearly satisfied by that which the testator himself has said, that it was his intention to exonerate the personal estate.

[*771]

Now, upon the face of this instrument, although there is great difficulty in reconciling this particular clause with the rest of the will, so far from finding it to be manifest that the testator intended to exonerate the personal estate from the burthen of this mortgage debt, I find that which amounts to a plain declaration to the contrary. For I cannot possibly reconcile such an intention with the declaration that his personal estate is to be subject to the payment of his just debts, except such as are specially excepted therefrom.

(1) 8 R. R. 124 (11 Ves. 179).

BICKHAM   It was argued, on behalf of the defendants, that by describing
v.
CRUTTWELL. the debt as money borrowed on mortgage of the houses by
Orchard, of whom he purchased the same, the testator has
himself told us that he did not consider it as his own debt,
and therefore that it was not necessary for him to except it.
This mode of expression, however, as I observed when going
through the history of the transaction, is not at all inconsistent
with the circumstances of the case, or with the notion that the
debt was really the testator's debt, and was so treated and
considered by himself; and the word "purchased," though
perhaps not quite accurate in fact, correctly enough describes
the form which the transaction assumed.

[772]   We must presume that the testator was cognizant of the rule
of law; and if he knew the law at all, he must have known that
he could not exonerate the personal estate from the burthen
of his debts, unless he so expressed himself as to lead the Court
to the fair conclusion, from the language which he used, that
such was the intention which he meant to express.

I am quite satisfied that the debt in question was the testator's
debt; and if it was his debt, he must have known, or be
presumed to have known, that his personal estate could only
be relieved from it by an express declaration, or by words
raising a necessary inference to that effect. He has not so
done with respect to this debt—he has done so with respect
to other mortgage debts, and therefore I think that the ordinary
rule must prevail (1).

———

1838.   STANLEY *v.* THE CHESTER AND BIRKENHEAD
June 23.   RAILWAY COMPANY.
———
Lord   (3 My. & Cr. 773—783 ; S. C. 1 Rail. Cas. 58.)
COTTENHAM,
L.C.   The B. and C. Railway Company agree with the plaintiff to give him,
[773]   for fourteen acres of land, 20,000*l.*, to be paid by instalments; other
parties, called the C. and B. Railway Company, at the same time start
a rival line, and both Companies go to Parliament. In committee it is
agreed that the merits of both lines shall be referred to two members
of the committee, and the solicitors for the rival Companies at the same
time sign an agreement, by which it is stipulated, that the adopted
Company shall take the engagements with landholders, into which the

(1) See *Noel* v. *Lord Henley*, 26 R. R. 660 (7 Price, 241).

STANLEY
v.
THE
CHESTER
AND BIRKEN-
HEAD
RAILWAY
COMPANY.

rejected Company may have entered; and to this agreement the sanction of two members of each Company, and also of the plaintiff, is subsequently obtained, and is signified by a written memorandum of approval. The C. and B. Company is adopted, and incorporated by Act of Parliament. Their line will require sixteen acres of the plaintiff's land in a different place. The plaintiff files a bill against the C. and B. Company, stating these facts, and seeking to compel them to keep the agreement entered into by him with the B. and C. Company; and to restrain the C. and B. Company from entering upon any lands belonging to him, till after payment of the first instalment, which is already due; and from proceeding, after subsequent instalments became due, till such instalments shall have been paid. The defendants demur generally to the bill. Demurrer over-ruled.

THE bill, which was filed on the 12th of May, 1838, stated that in the latter part of the year 1836, certain persons were preparing to form a Company to make a railroad from Chester to Birkenhead, and were intending to apply for an Act of Parliament to enable them so to do, and that they proposed to call themselves "The Chester Junction Railway Company," but afterwards altered their name to that of "The Birkenhead and Chester Railway Company:"

That the line of railway proposed to be formed by the intended Company was to pass through certain parts of the plaintiff's estates, and would have been injurious to, and destructive of, his property; and that he was therefore, in the first instance, much opposed to the formation of that railway:

That William Spurstow Miller, in the character of solicitor for the promoters of the intended railway, made *overtures to the plaintiff for his consent, and that, after some negotiation, the plaintiff undertook to give his consent to the Company for the proposed line of railway, and to permit them to form the same through his estates, on terms [which were subsequently reduced into writing, and signed by W. S. Miller for the Company, and by Richard Blundell for the plaintiff. The agreement, dated the 17th of January, 1837, fixed the purchase-money at 20,000*l.*, and defined the line of the intended railway.] [*774]

That about the same time at which the scheme for forming the Company, to be called "The Birkenhead and Chester Railway Company," was set on foot, another proposal was made by other parties for forming a railway between the same points—Chester and Birkenhead—but by a different line, and that it was proposed by them that application should be made to Parliament for [775]

STANLEY
v.
THE
CHESTER
AND BIRKEN-
HEAD
RAILWAY
COMPANY.

forming them into a Company, with powers to make such railway, and which should be called "The Chester and Birkenhead Railway Company:"

That the proposed line of the proposed Chester and Birkenhead Railway also passed through the plaintiff's estates, and that to such line the plaintiff dissented:

That Joseph Mallaby was the solicitor for the intended Chester and Birkenhead Railway Company, and was authorised to act for them; and that two bills were in the session of 1837 introduced into the House of Commons, the one for forming the line which was to be called the Birkenhead and Chester Railway, and the other for forming the line which was to be called the Chester and Birkenhead Railway:

That both the bills were referred to the same committee of the House: and that in the course of their examination of the respective merits of the rival lines, one of the members of the committee proposed that it should be referred to Lord Sandon and Mr. Wilson Patten, two members of the committee, to determine which of the two lines should be adopted:

[776]   That such proposal was assented to by the promoters of the two bills respectively, and an entry of the fact of such agreement for *reference* was made in the minutes of the proceedings of the committee:

That before the committee adjourned for the day on which such proposal was made and agreed to, an agreement was made and signed by the respective solicitors for the two bills in the following terms:

"It is agreed by the undersigned solicitors of the Chester and Birkenhead, and Birkenhead and Chester Railways, for and on behalf of their respective clients, that the merits of the two lines shall be submitted to Lord Sandon and Mr. Wilson Patten, who are to decide which line shall be adopted, and what ought to be done, for the accommodation of the different ferries, by the line selected. It is the basis of the agreement that the shareholders of the rejected line are to be at liberty, if they think proper, to take shares in the other line. And further, that the adopted line (1) so to take the engagements entered

(1) So in the Bill.

STANLEY
v.
THE
CHESTER
AND BIRKEN-
HEAD
RAILWAY
COMPANY.

into with the landholders by the rejected line ; 18th April, 1837.
JOSEPH MALLABY, solicitor for the Chester and Birkenhead Rail-
way ; W. S. MILLER, SAMUEL BRITTAIN, junior, solicitors to the
Birkenhead and Chester :"

 ̤That the referees made their award in favour of the Chester
and Birkenhead Railway.]

That upon such award being made, the Birkenhead and Chester
Bill was withdrawn, and the bill for making *a railway from
Chester to Birkenhead was passed by the House of Commons :

That the plaintiff, relying on the agreement made between
W. S. Miller on behalf of the Birkenhead and Chester Railway
Company, and Richard Blundell on the plaintiff's behalf, and
so as aforesaid agreed to be adopted by the Chester and Birkenhead
Railway Company, and not doubting that the same would be
faithfully adhered to and executed by the Chester and Birkenhead
Railway Company, assented to the bill for forming the Chester
and Birkenhead Railway, and took no part in the further
opposition that was made thereto in the House of Commons
or in the House of Lords :

That the Chester and Birkenhead Railway Bill passed the
House of Lords, and the Royal Assent was given thereto on the
12th of July, 1837 ;   *   *   *

The bill then proceeded to allege that the Chester and Birkenhead Railway Company had refused to perform the agreement
made between Miller and Blundell, and it charged that, by the
terms of the agreement for the reference to Lord Sandon and
Mr. Wilson Patten, the defendants adopted the agreement between
 ̤Miller and Blundell, and took upon themselves all the liabilities
under it of the promoters of the other line of railway ; and that
when the proposal for reference to Lord Sandon and Mr. Wilson
Patten was under consideration between *the several parties,
W. S. Miller, acting as solicitor and agent of the line afterwards
rejected, distinctly informed Mr. Mallaby, who was acting as the
solicitor and agent of the promoters of the line which was adopted,
and in the presence and hearing of Mr. Blundell, the plaintiff's
agent, of the existence of a contract or agreement with the plaintiff, and although Mr. Miller declined to name the exact sum
which, under such contract or agreement, was to be paid to the

[777]
[*778]

[*779]

STANLEY
v.
THE
CHESTER
AND BIRKEN-
HEAD
RAILWAY
COMPANY.

plaintiff, yet he informed Mr. Mallaby, and also two of the persons acting as a committee for the Chester and Birkenhead Railway Company, that the sum was more than 15,000*l.*, but would not exceed 20,000*l.*, and that it was after they had distinct knowledge to that extent of the contract or agreement with the plaintiff, that the agreement for reference to Lord Sandon and Mr. Wilson Patten was made and signed.

The bill further charged that by the line of road proposed to be formed by the Birkenhead and Chester Railway, only fourteen and a half statute acres of the plaintiff's land would have been taken, whereas, by the line to be formed by the defendants, sixteen and three-quarters statute acres were to be taken, and the rejected line was purposely laid down so as to avoid certain fox covers and preserves on the plaintiff's estate, whereas the present line of the defendants went through and destroyed two fox covers and preserves; and, in other respects, the line of the defendant's railway did much greater injury to the plaintiff and his estate, than would have been done by that line of railway, the formation of which was the subject of the agreement.

The bill prayed, that it might be declared that the agreement of the 17th of January, 1837, was binding upon the defendants, [*780] and that under it they were *bound to pay to the plaintiff, at the time and in the manner therein mentioned, the sum of 20,000*l.*; and that they might be decreed specifically to perform that agreement. * * *

To this bill the defendants put in a general demurrer, which the VICE-CHANCELLOR over-ruled, and the defendants thereupon appealed to the Lord Chancellor.

Mr. Jacob, Mr. Wigram, and *Mr. Walker,* in support of the [781] demurrer, contended that * * it was impossible to suppose that Sir T. Stanley meant to assert the extravagant proposition that the defendants were bound to take the fourteen and a half acres which were situate on the line which the railway would not now pursue; and that it was impossible to maintain that Sir T. Stanley was entitled to the benefit of the agreement between the solicitors of the rival Companies, to which he was

Stanley
v.
The
Chester
and Birken-
head
Railway
Company.

no party, even although his solicitor, or even he himself, might have written " approved " at the foot of that agreement. They insisted that, even supposing the agreement between the solicitors of the rival Companies to be a contract of indemnity between the two Companies, yet the agreement which Sir T. Stanley sought to enforce was an agreement which was to be performed by the rejected Company, only in the event of their Act of Parliament passing and their intended line being sanctioned. They further observed that the plaintiff did not offer to give up the sixteen acres, and that he might say, at the hearing, that he never intended to give them up.

The Lord Chancellor :

The question for me to consider (arising as it does upon a general demurrer), is whether the bill does or does not state a case which, if proved, will, at the hearing, entitle the plaintiff to some relief. The case, as it appears on the face of the bill, is one of the grossest frauds I have ever seen attempted. I have *nothing to do with the question whether Sir T. Stanley (the plaintiff) has or has not an extravagant bargain. Sir T. Stanley entered into a certain contract with an intended Railway Company ; [His Lordship read the substance of the contract] ; but it being a matter of contest between that Company and this which of them should have an Act of Parliament, an agreement was entered into between the two Companies, pending this contest, by one of the terms of which it was provided that the adopted line should take the engagements entered into with the landholders by the rejected line. [His Lordship read this agreement.] The plaintiff is no party to this agreement, but the allegation is, that it was approved and adopted by the promoters of the two Companies, and by the plaintiff, and that such approval was testified by the agreement being signed by two persons on behalf of each of the Companies, and by the plaintiff himself, through the instrumentality of an agent. What could be the meaning of the arrangement so made, if it was not that the plaintiff was to look for performance of his contract to the existing Company, instead of to the rejected Company ? [His Lordship read the allegation.]

[*782]

STANLEY
v.
THE
CHESTER
AND BIRKEN-
HEAD
RAILWAY
COMPANY.

It could mean but one of two things; viz., either that the agreement already existing between the plaintiff and one of the Companies should be considered as if entered into between himself and that Company which should be actually selected by Parliament; or that, in order to relieve the Company which should not succeed in obtaining an Act of Parliament, the contracts of that Company should be executed by the Company selected: and then, the Company selected having obtained the concurrence of the plaintiff in that agreement—although it certainly is not distinctly alleged that he assented to the bill on the faith of it—it is said that if you look to the original agreement, the land was to be taken only in *case the rejected Company succeeded in getting an Act of Parliament; and therefore we, the defendants, will exercise the adverse powers of our Act of Parliament independently of that agreement.

[*783]

Would any court of equity permit the Company first to obtain the concurrence of the plaintiff in an agreement like this, and then to turn round and say they will disregard it altogether, and put in force the adverse powers of the Act, as if no such agreement was in existence?

I have no hesitation in saying, that, on the face of the bill, there does appear such a case as will entitle the plaintiff to some relief. I cannot suppose that the Company, as a body, will adopt a course which no individual member of the Company would adopt. If I were to allow the demurrer, I should be saying that the Company might go upon the plaintiff's land, and give him for it only what a jury might award.

Demurrer over-ruled.

Mr. *Temple* and Mr. *Loftus Lowndes* were counsel for the plaintiff, but were not called upon.

GREENHALGH *v.* THE MANCHESTER AND BIR-MINGHAM RAILWAY COMPANY.

(3 My. & Cr. 784—800; S. C. 8 L. J. (N. S.) Ch. 75; 2 Jur. 1035; 3 Jur. 693; 1 Rail. Cas. 68.)

1838.
Dec. 5, 6, 13.
———
Lord
COTTENHAM,
L.C.
[784]

The owner of land upon which a Railway Company empowered by Parliament are about to enter, is not entitled to an interlocutory injunction to restrain them from so entering, if by his silence and conduct he has permitted the Company to carry on their works upon the supposition that they were entitled to enter on and take the land in question.

IN the latter part of the year 1836, two joint stock Companies were projected for the construction of distinct and independent lines of railway, to proceed from Manchester towards the south. One of these lines, to which was given the name of "The Manchester South Union Railway," was to terminate at Tamworth in Warwickshire: the other, under the name of "The Manchester, Cheshire, and Staffordshire Railway," was intended to connect the town of Manchester with the Grand Junction Railway, which it was to join near a place called Rickerscote in the county of Stafford.

The subscribers to the respective undertakings immediately adopted the usual measures for carrying their schemes into effect, by forming provisional committees, by appointing solicitors, agents, and engineers, by entering into contracts with the owners of property situate on the proposed lines, and by giving the requisite notices of their intention to apply for Acts of Parliament to confer on them the powers and privileges of incorporated Companies.

On the 14th of February, 1837, the plaintiff, who was a proprietor of land in the township of Ardwick, and lying in the proposed line of the Manchester South Union Railway, entered into an agreement, in writing, with three of the provisional committee of that undertaking, acting on behalf of themselves and the other subscribers, by which he agreed, at the price and upon the terms therein stated, to sell and convey to the Company *the fee simple of two plots of land therein described, and containing together 7,040 square yards; and it was thereby, among other things, provided that, in case the Act for incorporating the subscribers as a Company should not pass during the then

[*785]

present session of Parliament, it should be lawful for the
subscribers to vacate the agreement, on giving the plaintiff three
months' notice, and paying rent for the land up to the expiration
of such notice: and further, that, in the event of any other
Company obtaining an Act, for the purposes of which it might
become necessary or desirable to sell the land to such company
before the South Union Company should obtain their Act, or in
the event of the purchase not being completed within two years,
the plaintiff should be at liberty to vacate the agreement upon
giving three months' notice.

In the parliamentary session of 1837, two bills were
accordingly introduced into the House of Commons, one for
constituting the Company which was to be called "The Manchester South Union Railway Company," and the other for
constituting the Company which was to be called "The Manchester, Cheshire and Staffordshire Railway Company." To the
former of those bills the plaintiff was an assenting party. Both
bills were referred to the same committee of the House, and,
after some investigation into the comparative merits of the
respective lines, the committee recommended that the two bills
should be consolidated, and that the subscribers to the two
undertakings should be united so as to form one Company. The
necessary arrangements were made for carrying this recom-
mendation into effect; and an agreement in writing was, in the
month of May, 1837, entered into and adopted by persons duly
authorised to act on behalf of the promoters of the respective
[*786]   undertakings. By one of the clauses in that agreement, *it was
provided, that in every case where either Company should have
entered into any contracts or engagements with landowners
whose property might be affected by whichever of the two projected lines might be adopted, though in a somewhat different
mode, and the Company projecting the accepted line should not
(though the other Company might) have made contracts with
individual landowners, the contracts so entered into by the
Company proposing the rejected line, should be adopted by the
united Company, having regard to the different modes in which
the property might be affected by the adopted line. On the
13th of May, 1837, a copy of this clause in the agreement was

sent to the plaintiff by the solicitors acting on behalf of the united Company.

In pursuance of the arrangéments before mentioned, leave was given to consolidate the two bills, which was accordingly done; and the committee then reported to the House of Commons that the line adopted in the consolidated Bill was partly that proposed for the Manchester, Cheshire and Staffordshire Railway, and partly that proposed for the Manchester South Union Railway. So far as the plaintiff's land was concerned, the line adopted was the line which had been proposed to be taken by the Manchester, Cheshire and Staffordshire Railway; and the plaintiff, relying, as he stated in one of his affidavits in this cause, on the before mentioned clause in the agreement of May, and on the faith that the united Company were bound to perform the contract of the 14th of February, 1837, instead of opposing, gave his assent to the new bill. On this point, however, the affidavits were conflicting, there being some evidence to show that the plaintiff's name was not included among the assents, but was returned in the list as neutral. The new bill afterwards passed both Houses of Parliament, *and finally received the Royal assent on the 30th of June, 1837. By the Act so passed, the persons therein named, and all other the subscribers to the two proposed railways, were incorporated under the name of "The Manchester and Birmingham Railway Company," for making and maintaining the railway therein described; and the usual powers for purchasing and holding lands for the purposes of the undertaking, were thereby conferred on the Company. Shortly after the passing of the Act, some written communications passed between the plaintiff, or his solicitor, and the solicitors of the new Company, with reference to his contract with the South Union Company; and, on the 7th of October, 1837, he received from the chairman of the provisional committee of the proposed South Union Railway Company, a formal notice, dated the 18th of September, that the subscribers to the agreement between that Company and the plaintiff, would vacate that agreement as on Christmas Day then next. On the 5th of December, in the same year, he received a letter from the chairman of the board of directors of the

GREEN-
HALGH
v.
THE
MANCHESTER
AND BIR-
MINGHAM
RAILWAY
COMPANY.

[*787]

GREEN-
HALGH
r.
THE
MANCHESTER
AND BIR-
MINGHAM
RAILWAY
COMPANY.

Manchester and Birmingham Railway Company, informing him
that the Company's engineers were about to enter upon his land,
for the purpose of staking out the line, and taking the levels and
surveys by which the quantity of ground required by the Company would be determined; and that as soon as the chief
engineer should have reported to the Directors what portion of
his property would be required for the railway, they were
desirous of treating with the plaintiff for the purchase of it.

On the 23rd of January, 1838, the plaintiff sent a letter to the
chairman of the Manchester and Birmingham Railway Company,
in which he inquired whether the Company intended to hold
him to his contract with the projectors of the South Union line,
and if not, *what quantity of his land they would require. The
terms of this letter are fully stated in the judgment. On the
15th of June, 1838, a communication was made by the plaintiff's
solicitor to the solicitor for the Manchester and Birmingham
Railway Company, contending that the contract of the 14th of
February, 1837, was binding on the Company, and refusing to
treat with them on any other basis, and at the same time
threatening to take proceedings to enforce the contract; and on
the 26th of the same month, the solicitor for the Company
stated, in reply, that any such proceedings would be resisted.

[*788]

On the 6th of August, 1838, the plaintiff was served with a
notice from the Manchester and Birmingham Railway Company,
stating that the Company intended, under the provisions of their
Act, to take the land of the plaintiff described and delineated in
a schedule and plan annexed, and requiring him to treat with
them for the sale of such land, and also for any compensation he
might claim; and intimating that, in case of his refusal to do so
within ten days, a jury would be impannelled, to assess the
value of such land, and also such compensation.

The plaintiff thereupon filed the present bill against the
Manchester and Birmingham Railway Company, praying a
declaration that the agreement of the 14th of February, 1837,
with the subscribers to the Manchester South Union Railway,
was binding upon the defendants; and that they might be
compelled specifically to perform it; and that an injunction
might, in the meantime, be issued to restrain them from taking

any proceedings in respect of his land under the powers contained in their Act of Parliament.

GREEN-
HALGH
v.
THE
MANCHESTER
AND BIR-
MINGHAM
RAILWAY
COMPANY.

[789]

An *ex parte* injunction, obtained during the long vacation, was afterwards, upon argument, dissolved by his Honour the VICE-CHANCELLOR, principally on the ground that the projectors of the South Union Line, having failed in obtaining their Act of Parliament, and having afterwards determined their contract with the plaintiff by a notice, the plaintiff had no equity to enforce that contract against the new Company.

The plaintiff appealed against his Honour's order dissolving the injunction.

Upon the appeal-motion before the Lord Chancellor, the argument proceeded partly on the ground upon which his Honour had rested his judgment in dissolving the injunction, and partly also on the conduct and dealings of the plaintiff with the defendants, and with other persons, relative to his land, subsequently to the passing of the Act of Parliament, and which, it was contended, were of such a nature as to deprive the plaintiff of any title to the interlocutory interposition of the Court by injunction. The material circumstances constituting this part of the case, and upon which exclusively the LORD CHANCELLOR disposed of it, are stated in his Lordship's judgment.

Mr. Wigram and *Mr. Sharpe*, for the plaintiff.

The *Solicitor-General, Mr. Knight Bruce, Mr. Koe*, and *Mr. Loftus Lowndes*, for the defendants.

THE LORD CHANCELLOR :

This case, though it occupied two days in discussion, and the affidavits are exceedingly numerous, and branch *out into a variety of facts and statements, many of which are utterly irrelevant, turns entirely upon two questions; first, whether the Company which obtained the Act, and is now the existing Company, is or is not bound by the contract entered into by the projectors of the South Union Company ; and secondly, whether, if the plaintiff ever had any right against the existing Company, anything has taken place to prevent him from asserting that right by means of an interlocutory injunction.

GREEN-
HALGH
v.
THE
MANCHESTER
AND BIR-
MINGHAM
RAILWAY
COMPANY.

In the view which I take of the case, it is not necessary for me to give any opinion upon the first point: and I am not sorry to be relieved from that duty; for the question is one of very great nicety and difficulty, and therefore not to be decided, except in a case in which it is absolutely necessary, for the purposes of justice, that it should be decided. And I find in this case what appear to me to be very safe grounds upon which to dispose of it, without at all touching upon that point; and, for the purpose of explaining the grounds of my decision, I will assume that the plaintiff had a right against the existing Company, which he might have enforced in the manner alleged by the bill. I assume that for the purpose of argument merely, and not for the purpose of laying down any rule as to any future case which may occur.

The second question then is, supposing that right to have existed when the Act of Parliament passed, in June, 1837, whether anything has since taken place between the parties, that is to say, between the month of June, 1837, and the month of June, 1838, when the contest between the parties arose, to deprive the plaintiff of the right to the protection of this Court by injunction. The right, if it existed, of course existed at the time when the Act passed. Now the right is not, properly [*791] speaking, *a right of contract, but rather arises out of the contract; for neither in this case, nor in the case of *Edwards* v. *The Grand Junction Railway Company* (1), was it a matter of contract; but the equity is this, that what has subsequently taken place, and the position in which the parties stand, give the party seeking the benefit of the contract a right to the interference of this Court, by virtue of an equity which induces the Court to prevent the Company from exercising their legal right, unless upon the terms of adopting and giving effect to the contract which has been entered into by other parties.

In considering how far a party has, by his own conduct, lost the benefit of an equity to which he was once entitled, it is obvious that very different considerations attach to a case in which a party has been all along cognizant of his rights, from those which attach to a case in which he was not so cognizant.

(1) 43 R. R. 265 (1 My. & Cr. 650).

If the case should arise in which both parties were ignorant of the right which one of them, had he been aware of it, might have asserted, it might be open to considerable question how far that ignorance ought to prejudice him. But if the plaintiff is cognizant of his right, of course he cannot be heard to say that he did not assert it sooner in consequence of his not being aware of the advantage to be derived from asserting it. The plaintiff has relieved the Court from this difficulty: for in a late affidavit, filed so recently as the 24th of November last, he states that amongst his papers he found a letter which he sent on the 7th of October, 1837, to the solicitor of the South Union Company, when he first received notice of the intention of that Company to determine the tenancy created by his contract. In this letter, sent in answer to the notice, he says, "I take the liberty to object to it, principally for two reasons, which *at first view your own mind will admit as valid; first, because, if your ideas be correct, that you can vacate the agreement, the term of contract cannot expire before March next, as your notice was not delivered until to-day, being eight days after the quarter day; but secondly, and mainly, because you are not at liberty, as you and your clients well know, to annul the agreement, as the Act has been obtained, and the respective shareholders, as recent advertisements attest, are, each and all, amenable in law to the united acts of the amalgamated Company, or the prior respective acts of each Company." So that he tells us in his own affidavit that, on the 7th of October, 1837, he was aware of his equity, and was prepared to assert it. Whether that were so or not might be a matter of some doubt, if it were material to inquire into the accuracy of that statement—I say the *accuracy*, because I find an attempt to support the statement by evidence which throws infinite doubt upon the truth of it altogether. The plaintiff not only himself swears to a letter not forthcoming, which he never adverted to before, though this is the third affidavit he has made; but he attempts to establish and confirm it by the affidavit of Thomas Wilson, his shopman, who swears to a copy of the letter, without saying he ever read or compared it. Wilson says that he was employed to deliver the letter, and that the following is a copy of such letter; and he then sets out a

GREEN-
HALGH
v.
THE
MANCHESTE
AND BIR-
MINGHAM
RAILWAY
COMPANY.

[*792]

GREEN-
HALGH
v.
THE
MANCHESTER
AND BIR-
MINGHAM
RAILWAY
COMPANY.

copy in the same words as are to be found in the plaintiff's affidavit, without giving any explanation or information as to how
he is enabled to make the affidavit, and swear to the words of a
letter which he was only employed to deliver. Still it may be
true; but it is not material to inquire into its truth, because,
after having made that statement, the plaintiff is precluded from
saying that he was not perfectly aware, in the month of October,
[*793]   1837, of the equity which he is now seeking to assert; and *his
conduct therefore must be looked at as the conduct of a party
fully cognizant of his rights.

In considering the evidence, two things must be borne in
mind, namely, the fact, undisputed, that, upon the union of the
two Companies, it was part of the arrangement between them,
that the Company which Parliament might sanction should, as
far as was practicable and consistent with their scheme, adopt
all contracts made by the other parties: and secondly, that,
quite independently of enforcing the contract for the purpose of
completing the purchase of the plaintiff's land, there was a
question existing (adverted to indeed in that very letter), between
the plaintiff and the South Union Company, not as to the completion of the purchase, but as to the continuance of the tenancy,
a question that depended upon the validity of the notice to quit.
Now that arrangement, forming part of the contract, appears
to have been communicated to the plaintiff. If, therefore, he
thought he had a right to enforce the contract, he must have
been, at all events, aware, that there was a chance, at least, that
the Company which obtained the sanction of Parliament, and
was brought into legal existence by the Act, might, to a certain
degree, adopt the contract into which he had entered with the
South Union Company. Nothing had passed to prevent them
from adopting the contract, if they thought it expedient to do so.
It was a point not decided, but remaining entirely open, whether,
if the plaintiff had not a right to enforce his contract in equity,
he might not still obtain the benefit of it, from the new Company
choosing to take it upon themselves.

Now, on the part of the defendants, the Company, certain
facts are stated, which, if left unexplained, undenied, unqualified,
[*794]   and not in some way or other *displaced by the statements on

the part of the plaintiff, would, I apprehend, be quite conclusive against the right which the plaintiff is now asserting.   In the December following the passing of the Act, the usual course was adopted : circular notices were sent intimating to all persons who received them, and amongst others to the plaintiff, the intention of the Company to proceed under the powers of the Act of Parliament.   In January, 1838, that notice was followed by marking out the land to be taken.   In the month of May other transactions take place : between January and May whatever was necessary to be done prior to the actual commencement of the work was done; the line was surveyed, and the ground marked out; and in the course of that time the plaintiff is stated to have applied on various occasions to the officers of the Company, to know what quantity of his land they would require in carrying their Act of Parliament into operation.   It is also proved, that in treating with a brickmaker, a conversation took place which would show that he contemplated dealing with the land as his own property, except only as to so much as the Company might require for their line.

These facts, which are not a matter of dispute, would bring the plaintiff into this position, viz., that with knowledge of his supposed equity, he not only permitted the defendants to act in exercise of their legal rights, and therefore without reference to his contract, but permitted them to proceed to a considerable extent in the execution of their intended line; whereas, as is stated, and not contradicted, if it had been thought expedient, and the plaintiff had asserted his right, it would have been quite as easy for the Company, under the provisions of the Act, to adopt a line which would have avoided any contact with the plaintiff's land.   The affidavits filed on the *part of the Company [*795] fall short in not stating what the Company actually did; but it is obvious from what is stated, that a great deal must have been done between January and June, when the plaintiff first asserted his right to an injunction.   The mere expense of engineering in marking out the line of railway over the plaintiff's land, though probably not much in itself, was necessarily connected with the whole line, the engineering expenses of which must have gone to a very considerable extent.   Then in May advertisements

GREEN-
HALGH
v.
THE
MANCHESTER
AND BIR-
MINGHAM
RAILWAY
COMPANY.

GREEN-
HALGH
v.
THE
MANCHESTER
AND BIR-
MINGHAM
RAILWAY
COMPANY.

were published for receiving tenders for contracts for the works, although the affidavits do not state that any such contracts were made.

The plaintiff meets this case by saying, that whatever the Company may have done was not induced by anything which he did; that he was not only aware of his right, but that he uniformly declared his intention of acting upon it, and frequently and openly communicated that intention to the Company; and that whatever they did, therefore, was done with their eyes open. This was in argument put in the form of a statement, perfectly true in fact, that the parties with whom the contract was made, and with whom these communications took place, namely, the projectors of the South Union line, had become actually members of the incorporated Company under the Act of Parliament, and that the notice brought home to them in the one character must necessarily affect them in the other. So far as notice and knowledge go, that observation is perfectly true; but the question between these parties is not one of notice or knowledge: it depends upon the dealings of the plaintiff with those who represented the two Companies. If the plaintiff communicated to the Directors of the South Union Railway Company an intention of enforcing against them in that character any rights he might be entitled to, and if, *dealing with those who represented the existing Company under the Act, he not only abstained from making any claim on that body, but permitted them to proceed, and became, by communications with them, a party to an understanding that they were at liberty to proceed without being in any way affected by his contract with the South Union Company, that would deprive him, not of the right of enforcing the contract against the South Union Company, but of the right which he now asserts, of interfering with the operations of the new Company under the authority of the Act of Parliament.

[*796]

A great part of the evidence which the plaintiff has adduced, consists of communications between himself and others, for the purpose of showing what was present to his own mind, and what his own intention was. Now, as I have before remarked, the question does not depend upon what was in the plaintiff's mind, but upon what was the effect of the course of conduct pursued by the plaintiff on the minds of those who constitute the existing Company. I cannot, however, but observe that the plaintiff's affidavits, and some other affidavits produced on his behalf, furnish very strong reason for supposing that what did take place was, not with reference to asserting a right against the Manchester and Birmingham Railway Company, but had a very different object, and was addressed to an entirely different subject. Bearing in mind that, according to his own allegation, the plaintiff always intended to assert his right against the existing Company ; and also bearing in mind that an agreement existed which made it probable, or at least possible, that he might have the benefit of a voluntary adoption by the existing Company of his contract with the South Union Company, expressions, I think, occur which show that he did not contemplate enforcing his contract adversely against the existing Company, but that he thought it *probable they would adopt the contract of the South Union Company. [The LORD CHANCELLOR here read and commented upon several passages in the affidavits which he considered as corroborating this view of the case.]

Then there is that on which there can be no mistake in point of fact; I mean the plaintiff's letter of the 23rd of January, 1838. That letter was addressed to the chairman of the new Company, and was in these terms : " Being applied to by a wealthy gentleman for the whole of my land, &c., in Ardwick, as marked blue on the accompanying plan, I respectfully presume to request that you, as chairman of the Manchester and Birmingham Railway Company, will kindly answer the subjoined queries. 1st. Does the United Company design to maintain the contract entered into between me and the South Union Company, or am I perfectly free from it by the notice sent. 2ndly. If the contract is not binding, please say as nearly as you can, what quantity of my land, &c. will be required. 3rdly. As certain portions of my property are available by the Company, shall I subject myself to any legal difficulty by a disposal of the entire, if the application, as above, shall be urged. If an immediate reply cannot conveniently be given, by informing the bearer when, at the earliest, you will furnish it, you will greatly oblige yours, &c. J. GREENHALGH."

GREEN-
HALGH
v.
THE
MANCHESTER
AND BIR-
MINGHAM
RAILWAY
COMPANY.

[*797]

GREEN-
HALGH
v.
THE
MANCHESTER
AND BIR-
MINGHAM
RAILWAY
COMPANY.

Here then is a letter which, if there were any ambiguity in the transaction previously, would be quite sufficient to remove it. It is impossible to believe that the man writing that letter thought he had a contract with the Company which, as against them, he was entitled and able to enforce. He puts it to them in a manner quite consistent with the case of their having an option, not binding upon them, but of which he would be glad

[*798]

to *avail himself if they chose to exercise it, but utterly inconsistent with the notion of his having a right, or rather, intending to enforce that right adversely against them. In his affidavit he tells us he knew of his right; and yet here was a distinct communication, passing between the parties in January, 1838, in which he surrenders that right, putting it to them, what quantity of land they will take, and leaving it to them to say, whether they will perform the contract or not. Well, after that communication between the Company and the plaintiff, with that letter in their hands, setting them entirely at liberty, they proceed with their work—to what extent does not appear—till June, and never till the month of June is the plaintiff's title asserted. Upon that state of evidence, I have no hesitation in saying, that the plaintiff is not entitled to the injunction of this Court to prevent another party from carrying on the work which by his silence and conduct he has permitted that other to carry on, at all events, from January to June.

If I entertained more doubt than I do on this subject, I should be very much influenced by considerations similar to those which weighed with me in deciding the *Liverpool* case (1); because, where the question is as to interposing by injunction to protect a right which in itself is doubtful or disputed, it must always be considered on which side the balance of danger preponderates. If the contract be a contract binding on the existing Company— and that is the question between the parties—the plaintiff is not precluded from attempting to establish it. What the Company are doing, is to take part of the plaintiff's land under the powers of their Act of Parliament; and this, if done adversely against

[*799]

the plaintiff, *will not preclude him, should he establish his

(1) *The Attorney-General* v. *The Mayor of Liverpool*, 43 R. R. 176 (1 My. & Cr. 171).

GREEN-
HALGH
v.
THE
MANCHESTER
AND BIR-
MINGHAM
RAILWAY
COMPANY.

right at the hearing, from compelling them to take the whole of his land, under the contract. But if, on the other hand, the evidence were more doubtful than it is, the granting of the injunction in the mean time would certainly produce irreparable injury to the other party, in case it should ultimately turn out that the plaintiff has not that right which he asserts that he has. It cannot be supposed that the plaintiff should stop the defendants' works until this cause shall have been heard. At the same time the Company should be well aware that that would be no answer, if a claim can be established against them upon the contract. The case is only one in which there being a doubt what the ultimate rights of the parties will prove to be, the Court is in infinitely greater danger of doing injustice by granting the injunction than by refusing to grant it.

This case came before me, however, not properly by way of appeal from the judgment of the VICE-CHANCELLOR. His Honour dissolved the injunction without costs; and the parties have wisely added to their notice of motion that which amounts to a new motion, if I should be of opinion that the VICE-CHANCELLOR's decision was right. I say they have *wisely* done so; because, looking at the affidavits upon which the injunction was obtained, if the case were brought before me as a question of sustaining an *ex parte* injunction, I should have no hesitation in dissolving it upon the demerits of the affidavit upon which the injunction was obtained. My first ground would be the unqualified way in which the plaintiff states that his assent to the South Union line was used as a means of obtaining the Act; but what I should principally rely upon, if asked to sustain the *ex parte* injunction, is the way in which the plaintiff drops all mention of what took place after the month of *December, 1837. His affidavit, verifying the allegations of the bill, states, that subsequently to the 5th of December, 1837, an application was made to him to state what claim he made upon the Company; and then comes the letter of the 15th of June, 1838, representing that, from the month of December, 1837, to the month of June, 1838, he uniformly insisted upon his contract, and refused to treat upon any other basis; whereas there is clear evidence to the contrary. I consider this as a misrepresentation of what really took place;

[*800]

GREEN-
HALGH
v.
THE
MANCHESTER
AND BIR-
MINGHAM
RAILWAY
COMPANY.

and if that had been properly stated to the Court, the injunction would not have been granted.

The only doubt I have felt is with regard to costs.   The facts which are free from doubt are quite sufficient to induce me to refuse the motion ; but there are many very important facts, the truth of which it is impossible to ascertain in the present state of the cause ; and upon the whole, although I do not think that the conduct of the plaintiff has been such as the Court had a right to expect, particularly with regard to his first affidavit, I shall

Refuse the motion without costs.

IN THE KING'S BENCH.

SHAW *v.* ROBBERDS, HAWKES, AND STONE.

(6 Adol. & Ellis, 75—84; S. C. 1 N. & P. 279; W. W. & D. 94; 1 Jur. 6; 6 L. J. (N. S.) K. B. 106.)

1837.
Jan. 11.

[75]

Plaintiff insured premises against fire, by the description of a granary, &c., and " a kiln for drying corn in use," communicating therewith. By the conditions of insurance, the policy was to be forfeited unless the buildings were accurately described, and the trades carried on therein specified; and, if any alteration were made in the building, or the risk of fire increased, the alteration, &c., was to be notified and allowed by indorsement on the policy, otherwise the insurance to be void. The plaintiff carried on no trade in the kiln except drying corn; but, on one occasion, he allowed the owner of some bark, which had been wetted, to dry it gratuitously in the kiln, and this occasioned a fire, by which the premises were destroyed on the third day after the drying of the bark commenced. Drying bark was a distinct trade from drying corn, and more hazardous, and insurers charged a higher premium for bark kilns than corn kilns:

Held, that the assured was not precluded from recovering, either on the ground of an alteration of risk, or (in the absence of fraud) because the fire arose from his negligence.

Assumpsit on a policy of insurance against fire. The first count set out the policy, dated 29th March, 1830, which stated that the plaintiff had paid to the Norwich Union Fire Insurance Society 3*l.* 15*s.*, as premium for insuring 2,500*l.* on the property in the policy mentioned; that the defendants, being three directors, whose hands were subscribed to the policy, agreed that, while the premium should be paid, the capital stock and funds of the society should, according to the deed of settlement thereof, be liable to make good all loss by fire to the property therein described, not exceeding 1,400*l.*, " on a granary divided in the middle by a party wall, with a counting-house at the west end, all under one roof, brick and slate, and also a kiln for drying corn in use, attached to the outward walls of the granary, and communicating therewith by one door, the kiln built entirely of brick and iron, and tiled, except the spars of the roof and inside plastering; " 1,000*l.* on grain, pulse, seed and utensils in trust, in trade, on commission, or the plaintiff's own property, in the said divided granary; and 100*l.* on a warehouse, described in the policy; and by a memorandum, afterwards indorsed, it

SHAW
v.
ROBBERDS.

[*76]

was declared that 1,350*l.* of the 1,400*l.* was insured on the granary and counting-house, and 50*l.* on the kiln: the declaration then alleged that certain conditions were *indorsed on the policy, some of which were set out. The third was as follows: " Persons insuring will forfeit their right to the sums secured by their policies, unless the buildings insured, or containing the goods insured, be accurately described, the trades carried on therein specified, and the nature of the property correctly stated, so that it may be placed under proper classes, and charged at the appropriate rates of premium ; and if a building contain any stove or oven (used in the process of manufacture), kiln, furnace, or steam engine, or any process of fire-heat be carried on therein, other than the ordinary risk of common fires in private houses, the same must be noticed in the policy, or it will be void in respect to such building and the goods therein." The sixth was as follows: " If any alteration or addition be made in or to the building or covering of any premises insured, or in which any insured property is contained, or the risk of fire to which such building is exposed, be by any means increased, or if any furniture or goods be removed into other premises, such alteration, addition, increase of risk, or removal, must be immediately notified and allowed by indorsement on the policy (the indorsement being duly made and signed by one of the society's secretaries or agents), otherwise the insurance, as to such buildings or goods, will be void." The declaration then alleged the payment of premium, mutual promises, interest in the plaintiff to the amount insured, and that afterwards, to wit 13th December, 1832, the said granary, counting-house, and kiln, grain, pulse, seed, and utensils, were burnt; that, at the time of making the policy, the premises were accurately described, the trade carried on therein specified, and the nature of the property correctly stated: compliance *with other conditions (not material here) on the part of the plaintiff was also alleged. Breach, that neither the defendants nor the society had paid the 2,500*l.*, or made good the loss, &c.

[*77]

Plea, *Non assumpsit* (1).

On the trial before Lord Denman, Ch. J., at the London sittings

(1) The declaration was entitled of August 11th, 1833,

after Trinity Term, 1835, the following facts appeared (1). The
plaintiff, who was a corn merchant, effected the policy described
in the declaration, on premises at Lynn in Norfolk. He was in
the habit of using the kiln to dry corn, and for no other purpose.
In 1832 a vessel, laden with oak-bark, was sunk near Lynn. The
owner of the bark requested the plaintiff to allow him to dry it
on his premises. The plaintiff consented ; and the owner of the
bark, being allowed to dry it gratuitously, commenced drying it
in the above mentioned kiln. No notice of this was given to the
insurers. The fire in the kiln, for drying the bark, was not
larger than that usual in the case of drying corn. While the
bark was drying, on the third day after the commencement of
that process, the kiln and all the premises insured took fire and
were consumed. It was proved that insurance offices require a
higher premium in the case of bark-kilns than in that of corn-
kilns. The LORD CHIEF JUSTICE desired the jury to say, first,
whether drying bark and drying corn were different trades ;
secondly, whether drying bark was more dangerous than drying
corn ; thirdly, whether the fire was occasioned by drying the
bark. The jury found that *the trades were different, that   [*78]
drying bark was the more dangerous, and that the fire was
occasioned by drying it. His Lordship then directed a verdict
for the defendants, reserving leave to move for a verdict for the
plaintiff, for the whole sum claimed, or for such part as the
Court should think him entitled to recover. In Michaelmas
Term, 1837, *Sir J. Campbell*, Attorney-General, obtained a rule
accordingly.

[The case having been argued in Michaelmas Term last, the
Court took time for consideration.]

LORD DENMAN, Ch. J. now delivered the judgment of the Court (2) :   [81]

This was an action upon a policy of insurance against fire.
There were two subjects of insurance : certain buildings including a dwelling-house, " and also a kiln for drying corn in use,

SHAW
v.
ROBBERDS.

(1) Some argument took place respecting the communications between
the parties, which led to effecting the
policy, as showing the view taken by
the insurers of the degree of risk ;

but, as the judgment proceeded on
other grounds, this is not noticed in
the report.

(2) Lord Denman, Ch. J., Patteson,
Williams, and Coleridge, JJ.

attached to the outward walls of the granary, and communicating
therewith by one door, the kiln built entirely of brick and iron."
Both were destroyed by the fire. The policy was subject to the usual
conditions: amongst which the third provided that, if there were
any mis-representation in the description of the premises, the
policy should be void; and the sixth that, if any alteration were
made, either in the buildings or the business carried on therein,
notice should be given to the insurers, an additional premium, if
required, paid, and an indorsement made on the policy; otherwise
the policy should be void.

It appeared in evidence that the kiln had been constantly used
for the purpose of drying corn only; but that, in the year 1832,
a vessel laden with bark having been sunk in the river near the
premises, and the bark wetted, the plaintiff had allowed the bark
to be dried in his kiln, as a favour to the owner of it. No notice
was given to the insurers. No greater fire than usual had been
made; but, in the course of drying the bark, the kiln took fire,
and both the kiln and the other premises were burned down.

[82]   The jury found that corn-drying and bark-drying are different
trades, that the latter is more dangerous than the former, and
that the loss happened from the use of the kiln in drying the
bark. A verdict was entered for the defendants, with leave to
the plaintiff to move to enter a verdict for him, either for the
whole amount of the loss, or, at least, for the value of the kiln.

The third and sixth conditions were relied on in argument by
the defendants; and it was contended that the facts here show
either a mis-description of the kiln within the third condition,
or a change of business within the sixth. The two conditions
together were also said to amount to a warranty that nothing
but corn should ever be dried in the kiln; and what has occurred
was likened to a deviation in the case of a marine insurance.
It was proved, at the trial, that a much higher premium was
regularly exacted by insurance offices for a bark-kiln than for
a malt-kiln. The argument, therefore, was, that the premises
were not truly described in the policy, or that the trade carried
on there had been altered at the time of the fire without notice
to the insurance office.

We are, however, of opinion that neither of the conditions

applies to this case.   The third condition points to the description of the premises given at the time of insuring; and that description was in this instance perfectly correct.   Nothing which occurred afterwards, not even a change of business, could bring the case within that condition, which was fully performed when the risk first attached.

The sixth condition points at an alteration of business, at something permanent and habitual; and, if the plaintiff had either dropped his business of corn-drying, and *taken up that of bark-drying, or added the latter to the former, no doubt the case would have been within that condition.   Perhaps, if he had made any charge for drying this bark, it might have been a question for the jury whether he had done so as a matter of business, and whether he had not thereby (although it was the first instance of bark-drying) made an alteration in his business, within the meaning of that condition.   But, according to the evidence, we are clearly of opinion that no such question arose for the consideration of the jury; and that this single act of kindness was no breach of the sixth condition.

[*83]

The case of *Dobson* v. *Sotheby* (1) was decided by Lord TENTERDEN upon the same principle, and is an authority nearly in point upon this part of the case.   No clause in this policy amounts to an express warranty that nothing but corn should ever be dried in the kiln; and there are no facts, or rule of legal construction, from which an implied warranty can be raised.

Neither does the principle on which a deviation puts an end to a marine insurance, viz. that the risk insured against is not the same as that incurred, and that the assured have no right to vary it, apply to the present case.   This policy, by the sixth condition, expressly provides for such alterations or deviations as the parties deem material.   For the reasons already given, we think that the facts of this case do not bring it within that condition; and anything short of that cannot be considered as an alteration or deviation under this contract.

One argument more remains to be noticed, viz. that the loss

(1) 31 R. R. 718 (Moo. & Mal. 90).

SHAW
r.
ROBBERDS.
[*84]

here arose from the plaintiff's own negligent *act, in allowing the kiln to be used for a purpose to which it was not adapted. There is no doubt that one of the objects of insurance against fire is to guard against the negligence of servants and others ; and, therefore, the simple fact of negligence has never been held to constitute a defence.   But it is argued that there is a distinction between the negligence of servants or strangers and that of the assured himself.   We do not see any ground for such a distinction ; and are of opinion that, in the absence of all fraud, the proximate cause of the loss only is to be looked to.

For these reasons, we are of opinion that the rule must be made absolute, to enter a verdict for the plaintiff for the whole loss, as having been produced by causes which do not prevent the policy from attaching.

Rule absolute.

1837.
Jan. 11.
———
[84]

REX *v.* THE JUSTICES OF STAFFORDSHIRE.

(6 Adol. & Ellis, 84—103 ; S. C. 1 N. & P. 260 ; 6 L. J. (N. S.) M. C. 65.)

To a *mandamus*, calling on the justices and clerk of the peace of a county to allow rate-payers an inspection of certain orders of Sessions, concerning the expenditure of the county rate, and all accounts, &c., relating to such orders, it was returned that inspection of the orders had been given, but that the accounts were those of the treasurer and high constable, which had been passed at Sessions, and deposited with the clerk of the peace, according to stat. 12 Geo. II. c. 29, s. 8 (1) ; and that an abstract thereof had been published, according to stat. 55 Geo. III. c. 51, s. 18 (1) ; wherefore the inspection of such accounts had been refused : Held, a good return ; for that

1. Parties claiming merely as rate-payers have no right, by the above statutes, to inspect such accounts when passed and deposited.

2. Supposing the accounts, when so passed and deposited, to be public documents, the rate-payers have not such an interest in the contents as entitles them, independently of the statutes, to demand an inspection.

MANDAMUS, tested May 13th, 1835, directed to the justices and clerk of the peace of the county of Stafford.   The writ recited that, since December 31st, 1831, divers rates or

---

(1) The provisions of the Acts here referred to are consolidated and amended by the County Rates Act, 1852 (15 & 16 Vict. c. 81). The above case has been referred to as an authority on the common law right to the inspection of public documents by LINDLEY, L. J., in *Mutter v. Eastern and Midlands Ry. Co.* (1888) 38 Ch. Div. 92, 106, 57 L. J. Ch. 615, 621.—R. C.

assessments had been made by the said justices, on the
several townships and parishes of *that county lying within
their commission, under the statutes in that case &c., and
large sums levied by virtue of such rates; that divers orders
had been made by the justices, or some of them, for the
expenditure of such rates; and that several orders of Sessions
had been made thereon and relating thereto: and that, indictments or presentments having been made of Strynes and
Beamhurst bridges, certain orders of Sessions were thereupon
made by the said justices, or some of them, for taking down
and rebuilding the same, and for payment of divers large sums
in respect thereof and relating thereto: and that divers bills of
costs for business alleged to be done for the said county, and
divers accounts of disbursements made by the said clerk of the
peace, which were respectively comprised in the annual accounts
of the said county for the year 1833, amounting &c., were, by
two certain orders of Sessions made by the said justices, or
some of them, on January 2nd and April 10th, in the year
3 Will. IV., respectively allowed and directed to be paid by the
treasurer of the said county: and that divers applications had
been made to the said justices and clerk of the peace, by and on
behalf of divers inhabitants of the township of M. W., in &c.,
being one of the townships within the said county contributory
to the said rates, to permit the said inhabitants, being rated or
contributory to the said rates, or their attorney, "to inspect and
take copies of the said rates or assessments, and the orders made
for the expenditure thereof, and the several orders of Sessions
made thereon, and all accounts, proceedings, and documents
relating thereto, and of the said indictments or presentments
of Strynes and Beamhurst bridges, and of the orders of Sessions
for taking down and rebuilding the same, and for payment of
any sum or sums of money in respect thereof or of either of
them, with *the accounts relating thereto, and also of such
several bills of costs and disbursements" of the said clerk of
the peace; which said rates, &c. (referring to the several documents just mentioned), still remain in the custody or power of
the said justices and clerk of the peace, or some of them, but
that they had refused to allow such inspection or taking of

REX
v.
THE
JUSTICES OF
STAFFORD-
SHIRE.
[*85]

[*86

copies, "to the great damage and prejudice of the inhabitants of the said township, being rated" &c. The writ, therefore, commanded them, or such of them in whose custody or power the same might be, to permit and suffer the said rate-payers of M. W., and Abraham Flint, their attorney, to inspect and take copies of all the said rates or assessments made by the said justices since December 31st, 1831, and of all orders made for the expenditure thereof, and of the several orders of Sessions &c. (enumerating the other documents, as mentioned in the preceding clause of the *mandamus*), or that they should show cause &c.

Return. That the said justices and clerk of the peace had not refused the said inhabitants, or their attorney, &c., permission to inspect or take copies of the said rates and assessments, the orders for the expenditure thereof, the orders of Sessions made thereon, or the proceedings relating thereto; nor of the said indictments or presentments, or the orders of Sessions for taking down and rebuilding the same bridges, or for payment of any sum or sums in respect thereof or of either of them; but that Flint (on behalf of the said inhabitants of M. W.) had applied to the Sessions, before the issuing of the writ, for permission to inspect and take copies of (among others) the several documents last-mentioned ; that, by order of Sessions, July 2nd, 1834, permission had been granted to him, on behalf of the said inhabitants, to inspect and take

[*87]   copies of such last-mentioned *documents; and he had, in fact, been permitted to do so; and that his application was the only one that had been made on behalf of the inhabitants and rate-payers for permission to inspect and take copies of the documents in the return mentioned. The justices and clerk of the peace further returned, " that the only accounts or documents in the custody of us, or of either of us, relating to the said rates or assessments, are the within-mentioned bills of the clerk of the peace, and certain other accounts and vouchers of the treasurer and high constable of the said county, all of which have been passed by us, the said keepers of the peace and justices, at our respective Quarter Sessions for the said county, and all of which have been deposited with the clerk of the peace for the

said county, to be kept among the records of the said county, and to be inspected from time to time by us the said justices, according to the form of the statute in such case made and provided; and that a true and accurate abstract of the accounts of the receipts and expenditure of the said treasurer, under their several heads, signed by such of us the said justices as audited the same, hath been duly published once in every year in a public newspaper circulated in the said county: Wherefore we, the keepers of the peace and justices, and also the clerk of the peace within-mentioned, have refused to permit the said inhabitants and rate-payers, or any person on their behalf, to inspect or take copies of the within-mentioned accounts, and documents, and bills of the clerk of the peace, or any or either of them."

The return was argued in Michaelmas Term, 1836, on a *concilium*.

*   *   *   *   *

LORD DENMAN, Ch. J. now delivered the judgment of the COURT (1) as follows, first stating the substance of the *mandamus* and return :

[96]

This return raises the question, whether the ratepayers of any parish within a county have, as such, any right to inspect and copy the bills of charges of county officers, which, having been paid by the treasurer under orders of justices, have become items in his accounts, and, those having been passed at Sessions, and he having been discharged by order of Sessions, have been deposited by the clerk of the peace among the county records, in pursuance of stat. 12 Geo. II. c. 29, s. 8.

The existence of such right was contended for principally on three grounds.   1. Upon the authority of *Rex* v. *The Justices of Leicester* (2).   2. Because the bills in question were parcel of the orders in virtue of which they were paid, of which the inspection was conceded; but that such inspection was wholly nugatory unless it extended to the bills also.   3. Because the bills were public documents, which, by the common law, every one interested in them had a right to see; and that the provisions

(1) Lord Denman, Ch. J., Patteson, Williams, and Coleridge, JJ.   (2) 4 B. & C. 891.

REX
v.
THE
JUSTICES OF
STAFFORD-
SHIRE.

relative thereto, in stats. 12 Geo. II. c. 29, and 55 Geo. III. c. 51,
were either collateral to, or in affirmance of, and certainly did
not abridge, this right.

Prior to the passing of stat. 12 Geo. II. c. 29, the justices
in Sessions were authorised, by several Acts of Parliament, to
raise rates applicable to specific purposes. By that Act, one
general rate, applicable to all these purposes, and for such sum
as the justices shall think necessary, is directed to be from time
to time assessed and collected. The monies are to be received
by the treasurer (who is *appointed by them), and paid according
to their orders for any use or purpose to which the public stock of
the county is by law applicable; and no new rate is to be made,
until the justices are satisfied that three fourths of the money
collected by the preceding rate have been so expended. The
treasurer is to keep books and accounts of his receipts and payments, distinguishing the particular uses to which the payments
have been applied; and these, with the vouchers, he is to lay
before the justices at Sessions, and, after they have been there
passed, both are to be deposited with the clerk of the peace, who
is required to keep them among the records of the county, "to be
inspected from time to time by any of the said justices, within
the limits of their commissions, as occasion shall require, without
fee or reward." When the justices have passed the accounts,
their discharge by order of Sessions is to be allowed as a
sufficient acquittance to the treasurer, in any court of law or
equity, to all intents and purposes whatsoever. A limited appeal
to the Sessions is given against the proportions of the rate, but
not against the rate itself; and finally the jurisdiction of this
Court is restrained within certain limits by the twenty-first section,
as to the removal into it by *certiorari* of any rate, or orders or
proceedings at Sessions relating thereto.

[*97]

This Act was amended by stat. 55 Geo. III. c. 51, the principal object of which was to provide for the due proportioning of
the rate on the several parishes; but, by the eighteenth section,
the treasurer is required once in every year to publish, in some
one of the county newspapers, a true and accurate abstract of his
account, under its several heads, signed by the justices who shall
have audited the same.

These are the provisions of the statutes material to the present question, which we have stated thus at length, because they appear to us to furnish very cogent inferences as to the right now in dispute. No one can read the clauses without being satisfied that, subject to the limitations specified, the Legislature has placed the whole control, as to the imposition and expenditure of the county rate, in the Court of Quarter Sessions. And with regard to the particular matter of publicity, they provide specifically for the preservation of the vouchers, and for their inspection by a particular class, the members namely of the Court which controls the expenditure ; and provide also for information to be conveyed to the rate-payers in general, by the annual publication of the receipts and payments, in such a form as was deemed sufficient for the purpose.

This latter provision may perhaps throw some light upon the construction which the former ought to receive ; but, looking at the former by itself, it is difficult to understand why a specific provision should have been made for the inspection by the justices without fee or reward, if by the common law the same right (and it is that same right which is now claimed) existed in favour of every rate-payer. It is remarkable, moreover, that, in the same statute, 12 Geo. II. c. 29, s. 14, respecting the repairs of public bridges, banks, &c., a similar provision is made for the preservation and deposit of contracts for the repairs ; and, as to these, the purpose is declared to be the inspection, not only by the justices, but by "any person" "employed by any parish, township, or place, contributing to the purposes of this Act." The difference in the two clauses can hardly be conceived to have been unintentional.

It is also material to observe that the duty of preserving the vouchers appears to have been first created by stat. 12 Geo. II. c. 29. Upon examination of all the statutes recited in the preamble, no such enactment appears among them, though the provision for the absolute discharge of the treasurer, by the acquittance of the justices, is copied from one of them, 11 & 12 Will. III. c. 19, s. 2. Independently of the statute, we know of no direct obligation on the justices to preserve the vouchers of audited accounts, however prudent such a preservation might be : nor do we know of anything which should make it compulsory on

[99]

the clerk of the peace to receive such documents, and preserve
them among the county records. If this be so, and the statute
which first directs their preservation, and place of deposit, defines
also the purpose of such preservation, and the persons who are
to have access to them, what right can others have to inspect
them for other and undefined purposes ?

We are of opinion, therefore, upon a review of the provisions of
the statutes, that they raise a direct inference against the existence
of any such right. It is fitting, however, to consider the weight of
the argument independently of these provisions. It is alleged that
these are public documents, and that every one having an interest
in them has therefore a right to inspect them. It is not necessary
to inquire whether these are, strictly speaking, public documents;
and, though most of the cases cited on this point were examples
of the exercise of a power by the Court to compel one of two
litigating parties to make reasonable disclosures to the other, we
are by no means disposed to narrow our own authority to enforce
[*100]   by *mandamus* the production of *every document of a public
nature, in which any one of the King's subjects can prove himself
to be interested. For such persons, indeed, every officer appointed
by law to keep records ought to deem himself for that purpose a
trustee. But the difficulty is to see that the present applicants
have such an interest as brings them within the rule. During
the argument, we enquired what interest in the applicants was
relied on as entitling them to the inspection. In answer, it was
conceded that the rate-payers had no direct interest in ascertaining the expenditure of the by-gone rate, because, even if discovered
to be illegal, the monies paid by the treasurer could not be
recovered from him; and it is obvious that they could not be
recovered from the parties to whom they had been paid, nor from
the individual justices who had sanctioned the payments. But it
was said that, as the justices at Sessions were prohibited from
imposing a new rate until three fourths of the former had been
lawfully expended, the rate-payers were interested in ascertaining
the nature of such expenditure, to enable them to oppose the
imposition of a new rate. The answer to this is, that the rate-
payers as such cannot by law interfere in the matter. Let it be
assumed that the inspection prayed for should disclose an illegal

expenditure of a former rate, or the fact that more than one fourth of the former rate still remained unexpended in the treasurer's hands, still no rate-payer, as such, could be heard in the Court of Quarter Sessions to object to the imposition of a new rate: *Rex* v. *The Justices of Nottingham* (1). The subject-matter is not one which the rate-payer can bring before the Court as a litigant; nor is he, as such, a member of the Court.

The utmost, therefore, that can be said on the ground of interest, is that the applicants have a rational curiosity to gratify by this inspection, or that they may thereby ascertain facts useful to them in advancing some ulterior measures in contemplation as to regulating county expenditure; but this is merely an interest in obtaining information on the general subject, and would furnish an equally good reason for permitting inspection of the records of any other county: there is not that direct and tangible interest, which is necessary to bring them within the rule on which the Court acts in granting inspection of public documents. [101]

But it is contended that these vouchers are substantially parcel of the orders which relate to them. But what in truth is the form of the orders, and whether the vouchers are or are not by any reference or otherwise so incorporated with them as to become parcel of them, is not disclosed either in the writ or return. The applicants, prior to the date of the writ, had a full opportunity of inspecting the orders; it is therefore their fault that we have not this information; the language of their own writ raises a presumption against them; and there is every reason to suppose that in truth the orders are perfect instruments without the vouchers.

Lastly, however, we are strongly pressed with the authority of *Rex* v. *The Justices of Leicester* (2), in which Lord TENTERDEN and this Court made a rule absolute in the very terms of the present. The great authority attached to that decision rendered it necessary for us to grant the writ, and see what return should be made, that the principles on which it rested might undergo the *most deliberate revision. We cannot adopt the argument urged at the Bar, by which that case was sought to be distinguished from this: [*102]

(1) 3 Ad. & El. 500.   (2) 4 B. & C. 891.

REX
v.
THE
JUSTICES OF
STAFFORD-
SHIRE.

because, though the refusal of the justices there was too extensive, and the return therefore properly quashed, the Court obviously intended to decide the present question also. After much consideration, we think in that respect it cannot be supported. It is observable that, although the material arguments at the Bar against the *mandamus* received no answer from the other side, and no reason is stated for the judgment of the Court, yet it appears that no argument was permitted upon the return. Our brother LITTLEDALE, who was a member of the Court at the time, permits us to say that he disapproves of that case.

Upon the whole, we conclude that this return is sufficient in law. Much has been said upon the practical irresponsibility which our decision may occasion as to the expenditure of the county rate by the justices. If this consequence really flowed from our refusal of the writ, that would be no reason with us for straining the law to prevent it: the law must be altered by the proper authority, if too much discretion is now vested in the Court of Quarter Sessions.

But in truth, considering the number of the magistracy in every county, the large attendance usual on the days of transacting the county business, that the Court in which it is transacted is an open Court, that all these accounts are there publicly considered, and an abstract of the whole expenditure afterwards publicly circulated, and that the law is most explicit as to the matters to which the county rate is applicable, it appears to us
[*103] very unreasonable to apprehend any evil consequences *from holding that the magistrates are not compellable to grant to rate-payers generally this inspection. If any abuse exists, it can hardly be supposed that, among so many, no one magistrate will be found to bring the order before this Court; and the law has given already to him every advantage which the granting of a peremptory *mandamus* would afford to the present applicants.

On the other hand, no slight inconvenience might result from holding that, in every county, all its thousands of rate-payers, with no other interest, and without fee or reward, have a right to the inspection now contended for. Nor can we believe that such a power would have been given by doubtful implications.

We disclaim, however, the being influenced on either side by these considerations, and have attended only to the legal principles which appear to us applicable, in pronouncing that the return is sufficient.

Judgment for the defendants.

HAYWARD *v.* PHILLIPS.

(6 Adol. & Ellis, 119—129; S. C. 1 N. & P. 288; W. W. & D. 1; 1 Jur. 102; 6 L. J. (N. S.) K. B. 110.)

Declaration in covenant upon an indenture, alleged one breach by non-payment of rent, and three by not repairing, &c. Pleas; first, that the indenture was obtained by fraud; and, next, performance as to the several breaches. The plaintiff traversed the fraud, and joined issue on the pleas of performance, except that there was an omission to perfect the issue on the fourth plea. By order of Nisi Prius, it was directed that the jury should give a verdict for the plaintiff on the first issue, and damages assessed on the first breach at 10*l.*, and costs 40*s.*, subject to the award of an arbitrator, to whom the cause and all matters in difference were referred, to order and determine what he should think fit to be done by the parties, respecting the matters in dispute, with liberty for him to amend the record, and to direct what should be done between the parties: the costs of the cause to abide the event of the award, and the costs of the reference and award to be in the arbitrator's discretion. The award recited that the only matter in difference, besides the cause, was a claim of 20*l.* rent; and the arbitrator awarded that the verdict on the first issue, and the assessment of 10*l.* on the first breach, should stand, and found for the plaintiff on the three other issues, and assessed damages upon each, directing the verdict to be entered for the aggregate of the damages on the four breaches; he also directed that the defendant should pay 20*l.* for rent, and that the plaintiff should expend 193*l.* 6*s.* in repairs, for which purpose he should have power to enter on the premises; and that the defendant should pay the costs of the reference and award:

Held, that the award was entirely bad, the arbitrator having no power to increase the verdict, and, therefore, not having determined the matter in dispute.

Held, also, that the defendant did not waive the objection to the award, by permitting the plaintiff to enter and perform the repairs.

Nor by attending the taxation of costs in Hilary vacation.

Nor by applying to the plaintiff in Hilary vacation for delay of execution, which application was acceded to by the plaintiff on terms which the defendant did not accept.

The rule to set aside the award was drawn up on reading "the affidavit of the defendant, and the paper writing thereto annexed;" and the affidavit in support of the rule stated facts to show that the paper writing was a copy of the award: Held sufficient.

SIR *W. W. FOLLETT* had obtained a rule in Easter Term, 1836, drawn up on reading "the affidavit of the defendant, and

the paper writing thereto annexed," calling upon the plaintiff to
" show cause why the award made between the parties should not
be set aside on the grounds ; first, that the arbitrator has
exceeded his authority in awarding a larger amount of damages
than he had power to award by the order of reference ; secondly,
that he has exceeded his authority in awarding damages to the
amount of 249*l.* 3*s.* on the second breach ; thirdly, that he has
also exceeded his authority in directing 193*l.* 6*s.* to be expended
in repairs."

[120]   An affidavit by the defendant stated the reference (as hereafter
set out in the recital of the award), and that the paper writing
annexed to the affidavit was, or contained, as the deponent
believed, a true copy of the award, the deponent having been
served with the same by the attorney of the plaintiff. The following facts appeared by the recital of the award.   The action was
brought in this Court ; and the declaration was on an indenture
between the plaintiff and defendant, whereby the plaintiff
demised to the defendant a cottage and other premises for a term
not yet expired, at a certain rent, with covenants to pay the rent,
to repair during the continuance of the demise, to paint, and to
repair within three calendar months after notice of defects : the
breaches in the declaration were, first, that 10*l.* of rent was in
arrear ; secondly, non-repair ; thirdly, that defendant did not
paint according to his covenant ; fourthly, that he did not repair
after notice : the defendant pleaded, first, to the whole action,
that the indenture was obtained by fraud ; and then, to the
several breaches, performance : the plaintiff denied the fraud ;
and, on that fact, and the pleas of performance, issues were
joined, except that there was an omission to perfect the issue on
the fourth plea.   By an order of Nisi Prius it was ordered that
the jury should give a verdict for the plaintiff on the first issue,
and damages assessed on the first breach, 10*l.*, and costs 40*s.*,
subject to the award of the arbitrator, to whom the cause and all
matters in difference between the parties were referred, to order
and determine what he should think fit to be done by the parties
respecting the matters in dispute, with liberty for the arbitrator
[*121]   to amend the record, and to direct what should *be done between
the parties, except cancellation of the lease ; the costs of the

cause to abide the event of the award, and the costs of the reference and award to be in the discretion of the arbitrator. The only matter in difference between the parties, besides the cause, was a claim for 20*l.* rent. The arbitrator amended the record.

The award was as follows: That the verdict already entered up on the first issue should stand; and that the assessment of 10*l.* on the first breach should also stand; that the defendant did not repair, as alleged in the plea to the second breach, and the arbitrator assessed the damages thereupon at 249*l.* 3*s.*; that the defendant did not paint as alleged in the plea to the third breach, and the arbitrator assessed the damages thereon at 1*s.*; that the defendant did not repair as alleged in the plea to the last breach, and the arbitrator assessed the damages thereon at 1*s.* "For which said several sums of 10*l.*, 249*l.* 3*s.*, 1*s.*, and 1*s.*, amounting together to the sum of 259*l.* 5*s.*, the verdict is to be for the plaintiff, over and above his costs," &c. The arbitrator further ordered that the defendant should pay to the plaintiff, on &c., at &c., 20*l.* for rent (being the matter in difference besides the cause), and that the plaintiff should in three months, at his own cost, repair the premises (as specified in the award), and lay out on such repairs 193*l.* 6*s.*; and, to enable him to do such repairs, should have power to enter on the premises without prejudice to his right to recover the rent; and that the costs of the reference and award should be paid by the defendant.

The affidavit in answer stated that the award was dated 22nd January, 1836, and that, on the 23rd of *January, the plaintiff's attorney, having received notice on that day from the clerk of the arbitrator, took it up, and, on the same day, left at the arbitrator's chambers, for the defendant or his attorney, a copy which the arbitrator had caused to be made for the defendant: that, on the 28th of January, and not before, no motion having been made or notice given on behalf of the defendant of any intention to object to the award, the plaintiff employed a builder to perform the repairs mentioned in the award, which were thereupon commenced, and that the plaintiff was liable to the expense thereof, amounting to 193*l.* 6*s.*: that, about January 29th, the plaintiff's attorney told the defendant's attorney of the plaintiff's having so employed the builder, and

HAYWARD   that the defendant's attorney did not then intimate any objec-
   v.   tion to the award, or intention to apply to set it aside : that
PHILLIPS. notice of taxation of costs was given, on the 1st of February,
1836, to the defendant's attorney, who attended the taxation on
the 2nd of February, and also the signing of the judgment upon
the verdict directed by the award, and did not object to the
award or the verdict, or intimate any intention to interfere with
it : that, on the said taxation, the defendant's attorney requested
the plaintiff's attorney not to issue execution for a week ; that
the plaintiff's attorney in consequence delayed issuing execution,
and applied to the plaintiff for his consent ; and that, afterwards,
with the plaintiff's assent, he offered to agree to the request of
the defendant's attorney, on condition that the defendant would
waive the necessity of a personal demand for the 20l. awarded
as a matter in difference : that the defendant's attorney agreed
to consult his client on this point : but it did not appear from
[*123]   the affidavit that any *answer had been returned : that, on
February 9th, the defendant took out a summons to show cause,
at Chambers, why proceedings should not be stayed till the fourth
day of Easter Term, 1836, to enable the defendant to apply to
the Court to set aside the award ; that, on February 16th, the
summons was heard before Patteson, J., who, on the ground
that he considered the application too late, refused to grant it,
except upon condition that the defendant should bring 438l. into
Court within one week ; that the learned Judge made a conditional order for staying proceedings accordingly : that the money
was not paid in within the time : that the plaintiff issued
execution : and that, on February 19th, the defendant took out
a summons for further time to pay the money into Court, which
was discharged by PATTESON, J. on the 20th.

[After argument :]

[128]   LORD DENMAN, Ch. J. :

It is clear that this award cannot be sustained. The arbitrator
had no power to direct a verdict to be entered, without having
such authority conferred in express terms. *Donlan* v. *Brett* (1)
is conclusive.

(1) 41 R. R. 453 (2 Ad. & El. 344).

LITTLEDALE, J. :

I am of the same opinion. Besides *Donlan* v. *Brett* (1), *Bonner* v. *Charlton* (2) shows that the arbitrator had not the power which he has assumed. * * *

WILLIAMS, J. :

I am of the same opinion. The arbitrator has clearly exceeded his power.

COLERIDGE, J. :

Donlan v. *Brett* (1) is decisive on two points : first, that the arbitrator here had no power to order a verdict to be entered ; secondly, that his making such an order cannot be construed as an order to pay the money. * * It was also contended that the objection to the award had been waived. I do not think that has been satisfactorily made out. The facts come merely to this : that the defendant's attorney, on notice, attended the taxation ; and, afterwards, to prevent his client from being pressed, endeavoured to obtain an indulgence as to time on the best terms he could get. The facts did not amount to any thing like what ought to be required to establish a waiver.

John Jervis then suggested that the award should be set aside only as to part, being good for a part.

Per CURIAM : We think it bad altogether.

> *Rule absolute for setting aside the award, the defendant undertaking not to bring any action, and the plaintiff to be at liberty again to proceed to trial.*

(1) 41 R. R. 453 (2 Ad. & El. 344).   (2) 7 R. R. 668 (5 East, 139).

1837.
Jan. 12.

REX *v.* TINDALL AND OTHERS.

(6 Adol. & Ellis, 143—152; S. C. 1 N. & P. 719; 6 L. J. (N. S.) M. C. 97.)

[143]

Indictment for a nuisance, by erecting and continuing piles and planking in a harbour, and thereby obstructing it and rendering it insecure. Special verdict, that, by the defendant's works, the harbour is in some extreme cases rendered less secure:

Held, that the defendant was not responsible criminally for consequences so slight, uncertain, and rare, and that a verdict of not guilty must be entered.

INDICTMENT for a nuisance. The first count stated that, before the committing &c., to wit, from time whereof &c. hitherto, there has been, and was, and still is, a certain ancient port and harbour, commonly called the harbour of Scarborough, in the county of York, to wit at Scarborough within the said county, used by the liege &c. for the purposes of safe and commodious navigation, for the importation and exportation of goods, and for the receiving and sheltering, in times of tempests and other times of danger and distress of weather, ships and vessels navigating to and along the northern coasts of that part of the United Kingdom called England, and to and from the eastern seas and other places: that the defendants, well knowing &c., on 1st February, 10 Geo. III., and on divers other days and times between that day and the day of the taking of this inquisition, to wit, on each and every day between &c., with force &c., within the said county of Y., to wit at &c., unlawfully, wilfully, and injuriously, did erect, place, fix, put, sink, and set, in the said port and harbour, and in the sea near to the shore within the said port and harbour, divers stages, erections, and buildings, projecting into the said port and harbour, composed of piles, posts, planks, and timber, and also divers large quantities of earth, stones, sand, and rubbish, to wit, 100,000 cart loads of &c.; and unlawfully and injuriously kept and continued, and caused and procured to be kept and continued, the said stages, &c., so projecting into the said port and harbour as aforesaid,

[*144]

and *the said piles, &c., so erected, &c., in the said port and harbour, and in the sea near to the shore in the said port and harbour, for a long space of time, to wit from thence hitherto, within the county aforesaid, to wit at &c.; and thereby, during the time aforesaid, greatly obstructed, choked up, narrowed, and

otherwise injured the said port and harbour, and rendered the
same insecure and incommodious, whereby the said port and
harbour then and there became, and was, and from thence hath
been, and still is, greatly obstructed and choked up, narrowed,
and rendered insecure and incommodious, so that the liege &c.
of George III., could not, and the liege subjects of George IV.,
during the reign of &c., could not, and the liege subjects of
William IV., now King, during the reign of &c., and other
persons, could not, nor yet can, use the said port and harbour
for the exportation and importation of goods and merchandizes
there, and for the receiving and sheltering of ships and vessels
in times of tempests, and other times of danger and distress of
weather, and for other purposes of safe and commodious navigation, and could not and cannot use the said port and harbour
without imminent hazard and danger of destruction of their
ships, lighters, boats and other vessels, and danger and peril of
the lives of those navigating the same, and loss and damage
of the goods and merchandizes laden on board thereof, to the
great damage and common nuisance of all the liege &c. and
other persons using the said port and harbour, as aforesaid;
against the peace of his said late Majesty King George III., his
crown and dignity; also against the peace of his said late
Majesty King George IV., his crown &c.; also against the peace
of our said lord the now King, his crown &c.

The second count stated that, before the committing &c. (not   [145]
saying from time immemorial), there was, and still is, a certain
other ancient harbour, &c. (not stating it to be a port); and that
the defendants unlawfully, &c., did erect, &c., in the said last-
mentioned harbour, divers stages, &c. (not stating that they
projected into the harbour), composed of piles, &c., and also
divers large quantities of earth, &c., to wit 100,000 cart loads
&c., and unlawfully and injuriously kept and continued &c.,
and thereby &c. (describing the injury to the " harbour " as to
the "port and harbour " in the first count).

The third count was like the second, except that it omitted
all the statements relative to the importation and exportation
of goods.

The fourth count stated that there was, and from time

whereof &c. had been, an ancient harbour; and in other respects was like the third count.

The fifth count stated the harbour, &c. (not port), to be adjoining to the town of Scarborough, and omitted all the statements relative to the importation and exportation of goods ; and charged that the defendants unlawfully, &c., did erect, &c., in the said last-mentioned harbour divers stages, &c., projecting into the said last-mentioned harbour, composed of piles, &c., and also divers large quantities of earth, &c., to wit 100,000 cart loads &c., and unlawfully and injuriously kept and continued &c., and thereby &c. (as before, *mutatis mutandis*).

The sixth count described the commencement of the nuisance, by " divers persons," as in the first count ; and charged that the defendants, well knowing &c., on the said 1st of February, &c., and for a long time afterwards, to wit from the day and year last aforesaid *until the taking of this inquisition, unlawfully, &c., kept and continued, and caused &c., the last-mentioned stages, &c.

[*146]

The seventh count recited the existence and use of the harbour as in the third count ; and charged the creation of the nuisance, described as in the fifth count, by divers persons, and its continuation by the defendants.

The eighth count charged that the defendants, on the said 1st of February, &c , and on divers other &c., wrongfully and injuriously did choak up and greatly obstruct a certain other ancient harbour within the said county of York, to wit at Scarborough in the said county, by casting and throwing into the same divers large quantities of timber, earth, stones, and sand, to the great danger and common nuisance of all the liege &c., against the peace &c.

Plea, Not guilty.

On the trial before Lord Denman, Ch. J., at the Yorkshire Summer Assizes, 1833, a special verdict was found to the following effect.

That, during all the time within mentioned, there was an ancient port and harbour, commonly called the harbour of Scarborough, in the county of York, much used and frequented, for the purpose as well of shelter as of repairs, by ships and vessels navigating along the northern coast of this kingdom ;

and that the prosecutors of the indictment are the commissioners for executing the powers and authorities contained in
certain Acts of Parliament hereinafter mentioned. The verdict
then set forth certain provisions of several Acts of Parliament
respecting.the management of the harbour and the power of the
commissioners, namely, stat. *5 Geo. II. c. 11, stat. 25 Geo. II.
c. 44, stat. (U. K.) 41 Geo. III. c. 69 (local and personal, public),
stat. 46 Geo. III. c. 33 (local and personal, public), stat. 3 Geo. IV.
c. xxii. (local and personal, public) ; and the verdict then found
that, in and subsequently to the year 1817, the commissioners,
with a view to improve and preserve the said harbour, did cause
the same to be excavated, by removing divers large quantities of
sand from the bottom thereof, and thereby the said harbour hath
been deepened about four feet all along the upper part of the
harbour ; and that this process of excavation and deepening was
carried on by the commissioners, amongst other places, within
from ten to twenty feet of, and immediately before, the line of
the piles hereinafter mentioned : that, in 1819, the commissioners, with a view further to improve the harbour, removed
a pier called an island pier, which had previously stood in the
harbour, and, in 1820, erected or completed the pier called the
western pier, being the same mentioned in stat. 3 Geo. IV.
c. xxii., and that, by such excavation, the harbour was materially
improved, and rendered more secure and commodious for shipping: that, for many years previously to 1817, the defendants
were, and thence have been, and at the respective times of
committing the acts within complained of were, the owners of
certain premises on the edge of the upper part of the harbour
which premises, during all the time hereinbefore mentioned, had
been used and enjoyed by the said defendants as a ship building
yard, and for the purpose of building and repairing ships therein,
and, for 200 years last past and upwards, had been used and
enjoyed in like manner, and for the like purpose, by the owners
thereof for the time being: that, during the space of seventy
years last past and upwards, divers piles have *been placed and
driven into the sandy bottom in face of the said yard and premises
of the defendants ; upon which piles, plank stages, during all
the time aforesaid, have been erected and placed by the owners

REX
v.
TINDALL.

[*147]

[*148]

Rex
v.
Tindall.

for the time being of the yard and premises, and timber and other materials used in building and repairing ships kept thereon ; and the same, during the time aforesaid, have been and are proper and necessary for the purpose of carrying on the business of building or repairing ships on the said yard and .premises : that, until the planking of the same by the defendants as hereinafter mentioned, the said piles had always stood at certain distances from one another, and that the water might flow freely between them, and might spend itself on the sloping beach : that the defendants, in order to protect their said premises, afterwards, to wit, on 1st January, 1826, and on divers other days and times between that day and 1st January, 1828, connected together the said piles, by nailing transverse planks from pile to pile, and inclosed the area contained within the said piles, the same being thus rendered impervious to the tide, and presenting perpendicular lines of frontage, five feet high from the sand ; and at ordinary spring tides there is now, at high water, a depth of from two to three feet of water against and along the said frontage: that, by the aforesaid works of the commissioners, a greater rush of tide was and thence hath been caused to and against the beach and sand in front of the said ship building yard and premises of the defendants than had ever previously been experienced, insomuch that, by reason thereof, the land was washed down from before the front of the said yard and premises of the defendants ; and the said yard and premises, and their plank stages aforesaid, at the times of the defendants

[*149]

committing *the acts within complained of, had become and were thereby in danger of being swept away by the sea: that, "by the defendants' works, the harbour is in some extreme cases rendered less secure :" that the said defendants have done nothing more than is necessary to protect their property against the sea, in consequence of the alterations made by the commissioners.

The case was argued in Trinity Term last (1).

Alexander, for the Crown, contended, first, that the acts of the commissioners were lawful ; secondly, that the defendants

(1) June 1st, 1836. Before Lord Denman, Ch. J., Littledale, Patteson, and Williams, JJ.

were not entitled to interfere with the public rights in the
harbour, even if the acts of the commissioners were illegal;
thirdly, that the finding of the jury showed a legal nuisance,
inasmuch as an injury was done to the harbour, and as none of
the facts stated in the verdict afforded an answer.

Cresswell, for the defendants, contended, first, that every
count charged the act to have been committed in the harbour,
but that the verdict did not support this; secondly, that no
public right was shown legally to exist which made the acts of
the defendant unlawful; thirdly, that, at any rate, a contingent
or trifling injury, like that shown by the verdict, was not the
subject of indictment.

Alexander, in reply, contended that to render the harbour
less commodious in extreme cases, as, for instance, of violent
tempest, was a nuisance.

The following authorities were cited: *Rex* v. *Pease* (1). Hale,
de Portibus Maris, c. 7 (2). Hale, de Jure Maris, c. 6 (3).
The Attorney-General v. *Burridge* (4). *The Attorney-General* v.
Parmeter (5). *The Attorney-General* v. *Richards* (6). *Rex* v.
Lord Grosvenor (7). *Rex* v. *Russell* (8). *Rex* v. *Ward* (9). *Rex*
v. *Trafford* (10). *Trafford* v. *Rex* (11). *Rex* v. *The Commissioners of Sewers for Pagham, Sussex* (12). Hale, de Portibus
Maris, c. 6 (13). Hale, de Jure Maris, c. 4 (14). HOLROYD, J. in
Blundell v. *Catterall* (15). *Ball* v. *Herbert* (16). Note (1) to Co.
Litt. 261 a. *Sutton* v. *Clarke* (17). 2 Roll. Abr. 564. Trespass (I.)
pl. 1. *Chichester* v. *Lethbridge* (18). *Williams's* case (19). Hawk.
P. C. B. 1, c. 60, s. 28. *Regina* v. *Watts* (20). Domat,

[150]

RXX
v.
TINDALL.

(1) 38 R. R. 207 (4 B. & Ad. 30).
(2) Harg. L. T. 83.
(3) Harg. L. T. 36.
(4) 24 R. R. 705 (10 Price, 350).
(5) 24 R. R. 723, 745 (10 Price, 378, 412).
(6) 3 R. R. 632 (2 Anstr. 603).
(7) 20 R. R. 732 (2 Stark. 511).
(8) 30 R. R. 432 (6 B. & C. 566).
(9) 43 R. R. 364 (4 Ad. & El. 384).
(10) 1 B. & Ad. 874.

(11) 34 R. R. 680 (8 Bing. 204) Ex. Ch.
(12) 32 R. R. 406 (8 B. & C. 355).
(13) Harg. L. T. 73.
(14) Harg. L. T. 12.
(15) 24 R. R. 353 (5 B. & Ald. 268, 303).
(16) 1 R. R. 695 (3 T. R. 253).
(17) 16 R. R. 563 (6 Taunt. 29).
(18) Willes, 71.
(19) 5 Co. Rep. 72 b.
(20) 1 Salk. 357.

book 2, tit. 8, s. 1, art. 11 ; s. 3, art. 6, 9.   *Turbervil* v.
Stamp (1).   *Wilkes* v. *Hungerford Market Company* (2).

As the judgment of the COURT proceeded exclusively on the
slightness of the injury in degree, and the uncertainty of its
occurrence, it is not thought necessary to report the arguments
at length.

Cur. adv. vult.

LORD DENMAN, Ch. J. now delivered the judgment of the
COURT :

[151]   This is an indictment for an alleged nuisance in the harbour
of Scarborough.   The indictment, in all the counts, charges the
defendants with having erected or continued certain piles and
planking in the harbour, and thereby obstructed and rendered
it insecure.

The special verdict in substance finds that the defendants are
owners of premises used as a yard for ship-building on the edge
of the upper part of the harbour ; that the piles in question
have been erected and driven into the sandy bottom in face of
the said yard and premises, during the space of seventy years ;
and that the water might flow between the piles until the
planking was placed there.   It then finds that the commissioners
under certain Acts of Parliament erected works and deepened
the harbour, so as to cause a greater rush of water against the
defendants' premises than formerly, to the extent of washing
away the soil and threatening destruction to their building yard :
that the defendants, in order to protect their property, placed
transverse planking in front of the piles, and have done nothing
more than was necessary to protect their property against the
sea in consequence of the alterations made by the commissioners.
It then finds, that by the defendants' works the harbour is in
some extreme cases rendered less secure.

The COURT has considered much, whether this verdict is not
so imperfect as to make it necessary to award a *venire de novo ;*
but, upon the whole, we think that the facts are so found as to
enable us to give our judgment upon them.

It is not indeed *expressly* found that the piles or planking are

(1) 1 Salk. 13.   (2) 2 Bing. N. C. 281.

in the harbour at all, which is the charge in the indictment;   REX
but, assuming that this may be collected from the whole verdict,   *v.*
the question will be, whether *the effect produced by them is   TINDALL.
sufficiently described to enable the Court to say that the   [*152]
defendants' works are or are not in law a nuisance.

Doubtless the expression " that by the defendants' works the
harbour is in some extreme cases rendered less secure " is vague
and indefinite; but it is sufficient to convey to the mind that
the defendants' works, even when other causes concur with them
and produce their worst result, do but diminish the security of
the harbour, possibly, in the least possible degree, on very rare
occasions, and under undefined circumstances.

Now, without deciding at all how far the conduct of the
defendants could under the circumstances be justified, if their
works of themselves injured the harbour or rendered it insecure,
or even if, combined with other things, they had that effect
generally, we think that the jury must be taken to ask by their
special verdict for our decision, whether such consequences as
are therein stated must amount to a nuisance. We do not think
that they *must*, but hold, on the contrary, that no person can be
made criminally responsible for consequences so slight, and
uncertain, and rare, as are stated by this verdict to result from
the works of the defendants. A verdict of Not guilty must
accordingly be entered.

Verdict of Not Guilty entered.

REX *v.* OCTAVIUS MASHITER, Esquire (1).

(6 Adol. & Ellis, 153—167; S. C. 1 N. & P. 314; W. W. & D. 173; 6 L. J.
(N. S.) K. B. 121.)

1837.
Jan. 13.
—
[153]

The word "inhabitants" in a charter has not in itself any definite
legal meaning, but must be explained, in each case, extrinsically, as
by evidence of usage, or by reference to the context and objects of the
charter.

Where, by charter, a justice of peace was to be elected by the "tenants
and inhabitants" of a manor, and, on motion for a *quo warranto* information against a party elected to that office, the unsuccessful candidate
complained that the votes of "inhabitants," "not actual householders,"

(1) Compare *R.* v. *Davie*, p. 494, *post* (6 Ad. & El. 374).—R. C.

had been rejected, alleging that a sufficient number of such votes had been tendered on his side to give him a majority:

Held, that the motion was not sustained, inasmuch as the relator did not show what class of persons was, in this case, comprehended under the words "inhabitants, not householders," and that votes were tendered, from that class, sufficient to carry his election.

THESIGER, in last Easter Term, obtained a rule *nisi* for a *quo warranto* information requiring the defendant to show by what authority he claimed to be a justice of the peace for the liberty, lordship, or manor, of Havering-atte-Bower in Essex. The affidavits in support of the rule set out in part a charter of 5 Edward IV., reciting and granting as follows:

"Whereas the lordship or manor of Havering-atte-Bower, in the county of Essex, is of ancient demesne of the Crown of England, and all the lands and tenements holden of the said manor, and real and mixed actions, in, upon, and concerning the same lands and tenements or any parcel of them, arising or to arise, are pleadable, and have been pleaded, in the court unto the said manor belonging, before the steward and suitors of the same court for the time being, and not elsewhere, and have ever been accustomed, since the time whereof no memory of man is to the contrary, in the same court to be pleaded, and determined as of all other lands holden in ancient demesne, time out of mind, ought and is accustomed to be done; and now, having heard by the lamentable complaints of the tenants and inhabitants of the said lordship or manor, in what sort they have been, and now are, out of the said lordship, in other courts than in the aforesaid court before the steward and suitors of the same,

[*154] in and concerning divers actions and plaints, *of and upon divers lands and tenements, which heretofore have arisen and daily do arise or happen within the said lordship, many times by their ill-willers troubled, vexed, grieved, and molested, to the no small loss and grievance of them the said tenants and inhabitants, and to the hazard of their utter undoing, unless they be by us relieved in this behalf, whereupon they have been humble petitioners unto us that we would provide remedy for them in the premises; we, having a tender compassion of these their humble petitions in this behalf, out of our especial grace have granted, and by these presents do grant, to the above named

tenants and inhabitants which now are, and for the time hereafter shall be, and to their heirs and successors, that they shall
not be forced, compelled, or bound to answer, before any justices,
judges, or commissioners of us or our heirs, in any real, personal,
or mixed actions, arising, or to arise, of, in, or upon the lands
and tenements aforesaid, holden of that aforesaid manor, or of
any parcel thereof, as is before said, in any other courts, out
of the said lordship or manor, than in the court of the manor
aforesaid before the steward and suitors of the same for the
time being, but that all such actions and plaints, and pleas
thereof, shall be there determined and proceeded in, according
to the custom of the said manor, before the steward and suitors
of the aforesaid court, in the same court of the manor aforesaid.
And we will and grant that the steward and suitors of the court,
aforesaid, for the time being, shall and may have full power and
authority to hear and determine, by plaints to be levied and
prosecuted in the same court, pleas of debts, accompts, covenants,
respasses, as well by force and arms committed as otherwise,
detention of chattels, *and all other contracts whatsoever,
within the lordship or manor aforesaid made, done, or arising,
although the same debts, accompts, covenants, trespasses,
chattels, and other contracts, do amount unto, or exceed the
sum or value of 40s." "And furthermore" we "do grant unto
the aforesaid tenants and inhabitants, and to their successors,
that the steward of the said manor for the time being, so long as
he shall continue in the same office, and one of the discreetest
and honestest tenants or inhabitants aforesaid, to be from time
to time chosen by them, the tenants and inhabitants and their
successors, shall be for us and our heirs justices of the peace,
and keepers of our peace, to be kept within the said manor of
Havering aforesaid, and as justices of us and of our heirs, to
hear all felonies, trespasses, and all other unlawful acts whatsoever, committed, or to be committed, within the said manor;
and shall have full power and authority to enquire of all and
singular articles, as well concerning labourers, artificers, butchers,
tanners, makers of cloth and of caps, as of all other things
whatsoever, which any other of our justices of the peace, or
keepers of our peace, in other places out of the lordship aforesaid

REX
v.
MASHITER.

[*155]

28—2

in the said county of Essex, have power to enquire of, and to determine all and singular the same, and all other things to do and execute which any other such justices of the peace and keepers of the peace in other places may do, or any ways execute ; yet, notwithstanding, they shall no way proceed to the trial of any treason or felony within the lordship aforesaid without our special mandate." And the justices of the county were not to meddle with any thing committed or arising within the manor. The charter also granted to the said tenants and inhabitants, their heirs and successors, *to have a fair every year, &c., with a pie poudre court to be holden before a steward for the time being, to be nominated by the tenants and inhabitants, their heirs and successors, to keep such court. "And furthermore we will, and by these presents do grant unto the same tenants and inhabitants, their heirs and successors, that they shall be able persons and capable in the law to receive, have, and accept all and singular the privileges, liberties, and authorities, and franchises aforesaid, and the same to enjoy to them and their aforesaid heirs and successors for ever as is above said," &c.

[*156]

This charter was ratified by Queen Mary ; and Queen Elizabeth, by charter of the thirtieth year of her reign, ratified the preceding ones, and did "grant, constitute, and declare, that the tenants and inhabitants of the same lordship or manor of" &c. "are and shall be one body corporate or politic of themselves in due fact and name, and shall have perpetual succession ; and that they and their successors for ever shall and may be styled, termed, and called by the name of tenants and inhabitants of the lordship or manor of Havering-atte-Bower in the county of Essex ; and we by these presents do, for us, our heirs and successors, really and fully, erect, make, ordain, and create them one body corporate and politic, by the name of the tenants and inhabitants of" &c., "and that by the same name they shall and may have perpetual succession." These charters were confirmed and renewed in subsequent reigns.

The affidavits further stated that a court of ancient demesne was holden for the said lordship or manor, on February 11th, 1836, pursuant to notice, addressed to the tenants and

inhabitants, for the election of a justice of the peace pursuant
to charter; that the defendant *Octavius Mashiter and Edward
Young Hancock were candidates, and, the show of hands being
in favour of the latter, a poll was demanded; that, on the first
day of polling, "several persons claimed to vote as inhabitants
of the said liberty, manor, or lordship, but whose votes were
objected to on the ground that such persons were not householders; and thereupon the court directed the votes of all such
persons to be entered as tendered votes only;" that, on the
close of the poll on the second day, 341 votes were recorded for
Hancock, and 455 for Mashiter, "and that, in addition thereto,
218 persons, all of whom were, as deponent" (Hancock) "verily
believes, inhabitants of the said manor or lordship, though not
actual householders therein, claimed to be entitled to vote, and
that 170 of such persons tendered their votes in favour of
deponent, and forty-eight in favour of the said Octavius
Mashiter;" that all the tendered votes for Hancock were
ultimately rejected; and that the defendant was declared duly
elected; but that, if the tendered votes had been received, he
would have had a majority of eight; that the courts of ancient
demesne for the election of justices had always been open to and
attended by the tenants and inhabitants, without distinction as
to householders; that no former instance had been found of a
contested election; but that, in books containing minutes of the
proceedings at the above courts, there were entries of certain
persons having been chosen " justice for the people ; " and
others stating the election of such justice by " the tenants and
inhabitants whose names are hereunto subscribed;" and that
among such names were those of several persons who, at the
time of such elections, were not householders nor (as was
believed) tenants of the said liberty or manor.

The affidavits in opposition to the rule stated that Mashiter
had the majority of tenants of the manor, both resident and non-
resident, and the majority of householders; that the alleged
majority for Hancock consisted of persons who were neither
tenants of the liberty or manor, nor householders, nor owners
or occupiers of any house or land, within the same, nor assessed
or rated to the poor or any other rate or tax; that, of his voters,

REX
v.
MASHITER.

many more than such alleged majority were lodgers only; and that thirteen of them were persons receiving parochial relief at the time of the election.

Sir W. W. Follett now showed cause :

The relator does not show that he had a majority of voters. He claims a majority of "inhabitants," but not of inhabitants according to any given definition. "Inhabitants," in a charter, has never been taken to mean simply any person who happened to be resident at a particular time. Some qualification has constantly been adopted in the construction of the word. Lord HARDWICKE lays it down, in *Fludier* v. *Lombe* (1), that a lodger cannot be said to be an inhabitant. Lord COKE says, upon the word "inhabitants" in the Statute of Bridges (2), 2 Inst. 702, that it is "the largest word of its kind," and, 703, that "every person that dwelleth in any shire, riding, city, or town corporate, though he hath but a personal residence, yet is he said in law to be an inhabitant, or a dweller there, as servants, &c. But this statute extendeth not to them, but to such as be householders."

[*159]

In *Rex* v. *Adlard* (3), where many authorities *on the subject are collected, ABBOTT, Ch. J. observes, that the word "inhabitant" "varies in its import, according to the subject to which it is applied." The Court there held that a non-resident occupier could not be liable, as inhabitant, to serve the office of constable; but, on the other hand, it could not have been said that a person was liable to serve who merely happened to be in the parish, and was not an occupier. In *The Attorney-General* v. *Parker* (4) Lord HARDWICKE, after stating that "inhabitants" is a still larger word than "parishioner," observes that, in that case, some sort of limitation was allowed by both sides to have been put upon the generality of the grant there in question, and says further that, if the grant had stood unrestricted at all, he should have thought it not unreasonable to restrict the terms "parishioners and inhabitants" to inhabitants paying scot and lot. He adds that he was of that opinion in *The Attorney-General* v. *Dary* (5), and that he there thought "*inhabitants*

(1) Ca. temp. Hard. K. B. 308.   (4) 3 Atk. 576.
(2) 22 Hen. VIII. c. 5, s. 3.   (5) 2 Atk. 212 (not S. P.)
(3) 4 B. & C. 772.

ought to be restrained to persons paying scot and lot." In *The Attorney-General* v. *Forster* (1) Lord ELDON said, of the word "inhabitants," that there was none "capable of a larger or more limited interpretation;" observing, "It was decided in Lord Coke's time, that a man, living in Cornwall, may to many purposes be an inhabitant of London; that is, by having property liable to the repair of bridges." Now, if the word be capable of such various constructions, the person who makes an application like the present, on the ground that a majority of "inhabitants" voted for him, ought to show in what sense he uses the word. His affidavit, on this point, should be framed *so precisely that perjury might be assigned upon it if necessary.

Thesiger, contrà, was then called upon by the COURT to answer this objection:

All persons were entitled to vote, who came within the full sense of the word "inhabitants." Wherever a qualified construction has been put upon that term, there has been usage to explain it. The affidavits here show the real dispute to have been whether persons, to be qualified as inhabitants, must be householders. There was no usage warranting such a restriction. In *The Attorney-General* v. *Parker* (2) (referred to in *Withnell* v. *Gartham* (3), by LAWRENCE, J.), in *The Attorney-General* v. *Forster* (4), and in *The Attorney-General* v. *Newcombe* (5), usage was recognised as the ground upon which a limited interpretation was to be put upon a right given to "inhabitants."

(COLERIDGE, J.: Who do you say are qualified here, according to the full sense of the term?)

All resiants or indwellers.

(COLERIDGE, J.: Any person, who may have come in the night before?)

If he came *animo morandi*. No limitation can be inferred here from the expressions and objects of the charters. That of

(1) 10 Ves. 339.
(2) 3 Atk. 576.
(3) 6 T. R. at p. 398 (see 3 R. R. 218).
(4) 10 Ves. 335.
(5) 14 Ves. 1.

REX
v.
MASHITER.

[*160]

Edward IV. recites the complaint made by the tenants and
inhabitants, of their being drawn into courts other than that
of the steward and suitors of the manor, in actions and plaints
" of and upon divers lands and tenements." But the subsequent
grant of a court was not necessary for the relief of tenants in
ancient demesne, who, at the common law, were not compellable
to appear in any court out of the manor ; and the powers given
[*161] by the charter *to the court constituted are not limited in a
manner corresponding to the complaint before pointed out, but
extend generally to pleas of debts, accounts, covenants, trespasses
by force and arms or otherwise, detention of chattels, and all
contracts, within the manor made, done, or arising. The justices
to be appointed have authority to enquire of articles of labourers,
and of all other things which other justices elsewhere may
inquire of. And the charter establishes a fair and a pie-poudre
court. From all these circumstances it must be concluded that
the benefits of the charter, generally, were designed, not merely
for the tenants in ancient demesne, but for all persons happening
to reside within the ambit of the manor. The intent was to
bestow upon these the benefits of a court leet, which, Lord Coke
says, 2 Inst. 71, was established " for the ease of the people,
and specially of the husbandman, that each of them might the
better follow their business in their several degrees." " So as
the tenants and resiants should have the same justice, that they
had before in the tourn, done unto them at their own doors."
" Tenants and inhabitants," in the charter, are spoken of in the
same sense as " tenants and resiants " in this passage.

> *Sir W. W. Follett, contrà,* was then desired to continue
> his argument :

It has not yet been shown that any precise legal meaning
attaches to the term " inhabitants." If it means residents,
even for a week preceding the election, it is not proved that Mr.
Hancock had the majority. Whoever may be considered as
inhabitants, it ought to appear that, of such, a majority voted
for him. No definition of the word " inhabitants " has been
[*162] cited. If it imply something less than residency, *will it be
said that any persons happening to pass through the town, as

soldiers on a march, or postillions driving a carriage, are qualified? Or that persons coming in for the sole purpose of voting would be so? No instance can be given in which "inhabitant" has been held to mean any thing less than an occupier. The election here in dispute is that of a justice of peace. The conservators of the peace were anciently elected by the freeholders, the persons who occupied the land; and the freeholders still elect coroners. The justice here is to be chosen from the "tenants or inhabitants aforesaid." It would follow from the argument on the other side that a person coming by mere chance into the liberty, even a beggar, might be elected justice; for the same restriction applies, or does not apply, to electors and elected. Where a privilege is conferred upon the men or inhabitants of a place, as the right of electing members of Parliament, or exemption from toll, it is always understood as attaching to persons who are at least occupiers. In a case in Bosanquet and Puller (1) it was decided that freemen of the city of London were not exempt from toll, unless they were inhabitants, and paying scot and lot.

Thesiger, in support of the rule :

Four descriptions of persons are shown to have voted in this election: tenants, resident and non-resident, inhabitant house-holders, and inhabitants not householders. Tenants non-resident cannot be objected to; and, if the terms "tenants *and inhabitants" do not limit the qualification to resident tenants, it seems difficult to say that the same words confine it to inhabitants who are occupiers. "Inhabitants" and other similar words are known and definite terms in the law, and so treated in many books; thus it is said, that the "parishioners or inhabitants, or *probi homines* of Dale," "are not capable to purchase lands; but goods they are, unless it were in ancient time when such grants were allowed:" Co. Litt. 3 a. "By the forest law a grant made of a privilege within the forest to all the inhabitants

[*163]

---

(1) See *The Corporation of London v. The Corporation of Liverpool*, 1 Bos. & P. 522, *n.*, to *The Mayor of London v. The Mayor of Lynn Regis*, in which latter case the same point was discussed, but not decided. See the latter case, at earlier stages, 1 H. Bl. 206, and 4 T. R. 144.

REX
v.
MANHITER.

being freeholders within the forest or such other commonalties not incorporated, is good : " 4 Inst. 297.   In *Russell* v. *The Men of Devon* (1) Lord KENYON says, " I do not say that the inhabitants of a county or hundred may not be incorporated to some purposes ; as if the King were to grant lands to them, rendering rent, like the grant to the good men of the town of Islington ; " and an *Anonymous* case (2) in Dyer is referred to.   In the absence of such usage as appeared in the cases cited on the other side, "inhabitants " may well be taken to mean persons who come to a place, not, perhaps, to reside permanently, but with the same intention to inhabit, to stay and abide, as appeared, for instance, in *Rex* v. *Woolpit* (3).   Some weight must be ascribed, in the present case, to the minutes of former elections, in which persons sworn not to have been occupiers were permitted to subscribe declarations beginning "We, the tenants and inhabitants."

LORD DENMAN, Ch. J. :

[*164]

I was at first alarmed at some of the consequences which might have resulted from a *refusal to grant this rule ; and I am not now prepared to say that a person, to be qualified to vote in these elections, must be an occupier.   But, to dispossess the party who has been declared elected, we must see a clear right in some other. It is said here that Hancock was rightfully elected by the majority of persons not householders : and that the being a householder or not was the criterion by which the admissibility of votes was tried.   But, to prove that he had a legal majority, Hancock must point out the description of persons in whom the legal right to vote subsisted, and who made up such majority.   Now he makes it up merely by stating that a hundred and seventy persons tendered their votes for him, all of whom, as he believes, were inhabitants of the manor, though not actual householders therein.   The case is thus thrown upon the word "inhabitants."   But it is clear that that is a word of such uncertain legal meaning that the party relying upon it ought to have a construction of his own to put upon it, and should be prepared to sustain that construction,

(1) 1 R. R. 585 (2 T. R. 667, 672).   (3) 4 Ad. & El. 205.
(2) 1 Dyer, 100 a, pl. 70.

and to show that, according to it, he has a rightful claim. REX
That has not been done here; and therefore the question of right *v.*
is not properly brought before us. It is contended that the word MASHITER.
"inhabitants" has, of itself, a definite legal meaning; but the
authorities cited do not show this. LAWRENCE, J., in *Withnell* v.
Gartham (1), say's that, in the case before Lord Hardwicke, great
inconvenience would have arisen from giving the "full sense" to
the word "inhabitants," and that Lord HARDWICKE thought it
must be construed according to usage, where that could be
ascertained; but LAWRENCE, J. does not state *what the full   [*165]
sense would have been. In *Russell* v. *The Men of Devon* (2),
which was a case under very different circumstances from the
present, Lord KENYON referred to a ruling of BROMLEY, Ch. J.
and others, reported in Dyer (3); but the only result of that is
that, if the Queen grant land by charter "to the good men of
Islington," without saying "to have to them, their heirs, and
successors," the charter creates a good corporation for that
purpose. It is not to be inferred that BROMLEY, Ch. J., at the
time when he so held, entertained any definite idea as to the legal
meaning of "good men" or "inhabitants."

LITTLEDALE, J.:

It is difficult to assign a meaning to the word "inhabitants."
Under the Statute of Bridges it means persons holding lands in
the county. In the grant of a way over a field to church it would
extend to all persons in the parish. It must be taken according
to the subject-matter, and be explained, as circumstances allow,
sometimes by usage, sometimes by the context or object of a
charter. It cannot be said to have any fixed meaning. It
ought, therefore, to have been shown, on this application, who,
beyond tenants, were meant by the words "tenants and inhabitants." It might be lodgers, inmates, servants, or, perhaps,
other descriptions of persons. Those who rely upon the term
ought to have shown what was the character of those whom
they seek to introduce under it.

(1) 6 T. R. at p. 398 (see 3 R. R.   (2) 1 R. R. 585 (2 T. R. 667, 672).
218).   (3) 1 Dyer, 100 a, pl. 70.

WILLIAMS, J. :

[*166]   We could not disturb this election unless we saw reason to
conclude that it had been improperly *decided.   It ought
to have been shown that the word "inhabitants" here had
some definite meaning attached to it; or at least it should
have appeared by affidavit what were the particular qualifica-
tions of those whose votes were tendered and rejected; so that,
if possible, we might have formed a conclusion as to the right
upon which the claim of parties to vote as inhabitants was
grounded.   The word is uncertain in itself; and here no fixed
meaning has been assigned to it from which we can infer that
a majority of legal votes was given for any other than the person
actually elected.

COLERIDGE, J. :

Before we could grant a rule like this we ought to see a clear
primâ facie case.   Here it appears only that the relator would
have had a majority by the reception of persons who were
inhabitants but not householders.   Then it is contended that
the word "inhabitants" by itself, unless restrained by custom,
or the context of the grant, has, in law, a definite meaning, and
that it must here be taken in the full legal sense.   If this be so,
perhaps a case is made out for granting the rule.   But I cannot
go along with these propositions.   Any lawyer, who was asked
the interpretation of the word "inhabitants," would say "I must
see where it is used, for, by itself, it has no definite meaning."
If its signification varies we must resort to the context for
explanation.   Then it is contended that, according to the context of this grant, the word must mean all persons being in the
place *animo morandi*.   But, in the first place, if that be so, the
affidavits ought to have shown that Hancock had a majority by
the votes of persons, not merely passing through, but inhabiting
[*167]   *animo morandi*, in which case the party opposing the *rule might
have given a direct answer to that allegation; and, secondly, I do
not think the context of this charter clearly shows that the interpretation suggested is the proper one.   The rule must, therefore,
be discharged.

Rule discharged.

DOE d. HICKMAN v. HASLEWOOD.

(6 Adol. & Ellis, 167—179; S. C. 1 N. & P. 352; W. W. & D. 116; 1 Jur. 1138; 6 L. J. (N. S.) K. B. 96.)

By a will, apparently drawn by an illiterate person, testator bequeathed to his wife, her heirs and assigns for ever, all the residue of his goods, chattels, and personal estate; and likewise made her full and sole executrix of the freehold house, situate in, &c. No other person or property was specified in the will, nor any executor appointed, except as above :
Held, that the wife took a fee in the house.

EJECTMENT for a house in Middlesex. On the trial before Lord Denman, Ch. J., at the Middlesex sittings after Michaelmas Term, 1835, a verdict was found for the plaintiff, subject to a case, the material parts of which are as follows :

George Haslewood, being seised in fee of the said house, made his will as follows (1) :

"I George Haslewood, of Swallow Street, No. 50, in the parish of St. James, Westminster, being of sound " &c., " do make and ordain this for my last will and testament, in manner and form following : viz., I give and bequeath unto my wife Ann Haslewood, to her heirs and assigns for ever, all the residue of my goods, chattels, and personal estate, whatsoever and wheresoever, and also all my right, title, and interest of, in, and to all and every sum and sums of money whatsoever which now is, are, or shall be due to me upon and in virtue of any will, bond, or other securities; and I do likewise *make my wife, the said Ann Haslewood, full and sole executrix of the freehold house, situated in Great Queen Street, No. 15, in the parish of St. Giles in the Fields, being the north side of the street, in the county of Middlesex. This my last will and testament hereby revoking all former wills by me made. In witness whereof," &c. (Signed and sealed by the testator, and dated June 4th, 1805.)

[*168]

The testator died in December, 1805, leaving Ann Haslewood, his widow, him surviving. The testator and his wife lived in the house until and at the time of his death; and the widow afterwards continued in possession until her death, which took place in November, 1833. The lessor of the plaintiff was her nephew and heir-at-law.

(1) The testator's own name, and many other words in the will, were mis-spelt.

The questions for the opinion of the Court were, first, whether Ann Haslewood took an estate in fee-simple under the will of her husband ; secondly, whether, on the facts of the case, the plaintiff is entitled to recover. The case was argued in Michaelmas Term last (1).

Sir W. W. Follett, for the plaintiff:

Ann Haslewood took a fee-simple in the house, the intention of the will being clear, though untechnically expressed ; for the testator undoubtedly meant to give her a full and absolute interest. A bequest of personalty to a man's heirs will carry the absolute property to the next of kin ; at least this seemed to be the inclination of the opinion of Sir R. P. ARDEN, M. R., in *Holloway* v. *Holloway* (2). *The first part of the will here is clearly meant to give the personalty to the wife absolutely. The Court always collects the meaning of the testator, without insisting upon accurate legal phraseology ; as in *Doe* d. *Tofield* v. *Tofield* (3). It will be admitted that the intention was that the wife should take some estate in the house ; but what estate can be given to her except a fee ? She was to have the same power over the realty that an executor has over the personalty ; that is, an absolute power. It is held, indeed, that, if a testator devise land to A., without adding more, A. takes only a life-estate : that seems to be the only exception from the general rule of following the intention ; but the Court allows any strong evidence of intent to take a case out of the exception, as in *Loveacres* d. *Mudge* v. *Blight* (4), where the words " freely to be possessed and enjoyed " were held to carry the inheritance. These words do not furnish such strong evidence of the intention as the words in the present will ; and Lord MANSFIELD'S remarks apply. In *Rose* d. *Vere* v. *Hill* (5) a devise to five children of the devisor, " and the survivors and survivor of them, and the

[*169]

---

(1) November 18th, 1836, before Lord Denman, Ch. J., Patteson, Williams, and Coleridge, JJ. Besides the points discussed in the text, a question arose as to an alleged adverse possession : but, as the judgment of the Court proceeded upon another ground, the facts and arguments relating to this point are not reported.
(2) 5 R. R. 81 (5 Ves. 399).
(3) 10 R. R. 496 (11 East, 246).
(4) 1 Cowp. 352.
(5) 3 Burr. 1881.

executors and administrators of such survivor, share and share
alike, as tenants in common, and not as joint tenants," was held
to give a tenancy in common in fee ; and WILMOT, J. there said
that "executors" is equivalent to "heirs," in a will. In *Roe
lessee* of *Shell* v. *Pattison* (1) the words "I leave all the remainder
in the above stocks with my freehold property to my sister" were
held to give a fee ; Lord ELLENBOROUGH saying that "it was
clearly the intention of the testator *to give as absolute an   [*170]
estate and interest in his freehold property as in his stock ; "
and that "there are no words of such an inflexible nature as will
not bend to the intention of a testator, when it can be collected
from the context of his will." In *Doe* d. *Gillard* v. *Gillard* (2)
the words, " I make R. G. my whole and sole executor of all my
lands for ever," were held to give a fee.

(COLERIDGE, J. referred to *Piggot* v. *Penrice* (3).)

The cases where words making a party executor of lands have
been held to pass no inheritance, will be found to be cases where,
as in *Piggot* v. *Penrice* (3), the devise is not of specific land, as
here, but of estates generally.

(LORD DENMAN, Ch. J. referred to *Clements* v. *Cassye* (4) and
Shaw v. *Bull* (5).)

It may be doubted whether *Shaw* v. *Bull* (5) would now be decided
in the same way. At any rate, where the intent to give the specific
property to the executrix is clear, as here, the case does not apply.
There is no alternative between giving the fee and rejecting the
clause altogether.

(PATTESON, J.: In *Tayler* v. *Web* (6) it was held that the words,
I make my cousin G. B. my sole heir and my executor, passed a
fee : you contend that making a person a sole executor only does
the same.)

(1) 16 East, 221.
(2) 5 B. & Ald. 785.
(3) Prec. Chan. 471.
(4) Noy, 48.

(5) 12 Mod. 593 ; *S. C.* 2 Eq. Ca.
Abr. 320, pl. 8.
(6) Style, 301, 307, 319 ; and see
Marret v. *Sly*, 2 Sid. 75.

DOE d.
HICKMAN
r.
HASLEWOOD.

If a person be made executor of specific land, that is the effect: as a devise making a man sole heir of a leasehold would give him the absolute property in the chattel.

(PATTESON, J.: If "executrix" in this will means devisee, there is no executor named; for the wife is not made executrix generally.)

She would be administratrix *cum testamento annexo*.

[171]   *Butt, contrà:*

This is, at the most, a gift of the house to the executrix : that passes only a life-estate, for want of words of inheritance. In *Loveacres* d. *Mudge* v. *Blight* (1) the will commenced with the words "as touching such worldly estate," &c.: the word "estate" has been · held to pass a fee. But that case is at variance with the later case of *Denn* d. *Gaskin* v. *Gaskin* (2). In *Doe* d. *Gillard* v. *Gillard* (3) the debts, legacies, and funeral expenses were charged on the realty; so that it was necessary for the executor to have a fee. So, in *Rose* d. *Vere* v. *Hill* (4), the executors. who were devisees, were, in the first place, to pay the debts . this charge has often been held to give a fee by implication: *Doe* d. *Willey* v. *Holmes* (5), *Goodtitle* d. *Paddy* v. *Maddern* (6), *Doe* d. *Beezley* v. *Woodhouse* (7).   In *Goodright* d. *Drewry* v. *Barron* (8) the words were "as touching such worldly estate " &c., with a devise following, and then "also I give and bequeath to my wife Elizabeth, whom I likewise make my sole executrix, all and singular my lands, messuages and tenements, by her freely to be possessed and enjoyed." This was held to give a life-estate only. In *Clements* v. *Cassye* (9) "I make my wife executrix of all my goods and lands " was held to give her such lands only as she might have as executrix. In *Piggot* v. *Penrice* (10) the words were more in favour of the executor than here; for the gift was of "all my

(1) 1 Cowp. 352.   (6) 4 East, 496.
(2) 2 Cowp. 657.   (7) 4 T. R. 89.
(3) 5 B. & Ald. 785.   (8) 11 East, 220.
(4) 3 Burr. 1881.   (9) Noy, 48.
(5) 8 T. R. 1.   (10) Prec. Chan. 471.

goods, lands, and chattels." In *Denn* d. *Moor* v. *Mellor* (1) the words were " all the rest of my *lands, tenements, and hereditaments " &c., " I give, devise, and bequeath the same unto my wife," who was also made sole executrix : this was held to pass only a life-estate. A similar decision, given upon the same facts, in *Doe* d. *Mellor* v. *Moor* (2), was reversed in the Exchequer Chamber, *Denn* d. *Mellor* v. *Moor* (3) ; but the decision of the Exchequer Chamber was reversed, and that of the King's Bench affirmed, in the House of Lords: *Moor* v. *Denn* d. *Mellor* (4). In *Doe* d. *Ashby* v. *Baines* (5) a testator devised to his daughter, being his sole executrix, " all and singular my lands, tenements, and messuages, by her freely to be possessed and enjoyed : " this was held to give only a life-estate. The heir cannot be disinherited except by plain words.

DOE d.
. HICKMAN
c.
HASLEWOOD
[*172]

Sir W. W. Follett, in reply :

It appears from Co. Litt. 9 b, that the rule as to words of inheritance being requisite never prevails against the manifest intention of a devisor. This passage from Coke is referred to in Cruise's Digest, Devise, ch. xi. ss. 5, 6 (6) ; and numerous authorities to the same effect are collected in that chapter. In *Trent* v. *Hanning* (7) a testator, after charging his real estate, appointed three persons " as trustees of inheritance for the execution hereof ; " and this was held to carry a fee. In *Doe* d. *Penwarden* v. *Gilbert* (8) a testatrix, after devising and bequeathing to J. G. all her lands, particularly those called B. and B., added, " and all the rest and residue of my goods and chattels, personal and testamentary estate and effects whatsoever I give and bequeath unto the said J. G., *whom I make whole and sole executor of this my last will and testament ; " and J. G. was held to take a fee in B. and B.

[*173]

(*Butt* : DALLAS, Ch. J. there says that, but for the concluding words, and the introductory ones, " as for my temporal estates and effects," there would have passed a life-estate only.)

(1) 5 T. R. 558.   (5) 2 Cr. M. & R. 23 ; 5 Tyr. 655.
(2) 6 T. R. 175.   (6) Vol. vi. p. 208, 4th ed.
(3) 1 Bos. & P. 558.   (7) 7 East, 97.
(4) 2 Bos. & P. 247.   (8) 3 Brod. & B. 85.

Numerous cases of fees passing without words of inheritance are collected in Harrison's Digest, Will, part II., vii.

LORD DENMAN, Ch. J. now delivered the judgment of the COURT. After stating the case, his Lordship proceeded as follows:

The question is, whether, under the will above set forth, Ann Haslewood took an estate in fee-simple.

Upon the argument of this case many cases were cited, not, we think, (with one exception), as being in their circumstances similar, and, therefore, bearing directly upon this, but rather in illustration of the general principle upon which our decision ought to be founded.

We have referred to those cases, and perused them, and are clearly of opinion that none can be considered to be directly decisive of this point. We could not fail to observe, however, upon that perusal, a constant reference to the principle upon which this and every other will is to be construed, viz., that "every case of this sort depends upon its own peculiar circumstances; for, in every case, the question is one of construction to be made on the whole of the will; every case, therefore, is individual:" DALLAS, Ch. J., in *Doe* d. *Penwarden* v. *Gilbert* (1), cited at the Bar.

[174] The question for our decision seems to depend upon two points: first, whether the intention of the testator can be clearly and satisfactorily collected from the will; secondly, whether we are enabled, consistently with the rules of law, to carry that intention into effect.

Upon the first point, it is to be observed that it does not appear that the testator was possessed of any other property beyond that which is noticed by his will; nor can we perceive an allusion to any other object of his bounty except his wife. Moreover, in the earlier clause of the will, all the testator's personal property, including everything due to him upon securities of every kind, is (though the word "heirs" is there as much misapplied as the word "executors" to the freehold house) beyond all doubt bequeathed to the wife.

Having thus completed his purpose with respect to the whole

(1) 3 Brod. & B. at p. 88.

of his personalty, the will immediately proceeds to notice the only remaining property of the testator, his freehold house, No. 15, Great Queen Street, in the parish of St. Giles. For what purpose, then, can we suppose that the house was introduced into the will at all? Why is it mentioned in immediate connexion with property most certainly disposed of, if he meant to die intestate with respect to it? We can discover no other probable or reasonable supposition but that the house was introduced into the will with the intention of disposing of it; and, if so, there is no other conclusion possible but that he meant the disposition to be in favour of his wife.

We therefore think that, by the words "I do likewise make my said wife full and sole executrix of the freehold house," &c., the testator did intend to devise that house to his wife; and that (however inartificially *he has executed his purpose) he fully believed that he had done so. Whatever effect can reasonably be given to the word "likewise," we are not, we think, authorised to reject and expunge, as wholly insignificant and unmeaning, a clause in the will in which, we have no doubt, the testator himself thought his meaning had been most fully, and even learnedly, expressed. And, if this clause must be retained, as we are of opinion it must, it seems impossible to say that the testator did not intend to give to his wife *some* interest; and, if so, there is not only nothing to limit the intention to giving her anything less than "the full and sole" dominion over the house in question, or, in other words, an estate in fee-simple therein, but the term "full and sole executrix," as it would import the grant of the entire interest and dominion in and over property whereto it is correctly applicable, evinces an intention to grant no less in that to which it is, through ignorance, misapplied. Thus much, therefore, as to the *intention* of the testator.

The solution of the first point has, we think, a very considerable effect in disposing of the second; indeed, the last argument, if correct, concludes the question; because we are aware of no authority (and none such has been suggested) which affects to impose a limit beyond which the Courts shall not proceed, in their favourable construction of wills, to carry into effect the intention of a testator.

DOE d.
HICKMAN
v.
HASLEWOOD.

[*175]

29—2

Words, which are supposed to have (and which really have, when correctly and technically applied) a precise and definite meaning, are bent and diverted continually from that meaning, if the sense of the will requires it. "Heirs," "issue," "son," &c., are familiar instances of the kind now alluded to. The word "legacy" must *be admitted to have a direct reference to a bequest of personalty, and not to a devise of land ; yet in the case of *Hardacre* v. *Nash* (1), in which, by the former part of the will, there had been 150*l*. each given to a son and daughter of testator, afterwards certain land to each, and afterwards it was provided that, upon their death, in the wife's life-time, those "legacies" that had been left them should return to his wife, Lord KENYON thus states and deals with the argument arising from the proper meaning of the word : "Considerable stress was laid on the word 'legacies,' and it was argued" "that that word was an appropriate term, applicable to personal estate only : but the same technical and correct expressions are not to be expected from unlettered persons as are usually found in wills drawn by professional men. Even if there were no decision warranting us in saying that the word 'legacy' may be applied to a real estate, if the context required it, I should have had no difficulty in making such a determination for the first time." His Lordship then adds, that such a construction had been put upon it in the case of *Hope* d. *Brown* v. *Taylor* (2), as it had most undoubtedly, upon the short ground that it was "most agreeable to the intention of the testator in this case, to construe the word legacy to extend to land." The case of *Doe* d. *Tofield* v. *Tofield* (3), however, carries the principle as far, perhaps, as can be necessary for the decision of this, or, indeed, any other case. The only question was (as stated in the judgment delivered by the COURT) whether freehold lands passed under the words, "all my personal estates ; " and the Court had no hesitation in saying that the lands did *pass by that description. One only case (the excepted one before alluded to) we understood to be adduced, as in point, for the purpose of showing that, whatever may be the probable conjectures, the Court cannot

[*176]

[*177]

(1) 2 R. R. 691 (5 T. R. 716).   (3) 10 R. R. 496 (11 East, 246).
(2) 1 Burr. 268.

or, at least, ought not to infer that a fee passed to the wife in
this case, because the same inference has been before repudiated
under similar circumstances.   This case is *Piggot* v. *Penrice* (1).
We, however, are so far from thinking that it is in point, that
the manifest distinction between the cases, and even the reasoning of the LORD CHANCELLOR, seem clearly to lead to a conclusion
in favour of the lessor of the plaintiff.   The question in that
case arose, entirely, upon the following words : I make my niece
" executrix of all my goods, lands, and chattels ; " and it was
whether, under those words, any lands would pass.   Now, before
we refer to the reasons of the LORD CHANCELLOR, it is impossible
not to perceive the extreme dissimilarity between that case and
the present.   There the word " lands " is placed in the midst of
words strictly and legally referable to the character of executrix :
in the present case, no personalty is alluded to in the clause in
question, but the wife is made " sole and full executrix " (after a
bequest of the personalty) of a freehold house only.   The LORD
CHANCELLOR, in reasoning upon the case for the purpose of
showing that the heir could not, upon such uncertainty, be
disinherited, does not rest upon the effect of the word " lands "
being neutralised by its juxtaposition with personalty, but
proceeds to observe that the word " lands " was not to be rejected
as useless, for, probably, there might be rents in arrear of these
lands, and, by making her *executrix of her (testatrix's) lands,
those rents would pass.   Now, in this view of the case there was
no inference whatever to be drawn in favour of an intention that
land should pass.   Of course it furnishes no argument against
giving that effect to words which make that intention clear.

The word " executrix " happens to have received a sufficient
construction in two other cases.   In *Clements* v. *Cassye* (2) the
devise was of Blackacre and Whiteacre to the wife for life,
remainder in Blackacre to B. in fee, the remainder in Whiteacre
not being given over.   " Item, I make my wife executrix of all
my goods and lands."   But here the limited devise of land,
followed by the combination of land with goods, was justly
thought to negative the intention of devising the remainder in
Whiteacre to the wife.

(1) Prec. Chan. 471.   (2) Noy, 48.

In *Shaw* v. *Bull* (1) the testator, seised of five houses, devised four specifically to several persons, one of these four to his wife in fee, charged with legacies : finally, "all the overplus of my estate to be at my wife's disposal, and make her my executrix." The Court was divided in opinion ; NEVILL, J. thinking that a fee passed to the wife in the fifth house also. The Chief Justice TREVOR and POWELL and BLENCOWE, JJ. differed, not because the words were incapable of passing the fee, if the intent were clear, but because they thought the intent negatived by the other provisions.

The last case which we shall notice is that of *Thomas* v. *Phelps* (2), and we do so, partly because the testator had made nearly the same indiscriminate abuse of terms as in the present instance, and because the MASTER OF *THE ROLLS treats very lightly such abuse and confusion. In that case, the testator had given a certain lease to his son, James Phelps, and then added, "Him and my daughter Elizabeth Phelps I do make, constitute, and appoint my joint executor and executrix of this my will and testament, of all that I possess in any way belonging to me, by them freely to be enjoyed or possessed," "only my household furniture, which I give to my daughter who lives the longest single," &c. Upon this will, the argument was that, the gift being to an executrix, she can only take personal property, and, further, that, if the clause could pass a freehold, there were no words of limitation to carry it beyond a life estate. The MASTER OF THE ROLLS observed that it was the will of a person who had not the advantage of professional assistance, and was plainly ignorant of the nature and character of the office of executor, "and of the distinction between real and personal estate, as it regards that office." He then adverted to the words above set forth, and said that they were equivalent to a gift of all the testator's property, and would pass *all* the testator's interest in that estate.

[*179]

Upon the whole, we are of opinion that the intention of the testator clearly was to give to his wife, Ann Haslewood, the freehold of the house in question ; and, further, that the words

(1) 12 Mod. 593 ; *S. C.* 2 Eq. Ca.   (2) 28 R. R. 120 (4 Russ. 348).
Abr. 320, pl. 8,

in the will are sufficient to carry that intention into effect; and that no rule of law will be contravened by our giving judgment for the plaintiff.

Postea to plaintiff (1).

DOE D. JOHN PRATT AND ANOTHER *v.* WILLIAM PRATT AND OTHERS.

(6 Adol. & Ellis, 180—185; S. C. 1 N. & P. 366; 6 L. J. (N. S.) K. B. 101.)

> P. by his will directed that his debts and funeral expenses should be paid by his executor thereinafter named, and, after giving two life annuities of 2l. 10s. each, and a bequest of 5s. to J. P., his heir-at-law, he appointed W. P. his sole executor of his houses and land situate at F.:
> Held, that the houses and land at F. passed to W. P., and that he took an estate in fee.

THIS ejectment for messuages, lands, &c., at Flixton, Yorkshire, was tried before Parke, B., at the York Spring Assizes, 1835. The question was, whether John Pratt, the lessor of the plaintiff, was entitled as heir-at-law, or the defendant William Pratt, as devisee of Thomas Pratt, who died seised of the freehold and inheritance of the premises in 1833. By his will, dated August 30th, 1830, the said Thomas Pratt, being then seised in fee of the said premises, directed that all his debts and funeral expenses should be paid and discharged by his executor thereinafter named; and, after giving and devising to his sister Alice Hall an annuity for her life of 2l. 10s., and to his niece Ann Pratt an annuity for her life of 2l. 10s., and after giving to his nephew John Pratt the lessor of the plaintiff the sum of 5s., to be paid at the end of twelve months next after testator's decease, he added, "I appoint my nephew William Pratt my whole and sole executor of all my houses and land situate at Flixton, in the county of York." On the trial, *Piggot v. Penrice* (2) was cited for the plaintiff; and, on the authority of that case, the learned Judge directed a verdict for him, giving leave to move to enter a verdict for the defendant. A rule *nisi* was obtained accordingly; and, in Michaelmas Term last (3),

(1) See the next case.
(2) Prec. Chan. 471.
(3) November 17th. Before Lord

Denman, Ch. J., Patteson, Williams, and Coleridge, JJ,

Alexander and *Wightman* showed cause :

The words appointing William Pratt executor of all the testator's houses and land at Flixton cannot give the executor an interest in freehold lands ; the premises in question were therefore undisposed of by the will, and descended to the lessor of the plaintiff as heir. Words of devise are construed strictly in favour of the heir-at-law. As to the construction of these particular words, *Piggot* v. *Penrice* (1) is in point, and agrees with former decisions : *Clements* v. *Cassye* (2), *Rowse* v. *Stanning* (3). *Shaw* v. *Bull* (4) is to a similar effect, though the word " estate," there used, would now be held to pass the fee. Other authorities are collected in Com. Dig. Devise, (N. 3).

(COLERIDGE, J. mentioned *Doe* d. *Gillard* v. *Gillard* (5).)

There the will imposed charges on the executor, which could not be met unless the freehold in question was devised to him. Here it does not appear that any of the charges could affect the realty. The debts would be paid out of the personalty, so far as the assets would go ; but the executor would not be chargeable further. In *Doe* d. *Ashby* v. *Baines* (6) it was held that a devise of all the testator's lands, tenements, and messuages to his executrix, following a direction that she should pay his debts and funeral expenses, did not give her an estate in fee. The annuities here are not charged on the realty ; and an annuity out of personalty is only a general pecuniary legacy, the payment of which must depend upon the sufficiency of the personal

estate : *Hume* v. *Edwards* (7) ; with which *case *Davies* v. *Wattier* (8) is consistent in principle. The present annuities are simply left to the parties : there is not even a direction to the executor which might be construed as obliging him to pay them otherwise than in the ordinary course of administration. The gift of 5s. to the heir-at-law is not conclusive, if he is not

(1) Prec. Chan. 471.
(2) Noy, 48.
(3) 1 Roll. Abr. 613, Devise (N),
pl. 1.
(4) 12 Mod. 593 S. C. 2 Eq. Ca.

Abr. 320, pl. 8.
(5) 5 B. & Ald. 785.
(6) 2 Cr. M. & R. 23 ; 5 Tyr. 655.
(7) 3 Atk. 693.
(8) 1 Sim. & St. 463.

disinherited by the other clauses of the will: *Denn* d. *Gaskin* v. *Gaskin* (1). Where executors or trustees have been held to take the fee without express words for that purpose, it has been because the declared intent of the testator, as to some duty to be discharged by them, could not else have been accomplished. That was so in *Doe* d. *Gillard* v. *Gillard* (2), *Anthony* v. *Rees* (3), and *Loreacres* d. *Mudge* v. *Blight* (4) ; but is not so here.

(PATTESON, J.: According to your construction, no effect is given to the words " and land," in this will.)

The same objection was made, but did not prevail, in *Piggot* v. *Penrice* (5).

Cresswell and *Starkie*, contrà :

In *Rowse* v. *Stanning* (6) there was a lease for years which was held to satisfy the words of devise to the executors. No such fact appears here. In *Clements* v. *Cassye* (7) the testator devised Whiteacre and Blackacre to his wife for life, remainder over, as to Blackacre, in fee, and made his wife executrix of all his goods and lands; and it was held that the fee in Whiteacre did not pass to her. That case would have resembled the present, if he had made her executrix of all his goods, and of his lands called Whiteacre ; and *the result would probably have been in favour   [*183]
of the executrix. *Shaw* v. *Bull* (8) is contained in a book of bad authority, and the limited construction there of the word " estate " cannot now be supported. *Piggot* v. *Penrice* (5) does not show that the word "lands," used as it is here, will not pass a fee to the executor. "Lands" there occurred between the words " goods " and " chattels." And it has been doubted whether the construction in that case was not incorrect, as giving, in reality, no effect to the word " lands " (9). It is

(1) 2 Cowp. 657.
(2) 5 B. & Ald. 785.
(3) 37 R. R. 626 (2 Cr. & J. 75;
2 Tyr. 100).
(4) 1 Cowp. 352.
(5) Prec. Chan. 471.

(6) 1 Roll. Abr. 613, Devise (N),
pl. 1.
(7) Noy, 48.
(8) 12 Mod. 593.
(9) See 2 Powell on Devises, 173,
c. 10, s. 3, 3rd ed. by Jarman.

contended here that the debts are not charged upon the real estate ; but they are so, if the lands are left to the executor. There could be no doubt of this if the testator had said, " I make William Pratt executor of all my lands, and charge him to pay my debts ; " not providing any particular fund. The position of the clauses here cannot make a difference in that respect. In 2 Powell on Devises, after stating (p. 654) that, where the debts are directed to be paid by the executors, " unless land be devised to them, it will be presumed that the payment is to be made exclusively out of funds which by law devolve upon them in that character : " it is added (p. 657 (1)), " where, however, the executor is devisee of the real estate, a direction even to him (though describing him as such), to pay debts or legacies, will, it seems, cast them upon the realty ; " and *Awbrey* v. *Middleton* (2), and *Alcock* v. *Sparhawk* (3), are cited. The effect of a charge on the person of the devisee is discussed by the COURT in *Goodtitle* *d. *Paddy* v. *Maddern* (4). The amount of charge is not material. In the present case the debts are to be paid by the " executor hereinafter named ; " and William Pratt is named afterwards as " executor," specifically, " of all my houses and lands situate at Flixton ; " the charge being thus pointed to the very premises now in dispute. In *Thomas* v. *Phelps* (5) a devise appointing J. and E. " executor and executrix " " of all that I possess, in any way belonging to me, by them freely to be enjoyed or possessed, of whatsoever nature or manner it may be," was held to pass the fee. The words here used are not less distinct. *Doe* d. *Gillard* v. *Gillard* (6) is an authority for the defendant. The intention, which was relied upon there, is equally clear in the present case. The words there were " sole executor of all my lands for ever ; " but the last two words could not, at any rate, raise an important distinction, as the quantity of estate here would not affect the result of the cause.

[*184]

Cur. adv. vult.

(1) Ch. 34.
(2) 4 Vin. Abr. 460, Charge (D), pl. 15; *S. C.* 2 Eq. Ca. Abr. 497, pl. 16.
(3) 2 Vern. 228; *S. C.* 1 Eq. Ca.
Abr. 198, pl. 4.
(4) 4 East, 496.
(5) 28 R. R. 120 (4 Russ. 348).
(6) 5 B. & Ald. 785.

LORD DENMAN, Ch. J. now delivered the judgment of the COURT:

This was a motion by leave to enter a verdict for the defendant, as devisee of premises under a will, which, after directing all the testator's debts and funeral expenses to be paid by his executor, giving several annuities for life, and bequeathing five shillings to the plaintiff, who was his heir-at-law, concluded by appointing the defendant his whole and sole executor of all his houses and land, situate at Flixton.

We do not think it needful to go into the authorities *which have been so recently considered by the Court, in the case between *Hickman* v. *Haslewood* (1). It was admitted by the learned counsel for the plaintiff, and is perfectly clear, that, if the defendant took any interest, it must be a fee simple; and no man, applying common sense to the construction of the will, can doubt that the estate was given to the defendant. No decided case opposes any obstacle to our arriving at this conclusion; and the rule must be made absolute.

Rule absolute.

Doe d.
PRATT
v.
PRATT.

[*185]

BROWN, MANAGER OF THE AUSTRALIAN COMPANY, *v.* THORNTON (2).

(6 Adol. & Ellis, 185—193; S. C. 1 N. & P. 339; W. W. & D. 11; 6 L. J. (N. S.) K. B. 82.)

1837.
Jan. 16.

[185]

In Batavia, charter-parties are entered into by the instrument being written in the book of a notary (he being a public officer, according to the Dutch law, which prevails in Batavia) and there signed by the parties. The notary makes copies, which he signs and seals, and which the principal officer of the Government of Java signs, upon proof of their being executed by the notary. Then one copy is delivered to each party. In the Courts of Java, in order to prove the charter-party, it is requisite to produce the notary's book; but this book is never allowed to be taken out of Java; and, in Dutch Courts out of Java, faith is given to the above copies, as to an original.

Held, that, in English Courts, such copies are not receivable, either as originals or as secondary evidence of the charter-party. At all events, not without proof that they were made at the time of entering into the original charter-party, and in the presence of the parties.

ASSUMPSIT. The first count of the declaration (dated Michaelmas Term, 1 Will. IV.) stated that the defendants were indebted

(1) *Ante*, p. 445.
(2) 14 & 15 Vict. c. 99, s. 7, does

not seem to include a case of this kind.—F. P.

BROWN
v.
THORNTON.

[*186]

[*187]

to the Australian Company of Edinburgh (1) in 3,000l. for freight, in respect of the carriage of goods by the Company in the ship *Portland*. Promise to the plaintiff: breach, non-payment. The second count stated that the Company, on 25th September, 1825, were possessed of the ship *Portland*, then at Batavia; that on that day, at Batavia, a charter-party *was made by one William Phillips, as agent of the defendant, and Christopher Mood, master of the ship, on behalf of the Company. The charter-party was then set out, whereby (among other things) it was agreed that the Company should let, and the defendant take, the ship to freight; the port of discharge to be London or Antwerp, at defendant's option: the rate of freight was also specified in the charter-party, as set out in the declaration. The declaration alleged mutual promises, performance on the part of the plaintiff, lading of the ship by the defendant, and delivery of the cargo by a Mood, according to the defendant's order, at Antwerp. Breach, non-payment of freight to the plaintiff. The third count was like the first, except that the debt was stated to be to the plaintiff.

Plea, *Non assumpsit*.

On the trial before Lord Denman, Ch. J., at the London sittings after Trinity Term, 1835, it appeared that the defendant, in answer to a bill filed in Chancery, had admitted that he had ordered the cargo to be delivered at Antwerp, that it had been delivered accordingly, and that he was in possession of the bill of lading under which the goods were shipped, and of a copy of the alleged charter-party. Certain letters were produced, written by or to the defendant, referring to the chartering of the ship and the shipping of the goods; but no letter from the defendant stated the rate of freight. On the bill of lading being called for, it was produced by the defendant; and it stated that the goods were shipped by Robert Thornton, to be delivered unto Richard Thornton, Esq. (the defendant), or to his assigns, "he or they paying freight as per charter-party." To prove the charter-party (which the defendant had notice to produce), *the plaintiff put in a copy, not signed by the parties, under the notarial seal and signature of a person who was proved to be a notary at Batavia,

_____

(1) The Company sued in the name   5 Geo. IV. c. lxxi. (local and personal.
of the present plaintiff, under stat.   public).

and also under the signature of the acting Governor of Java. It BROWN
v.
THORNTON. was proved that, under the Code Civil, which, as constituting a part of the Dutch law (1), prevails in Batavia, the notary is a public officer, and that contracts of charter-party are entered into at Batavia by the contract being entered in the notary's book, and there signed by the parties; that the notary makes out two copies, which he signs and seals, and which are afterwards signed by the chief officer of the Government (the signature of the notary having been proved before him), and that one of these copies is delivered to each of the parties; that the copy now produced was such a copy, and that the seal and both signatures were genuine; that, in the Courts of Java, in order to prove the contract, the notary's book is produced, but that, in Dutch Courts out of Java, the copies so authenticated are received, and full faith given to them, as evidence of the original, which is not allowed to be taken out of the island. The defendant's counsel contended that the copy was not evidence; but his Lordship admitted it, giving leave to move for a nonsuit. Verdict for the defendant. In Michaelmas Term, 1835, *Cresswell* obtained a rule *nisi* for entering a nonsuit.

> *Sir J. Campbell*, Attorney-General, and *W. H. Watson*, now
> showed cause:

The contract is proved by the bill of lading, and by the admissions and correspondence: the charter-party is wanted only to show the amount of freight; at any rate, therefore, there must be nominal *damages, and there can be no nonsuit (2). [*188] But the copy of the charter-party was admissible. It is, properly speaking, an original. The evidence goes the length of showing that the notary is, according to the understanding at Batavia, the agent of both parties, not only to enter the contract, but to deliver copies to each: such copies are therefore in the nature of original documents, mutually delivered by the parties themselves. They resemble bought and sold notes. The plaintiff does not contend that the Dutch law of evidence is to be applied here, but

(1) See Code Civil, livr. iii. tit. iii. ch. vi., and especially s. 1, § iv.

(2) It was also argued that the answer in Chancery admitted the terms of the charter-party: but it appeared that the admission did not go to this extent.

that the meaning of the parties is to be collected from what they have done where the Dutch law prevails, and from the understanding which they must necessarily have had of the effect of their acts. This is as if the notary had been authorised to deliver these instruments by powers of attorney. That he also enters the contract in a book in the first instance, cannot alter this view of the case. *Appleton* v. *Lord Braybrook* (1) and *Black* v. *Lord Braybrook* (2) will be relied upon on the other side. There it was held that a judgment of the Supreme Court of Jamaica was not proved by a copy signed by the clerk of that Court, though it was proved that such copies were received as evidence in Jamaica. But there the copies were not under the seal of the Court: there was only the great seal of the island annexed to a certificate that C. was a notary public, and secretary of the island; and C.'s certificate to the identity of the clerk who signed the copy. That case shows only that the law

[*189]   of proof which prevails in a *foreign Court is not to supersede the English law of evidence in the Courts here: but this the plaintiff does not contend for. The interpretation of the act of the parties must be governed by the effect given to it at the place: the effect of all contracts depends upon the *lex loci*. The copy may also be received on the ground that the notary was a public officer, authorised to make it; instruments so made are receivable as acts of a public nature.

Cresswell, contrà :

The whole action depends on the contract; and, as it appears, from the references to the charter-party, that the specific terms of the contract are contained in that instrument, the plaintiff must be nonsuited unless he prove it. The original contract must be that which the parties signed, namely, that which was entered in the notary's book. These copies are not signed by the parties; they are not therefore in the nature of duplicate originals. When they were made does not appear. Then it is said that the parties have authorised the notary, as their agent, to confer upon this instrument the effect of an original. No

(1) 18 R. R. 294 (6 M. & S. 34;   (2) 6 M. & S. 39; 2 Stark. 7.
2 Stark. 6).

doubt this might be done by a power of attorney. But here, even adopting the argument on the other side, the parties have only authorised the notary to give to the instrument the effect which it would have by the Batavian law; and that effect is merely to make it evidence in Dutch Courts; for the Batavian law cannot make it evidence in English Courts. It might as well have been contended, in *Appleton* v. *Lord Braybrook* (1), and *Black* v. *Lord Braybrook* (2), *that the parties, by appearing in the Court at Jamaica, authorised the clerk to make copies of the judgment evidence all over the world. Those cases are in accordance with *Alves* v. *Bunbury* (3). Then it is argued that the instrument is receivable, because it appears that the notary is a public officer authorised to make such instruments. But that principle applies only where the instrument derives its validity from its being the act of the officer; and then the instrument proves only that of which the validity depends upon the act. Thus the indorsement of the date of enrolment of a bargain and sale, by the clerk of the enrolments, is a record, and conclusive as to the date (4). So the chirograph of a fine is evidence of a fine, because the chirographer is the proper officer to give out copies: the fine is not complete without the chirograph (5): but the proclamations are not proved by the chirograph (6), because the chirographer is not appointed to copy the proclamations.

(*R. V. Richards*, on the same side, was stopped by the COURT.)

LORD DENMAN, Ch. J.:

It is clear that the plaintiff cannot recover, unless the contract be proved. Now the contract for freight refers to the charter-party; and so does all the evidence which is produced. The charter-party, therefore, is necessarily connected with the other evidence, and must be proved. The original charter-party is that signed by the parties in the notary's book. The notary has

BROWN
v.
THORNTON.

[*190]

(1) 18 R. R. 294 (6 M. & S. 34; 2 Stark. 6).

(2) 6 M. & S. 39; 2 Stark. 7.

(3) 4 Camp. 28.

(4) *Rex* v. *Hopper*, 18 R. R. 641 (3 Price, 495).

(5) See *Newis* v. *Lark*, or *Scolastica's* case, Plowd. 410.

(6) See MANSFIELD, Ch. J., in *Waldron*.v. *Coombe*, 12 R. R. 629 (3 Taunt. 162, 166; Bull. N. P. 229, 230).

the privilege of giving out the copies. To *these copies full faith is given in Dutch Courts, but not to the exclusion of the original; for at Java, where the original book is, it must be produced. But, at Rotterdam, full faith is given to the copies. That, however, is very different from saying that the copies, even by the Dutch law, are binding evidence in general: they constitute perfect evidence only in the places where the original cannot be procured. At the trial I thought that the evidence might be admitted; and I should be glad if I could think so still. It is said that the officer is an agent authorised by both parties to give the copies. If these copies were identified as copies taken at the time when the original was entered in the notary's book, that might possibly be so; but here we have no proof that the copies were not taken six months after. There is, therefore, nothing to give the copies the weight of evidence, except the Dutch law; and, as was decided in *Appleton* v. *Lord Braybrook* (1), and *Black* v. *Lord Braybrook* (2), we cannot here adopt a rule of evidence from foreign Courts. *Mr. Cresswell* drew a proper distinction between the consent of the parties as to the effect of the copy in the Dutch Courts, and as to its effect elsewhere. The rule must be made absolute.

WILLIAMS, J. (3) :

I am compelled, not very willingly, to adopt the same opinion. I was a good deal struck with the argument that the notary, in giving out the copies, acts as the agent of both parties. But, upon consideration, I think it impossible to adopt that argument :

the parties go before the notary in compliance *with the custom, or if you please with the law, of the country where the transaction takes place : but they enter into no agreement to give to the document a validity or construction which it would not be entitled to from its own nature. It is impossible not to see that the entry in the notary's book is the original. The question, therefore, is, whether it be authenticated according to our law. The plaintiff did not show that, by the law of Batavia, any

(1) 18 R. R. 294 (6 M. & S. 34;   (3) Littledale, J. was absent, on
2 Stark. 6).   account of indisposition.
(2) 6 M. & S. 39; 2 Stark. 7.

person had an authority to give out copies, analogous to the BROWN
v.
THORNTON. authority that is given where office copies are admissible in England. In Buller's Nisi Prius (1) it is said, with reference to an office copy, " Here a difference is to be taken between a copy authenticated by a person trusted for that purpose, for there that copy is evidence without proof; and a copy given out by an officer of the Court, who is not trusted for that purpose, which is not evidence without proving it actually examined. The reason of the difference is, that where the law has appointed any person for any purpose, the law must trust him as far as he acts under its authority; therefore the chirograph of a fine is evidence of such fine, because the chirographer is appointed to give out copies of the agreements between the parties that are lodged of record." But it is added, " Where the fine is to be proved with proclamations (as it must be to bar a stranger), the proclamations must be examined with the roll, for the chirographer is authorised by the common law to make out copies to the parties of the fine itself, yet is not appointed by the statutes to copy the proclamations, and therefore his indorsement on the back of the fine is not binding." The *Attorney-General* *contends that the other [*193] evidence is sufficient without the charter-party : but I think that proof of the charter-party is a necessary foundation for all the other evidence that has been given.

COLERIDGE, J. :

The plaintiff could not maintain the action without some evidence of the charter-party. The question, therefore, is merely one of evidence, and must be decided by the law of this country, although the transaction took place in a foreign one. The general rule here I need not state : the question is, whether it be satisfied. It is argued that this is not a copy, but an original. That certainly would make out the plaintiff's case to the full extent; but I think that it is not the fact. An entry is made in the notary's book, which the parties sign. After that, the notary gives out copies : it does not appear when ; nor whether this is done in the presence of the parties. It is clear that the entry in the notary's book is the original contract; and that is not

(1) P. 229.

produced. It is not denied that secondary evidence might be
given ; but has that been done ? There were two ways of giving
it. First, a copy by the public officer of a court, employed for
that purpose, might be produced, which is not done here ; or,
secondly, copies might be produced made by some person
authorised by the parties to give copies which should bind each.
We cannot go beyond this. But what the parties have done
here can have merely the effect attributable to it by the law
prevailing in the country where the transaction took place.

Rule absolute.

———————

DOE D. GRATREX AND HOFFMAN *v.* HOMFRAY.

(6 Adol. & Ellis, 206—209 ; S. C. 1 N. & P. 401 ; 6 L. J. (N. S.) K. B. 132.)

Devisor, being seised in fee of land, devised it " to the uses hereinafter
declared ; that is to say, to the use and intent that D. shall receive and
take the rents, &c., and pay the same to J. for the term of his natural
life ; and, after J.'s decease, I give and devise the same premises to the
heirs of the body of J. ; and, in default of such issue, I give and devise
the same premises to C. and the heirs of her body ; and, in default of
such heirs, I give and devise the same " to K. in fee :

Held, that a legal estate passed to D., the trustee, though there was
no direct devise to him, and though there were no trustees to preserve
contingent remainders.

EJECTMENT for messuages and land in Brecknockshire. On the
trial before Patteson, J., at the Brecknockshire Summer Assizes,
1835, the following facts appeared :

John Jones, being seised in fee of the premises in question,
made his will, dated 13th of July, 1825, which contained the
following clause : " I give and devise all those my freehold
messuages, farms, and lands, with their respective appurtenances,
called " &c. (not the premises in question), " unto my said son,
James Jones, to hold unto my said son, James Jones, his heirs
and assigns, for ever. Also all other my freehold estates,
situated " &c. (including the premises in question), " with their
respective appurtenances thereunto belonging, and every part
thereof, to the uses hereinafter declared and expressed concerning
the same ; that is to say, to the use and intent that the Rev.
Richard Davies, Archdeacon of Brecon, and Walter Lewis, of
Trevecca in the said county of Brecon, minister of the gospel,

their executors and administrators, or the executors or administrators of the survivors of them, shall and may receive and take the rents, issues, and profits of the above-mentioned estates, and pay the same to my said son, James Jones, for and during the term of his natural life; and, from and immediately after the decease of my said son, James Jones, then I give and devise the same premises, and every part thereof, to the heirs of the body *of my said son, James Jones, lawfully to be begotten; and, in default of such issue, then I give and devise the same premises, and every part thereof, to my daughter, Catherine Jones, and the heirs of her body lawfully begotten; and, in default of such heirs, then I give and devise the same " to another son, John Jones, in fee.

[*207]

The devisor died in 1826; and afterwards, in the same year, Archdeacon Davies, the trustee, executed a deed of renunciation. A suit in Chancery was afterwards instituted to change trustees and the estates devised to the trustees were duly conveyed, in 1833, to the lessors of the plaintiff, by Walter Lewis. The learned Judge, being of opinion that the will gave a legal estate to the trustees, directed a verdict for the plaintiff, reserving leave to the defendant to move for a nonsuit. In Michaelmas Term, 1835, *Evans* obtained a rule accordingly.

Chilton and *E. V. Williams* now showed cause (1):

It is clear that some legal estate is given to the trustees; and that is sufficient to entitle the plaintiff to a verdict. The rule is that, where land is given to a trustee, in trust to permit the cestui que trust to take the rents, that is a legal use executed in the cestui que trust; but that, if the land be given to the trustee, in trust to receive the rents and pay them over to the cestui que trust, the trustee has the legal estate, because otherwise he cannot perform the trust. This distinction appears from *Doe d. Leicester* v. *Biggs* (2). There the will directed the trustee to pay to, or permit the cestui que trust to take, the rents: and *it was held that the legal estate passed to the cestui que trust,

[*208]

(1) Before Lord Denman, Ch. J., and Williams, J. Littledale and Coleridge, JJ. were absent on account of indisposition.

(2) 11 R. R. 533 (2 Taunt. 109).

because the word "permit" came after the word "pay," and must therefore, in a will, prevail. If the order had been inverted, the trustee, as appears by the judgment, would have had the legal estate. The rule was taken for granted in *Garth* v. *Baldwin* (1). The same principle was admitted in *Robinson* v. *Grey* (2), where *Jones* v. *Lord Say and Sele* (3) was cited. The cases are collected in note (17) to *Jeffreson* v. *Morton* (4). If the intention be collected from other parts of the devise, this construction is strengthened; for, in the commencement, a different property is given to the first cestui que trust.

Evans, contrà :

The distinction is as suggested on the other side; but it does not apply to the present case, because here is no devise to the trustees at all. And, further, there is no estate in the trustees to preserve contingent remainders. Immediately on the death of James Jones, the estate goes over to the heirs of his body; so that no purpose of the will is effected by giving to the trustees a legal estate. The defendant does not deny that the trustees must take such an estate as will enable them to effect the purposes of the will.

Cur. adv. vult.

Lord Denman, Ch. J., on a subsequent day of this Term (January 23rd), delivered the judgment of the Court :

It is enough to say that, on the argument of this case before my brother Williams and myself, we thought that it fell within the numerous class where it has been *held that a devise to trustees to pay over the rents vests the estate in such trustees.

That the devise is not directly to the trustees, but " to the use and intent that they may receive " &c., appears to us to make no difference; nor the absence of a devise to trustees to preserve contingent remainders.

It was observed that the will required nothing to be done by the trustees; and it is true that nothing is to be done beyond

[*209]

(1) 2 Ves. Sen. 646.
(2) 9 East, 1.
(3) 8 Vin. Abr. 262, Devise (C. b),
pl. 19.
(4) 2 Wms. Saund. 11 b.

paying: but this has been held sufficient, and must be taken to be the present law; *Doe* d. *Leicester* v. *Biggs* (1). My brother PATTESON was of this opinion on the trial, and, on consideration, retains it. The rule for a nonsuit must, therefore, be discharged.

Rule discharged.

DOE D. REED *v.* ALICE HARRIS (2).

(6 Adol. & Ellis, 209—218; S. C. 1 N. & P. 405; 6 L. J. (N. S.) K. B. 84.)

Under the Statute of Frauds, 29 Car. II. c. 3, s. 6 (see now the Wills Act, 1837, 1 Vict. c. 26, sect. 20), a will of freehold is not legally revoked, if the testator, intending to destroy it, throws it on the fire, and another person snatches it off, a corner of the envelope only being burnt; and such person afterwards, being urged by the testator to give up the will, promises to burn it, and pretends to have done so.

The cancellation of a will, under s. 6 of the Statute of Frauds, may be proved in any manner consistent with the general law of evidence, the statute not introducing any new rule of proof. The defacing of it, therefore, may be shown by proving the declaration of any person whose assertion would be evidence against the party setting up the will; and it is not necessary that the will, if produced, should bear visible marks of having been defaced.

EJECTMENT for messuages and other premises. On the trial before Patteson, J., at the Glamorganshire Summer Assizes, 1835, it appeared that the lessor of the plaintiff claimed as son and heir-at-law, the defendant as devisee, of John Reed. The will was duly executed in August, 1832. The testator died December 31st, 1834. *He was an old and infirm man: the defendant was his niece, and lived with him as his housekeeper. She exercised great influence over him; but it appeared that they had violent quarrels, and that he sometimes spoke of her to other persons in very abusive terms, and said that he feared danger to his life from her. A witness named Esther Treharne, who had been the testator's servant, stated that, about a month before he died, she was shaking up the cushion of his easy-chair, and observed, under the cushion, a folded paper. It was brown or cartridge paper, and the corner of it was burnt. Shortly after, on the same day, Alice Harris went out; and, while she

[*210]

(1) 11 R. R. 533 (2 Taunt. 109).   P. D. 251, 253, 46 L. J. P. D & A.
(2) See on parallel question, *In re*   66.—R. C.
Harris, Cheese v. *Lovejoy* (1877) 2

was away, the testator inquired for the paper: the witness told
him where she had seen it, upon which he exclaimed that Alice
had gone away with the will; and, on his then removing the
cushion, the will appeared no longer. He then told the witness
that he had sent Alice Harris to fetch the will to him, that he
had looked into it, and that, when he had seen it, he had thrown
it on the fire; and that Alice had "scramped" it off the fire.
This appeared to have taken place the evening before. After
the above conversation, Alice Harris returned; and, when she
and the testator retired at night (both sleeping in the same
room), the witness heard a quarrel, and blows; and, upon her
going into the room, the testator said that Alice Harris would
not give him his will. Alice went down stairs with the witness,
and the latter urged her to give up the will; but she said she
would not; that she had given it him last night, and he threw
it on the fire; and that she would rather have the pleasure
of burning it herself, and would do so the next morning. After
this conversation she returned to the testator, on the witness's
persuasion, begged his pardon, and promised to burn the will
[*211] the following morning. The *next morning, the witness, going
into the kitchen where Alice and the testator were, heard Alice
say, "There, every thing is finished;" and the testator then told
the witness that Alice had thrown the will upon the fire. The
witness doubting it, he said, "She threw something with writing
upon it on the fire; but I did not have it in my hand to look at
t." The witness answered, "I do not think she has thrown it;"
and the testator said, "I do not care; I will go to Lantwit, if I
am alive and well, and make another will;" adding that Alice
Harris should not have his property, and that he had a son
nearer to him than her. He also said (as he did on many other
occasions) that the will was one made by Alice and Mr. R. (the
attorney who prepared it), and that R. was a thief, and wanted,
with Alice, to get every thing he had. Alice Harris, in an
affidavit exhibited in the Prerogative Court, stated that, on
January 1st, 1835, she found the will in a trunk used by the
testator for holding his deeds and papers, and kept in his
dressing-room. The will produced on the trial had no mark of
fire. It did not appear that any envelope had been found upon

it. The plaintiff's counsel contended, first, that the testator had been prevailed upon to execute the will by importunities of such a nature as to deprive him of his free agency; and, secondly, that, assuming the will to have been properly executed, the evidence showed a cancellation within the Statute of Frauds, 29 Car. II. c. 3, s. 6. The learned Judge stated to the jury, on the latter point, that, if they believed the evidence of Esther Treharne, and were satisfied that the testator threw the will on the fire intending to burn it, that Alice Harris took it off against his will, that he afterwards insisted on its being thrown on the fire again, with intent that it should be burnt, and *that she then promised to burn it, there was a sufficient cancellation within the statute. The jury found for the plaintiff, not stating the grounds of their verdict. In the ensuing Term a rule *nisi* was obtained for a new trial, on account of mis-direction on the two points above stated. It was also objected that the evidence of cancellation was not of a proper kind; the fact being proved only by declarations, and not by the testimony of eyewitnesses, or by marks of cancellation on the will itself; and *Willis* v. *Newham* (1) was referred to as an analogous case.

[*212]

Chilton and *James* now showed cause:

(The COURT desired them to direct their attention to the point of cancellation, since it could not be assumed that the jury had left that part of the case out of consideration in giving their verdict; and, if the verdict was not sustainable upon that, there must be a new trial.)

The revocation of this will was complete. The facts proved are as conclusive as those in *Bibb* d. *Mole* v. *Thomas* (2), where the will was held to be effectually cancelled. No reference appears to have been made there to the mode of proof; nor does the statute, among the alterations which it introduces, make any in this respect. It is true that, in *Willis* v. *Newham* (1), the Court of Exchequer held that a verbal acknowledgment of having paid interest was not an answer to the Statute of Limitations within Lord Tenterden's Act, 9 Geo. IV. c. 14. But the judgment

(1) 3 Y. & J. 518. [Overruled, L. J. Ex. 238.]
Cleave v. *Jones* (1851) 6 Ex. 573, 20   (2) 2 W. Bl. 1043.

in that case proceeded on a comparative view of the enacting clause and the proviso under discussion in the particular statute ; and the fact proved was no more than an acknowledgment of an acknowledgment, payment of *interest amounting itself to no more than an acknowledgment. And in *Haydon* v. *Williams* (1) it was held that, where a written promise, sufficient to bar the statute, had been given and lost, oral evidence of the contents might be given, as in the case of other written instruments. An oral report of something said might, in a case like the present, be within the mischief provided against by the statute ; but not so the statement of an act done. The declaration of the defendant herself as to what she witnessed was, at all events, evidence. Nor can it be a necessary ingredient in the proof that the will should exhibit marks of cancellation to the eye. If it had been obliterated with ink, and the ink removed by a chemical process, or if it had been torn to pieces and joined together again, so that the tearing was imperceptible, there would still be a sufficient cancellation.

(WILLIAMS, J. : No doubt there would.

PATTESON, J. : In such a case the act would have been perfect at one time.

LORD DENMAN, Ch. J. : I think it is not doubtful that the evidence of cancellation may be of any description ; but what we wish to see here is that the evidence makes out the fact of cancellation.)

In *Bibb* d. *Mole* v. *Thomas* (2) the language of the COURT is, " Revocation is an act of the mind, which must be demonstrated by some outward and visible sign or symbol of revocation. The statute has specified four of these ; and if these or any of them are performed in the slightest manner, this, joined with the declared intent, will be a good revocation. It is not necessary that the will, or instrument itself, be totally destroyed or consumed, burnt, or torn to pieces." " Throwing it on the fire, with an intent to burn, though it is only very slightly *singed

[*214]

(1) 33 R. R. 415 (7 Bing. 163).   (2) 2 W. Bl. 1043.

and falls off, is sufficient within the statute." It is enough
therefore, in this case, that the packet containing the will was
thrown on the fire with intent to revoke, and the envelope partly
burnt or singed. The outward sign of an intended revocation
is all that the statute requires. It cannot be necessary that the
written part of the will should have received the marks of fire ;
nor is it of any importance whether those marks were made on
the envelope or on the outside sheet, or whether they were of
greater or less extent. If it be so, where is the line to be drawn ?

(COLERIDGE, J. : You contend that singeing the envelope with
intent to revoke is " burning " the will within the words of the
statute.)

In *Doe* d. *Perkes* v. *Perkes* (1), where the doctrine of *Bibb*
d. *Mole* v. *Thomas* (2) was recognised, the COURT considered
the question to be, whether the testator had accomplished his
intention of cancelling as far as lay in him, or had been stopped,
and desisted from his purpose. Applying that test here, the
testator had done all in his power to burn the will, and never
changed his purpose : the entire burning was prevented merely
by the fraud of another person.

(PATTESON, J. : Is not it the same, in effect, as if he had been
struggling to throw the will into the fire, but some one had held
him back ?)

John Evans and *E. V. Williams, contrà*, were stopped by
the COURT.

LORD DENMAN, Ch. J. :

The Statute of Frauds requires that a will shall be executed
with certain solemnities ; and, after prescribing these, directs
how it shall be revoked ; and that is by certain acts, which are
specified. *In the present case, there is no evidence that any   [*215]
one of those acts has been done. It is impossible to say that
singeing a cover is burning a will within the meaning of the
statute. The terms used in the sixth section show that to assert
this would be going a length not contemplated in the statute.

(1) 22 R. R. 458 (3 B. & Ald. 489).   (2) 2 W. Bl. 1043.

The acts required are palpable and visible ones. Cases may, indeed, be put where very little has been done, as a slight tearing and burning, and yet a revocation has taken place; but the main current of the statute is against the argument from such cases. The intention seems to have been to prevent inferences being drawn from such slight circumstances. In *Bibb* d. *Mole* v. *Thomas* (1) the will was slightly torn and slightly burnt: and the COURT said that the case fell within two of the specific acts described by the statute; there was both a burning and a tearing. Doubt might be entertained now whether the proof there given would be sufficient as to these; but, as the COURT considered what was done to have been a burning and a tearing, the case shows at least that they did not think the acts required by the statute could be dispensed with by reason of the conduct of a third party. In *Doe* d. *Perkes* v. *Perkes* (2) the testator's hand was arrested while he was in the act of tearing the will: he submitted to the interference; and the intention of revoking was itself revoked before the act was complete. There it was properly left to the jury to say whether the testator had done all he intended or not. Neither of these cases at all approaches the present. It would be a violence to language, if we said here that there was any evidence to go to the jury of the will having
[*216] *been burnt. Great inconvenience would be introduced by holding that there may be a virtual compliance with the statute; but there is none in saying that, if a testator perseveres in the intention of revoking his will, he shall fulfil it by some of the means pointed out in the statute; that he shall revoke the will, if not in his possession, by writing properly attested; or cancel it, if in his power, by some of the other acts which the statute prescribes.

PATTESON, J.:

I am quite satisfied that I left this case wrongly to the jury. I did not see the distinction between the present case and *Bibb* d. *Mole* v. *Thomas* (1), as I ought. There something had been done which the Court considered to be a burning and a tearing of the will. The testator is described, not as having merely done

(1) 2 W. Bl. 1043.　　　　(2) 22 R. R. 458 (3 B. & Ald. 489).

something to the corner of the will, but as having given it "something of a rip with his hands," and so torn it "as almost to tear a bit off." It is plain that, on the production of the instrument, it would appear (though I do not think that important) that there had been some tearing of the will itself. As the Act says that there must be a tearing or burning of the instrument itself, a mere singeing of the corner of an envelope is not sufficient. To hold that it was so would be saying that a strong intention to burn was a burning. There must be, at all events, a partial burning of the instrument itself: I do not say that a quantity of words must be burnt; but there must be a burning of the paper on which the will is. I am quite satisfied that I was wrong in my direction to the jury.

WILLIAMS, J.:

We must give effect to a statute as providing for cases of ordinary occurrence, and not for any that may be put. It is argued that, if a testator throws his will on the fire with the intention of destroying it, and some one, without his knowledge, takes it away, that is a fraud which ought not to defeat his act. But so it might be said that, if the testator sent a person to throw it on the fire, and he did not, the revocation was still good. Where would such constructions end? The effect of them would be to defeat the object of the statute, which was to prevent the proof of a cancellation from depending on parol evidence. The will must be torn or burnt; and the question will always be whether that was done with intention to cancel: how much should be burnt, or whether the will should be torn into more or fewer pieces, it is not necessary to lay down.

COLERIDGE, J.:

The kind of construction which has been insisted upon would lead to a repeal of the statute on this subject, step by step. The statute, for wise purposes, does not leave the fact of cancellation to depend on mere intent, but requires definite acts. In the making of a will, if the proper signatures were not affixed, no explanation of the want of signatures could be received; and so, when a will has been made, to revoke it, there must be some act

Dom d.
REED
v.
HARRIS.

coupled with the intention of revoking, to bring the case within the sixth section. The question is put, whether the will must be destroyed wholly, or to what extent? It is hardly necessary to say : but there must be such an injury with intent to revoke as destroys the entirety of the will ; because it may then be said

[*218]

that the instrument no longer exists as it was. *Here the fire never touched the will. It can only be said that the testator's intention to cancel was defeated by the fraud of another party. But, to instance another case under the same clause of the statute, suppose the testator had written his revocation, and that, by the act of some other party, he had been prevented from signing, or the witnesses had been prevented from attesting it ; could it be said that the testator had done all that lay in him, and therefore the act of revocation was complete? We must proceed on such a view of the statute as accords with common sense.

Rule absolute (1).

———————•———————

1837.
Jan. 27.
———
[339]

REX *v*. THE MAYOR, ALDERMEN, AND BURGESSES OF THE BOROUGH OF BRIDGEWATER (2).

(6 Adol. & Ellis, 339—348 ; S. C. 1 N. & P. 466 ; 6 L. J. (N. S.) M. C. 78.)

Before and until the Corporation Act (5 & 6 Will. IV. c. 76)(3) T. was common clerk, prothonotary, and clerk of the peace of the borough of B. during good behaviour ; and acted as clerk to the justices of the borough, as by usage the common clerk had always done, either, as T. alleged, incidentally to the office of common clerk, or, as was alleged in answer, by appointment of the justices ; the office of clerk to the justices not being mentioned in the charters or muniments. After the Act passed he was appointed town clerk ; and afterwards, upon a separate commission of the peace being granted to the borough, another person was appointed clerk to the justices, by the justices under that commission :

Held, that T. was entitled to compensation under sect. 66, for the loss of the emolument derived from the place of clerk to the justices.

Although, after the appointment of the new clerk to the justices,

(1) In a subsequent case between the same parties, upon nearly the same evidence, it was decided (Hil. T. 1838, 8 Ad. & El. 1) that the will was revoked as to copyhold lands. [But that decision is of no importance in regard to wills coming under the Act of 1837.—R. C.]

(2) Cited in judgment of the COURT in *R.* v. *Local Government Board* (1874) L. R. 9 Q. B. 148, 151, 43 L. J. Q. B. 49, 51.—R. C.

(3) Repealed by Municipal Corporations Act, 1882 (45 & 46 Vict. c. 50).—R. C.

a Court of Quarter Sessions was granted to the borough, and T. was appointed clerk of the peace.

Semble, that, if the Lords Commissioners of the Treasury order compensation to a party not holding an office which falls within sect. 66, this Court will not enforce the order by *mandamus* to the corporation.

But they will grant such *mandamus* where the Lords Commissioners have ordered compensation to a party holding such an office.

SIR *W. W. FOLLETT* had obtained a rule in this Term, calling upon the mayor, aldermen, and burgesses of the borough of Bridgewater to show cause why a *mandamus* should not issue, commanding them to prepare and execute a bond under the common seal of the borough, conditioned for the payment to John Trevor of the yearly sum of 101*l.* 2*s.* 4*d.*, the first of such yearly payments to be made on the 15th of February next.

The rule was obtained upon Trevor's affidavit to the following effect. On the 1st August, 1833, he was duly elected and sworn common clerk, prothonotary, and clerk of the peace of the borough of Bridgewater, under the charters of the borough, and entered upon the *office, and undertook its duties. The office of clerk to the justices of the borough was incident and appurtenant to this office, and had been usually held in conjunction therewith and attached thereto; and the average of the annual emoluments of the office of clerk to the justices, for five years, was 152*l.* 8*s.* 8*d.* Trevor continued to hold all the offices till 26th December, 1835, when a new town council was elected, under stat. 5 & 6 Will. IV. c. 76. On 1st January, 1836, he was appointed town clerk. On 22nd January, 1836, a separate commission of the peace for the borough was granted to four persons. On 15th February, 1836, another person was appointed clerk to the justices, and he always acted afterwards, Trevor having performed the duty up to that time. On 27th February, 1836, Trevor delivered to the treasurer of the borough a statement of his claim for compensation for the loss of the office of clerk to the justices; wherein he alleged that, before the passing of the Act, he was entitled to, and received, all the emoluments of the office; which office he stated himself to be entitled, under the ancient charters of the borough and parish, to hold during good behaviour: and he claimed 1,923*l.* 13*s.*, as being the price of a Government annuity of 101*l.* 12*s.* 4*d.* for his life. The

[*840]

town council appointed a committee to examine into the claim ;
and, on their report, disallowed it entirely, by a resolution,
stating, as the grounds, "it not having been a borough office,
the claimant never having been appointed to such an office, and,
even if he had, that a clerk to justices has no legal hold upon
his office, as he is only acting to assist the justices during
pleasure." Trevor appealed to the Lords Commissioners of the

[*341]

Treasury, who ordered and determined that he was *entitled to
101*l.* 12*s.* 4*d.* per annum for his life; upon which he demanded,
by letter to the mayor, a bond for that sum to be paid to him
out of the borough fund for his life. The town council referred
the matter to a committee ; and Trevor afterwards, by letter
to the mayor and town council, again demanded the bond,
threatening legal proceedings in case of their refusal to execute
and deliver it before the first day of Hilary Term, 1837 ; and
afterwards, by another letter to the then town clerk, tendered a
bond for execution. The town council sent in a memorial to the
Lords Commissioners, praying them to rescind their former
order ; but they adhered to it, stating, as the reason, that
Trevor had been deprived of his office by the operation of the
Municipal Corporation Act. The town council, however, took
no steps in the matter.

The present town clerk of the borough (Trevor having been
displaced from that office, on 30th July, 1836, before he applied
for the rule) made affidavit, in answer, that, to the best of his
knowledge and belief, and so far as he had been able to ascertain
by a careful inspection of the charters or other muniments of
the corporation, or otherwise, no mention was made therein of
any such office as clerk to the justices of the borough ; that,
although, as he believed, the duties of clerk to the justices were
performed by the town clerk or common clerk of the borough,
yet the appointment was derived from the justices only, and not
from the corporation : that Trevor was appointed clerk of the
peace in 1833, and continued to fill that office till 1st May, 1836,
when it became extinct, by stat. 5 & 6 Will. IV. c. 76, s. 107 :
that the town council, elected under the provisions of the Act,

[*342]

petitioned for and obtained a commission for holding a *separate
Court of Quarter Sessions ; and that, in June, 1836, the town

council re-appointed Trevor clerk of the peace, which office he had held ever since.

REX
v.
THE
MAYOR,
OF BRID
WATE

[346

[After argument :]

LORD DENMAN, Ch. J. :

The whole question is, whether this applicant has been deprived of a beneficial corporate office by the operation of the Act. We are not to put too close a construction on the word " office." The affidavit of Trevor states that he held the office of clerk to the justices as incident and appurtenant to the office of town clerk, and received the emoluments. I am of opinion, therefore, that he was entitled to compensation; and that the Lords Commissioners had jurisdiction. It is true that, at the time he presented the memorial upon which the Lords of the Treasury have adjudicated, Mr. Trevor was still town clerk; and it is argued that, if the office of clerk to the justices be incident to that of town clerk, he continued to hold the former office as long as he was town clerk. But the statute comes in, and destroys the incident. By means of the statute, therefore, Trevor has *lost the office which he held in conjunction with that of town clerk; and, this being the case, the Lords Commissioners had jurisdiction as to the amount of compensation. I do not say that, if this Court saw the office in question not to be a borough office, they would enforce the compensation granted by the Lords Commissioners. I rather think that they would not.

[*347

WILLIAMS, J. (1) :

I am of the same opinion. This may, in some sense, possibly be considered as no office; but not in the sense used in the Act. The effect of the sixty-sixth section, especially that part of it in which the party claiming is directed to distinguish " the office, place, situation, employment, or appointment," seems to be, that a reasonable interpretation is to be given, and that the word " office " must be understood in a greater latitude than an office strictly legal. Then it becomes a question merely whether, by the Act, this gentleman lost perquisites and emoluments

(1) Littledale, J. was absent.

which were previously attached.   Now it is clear that, as common clerk of the borough, he was *ipso facto* clerk to the justices.   The case *Ex parte Sandys* (1) did not turn upon an Act of Parliament.   Here the statute gives compensation to any party holding " any office of profit."   The Lords Commissioners had therefore jurisdiction.

COLERIDGE, J.:

It seems to me that the *Attorney-General* was right in putting his objection on the ground that the order of the Lords Commissioners was a nullity; for, if it be not so, it is final.   If facts were made out which would render it a nullity, I should hesitate [*348]   long *before I agreed that they could give themselves jurisdiction. It seems a condition precedent to their having jurisdiction, that the party applying should have held an office : and perhaps they cannot decide whether he did or not.   But I think that this was an office, in the strictest sense.   Trevor was an officer before the Act : the town clerk is named in the charter ; and this office seems to have been held during good behaviour : it is abolished by the Act; and 'the present office of town clerk is totally new. Suppose Trevor had never taken the new office, would he not have had compensation ?   No doubt he would.   Then what would have been the measure of the compensation ?   He would have said, I was common clerk, and did the duties of that office ; and, as such clerk, by the usage of the borough, I did other duties, for which I received fees.   He would then have had compensation for all.   But, as he is appointed town clerk afterwards, the compensation is limited to those emoluments which were received for duties subordinate and incidental to the old office.   There is, then, a claim in respect of an office, in the strictest sense.   But, again, I agree with the rest of the Court that it is not necessary that there should be an office, strictly speaking.   Looking at the words of sect. 102, where the words are " office of clerk to the justices," it is clear that the word is not used there in the strict sense in which we find it employed in our law books, but in the general and liberal sense of a place to which duties and profits are attached.   *Rule absolute.*

(1) 4 B. & Ad. 863.

REX *v.* The MAYOR, ALDERMEN, and BURGESSES of the CITY and BOROUGH of OXFORD.

[6 Adol. & Ellis, 349—354 ; S. C. 1 N. & P. 474 ; 6 L. J. (N. S.) K. B. 103.)

If a councillor of a corporation be ousted, and another elected in his stead, and such election be merely colourable, a *mandamus* will go to permit the ousted party to exercise his office, but not to restore him to his office.

If such ouster and election be *bonâ fide*, the Court will not grant a *mandamus* in favour of the party displaced : the proper proceeding is by *quo warranto* against the party holding the office *de facto.*

Quære, whether, if a party be elected a councillor, and duly qualified at the time of his election, and his name be afterwards improperly omitted in the burgess-list before his time of service as a councillor is expired, such omission vacate the office of councillor.

BINGHAM had obtained a rule in this Term, calling upon the mayor, aldermen, and burgesses of the city and borough of Oxford to show cause why a *mandamus* should not issue, directing them to restore John Towle to the place and office of a councillor of the said city and borough. The facts were as follows. In January, 1836, Towle was elected a councillor for the south ward of the corporation, which, by schedule (A) of stat. 5 & 6 Will. IV. c. 76 (1), has five wards and thirty councillors. Towle had duly subscribed a declaration of his acceptance, and of his qualification, and had acted ; and he alleged that he was entitled to remain in the office till 1st of November, 1837. On the 28th of October, 1836, Mr. Butler, the then mayor, affixed to the church-door of St. Mary's, Oxford, a notice that there was an additional vacancy of a town councillor in the south ward, occasioned by Towle ceasing to be a burgess ; and that, of the three persons to be elected in this ward, the one having the lowest number of votes would be councillor to fill up the said vacancy ; and, on 2nd of November, he affixed another notice, making known the result of the election of councillors ; of which notice the following is an extract.

"South Ward. [350]

"Mr. John Hastings - - - - - -	203
Mr. Charles Butler - - - - - -	146
Mr. Thomas Dry, in the room of Mr. Towle -	119

(1) Repealed by the Municipal Corporations Act, 1882 (45 & 46 Vict. c. 50), s. 5.

REX
r.
THE
MAYOR, &C.
OF OXFORD.

Towle deposed that, at the time of his election as councillor, he was duly enrolled as a burgess; that he had continued to be rated for premises situate in the city and borough, and was fully entitled to be on the burgess-roll; that he had been an inhabitant householder for the last ten years and had not become insolvent, or bankrupt, or compounded with his creditors, or absented himself for six months since his election, nor had the council declared his seat vacant or office void; and that he was worth 1,000*l.*, over and above what would pay his debts, and was above thirty years of age.   On the 9th of November, 1836, he attended a meeting of the council; but the then mayor, Mr. Butler, refused to permit him to speak, or to take any part in the proceedings; and afterwards the present mayor, Mr. Sadler, refused to permit him to exercise his functions as councillor.

From the affidavits in answer to the rule it appeared that the overseers of the several parishes of the borough delivered in the burgess-lists to the town clerk on September 6th, 1836; that Towle's name was not on any of the lists; and that he had not applied to the town clerk, nor at his office, to inspect any of the lists, nor given notice of the omission of his name, nor claimed to have it inserted.   There were also statements as to the time of printing and exhibiting the lists; but they are not material to the decision.

Sir J. Campbell, Attorney-General, and *Amos* now showed cause. * * *

[351]   *Bingham, contrà.* * * *

[352]   WILLIAMS, J. (1):

It is not necessary to enter into the question whether, under sect. 28 (2), the party is entitled to hold the office; for the assumption necessarily made in support of the rule is that he actually is in the office now, having never been displaced; and, on that ground, no *mandamus* can be necessary to restore him.

(1) Lord Denman, Ch. J. and   (2) 5 & 6 Will. IV. c. 76.
Littledale, J. were absent.

COLERIDGE, J. :

I am of the same opinion. Looking at the facts agreed on by both parties, this rule appears to me either in part or wholly misconceived. Supposing all that has been done by the mayor and corporation, in regard to the election of Dry, to be merely colourable and void, and there to be no more than an exclusion *de facto* of Towle from the exercise of his office, a *mandamus* might go, without infringing upon the rule laid down in *Rex* v. *The Mayor of Colchester* (1) ; for then there would be a wrongful exclusion *de facto* of the one, and yet the office not filled by the other (2). But, as this is a case in which Towle has once been in full possession, and asserts that the office is still full of him *de jure*, the *mandamus* only ought to be to command the restoration of him to that of which he has been deprived, his seat and voice in the council. I am not, however, prepared to say that what has been done is merely colourable and void. No want of good faith is imputed. The election of Dry, if wrongful, has proceeded upon an erroneous yet honest misconstruction of the statute ; and, under the same impression, Towle has been supposed to have ceased to be a councillor. If so, I cannot pronounce at once that Dry is not actually in the office ; and, if he be, it is clear that no *mandamus* will lie, and that the proper remedy for Towle, in the first instance, is by *quo warranto* to oust Dry. In *Rex* v. *The Mayor of York* (3) two persons claimed to have been legally elected as recorder : the corporation had certified the election of one to the Secretary of State *for the approbation of the Crown ;

[*354]

and this Court thought that a proper case for a *mandamus* to the corporation to put the corporate seal to the election of the other, in order that the title of the contending parties might be tried on the return. But there the office was not *de facto* full of either party : the certificate was only a step towards the completion of the title ; and the Crown had not signified its approbation.

Rule discharged.

(1) 1 R. R. 480 (2 T. R. 259).
(2) See the observations of Lord MANSFIELD, in *Rex* v. *Bankes*, 3 Burr. 1454: also *Rex* v. *The Mayor,*

Bailiffs, and Burgesses of Cumbridge, 4 Burr. 2008.
(3) 2 R. R. 501 (4 T. R. 699).

1837.
Jan. 28

355]

REX *v.* The COMPANY of PROPRIETORS of the NOTTINGHAM OLD WATER WORKS.

(6 Adol. & Ellis, 355—373; S. C. 1 N. & P. 480; W. W. & D. 166; 6 L. J. (N. S.) K. B. 89.)

By an Act, incorporating a Company for supplying the town of N. with water, the Company were empowered to continue, make, &c., water-works, weirs, and other like works in the parish of L., subject to the restriction after contained, and to enter upon all rivers, lands, &c., specified in the plans and books of reference, and to do all other things necessary for making, completing, &c., the water-works. The Company were empowered to agree for the purchase of lands, &c.; and tenants for life, &c., and owners and occupiers of lands through which the works were to pass, were to receive satisfaction for the value of the lands and the damages sustained in making the works; the amount to be settled, if necessary, by a compensation jury at Quarter Sessions, to be summoned by the Company's warrant to the sheriff on certain notice to the Company, and not without; and the jury were to assess purchase-money or compensation, and to settle what share should be allowed to any tenant or person having a particular interest. The Sessions were to give judgment for the sum awarded; and the verdict and judgment were to be registered among the records of the Quarter Sessions, and to be deemed records to all intents and purposes. A subsequent section directed the assessment of compensation for any damages not before provided for, accruing by reason of the execution of any of the powers in the Act; the sum assessed to be levied as directed with respect to damages before provided for. The Company, on payment, tender, &c., of the sums agreed upon or assessed, might enter on the lands, &c., but not before.

The Company, by alterations in a weir in L., across a river, raised the water so as to damage a mill in L., of which T. was tenant for life: neither the mill, nor the weir or its site, nor T.'s name, was specified in the books or plan, nor was the weir in the line of works there described; but that part of the river in which the mill and weir respectively lay was in the plan.

1. Held, that a *mandamus* lay to the Company, commanding them to issue their warrant for a jury to assess the damages sustained by T.

2. The jury, summoned in obedience to the *mandamus*, having assessed a compensation, and the Company refusing to pay the same, or the costs, Held, that a *mandamus* lay to enforce payment of the compensation, though the statute made the verdict and judgment records of the Quarter Sessions.

3. Held, also, that the Company, in showing cause against the rule for a second *mandamus*, were precluded from contending that the injury sustained by T. was not within the Act, or that all preliminaries necessary to support the first *mandamus* were not fulfilled.

4. That all formal preliminaries, essential to the verdict, must be presumed to have been fulfilled, in default of affidavit to the contrary.

5. That the jury, having assessed a compensation to T. without noticing

REX
v.
THE NOT-
TINGHAM
OLD WATER
WORKS
COMPANY.

the interest of any other person, it was not to be presumed, in the absence of any affidavit, that they had given such compensation for a larger interest than T. really had, or had overlooked any other person's interest.

SIR W. W. FOLLETT, in Easter Term, 1835, obtained a rule *nisi* for a *mandamus* to the Company of Proprietors of the Nottingham Old Water Works to issue *a warrant under their common seal to the sheriff of the county of Nottingham, commanding him to summon and return a jury of twenty-four &c., to appear before the justices of the peace at the next General Quarter Sessions for the said county, in order that a jury might be then and there empannelled, according to stat. 7 & 8 Geo. IV. c. lxxxii. (1), to assess the damages sustained by Sarah *Turner in

[*356]

[*357]

(1) Stat. 7 & 8 Geo. IV. c. lxxxii. (local and personal, public), entitled "An Act for more effectually supplying with water the inhabitants of the town and county of the town of Nottingham, and the neighbourhood thereof."

Sect. 1 recites that the inhabitants of Nottingham, for many years, have been supplied with water from the river Leen, by means of works constructed at the expense of the proprietors of such works, on ground demised to them for a long term; and it incorporates the proprietors by the name of "The Company of Proprietors of the Nottingham Old Water Works."

Sect. 2 empowers the Company "to continue, make, complete," &c., "water-works, houses," "reservoirs," "weirs," "pipes," &c., "in and near" "the several parishes or townships of Basford, Lenton" &c., "and from time to time to regulate, conduct, continue," &c., the same, and to discontinue the same, subject to the restriction after contained; and "to go enter and pass in, upon, over, under and through all or any of the rivers, brooks, streams, waters, highways," &c., "and all other lands and places of or belonging to any person or persons," &c., "mentioned and specified in the plans and books of reference hereinafter mentioned," (with exceptions not material here,) "and to set out and ascertain such part or parts thereof as they the said Company shall think necessary and proper for continuing, making," &c., "the said water-works," &c., "and all such other works" "as they shall think necessary for effecting the purposes aforesaid;" doing as little damage as may be, &c., "and making full satisfaction in manner hereinafter mentioned to the owners or proprietors of, and all persons interested in any lands, tenements or other hereditaments which shall be taken, used," &c., "or injured, for all damages to be by them sustained in or by the execution of all or any of the powers hereby granted; and this Act shall be sufficient to indemnify the said Company, and their deputies, servants," &c., "for what they or any of them shall do by virtue of the powers hereby granted, subject nevertheless to such provisoes and restrictions" as are after mentioned.

Sect. 3 recites that a map or plan, describing the intended reservoirs and line of pipes and other works, and the lands &c. upon or through

REX
v.
THE NOT-
TINGHAM
OLD WATER
WORKS
COMPANY.

[358]

her lands, tenements, hereditaments, and premises, by reason and in consequence of certain works done and erected by the said Company, in the execution of certain of the powers of the said statute.

By the affidavits in support of the rule, it appeared that Sarah

[*357, *n.*] *which they are made or intended to be carried, together with a book of reference containing a list of the owners thereof, have been deposited at the offices of the clerks of the peace in Nottingham and Nottinghamshire; and also another plan, describing a certain variation, &c.; and enacts that the maps or plans, and books shall remain in the custody of the clerks of the peace; "and the said Company in making such reservoirs," &c., "and other works, and laying such pipes as aforesaid, shall not deviate from the line described in the said first mentioned maps or plans, save as the same is varied or altered by the said second mentioned plans; and that the said Company in laying the said pipes through the parishes of Radford and Lenton aforesaid, shall not deviate from the line described in the said second mentioned plans."

Sect. 8 gives powers for the purchase and sale of lands, &c.

Sect. 11 enacts that the tenants for life or in tail, &c., owners, occupiers, &c., of any lands, tenements, or hereditaments through, in or upon, over or under which the works authorized by this Act are or are intended to be

[*358, *n.*] made, may accept and receive satisfaction for the value of such lands, &c., "and for the damages to be sustained in making and completing the said works, in such gross sums as shall be agreed upon" between them and the Company of Proprietors; and in case the Company and the parties interested in such lands &c. cannot or do not agree, the amount of such satisfaction or

compensation shall be ascertained by the verdict of a jury, as after directed.

Sect. 12. "And for settling all differences which may arise between the said Company of Proprietors and the several owners of or persons interested in any lands," &c., which the Company are by this Act enabled to take and make use of for the purposes thereof; be it further enacted, that if any "person or persons so interested, entitled or empowered or capacitated to sell as aforesaid, for and on behalf of himself," &c., "or of the person or persons entitled in remainder or reversion after them," &c., shall refuse to accept the "purchase-money recompence or other compensation" offered by the Company, and give written notice thereof to the Company within twenty-one days of the offer, with a request that the matter may be submitted to a jury, the Company shall, and they are hereby empowered and required, from time to time, to issue a warrant under their common seal to the sheriff of the county, &c., commanding him, and the sheriff is authorized and required, to empannel a jury of twenty-four, who are required to *appear at some Court of General or Quarter Sessions, or adjournment thereof, for the town or county of Nottingham; out of whom a jury of twelve shall be drawn, who shall "inquire of, assess and ascertain, and give a verdict for the sum or sums of money to be paid for the purchase of such lands," &c., tenements, or hereditaments, "and also the separate and distinct sum or sums

REX
v.
THE NOT-
TINGHAM
OLD WATER
WORKS
COMPANY.

[*359]

Turner was owner, as tenant for life, of a water-mill, in Lenton, in Nottinghamshire, on the river *Leen. In 1826 (after the commencement of her ownership) the Company were in possession

of money to be paid by way of recompence or compensation either for the damages which shall or may before that time have been occasioned and sustained as aforesaid, or for the future temporary or perpetual continuance of any recurring damages," &c.; "and the said justices shall accordingly give judgment for such purchase - money, recompence or compensation as shall be assessed by such jury, which said verdict, and the judgment thereupon to be pronounced as aforesaid, shall be binding and conclusive to all intents and purposes, upon all bodies politic," &c., and all other persons whatsoever.

Sect. 14 empowers the said juries to "settle what shares and proportions of the purchase-money or compensation for damages," to be assessed, "shall be allowed to any tenant or other person or persons having a particular estate term or interest in the premises, for such his her or their interest or respective interests therein."

Sect. 15 enacts, "that all the said verdicts and judgments, being first signed by the clerk of the peace," shall by him be "registered among the records of the Quarter Sessions for such town or county, and shall be deemed records to all intents and purposes: and the same, or true copies thereof, shall be allowed to be good evidence in all Courts whatsoever."

Sect. 18 enacts, that where a verdict shall be given for more money than the Company shall have offered as a recompence or satisfaction for any such lands, &c., or for any such estate, &c., "or for any damages that may have been sustained by any person or persons aforesaid," the cost of summoning, &c., the

jury, taking the inquisition, witnesses, and recording the verdict or judgment, shall be borne by the Company, and shall, in default of payment by them or their treasurers, be levied by distress and sale under the warrant of a justice of the town or county, which warrant the justice is authorized and required to issue; and where differences shall arise respecting the amount of the costs, the same shall be ascertained by a justice of &c., who is authorized and required to do so.

Sect. 20 enacts, that if "any person or persons sustain any damage in *his her or their lands, tenements, hereditaments or property, by reason of the execution of any of the powers given by this Act, and for which a compensation is not hereinbefore provided," such damages shall from time to time be assessed by a jury, "and the sum or sums of money to be paid for the same shall be recovered levied and applied" in the same manner as is directed with respect to such damages as are in the Act before provided for.

Sect. 21 enacts, that the Company shall not be obliged, nor any jury under this Act be allowed to receive and take notice of any complaint of injury or damage sustained by virtue or in consequence of the execution of this Act, unless notice in writing, stating the particulars of such injury or damage, and the amount of compensation claimed, shall have been given to the Company within three calendar months after the injury shall have been sustained, or the doing thereof shall have ceased.

Sect. 22 enacts, that on payment or tender of sums agreed upon, or assessed by a jury, within one calendar

[*359 n.]

of works for raising water from the Leen. The local Act passed on 14th June, 1827. About the end of 1830 the Company removed a weir, which had been placed across the river, to a part of the river higher up, and at the same time heightened the weir ; in consequence of which the working of the mill was obstructed, and the value of the property lessened. The Company were applied to for *compensation, and, in November, 1834, were formally required to issue a warrant to summon a jury for assessing the damage ; but they did not grant either.

Affidavit was made in answer, to the effect that neither the new weir, nor the site thereof, was specified or referred to in the plans or books of reference mentioned in the Act (sect. 3) ; that none of the plans or books showed that the Company sought, by virtue of the Act, to obtain the power of changing the site of the weir, or raising it, or in any way altering the height of the water in the Leen, or diminishing the power or value of the mill : that the weir was not in the line of works marked on either of the maps or plans ; and that no part of the estate through which that part of the river passed wherein the new weir stood, was specified or referred to in either of the books or plans. It was not, however, denied (and was assumed in argument) that the parts of the river Leen on which the mill and the new weir respectively stood were comprehended in the plans. It was also assumed that the new weir, as well as the mill, was in Lenton.

Hill and *Humfrey* showed cause in Michaelmas Term, 1835 (November 7th), and contended that the remedy sought for was

---

month after the same shall be agreed for or assessed, (with a provision in case the persons entitled cannot be found, &c.,) the Company may enter into such lands, and the same shall vest in them ; but before such payment, &c., the Company shall not dig or cut into such lands, &c., without leave in writing.

Sect. 108 enacts that no plaintiff shall recover in any action for any thing done in pursuance of this Act, unless he shall have given twenty-eight days' notice of action, nor if sufficient amends be tendered, &c.

Sect. 109 enacts, "that no action suit or information shall be brought commenced or prosecuted against any person" for any thing done in pursuance of this Act, or in execution of the powers, &c., made given &c. in by or under the same, unless certain notices be given, nor after certain times specified ; and other enactments as to the proceedings, &c., in such actions, are added. In case of the plaintiff's not succeeding, the defendants to have double costs.

REX
v.
THE NOT-
TINGHAM
OLD WATER
WORKS
COMPANY.

[*361]

not the proper one, for that the injury complained of was not occasioned by any act done under the compulsory powers of the statute, and, that being so, the process given by the statute was not applicable : *Rex* v. *The Hungerford Market Company* (*Ex parte Yeates*) (1), *Rex* v. *The Hungerford Market Company* (*Ex parte Eyre*) (2); but the complainant ought to *proceed by action, as in the case of an ordinary wrong. And they endeavoured to show that, the weir in question not being comprehended in the plans or books of reference mentioned in sect. 3, the work done upon it was not an execution of any power given by the Act. They urged that sect. 20 did not apply to any damages but such as arose from the execution of the powers given by the Act; and they cited *Scales* v. *Pickering* (3), as showing that such powers must be construed strictly. If this were a proper subject for compensation, the Company would be entitled to retain the weir, and be liable to no further complaint for the consequences.

Sir W. W. Follett, *contrà*, referred to sects. 2, 11, and 20, and argued that the last applied to the damage here complained of, inasmuch as sect. 2 enabled the Company to lay down weirs; and he observed that, although the weir was not in the plan, it was newly erected, under the powers of the Act, on a part of the river Leen which was in the plan; and that a particular specification of that or of the mill was not necessary for the purpose of enabling the Company to erect works in that part of the river which was in the plan.

LORD DENMAN, Ch. J.:

The erection of this weir seems directly within the powers given by the Act; and the Act might be pleaded by the Company in justification. This appears to be the very case contemplated by sect. 20.

PATTESON, J.:

The second section gives the power expressly.

(1) 1 Ad. & El. 668. (3) 4 Bing. 448.
(2) 1 Ad. & El. 676.

REX
v.
THE NOT-
TINGHAM
OLD WATER
WORKS
COMPANY.

[362]

WILLIAMS, J. :

The only doubt I felt was whether the clause as to the plans and books restricted the Company. But, as the part of the river in question is within the plan, I think it does not. It was not a matter of course, when the plans were made, that the weir should be erected.

COLERIDGE, J. :

The argument as to the plans and names of the owners falls to the ground as soon as we refer to sect. 20. As to the future consequential damages we need not decide now.

Rule absolute.

A *mandamus* issued accordingly, tested 7th November, 1835, in the terms of the rule. The jury were summoned ; and, at the Nottinghamshire Quarter Sessions in April, 1836 (the time having been enlarged by consent), assessed the damages of Sarah Turner at 500*l.* This sum, and the costs incurred in obtaining the *mandamus* and verdict, were demanded of the Company, but not paid. Sarah Turner then applied for a warrant of distress at the June Quarter Sessions, 1836 : the Sessions adjourned the consideration till the October Sessions, and then refused the warrant. A similar application was afterwards made to a single magistrate of the county, who refused to issue the warrant. The costs previous to the inquiry were sworn by the attorney for Sarah Turner to be 167*l.* 13*s.* 11*d.* ; and those incurred since, to be 73*l.* 13*s.* 4*d.* An offer was made on the part of Sarah Turner to refer the taxation to the clerk of the peace for Nottinghamshire, or the proper officer of this Court, or any indifferent professional man. The attorney also stated that the costs incurred since those already mentioned

[*363]

*would amount to a considerable sum. Upon affidavit of the above facts, *Sir W. W. Follett* obtained a rule in Michaelmas Term, 1836, calling upon the Company to show cause why a *mandamus* should not issue, commanding them forthwith to pay Sarah Turner 500*l.*, being the damages assessed by the jury ; and also 241*l.* 7*s.* 3*d.*, her costs of the inquiry.

Hill, N. R. Clarke, and *Whitehurst* now showed cause. * * *

Sir W. W. Follett and *Bourne*, *contrà*. * * *

REX
v.
THE NOT-
TINGHAM
OLD WATER
WORKS
COMPANY.
[367]
[369]

PATTESON, J. (1) :

This is an application to compel payment of 500*l*., compensation assessed by a jury, and of another sum for costs. It is clear that we are not bound to refuse the *mandamus* altogether, if we shall be of opinion that a part of the application may be granted. With respect to the costs, sect. 20 gives no directions, unless costs can be included under the words " sum or sums of money to be paid " for the damage done : such sums are to be levied in the same manner as is directed with respect to the damages before provided for ; and in sect. 18 there is a course prescribed for recovering the costs, in the case of a verdict being given for a higher compensation than the Company shall have offered. If, therefore, costs are here recoverable at all, they are recoverable by that method. There must, consequently, be no rule as to costs.

As to the 500*l*. I have some difficulty. If there be a specific remedy for this sum, we cannot grant the *mandamus*. Now, by sect. 12, the Court of Quarter Sessions is to give judgment for the sum assessed by the jury, which judgment is to be conclusive : and, by sect. 15, the clerk of the peace is to sign the verdicts and judgments, which are to be registered and to become records. It seemed to me at first that, if these were judgments of record, they might be enforced like judgments of other Courts, by the process of the Court itself, if it had any process proper for the purpose, and, if not, by action of debt. But, on looking to the Act, I doubt whether such a consequence can be admitted. These are not the ordinary records of the Quarter Sessions ; and I never heard of an action on a record of this *sort. The Quarter [*370] Sessions are a Court for this particular purpose ; no form of the record is prescribed, and I cannot tell what the form is to be. It is difficult to say in what form an action can be maintained upon it. Sections 12 and 15 contain no directions how the money is to be levied : only the 22nd section enacts that the Company, on payment as there prescribed, may take possession, and cannot act before. It seems that was thought sufficient

(1) Lord Denman, Ch. J. was absent.

REX
r.
THE NOT-
TINGHAM
OLD WATER
WORKS
COMPANY.

security for the compensation and damages provided for by sect. 12. By sect. 20 damages, for which compensation is not provided in the preceding part of the Act, are to be assessed by a jury. Nothing is there said of making a demand, or of offer to pay the damages. And then it is said, that such damages are to be levied as is directed with respect to the damages before provided for. I suppose it was taken for granted that there had been some previous provision for levying the damages mentioned in the earlier part of the Act. But there are no means of levying them; there can be no *fieri facias* or *levari facias*; neither can we remove the record by *certiorari* and enforce the judgment here. But the main argument in opposition to the rule was, that an action of debt would lie. I am not prepared to say whether that be so or not. But, as it is not clear that such an action does lie, we are bound to grant a *mandamus* in the absence of any other clear remedy.

Objections have been made to the regularity of the proceedings. I do not understand that the affidavits show irregularity, but only that there is no affidavit showing the regularity. This, however, we are not bound to require. We shall presume *omnia rite acta*, in pursuance of the *mandamus* which we granted.

[371]   Then it is said, that the applicant is only a tenant for life, and that the jury ought to have assessed and apportioned the damages for all parties interested. However that may be in the case of the purchase of lands by the Company, where all tenants having partial interests are entitled to compensation, it is not clear here that any one but the tenant for life had a right to complain : the injury might be merely temporary. Besides, the expression in sect. 20 is "any person or persons," not "all persons." Here the party has sustained a damage in respect of her land ; and if, in fact, it were one in respect of which the jury ought to have limited her compensation, that should have been pointed out to them at the time of the inquiry : and no complaint is made of the chairman's summing up. Under all the circumstances, I think the rule must be made absolute so far as respects the 500*l.*

The costs of the other *mandamus* cannot be included in this rule ; and there is a specific statutory provision respecting such costs.

WILLIAMS, J. :

REX
v.
THE NOT-
TINGHAM
OLD WATER
WORKS
COMPANY.

As to the costs, no precise or ascertained right can be shown. With respect to the objection on the ground of irregularity, no doubt, we should presume that notice was proved at the time of the inquiry, unless the contrary be shown. We must suppose that all has been rightly done : and, on the same ground, no objection appears to the form in which the compensation is given. The principal question is, whether there be any remedy besides *mandamus ;* and it is clear that, if there be, this rule cannot be made absolute. An order of Sessions, awarding the payment of money, can be enforced only by the circuitous process *of indictment. That gives no direct remedy. But the most important question is, whether, the fifteenth section enacting that the verdict and judgment "shall be deemed records to all intents and purposes," that operate as a legislative declaration that there is to be a remedy by action of debt upon the record. I am aware of no applicable instance. As, there-fore, I doubt whether there be any other efficient remedy, I think the *mandamus* should go. I am also influenced by a doubt which I feel, whether the Legislature could have intended to put the party to so cumbrous a course as an action of debt on the record, to recover that for which they were professing to give a summary remedy.

[*372]

COLERIDGE, J. :

Two requisites must concur to authorise this application ; a right, and an absence of any other remedy for enforcing it. Costs are asked for, both those of the previous *mandamus,* and those of the inquiry. Now, when costs of a rule are given, there is no remedy, except that arising upon the order of the Court. But here the costs asked for are claimed, not as matter of common law, but under specific statutory enactment. Then as to the 500*l.* damages. We must take it that the party has a specific right. Has she then a clear remedy? It is said, in opposition to the rule, that this is either a judgment like other judgments of the Court of Quarter Sessions, or in the nature of a judgment of a superior Court, and thus to be enforced by action of debt on the record. Now the judgment of a Court

REX
v.
THE NOT-
TINGHAM
OLD WATER
WORKS
COMPANY.

[*373]

of Quarter Sessions can be enforced only by indictment. That has been held not to be a beneficial remedy. All that could be obtained by it would be the fining or imprisonment of the party refusing, *which clearly would give no beneficial remedy to the party aggrieved. Then, as to the remedy by action of debt, can any one say that it clearly exists? The authority of 3 Blackstone's Com. 159, 160, was cited, but no decision; and the doctrine would certainly be now much disputed. As to the regularity of the proceedings, where a *mandamus* has issued, and the party makes no return, but consents to obey, can he say, upon an application for another *mandamus* ancillary to the first, that the first was irregular? We must suppose that the Sessions, in obedience to the *mandamus*, have done all that was necessary; and we cannot, therefore, intend that notice has not been duly given, or that the jury have gone beyond the proper limit in the compensation which they have awarded.

Rule absolute, as to the 500l.

———————

REX *v.* SIR HUMPHREY PHINEAS DAVIE AND OTHERS.

(6 Adol. & Ellis, 374—387.)

By charter of Edw. VI., it was granted that the inhabitants of the vill of S., within the parish of C., should have a chapel for all the said inhabitants, with a chaplain, to be paid out of the profits of the vicarage of C., and that they should elect chapelwardens. And that certain governors, appointed for the said vill pursuant to that charter, "unà cum assensu majoris partis inhabitantium ejusdem villatæ," should nominate and appoint the chaplain. The charter also provided that the "inhabitants" of S. should not be charged towards the support of the church of C. otherwise than the other inhabitants of C.

In 1836, the governors having, upon a vacancy, nominated a chaplain, gave notice to the inhabitants of S. that such nomination had been made, and required them to meet at a time and place named, for the purpose of assenting or dissenting. At such meeting, the resident payers of church and poor-rates, and no other persons, were admitted to vote. Some persons, not rated, tendered their votes. The majority of rate-payers assented to the nomination. On motion for a *mandamus* to the governors to elect a chaplain, on the ground that such election was void, it appeared that the two preceding nominations and elections, in 1814 and 1771, had been conducted in the same manner; aged persons deposed that they had always understood that to be the customary mode; and a decree of Lord HARDWICKE, in a suit relative to the chaplaincy of S. in 1741, was proved, in which the same course was prescribed as the proper one, but it did not appear, with certainty, by the decree, that the decision on this point was a judgment on any question litigated in the suit:

Held,

1. That the nomination by the governors, with a subsequent reference to the inhabitants for their assent, was a compliance with the words " unà cum assensu," &c.

2. That, referring to the context of the charter, and the proof given as to usage, the word " inhabitants," in this charter, might be construed as meaning " inhabitants paying church and poor-rates."

A RULE was obtained last Term, calling on the above-mentioned parties to show cause why a *mandamus* should not issue, commanding them, with the assent of the inhabitants of the vill or hamlet of Sandford, to nominate and appoint a chaplain to perform divine service in the chapel of Sandford aforesaid, in the room of Hugh Bent, clerk, deceased.

By a charter (in Latin) of 1 Edw. VI. (confirmed by Queen Elizabeth) the King, for the advancement of divine worship, and the better preservation and management of the goods, &c., of the parish church of Crediton in Devonshire, and for the instruction of children, *and for other causes moving him to incorporate certain of his subjects, inhabitants of the said parish of Crediton, for the universal advantage and common utility of all and each of the inhabitants of the said parish, &c., did grant to the said inhabitants, that for the future there should be perpetually in the said parish, from among the inhabitants thereof for the time being, twelve governors of the hereditaments and goods of the said church of Crediton, three of whom should always be on the part of the vill or hamlet of Sampford, in the said parish: and the said governors were made a perpetual corporation by the name of The twelve governors of the hereditaments and goods of the church of Crediton, otherwise Kyrton, in the county of Devon. The first twelve were nominated by the charter; vacancies were to be filled up by the remaining governors; so, however, that three should always be from among the inhabitants of Sampford.

In a subsequent clause, after reciting that the vill of Sampford was distant from the parish church of Crediton, so that the inhabitants of Sampford could not conveniently resort thither, it was granted that the chapel of St. Swithin of Sampford should for the future perpetually be a chapel annexed to the church of

REX
v.
DAVIE.

Crediton, for all the inhabitants of the said vill then being or
thereafter to be, for divine services, &c., to be ministered to
them in the said chapel by a chaplain; and that the inhabitants
of the vill should have the free power and faculty of burying in
the said chapel and the burial-ground thereof, &c., and should
have the use, occupation, and appointment of the said burial-
ground, and of certain other premises called the church-house,
priest's-house, &c.: and that the inhabitants of the said vill, or
[*376]   the major part of them, should elect chapelwardens *from and
among themselves, which chapelwardens should account to the
inhabitants of the vill as other wardens are accustomed to do
in other parishes of Devonshire.   The twelve governors were
to pay a stated salary to the chaplain out of the issues and
profits of the vicarage of Crediton, which were granted to them
by the same charter.

It was then further declared and ordered by the charter that
the three governors who shall from time to time be for the vill of
Sampford, "together with the assent of the major part of the
inhabitants of the said vill of S., shall nominate and appoint,
and shall be able to, and may, nominate and appoint, one chaplain to administer divine services and sacraments in the said
chapel of S., for the inhabitants of the said vill and hamlet of
S.; and that he may by those three of the twelve governors,"
&c., "together with the assent of the said major part of the
inhabitants of the said vill and hamlet of S., from time to time
be, for reasonable cause, expelled and amoved, and another put
by them in his place" (1).   Power was also given to the twelve
governors from time to time, without fraud or deceit towards the
inhabitants of Sampford, to make reasonable, equal, and indifferent ordinances and decrees for compelling the inhabitants of

(1) "Quod illi tres dictorum duodecim gubernatorum qui ex parte
villatæ de Sampford prædictâ de
tempore in tempus fuerint, unà cum
assensu majoris partis inhabitantium
ejusdem villatæ de S., nominabunt
et appunctuabunt ac nominare et
appunctuare valeant et possint unum
capellanum ad divina servitia," &c.,
" ministrandum in capellâ de Samp-

ford prædictâ pro inhabitantibus
villatæ et hameletti de Sampford
prædictâ, et per illos tres dictorum
duodecim gubernatorum qui ex parte
villatæ " &c. "fuerint, unà cum
assensu prædictæ majoris partis
inhabitantium ejusdem villatæ,"
&c., "de tempore in tempus pro
rationabili causâ expellatur," &c.

the parish of Crediton to be assisting with their goods according to their power in all things *which should be necessary or opportune for the repairs and maintenance of the church of Crediton, and for all other needs of the said church, as often as should be requisite, so that the inhabitants of the said vill and hamlet of Sampford, or any of them, shall not be charged, nor shall they, or any of them, be chargeable otherwise or in any other manner whatsoever than the rest of the inhabitants of the said parish of Crediton.

The said vill of Sampford is now a parish by reputation, and commonly called Sandford (1). The Rev. Hugh Bent, the chaplain of Sandford, having died in June, 1836, the three governors on the part of Sandford, against whom the present motion was made, without any assent of the major part of the inhabitants of Sandford, nominated the Rev. Charles Gregory to be chaplain, and placed the following notice on the church door of Sandford. " We the undersigned " (the three governors for Sandford) " do hereby give notice to the inhabitants of the said vill or hamlet, that we have nominated the Rev. Charles Gregory of " &c. " to be the chaplain to perform divine service in the chapel of Sandford aforesaid, in the room of the Rev. Hugh Bent, late of " &c., " deceased. And we do hereby also give notice to the said inhabitants to meet in the said chapel, on " &c., " immediately after the evening service, in order that they, or the major part of them who shall be present at such meeting, may assent or dissent to such nomination. Given," &c.

The meeting was held, June 26th, 1836; one of the three governors was called to the chair; and the name of each resident rate-payer was then called from the poor-rate of Sandford, and every such rate-payer, upon answering, was asked whether he assented or dissented, and the answer taken down. When the resident rate-payers had been called over, it was submitted to *the chairman, on behalf of some of the inhabitants, that the non-resident rate-payers and non-rated inhabitants ought to be called over; but the chairman refused to call them. Three inhabitants, not rated to the poor, were then tendered to declare their dissent, and more

REX
v.
DAVIE.
[*377]

[*378]

(1) [This is the only form given in Donn's map of Devon, 1765. There are three other Sampfords in Devonshire.—F. P.]

were ready to do so, but the three votes were rejected. The numbers were given out as follows : " Assents 39, dissents 32 : " and Mr. Gregory was declared to be elected. A *caveat* was entered against the granting him a license.

In opposition to the rule affidavits were filed, stating that at the time of the above election the same persons were rated to the church and to the poor; that no rate-payers who were non-resident tendered their votes, and only five were present; that, on the respective appointments of the Rev. Hugh Bent (Mr. Gregory's immediate predecessor) in 1814, and the Rev. George Bent (1) (the immediate predecessor of Hugh Bent) in 1771, the same course was adopted as on the present appointment, that is, that the three governors nominated the chaplain, and then gave notice to the inhabitants to meet for the purpose of assenting or dissenting; and that, upon such meeting, the persons who voted were the inhabitants of Sandford paying to church and poor; and several of the deponents (among whom were persons more than eighty years old) stated that they had always heard and understood, and believed, that the custom in Sandford was to elect chaplains in this manner. It was also sworn (upon information and belief) that the churchwardens for Sandford were elected by none but the resident payers of church and poor-rates.

[*379] To these affidavits was added, on behalf of the *parties showing cause, a verified copy of a decree by Lord HARDWICKE, of July 27th, 1741. The decree set forth a petition exhibited before the Lord Chancellor, June 2nd, 1741, by Robert Read and Daniel Brown, two of the then governors for Sandford, and William Barter, clerk. By the recitals of the petition, stated in the decree, it appeared : That, in 1731, an information was exhibited in the Court of Chancery by the *Attorney-General*, at the relation of John Bremridge and two others, against the twelve governors of Crediton, Sir John Davie, Bart., and two others (the governors for Sandford), Theophilus Blackhall and James Lang, clerks, and others, which information set forth that, in 1730, the then governors for Sandford had proceeded, on a vacancy, to the election of a chaplain, and that two governors, with the minority

(1) George Bent was stated in one   in the room of Mr. Barter ; see p. 500
of the affidavits to have been chosen   *post.*

of the inhabitants of Sandford, had voted for Blackhall, and one
governor, with the majority of the inhabitants, for Lang; whereupon a dispute had arisen, and the prayer of the parties exhibiting
the information was, that the trust reposed in the said governors
by the charters of Edw. VI. and Elizabeth might be performed,
&c.   It further appeared that an answer to the information had
been filed, an issue joined, and depositions published; and that,
in 1736, a certain decree was made thereon: That, two of the
governors for Sandford having died, two new ones were appointed
and made parties to the cause, after which a rehearing was
obtained, and a decree was made, July 25th, 1737, that neither
Blackhall nor Lang was duly nominated or appointed; and that
the governors for Sandford should forthwith nominate a chaplain,
and should thereupon give public notice to " the inhabitants of
the said village or hamlet " by affixing such notice on the chapel
door, &c., signifying to the inhabitants the name of the person
*so nominated, and that they should meet, &c., on &c., in order
that they or the major part of them which should be present at
such meeting might assent or dissent to such nomination; and,
in case they or the major part of them should assent thereto, the
person so nominated was to be admitted, &c.; but, if they or
the majority should dissent, either side might apply to the Court
for further directions: That, two of the governors for Sandford
having died before any further proceedings took place, and one
of the governors chosen in their stead refusing to act, a bill of
revivor and supplemental bill was exhibited in 1738, and a
decree thereupon made, ordering, among other things, that a
new governor should be elected, and that the decree of 1737
as to the appointment of a chaplain should then be carried into
execution: That proceedings were thereupon taken (which it
is unnecessary to state), terminating in the election of a chaplain:
That, on petition by the new chaplain and one of the governors
for Sandford, that such chaplain might be admitted, the LORD
CHANCELLOR, upon the hearing, decreed the nomination and
election void, on the ground that it had been proceeded in by
two of the said governors for Sandford with the assent of the
majority of the inhabitants, but without giving notice to the
third governor; and he decreed further, that (the last-mentioned

REX
r.
DAVIE.

[*380]

32—2

REX
v.
DAVIE.

governor being dead since the election) a new governor should
be elected according to the charter, &c., and that the three
should then proceed to nominate a chaplain with the assent of
the major part of the inhabitants of Sandford, according to the
charter and to the former decree in the said petition mentioned,
"and that the right of assenting or dissenting to such nomination
was only in the inhabitants of the said hamlet paying the rates
[*381] and assessments for the poor and *chapel within the said hamlet:"
That a new governor was then elected, and that the three then
met, and two of them, Robert Read and Daniel Brown, did, as
far as in them lay, nominate a chaplain, William Barter; but
the third governor, without giving any reason, refused to join in
the nomination: That the two assenting governors then gave
notice to the inhabitants (according to the decree of July, 1737),
in pursuance of which all or the greater part of the inhabitants
within Sandford, "who were payers or owners or occupiers of land
charged to the rates and assessments of the said vill or hamlet,"
attended the meeting, and, the nomination being read to them by
the two last-mentioned governors, proceeded to a new election
of a chaplain, and assented to the nomination of the petitioner,
William Barter; "that not one of the inhabitants then present dissented;" and that only the third governor and a few of the other
inhabitants were absent: That Barter, notwithstanding such
nomination and assent, was kept out of possession of the chapel
&c.: And the prayer of the recited petition of June, 1741, was,
that Barter might be admitted to the chaplaincy &c., and that the
twelve governors might pay him his salary from the time of election. The LORD CHANCELLOR, after the above recitals, declared
by his said decree of July 27th, 1741, that he was of opinion that
Barter was duly nominated and appointed, and ordered that he
should be admitted to the said office, and the salary paid &c.

Sir W. W. Follett and M. Smith, now showed cause. * * *

[383]   Sir F. Pollock and Rogers, contrà. * * *

[385]   LORD DENMAN, Ch. J.:

The ground of this motion is that the election of June 26th,
[*386] 1836, was a nullity, and *that the office of chaplain is still vacant;

we are, therefore, called upon to grant a *mandamus* for filling it
up.   To warrant this proceeding, the nullity of the present
appointment ought to be very clearly made out.   Now it is contended, first, that, on a right construction of the words "unà
cum assensu," the nomination ought to have had the assent
of the inhabitants, whereas the nomination was made by three
governors only, and the inhabitants were merely called upon to
express their assent or dissent subsequently; and that this is
inconsistent with the charter.   But I am of a contrary opinion.
It is more convenient that the present course should be taken,
than that the inhabitants should be called upon to assent or
dissent at the time of nomination, being thus required to judge
of the party's fitness at the time when they are first acquainted
with his being proposed.   I think that "unà" in this charter
does not mean that the assent shall be at the same time as the
nomination, though it is essential to the appointment, and, if it
be not given, the governors must nominate again.   Then as to
the sense of the word "inhabitants."   We have decided lately,
in *Rex* v. *Mashiter* (1). that that word must receive its interpretation from circumstances; and usage here supports the
construction which has been acted upon.   It is indeed contended
that the usage, restricting the right of assent to the payers
of poor-rates, cannot have existed before 43 Elizabeth: but I am
not sure of that.   There probably were levies for the poor before
the statute 43 Eliz. c. 2.   And, if there be proof of usage, we
must consider it to have been according to the charter.   *Then
as to the proof; we have two instances of elections by the assent
of the rate-payers only, and the opinion expressed, in *The
Attorney-General* v. *Davy* (2), by Lord HARDWICKE, whose rule
of construction seems to be approved of by Lord ELDON, in *The
Attorney-General* v. *Newcombe* (3).   We do not know all the circumstances of *The Attorney-General* v. *Davy* (2); but we must
suppose that the opinion there expressed by Lord HARDWICKE
had reference to some particulars which were before him in
the suit, and that he thought the restricted right sufficiently
established from early times.

[*387]

REX
v.
DAVIE.

(1) P. 433, *ante* (6 Ad. & El. 153).   Sen. 43.
(2) 2 Atk. 212; 3 Atk. 577; 1 Ves.   (3) 14 Ves. 1.

REX
v.
DAVIE.

WILLIAMS, J. (1) :

I am of the same opinion. I think that "unà cum assensu" does not necessarily mean that the assent should be given *pari passu* with the nomination. It is merely Latin of a certain kind for "together with the assent;" and the nomination is made together with the assent, if the assent be afterwards given by vote. On the construction of the word "inhabitants" I agree with my Lord.

Rule discharged.

1837.
Jan. 30.

[388]

REX v. THOMAS RAYMOND BARKER, ESQUIRE, AND OTHERS, JUSTICES OF BUCKINGHAMSHIRE.

(6 Adol. & Ellis, 388—391; S. C. 1 N. & P. 503; W. W. & D. 162.)

By an Act for rebuilding a parish church, certain trustees were empowered to borrow money, and for payment thereof to make rates "on the full annual rent or value of the houses, warehouses, shops, buildings, lands, tenements, and hereditaments rated or rateable for the relief of the poor of the said parish of" &c., "on all and every the tenants or occupiers of the said parish." In case of non-payment, the Act gave a power of distress, under warrant, which any justice of the county was authorised and required to grant, on certain proof:

Held that, under the first-mentioned clause, a lessee and occupier of tithes was rateable in respect of them, tithes being rated to the poor within the parish.

And that justices of the county, who had refused a warrant on the ground that tithes were not rateable under the Act, ought to be compelled by *mandamus* to grant it.

GUNNING in the last Term obtained a rule *nisi* for a *mandamus*, commanding T. R. Barker, Esq., and two others, justices of Buckinghamshire, to grant a warrant for levying by distress upon the goods of Henry Webb 31*l*., assessed upon him by a rate made in pursuance of stat. 1 Will. IV. c. lvii. (local and personal, public), for taking down and rebuilding the parish church of Great Marlow.

The Act (by sect. 32) empowered certain trustees to raise money for the purposes therein mentioned, by loan or annuity, and (sect. 40) to make a rate or rates, not exceeding &c., "on the full annual rent or value of the houses, warehouses, shops,

---

(1) Littledale, J. was absent on account of indisposition; Coleridge, J. was in the Bail Court; Patteson, J. sitting at Nisi Prius.

buildings, lands, tenements, and hereditaments rated or rateable for the relief of the poor of the said parish of Great Marlow aforesaid, on all and every the tenants or occupiers of the said parish," to be appropriated in payment of such annuities and of principal and interest of the sums so borrowed. On non-payment of the rate, and after demand and summons, &c., the Act (sect. 42) gave a power of distress under warrant, which it was declared lawful for any justice of the county, and such justice was by that clause "authorised and required," to grant, on certain proof. Sect. 54 gave an appeal against the acts of *trustees or of justices. The trustees, on December 3rd, 1835, made a rate pursuant to the Act, and thereby assessed Henry Webb at the said sum of 31l., for tithes of the parish, of which tithes he was lessee and occupier. Tithes arising within the parish were rateable and rated there to the poor. The church-wardens (whose duty it was under the Act) demanded payment of Webb, which he refused ; and they then, after taking the other steps pointed out by the Act, requested the above-mentioned three justices, assembled in Petty Sessions, to issue their warrant for levying the 31l. by distress. The justices refused, on the ground (previously alleged by Webb) that tithes were not rateable under the Act. Webb had not appealed against the rate within the time limited by sect. 54.

[*389]

Sir W. W. Follett and *Phillimore* now showed cause :

An owner or lessee of tithes is not liable to church rate unless by statute, because the tithes are already charged with the burden of repairing the chancel. And there is no reason for supposing it intended, by the statute in question, to lay the double burden upon these tithes. The subjects of rate enumerated in sect. 40 are "the houses, warehouses, shops, buildings, lands, tenements, and hereditaments," rated or rateable to the poor in Great Marlow. Where general words, in such a clause, follow words of a more limited import, the larger ones are qualified, in construction, by those which precede. In *Rex* v. *The Manchester and Salford Waterworks Company* (1) the meaning of the word "tenement" was limited conformably to

(1) 1 B. & C. 630.

this rule (which is recognised *in *Rex* v. *The Trustees for paving Shrewsbury* (1)), and with a reference to the objects of the Act, as shown by several of its clauses (2). The word "tenement" is used in sects. 44 and 46 (3) of the Act now before the Court, in a manner which makes it, there, clearly inapplicable to tithes. And in *Phillips* v. *Jones* (4) it was held that tithes would not pass by a release of "hereditaments" belonging to messuages and lands. In stat. 32 Hen. VIII. c. 7, s. 7, "tithes" and "lands, tenements, or other hereditaments," are used in wholly distinct senses. The qualifying words "rated or rateable for the relief of the poor" seem applicable to "hereditaments" only. At all events, the "tenements and hereditaments" spoken of must be considered as including only things *ejusdem generis* with those specified before. If there be even a reasonable doubt in this case, whether or not the magistrates would be justified in acting, -the Court will not grant a *mandamus*.

Kelly, contrà :

It is not necessary to dispute the principles of construction laid down in the cases which have been cited. But here the general words "tenements and hereditaments" are followed by others which fix their meaning, "rated or rateable for the relief of the poor;" and the rate upon the rent or value of such tenements and hereditaments is to be laid "on all and every the tenants and occupiers of the said parish." Any argument from the general law, as to liability in respect of tithes, is out of

place here, since the question arises *upon a statutory provision made on purpose to facilitate rating by regulating the assessment according to the poor-rate. The supposed doubt in this case ought not to excuse the justices, there being an appeal clause in the statute: *Rex* v. *Trecothick* (5).

LORD DENMAN, Ch. J. :

It would be repealing the statute to say that the words "tenements, and hereditaments rated or rateable for the relief of the

(1) 37 R. R. 409 (3 B. & Ad. 216).
(2) *Sir W. W. Follett* also referred to a case of the same class, not then reported, probably *Colebrooke* v. *Tickell*, 43 R. R. 520 (4 Ad. & El. 916).

(3) It is not thought necessary to extract these.
(4) 3 Bos. & P. 362.
(5) 41 R. R. 460 (2 Ad. & El. 405).

poor of the said parish," do not include this property. Acting, therefore, upon the principle that the Court will not grant a *mandamus* which would expose justices to danger, but that it must put them in motion where they clearly ought to proceed, I think we must order that this *mandamus* should go. We should have wished to consult our brothers who are absent; but, having no doubt upon the point, and there being so many other subjects before us for discussion, we think we ought not to delay pronouncing our judgment. The rule must be absolute.

WILLIAMS, J. (1) concurred.

Rule absolute.

REX *v.* PAYN.

(6 Adol. & Ellis, 392—407; S. C. 1 N. & P. 524; W. W. & D. 142; 1 Jur. 54; 6 L. J. (N. S.) M. C. 62.)

The treasurer of a county in possession of books containing the entries of his accounts, with the discharges signed by the magistrates as directed by statute, which also directs the accounts and vouchers to be deposited with the clerk of the peace to be kept with the county records, may be compelled by *mandamus* to deposit the books with the clerk of the peace accordingly: although the discharges are claimed by the treasurer as necessary for his own personal exoneration, and that of his father, the late treasurer.

The *mandamus* issued, reciting the book to be in the defendant's custody, power, and control; and was tested the day on which the rule for the *mandamus* was made absolute. Return, that the book was not at the time of the *teste*, nor since, nor at the time of the return, in the custody, &c. The COURT refused to take the return off the file, or quash it, on motion, upon affidavit of the facts as above stated, and of the belief of deponents that the defendant's object was to evade the process of the Court.

But the COURT refused the defendant the costs of the last motion, though moved with costs.

SIR JOHN CAMPBELL, Attorney-General, obtained a rule in last Term, calling upon William Payn, the treasurer of Berkshire, to show cause why a *mandamus* should not issue commanding him to deposit with the clerk of the said county the two books containing his accounts of the sums of money received and paid by him as such treasurer from the date of

1837.
Jan. 30.
——
[392]

_____

(1) Littledale, J. was absent on account of indisposition; Coleridge, J. was in the Bail Court; Patteson, J. sitting at Nisi Prius.

REX
v.
PAYN.

his appointment, and which accounts had been passed by the justices in Quarter Sessions (1).

The rule was obtained at the instance, and on the joint affidavits, of two justices of the county. They deposed that the defendant was appointed in 1822; and that, from the early part of 1825 up to Epiphany Sessions, 1835, he passed his

[*393]

accounts by producing to a *committee of the justices, called the Finance Committee, certain books, one from the date of his appointment to 1833, the other from thence to the time of making the affidavit, represented by him to contain a true account of sums received and paid, and distinguishing the uses to which the sums were applied, with such vouchers as he thought proper; and that such accounts had been passed by the justices, and the books and vouchers returned to the defendant: that he had passed no other accounts till Epiphany Sessions, 1836: that none of the accounts so passed and entered in the said books had been deposited with the clerk of the peace, or formed part of the county records: that, from his appointment to July, 1825, the defendant published an annual abstract of his accounts, and since then a quarterly abstract, which abstracts had been deposited by him with the clerk of the peace, together with such vouchers as the defendant thought fit. The affidavits then stated certain inaccuracies and omissions in the defendant's accounts, appearing, as was alleged, from the above abstracts; and one of the deponents stated that, if the abstracts were correct (which he had no means of knowing, from the accounts not being deposited), certain receipts had been omitted, and certain payments twice charged: and items were specified in support of this. It was added that the treasurer had disclaimed being bound by the abstracts, and had said that he would be bound only by his books, which were correct. The deponents also stated that they believed the accounts could not be understood, and did not know what steps the justices should adopt, till the accounts in the books were deposited; and that they had demanded that the books should be deposited, but defendant had refused.

(1) See stat. 12 Geo. II. c. 29, ss. 7, 8, 9; stat. 55 Geo. III. c. 51, s. 18.   (Compare the County Rates Act, 1852 (15 & 16 Vict. c. 81), ss. 1, 51.—R. C.)

The defendant, in answer, made affidavit that he had delivered
to the magistrates, at the time for passing the accounts, the bills
for all his disbursements, with the receipts for the payments,
and separate accounts of his own receipts, such as the clerk of
the peace's account of sums levied for the county rates, &c.:
that he had also kept books of entries, being the two books in
question, of the several sums respectively received and paid by
him: that these books were examined by the justices with
the separate accounts of receipts and disbursements above
mentioned, at the time of passing the accounts; and that the
magistrates, on finding the books of entries correspond with such
separate accounts, had been in the habit of signing his discharge
in the said books, which were then returned to the defendant:
that he had no other discharge from the justices: that, since the
Epiphany Sessions, 1836, a duplicate of the entries in the book
had been deposited with the clerk of the peace: and that one of
the two books mentioned in the rule contained also the entries
and discharges of the defendant's father, who had been his
immediate predecessor in office. The defendant then gave
explanations as to the inaccuracies in the accounts stated to
appear from the abstracts, and alleged facts for the purpose of
showing that the imputations against the accounts were groundless, to the knowledge of the parties now applying, and that
material circumstances on this part of the case had been kept
back or misrepresented in their affidavits. There were numerous
affidavits by magistrates, confirming the above statements, and
alleging that the separate accounts and vouchers, examined by
the magistrates, had been deposited with the clerk of the peace,
and were still in his custody.

Talfourd, Serjt., *Thesiger*, and *T. F. Ellis* now showed   [395]
cause. * * *

Sir John Campbell, A.-G., with whom were *Sir W. W. Follett*   [399]
and *F. Robinson*, contrà, was stopped by the Court.

LORD DENMAN, Ch. J.:

This rule must be made absolute. By mistake, or from some
other cause, the magistrates and the treasurer have both done

RΕΧ
v.
PAYN.
[394]

wrong. I disclaim entering into the general merits of the case.
It is enough that a public duty is left unperformed, by a public
officer keeping back documents of which he obtained custody in
that character. It is quite clear that these books of entries were
the accounts passed. After the defendant had delivered them
in, he had no right to take them away; and the magistrates had
no right to leave them in his hands; nor has he a right to
keep them now. The public are represented, not merely by the
justices present when the accounts are passed, but by all the
justices of the county: and any individual justice has a right,
at all times, to inspect those accounts. We can enter into no
question between the individuals applying and the defendant.
It is said that the defendant has a right to retain the books,
because they contain his discharges and those of his father.
But the book is a public document; and he cannot render it
[*400]   private by *having such discharges written in it. Whatever
inconvenience this puts him to arises from his own fault. The
cases cited are totally inapplicable. In *Rex* v. *Jeyes* (1) the
defendant was the servant of the magistrates; and the COURT
refused to place itself in the situation of the magistrates to make
their officer perform his duty. But here both the magistrates
and their officer have made a mistake, the result of which is that
the public are kept from that to which they have a right. The
treasurer, by keeping the books, contravenes the express provisions of the Act; and, that being so, it is a duty we owe to
the public to make this rule absolute.

WILLIAMS, J. (2) :

The only doubt in my mind has been, whether the defendant
was the proper party to whom the *mandamus* should go. It was
suggested that the duty of depositing was incumbent on the
magistrates; and there may be very great weight in that argument, inasmuch as the accounts were delivered in to them. It
is urged that the proper remedy against the treasurer is indictment. Now, in *Rex* v. *Bristow* (3), and in other cases brought
before us, there was an order for the payment of money; and

(1) 3 Ad. & El. 416.   (3) 3 R. R. 144 (6 T. R. 168).
2) Littledale, J. was absent.

an indictment would lie for disobeying that order; and Lord
KENYON expressly relied upon that.   But here the magistrates
have returned the book to the defendant: I am not prepared to
say that, after that, they can make any order upon him.   If not,
they are not parties against whom a *mandamus* could issue; and,
then, is not the defendant the proper party?   The case is clearly
within stat. *12 Geo. II. c. 29; and, if no indictment lies, there
would be no remedy if the *mandamus* were refused.   Allusion
has been made to the hardship of the defendant's situation.   I
cannot enter into that; but I trust that he will find no difficulty.
The book will be as safe among the county records as in his
own custody.

COLERIDGE, J.:

There can be no doubt that these books are really the accounts:
they are offered and received as such, and the discharge entered
in them.   It has been argued that the accounts were those
separate documents which, in truth, were no more than the
materials for an account.   The treasurer is not merely to throw
before the magistrates his bills and vouchers, but to present a
clear statement of receipts and payments.   It is urged that the
affidavits of the applicants contain many misrepresentations
and suppressions.   But, if statements remain uncontradicted
sufficient to warrant the application, we must proceed upon
them.   The defendant's counsel probably had in view the rule
which prevails where a criminal information is moved for: but
in a case like the present there is no such rule.   My only doubt
was whether *mandamus* be the proper remedy.   The result of
the cases cited appears to be merely this: that, where we find
a public officer, who has received an order from his masters or
any competent authority, and who upon disobeying that order
will be liable to indictment, we do not proceed by *mandamus*.   The
Court leaves the case to the ordinary remedies, not because the
party is too low, but because he has received an order from
competent authority.   Here the magistrates have issued no
order; and this distinguishes the case from *Rex* v. *Bristow* (1),
and *Rex* v. *Jeyes* (2), in one of which *there was an order by the

(1) 3 B. R. 144 (6 T. R. 168).   (2) 3 Ad. & El. 416.

REX
v.
PAYN.

[*401]

[*402]

REX
v.
PAYN.

magistrates, and in the other an order by the Judge of Assize. Then the question with me was, whether the first step should have been for this Court to issue an order on the magistrates to compel them to make an order, disobedience to which might be the subject of an indictment. But the long received practice appears to have been for the magistrates, after having the book in their possession, to return it; and it is doubtful whether the Court can compel them to make an order to restore the books. I have no doubt, however, that we have power to compel a public officer to deposit a public document where the statute directs it to be deposited: and the moment the defendant delivered to the justices his accounts in these books they became public documents. And, when they are in a place of public custody, he may always have access to them for his protection.

Rule absolute.

The *mandamus* issued accordingly, tested 30th January, 7 Will. IV., the day on which the above rule was made absolute. It recited the appointment of the defendant in 1822, receipt and payment of moneys by him, &c., and that he ought to have delivered in accounts, &c., which, after being passed, ought to have been deposited with the clerk of the peace; that they had been delivered in by him, by his producing and delivering in certain accounts in two several books, as and for the true and correct accounts, &c., which accounts, so contained and set forth in the said books, had been from time to time passed as and for the true and exact accounts; that the said accounts so contained, &c., in the said books, and so passed, had not, nor had the said books or either of them, ever been deposited by the defendant or any other person with the clerk of the peace, although the defendant had been required, &c.; "and although the said books, so containing such passed accounts as aforesaid, still remain in your custody, power, and control, in contempt" &c.: the writ then commanded the defendant to deposit, or cause to be deposited, with the clerk of the peace, the said several books, or show cause, &c.

Return. "That I did deposit with the clerk of the peace, on the 25th day of February now last past, one of the books in

[*403]

the within writ mentioned ; " and " that no other of the said books was, on the 30th day of January, in the seventh year of the reign of our Lord the now King, nor has since that day, at any time hitherto, been, nor is now, in my custody, power, or control ; therefore I am unable " &c.

In Easter Term following (5th May, 1837), *Sir John Campbell*, Attorney-General, obtained a rule calling on the defendant to show cause why the return should not be taken off the file of the Court, and why the defendant should not pay the costs of that application.   The rule was obtained on reading all the affidavits filed on the former occasion, and also a further affidavit by the justices who made the former application.   This affidavit gave an account of some of the former proceedings, and alleged that the defendant had not, by himself or his counsel, denied the possession of both the books on the discussion of the former rule, but had insisted on his right to retain them ; that the book not deposited contained that portion of the accounts which appeared most objectionable ; that the deponents believed it to be essential to the *due examination of the accounts that   [*404] this book should be deposited ; and that " they do not know whether the said William Payn has ever, in fact, parted with the possession of the said last-mentioned book, or whether he still has the same in his actual custody ; but, if the same be not, in fact, still in the possession and custody of the said W. P., the deponents believe that the said W. P. has parted with the same since the said rule *nisi* was granted, for the purpose of eluding the command of this honourable Court, and of defeating the ends of justice."   The *Attorney-General* cited *Rex* v. *The Justices of Leicester* (1).

Thesiger (with whom were *Talfourd*, Serjt., and *T. F. Ellis*) showed cause in Hilary Term following (2) :

If it be intended to deny the allegation in the return (which the affidavit does not in fact do), the prosecutors should have traversed the return, or brought an action for a false return. The Court will not try the question of fact on affidavit.   If it be

(1) 4 B. & C. 891, 896, *n.*   (2) January 18th, 1838.

intended to treat the return as a contempt, upon the matter shown in the affidavits, there should be a motion for an attachment. But the affidavits show no contempt. If it be contended that the return is bad on the face of it, the affidavits cannot be used: and then the question is, first, whether the Court will allow such a question to be discussed on this application; and, secondly, whether the return be not good, on the authority of *Rex* v. *Round* (1). On the first point, *Rex* v. *The Justices of Leicester* (2) is an authority: but there the return was bad upon the face of it; there is no authority for taking a return off the file upon affidavit.

(He was then stopped by the COURT.)

[405]

Sir J. Campbell, Attorney-General, *Sir W. W. Follett*, and *F. Robinson, contra :*

As to the form of the application, it is competent to the Court to quash a bad return, which is tantamount to taking it off the file; or, if it be not tantamount, the rule may now be so moulded (3), though a *mandamus* could not (4). The return was quashed in *Rex* v. *The Justices of Leicester* (5). The same course was pursued in *Rex* v. *The St. Katharine Dock Company* (6).

(LORD DENMAN, Ch. J.: That was owing to particular circumstances, under which the Court thought it best to hear the application.)

In *Rex* v. *Round* (7) the *mandamus* was to deliver all books of accounts, &c., in the custody of the defendant: here it is to deposit two specific books. And here the return applies only to the *teste* of the *mandamus;* whereas, in *Rex* v. *Round* (7), the defendant returned that he had no books in his custody when the demand was made.

---

(1) 4 Ad. & El. 139.
(2) 4 B. & C. 891, 896, *n.*
(3) *Rex* v. *The Justices of Leicester,* 4 B. & C. 895.
(4) *Rex* v. *The Church Trustees of St. Pancras,* 3 Ad. & El. 535.

(5) 4 B. & C. 891, 896, *n.*
(6) 38 R. R. 260 (4 B. & Ad. 360). It has been ascertained that there were no affidavits in either of these two cases.
(7) 4 Ad. & El. 139.

(LITTLEDALE, J.: My brother PATTESON thought that part of the return superfluous.)

The defendant here ought to have shown what he had done with the books. But, further, the affidavits prove the return to be evasive and contemptuous. The defendant resists the rule for a *mandamus* on the ground that he claims the custody; and then he returns to the *mandamus* by denying the custody. In Willcock on Corporations, 406, it is said that, if a return "attempt to show an incapacity to obey the writ by reason of the change of circumstances, it must appear that there was no fraud or stratagem on the part of the defendant."

(COLERIDGE, J.: Does not that arise on the face of the return?) [406]

In 5 Bacon's Abr. 282, Mandamus (I) (1), it is laid down that, "As every *mandamus* issues upon a supposal of some breach and disobedience of the law, or neglect of duty in the person to whom it is directed, the return thereto must be certain to every respect; and therefore it is said not to be sufficient to offer such matter as the party may falsify in an action, but also such matter must be alleged, that the Court may be able to judge of it, and determine, whether the party's conduct be agreeable to law or not." In *Rex* v. *Robinson* (2) the *mandamus* was to elect a mayor, to be chosen out of the aldermen. The return was that there were no aldermen; and the Court was moved for an attachment against the defendant, for that this was rather a banter than a return. The Court at first inclined to put the prosecutor to his traverse or action for false return; but afterwards granted the rule, saying, "If it appears this was a frivolous return, and purposely made to avoid the justice of the Court, an attachment shall go." This is a milder proceeding.

LORD DENMAN, Ch. J.:

I think that we ought not to have granted this rule. It must be discharged.

LITTLEDALE, PATTESON, and WILLIAMS, JJ. concurred.

(1) 7th ed.   (2) 8 Mod. 336.

REX
v.
PAYN.

[*407]

Talfourd, Serjt. applied for costs, on the ground of the rule having been moved with costs; and he remarked that in *Rex* v. *Round* (1), where the costs were refused on the ground that the return should have been fuller, *the question was raised in the regular course, by argument on the return.

Per CURIAM: We think this is not a case for costs.

Rule discharged without costs.

1837.
Jan. 31.

[407]

SOWELL *v.* CHAMPION, NICHOLAS TOLMIE TRESIDDER, AND WHITE.

(6 Adol. & Ellis, 407—419; S. C. 2 N. & P. 627; W. W. & D. 667; 7 L. J. (N. S.) K. B. 197.)

In trespass for taking goods under process, upon a regular judgment, but in a place to which the process did not run, the plaintiff may recover the whole value of the goods, and not merely the amount of damage which he has sustained by their being taken in a wrong place.

The COURT refused to grant a rule *nisi* for a new trial on the ground that the verdict was against evidence, where the damages fell below 20*l*., though the case was stated to be of general importance as relating to the boundaries of a jurisdiction.

Attorneys (partners) delivered to a bailiff, for the purpose of being executed, a precept, issued from a local Court, indorsed with the attorneys' names, and directing a levy upon goods within the jurisdiction. The attorneys carried on business at Falmouth; and the party to be levied upon had had, for many years, a house and goods at Penryn, and was not known to have a residence or property elsewhere. The levy was made in that house. The attorneys had sent a message to the debtor, as to the time at which the bailiff would levy; and the bailiff while levying, said that he was employed by those attorneys. In an action against them and the bailiff for unlawfully levying, the attorneys pleaded, 1. Not guilty: 2. A justification under the process: the bailiff pleaded the justification only: the plaintiff replied, that the house was not within the jurisdiction; and issues were joined thereon.

Held, 1. That the attorneys were not entitled to an acquittal at the close of the plaintiff's case, in which the facts had appeared as above stated.

2. That, on the close of the whole case, nothing material having been added except that the defendants, (though they proved a regular judgment), failed to bring themselves within the jurisdiction, the Judge ought to have told the jury that there was no evidence to implicate the

(1) 4 Ad. & El. 139.

attorneys. And this, even assuming them to have known that the bailiff intended levying at the house in question; although, if they had known also that the house was beyond the jurisdiction, they might possibly have been considered joint trespassers with the bailiff.

TRESPASS for breaking and entering plaintiff's dwelling-house, and taking his goods therein.

Plea by Champion. That within the manor of Penryn Forryn, in Cornwall, there now is, and from time whereof &c., hath been, a certain court of record holden in and for the said manor, from three weeks to three weeks, before the steward of the said Court, for the trying and determining of all personal actions and pleas of trespass on the case arising within the said manor, to be commenced by plaint in the said Court to be levied: that one Robert Tresidder levied a plaint in the said *Court against the said Richard Sowell (the now plaintiff) for causes of action arising within the jurisdiction, and such proceedings were thereupon had in that Court, that R. Tresidder, by the judgment of that Court, recovered in such plea against Sowell 11*l*. 18*s*. 8*d*. for his damages, &c., as by the record &c.: that R. Tressider, for obtaining satisfaction of the same, sued out of the said Court, according to the custom thereof, a precept directed to the bailiff of the manor, and to the defendant Champion and two others, commanding them, and every and either of them, that of the goods and chattels of the said R. Sowell within the said manor they or one of them should cause to be levied the damages aforesaid, which the said R. Tresidder had recovered; and which precept, before the delivery thereof to Champion, was duly indorsed to levy the whole, with incidental charges, &c.: that the precept was delivered to Champion, who was the bailiff of the manor and an officer of the said Court, to be executed: by virtue of which precept he, so being and as such bailiff, afterwards, &c., peaceably entered into the said dwelling-house, &c., the outer door being open, and the said dwelling-house being then situate in the said manor, and within the jurisdiction of the said Court, in order to seize, &c., and did then and there seize, &c., the said goods, &c., the same then and there being in the said dwelling-house and within the said manor and jurisdiction, for the purpose of levying, &c., and in so doing did necessarily, &c., as it was

[*408]

33—2

lawful &c.: and that Sowell afterwards, and before the moneys
were levied, paid Champion, so being such bailiff, the said
damages, whereupon he gave up the goods to Sowell, who
accepted the same. Verification.

Pleas by N. T. Tresidder and White. 1. Not guilty. 2. The
[*409] same as Champion's plea, but adding to the statement *of his
entry as bailiff that N. T. Tresidder and White entered as his
servants, and by his command ; and stating the goods to have
been relinquished by Champion, and by N. T. T. and W. as his
servants, and by his command, and with the consent and license
of Sowell. Verification.

Replication to Champion's plea. That the said dwelling-house
in which &c., at the said time when &c., was not situate in the
said manor, and within the jurisdiction of the said Court in the
said plea mentioned, in manner and form &c. Conclusion to
the country. Joinder. To the second plea of Tressider and
White there was a like replication, and joinder thereon.

On the trial before Coleridge, J., at the Cornwall Summer
Assizes, 1835, it was proved, on behalf of the plaintiff, that
Champion, as bailiff, had levied upon certain goods of the plaintiff under a precept of the above Court indorsed with the names
of the defendants N. T. Tressider and White, who were attorneys,
in partnership, living at Falmouth. The plaintiff's house, in
which Champion levied, was in Penryn : he had lived there
many years ; and it appeared, as far as the evidence on this
subject went, that he had no house or goods at any other place.
Evidence was given that N. T. Tresidder had spoken to his
brother (at what time did not precisely appear) about levying
this execution, and that he had one day sent word to the plaintiff that the levy would not be made on that day, as Champion
was not at home. It was then proved that Champion, when
making the levy, stated that he was employed by N. T. Tresidder
and White. The plaintiff's case, as against these parties, being
closed here, their counsel urged that an acquittal should be
immediately taken as against them, there being no evidence
[*410] *that they had authorised a levy on the premises in question,
whether situate within or without the jurisdiction. The learned
Judge refused to direct an acquittal. The case for the defendants

was then gone into. The judgment against Champion was proved; and the defendants' counsel contended, first, that the precept was regular, being founded on a regular judgment, and directing a levy within the jurisdiction; and that the defendants N. T. Tresidder and White (who were attorneys for Robert Tresidder in the cause in the manor Court) had given no specific direction to Champion as to the place where he should levy; which part of the case remained as it had stood at the close of the plaintiff's evidence. It was further contended that the plaintiff's house, where Champion made the levy, was, in fact, within the jurisdiction of the Court of Penryn Forryn; and on this latter point a good deal of evidence was given. The learned Judge left it to the jury to say, first, whether N. T. Tresidder and White directed Champion to levy in the house in question; and, secondly, whether the house was within the manor of Penryn Forryn; and he stated that, if they found for the plaintiff on these points, the damages would be the amount levied, 18*l.* 11*s.* 8*d.* The jury found for the plaintiff on both the points left, and assessed the damages as directed by the learned Judge. Leave was given to move to enter a verdict for N. T. Tresidder and White, if this Court should be of opinion that there was no evidence to go to the jury of their having employed Champion to levy at the house in question.

Crowder, in the ensuing Term, November 5th, 1835, moved accordingly. He, at the same time, moved, on behalf of Champion, for a new trial, on the ground that *the learned [*411] Judge had misdirected the jury as to the amount of damages; contending that, as the goods were taken under a valid judgment and precept, for a debt not now denied to have been due, the true measure of damages was the injury, if any, which the now plaintiff had suffered by having his goods taken in an improper place.

(COLERIDGE, J.: Damages were pressed for; and I told the jury that the plaintiff must be replaced in the situation in which he was before the levy.)

Crowder also moved for a new trial, on the ground that the verdict was against evidence as to the extent of the manorial

SOWELL
v.
CHAMPION,

jurisdiction; and he urged that, although the damages were below 20*l.*, the question, affecting the general interest of a district, was important enough to warrant a departure from the general practice on the subject of new trials.

LORD DENMAN, Ch. J. :

On the first point I think there ought to be a rule. As to the amount of damages, I am of opinion that the learned Judge left the question in the manner most favourable to the defendants. Parties are not to extort even what is justly due, by the improper execution of a warrant. It might lead to the most fatal consequences if we were to hold otherwise. The person who takes upon him to exact money by an authority which he does not possess is bound to repay what he has so levied. As to the question upon the evidence of jurisdiction, I regret that we should be obliged to refuse a rule for a new trial, in a case affecting the general interests of a neighbourhood ; but I think the apprehension of that inconvenience in a particular case ought not to make us depart from the regulation which has been laid down in cases where the damages fall below 20*l.*

[412]   PATTESON, J. :

I am of the same opinion. As to the amount of damages, the reduction would not perhaps be mischievous in the present case ; but I am afraid of the principle that would be established if we held that, where money has been levied by an illegal course of proceeding, the damage to be taken into consideration is only the amount of injury actually sustained. All kinds of irregularities would follow if such a doctrine were admitted.

WILLIAMS, J. :   •

To admit the proposed mode of estimating damages would be, in effect, allowing the illegal proceeding to stand good. The only way to deal with it is to set aside what has been done altogether.

COLERIDGE, J. concurred.

Rule nisi granted, to enter a verdict for Tresidder and White.

[After argument:]

LORD DENMAN, Ch. J., now delivered the judgment of the Court:

This case turns upon the question, whether the defendant Champion, being the bailiff for executing process within an inferior jurisdiction, was directed by the other two defendants, being the attorneys who sued out the process, to make a levy in the plaintiff's house, which was proved to be out of the jurisdiction. The rule was granted on a doubt whether there was any evidence of such specific direction.

All the defendants pleaded not guilty; and, secondly, a justification, under the judgment and *fi. fa.*, averring the plaintiff's house to be within the jurisdiction. The plaintiff contented himself at first with proving the goods seized, and that they were taken by the defendant Champion, under a precept handed to him by the defendants Tresidder and White. At the close of this case, the counsel for Tresidder and White applied to the learned Judge to direct their acquittal, which, we think, he properly refused. The ground for the application was the alleged absence of any evidence against them to make them co-trespassers; but this ground, if true in fact, would by itself have been wholly insufficient to warrant it. The application to a Judge, in the course of a cause, to direct a verdict for one or more of several defendants in trespass is strictly to his discretion; and that discretion is to be regulated, not merely by the fact that at the close of the plaintiff's case no evidence appears to affect them, but by the probabilities whether any such will arise before the whole evidence in the cause closes. There is so palpable a failure of justice, when the evidence for the defence discloses a case against a defendant already prematurely acquitted, that *such acquittal ought never to take place, but where there is the strongest reason to believe that such a consequence cannot follow. In the present case, we think that if, in truth, there had been nothing for the jury to consider, as against these two defendants, the Judge would have exercised a sound discretion in refusing to direct their acquittal when the application was made; but we are of opinion that, until the judgment was put in, and they appeared to be acting as attorneys in the execution

[*416]

of a judgment, they could be considered only as directing a seizure of the plaintiff's goods without any authority ; and although the direction was, in terms, to seize within one jurisdiction, and the seizure was, in fact, made in another, yet it was open for the jury, as against wrong doers, to consider, upon the evidence, whether they did not direct the seizure to be made in that place in which they certainly knew that it would take place.

The defendants then attempted to establish their justification, but failed : they proved, however, a judgment against the plaintiff, and an execution regular in all respects, except that the plaintiff's house was not within the jurisdiction. In the course of this evidence, however, it clearly appeared that the two attorneys had merely handed the precept to the bailiff to be executed ; and it was now contended that they were not liable to an action of trespass, if he acted beyond the bounds of his franchise, which it was his duty to know, and not their's. The plaintiff not disputing this general proposition, contended that the attorneys had, in effect, taken upon themselves to order the bailiff to enter the plaintiff's house. The circumstances relied upon to prove this proposition were that, all these persons living near together and being acquainted, and the plaintiff having

[*417] *notoriously no other house than this, and no goods but what were in this, the bailiff must have understood the attorneys, when he received the precept from them, to intend that he should make the seizure in that identical house : and, further, that one of the attorneys sent a message to the plaintiff to inform him that Champion was about to be absent a short time, and would not levy on that day. The special pleas, pleaded by all the defendants, were also strongly urged, as showing that they all avowed and justified the fact of levying at the plaintiff's house ; Tresidder and White thus adopting the act of Champion, as, indeed, they might fearlessly do, if they believed their own plea that the house was within the jurisdiction.

Upon consideration these grounds appear to us all insufficient.

1. The attorney, who places a writ for execution in the hands of an officer, does a lawful act, though he may be fully persuaded that the officer will be likely to execute it in some particular

place which may turn out, upon inquiry, to be out of his jurisdiction. The attorney's opinion upon such a point is immaterial,
unless he induces the officer to act upon it. He is not bound to
form any: the officer must, at his peril, act where he has the
power. We think that the circumstances of the case go no
further than to show that, when the attorney gave the precept,
he thought it would be executed at the plaintiff's house, without
directing or authorising it.

2. If it could be pressed even to the extent of implying that
the attorney knew the bailiff intended to do so, we cannot say
that is any evidence of his giving such authority. The bailiff
may have told him his intention, *and the attorney may have
either thought him right, or not thought about the matter.
That the bailiff's intention originated with some act or word
of the attorney is not at all evidenced by the knowledge now
supposed. If, indeed, the bailiff had communicated his intention, with respect to a house that the attorney knew to be out
of the jurisdiction, his acquiescence in an act he must have
known to be illegal might possibly have made him a joint
trespasser. But every thing here makes it impossible to doubt
the attorney's *bond fide* belief that the house was within the
jurisdiction.

3. Furthermore, the plaintiff argues the co-operation of all
the defendants in the unlawful entry of the plaintiff's house
from the special pleas. He contends that, if the attorney gave
no special directions to the bailiff, he would have rested on the
general issue, and not have defended himself by asserting the
lawfulness of the act, as done within the jurisdiction. The
introduction, however, of a special plea on the record can
furnish no evidence in answer to the general issue. A defendant, by adducing evidence on a second plea, may strengthen
against himself a case already made on the first; but he
makes no such case by the mere averments or admissions in
such plea.

Upon the whole, therefore, we think that, at the close of the
case, as the two defendants Tresidder and White would have
been entitled, if sued without Champion, to a nonsuit, they were
entitled to a positive direction from the Judge to the jury that

[*418]

they ought to find a verdict in their favour; and that he was mistaken in leaving it at all as an open question for their consideration. It follows that, as these defendants are to have the same benefit now as if the Judge had given that strong direction, and a verdict had passed in their favour, *a verdict of Not guilty ought now to be entered for them.

Rule absolute.

IN THE EXCHEQUER CHAMBER.

(ERROR FROM THE KING'S BENCH.)

1837.
Feb. 6.

[438]

HITCHCOCK *v.* COKER (1).

(6 Adol. & Ellis, 438—457; S. C. 1 N. & P. 796; 2 H. & W. 464; 6 L. J. (N. S.) Ex. 266.)

Declaration, in assumpsit, that, before and at the time of the promise, plaintiff was a druggist, and had taken defendant into his service as assistant, at an annual salary, on condition (among other things) that defendant should enter into and perform the agreement after mentioned : that defendant, in consideration of the premises, and in performance of the condition, by an agreement, reciting as above, agreed with plaintiff that, if defendant should at any time thereafter exercise the trade or business of a chemist and druggist in the town of T., or within three miles thereof, defendant should pay plaintiff 500*l.* as liquidated damages. Allegation of mutual promises to perform the agreement; and that defendant exercised the trade within T. Breach, non-payment of 500*l.* Verdict for plaintiff, on *non assumpsit.*

Held, by the Court of Exchequer Chamber (on error from the Court of K. B., in which judgment had been arrested),

1. That there was a legal consideration for the contract.

2. That the Court could not enter into the question, whether the consideration was equal in value to the restraint agreed to by the defendant.

3. That the restraint was not shown to be unreasonable or oppressive by the circumstance that its duration was not limited to the life of the plaintiff, or to the time during which he should carry on the business.

Judgment for the plaintiff.

ASSUMPSIT. The declaration stated that, before and at the time of making the agreement and the promise of defendant thereinafter mentioned, the plaintiff was a druggist, and had taken defendant into his service as an assistant in his said

---

(1) Cited by LINDLEY, M. R., and followed in *Haynes* v. *Doman* [1899] 2 Ch. 13, 30, 68 L. J. Ch. 419, 421, 80 L. T. 569, C. A.; a case in which all the principal modern authorities are cited and considered.--R. C.

trade, at a certain annual salary, upon condition (amongst other things) that defendant should enter into and observe and perform the agreement thereinafter contained : that, in consideration of the premises, and in performance of the said condition, to wit on 12th of April, 1832, by a certain agreement then made by and between defendant of the one part and plaintiff of the other, (after reciting that plaintiff had taken defendant into his service as an assistant at a certain annual salary, upon condition, amongst other things, that defendant should enter into and observe and perform the agreement thereinafter contained) the defendant did, in and by the said agreement, promise and agree to and with the plaintiff that, if defendant should at any time thereafter, directly or *indirectly, either in his own name or in the name of any other person, use, exercise, carry on, or follow the trades or businesses of a chemist and druggist, or either of them, within the town of Taunton, in the county of Somerset, or within three miles thereof, then defendant, his executors, &c., should or would, on demand, pay plaintiff, his executors, &c., 500l., as and for liquidated damages ; and the said agreement being so made as aforesaid, afterwards, to wit on &c., (mutual promises to perform the agreement) : and, although &c. (allegation of performance by plaintiff), yet defendant hath not performed the said agreement on his part, but, on the contrary, afterwards, and after the making the said agreement, to wit 21st of April, 1832, defendant in his own name used and exercised, carried on and followed, the trades and businesses of a chemist and druggist within the said town of T., in the said county of S., contrary to the said agreement : and, although plaintiff afterwards, to wit 20th of January, 1835, demanded of defendant the said 500l., yet defendant, not regarding &c., hath not as yet paid &c. Plea, *non assumpsit.*

[*439]

On the trial before Gurney, B., at the Somersetshire Spring Assizes, 1835, the jury, by agreement of the parties, found a verdict for the plaintiff, assessing the actual damages at 500l., whether the 500l. in the agreement mentioned was to be considered as liquidated damages or a penal sum. In Easter Term, 1835, *Erle* obtained a rule, in the Court of King's Bench, to show cause why judgment should not be arrested.

HITCHCOCK
v.
COKER.

[*440]

Bompas, Serjt. and *Crowder* showed cause in Easter Term last (1) :

The agreement recites that the plaintiff *had taken the defendant in consideration of his performing the agreement; and then there are mutual promises to perform, which are the consideration for each other. The promise alleged in the declaration to be broken is, therefore, on the whole, upon an executory consideration. It is not as if the defendant had promised in consideration of the plaintiff having taken him. The general question is, whether the restraint of trade here be larger than the law will sanction. Some cases are collected in Com. Dig. Trade (D 3), and in note (1) to *Hunlocke* v. *Blacklowe* (2). The leading case is *Mitchel* v. *Reynolds* (3). There a bond not to carry on the trade of a baker within a parish was held good ; and PARKER, Ch. J. said that, whether by promises or bond, a general restraint was bad, but a restraint as to a particular place good, if there appeared a sufficient consideration. Many parishes are larger than the space to which the present contract extends. In *Wickens* v. *Evans* (4) parties mutually agreed to abstain from interfering with each other in large districts of England, and it was held good. In *Horner* v. *Graves* (5) an agreement not to practise as a dentist within 100 miles of York, without the plaintiff's consent, while the plaintiff should be practising as a dentist, was held bad, on the ground that the restraint was larger than was needed for the plaintiff's protection.

(COLERIDGE, J.: Here the agreement restrains the defendant, though the plaintiff should leave the place, or quit practice, or die.)

[*441]

The agreement would probably be construed as a personal contract, expiring *with the lives of the parties. Besides, the plaintiff might choose to bargain for a restraint enabling him to sell his practice, or to bequeath it. Many of the agreements

(1) April 30, 1836, before Lord Denman, Ch. J., Littledale, Patteson, and Coleridge, JJ.
(2) 2 Wms. Saund. 156.
(3) 1 P. Wms. 181. See notes on

S. C. in 1 Smith's Leading Cases, p. 181.
(4) 32 R. R. 806 (3 Y. & J. 318).
(5) 33 R. R. 635 (7 Bing. 735).

which have been held good were in this form. In *Davis* v.   HITCHCOC
Mason (1) a bond conditioned that the defendant, who had been   *v.*
taken as assistant to the plaintiff, a surgeon and apothecary,   COKER.
should not practise within ten miles of Thetford, was held good.
There the consideration was like that in the present case, even
if it be held executed. In that case there was no limitation of
the contract to the duration of the plaintiff's practice or life:
and there was none such in *Chesman* v. *Nainby* (2), or in *Hayward*
v. *Young* (3), where the restraint extended over twenty miles.
In *Young* v. *Timmins* (4) the restraint was held to be bad, as
being without adequate consideration, the one party being
restrained from working without the consent of the other, who
was not bound to find work, and was expressly allowed to employ
others, and rescind the agreement at three months' notice.
When it is said that there must be adequate consideration, it is
not meant that the Court will inquire whether the party sub-
mitting to the restraint made a judicious contract. There must
be a legal consideration to support the promise; and the cases
decide that the taking into service is such. In *Mitchel* v.
Reynolds (5) one test put is the advantage to the party who
imposes the restraint. In *Homer* v. *Ashford* (6) it was held
sufficient, on general demurrer, that the declaration stated the
covenant to be " for the considerations *therein mentioned."   [*442]
This shows that the magnitude of the consideration moving the
party promising is not to be weighed by the Court, if there be
some legal consideration.

Erle and *Kinglake, contrà :*

No consideration appears for the agreement itself, except that
the plaintiff had taken the defendant into his service: that is an
executed consideration, and without a request. Mutual promises
form a good consideration, where the agreement itself is good;
but, according to the cases, an agreement in restraint of trade
must itself be upon good consideration. It makes no difference

---

(1) 2 R. R. 562 (5 T. R. 118).   (3) 2 Chitty, 407.
(2) 2 Str. 739; *S. C.* 2 Ld. Ray. (4) 1 Cr. & J. 331; 1 Tyr. 226.
1456; *S. C.* in error, in Dom. Proc. (5) 1 P. Wms. 190, 191, 192.
1 Br. P. C. 234 (2nd ed.).   (6) 28 R. R. 634 (3 Bing. 322).

HITCHCOCK
v.
COKER.

that the agreement states the plaintiff to have taken the defendant
on condition that the latter would perform an agreement not then
existing.   But, independently of this objection, there is no consideration unless the plaintiff part with, or the defendant receive,
some advantage.   Here the plaintiff is bound to nothing, and
the defendant gets nothing.   At all events the consideration
is not adequate to the restraint.   In *Mitchel* v. *Reynolds* (1)
PARKER, Ch. J., says, "Where a contract for restraint of trade
appears to be made upon a good and adequate consideration,
so as to make it a proper and useful contract, it is good."   In
Gale v. *Reed* (2) Lord ELLENBOROUGH says, "The restraint on one
side meant to be enforced should in reason be coextensive only
with the benefits meant to be enjoyed on the other;" and he
adds that the Courts will so construe the agreements as to make,
if possible, the benefits coextensive.   Therefore a mere technical
consideration is not enough.   In an *Anonymous* case in Moore (3),

[*443]

it was held that no *action lay on a bond, by an apprentice of a
mercer of Nottingham to his master, not to exercise the trade in
Nottingham for four years.   In another *Anonymous* (4) case in
the same book, a bond conditioned not to exercise the trade of
a blacksmith in South Mims was held bad.   No consideration
appeared in these cases; and the Court presumed none, though
the contracts were under seal.   In *Chesman* v. *Nainby* (5) the
Court thought there was ground for inferring a covenant to
instruct for three years.   In *Horner* v. *Graves* (6) the Court
adverted to the question of the slenderness of consideration as
a proper test, though the decision was principally on another
point.   Further, an agreement of this sort, to be good, must not
be oppressive; which it is, if it impose a restraint greater than
is necessary for the plaintiff's protection (7).   Here the time
during which the defendant is restrained is longer than the
plaintiff can require, inasmuch as it is not put an end to by the
plaintiff's death or retirement from business.   Suppositions have

---

(1) 1 P. Wms. 186.

(2) 9 R. R. 376 (8 East, 80).

(3) Moore, 115, pl. 259.

(4) Moore, 242, pl. 379; *S. C.* 2
Leon. 210.

(5) 2 Str. 739; *S. C.* 2 Ld. Ray.

1456; *S. C.* in error, in Dom. Proc.
1 Br. P. C. 234 (2nd ed.).

(6) 33 R. R. 635 (7 Bing. 735).

(7) Per CURIAM, in *Horner* v.
Graves, 33 R. R. at p. 642 (7 Bing.
743.)

been made for the plaintiff, upon which it might possibly be for
his benefit that the restraint should not be put an end to by his
own death or ceasing to carry on the business : but the restraint
is general, and will, if the agreement be upheld, operate whether
those suppositions be verified or not. The objections hitherto
have been made principally to the extent of space to which the
contract extended : but its duration is manifestly as much a test
of *its reasonableness. In *Davis* v. *Mason* (1) and *Homer* v.
Ashford (2) the duration was limited to fourteen years : in
Mitchel v. *Reynolds* (3) to five. It does not appear whether there
was a limit in *Hayward* v. *Young* (4). If the agreement here be
construed as limited to the time during which the defendant
should remain in the plaintiff's service, the declaration is bad,
for want of an allegation that the defendant was still in the
service. So if it be construed as limited to the life of the
plaintiff, or his carrying on trade by himself or his executors or
assigns, the corresponding allegations are wanting.

HITOHOOOK
v.
COKER.

[*444]

Cur. adv. vult.

LORD DENMAN, Ch. J., in Trinity Term last (May 25th), delivered
the judgment of the Court of King's Bench. After stating
the nature of the motion, his Lordship said :

Some minor objections were taken to the declaration, which it
is unnecessary to notice, as we are of opinion that the agreement
itself is illegal.

The law upon this subject has been settled by a series of
decisions, from *Mitchel* v. *Reynolds* (3) to *Horner* v. *Graves* (5) ;
viz., that an agreement for a partial and reasonable restraint of
trade upon an adequate consideration is binding, but that an
agreement for general restraint is illegal. What shall be considered as a reasonable restraint was much discussed in the case
of *Horner* v. *Graves* (5) ; where the CHIEF JUSTICE of the Common
Pleas observed (6), "We do not see how a better test can be
applied to the question whether reasonable *or not, than by considering whether the restraint is such only as to afford a fair

[*445]

(1) 2 R. R. 562 (5 T. R. 118).
(2) 28 R. R. 634 (3 Bing. 323).
(3) 1 P. Wms. 181.

(4) 2 Chitty, 407.
(5) 33 R. R. 635 (7 Bing. 735).
(6) 33 R. R. at p. 642 (7 Bing. 743).

protection to the interests of the party in favour of whom it is
given, and not so large as to interfere with the interests of the
public. Whatever restraint is larger than the necessary protection of the party, can be of no benefit to either, it can only be
oppressive; and if oppressive, it is, in the eye of the law, unreasonable. Whatever is injurious to the interests of the public is
void, on the grounds of public policy." It may indeed be said
that all such agreements interfere in some degree with the public
interest; and great difficulty may attend the application of that
test, from the variety of opinions that may exist on the question
of interference with the public interest which the law ought to
permit. But, on the other hand, it appears quite safe to hold
that the law will not enforce any agreement for curtailing the
rights both of the public and the contracting party, without its
being necessary for the protection of him in whose favour it
is made.

In that case, the question arose upon the distance to which
the restraint extended: here it arises upon the time.   The
agreement as to time is indefinite; it is not limited to such time
as the plaintiff should carry on business in Taunton, nor to any
given number of years, nor even to the life of the plaintiff: but
it attaches to the defendant so long as he lives, although the
plaintiff may have left Taunton, or parted with his business,
or be dead. None of the cases in the books turn upon this
question; it is indeed alluded to in *Chesman* v. *Nainby* (1); and

[*446] the counsel for the plaintiff below, *arguendo*, *seems to admit
that the bond on which that action was brought could not be put
in force for a breach after the death of the obligee: but the
breach was assigned on another part of the condition, and held
good. In the present case, the agreement, not being under seal,
and not being divisible, if bad in part, is bad altogether. In
the absence of any authority establishing the validity of an
agreement thus indefinite in point of time, and trying the
reasonableness of it by the test above alluded to, we think that
the restraint is larger than the necessary protection of the party
in favour of whom it is given requires, and that it is therefore

(1) 2 Str. 739; *S. C.* 2 Ld. Ray. 1456; *S. C.* in error, in Dom. Proc.
1 Br. P. C. 234 (2nd ed.).

oppressive and unreasonable. The consideration for this agree- HITCHCOCK
ment appears to have been trifling; but, even if it had been   *v.*
much more valuable, the same result would have followed. The   COKER.
judgment must be arrested.

Rule absolute.

Error having been brought in the Court of Exchequer
Chamber, the case was argued on Saturday, November 26th,
1836, before Tindal, Ch. J., Lord Abinger, C. B., Gaselee and
Vaughan, JJ., Bolland and Alderson, Barons.

> *Sir W. W. Follett*, for the plaintiff in error (the plaintiff
> below):

The plaintiff was not bound to take the defendant into his
service: his doing so, therefore, constitutes a good consideration:
the defendant has learned the secrets of the business, and has
become acquainted with the customers. The objection as to the
restraint being larger than is beneficial to the plaintiff was for
the parties themselves to consider: but, in fact, it is not larger.
First, as to the magnitude of the consideration, *there is here a   [*447]
full consideration in fact: but it is necessary only that there
should be a consideration capable of legally supporting an agreement: the magnitude of its value, provided there be a legal
value, the Court cannot consider. This is all that the *dicta* to
be found (for instance) in *Mitchel* v. *Reynolds* (1), *Horner* v.
Graves (2), *Davis* v. *Mason* (3), *Gale* v. *Reed* (4), and *Young* v.
Timmins (5) can mean.

(ALDERSON, B.: If the consideration were so small as to be
colourable, the agreement would be bad.)

That is the full extent to which the *dicta* can be held properly
to go. The language which has been supposed to touch upon
the amount of consideration had reference to the cases of
bonds, where no consideration at all appeared, as in the case of
the dyer who gave a bond without consideration (6). In *Horner* v.

(1) 1 P. Wms. 181.
(2) 33 R. R. 635 (7 Bing. 735).
(3) 2 R. R. 562 (5 T. R. 118).
(4) 9 R. R. 376 (8 East, 80).
(5) 1 Cr. & J. 331; 1 Tyr. 226.

(6) Year B. Pasch. 2 Hen. V. fol. 5,
B. pl. 26; agreed to per CURIAM,
in the *Anonymous* case, Moore, 242,
pl. 379; *S. C.* 2 Leon. 210; and see in
Mitchell v. *Reynolds*, 1 P. Wms. 193.

HITCHCOCK
v.
COKER.

Graves (1) the amount of consideration was not the ground of decision.   Secondly, the extent of the restraint is reasonable. In *Horner* v. *Graves* (1) the restriction was thought to extend to a distance which could not be of any benefit to the plaintiff.

(LORD ABINGER, C. B.: I should have thought that both questions were for the jury.)

[*448]

It is difficult to see how the questions can be raised on the record.   In *Bunn* v. *Guy* (2) the restriction of an attorney's practice extended to London and 150 miles round, and yet was held valid.   Here the objection is to the time.   The policy of the English law admits of restraints unlimited *as to time : for, under the ancient corporate system, the carrying on trades within certain limits by any but a privileged class was often prohibited without any such limitation.   The restraint here does not extend beyond the defendant's life.   These restraints commonly originate in contracts of service, in partnerships, and in sales of good-will.   The restriction may be unlimited, as to time, in any of these cases.   If the plaintiff had sold the good-will to a stranger, could it have been unreasonable that he himself should have been restrained for life, without reference to the vendee's life, since the vendee might afterwards wish to sell it?   Or why should not the plaintiff have the power of bequeathing it?   Good-will has been treated as assets in the hands of an executor (3).   So, if one partner quit a partner-ship on terms, it is reasonable that he should agree, for his own life, not to be a competitor with the remaining partners, or any new partners or assignees.   There is no authority for the limita-tion contended for, except the argument of counsel in *Chesman* v. *Nainby* (4), and the apparent concession of the opposite counsel, the point not being raised in the cause.   If it be necessary to confine the restraint to the plaintiff's life, then a restraint for fourteen years only, without reference to the life, would be bad : but it was held good in *Davis* v. *Mason* (5) and *Homer* v. *Ashford* (6).

(1) 33 R. R. 635; 7 Bing. 735.   (2nd ed.).
(2) 7 R. R. 560 (1 Smith, 1 ; 4 East,   (4) 2 Str. 743, 744.
190).   (5) 2 R. R. 562 (5 T. R. 118).
(3) See 2 Williams on Executors,   (6) 28 R. R. 634 (3 Bing. 323).
1178, *n.* (*p*), pt. iv. book 1, ch. i.

In *Mitchel* v. *Reynolds* (1) no such limitation is laid down in the judgment; and there the contract was for five years generally, without reference to the life of any party. In **Bunn* v. *Guy* (2) and *Hayward* v. *Young* (3) there was no limitation as to time. In *Bryson* v. *Whitehead* (4) Sir JOHN LEACH, Vice-Chancellor, enforced an agreement by a trader, upon selling a secret in his trade, to restrain himself for twenty years absolutely from the use of such secret, and said that he might "restrain himself generally." The limitation as to time might have been insisted on in *Capes* v. *Hutton* (5), but was not. The reporter's note on *Williams* v. *Williams* (6) collects the cases as to contracts in restraint of trade, but does not mention the question of duration. If the want of limitation to the life of the plaintiff render the defendant liable to the plaintiff's executors, that must be on the ground that the restraint becomes part of the plaintiff's personal estate: if so, the contract is not longer than is beneficial to the plaintiff. Further, the contract is for the defendant to pay 500*l.* if he practise. The plaintiff might, if he pleased, have demanded the sum absolutely for taking the defendant into his service at all: why then may he not make the payment depend upon the defendant's abstaining from practice? On a contract, shaped as this is, perhaps a court of equity would not restrain a party from practising, but would treat the agreement as simply a condition attached to the payment of the money.

Erle, for the defendant in error (the defendant below):

First, contracts in restraint of trade are void *primâ facie*: but, where the consideration is adequate, it is an excepted case, and they are then allowed: *Mitchel* v. *Reynolds* (7). Here there is not such a consideration. The **service is paid for by the salary, which must be presumed to be no more than adequate to the service, and which cannot form a consideration for the restraint. The agreement is made after the relation of master and servant

[*450]

(1) 1 P. Wms. 181.
(2) 7 R. R. 560 (1 Smith, 1; 4 East, 190).
(3) 2 Chitty, 407.
(4) 1 Sim. & St. 74.
(5) 26 R. R. 102 (2 Russ. 357).
(6) 2 Swanst. 254.
(7) 1 P. Wms. 181.

HITCHCOCK
v.
COKER.

is entered into: the consideration is therefore executed; and there is no request. But, supposing a legal consideration to exist, there is no adequate one; this has been always required to take the case out of the rule invalidating such contracts; and the Courts will notice the adequacy or inadequacy. The expressions of the Judges can be no otherwise construed.

(ALDERSON, B. referred to the language of Lord KENYON, in *Davis* v. *Mason* (1).)

There the introduction is put as a "fair" consideration. In *Mitchel* v. *Reynolds* (2) the words of the Court are, "upon a good and adequate consideration, so as to make it a proper and useful contract."

(LORD ABINGER, C. B.: Do you say a bond would be bad, if it were conditioned for any abstinence from trade and no consideration appeared?)

The COURT, in *Mitchel* v. *Reynolds* (3), say, in answer to such a question, "Wherever such contract *stat indifferenter*, and for aught appears, may be either good or bad, the law presumes it *primâ facie* to be bad." In the two *Anonymous* cases (4) (5) in Moore, bonds were held void: yet, in the technical sense, a bond is presumed to be upon consideration. In *Jelliet* v. *Broad* (6) a promise, for a good consideration, not to trade in a particular place, was upheld; but *Leggate* v. *Batchelour* (6) was there cited and approved of, in which a bond on a condition not to trade in Canterbury or Rochester for four years, no *consideration appearing, was held bad.

[*451]

(ALDERSON, B.: In *Jelliet* v. *Broad* (6) the consideration was the sale of goods for 200*l.*: it might be argued that the goods were to be presumed worth the money.)

Prugnell v. *Gosse* (7) seems to show that the adequacy of the consideration must be discussed. In *Young* v. *Timmins* (8) the

(1) 2 R. R. 562 (5 T. R. 120).   Leon. 210.
(2) 1 P. Wms. 186.   (6) Noy, 98.
(3) 1 P. Wms. 192.   (7) Aleyn, 67.
(4) Moore, 115, pl. 259.   (8) 1 Cr. & J. 331; 1 Tyr. 226.
(5) Moore, 242, pl. 379; S. C. 2

judgment turned entirely on the question of adequacy of consideration: there was a clear technical consideration, yet the contract was held bad.

(ALDERSON, B.: One party had the power to determine the contract, so that he gave up nothing: here there is an annual salary, which implies at least a contract for a year.)

It does appear that the plaintiff could not discharge the defendant; nor that the defendant was still in the plaintiff's service when he signed the agreement. In *Gale* v. *Reed* (1) Lord ELLENBOROUGH enquires, whether the consideration be "adequate," whether "the restraint on one side" be "co-extensive only with the benefits meant to be enjoyed on the other," whether "the compensation and restraint" be "commensurate with each other." So in *Chesman* v. *Nainby* (2) the question is discussed on the commensurability of the consideration with the restraint. The same criterion was recognised in *Horner* v. *Graves* (3). Assuming, then, that principle, it cannot be said that the being taken into service at an annual salary, at a time past, is a consideration adequate to a promise by a party to abstain during his whole life from exercising the business in the prescribed limits. Secondly, the restraint is more than is necessary for the plaintiff's protection. It is said that the plaintiff may wish *to sell or bequeath: but nothing of that kind appears: and, on that supposition, the contract should still have been limited to such time as the plaintiff, or his executors, administrators, or assigns, should carry on the business.

[*452]

Sir W. W. Follett, in reply:

There are many expressions which at first sight appear to warrant the argument that the Court will measure the adequacy of the consideration to the restraint; but no decision has turned upon the degree. In *Prugnell* v. *Gosse* (4) the words are "no consideration," and "a consideration." PARKER, Ch. J. clearly

(1) 9 R. R. 376 (8 East, 80).
(2) 2 Str. 739; *S. C.* 2 Ld. Ray. 1456; *S. C.* in error, in Dom. Proc.
1 Br. P. C. 234 (2nd ed.).
(3) 33 R. R. 635 (7 Bing. 735).
(4) Aleyn, 67.

HITCHCOCK
v.
COKER.

speaks only of technical adequacy in *Mitchel* v. *Reynolds* (1) ; yet he uses the word " adequate," which is the expression of the Judges, in *Young* v. *Timmins* (2), insisted on here for the defendant. In *Wickens* v. *Evans* (3) HULLOCK, B. uses the words " sufficient consideration," but afterwards " no consideration," which shows that the technical sufficiency was meant. The expression of the COURT in *Horner* v. *Graves* (4) is "good and sufficient." It is said that the plaintiff might discharge the defendant : but in *Davis* v. *Mason* (5) such a discharge was admitted on the record. As to the technical objections to the consideration, the original agreement, at the commencement of the service, clearly is that the plaintiff shall take the defendant into service, and that the defendant shall promise : the agreement is afterwards reduced into writing.

(LORD ABINGER, C. B. : Suppose the plaintiff to die without assigning the business : who is to sue ?)

The executors, if any action would lie.

Cur. adv. vult.

[453]

TINDAL, Ch. J. on this day delivered the judgment of the COURT:

The ground upon which the Court of King's Bench held, after a verdict obtained by the plaintiff in this case, that the judgment of that Court ought to be arrested, was, that the agreement set out upon the record, and upon which the action was brought, was void in law, being an agreement in unreasonable restraint of trade. For, although the inadequacy of the consideration, upon which the agreement was entered into, was urged in argument as one reason for holding the agreement to be void,—and, in the delivering the opinion of the Court, some reference was made to that objection,—yet it is manifest that it formed no part of the ground upon which the Court refused to give their judgment in favour of the plaintiff.

The consideration for the agreement in question appears to have been, the receiving of the defendant into the service of the

(1) 1 P. Wms. 185, 186.
(2) 1 Cr. & J. 331 ; 1 Tyr. 226.
(3) 32 R. R. 806 (3 Y. & J. 318).

(4) 33 R. R. 635 (7 Bing. 735).
(5) 2 R. R. 562 (5 T. R. 118).

plaintiff as an assistant in his trade or business of a chemist and
druggist, at a certain annual salary.   And the agreement, on the
part of the defendant, founded upon such consideration, is that,
if he should at any time thereafter, directly or indirectly, in his
own name or that of any other person, exercise the trade or
business of a chemist and druggist within the town of Taunton,
in the county of Somerset, or within three miles thereof, then
that the defendant should, on demand, pay to the plaintiff, his
executors, administrators or assigns, the full sum of 500*l.* as and
for liquidated damages.

The ground upon which the Court below has held this restraint
of the defendant to be unreasonable is that it operates more
largely than the benefit or protection *of the plaintiff can possibly
require ; that it is indefinite in point of time, being neither
limited to the plaintiff's continuing to carry on his business at
Taunton, nor even to the term of his life.   We agree in the
general principle adopted by the Court, that, where the restraint
of a party from carrying on a trade is larger and wider than the
protection of the party with whom the contract is made can
possibly require, such restraint must be considered as unreasonable in law, and the contract which would enforce it must be
therefore void.   But the difficulty we feel is in the application of
that principle to the case before us.   Where the question turns
upon the reasonableness or unreasonableness of the restriction of
the party from carrying on trade or business within a certain space
or district, the answer may depend upon various circumstances
that may be brought to bear upon it, such as the nature of the
trade or profession, the populousness of the neighbourhood, the
mode in which the trade or profession is usually carried on ; with
the knowledge of which, and other circumstances, a judgment may
be formed whether the restriction is wider than the protection
of the party can reasonably require.   But with respect to the
duration of the restriction the case is different.   The good-will
of a trade is a subject of value and price.   It may be sold,
bequeathed, or become assets in the hands of the personal representative of a trader.   And, if the restriction as to time is to be
held to be illegal, if extended beyond the period of the party by
himself carrying on the trade, the value of such good-will,

considered in those various points of view, is altogether destroyed.
If, therefore, it is not unreasonable, as undoubtedly it is not, to
prevent a servant from entering into the same trade in the same

[*455] town in which his master *lives, so long as the master carries
on the trade there, we cannot think it unreasonable that the
restraint should be carried further, and should be allowed to
continue, if the master sells the trade, or bequeaths it, or it
becomes the property of his personal representative; that is, if it
is reasonable that the master should by an agreement secure himself from a diminution of the annual profits of his trade, it does
not appear to us unreasonable that the restriction should go so far
as to secure to the master the enjoyment of the price or value for
which the trade would sell, or secure the enjoyment of the same
trade to his purchaser, or legatee, or executor.   And the only effectual mode of doing this appears to be, by making the restriction
of the servant's setting up or entering into the trade or business
within the given limit co-extensive with the servant's life.

And, accordingly, in many of the cases which have been cited,
the restriction has been held good, although it continued for the
life of the party restrained.   And, on the other hand, no case
has been referred to, where the contrary doctrine has been laid
down.   In *Bunn* v. *Guy* (1) a covenant by an attorney, who had
sold his business to two others, that he would not, after a certain
day, practise within certain limits, as an attorney, was held good
in law, though the restriction was indefinite as to time.   In
Chesman v. *Nainby* (2) (in error) the condition of the bond was
that Elizabeth Vickers should not, after she left the service of
the obligee, set up business in any shop within half a mile of the
dwelling-house of the obligee, or of any other house that she,

[*456] *her executors or administrators, should think proper to remove
to, in order to carry on the trade; and in that case the contract
was held to be valid, though the restriction was obviously
indefinite in point of time, and although one of the grounds on
which the validity of the contract was sought to be impeached
was, that the restriction was for the life of the obligor.   Again,

(1) 7 R. R. 560 (1 Smith, 1; 4 East,   (2nd ed.); *S. C.*, in K. B. 2 Str. 739;
190).   2 Ld. Ray. 1456.
    (2) In Dom. Proc. 1 Br. P. C. 234

in *Wickens* v. *Evans* (1) the agreement in restraint of trade was made to continue during the lives of the contracting parties; and no objection was taken on that ground.

HITCHCOCK
v.
COKER.

We cannot, therefore hold the agreement in this case to be void, merely on the ground of the restriction being indefinite as to duration, the same being in other respects a reasonable restriction.

But it was urged, in the course of the argument, that there is an inadequacy of consideration, in this case, with respect to the defendant; and that, upon that ground, the judgment must be arrested. Undoubtedly in most, if not all, the decided cases, the Judges, in delivering their opinion that the agreement in the particular instance before them was a valid agreement, and the restriction reasonable, have used the expression, that such agreement appeared to have been made on an adequate consideration, and seem to have thought that an adequacy of consideration was essential to support a contract in restraint of trade. If by that expression it is intended, only, that there must be a good and valuable consideration, such consideration as is essential to support any contract not under seal, we concur in that opinion. If there is no consideration, or a consideration of no real value, the contract in restraint of *trade, which in itself is never favoured in law, must either be a fraud upon the rights of the party restrained, or a mere voluntary contract, a *nudum pactum*, and therefore void. But, if by adequacy of consideration more is intended, and that the Court must weigh whether the consideration is equal in value to that which the party gives up or loses by the restraint under which he has placed himself, we feel ourselves bound to differ from that doctrine. A duty would thereby be imposed upon the Court, in every particular case, which it has no means whatever to execute. It is impossible for the Court, looking at the record, to say whether, in any particular case, the party restrained has made an improvident bargain or not. The receiving instruction in a particular trade might be of much greater value to a man in one condition of life than in another; and the same may be observed as to other considerations. It is enough, as it appears to us, that there actually is a consideration for the bargain; and that such consideration is a legal

[*457]

(1) 32 R. R. 806 (3 Y. & J. 318).

HITCHCOCK
v.
COKER.

consideration, and of some value. Such appears to be the case in the present instance, where the defendant is retained and employed at an annual salary. We therefore think, notwithstanding the objections which have been urged on the part of the defendant, that the plaintiff has shown upon the record a legal ground of action ; and, having obtained a verdict in his favour, that he is entitled to judgment.

Judgment for the plaintiff.

1837.

[469]

PICKARD *v.* SEARS AND BARRETT (1).

(6 Adol. & Ellis, 469—474 ; S. C. 2 N. & P. 488.)

In an action of trover, it appeared that, plaintiff being the legal owner of the goods in question, they were seized while in the actual possession of a third party, under an execution against such third party, and sold to defendant: Held, that, under a plea denying plaintiff's possession, defendant might show that plaintiff authorised the sale ; and that a jury might infer such authority from the plaintiff consulting with the execution creditor as to the disposal of the property, without mentioning his own claim, after he knew of the seizure and of the intention to sell.

TROVER for machinery. Pleas : First, Not guilty : Secondly, That the plaintiff was not possessed, &c. Issues on both pleas.

[470]

On the trial before Lord Denman, Ch. J., at the London sittings after Trinity Term, 1835, it appeared that the property was taken by the sheriff of Surrey, under a *fi. fa.* issued against Metcalfe in April, 1834, at the suit of Hill, and was sold by the sheriff to the defendants in August, 1834. It was not disputed that the property had originally belonged to Metcalfe, and that he in fact was in possession at the time of the seizure. The plaintiff proved the execution of an indenture of mortgage, dated 15th January, 1834, between Metcalfe of the first part, and himself of the second ; whereby, in consideration of 913*l.* 11*s.* 6*d.*, paid to Metcalfe by the plaintiff, the land and house where the machinery was, together with the machinery itself, and all the right, title, and interest of Metcalfe therein, were assigned to the

---

(1) The general principle enunciated in the judgment of Lord DENMAN is referred to, expressly or impliedly, in many other cases, of which, as among the more recent, it may suffice to mention *Colonial Bank* v. *Cady* (H. L. 1890) 15 App. Cas. 267, 60 L. J. Ch. 131, and *Henderson* v. *Williams* [1895] 1 Q. B. 521, 64 L. J. Q. B. 308, C. A.; and, as one of the most important, *Freeman* v. *Cooke* (1848) 2 Ex. 654, 18 L. J. Ex. 114.—R. C.

plaintiff, his executors, &c., subject to a proviso for redemption on payment to the plaintiff, his executors, &c., of the said sum of 913*l*. 11*s*. 6*d*., with interest, on the 15th of January, 1835; with a covenant that, if default should be made in payment, it should be lawful for Pickard to enter upon the messuage, &c., and take possession of the goods, &c. Notice of this deed was given by the plaintiff to the defendants, after the sale by the sheriff; and possession of the property was demanded of them, and refused. By the evidence of Hill's attorney, it appeared that, after the seizure, the plaintiff had repeatedly conversed with the witness, sometimes in Metcalfe's presence, referring to the seizure, and had never made any claim to the goods, though he stated that Metcalfe was his debtor for about 500*l*., and frequently consulted with the witness as to the best way of disposing of the property: that, after a negotiation for sale had gone off, the witness had advised the plaintiff and Metcalfe *to try to raise 1,000*l*. to pay off the execution creditor, and the remainder to go to carry on the business: that the plaintiff had named a party, from whom it was attempted, but without success, to obtain the money; and that the witness had told the plaintiff that the defendants were about to purchase the property. It was not disputed that the mortgage was made *bonâ fide*, nor that the defendants had purchased *bonâ fide* and without notice of the mortgage. The defendant's counsel applied to the Lord Chief Justice to amend the pleas by inserting a plea of leave and licence; which was refused. They then suggested that it should be left to the jury whether the plaintiff had concurred in the sale: but his Lordship was of opinion that there was no evidence of such concurrence, and directed the jury to find for the plaintiff, if they thought that the mortgage was a *bonâ fide* transaction. Verdict for the plaintiff. In Michaelmas Term, 1835, *Sir F. Pollock* obtained a rule *nisi* for a new trial.

Erle and *Sewell* showed cause in Hilary Term last (1):

The articles were in Metcalfe's possession according to the intention of the mortgage deed; there was no badge of fraud. The property was in the plaintiff, and never passed to the defendants. This is the only question open on the pleadings,

(1) January 16th. Before Lord Denman, Ch. J., Williams and Coleridge, JJ.

PICKARD
v.
SEARS.

[*472]

no doubt being raised as to the conversion, which alone can be disputed on the first plea.   Now the fact, that the plaintiff made no objection when the sale was going to take place without his knowledge, could not divest him of the property.   *He was not bound to interfere.   The plaintiff's consent, if material to the defence, should have been pleaded.

Sir F. *Pollock* and *Cleasby, contrà :*

The sale took place with the knowledge of the plaintiff, and virtually by his authority.   He had full power to authorise a sale, either generally, or to a particular party ; and his acts went far enough to give the authority.   Then he cannot dispute that the sale was valid, and transferred the possession, so as to support the second plea.   His conduct induced the attorney of the execution creditor to change the situation of the parties ; and the case resembles that of admissions made, upon which the party to whom they are made acts so as to change his situation ; there he who makes the admission is estopped from disputing the fact admitted ; judgments of the Court of K. B. in *Graves* v. *Key* (1) and *Heane* v. *Rogers* (2).   The jury should, therefore, have been asked whether the plaintiff authorised the sale.

Cur. adv. vult.

LORD DENMAN, Ch. J., in this Term (April 27th), delivered the judgment of the COURT :

This was an action of trover for machinery and other articles, brought by a mortgagee of one Metcalfe, the former owner, against a purchaser from the sheriff, under an execution levied against the former owner.   The pleas were: first, Not guilty : second, That plaintiff was not possessed of the property as his own.   Sufficient evidence of a *bonâ fide* mortgage was adduced to prove that the property had been assigned to the plaintiff some *months before the execution ; and no doubt was ultimately made that the property was in fact his.   The mortgagor had however remained in possession, carrying on his trade, till the execution issued : and the defendant made it plainly appear that, even after the sheriff had entered, and even after the plaintiff

[473]

(1) 3 B. & Ad. 318, *n.*   (2) 9 B. & C. 586.

knew that a sale was in contemplation, he had come to the premises, and given no notice of his claim; on the contrary, he called on the execution creditor's attorney, with the mortgagor, and consulted him about the state of affairs, and the course to be taken. He stated, indeed, that he was Metcalfe's creditor to the amount of 500l., but never spoke of the mortgage, or claimed the goods as his own, though the attorney told him that he had some intention to sell them. The defendant purchased *bonâ fide*, and in total ignorance that the plaintiff had any interest. The bill of sale was executed on the 12th of August, the plaintiff's first application was made in December, when he demanded the sum advanced; which being refused, he demanded the goods : they were refused also.

The difficulty was, to give the defendant the benefit of these facts under the pleas on the record. After I had summed up the evidence, an application to amend by introducing a plea of leave and licence was, for obvious reasons, refused.

The defendant's counsel then contended that the plaintiff's conduct amounted to a concurrence in the sale, so as to make him in truth the vendor, and divest the property. I thought there was no evidence of this; and declined to take the jury's opinion, whether the facts proved it. We granted a rule for a new trial, being *desirous of considering whether this view of the case ought not to have been submitted to the jury. [*474]

Much doubt has been entertained whether these acts of the plaintiff, however culpable and injurious to the defendant, and however much they might be evidence of the goods not being his, in the sense that any persons, and amongst others the defendant, would be naturally induced thereby to believe that they were not, furnished any real proof that they were not his. His title having been once established, the property could only be divested by gift or sale ; of which no specific act was even surmised.

But the rule of law is clear, that, where one by his words or conduct wilfully causes another to believe the existence of a certain state of things, and induces him to act on that belief, so as to alter his own previous position, the former is concluded from averring against the latter a different state of things as existing at the same time ; and the plaintiff, in this case, might

PICKARD
v.
SEARS.

have parted with his interest in the property by verbal gift or sale, without any of those formalities that throw technical obstacles in the way of legal evidence. And we think his conduct, in standing by and giving a kind of sanction to the proceedings under the execution, was a fact of such a nature, that the opinion of the jury ought, in conformity to *Heane* v. *Rogers* (1) and *Graves* v. *Key* (2), to have been taken, whether he had not, in point of fact, ceased to be the owner. That opinion, in the affirmative, would have decided the second issue on the record in the defendant's favour.

Rule absolute.

1837.
April 19.
———
[486]

JONES *v.* LITTLEDALE AND OTHERS (3).

(6 Adol. & Ellis, 486—491 ; S. C. 1 N. & P. 677 ; 6 L. J. (N. S.) K. B. 169.)

L. & Co., brokers at Liverpool, sold hemp by auction at their rooms, and gave an invoice, describing the goods as " bought of L. & Co.," and received part of the price, but failed to deliver the goods. An action being brought against them by the purchaser for the non-delivery, and for money had and received,

Held, that L. & Co. had made themselves responsible as sellers, by the invoice ; and could not defend themselves by evidence tending to show that they sold as agents, and had intimated that fact before and at the time of the sale, and that, the principals being indebted to L. & Co., the invoice had been made out in their names, according to a custom of brokers in Liverpool, to secure the passing of the purchase-money through their hands.

ASSUMPSIT for not delivering a quantity of hemp, alleged to have been bought by the plaintiff of the defendants at the price of 155*l.* 14*s.* 11*d.* There was also a count for money had and received, and on an account stated. The defendants pleaded to the first count, and all but 52*l.* in the second count, *non*

[*487] *assumpserunt ;* *and as to that 52*l.* a tender. The particulars of demand claimed 155*l.* 14*s.* 11*d.*

On the trial before Patteson, J., at the last Liverpool Assizes,

(1) 9 B. & C. 586.

(2) 3 B. & Ad. 318, *n.*

(3) Distinguished in *Holding* v. *Elliot* (1860) 5 H. & N. 117, 29 L. J. Ex. 134, where there was sufficient evidence that the invoice was not the record of the contract. The principle that the agent con-

tracting in his own name is bound by the form of the contract is confirmed by *Higgins* v. *Senior* (1841) 8 M. & W. 834, 11 L. J. Ex. 199 ; *Calder* v. *Dobell* (Ex. Ch. 1871) L. R. 6 C. P. 486, 40 L. J. C. P. 224 ; and *Fleet* v. *Murton* (1871) L. R. 7 Q. B. 126, 41 L. J. Q. B. 49.—R. C.

it appeared that the plaintiff had (in 1836), bought, by auction, at the rooms of the defendants, who were brokers at Liverpool, the hemp in question, to be paid for at certain times then agreed on : that the defendants afterwards sent an invoice of the goods, headed,

" —— Jones,

Bought of J. and H. Littledale,

Sixty-four bales of hemp. Payment fourteen days and six months. Received on account 100*l.* October 31.

Settled November 26.

(Signed by defendants' clerk.)

That the plaintiff, on the 31st of October, paid the defendants 100*l.*, and afterwards, on the 26th of November, the residue, 52*l.* ; and on the latter day asked for a delivery order. An order on Messrs. Coupland and Duncan was given him, which on presentation the same day was refused ; and one of the defendants, being applied to, said that he would see his attorney, and procure the delivery ; but the defendants never did procure the delivery. In answer, the defendants offered to prove that the hemp was advertised in two newspapers, which the plaintiff was in the habit of seeing, for sale, at the rooms of the defendants, brokers, with a reference to Coupland and Duncan, merchants (1). That it was sold by auction at the defendants' rooms, under printed conditions of sale, describing the defendants *as the seller's brokers, but not mentioning the name of the seller : that the defendants had made advances to Messrs. Coupland and Duncan on these and other goods ; and that the custom at Liverpool was for brokers, when they had made advances, to deliver invoices in their own names, in order to secure the passing of the purchase-money through their hands : That Messrs. Coupland and Duncan became bankrupts, and that a fiat issued on the 25th of November (2). The learned Judge thought that these facts, if proved, constituted no defence to the action ; and directed a verdict for the plaintiff.

[*488]

---

(1) The advertisement, after describing the goods, added, "Apply to Coupland and Duncan, merchants, or Littledale & Co., brokers."

(2) It was admitted, on the trial, that the defendants had tendered the 52*l.*

Cresswell now moved (1) for a rule to show cause why there should not be a new trial, on the ground of misdirection :

The evidence which it was proposed to offer would have been a good defence, and should have gone to the jury. If the plaintiff knew that the defendants were selling for Coupland and Duncan, he has no right to recover against the defendants. This was a sale by brokers for a declared principal : the terms of the invoice could not alter the contract entered into by that sale. The invoice is not the contract.

(COLERIDGE, J. : Do not the brokers, by such a dealing as this, undertake that they have a right to deliver ?)

If they do, and have not the right, they may be liable on a declaration adapted to those circumstances. Had the plaintiff here made his payment at the fourteen days he would probably have obtained the goods, for Coupland and Duncan were still [*489] solvent. *Moore* v. *Clementson* (2) shows that parol *evidence may be received to prove who was the real principal in a sale of goods, though an invoice may have been given in which that party was not named ; a fact upon which Lord ELLENBOROUGH, in that case, thought no stress was to be laid.

(PATTESON, J. : Such evidence is admissible to charge a party not mentioned in the invoice ; but can it also be received to exonerate the seller named in the invoice, when he is sued as such ?)

If once admitted, it must be available in either case. As to the counts for money had and received, the 52*l.* received by the defendants after the bankruptcy was tendered back ; and, with respect to the 100*l.*, if Coupland and Duncan were the owners of the goods, and sold them through the defendants as brokers, and the defendants received this money with their sanction, the payment was virtually a payment to Coupland and Duncan : *Warner* v. *M'Kay* (3) explains the law on this subject.

(1) Before Lord Denman, Ch. J., Littledale, Patteson, and Coleridge, JJ.
(2) 11 R. R. 653 (2 Camp. 22).
(3) 1 M. & W. 591 ; Tyr. & Gr. 965.

(PATTESON, J.: According to your view of the case, what need had the plaintiff of a delivery order?)

Probably it was a voucher to Coupland and Duncan that the defendants had been paid. The defendants, not having the advantage of a lien, may have arranged with the owners that the goods should not be given up without such voucher.

Cur. adv. vult.

LORD DENMAN, Ch. J., on a subsequent day of the Term (May 5th), delivered the judgment of the Court. After having stated the pleadings, and the facts as they are above set forth, his Lordship said,

On moving to set aside this verdict, the counsel for *the defendants argued that the sale by auction was the contract, from which, and the previous advertisement, it was apparent that the plaintiff knew that the defendants were only agents, and who the principals were, and that the learned Judge should have left to the jury to say whether the contract was made with the defendants, or the principals; urging also that, if the purchase-money had been paid at the proper time, the plaintiff would have obtained the goods; and contending that the 100*l.* must be taken as paid·to the principals, and might be proved under the fiat against them, and that the 52*l.*, paid after the fiat, had been tendered. And he cited *Moore* v. *Clementson* (1), to show that the form of the invoice made no difference, but evidence was admissible to show who was the real contracting party; contending that, from the evidence of the facts and the custom, the invoice had the same effect as if it had stated that the plaintiff bought of the defendants for Coupland and Duncan, payment to be made to the defendants.

There is no doubt that evidence is admissible, on behalf of one of the contracting parties, to show that the other was agent only, though contracting in his own name, and so to fix the real principal; but it is clear that, if the agent contracts in such a form as to make himself personally responsible, he cannot afterwards, whether his principal were or were not known at the time of the contract, relieve himself from that responsibility. In this

[*490]

(1) 11 R. R. 653 (2 Camp. 22).

case there is no contract signed by the sellers, so as to satisfy
the Statute of Frauds, until the invoice, by which the defendants
represent themselves to be the sellers: and we think that they
are conclusively *bound by that representation. Their object in
so representing was, as appeared by the evidence of custom, to
secure the passing of the money through their hands, and to
prevent its being paid to their principals ; but in so doing they
have made themselves responsible; and we think it impossible
to read the invoice in the sense proposed.
                                                    Rule refused.

DOE d. PETER BECK *v.* JOHN HEAKIN.

(6 Adol. & Ellis, 495—499 ; S. C. 2 N. & P. 660.)

1. In ejectment by a party claiming to be devisee of a manor, the
facts of the devisor having held a court thirty-five years ago, and the
lessor of the plaintiff on several occasions since his death, and of appointments of gamekeepers, are *primâ facie* proof, both that a manor exists,
and that the lessor of the plaintiff is the lord, without the production of
court rolls or any documentary evidence of courts having been held.

2. The will recited that the devisor had charged the land with 3,000*l.*
on his daughter's marriage ; then followed a devise to trustees to keep
down the interest and apply the surplus rents as directed, till the lessor
of plaintiff should come to the age of twenty-three, and then to him,
subject to the charge : Held, that this did not show a legal estate out
of the lessor of the plaintiff.

3. The premises in dispute had been inclosed from the waste, with the
knowledge of the lord, ten years before the action was brought. Three
days before the action was brought, the lessor of the plaintiff broke down
the fences : Held to be a sufficient revocation of any licence which could
· be presumed from previous acquiescence.

EJECTMENT for messuages and lands in Shropshire. On the
trial before Bolland, B., at the last Shrewsbury Assizes, the
following facts appeared. The lessor of the plaintiff was second
son of Peter Beck, deceased, whose will was put in, and contained the following clause : " Whereas, on the marriage of my
daughter, Mary Darnsward, I charged my Hope estate with the
sum of 3,000*l.*, I will and devise unto my trustees hereinafter
named, their heirs and assigns, all that my manor of Hope,"
" with the several farms," &c., " thereunto belonging, to hold
unto my said trustees, their heirs and assigns, upon trust that
they do and shall keep down the interest of the sum of 3,000*l.*

charged thereon in favour of my said daughter Mary, by virtue
of her marriage settlement, and to apply the residue of such
rents and profits in aid of my personal estate, until my son
Peter attains the age of twenty-three years; and, upon his
attaining that age, I give and devise the same manor and
premises to him and his heirs absolutely, subject nevertheless to
the said sum of 3,000l. charged thereon in favour of my said
daughter Mary Darnsward, her children, and issue.'" Three
persons, of whom the lessor of the *plaintiff was one, were then
named trustees and executors of the will. The lessor of the
plaintiff had attained the age of twenty-three. In order to show
the existence of, and property in, the manor of Hope, it was
proved that Peter Beck, the father, had held a court about
thirty-five years ago. The father died in 1824; and, subsequently, the lessor of the plaintiff had held meetings which, on
his part, were represented as courts; but it was denied on the
other side that they were so. Some deputations of gamekeepers,
filed with the clerk of the peace, were put in, one of which was
in the name of the trustees under the will. No court rolls were
produced. It was proved that the land in question, which consisted of about four acres, was formerly part of the waste of the
manor. It had been inclosed, and a cottage built on it, about
ten years before the commencement of the action. The lessor
of the plaintiff lived near the premises, but offered no interruption; except that, three days before the service of the declaration
in ejectment, he broke down the inclosures. On this evidence,
the defendant's counsel contended that no manor was shown to
exist; that at any rate the legal estate, under the will, was not
shown to be in the lessor of the plaintiff solely; and that there
was ground for presuming a licence, which could not be revoked
by an interruption taking place so short a time before the commencement of the action. The learned Judge was of opinion
that a *primâ facie* case was made out for the plaintiff, but reserved
leave to move for a nonsuit. Verdict for the plaintiff.

Godson now moved to enter a nonsuit:

First, there was not sufficient evidence to go to the jury of the
*existence of a manor at all, without the production of court rolls,

DOE d.
BECK
v.
HEAKIN.

[*496]

[*497]

Doe d.
Beck
v.
Heakin.

or, in their absence, without at least constant acts done, showing notoriety of the alleged manorial rights, and acquiescence in them. Secondly, the will gives the land to the lessor of the plaintiff, subject to a charge. Now the precise nature of the charge did not appear: but it may be assumed that it was created by giving a term, or some legal estate. That being so, the lessor of the plaintiff would have only an equitable title.

(Coleridge, J.: Why might not the charge be a rent-charge?)

It is of a sum in gross, not an annual payment. If, contrary to the more ordinary mode, the charge was such as not to affect the legal estate, it was for the lessor of the plaintiff to show its nature. He cannot be said to have made out his title, when he claims under a will which shows no title, except on the supposition that a charge, the existence of which in some shape he admits, confers no legal estate. Thirdly, it appears from *Doe d. Foley* v. *Wilson* (1) that a licence to the defendant was to be presumed, and that this is a good defence in the absence of a revocation. An interruption, made immediately before, and for the purpose of, the action, cannot have the effect of a revocation.

Cur. adv. vult.

Lord Denman, Ch. J., in the same Term (May 5th), delivered the judgment of the Court: After stating the nature of the application, his Lordship said:

[*498]   The lessor of the plaintiff had recovered a verdict at *the trial, claiming the land in question as parcel of the waste of his manor. It was objected, at first, that he had given no evidence of a manor, or of his being the lord, because he had produced no court rolls nor any other documentary proofs of the holding of courts: but this last was certainly not necessary; and the parol evidence, that his father had held a court thirty-five years ago, and he himself on several occasions more recently, with proof of the appointments of gamekeepers by deputation, were clearly sufficient *primâ facie* evidence of both facts.

It was next objected, the lessor of the plaintiff having put in

(1) 11 East, 56.

his father's will, that he had thereby shown the legal estate out of himself. The will was stated to recite some subsisting charges, and then to devise to trustees to keep down the interest on them, and apply the surplus rents as therein directed until the lessor of the plaintiff should attain the age of twenty-three: and then it devised to him, subject to the before-mentioned charges. We think we cannot infer, from this statement, that any legal estate was outstanding in the incumbrancers; but that the more reasonable presumption is that which accords with the very words of the will.

Lastly, it was said that, as the cottage had been built on land inclosed from the waste, and there was evidence of this having been done with the knowledge of the lord, a licence at least must be presumed; and that it had not been properly revoked before action brought. The lessor had proved that, a very short time, a few days only, before the action brought, he and his servants had entered on the inclosure, and broken down the hedges in several places. It appears to us that this *act, the purpose of which was unambiguous, was evidence from which the jury were warranted in finding a revocation of the licence. Such revocation might be by act *in pais*, or by parol; and no precise time is limited by law as necessary to intervene between it and the commencement of the action which treats the party in possession as a trespasser.

[*499]

We think there should be no rule.

Rule refused.

TERRY AND OTHERS *v.* PARKER (1).

(6 Adol. & Ellis, 502—508; S. C. 1 N. & P. 752; W. W. & D. 303; 6 L. J.
(N. S.) K. B. 249.)

1837.
April 20.

[502]

If the drawer of a bill of exchange have no effects in the hands of the drawee at the time of drawing the bill, and of its maturity, and have no ground to expect that it will be paid, it is not necessary to present the bill at maturity; and, if it be presented two days after, and payment be refused, the drawer is liable.

ASSUMPSIT. The first count of the declaration stated that defendant heretofore, to wit, 16th May, 1836, made his bill of

(1) Confirmed by Bills of Exchange Act, 1882 (45 & 46 Vict. c. 61), s. 46 (2) (c).—R. C.

exchange, directed to John Twist, for 232*l.* 2*s.* 2*d.*, payable to
defendant's order six'months after date, which period had elapsed
before the commencement &c., and indorsed it to one Kirkby,
who indorsed it to the plaintiffs. "And the plaintiffs aver that,
at the time of the making of the said bill of exchange as aforesaid, and from thence until and at the end of the day on which
the said bill became due and payable, according to the tenor
and effect thereof, and from thence until and at the time of
the presentment thereof hereinafter mentioned, he, the defendant, had not in the hands of the said John Twist any effects
of him the defendant for the payment, by him the said John
Twist, of the money in the said bill specified, or any part thereof;
nor had he, the defendant, at the time of the making of the
said bill as aforesaid, nor from thence until the end of the day
when the same became due as aforesaid, nor from thence until
the presentment thereof hereinafter next mentioned, any reasonable grounds to expect that the said John Twist could have any
such effects, or that the said John Twist, or any other person or
persons whatsoever, would pay the said money in the said bill
specified, or any part thereof, upon the presentment of the same
bill to the said John Twist for payment; nor has he, the
defendant, sustained any damage by reason of the said bill not

[*503]   having been *presented on the day when the same became due,
or until the presentment thereof hereinafter mentioned, or by
reason of his, the defendant's, not having had notice of the said
bill being presented on the day when the same became due,
and being dishonoured, or by reason of the defendant's not
having had notice of the presentment hereinafter mentioned,
and the non-payment of the said bill upon such presentment,
until he, the defendant, had the notice hereinafter mentioned;
and the plaintiffs further say that, after the said bill became
due, and before the commencement of this suit, to wit"
21st November, 1836, "the said bill was presented to the said
John Twist for payment," &c.; that John Twist refused to pay;
that the whole is now due; and that, after the said presentment and refusal, and before the commencement &c., to wit on
the day and year last aforesaid, the defendant had notice of the
said presentment and refusal.

Third plea to the first count. That Richard Pullen, before and at the time of making the bill, was liable to defendant to the amount of a large &c., to wit the sum specified in the bill; that there were mutual accounts between Pullen and Twist; and that thereupon Pullen requested defendant to draw, and Twist to accept, the bill, for and on account of the liability of Pullen to defendant; whereupon defendant, upon the faith and credit of the said acceptance of Twist, and believing that the bill would be paid when due if duly presented to Twist, drew the bill, and Twist accepted it, for and upon account of the said liability of Pullen to the defendant; that the bill was not presented for payment when due, according to the tenor &c.; and that defendant, *by reason of the non-payment, and of his not having had notice of the bill being presented when it became due, is likely to lose the amount specified in the bill, and the amount for which Pullen was so liable to him: verification. Replication: that Pullen was not liable to defendant; that defendant did not make or draw, nor Twist accept, the bill for or upon account or in payment of a liability of Pullen to defendant; nor did defendant make or draw the bill upon the faith or credit of the said acceptance of Twist, in manner &c.: conclusion to the country.

[*504]

Fourth plea to the first count. That defendant had in the hands of Twist, at the time the bill became due, effects for the payment of the bill, to wit effects to the value of the money in the bill specified: conclusion to the country.

Fifth plea to the first count. That, before and at the time of drawing the bill, there were accounts between defendant and Twist; and that defendant drew the bill on Twist, and Twist accepted the same, for and upon good and valuable consideration between Twist and defendant; and that defendant fully expected that Twist would pay the bill when the same became due, according to the tenor &c.: verification. Replication: that defendant did not draw the bill on Twist, nor did Twist accept the same for or upon good and valuable consideration between Twist and the defendant; nor did defendant expect that Twist would pay the bill when it became due, in manner &c.: conclusion to the country.

TERRY
v.
PARKER.

On the trial before Alderson, B. at the last York Assizes, a verdict was found for the plaintiffs on all the issues.

[505]

Cresswell now moved (1) for a rule to show cause why judgment should not be arrested, or a nonsuit entered :

The question is, whether the want of effects in the hands of the drawee be an excuse for non-presentment. It is not necessary to deny that notice to the drawer of dishonour is excused by the fact of his having had no effects in the hands of the drawee at the times of the drawing of the bill and of its maturity. But it has never been held that this excuses presentment for payment, which cannot be dispensed with even by the insolvency or bankruptcy of the drawee. It is true that in *De Berdt* v. *Atkinson* (2) it was held that, where the payee of a promissory note, made without consideration, knows that the maker is insolvent, the indorsee, upon dishonour, may sue the payee, though presentment be not made till the day after maturity, nor notice given till five days after the dishonour. There EYRE, Ch. J. said that the ground on which an early demand is necessary is that, if delay take place, " the effects may be gone out of the hands of the acceptor." But, if presentment be necessary at all, it must be made at the time of maturity; the true reason for requiring presentment being that the drawer's engagement is only conditional : he is to pay if the drawee be requested, at the maturity of the bill, to pay, and refuse to do so, and notice be given. The drawer has, under all circumstances, a right to the chance of the drawee paying at maturity. It has been lamented that any excuse of notice has ever been admitted. Lord KENYON refused to receive evidence that want

[*506]

of notice *had caused no injury (3).

(LORD DENMAN, Ch. J.: In *De Berdt* v. *Atkinson* (2), it seems to be assumed that a drawer who has no effects in the drawee's hands can gain nothing by presentment at maturity.)

That assumption can, at any rate, not be universally made: in the case of a solvent drawee being willing to honour the bill at

(1) Before Lord Denman, Ch. J.,   (2) 2 H. Bl. 336.
Patteson and Coleridge, JJ.   (3) *Dennis* v. *Morrice*, 3 Esp. 158.

the time of maturity, but afterwards becoming insolvent before
presentment, the drawer is a loser by the *laches*. Perhaps
De Berdt v. *Atkinson* (1) may be distinguished from the present
case on the ground that the instrument there was not a bill
of exchange, but a promissory note; possibly the engagement of
the maker of a promissory note is less conditional than that
of the drawer of a bill. The Court, there, seems to have considered that some presentment was necessary, only that the
circumstances dispensed with the necessity of presenting at the
regular time. But no distinction can be made between omitting
to present at the regular time, and omitting to present altogether.
If the length of time which elapses be held material, then the
inquiry, which Lord KENYON refused to permit, will become
necessary. And, even as to notice, *De Berdt* v. *Atkinson* (1)
cannot be supported; for the principle of the decision would
show that the bankruptcy of the drawee would dispense with
notice to the drawer, which is contrary to *Rohde* v. *Proctor* (2).

(LORD DENMAN, Ch. J. referred to *Boultbee* v. *Stubbs* (3), and
Ex parte Rohde (4).

PATTESON, J.: *Hopley* v. *Dufresne* (5) seems rather in your
favour: there a *waiver was relied on, which would not have   [*507]
been required unless presentment had been necessary.)

Cur. adv. vult.

LORD DENMAN, Ch. J., on a subsequent day of the Term (May 5th),
delivered the judgment of the COURT as follows:

The question in this case is, whether want of effects in the
hands of the drawee excuses the holder of a bill of exchange
from the necessity of presenting the bill for payment, as well as
of giving notice of dishonour to the drawer.

Many cases establish that notice of dishonour need not be
given to the drawer in such a case; and the reason assigned is,
because he is in no respect prejudiced by want of such notice,

TERRY
v.
PARKER.

(1) 2 H. Bl. 336.
(2) 28 R. R. 369 (4 B. & C. 517).
(3) 11 R. R. 141 (18 Ves. 21).
(4) Mont. & Mac. 430.
(5) 13 R. R. 463 (15 East, 275).

TERRY
v.
PARKER.

having no remedy against any other party on the bill.   This reason equally applies to want of presentment for payment, since, if the bill were presented, and paid by the drawee, the drawer would become indebted to him in the amount, instead of being indebted to the holder of the bill, and would be in no way benefitted by such presentment and payment.

No case directly in point seems to have been decided.   The case of *De Berdt* v. *Atkinson* (1) was an action on a promissory note against the payee and indorser, who had lent his name, knowing that the maker was insolvent ; and it was held that he was not discharged by the note not having been presented till the day after it was due, and notice of dishonour not having been given for several days.   But that case can hardly be supported,

[*508]

*inasmuch as the defendant was not the party for whose accommodation the note was made ; on the contrary, he lent his name to accommodate the maker.   Neither is the case of *Hopley* v. *Dufresne* (2) an authority the other way ; for, although that was a case of an acceptance for the accommodation of the defendant, Lord ELLENBOROUGH nonsuited the plaintiff, because the bill was presented to the acceptor's bankers after banking hours ; yet that nonsuit was set aside on the ground of there being evidence of a subsequent waiver ; and the point, whether the drawer was entitled to object to the want of due presentment, was not determined.

It appears to us that the same reason applies to want of presentment, as to want of notice of dishonour, and therefore that the same rule ought to prevail with respect to want of effects operating as an excuse : and the rule to arrest judgment must be refused.   *Rule refused.*

1837.
April 20.

[509]

REX *v.* THE INHABITANTS OF SCARISBRICK.

(6 Adol. & Ellis, 509—515 ; S. C. 1 N. & P. 582 ; W. W. & D. 246 ; 6 L. J. (N. S.) M. C. 103.)

The township of S. was indicted for not repairing a road in S., on a custom alleged and proved, that all the townships in the parish in which S. was situate repaired their own roads in general.   In answer, it was shown that the township of N., in another parish, was adjacent to S. ; and that an agreement had been made, 250 years before, between the

(1) 2 H. Bl. 336.   (2) 13 R. R. 463 (15 East, 275).

then owner of all S. and the then owner of all N., whereby the boundary between the properties was marked out, and the owner of S. agreed to allow to the owner of N., and the rest of the inhabitants of N., a road through S., of which S. was to repair part, and N. another part, being the subject of the indictment; and that further assurance for the performance of the agreement should be made by a sufficient lawyer. It was also shown that afterwards the owner of S. filed a bill for specific performance against the owner of N., the event of which did not appear; but that the owners of lands in N. had ever since repaired in conformity with the agreement:

Held, not to be evidence for a jury of an instrument binding the owner of N., and all claiming through him, to repair, assuming that such a conveyance could have been made so as to exonerate the inhabitants of S.

INDICTMENT against the township of Scarisbrick, in the parish of Ormskirk, Lancashire, for not repairing a common highway in the said township, stated to be 340 yards in length. The first count charged a custom for the township to repair the roads within it; the second, a custom for all the townships in the parish of O. to repair within such townships respectively. Plea, Not guilty.

On the trial before Patteson, J., at the last Liverpool Assizes, evidence was given of the non-repair, and that the custom was for each township to repair its own roads. The township of Scarisbrick was adjacent to the township of North Meols, in the parish of North Meols, Lancashire; and the road in question ran through Scarisbrick, from the boundary between the townships of North Meols and Scarisbrick. The defendants offered in evidence a document headed, " Articles covenanted, condescended, concluded and fully agreed upon, the 6th day of July," &c., 33 Eliz., and purporting to be made between Edward Scarisbricke of Scarisbrick, in the county of Lancaster, on the one part, Barnaby Kitchen and John Bold of the North Meoles, within the said county, Esqrs., *and Hugh Hesketh of Rufforde,   [*510] in the said county, Gentleman, on the other part; "for and concerning the division of a certain moss, lying between the lordship of Scarisbrick and the North Meales, known by the name of the Ottersties Moss, and the Meales Moss." The articles described a boundary agreed upon between the parties, for themselves and their heirs for ever, for the partition of the moss between Edward Scarisbricke, on the one side, and Kitchen, Bold, and Hesketh on the other, namely a ditch (in the direction of a former boundary); for the maintenance of which the articles provided. They then went on as follows: "It is further agreed that, in consideration of which partition to be made and done in manner and form aforesaid, the said Edward Scarisbricke is contented to grant, permit, and suffer, and to allow unto the said parties, every of them, and their heirs, and to the rest of the inhabitants of the North Meales, a convenient highway and free passage of eight yards broad unto the town of Ormskirk, through his part and portion of the said moss, over a certain coppe which heretofore had been ditched and cast up by the consent and agreement of the said parties for the said way, containing in length from the Ottersties ditch unto the remaining ditch at the end of the Meales Fields, accordingly as the coppe and way leadeth, fourteen score and eight roods, or thereabouts, whereof the said É. S. is contented to make or·cause to be made the one half thereof, passable for horse and man; and that the said B. K., J. B., and H. H., shall likewise make or cause to be made the other half thereof towards the Meales passable for horse and man, as is aforesaid. It is further agreed between the said

[*511]
parties that, whereas the one half of the coppe *or highway leading through that portion of moss from the said ditch or boundary towards the Meales allotted and fallen unto the said B. K., J. B., and H. H., according to the partition made by consent as is aforesaid, doth not contain in length to the number of sevenscore and four roods, which is measured to be the full half part of the said coppe reserved for the said highway as is aforesaid, therefore the said B. K., J. B., and H. H., do covenant and grant, for them and every of them, by these presents, to make or cause to be made passable for horse and man, as is aforesaid, so much of the said coppe or highway from the said ditch or boundary towards Ottersties ditch, being within the portion of the said moss belonging to the said E. S., as will contain or comprehend the full number of forty roods to make good that part of the coppe which leadeth towards the Meales Fields, to be full seven score and four roods as is aforesaid. And finally it is concluded and agreed " between the said parties, "for the better establishing and performing of all and singular the premises before set down and declared in and by these presents, that there shall be a good and sufficient lawyer, indifferently

elected and chosen at and before Michaelmas next, upon all their
costs and charges, to make and set down such further assurance
for the performance of these articles as by him shall be thought
most meet and convenient in that behalf. In witness" &c.
(Signed by EDWARD SCARISBRICKE.) Evidence was also offered,
to show that, at the time of the agreement, Edward Scarisbricke
was owner of the whole of the township of Scarisbrick, and that
Kitchen, Bold, and Hesketh were the owners of the whole of the
township of North Meols. And that, in 1631, a bill was filed, in
the Duchy Court of Lancaster, *by the then owners of the township of North Meols, against Edward Scarisbrick, the descendant
of the party to the agreement, and who then was, and had for
several years been, owner of the property, and had come of age
about this time. The object of the bill was to compel him to
repair the part of the road in Scarisbrick which he was liable to
repair by the agreement. Proof was likewise offered that Edward
Scarisbrick, the then defendant, put in an answer, alleging,
besides other facts, that there were no fit materials of sand, gravel,
or the like in Scarisbrick, nor nearer than North Meols. Proof was
further offered, that a commission issued to examine witnesses.
No further evidence of proceedings in this suit could be obtained;
but it appeared, from the evidence produced for the Crown, that,
as far back as could be remembered, the inhabitants of North
Meols had repaired the road from the boundary between the two
townships, to a stone (which was marked "Meols" on the side
towards North Meols, and "Scarisbrick" on the other side), being
the distance agreed upon in the articles, within about twenty yards,
taking the materials from North Meols. This part was the part
indicted. Upon the above evidence, the counsel for the defendants
contended that there was enough to raise a presumption for the
jury that the owner of the lands in North Meols was liable to
repair this part, *ratione tenuræ*. The learned Judge was of a
contrary opinion, and directed a verdict for the Crown.

> *Cresswell* now moved for a new trial, on the ground of
> misdirection :

There was evidence, to go to the jury, of this defence, which
might be set up under the general issue, on behalf of a township;

REX
v.
THE INHABI-
TANTS OF
SCARIS-
BRICK.

[*512]

REX
v.
THE INHABI-
TANTS OF
SCARIS-
BRICK.
[*513]

note (10) to *Rex* v. *Stoughton* (1). It is true, in general, that, where the origin of a road is not shown, it will be presumed to be immemorial; and the *dictum*, that a liability to repair *ratione tenuræ* must be immemorial, properly applies to such cases : but a liability to repair *ratione tenuræ* may be set up, which is not immemorial, if the liability can be shown to have arisen at the time when the road was originally constructed, and upon a sufficient consideration. The liability by reason of tenure is explained in Callis on Sewers, 117. In *Porter's* case (2), there referred to, Lord Coke says "that any man at this day may give lands, tenements, or hereditaments to any person or persons and their heirs," for reparation of "highways, bridges, causeways," &c. *The Mayor and Burgesses of Lyme Regis* v. *Henley* (3) is an instance of a liability originating in a grant from the Crown ; and many other cases are collected in the argument there (4). Now, here, the grant of the road by the owner of Scarisbrick would be a full consideration for a charge upon the lands of the other party. The only question then is, whether a jury might not, if they thought fit, have presumed that the agreement was carried into effect by a legal instrument, prepared by a lawyer as contemplated in the agreement, and binding the lands. The presumption is much strengthened by the fact that, after the agreement, a bill is filed for a specific performance ; from which time the practice has been as it would have been had such an instrument been executed. If *such a deed were executed, then all parties holding the land, however divided, through the parties to the deed, would be bound.

(PATTESON, J. : I was struck, at the trial, with the case of *Rex* v. *The Mayor of Liverpool* (5).)

There no presumption of an agreement was shown.

(LORD DENMAN, Ch. J. : What lands do you say were assigned, subject to the liability? The lands belonged, in the first instance,

(1) 2 Wms. Saund. 159 a.   affirming 3 B. & Ad. 77. 5 Bing. 91).
(2) 1 Co. Rep. 26 a.   (4) 3 B. & Ad. 86.
(3) 37 R. R. 125 (2 Cl. & F. 331 ;   (5) 6 R. R. 546 (3 East, 86).
8 Bligh, N. S. 690 ; 1 Bing. N. C. 222 ;

to the parties whom you suppose to have taken subject to the charge.)

There would be no difficulty in the parties conveying their lands, and taking back a reconveyance with the charge. The Courts have gone so far as to presume an Act of Parliament to explain an usage: this is much less violent.

LORD DENMAN, Ch. J.:

We need not here decide whether such a liability as that contended for must be immemorial. But we cannot admit such a presumption of fact as that set up. No reasonable ground is shown for believing that such a machinery has been constructed. A Judge does not do his duty if he leaves the jury to presume that of which he himself does not believe the existence.

COLERIDGE, J. (1):

I am quite of the same opinion. If the Judge had merely left it to the jury whether they believed the conveyance to have been made, actually and in fact, the verdict would clearly have stood just as it does now. Where acts shown to have been performed would have been illegal, unless some suggested transaction had occurred, there is strong ground for telling a jury that it is probable that the occurrence *really took place. But, here, [*515] it is much more likely that something took place between the parties which did not bind them, and which therefore could not have constituted a legal defence, than that all the cumbrous machinery existed which has been supposed. It would have been idle to put such a matter to the jury.

PATTESON, J.:

I do not see that I could have left it to the jury. Every man would have seen that it was quite palpable that no such machinery existed.

Rule refused.

(1) Littledale, J. was absent, in consequence of a domestic affliction.

1837.
April 21.
———
[525]

THOMAS *v.* JENKINS.

(6 Adol. & Ellis, 525—529; S. C. 1 N. & P. 587; W. W. & D. 265; 1 Jur.
261; 6 L. J. (N. S.) K. B. 163.)

On a question of boundary between two estates, if evidence has been given that the boundary of the estates is the same as that between two hamlets, evidence of reputation as to the boundary of the hamlets may be adduced for the purpose of proving that of the estates; and the jury may be desired to take into consideration the latter evidence if they are satisfied with the first.

REPLEVIN for taking cattle. Avowry and cognizances, averring the cattle to have been distrained damage-feasant. Pleas in bar, traversing the title, as pleaded, to the place in which &c. Issues thereon. On the trial before Coleridge, J. at the Glamorganshire Spring Assizes, 1837, the material question was as to the boundary dividing the estate which comprised the *locus in quo* from another estate. An old witness, who was called for the defendant, swore that he had kept cattle on the first mentioned estate, and turned off those of other people; that his father at that time was tenant of the estate; that his father and brother told him what line of boundary he was to keep, and that he had acted accordingly in keeping the boundary; that his father and brother were over-seers of the hamlet of Glyncorrwg; and that the boundary of the estate was the same as that of the hamlet. He was then asked whether he had heard from old persons, since dead, what was the boundary of the hamlet. The question was objected to, as an attempt to prove the limits of a private estate by reputation. COLERIDGE, J. held the evidence admissible; and the witness then stated what he had heard as to the boundary of the hamlet: and other evidence was afterwards given on the same point. In summing up, the learned Judge left the evidence of reputation, as to the boundary of the hamlet, to the jury, but desired them not to take it into consideration unless they were satisfied that the boundary of the estate was the same with that of the hamlet. Verdict for the defendant.

[526]   *Chilton* now moved for a new trial:

The evidence of reputation, as to the boundary of the hamlet, was inadmissible here, being offered, in reality, upon a question of boundary between private estates. The inquiry was indeed introduced by a question whether the boundary of the estate comprising the *locus in quo* was not the same with the boundary of the hamlet; but evidence ought not to be thus indirectly let in, which cannot be given directly. The issue here was on a private right; the plaintiff was not prepared, by the pleadings or by the admissions (1), to meet evidence as to the limits of the hamlet. Evidence of reputation is undoubtedly admissible as to the boundaries between parishes and hamlets; but the rule in favour of this seems limited to cases where such boundaries are the subject of litigation between the public bodies which they immediately concern. The language of Lord ELLENBOROUGH in *Weeks* v. *Sparke* (2) favours this view of the subject.

(COLERIDGE, J.: It is said there, by DAMPIER, J., that, " in all cases where reputation is admitted in evidence, it is necessary to lay a foundation for its admission : " that necessity, therefore, is no objection to the admissibility.)

In 1 Starkie on Evidence, 156 (3), it is laid down that " Evidence of reputation, subject to the *limitations already stated, is admissible upon questions as to the boundaries of parishes, manors, or other districts in which many persons possess an interest: " and in 1 Phillipps on Evidence, 236, Book 1, Part i. c. 7, s. 7 (4), it is said that, " In questions concerning public rights, common reputation is admitted to be evidence; for such rights, being matters of public notoriety and of great local importance, become a continual subject of discussion in the neighbourhood, where all have the same means of information and the same interest to ascertain the claim." These passages appear to contemplate cases where the question both relates to a public

[*527]

(1) The parties had agreed " to admit respectively on the trial, the general title of the defendant, and of those under whom he claims, as stated in the pleadings, and the general title of the plaintiff as tenant, and of the Earl of Dunraven as landlord, of the Pencae and Blaennanthir farms and sheepwalks : and that the only question to be raised on the trial" " shall be, whether the land in dispute, which is coloured pink in the maps exchanged between the parties," "is parcel of the Corrwgfychan sheepwalk, or parcel of the Pencae and Blaennanthir sheepwalks."

(2) 14 R. R. 546, 550 (1 M. & S. 679, 686). He read the judgment of Lord ELLENBOROUGH from " The admission" to " received in evidence."

(3) 2nd ed.

(4) 6th ed.

THOMAS
v.
JENKINS.

boundary, and arises between the parties concerned in such boundary. The notoriety which prevails as to the limits of a parish cannot be relied upon as to those of a farm, which are subject to fluctuation. The ground upon which the Courts have excluded evidence of reputation on the subject of private rights, are pointed out in 1 Phillipps on Evidence, 239, Book 1, Part i. c. 7, s. 7 (1) ; and *Doe* d. *Didsbury* v. *Thomas* (2), *Richards* v. *Bassett* (3), *Talbot* v. *Lewis* (4), *Crease* v. *Barrett* (5), and *Rex* v. *Antrobus* (6), show the extent of the rule. The evidence in question here could not have been receivable unless it had been agreed, or put beyond doubt, that the farm and hamlet had the same boundary. Reputation could not be in any degree made available to show what the boundary of the farm was.

LORD DENMAN, Ch. J. :

[*528]

Notwithstanding the observations of Lord ELLENBOROUGH which have been referred *to, I think there is no doubt in the present case. Reputation is clearly evidence as to the boundary of a parish. The question is, whether in this case it was admissible as a medium of proof. Now I think that, the fact being once before the jury, that the boundaries of the farm and of the hamlet were identical, any legitimate mode of proving the boundary of the hamlet was allowable in the case. The answer of the witness, that the two boundaries were the same, was admitted without objection. It is true that the boundary of a farm may shift; but the answer here given applied to one state of the premises, and that appeared to have continued from as far back as living memory could reach. Then it is the same as if the estate had been originally sold with an express reference to the boundary of the hamlet: and, being so, that the boundary might properly be proved by any evidence applicable to the subject.

(1) 6th ed.
(2) 12 R. R. 533 (14 East, 323).
And see *Morewood* v. *Wood*, 12 R. R. 537 (14 East, 327, *n.*).
(3) 34 R. R. 529 (10 B. & C. 657).

(4) 40 R. R. 634 (1 Cr. M. & R. 495; 5 Tyr. 1).
(5) 40 R. R. 779 (1 Cr. M. & R. 919; 5 Tyr. 458).
(6) 2 Ad. & El. 793.

PATTESON, J. (1) :

The point in dispute on the trial was a very simple one, namely, whether the place in which the cattle were taken was or was not parcel of a certain estate : and that was, of course, to be determined by any evidence which could be admissible upon such a question.   On this precise question, evidence of reputation was clearly not admissible ; but such proof is receivable to show the boundary of a hamlet ; and, that being so, I do not see how it could be excluded in the present case, when it was established that the boundaries of the hamlet and of the farm were the same.   *Mr. Chilton*, indeed, seems not to rest his objection on the ground that such evidence is at all events inadmissible, *but to contend that, before it can be let in, the boundaries must be shown beyond all doubt to have been identical.   That, however, would be trying the question twice over : and I think that, as soon as some evidence of the identity was given, this proof was receivable, the jury being cautioned by the learned Judge not to take it into consideration unless satisfied that the boundaries were the same.   If the identity of the boundaries had been proved by evidence of reputation, the case would have been different : but the witness called on this subject stated it positively, and not as matter of reputation ; and, that being so, the proof of reputation as to the boundary of the hamlet was let in, and supported the defendant's case, provided the jury were satisfied of the identity upon the witness's statement.

[*529]

COLERIDGE, J. :

This is a question of more novelty than difficulty.   When the witness was asked, " Have you heard from old people, now dead, what was the boundary of the hamlet," the only objection that could have been taken to that question was, that it was not relevant.   But it was shown to be so : and then the objection comes to this, that evidence shall not be given as to the boundary of a hamlet in the same mode as on other occasions, because the proof is, in the particular case, only subsidiary.   But I never heard that a fact was not to be proved in the same manner

_____

(1) Littledale, J. was absent.

when subsidiary, as when it is the very matter in issue. If the fact here was relevant, I think it was to be proved in the ordinary way.   *Rule refused.*

1837.
April 26.

[572]

STANNARD *v.* FORBES AND WIFE, EXECUTOR AND EXECUTRIX OF LOCK.

(6 Adol. & Ellis, 572—589; S. C. 1 N. & P. 633; W. W. & D. 321; 6 L. J.
(N. S.) K. B. 185.)

> Where an assignment of a lease for a term of years, if C. should so long
> live, contains an express covenant that the lease is valid and effectual, &c.
> notwithstanding any act, &c. of the assignor and those claiming under
> him, the fact that the term has been determined by the death of the
> *cestui que vie* is not a breach of the covenant.

COVENANT. On the trial of this cause at the Middlesex sittings in Michaelmas Term, 1834, a verdict was taken for the plaintiff, subject to the opinion of this Court on the following case :

[573]

The declaration stated that, whereas heretofore, to wit 26th February, 1825, by a certain indenture then made between George Scott, guardian of Georgiana Scott, of the first part, Seanah Stoe Clement, of the second part, and John Lock (the testator) of the third part, George Scott as to one undivided moiety of the messuage and premises, &c., thereinafter mentioned, &c., did demise unto John Lock, and the said S. S. Clement as to the other undivided moiety thereof did also demise unto J. Lock, the said messuage, &c., to hold one undivided moiety thereof, that is to say the moiety of the said Georgiana Scott, from 25th December then last past, for the term of eleven years, if Georgiana Scott should so long live, at and under a certain rent to her payable, and to hold the other undivided moiety for the same term, provided S. S. Clement should so long live, at and under a certain rent to her payable ; and J. Lock covenanted, amongst other things, to pay the said rents, &c.; by virtue of which indenture J. Lock entered into, and was possessed of, the said messuage, &c., for the term therein mentioned, and according to the tenor and effect thereof ; and, after the making of the same indenture, and in the lifetime of J. Lock, to wit 21st September, 1826, by a certain indenture

then made between J. Lock of the one part, and the plaintiff of
the other part (profert), reciting, amongst other things, that, in
and by the said indenture, George Scott had, as to the moiety of
Georgiana Scott, and S. S. Clement had, as to the other moiety,
demised and leased unto J. Lock, his executors, &c., the premises
in the said indenture mentioned, to wit &c., to hold the moiety
of Georgiana Scott unto J. Lock, his executors, &c., for the term
of eleven years, from the 25th December then last past, at *and
under a certain yearly rent clear of all &c., and to hold
the other moiety, belonging to S. S. Clement, from the same
25th December, for the same term of eleven years, at and under
the further yearly rent of 25*l.*; and also reciting that, by a
memorandum of agreement bearing date 26th day of August
then last, between J. Lock and the plaintiff, J. Lock had agreed
to sell unto the plaintiff the said messuage, &c., with the appurtenances, demised by the said indenture, for the residue of the
said term of eleven years, together with the good will of a certain
trade, &c., and that J. Lock had thereby further agreed to assign
over the said lease and good will to the plaintiff; J. Lock, for
the considerations &c., did then and there grant, bargain, sell,
assign, transfer, and set over, unto the plaintiff, his executors,
&c., the said messuage, &c., to have and to hold the said
messuage, &c., unto the plaintiff, his executors, &c., from
29th September next ensuing the date, for and during all the
rest, residue, and remainder, which should be then to come and
unexpired, of the said term of eleven years therein, subject
to payment of the yearly rents, and performance of the covenants, &c., in and by the recited indenture of lease reserved and
contained, which from the said 29th September then next
ensuing, on the tenant, lessee, or assignee's, part and behalf,
were or ought to be paid, kept, &c.   And J. Lock, for himself,
his executors, &c., did, by the last-mentioned indenture, covenant,
promise, and declare, to and with the plaintiff, his executors,
&c., that (1), for and notwithstanding any act, deed, matter, or
thing whatsoever, by him the said J. Lock at any time theretofore
made, done, committed, or knowingly *occasioned, suffered, or
omitted, to the contrary, the recited indenture of lease was,

[*574]

[*575]

(1) Called the first covenant in the argument and judgment.

STANNARD
c.
FORBES.

at the time of the sealing and delivery of the said indenture between the plaintiff and J. Lock, a good, valid, and effectual lease in law and in equity, of and for the premises thereby demised ; and (1) that the same, and the term of eleven years therein expressed, were respectively in full effect, and in no wise forfeited, surrendered, assigned, determined, or otherwise become void or voidable, or prejudicially affected, in any manner howsoever, than by effluxion of time ; and that the yearly and other rents in and by the recited indenture of lease reserved, and also all taxes, &c., charged upon the premises, or the tenant or occupier, had been, and were, or would be, paid and satisfied, up to 29th September then next, and that the several covenants, conditions, and agreements therein contained, on the part of the tenant or lessee of the premises, had been well and truly performed and observed, down to the date of the indenture between J. Lock and the plaintiff ; and (2) also that, for and notwithstanding any such act, &c., he the said J. Lock had in himself full power, and lawful and absolute authority, to bargain, sell, assign, transfer, and assure the said messuage, &c., unto the plaintiff, his executors, &c., for and during all the residue and remainder, to come and unexpired by effluxion of time, of or in the said term of eleven years, according to the true intent and meaning of the same indenture ; and, further, that the plaintiff, his executors, &c., should or lawfully might, immediately after the execution thereof, and from time to time, &c., during the

[*576]

residue and remainder, &c., of the said term of eleven *years, peaceably and quietly enter, &c., and have or enjoy, &c., for and during such residue, &c., without any action, suit, eviction, hindrance, disturbance, or interruption whatsoever, of or by the said J. Lock, his executors, &c., or any person or persons then or thereafter rightfully claiming or possessing any estate, right, title, charge, or interest into, or out of, or upon, the said premises, or any part thereof, by, from, or in trust for him or them, or by or through his or their acts, deeds, defaults, means, consent, or privity ; and that free and clear, &c. (indemnified by John Lock, his executors, &c.), from and against all

(1) Called the second covenant in the argument and judgment.

(2) Called the third covenant in the argument and judgment.

former and other assignments, estates, rights, titles, trusts, interests, charges, payments, and encumbrances whatsoever, which, at any time theretofore, had been, or which at any time thereafter should or might be, committed, created, or knowingly occasioned or suffered, by him the said J. Lock, or any person or persons then or thereafter claiming or possessing any legal or equitable estate, right, title, trust, or interest, by, from, under, or in trust for him, save and except the rent, &c. (in the first indenture) ; and moreover that J. Lock, his executors, &c., and all and every other person or persons whosoever, lawfully claiming or possessing any legal or equitable estate, &c., under or in trust for him or them (covenant for further assurance). The declaration then averred that, after the making of the last-mentioned indenture, to wit 19th January, 1829, by indenture then made between the plaintiff and one Robert James, the plaintiff did bargain, sell, assign, &c., to James, his executors, &c., one equal undivided moiety of and in the same premises, &c., for the residue of the said term therein, provided the said Georgiana Scott and the said S. S. Clement should *so long respectively live ; and, confiding in the before-mentioned demise and covenants from and by J. Lock, did then and there thereby covenant and agree with Robert James, amongst other things, that the first-mentioned indenture of lease then was and continued a good and subsisting lease, and not surrendered, forfeited, or become void or voidable in any manner howsoever ; and also that he, the plaintiff, then had good right and absolute authority to grant, &c., such undivided moiety as last aforesaid, and also for quiet enjoyment, &c. That afterwards, to wit 16th August, 1829, by indenture likewise made between the plaintiff and R. James, the plaintiff did bargain, &c., to R. James, his executors, &c., the remaining moiety of and in the said premises, &c., for the terms aforesaid, respectively determinable as aforesaid, and covenanted with him in respect of the last-mentioned moiety (as of the former), that is to say, amongst other things, that the first mentioned lease was then still a valid and subsisting lease, and not forfeited nor rendered void or voidable in any manner however. Averment that, before the making of the indenture between J. Lock and the plaintiff,

[*577]

STANNARD
v.
FORBES.

S. S. Clement died ; whereupon, and whereby, the said lease and demise to the said J. Lock became and was voidable and void, and wholly ceased, ended, and determined, as to one undivided moiety of the same messuage, &c. : and thereupon and thereby George Scott became and was entitled to such moiety as last aforesaid : and the said G. Scott afterwards, and after the said assignments or demises to Robert James, to wit 30th April, 1831, entered into, and by due process of law ejected and expelled R. James from and out of, the same moiety, and kept him so

[*578]

expelled from thence hitherto, to the great damage of R. *James ; and thereupon, and by reason thereof, &c. ; averment that R. James sued plaintiff for breach of the covenants in the indentures between plaintiff and R. James, and recovered damages against him for having been so ejected, and costs ; and the plaintiff also incurred costs in respect of the action, amounting &c. Averment that, before the making of the said indenture between J. Lock and the plaintiff, J. Lock had notice of the death of S. S. Clement, but that plaintiff had no notice thereof until after the making of the indentures between the plaintiff and James.   And so the plaintiff saith that, by reason of the premises, and of the death of the said S. S. Clement as aforesaid, the said indenture between plaintiff and Lock was not, at the time of the sealing and delivery of the said indenture, a good, valid, and effectual lease ; and that the same, and the said term therein, were not, nor was either of them, in full effect and in no wise forfeited, surrendered, assigned, determined, or otherwise become void or voidable, or prejudicially affected, otherwise than by effluxion of time, in manner and form in the said covenant in that behalf expressed ; and, further, that J. Lock had not in himself such full power and lawful and absolute authority as in and by the before mentioned covenant in that behalf was expressed, in manner and form &c. ; and, further, that the plaintiff, his executors, &c. (like breaches of covenant for quiet enjoyment), contrary to the tenor, &c., of the covenants made by John Lock.

Pleas. First Not guilty.

Second, that the said George Scott did not enter into the said undivided moieties, &c., in manner, &c.

Third, that, before the making of the said supposed indenture
between J. Lock and the plaintiff, Lock had not *notice or knowledge of the death of S. S. Clement, in manner and form, &c.

Fourth, that the plaintiff has been, by J. L., his executors, &c.,
clearly and absolutely acquitted, exonerated, and discharged, or
otherwise, by and at the expense of John Lock, his executors,
&c., well and effectually protected, indemnified, and kept harmless, from and against all former and other assignments, &c.,
committed, created, &c., by J. Lock or any person, &c., claiming,
&c., by, from, under, or in trust for him, &c., save and except
the rents, &c.

The case then stated the facts of the indenture between Scott,
S. S. Clement, and Lock; the assignment by Lock to the plain-
tiff; S. S. Clement's death on 7th of September, 1825, and that
the jury found that Lock had notice of her death before
September, 1826; the plaintiff's entry and assignment to James;
James's eviction by George Scott upon a title accruing on S. S.
Clement's death; and that George Scott received from Lock, in
April, 1826, 50*l.*, for one year's rent due to one Hardisty (the
guardian of Joseph Clement, on whom S. S. Clement's moiety
had devolved) and himself, and afterwards received the rent of
James, and of Stannard, up to the time of the eviction, of both
moieties, as reserved by the lease of February, 1825. Assets
were admitted. The amount of damages, if recoverable, was to
be referred to arbitration.

The question for the opinion of the Court was, whether the
plaintiff was entitled to recover in this action against the
executors of Lock for breach of covenant?

The case was argued in Hilary Term (1).

[After argument, the COURT took time for consideration.]

LORD DENMAN, Ch. J., now delivered the judgment of the
    COURT:

After stating the facts as they appeared in the declaration, his
Lordship proceeded as follows.

The first question was, whether the covenant was restricted to

(1) January 24th, 1837. Before Lord Denman, Ch. J., Williams and
Coleridge, JJ.

the acts of Lock and those claiming under him. It has long
been established that, where, in a conveyance, express covenants
for warranty are introduced, none can be implied from the
general words of conveyance ; and that the Court has no other
duty to discharge than that of correctly construing the language
employed. In performing this task, on any particular occasion,
we are not likely to derive much assistance from the former
decisions that may be cited, as every instrument varies in some
respects from all others, and must be interpreted according to
its own language. It should seem that the true grammatical
sense of the words employed, when that can be ascertained,
must prevail ; and no case can be quoted in which our Courts
have thought themselves at liberty to act in direct contravention
of it. Such a course might indeed become necessary ; for a
deed may contain repugnant clauses : where these occur, the
authorities fully warrant us in comparing the clause under
immediate consideration with all which precedes and follows
it, even though not forming parts of the same sentence, and
with the nature of the obligations entered into, for the purpose
of discovering and effectuating the intention really expressed
by the parties. But, when we examine the covenant said to
have been broken by Lock by conveying the term after his title
had determined, and find it inseparably connected with the
preceding words, we do not feel the least difficulty as to the
grammatical meaning ; and that appears, on examination, to be
[*588]   conformable to the *general intention of the testator who entered
into the covenant.

All the covenants but the second are admitted to be restricted :
the second is in these terms. (His Lordship then read the
second covenant.) But the whole series of covenants is introduced by qualifying words, which (we cannot doubt) run through
both clauses of the sentence. The effect is, "I covenant that,
for and notwithstanding any act of mine, I have a right to
convey the term, and that the term is neither forfeited, surrendered, nor in anywise impaired, except by effluxion of time."
It was acutely remarked that these last words rendered the
restriction nonsensical, as effluxion of time could have been no
act of the covenantor. They are indeed unnecessary ; but from

that quality in legal documents too strong inferences cannot be
safely drawn. On the other hand, the absurdity of guarding himself from covenanting against any acts but his own, and in the same breath covenanting that the term was not affected by the acts of any person whatever, is glaring, and is rendered still more so by his repetition of the qualifying words after the succeeding covenant, which relates to the fact of clearing up arrears, &c., a fact with which his predecessors could have no concern. The same words are carefully incorporated in the residue of his covenants. The covenants in truth form one sentence, the first clause of which is restricted to the acts of the covenantor; the second omits to repeat the restriction; but the third refers to it by the expression "for and notwithstanding any such act, &c." If both parties had attentively scanned the language of the deed before completing the assignment, neither could have *believed the covenant to include any others than the testator and those claiming under him.

We feel it unnecessary to travel through the cases: that of *Browning* v. *Wright* (1) may however be referred to, as fully warranting the principle on which we act, and closely resembling the present case in the form of the covenant.

A second point was attempted to be raised from an additional fact in the case; viz., that, supposing the construction above stated to be right, there was still a breach of covenant by Lock, in paying rent to his lessor after knowledge that one of the lives had fallen. This act, it was said, would have the effect of converting his term into a tenancy from year to year, if done while the life continued, and could have no less, after the life had dropped. But, granting these premises for the sake of the argument, we think the conclusion does not follow, for the simple reason that the payment of rent made no difference whatever in Lock's interest which had previously expired. What he did was wholly inoperative, and could not therefore be a breach of his covenant.

For these reasons, we are of opinion that the plaintiff is not entitled to recover; and our judgment must be for the defendant.

Judgment for the defendant.

(1) 5 R. R. 521 (2 Bos. & P. 13).

REX *v.* The BIRMINGHAM and STAFFORDSHIRE
GAS LIGHT COMPANY (1).

(6 Adol. & Ellis, 634—644 ; S. C. 1 N. & P. 691 ; 6 L. J. (N. S.) M. C. 92.)

A local Act directed that the guardians of the poor, churchwardens,
and overseers of the parish of B. should, from time to time, but not
oftener than once in seven years, cause to be made a survey and valuation of the annual value of all houses, lands, tenements, and hereditaments in the parish, which might be amended from time to time by the
concurrence of a majority of the overseers ; and the poor rates were to
be made upon the annual value in such valuation, with power of appeal
to Quarter Sessions against the survey and valuation. Under another
local Act, a Gas Light Company laid down pipes in the parish, the soil
not belonging to the Company, and manufactured the gas out of the
parish.

In the valuation, they were entered for their mains, pipes, &c., for the
value at which the mains and pipes would let, and, for the land occupied
by the mains and pipes, at the value of the land to let for a pipeway.
In certain houses in the parish, there were steam engines and other
machinery affixed to the houses. These houses were valued at what they
were worth to let, without reference to the value which they derived from
the engines, &c. :

Held, that the valuation was bad.

On appeal by the Birmingham and Staffordshire Gas Light
Company against a survey and valuation made by the guardians
of the poor of the parish of Birmingham, and the churchwardens
and overseers of the said parish, the Sessions confirmed the
survey and valuation, subject to a case, which, so far as material
to the decision here, was to the following effect.

The case set out parts of stat. 1 & 2 Will. IV. c. lxvii. (local
and personal, public), entitled " An Act for better regulating the
poor within the parish of Birmingham," &c. (2), directing and

---

(1) Cited in the judgment of the
Court delivered by Cockburn, L. Ch.
J., in *Laing* v. *Bishopwearmouth* (1878)
3 Q. B. D. 299, 305, 47 L. J. M. C.
41, 44 ; and by Lord Esher, M. R.
in *Tyne Boiler Works Co.* v. *Overseers
of Long Benton* (1886) 18 Q. B. Div.
81, 89 ; 56 L. J. M. C. 8, 11.—R. C·

(2) Sect. 57 enacts, " That the said
guardians " (incorporated by sect. 1),
" churchwardens, and overseers of the
poor of the said parish of Birmingham
shall from time to time cause a survey

and valuation to be made of all
houses, lands, tenements, and hereditaments within the said parish of
Birmingham, and of the annual value
thereof, and for that purpose shall
employ any surveyor or surveyors "
&c.

Sect. 58 enacts, That " the sum
which shall be inserted in the said
survey and valuation as the annual
value of all houses, lands, tenements,
or hereditaments within the said
parish shall be taken and held to be

REX
v.
THE
BIRMINGHAM
AND STAF-
FORDSHIRE
GAS LIGHT
COMPANY.

[*635]

regulating the survey and valuation *of houses, &c., in the parish, for the purpose of rating.

In December, 1833, a survey or valuation was made under the direction of the guardians, churchwardens, and overseers, purporting to be a survey or valuation of all the houses, lands, tenements, and hereditaments within the parish. In this document the property of the Birmingham and Staffordshire Gas Light Company is thus described:

Birmingham and Staffordshire Gas Company.	For their gasholders and premises in Oxford Street, and mains and pipes within the parish.	Annual value. 2,480l. 0s. 0d.

The Company appealed duly against the survey and valuation, stating as the grounds of the appeal (among others) the objections noticed in the following argument.

It appeared in evidence that many persons, named in that behalf in the notice of appeal, were, at the time of the making of the survey or valuation, in the occupation of lands, houses, or buildings, to which pipes, steam engines, and various other

the annual value thereof for all the purposes of this Act; and all rates to be from time to time made by the churchwardens and overseers of the said parish for the relief of the poor, shall be made upon a fair and equal pound rate upon the annual value of all the lands, tenements, and hereditaments inserted in such survey or valuation."

Sect. 59 enacts That no alteration shall be made in the survey &c. without the concurrence of the major part of the overseers, under whose direction amendments or alterations, and additions of other rateable lands, &c., shall be inserted.

Sect. 60 enacts, "That no such survey and valuation shall be repeated or made oftener than once in every seven years from the time of making the first survey and valuation under the authority of this Act."

Sect. 101 enacts, "That in all cases where any body politic, corporate, or collegiate, or any person or persons, shall think himself aggrieved by any survey or valuation, or any rate for the relief of the poor," &c., such body politic, &c., may appeal to Quarter Sessions, giving certain notices, with the grounds of appeal, and complying with other requisites.

Sect. 102 enacts that, in cases of appeal, "the said justices upon hearing such appeal, where they shall see just cause of relief, shall and are hereby empowered to correct, alter, and amend such survey or valuation, or rate, in such manner only as shall be necessary for giving relief to the person so appealing, without quashing or wholly setting aside the same survey or valuation:" proviso, that the Court may wholly quash the same, and order a new survey and valuation, if they think this necessary to give relief to the party appealing.

REX
v.
THE
BIRMINGHAM
AND STAF-
FORDSHIRE
GAS LIGHT
COMPANY.

machinery for carrying on trades were affixed, being let into the ground, or otherwise attached to the freehold. If the steam engines and machinery for the purpose of manufacturing, affixed to houses and buildings, ought to be estimated in the present rate as forming part of the annual value of the houses and buildings, then the value of the houses and buildings would be increased beyond what they are rated at; as the annual value to let, of the lands, houses, and buildings mentioned in the notice of appeal, along with the steam engines and machinery, was, in point of fact, increased by the steam engines and machinery attached to them. These pipes, steam engines, and machinery were omitted in the survey or valuation, except as hereinafter mentioned. They were neither included in it specifically, as coming within the words houses, lands, tenements, and hereditaments, nor indirectly, as adding to the annual value of the lands, houses, and buildings to which they were so attached and affixed: the houses and buildings were valued at what they would be worth to let by the year (with a deduction of 20l. per cent. for repairs), reference being had to the purposes for which they were used, and to the additional strength and form of their construction for the purpose of allowing steam engines and other powerful machinery to be attached to them. The masonry and brick work for boilers, vats, and chimney stacks were included; but not the steam engines themselves: all machinery and apparatus used for

[*637]

the purpose of manufacturing, whether *fixed or not, was intended to be and was excluded from the survey or valuation. That was the principle upon which it was made.

The appellants were incorporated by stat. 6 Geo. IV. c. lxxix. (local and personal, public); and this Act formed a part of the case (1). In pursuance of this Act, they laid mains and pipes

(1) Sect. 1 incorporates the Company by the name of "The Birmingham and Staffordshire Gas Light Company." Sect. 2 enacts that the Company shall be established for producing gas for lighting the roads, streets, &c., in Birmingham, and other places named, in Warwickshire and Staffordshire.

Sects. 3, 4, enact, that there shall

be a capital stock divided into shares. Sect. 5 enacts, "That all shares in the said undertaking, and in the net profits and advantages thereof, shall be deemed personal estate, and not of the nature of real property, and shall be transmissible as such accordingly."

Sects. 48, 49, give the Company power to erect retorts gasometers,

REX
v.
THE
BIRMINGHAM
AND STAF-
FORDSHIRE
GAS LIGHT
COMPANY.

under the streets of the town of Birmingham, and have for many years supplied the town with gas by means of such mains and pipes. The whole of their gas is manufactured at West Bromwich, out of the parish of Birmingham, but conveyed into Birmingham by mains or pipeways. The appellants have no property whatever in the land in the streets in which their mains and pipes are laid, only a license to lay them from the commissioners under the Birmingham Street Act, in whom the soil is vested.

The annual value of the appellants' gas holders and premises in Oxford Street, and of their mains and pipes, was ascertained upon the following principle.

[638]

The buildings in Oxford Street, and land immediately connected with them, were valued as land and buildings, at what they were worth to let by the year, in the same way as the value of other lands and buildings in the parish was ascertained.

The gas holder, which contains the gas when made, and which is formed of brick and iron work sunk into the ground several feet, and raised several feet above the surface of the ground, was valued as a warehouse or building at what it was worth to let by the year.

The mains and pipes, and the land which they occupy, were valued by ascertaining the quantity of land through which they were laid, and then valuing that land, with reference to the value of the adjoining land, taking into consideration the purpose for which it is used. This value is an annual value to let for the purpose of a pipeway. The pipes and mains were separately valued at an annual rental, to let, deducting an allowance of 20*l*. per cent. for wear and tear in the same manner as the allowance for repairs in houses, the mains being considered as holders or

&c., and to sink and lay pipes, &c., and mains requisite for the supply of gas, requiring, in certain cases, the consent of owners and occupiers.

Sect. 53 empowers the Company to contract with the commissioners under stat. 52 Geo. III. c. cxiii. (local and personal, public, " for better paving, lighting," &c., " the town of Birmingham," &c.), and with their consent to erect retorts, gasometers, &c., and sink and lay pipes, &c., in such manner as the commissioners shall think necessary, and, with such consent, to break up the soil and pavements of streets, roads, &c., in Birmingham ; but not to enter into houses or lands without consent of owners or occupiers.

depositories from which the manufactured article is delivered to the consumers.

All these annual values were made with reference to the annual value of other houses, lands, and hereditaments in the parish, included in the valuation, except as stated in the case.

The questions for this Court were, 1, whether the gas holders, mains, and pipes, of the appellants ought to have been included [*639] in the survey or valuation. 2, *whether the survey or valuation is not bad in law, on account of such omissions as are mentioned in the case. 3, whether, supposing that the pipes and mains of the appellants are rightly included, the principle upon which their annual value has been ascertained is a correct one.

Hill and *Amos* in support of the order of Sessions :

First, the Company are rateable for the mains and pipes, inasmuch as they occupy the land by these means. The authorities on this point are conclusive, whatever exceptions have been admitted under the words of particular Acts : *Rex* v. *The Trustees for paving Shrewsbury* (1), *Rex* v. *The Manchester and Salford Water Works Company* (2), *Rex* v. *The Brighton Gas Light Company* (3), *Rex* v. *The Birmingham Gas Light and Coke Company* (4), *Rex* v. *The Corporation of Bath* (5), *Rex* v. *Bell* (6), *Rex* v. *The Chelsea Water Works Company* (7), *Rex* v. *Rochdale Water Works Company* (8). Secondly, the rate is not unequal, upon the ground of fixed machinery not being rated in other houses. The Company are rated for their property in question as occupiers of land. Now it is true that, under stat. 43 Eliz. c. 2, s. 1, occupiers, &c., are rateable for their personal property. But, by a "common impulse," as is said in 1 Nol. P. L. 223 (9), most parishes abstain from rating personal property, on account of the difficulty of ascertaining its amount, an objection recog-[*640] nised by Lord *Kenyon in *Rex* v. *Page* (10). There is thus an acknowledged distinction between the profits arising from the

(1) 37 R. R. 409 (3 B. & Ad. 216).
(2) 1 B. & C. 630.
(3) 29 R. R. 290 (5 B. & C. 466; 8 Dowl. & Ry. 308).
(4) 25 R. R. 483 (1 B. & C. 506; 2 Dowl. & Ry. 735).
(5) 13 R. R. 333 (14 East, 609).
(6) 7 T. R. 598.
(7) 39 R. R. 438 (5 B. & Ad. 156).
(8) 1 M. & S. 634.
(9) 4th ed.
(10) 2 R. R. 454 (4 T. R. 543).

permanent occupation of land, and those arising from the use of machinery. But for such distinction, overseers could not make an equal rate: and in this case the survey, which, by sect. 60 of stat. 1 & 2 Will. IV. c. lxvii., can be made once only in seven years, would be useless, unless made anew for each rate. Then all fixtures must be included, as well as fixed machinery. Neither would the difficulty be removed by striking out the rate here made on the Company's mains and pipes. For the same objection, if valid, might be made by any one rated in respect of his occupation of land; and a similar objection might be made, in any other parish, under stat. 43 Eliz. c. 2, which is more extensive in its terms than the local Act here. It will perhaps be argued that the property rated would go to the executor or tenant. That is questionable; but, if true, it would show merely that a hereditament may, regard being had to the object of the law in the particular case, be treated in some respects as personalty; just as, *in favorem vitæ*, a cupboard, press, &c., fixed to a house, are not treated as part of the house in a prosecution for burglary. Foster, in his remarks on *The Case of George Gibbons* (1), says that, in questions between the heir or devisee and the executor, these fixtures may with propriety enough be considered as annexed to, and parts of, the freehold, on the presumption that such was the intention of the owner; but that, in capital cases, such fixtures should be treated as mere moveables.

(COLERIDGE, J.: There are numerous cases in which fixed *machinery has been rated, as adding to the value of the house.)   [*641]

Stat. 43 Eliz. c. 2, s. 1, under which those cases were decided, imposes a rate according to ability of any kind; here the words are less comprehensive. It does not appear that in *Rex* v. *St. Nicholas, Gloucester* (2), the machine was rateable as other than personalty: in *Rex* v. *Hogg* (3) the machine was moveable. Those cases, therefore, if indeed they be now law, can be supported only by the generality of the provision of stat. 43 Eliz. c. 2, s. 1. The present case finds that the houses in the parish

REX
v.
THE
BIRMINGHAM
AND STAF-
FORDSHIRE
GAS LIGHT
COMPANY.

(1) Fost. C. L. 109.   S. C. Cald. 262).
(2) 1 R. R. 376, n. (1 T. R. 723, n.;   (3) 1 R. R. 375 (1 T. R. 721).

REX
v.
THE
BIRMINGHAM
AND STAF-
FORDSHIRE
GAS LIGHT
COMPANY.

are rated with reference to the purpose for which they are used : their value, therefore, *quâ* houses, has been fully taken : the only remaining question is whether the steam engines, &c., *per se*, are rateable. Now they are not hereditaments. In Termes de la Ley, (ed. 1708), Hereditaments are defined to be " touts ceux choses immoveable, soient ils corporeal ou incorporeal queux un home poet aver a luy et son heirs per voy de inheritance, et queux si ne sont auterment bequest veignant a celuy que est prochein de sank et nemy al executors ou administrators come chattels." The machines would go to the executor : *Lawton* v. *Lawton* (1), *Lord Dudley* v. *Lord Warde* (2), which cases are the stronger, because the fixtures there really derived their value from their application to the produce of the land. The executor's right was not adverted to in *Rex* v. *St. Nicholas, Gloucester* (3), or *Rex* v. *Lord Granville* (4), which is the strongest authority for the appellants.

[*642]   (COLERIDGE, J. referred to *Brown* *v. *Lord Granville* (5).)

In *Rex* v. *St. Dunstan* (6) the Court appeared to consider that, if the fixtures in question would have gone to the tenant, or executor, they could not have been considered as adding to the value of the land. It may be said that the pipes, being used for the purposes of trade, would also go to the executor ; and that, therefore, any argument founded on such a criterion fails to distinguish the two classes of property. But the answer is that, by the general law, fixtures do not go to the executor ; that exceptions can be made to this, only where the specific article has been held to be an exception ; and that there has been such a holding with respect to fixed machinery, but not with respect to pipes. *Winn* v. *Ingilby* (7) shows that the exceptions are not to be extended. And, as has been shown, property like that of the appellants has been always held to be realty. Further, it is by means of the pipeways alone that the land is used : the houses are not used by means of the engines alone.

(1) 3 Atk. 13.   (4) 32 R. R. 627 (9 B. & C. 188).
(2) Ambl. 113.   (5) 10 Bing. 69.
(3) 1 R. R. 376, n. (1 T. R. 723, n.;   (6) 4 B. & C. 686.
S. C. Cald. 262).   (7) 24 R. R. 503 (5 B. & Ald. 625).

Sir W. W. Follett, contrà :

No criterion is furnished by the fact that the machinery would go to the executor ; for, if that be true of the machinery it is true of the pipeways. Besides, sect. 5 of stat. 6 Geo. IV. c. lxxix. makes the shares in the Company's property personalty.

REX
v.
THE
BIRMINGHAM
AND STAF-
FORDSHIRE
GAS LIGHT
COMPANY.

(*Hill :* That has been decided to be no criterion in a question of rateability (1).)

Further, the gas-holders and pipeways are in effect rated with reference to the value the land acquires by the profit they produce ; that principle requires that the houses should be rated *according to the profit they produce ; and the fixed machinery yields a part of this. It is argued that, by common consent, personalty is not generally rated. But the appellants complain that this rule is applied unequally in the present case. The gas-holders and pipes are as much machinery as the engines. The cases in which fixed machinery has been rated have not been effectually distinguished. In *Rex* v. *The Proprietors of the Liverpool Exchange* (2) the COURT, after referring to *Rex* v. *Hogg* (3), and several other cases on the same point, say, "These cases establish the principle, that the advantages attendant upon a building, either in respect of the situation or the mode of its occupation, are to be taken into the account in estimating its rateable annual value, wherever those advantages would enable the owner of the building to let it at a higher rent than it would otherwise fetch ; but not the profits of a trade carried on in the building, and not enhancing its rent." Here a tenant would give more for the house on account of its added value arising from the fixed machinery. The principle was so applied in *Rex* v. *Lord Granville* (4) ; it was there admitted that the owner, if he occupied, should be assessed on the increased value, but the COURT held, further, that the mere occupier was so chargeable. There it might have been said that the tenant had the power of removal : the case is therefore stronger than the present. In *Rex* v. *Bilston* (5) it was held that a party was not rateable for

[*643]

(1) See *Rex* v. *The Dock Company of Hull*, 1 T. R. 219.
(2) 1 Ad. & El. 474.
(3) 1 B. R. 375 (1 T. R. 721).
(4) 32 B. R. 627 (9 B. & C. 188).
(5) 5 B. & C. 851.

REX
v.
THE
BIRMINGHAM
AND STAF-
FORDSHIRE
GAS LIGHT
COMPANY.

[*644]

an engine fixed to an iron-stone mine, because the mine itself was not rateable, and the engine was rateable only as part of *the mine.

(*Waddington*, on the same side, was stopped by the COURT.)

LORD DENMAN, Ch. J.:

This rate is bad on a ground which makes it unnecessary for us to discuss any other. It is expressly found that houses, to which machinery is attached, are not rated according to the increased value arising from the machinery. Such machinery constitutes a mode of occupying: that really is clear from the beginning to the end of all the cases on the subject. This principle has never been called in question; and, even where the machine has not been attached, a house has been held rateable in respect of it, if the value of the house was increased by the machine. In a case argued in last Hilary Term (1) the principle was never doubted; but it was only attempted to show that it did not apply to the particular case.

LITTLEDALE, PATTESON, and COLERIDGE, JJ., concurred.

> *Order of Sessions, on the appeal against the survey and valuation, quashed for insufficiency; and ordered, that the Court of Quarter Sessions do quash the said survey and valuation, or amend the same, in respect of the several omissions therein in the said order mentioned.*

REED v. COWMEADOW AND RUDGE (2).

(6 Adol. & Ellis, 661—663; S. C. at Nisi Prius, 7 Car. & P. 821.)

A party having apprehended another, and proceeded against him before a justice, under stat. 7 & 8 Geo. IV. c. 30, s. 24 (3), for a malicious injury to property, the justice dismissed the complaint, being of opinion that the party charged had acted under a reasonable supposition of right, according to the proviso of sect. 24. An action of trespass being brought for the arrest,

Held, that the defendant, if he acted under a *bonâ fide* belief that the

---

(1) Probably *Rex* v. *Guest*, argued in Hil. T. 1837; decided in Hil. T. 1838.

(2) See next case, and *Chamberlain* v. *King* (1871) L. R. 6 C. P. 474, 40

L. J. C. P. 273.—R. C.

(3) Since repealed. But see the Malicious Damage Act, 1861 (24 & 25 Vict. c. 97), s. 52.—R. C.

case fell within the statute, was entitled to notice of action under s. 41 (1);
and that, in default of notice, the jury on the trial might properly be
directed to find for the defendant, if they thought that he had acted
bonâ fide.

TRESPASS for assaulting and falsely imprisoning the plaintiff.
On the trial before Parke, B. at the last Spring Assizes at
Gloucester, it appeared that the plaintiff had pulled down part
of the chimney of a building in the defendant Cowmeadow's
possession; that Cowmeadow thereupon took the plaintiff and
(about five in the afternoon) delivered him into the custody
of a constable, the defendant Rudge, who, by Cowmeadow's
direction, kept him in charge till the next morning; that the
plaintiff was then dismissed without being taken before a magistrate, the defendant Cowmeadow having obtained a summons
for his attendance at a subsequent time; that the plaintiff and
Cowmeadow afterwards attended before a magistrate, and
Cowmeadow made a charge against the plaintiff under stat.
7 & 8 Geo. IV. c. 30, s. 24; and that the magistrate dismissed
the complaint, thinking that the plaintiff had acted under a
reasonable supposition of right within the meaning of the
proviso contained in that section.   No notice of action had been
given, and, on the trial, a nonsuit was contended for on this
ground.   The learned Judge refused to nonsuit; and in
summing up he stated to the jury that the plaintiff, having
acted under a colour of right, was in the same situation as if he
had actually had a right; but that the question, as to the point
of notice, was, whether the defendant Cowmeadow had acted
under *a bonâ fide* belief that he was proceeding in pursuance of   [*662]
the statute; for that, if he did so believe, he was entitled to
notice: and his Lordship left it to the jury, under the circumstances, whether Cowmeadow had entertained such *bonâ fide*
belief.   The jury found for the defendants.

Ludlow, Serjt., in this Term, moved for a new trial on the
ground of misdirection:

No notice was necessary, under sect. 41 of stat. 7 & 8 Geo. IV.
c. 30, because the act for which the plaintiff was arrested falls

---

(1) Since repealed.   But see the Malicious Damage Act, 1861 (24 & 25
Vict. c. 97), s. 52.—R. C.

within an exception, in the proviso of sect. 24, which takes the case entirely out of the statute.

(PATTESON, J. referred to *Beechey* v. *Sides* (1), and *Ballinger* v. *Ferris* (2).)

In *Beechey* v. *Sides* (1) the act with which the defendant had charged the plaintiff fell within sect. 20 of stat. 7 & 8 Geo. IV. c. 30, which does not contain any proviso like that of sect. 24.

(COLERIDGE, J. : You say that, if a party has arrested, supposing the case not to be within the exception of sect. 24, and it is within it, he is not entitled to notice.)

If the case is within the exception, the statute, as far as it regards notice, is as if it had not passed.

(COLERIDGE, J. : Suppose, instead of the enactment and exception in sect. 24, it had been provided that any person committing damage, &c., not under a reasonable supposition of right, shall be liable to be apprehended, and to pay a fine if convicted : do you say that a person who apprehended another, supposing him liable under that clause, would not be entitled to notice ?)

The clause requiring notice takes away a common law right, and its operation is not to be extended.

[663]   (PATTESON, J.: It does not take away the right of action ; it only makes notice a requisite.)

LORD DENMAN, Ch. J. :

Beechey v. *Sides* (1) is nearly in point ; and the doctrine of Lord TENTERDEN there is decisive of this case. There must be no rule.

PATTESON and COLERIDGE, JJ. concurred.

Rule refused.

(1) 33 R. R. 333 (9 B. & C. 806).   (2) 1 M. & W. 628 ; Tyr. & Gr. 920.

WEDGE v. THE HONOURABLE MAURICE FREDERICK FITZHARDINGE BERKELEY (1).

1837.
May 1.

[663]

(6 Adol. & Ellis, 663—669; S. C. 1 N. & P. 665; W. W. & D. 271.)

Under stat. 24 Geo. II. c. 44, s. 1 (2), a magistrate, sued for detaining goods on a suspicion of felony, is entitled to notice of action, if he proceeded under a *bonâ fide* belief that he was executing his duty, although it be proved that he had no reasonable ground of suspicion:

The *bona fides*, as well as the reasonableness of the suspicion, is a question for the jury.

And, if the plaintiff seeks to maintain his action without having given notice, it lies on him to cause the question of *bona fides* to be put to the jury.

TRESPASS. The declaration contained counts, 1. For assaulting plaintiff. 2. For taking from him a wheelbarrow and a sack of grass, &c. Plea, Not guilty. On the trial before Littledale, J. at the Lewes Summer Assizes, 1835, the following facts appeared. The defendant, a magistrate, met the plaintiff's son in the day-time wheeling a barrow of new-mown grass, in sacks. The defendant stopped the barrow, and asked what the sacks contained. According to the defendant's case, the plaintiff's son answered that it was no business of the defendant's; the son himself stated in evidence that he immediately told the defendant what was in the sacks, and told him also that a Mrs. Reynolds had given the plaintiff leave to cut it in a particular field. The defendant said that he believed it to be stolen property, and should seize it as such. The plaintiff came up during the conversation, and, according to the evidence *on his behalf, stated again the manner in which the grass had been obtained. The defendant had it wheeled away to his own premises; but afterwards, finding on inquiry that it had not been stolen, he offered it back. The plaintiff lived in the defendant's neighbourhood; he was a labourer in husbandry and looked after a farm; he had no land of his own. No notice of action was given under stat. 24 Geo. II. c. 44, s. 1. The defendant's counsel submitted that, for want of such notice, the plaintiff must be nonsuited. The learned Judge thought that there should have been notice, but he refused to nonsuit, giving leave, however, to move for a

[*664]

(1) See last case, and note, p. 580, *ante.*—R. C.

(2) Since repealed. See now the

Public Authorities Protection Act, 1893 (56 & 57 Vict. c. 61).—R. C.

nonsuit.   Evidence was then gone into for the defendant. LITTLEDALE, J., in summing up, stated to the jury that, the defendant being a magistrate, if he had reasonable ground of suspicion that the property was stolen, he was entitled to a verdict; but the learned Judge added that he saw no ground for such suspicion; leaving the question, however, with the jury. A verdict was given for the plaintiff on the count for an *asportavit*, damages, 5l.   In the ensuing Term a rule *nisi* was obtained for entering a nonsuit.

Turner now showed cause:

Notice of action is requisite, under stat. 24 Geo. II. c. 44, s. 1, in those cases only where the action is brought against a justice "for any thing by him done in the execution of his office." The act here complained of was not so done.   If a magistrate commits an error in a proceeding regularly before him, he is entitled to notice; but, if he sets aside legal forms, and, under colour of his office, stops a person on the high road, and detains property as stolen, merely upon his own view, he is entitled only

[*665] to the protection, *which a constable enjoys, that, if he has acted erroneously, he shall be excused on showing reasonable ground of suspicion.   The latitude given to a justice of peace, and to a constable, in this respect, is shown in 8 Hawk. P. C. 178, b. 2, c. 13, s. 18 (1), and 2 Hale's P. C. 86, 87, 90, part 2, c. 11 (2).   In *Cook* v. *Leonard* (3) BAYLEY, J. says: "If a magistrate act in a case which his general character authorises him to do, the mere excess of authority" does not deprive the "magistrate of that protection which is conferred upon those who act in execution of it; but where there is a total absence of authority to do any part of that which has been done, the party doing the act is not entitled to that protection."   And he proceeds to cite several of the cases in which notice of action to a magistrate has been held necessary or unnecessary.   Here the ground of protection fails; for there was no reasonable cause of suspicion, as the finding of the jury shows.   *James* v. *Saunders* (4), where the magistrate was held not entitled to notice, is like the present case.

(1) 7th ed. 1795.   (3) 30 R. R. 348 (6 B. & C. 353, 354).
(2) Ed. 1800.   (4) 38 R. R. 503 (10 Bing. 429).

(LITTLEDALE, J.: If the magistrate acted without reasonable cause, the plaintiff would be entitled to a verdict; but it may be a different question whether notice should not have been given.

WEDGE
v.
BERKELEY.

PATTESON, J.: You do not distinguish between right to do the act, and right to notice.)

If the magistrate acts without reasonable cause, he puts himself in the situation of any other individual, and must rest on such defence as the common law gives him.

(LORD DENMAN, Ch. J.: The observations of ALDERSON, J. and BOSANQUET, J. in *James* v. *Saunders* (1) apply here; for the *learned Judge in the present case was not asked to leave it to the jury whether or not the defendant acted *bonâ fide*.)

[*666]

The defendant's conduct showed that he could not be acting *bonâ fide*.

Platt, *contrà*:

No question was raised on the *bona fides*: the defence was put on the ground of right. But, if the magistrate acts *bonâ fide* in the plain execution of his duty, he is entitled to notice, even though the suspicion on which he acted may not prove justifiable. The object of notice is that he may tender amends if he has acted on a groundless suspicion. According to the argument on the other side, notice is to be given only where the suspicion was not groundless. In *Staight* v. *Gee* (2) Lord TENTERDEN held that a constable making an arrest for felony without reasonable cause was within the protection of stat. 21 Jac. I. c. 12, s. 5, which directs that actions against constables, for any thing done by virtue or reason of their offices, shall be brought in the county where such fact was done. In *Hopkins* v. *Crowe* (3), where the defendant was held not entitled to notice of action under stat. 5 & 6 Will. IV. c. 59, s. 19, it is clear that, if the party had been a constable or the owner of the horse which was injured, the Court would have considered it a proper enquiry whether he had

(1) 38 R. R. 503 (10 Bing. 431).   (3) 43 R. R. 476 (4 Ad. & El. 774).
(2) 2 Stark. 445.

WEDGE
r.
BERKELEY.

acted *bonâ fide*, and would have deemed him entitled to notice if he had so acted. The defendant here was a magistrate, and would have been justified in detaining the grass if he had done so on reasonable ground of suspicion ; he thought that he had such ground, and that he was doing his duty as a magistrate.   In *Cook* v. **Clark* (1) an officer who had entered a house, with a warrant, for the purpose of taking a person named in it whom he *bonâ fide* believed to be there, was held entitled to notice of action under stat. 46 Geo. III. c. 87, s. 21 (local and personal, public, Southwark Court of Requests Act), though the party was not in the house when he entered.

[*667]

LORD DENMAN, Ch. J.:

The defendant was entitled to notice of action if, when doing that which is complained of, he was acting " in the execution of his office," within stat. 24 Geo. II. c. 44, s. 1. If he had acted on a reasonable ground of suspicion that the property was stolen. he would have been entitled to a verdict; and the case went to the jury on that question, and they found against him. Now the question is, whether he acted in the execution of his duty, so as to be entitled to notice ; and I think he did, if, with some evidence before him, he really thought that property had been stolen, and seized what he believed to be so. At the end of the plaintiff's case the defendant's counsel moved for a nonsuit. It is clear that at that time the plaintiff did not rely upon the want of *bona fides*. Evidence was gone into for the defendant ; and the case went to the jury on the point as to reasonable suspicion. That, however, left open the question whether notice was necessary or not, which depends on the *bona fides*. If the plaintiff meant to say that the defendant acted in the execution of his office colourably, or to discharge an old grudge, or otherwise in bad faith, he should have required the learned Judge to put the question of *bona fides* to the jury; and, if they *had found against the defendant on that point, I should say that notice would not have been necessary. But that course was not taken : and therefore the rule must be absolute to enter a nonsuit for want of notice.

[*668]

(1) 10 Bing. 19.

LITTLEDALE, J.:

I think that the jury found a proper verdict; but that does not decide the present question. Whether the defendant is entitled to a verdict on the merits, and whether he is entitled to notice, are very different enquiries. If he had notice, and the merits were against him, he might tender amends. Had there been, in this case, any want of *bona fides* shown, or any proof that the defendant acted on a grudge, the case would not stand as it now does. But the evidence did not lead to any such conclusion. (He then recapitulated the principal facts.) It seems to me that the defendant acted *bonâ fide*; and that, being so, he was entitled to notice.

PATTESON, J.:

There were two points in question in this case; the *bona fides*, and the ground of suspicion. The question of *bona fides* was not put to the jury: but, if circumstances raise that question, there is no doubt that it is for the jury. The defendant applied for a nonsuit by reason of the want of notice, at the close of the plaintiff's case. The plaintiff did not then dispute the *bona fides*, or require that the opinion of the jury should be taken upon it. It must therefore have been assumed, at that time, that the defendant acted *bonâ fide*, supposing that he acted with authority. Then the statute 24 Geo. II. c. 44, s. 1, protects a magistrate for anything done "in the execution of his office;" that is, where he acts, *bonâ fide*, with the intention to execute *it. In general [*669] it has not been put to the jury whether the magistrate acted *bonâ fide*, because that has been assumed; but the question is for them. The defendant here is not entitled to a verdict, because reasonable ground of suspicion has been negatived; but the rule must be absolute for entering a nonsuit on account of the want of notice.

COLERIDGE, J.:

The distinction is clear between that which amounts to a defence and that which entitles to notice. The magistrate is entitled to notice where he has no defence on the merits, but where, in a matter within his jurisdiction, he has exceeded its limits (as if he has proceeded singly where another magistrate ought to have joined), acting, nevertheless, *bonâ fide*. Whether there was *bona fides*, and whether there was reasonable cause, are both questions for the jury. The first question has, in general, not been put, the *bona fides* being assumed; and I think it was assumed here. The defendant put it to the learned Judge, at the end of the plaintiff's case, that there should be a nonsuit for want of notice; but the plaintiff never proposed that the jury should be asked whether the defendant had acted *bonâ fide*; a question which the Judge would have put if required. The defendant must, at all events, have the benefit of the omission.   *Rule absolute.*

MAYALL AND OTHERS *v.* MITFORD AND OTHERS.

(6 Adol. & Ellis, 670—674; S. C. 1 N. & P. 732; W. W. & D. 310.)

Action against insurers, on a fire insurance policy upon the machinery of cotton mills, containing a warranty that the mills should be worked by day only. Plea, that a steam engine and horizontal shafts, being parts of the mills, were without defendants' consent worked by night, and not by day only :

Held bad, on motion for judgment *non obstante veredicto*, as not showing a breach of the warranty.

ASSUMPSIT on a policy of insurance against fire. The declaration set out the policy, which was on the machinery of certain cotton mills, and contained the following warranty (among others), "Warranted that the said mills were brick built, and slated; that they be warmed and worked by steam, lighted by gas, worked by day only, &c." Allegation (among others), that the said mills were brick built, and slated; that they were warmed and worked by steam, lighted by gas, worked by day only, &c. The declaration stated a loss by fire: breach, non-payment of the amount of loss.

First plea. That a certain steam engine and certain upright and horizontal shafts, then being respectively parts of the said mills in the said policy of assurance mentioned, after the making of the said policy of assurance in the said declaration mentioned, to wit 1st May, 1834, and on divers other times between that time and the destruction of the said premises by fire, as in the declaration mentioned, were, without the leave or consent of defendants, worked by night and not by day only. Verification.

Replication. That the said supposed steam-engine and shafts in that plea mentioned were not respectively parts of the said mills in the said policy of assurance mentioned ; and that the same were not, after the making of the said policy of assurance, without the leave or consent of defendants, worked by night and not by day *only, in manner and form &c. Conclusion to the country. Several other issues in fact were joined.

[*671]

On the trial before Lord Abinger, C. B., at the Liverpool Summer Assizes, 1835, a verdict was found for the defendants on the issue on the first plea, and for the plaintiffs on all the other issues. In Michaelmas Term, 1835, *Blackburne* obtained a rule *nisi* for judgment *non obstante veredicto* (1).

Cresswell, J. L. Adolphus, and *W. H. Watson,* now showed cause:

The first plea shows a breach of the warranty. In *Whitehead* v. *Price* (2) it was decided that the pleas did not show a breach of warranty, as they alleged only that the steam engine and parts of the gear were worked by night, while the words of the policy, according to their grammatical construction, imported merely that the buildings (constituting the mill) were worked by day only. Here the record shows that what was worked was part of the mill : the warranty therefore is broken, unless it can be said that a mill is not worked when a part of it is worked. And in *Whitehead* v. *Price* (2) there was only a description ; here there is an express warranty. A warranty must be strictly complied with ; *De Hahn* v. *Hartley* (3), *Newcastle Fire Insurance Company* v. *Macmorran* (4) : though substantial compliance with a mere description is sufficient: *Dobson* v. *Sotheby* (5), on the authority of which *Shaw* v. *Robberds* (6) *was decided. In this last case the decision turned upon the use of the kiln not being,

[*672]

---

(1) The rule was for a new trial, or judgment *non obstante veredicto*. Several points were discussed which the judgment of the Court renders it unnecessary to notice.

(2) 41 R. R. 767 (2 Cr. M. & R.

447 ; 5 Tyr. 825).

(3) 1 R. R. 221 (1 T. R. 343 ; 2 T. R. 186).

(4) 15 R. R. 67 (3 Dow, 255).

(5) 31 R. R. 718 (Moo. & Mal. 90).

(6) P. 407, *ante* (6 Ad. & El. 75).

MAYALL
v.
MITFORD.

on the evidence, habitual: here the plea follows the words of the warranty, and no such question arises. The warranty being actually broken, the extent is unimportant. The purpose for which any part of the mill was worked is immaterial: the warranty cannot be evaded by throwing a particular part out of gear. The object of an express warranty is to avoid subtleties of this kind. In *Shaw* v. *Robberds* (1) it was pointed out by the COURT that no clause in the policy amounted to an express warranty.

Sir J. Campbell, Attorney-General, (with whom were *Alexander*, *Wightman*, and *Tomlinson*,) *contrà*:

The meaning of the warranty clearly is that the mills are to be worked, as mills, by day only. But, if this plea disclose a breach, then any movement in any part of the machinery of the mill is a violation of the warranty, which cannot be contended. It might be necessary to work the engine for the purpose of repair, or for cleaning it, during the night: the warranty cannot be meant to provide against that. It does not follow, from the engine being part of the mill, that working the engine is working the mill. A warranty must have a reasonable interpretation: thus a warranty to sail with convoy is complied with if the vessel sail with convoy from the place of rendezvous, though she sail thither from the port of departure without convoy. The plea should have alleged that the mill was worked by night; then the question would have been, whether the evidence as to the working of the engine showed a working of the mill.

(He was then stopped by the COURT.)

[673]   LORD DENMAN, Ch. J.:

Whitehead v. *Price* (2) shows that there was no breach of warranty here, unless the mill was worked by night; then the question is, whether the plea is good which shows only that a part of the mill was so worked. I cannot say that from a part of the mill being worked it follows that the mill was worked. A part, for instance, might always be at work for supplying water;

(1) P. 407, *ante* (6 Ad. & El. 75).   (2) 41 R. R. 767 (2 Cr. M. & R. 447; 5 Tyr. 825).

would that be a breach? The foundation of the answer to the
declaration, therefore, fails, there being no allegation, in terms
of the warranty, showing a breach. There must be judgment
non obstante veredicto.

MAYALL
v.
MITFORD.

LITTLEDALE, J.:

I think the plea ought to have stated, in the terms of the
warranty, that the mill was worked by night. If issue had been
joined on such a plea, the question for the jury would have been,
whether the mill was, substantially, worked. Work may be
done during the night, by part of the mill, yet not by the mill,
and therefore not so as to cause a breach of the warranty,
although it was work without which the mill could not have
gone on.

PATTESON, J.:

All turns upon the meaning of the word "mills" in the
warranty. It is generally advisable, though I do not say that it
is always necessary, to plead a breach of warranty in its very
words; and then the question is, whether the evidence supports
a plea so worded. But I will not say that a plea might not have
been good here which alleged in substance that the work done
in the mill by day went on also by night. At *present, the plea   [*674]
is ambiguous; the work done might simply be a movement of
the machine for purposes different from those which I understand
the warranty to have in view, namely, the work usually carried
on by day.

COLERIDGE, J.:

This plea is bad, if it can be true consistently with no breach
of the warranty having been committed. Now, construe the
warranty by the rest of the policy. The policy is on the
machinery of cotton mills; the warranty, therefore, is against
the manufacture usually carried on in the mills being carried on
by night. The plea does not say what the work was which was
done by night, but simply that a part of the mills was worked.
It might not be necessary to show that every part of the
machinery worked by night; but the plea ought to show that so

much was worked that it might, with common sense, have been said that the mill worked by night. To say that the mere working of a part shows a working of the mill by night seems to me quite unreasonable.

Rule absolute for judgment non obstante veredicto.

1837.

[690]

PARTINGTON, GENT., ONE, &c. *v.* WOODCOCK.

(6 Adol. & Ellis, 690—699; S. C. 1 H. & W. 262.)

A mere notice to pay rent given by an assignee of the estate under an assignment prior to the creation of the tenancy, does not create the relation of landlord and tenant between the assignee and the tenant.

DEBT. The declaration stated that plaintiff heretofore, to wit September 2nd, 1830, demised to defendant, and defendant took

[*691]

of plaintiff, divers messuages, *&c., *habendum* to defendant, his executors, &c., from the day of the demise for seventy years then next ensuing, at the yearly rent of 40*l.* therefore payable by defendant to plaintiff by equal quarterly payments in the year, viz., &c. By virtue of which demise defendant, on 2nd September, 1830, entered &c., and was possessed &c., from thenceforth until and upon March 2nd, 1834, on which day 10*l.* for a quarter's rent, ending on that day, was due from defendant to plaintiff, and still is in arrear, &c., whereby an action &c.

Plea, that, before the making of the demise, to wit &c., plaintiff, being a prisoner within the meaning of stat. 53 Geo. III. c. 102, 54 Geo. III. c. 28, and 56 Geo. III. c. 102, petitioned the Insolvent Debtors' Court for his discharge, and the Court, on January 28th, 1818, adjudged him entitled to the benefit of the statutes, and ordered him to be discharged ; and that, by force of the first-mentioned statute, all the estate, right, &c., of the plaintiff of and in the premises, immediately after such adjudication, became and were assigned and transferred to Thomas Henry Ewbank, as assignee thereof, appointed by the Court, upon the trusts, &c. And " that, after the said plaintiff had been duly discharged according to the provisions of the said statute, and after the making of the demise in the said declaration mentioned (the said plaintiff having been authorized and permitted by the said T. H. Ewbank, as such assignee as aforesaid, PARTINGTON
r.
WOODCOCK. and by permission of the said Court after the said adjudication and discharge, and also by one George Shaw, who, afterwards and before the period hereinafter next mentioned, to wit on " &c., " had been appointed and substituted by the said Court in the place and stead of the said T. H. E. as such assignee as aforesaid, *to remain in the possession and management of the premises in the said declaration mentioned, and the said plaintiff having been also authorized and permitted by the said George Shaw as such assignee as aforesaid, and by the permission of the said Court, to make the said demise of the said premises to the said defendant), and before the said rent or any part thereof in the said declaration mentioned became due and payable, and before the commencement of this suit, to wit on the 23rd day of May, A.D. 1831, he the said defendant received from the said George Shaw, as such assignee as aforesaid, a certain notice and requisition that he the said defendant should thenceforth pay to the said G. S., as such assignee as aforesaid, all and every the rent and every part thereof that might and would then and thereafter accrue and become due and payable from the said defendant for and in respect of the said demised premises, and under and by virtue of the said demise in the said declaration mentioned ; " and also that, in default thereof, legal proceedings would be taken by Shaw, as assignee, against defendant, to recover such rent. Averment that the notice was never countermanded ; " And that by reason thereof he, the said defendant, became and was and still is liable and compellable, from time to time, to pay to the assignee or assignees of the estate and effects of the said plaintiff for the time being as well the said rent demanded by the said plaintiff in the said declaration, as all other the rent so reserved as aforesaid by the said demise, for and in respect of the said premises, as the same becomes and is due and payable, the reversion expectant on the determination of the said demise not being now vested in the said plaintiff, and the right and title of the said plaintiff to sue for and receive the said *rent so reserved by the said demise as aforesaid being, by reason of the said notice, wholly ended and determined." Verification.

[*692]

[*693]

PARTINGTON
v.
WOODCOCK.

Demurrer, assigning for causes that the plea is double, inasmuch as it indirectly denies that plaintiff had any thing in the premises during the period for which rent is claimed, and also states an eviction of defendant by Shaw; that the plea amounts to the general issue; that it is argumentative; that it does not specifically deny, or confess and avoid, &c.; and that it attempts to deny plaintiff's title to the premises, whereas defendant is estopped to deny the same, it appearing by the declaration that defendant enjoyed the same by virtue of the demise by plaintiff in the declaration mentioned. Joinder in demurrer. The demurrer was argued in Easter Term, (May 1st), 1835.

Kelly, in support of the demurrer, contended, first, that the plea, if it stated any defence, was in effect a plea of *nil habuit in tenementis*, and that this could not be pleaded even in the case of a demise without deed. Secondly, that, supposing such a defence admissible, the plea did not sufficiently deny the plaintiff's interest. On the first point, Note (1) to *Duppa* v. *Mayo* (1), *Wilkins* v. *Wingate* (2), *Doe* d. *Bristowe* v. *Pegge* (3), *Doe* d. *Hodsden* v. *Staple* (4), *Pope* v. *Biggs* (5), *Balls* v. *Westwood* (6), *Moss* v. *Gallimore* (7), and *Curtis* v. *Spitty* (8), were referred to by counsel and by the Court.

[*694]

(*Wightman*, for the defendant, said that he *should not contend that *nil habuit in tenementis* would be a good plea, but should maintain that the present plea was, in effect, a denial of any tenancy under the plaintiff at the time when the rent accrued.)

The plea does not amount to such a denial. The declaration alleges a demise by the plaintiff to the defendant: no other party is introduced. If the defendant meant to allege that the plaintiff demised on behalf of another person, and as his agent, that should have been stated.

(1) 1 Wms. Saund. 276 b.
(2) 6 T. R. 62.
(3) 1 T. R. 758, n.
(4) 1 R. R. 595 (2 T. R. 684).

(5) 32 R. R. 665 (9 B. & C. 245).
(6) 2 Camp. 11.
(7) 1 Doug. 279.
(8) 1 Bing. N. C. 15.

(LORD DENMAN, Ch. J.: If the assignee authorised the plaintiff
to demise, did not he likewise authorise him to receive the rents ?)

The plea merely alleges that, the plaintiff having been authorised and permitted by some person to make the demise stated in the declaration, the defendant received notice from that person to pay him the rent in future. The permission so alleged does not show that the lessor was agent to the party permitting. A permission might be given where none was requisite. And, supposing that the plea clearly showed a title in the assignee, and permission given by him to the plaintiff to demise, it does not follow that the assignee could, by a mere notice, countermand the permission.

(LORD DENMAN, Ch. J.: The plea does not allege any stipulation that the party giving permission should have power to determine the tenancy to the lessor.)

It cannot be contended that the assignee himself could have sued the defendant for rent due after the supposed countermand, the plaintiff having demised with the assignee's authority, and no notice having at that time been given to the tenant of the situation in which the plaintiff and the assignee stood. If the assignee could sue the tenant, he ought also to be liable to the tenant on the contract of demise; *but the tenant could not [*69 have had any remedy against him on that contract.

(LITTLEDALE, J.: The plea does not allege directly that the plaintiff demised by permission; it merely says, in a parenthesis, "the said plaintiff having been authorised and permitted" by the assignee to demise.)

All that appears on the plea as to title is that, in 1818, the then interest of the plaintiff vested in Shaw as assignee. Consistently with that allegation, the plaintiff may have taken a lawful title since 1818.

Wightman, contrà:

The object of this plea is, not to bring into question the title to the premises at the time of the demise, but merely to show

PARTINGTON   that the plaintiff cannot lawfully demand the rent now claimed.
WOODCOCK.   It is as if the tenant had pleaded that a mortgagor had demised
to him by permission of the mortgagee, and that the mortgagee
had given the tenant notice to pay him the rent, which would
have been an answer, according to *Pope* v. *Biggs* (1). A tenant
cannot dispute his landlord's title to demise ; but he may show
that the title was a defeasible one, and that a party having
paramount right to that of the landlord gave the tenant notice
to pay the rent to such party.

(PATTESON, J.: I never could see how notice could make the
mortgagor's tenant tenant to the mortgagee at the former rent.
There might, indeed, be a new tenancy created at the old rent,
where such notice was given and the rent paid accordingly.

LITTLEDALE, J.: If the lease was made subsequently to the
mortgage, I see no remedy the mortgagee could have against the
[*696]   tenant, on non-payment of *the rent, but to bring ejectment.

LORD DENMAN, Ch. J.: It strikes me that the sufferance in
this case makes a difference which is against you. You must
add to the facts of *Pope* v. *Biggs* (1) a permission to demise by
the party standing in the situation of mortgagee.)

If the mortgagee did suffer a demise to be made, he would not
forego his right of giving notice to the tenant; and, on giving
such notice, he might, at all events, recover for use and occupation, if the tenant held on ; and the rent reserved by the
mortgagor would be the measure of damages. In the case of a
lease made before the mortgage, the mortgagee might clearly
require a tenant to pay the rent to him as reversioner; the
assignee of an insolvent has similar rights ; and, where such
assignee has permitted the insolvent to demise after the
assignment, he may still call upon the tenant to pay the
rent to himself, if he finds the insolvent to be no longer a
trustworthy steward.

(LITTLEDALE, J.: Is not the effect of the plea here, that the
assignee, having an elder title, evicted the tenant by notice ?)

(1) 32 R. R. 665 (9 B. & C. 245).

It does not appear by the plea that the assignee could evict. The case, as stated, is like that of a lease made before mortgage.

(PATTESON, J.: Where the mortgagor has demised before the mortgage, there is a good lease subsisting at the time of the notice by the mortgagee. The case of a demise after the mortgage is different. In *Pope* v. *Biggs* (1) there might be a new tenancy created, if the proceedings of the mortgagee there can be considered equivalent to an ejectment; but I do not see how it could be said that the old rent continued.

LORD DENMAN, Ch. J.: If you say here that the assignee could not *evict the tenant, the case is so far unlike *Pope* v. *Biggs* (1) ; for there an eviction, or something equivalent, is assumed.)

[*697]

It is not necessary here to say what effect might have been given to the notice, because no actual proceeding took place; there was only a threat, upon which the rent was paid to the assignee. Supposing that, in this plea, the words in a parenthesis, from " the said plaintiff having been authorised," to " premises to the said defendant," were omitted, the plea would still be good. The title averred to have vested in the assignee in 1818 will be deemed to have still subsisted when the notice was given. The assignment of itself carried the property; and the presumption will be in favour of an outstanding title in the assignee, till proof is given to take it away : *Carr* v. *Burdiss* (2).

(PATTESON, J.: The plea here states that the assignee gave the defendant notice to pay him all the rent that should accrue " in respect of the said demised premises, and under and by virtue of the said demise " in the declaration mentioned, thus treating the previously mentioned demise by the plaintiff as still subsisting. Now, if that demise was made by the insolvent in his own name, I do not see how the assignee could come in as landlord, except by putting an end to the demise and commencing a new tenancy. I do not see how the rent claimed by the assignee could be rent under " the said demise." Unless

(1) 32 R. R. 665 (9 B. & C. 245).   (2) 1 Cr. M. & R. 782; 5 Tyr. 309.

PARTINGTON the previous demise is put an end to, you make the assignee or
WOODCOCK. mortgagee constructively party to a demise between others.)

[*698] At all events the words included in a parenthesis may be *left
out, and " under and by virtue of the said demise " treated as
surplusage. Unless the present defence can be made available,
the defendant may be held liable to pay the rent twice, to the
plaintiff, and to the assignee as superior landlord.

(LITTLEDALE, J. : If the words in a parenthesis are omitted,
it will at most appear only that the plaintiff demised to the
defendant, and that some one else, having the legal title, called
on him to pay the rent.)

BAYLEY, J., says, in *Pope* v. *Biggs* (1), " I have no doubt that, in
point of law, a tenant who comes into possession under a demise
from a mortgagor, after a mortgage executed by him, may consider the mortgagor his landlord so long as the mortgagee allows
the mortgagor to continue in possession and receive the rents ;
and that payment of the rents by the tenant to the mortgagor,
without any notice of the mortgage, is a valid payment. But
the mortgagee, by giving notice of the mortgage to the tenant,
may thereby make him his tenant, and entitle himself to receive
the rents."

(PATTESON, J. : That must mean that the mortgagor may make
him his tenant under a new tenancy.)

The learned Judge continues, " It is undoubtedly a well-esta-
blished rule, that a lessee cannot dispute the title of his lessor
at the time of the lease, but he is at full liberty to show that
the lessor's title has been put an end to." That must be by
notice from a party having superior title, to pay the rent to him.
Such notice had been given by such a party in the case then
before the Court. Then, according to the doctrine of BAYLEY, J.,
[*699] the present plea would be sufficient if the words *in a parenthesis were omitted ; and, if retained, they do not vitiate, for,

(1) 32 R. R. 665 (9 B. & C. 251).

by showing that the assignee was cognizant of the demise, they PARTINGTON
do not alter his right in point of law. *v.*
WOODCOCK.

If, however, the Court think the defence informally pleaded,
the defendant prays leave to amend.

Per CURIAM (1) :

> *Defendant to have leave to amend forthwith on pay-*
> *ment of costs : otherwise judgment to be entered*
> *for the plaintiff.*

GLAHOLM *v.* ROWNTREE AND MATCHETT, EXECUTORS OF CLARK.

1837.
May 3.

[710]

(6 Adol. & Ellis, 710—717; S. C. 2 N. & P. 557; 7 L. J. (N. S.) Q. B. 23.)

A testator, being indebted to R., deposited with him a policy of insurance on testator's life, as security for the debt, and for a further advance
then made by R. ; and died, leaving R. and M. his executors. R., still
holding the policy, applied to the insurers for the amount due on it
(200*l.*), which they refused to pay unless R. and M. gave a receipt for
it as executors. They did so, R. making protest that he signed as
executor, merely to satisfy the insurers. In an action by a judgment
creditor, to which the executors pleaded *plene administraverunt* except
as to 4*l.* (the surplus out of the 200*l.* after payment to R.) :

Held, that the executors were not chargeable with the 200*l.*, as assets,
but only with the surplus after payment to R.

DEBT, against the defendants as executors of John Clark,
deceased, on a judgment recovered by the plaintiff against Clark
in his life time. Plea, *plene administraverunt*, except as to 4*l.*
Replication, assets *ultra*. Issue thereon. On the trial before
Tindal, Ch. J., at the Newcastle Summer Assizes, 1835, the
following facts appeared.

Clark had effected a policy of insurance on his life for 200*l.*
Being indebted to one Price in the sum of 16*l.* 9*s.*, he deposited
the policy with him as a security. Afterwards, Clark being
indebted to the defendant Rowntree in a larger amount, Rowntree
agreed to pay off Price, and take the policy as a security. Clark
thereupon signed a memorandum as follows. "19th September,
1833. To Mr. William Rowntree. Sir, I hereby agree to deposit
with you my life policy with the Leeds and Yorkshire Insurance
Company for the sum of 200*l.*, as a security for any sum or sums

(1) Lord Denman, Ch. J., Littledale, Patteson, and Coleridge, JJ.

of money that I am or may be indebted to you." Clark gave notice to the Insurance Company that he had transferred his interest in the policy to Rowntree; and their agent, in reply, informed Clark that they had noted the "intended transfer" in their books, but were advised that a regular legal transfer was requisite. About the end of 1833, Clark went to prison, intending to take the benefit of the Insolvent Debtors' Act; but, before

[*711]

this *could be done, he died. During his imprisonment, Rowntree, having prepared a regular assignment of the policy, proposed that Clark should execute it; but he did not. By his will, dated January 31st, 1834, Clark left Rowntree and Matchett his executors. On the 17th of February they proved the will, and Rowntree gave notice to the Insurance Company as follows. "I hereby require you to pay over to me the sum of 200*l*., secured by you on the life of John Clark, formerly of " &c., " by your policy, No. 140, bearing date " &c., " which policy was assigned to me by the said John Clark in the month of December last, according to the notice already given to you, and entered on your books; and is now in my possession," &c. " W. ROWNTREE." The Company declined to pay except to a party showing title as executor; and, in consequence, another notice was given, in the names of both the defendants, beginning, "We, being the executors " &c., and accompanied by the probate. The Company's agent then offered, in payment of the 200*l*., bills indorsed to " Rowntree and Matchett, executors of John Clark ; " but, the defendants objecting, they gave bills generally indorsed. The Company insisted that a receipt should be signed by the defendants "as executors;" and they, in consequence, gave a receipt so worded; but Rowntree delivered a written protest to the Company's agent, stating that he signed as executor solely for the purpose of satisfying the Company and keeping them clear of litigation, and that he should not thereby compromise his claim to the money secured to him on the policy. It appeared on the trial that Rowntree had a just claim upon Clark to the amount secured, which would exhaust the proceeds of the policy, within 4*l*.; and

[*712]

that there were no assets beyond *that amount, if Rowntree was entitled to take credit for the sum so secured. A verdict was taken for the plaintiff, but leave given to move to enter a nonsuit.

In the next Term, *Cresswell* moved accordingly, and cited
2 Williams on Executors, 1179 (1), part 4, book 1, c. 1 (where it
is said that "chattels, whether real or personal, mortgaged or
pledged by the testator, and redeemed by the executor, shall be
assets in the hands of the executor, for so much as they are
worth beyond the sum paid for their redemption"), and the
authorities there referred to.   A rule *nisi* was granted.

Alexander and *Bliss* now showed cause:

The passage cited from 2 Williams on Executors, 1179, refers
to *dicta* in *Hawkins* v. *Lawse* (2) and *Alexander* v. *Lady Gresham* (3),
and to the case of *Harecourt* v. *Wrenham* (4).   These authorities,
so far as they bear upon the present case, can show only that,
where executors have redeemed a pledge of the testator with their
own monies, they are entitled to the amount by way of retainer.
The case in Year Book, 20 Hen. VII. (5), cited in *Alexander* v.
Lady Gresham (3), puts the executor's right upon this ground.
But executors cannot retain for their own debt against a debt of
superior degree.   The plaintiff here sues upon a judgment; the
defendants seek to retain money in effect paid by Rowntree and
Matchett to Rowntree in redemption of the testator's policy.
And, further, the defendants here, by receiving the 200*l.* expressly
as executors, have precluded themselves from *alleging that they
took it in any other right.   Not only has Rowntree accepted it in
the character of executor, but the other defendant, who had no
lien, has done so likewise.   They are now, therefore, estopped
from insisting upon Rowntree's lien, according to the principle
laid down in *Heane* v. *Rogers* (6).   By claiming as executors they
led creditors to look upon this fund as assets; they cannot now
alter the situation of such parties.   *Boardman* v. *Sill* (7) also
shows that the defendants cannot now claim in a new character.

(LORD DENMAN, Ch. J. : I cannot see what your client has to do
with the character in which they first claimed this money.   He

[*713]

GLAHOLM
v.
ROWNTREE.

(1) 2nd ed.
(2) 1 Leon. 154.
(3) 1 Leon. 224.
(4) Moore, 858. See *Harwood* v.
Wraynam, cited, 1 Roll. Rep. 56;
Harcock v. *Wrenham*, 1 Brownl. &
G. 76.
(5) Year B. Mich. 20 Hen. VII.
f. 2 B. pl. 5; f. 4 A, B. pl. 12, 14.
(6) 9 B. & C. 577; see p. 586.
(7) 1 Camp. 410, *n.*

GLAHOLM   is in no worse a situation than if they had said, "We claim to
v.   hold this money as trustees for Rowntree."
ROWNTREE.

PATTESON, J.: Suppose a third person had held the policy
under a lien, and the Insurance Company had refused to pay
him unless the executors would 'join in claiming the 200*l.*; could
not that party have compelled the executors to give him the
benefit of his lien ? The executors, in that case, would have
received the 200*l.* for the benefit of the third person, to the
extent of his claim, and the surplus would be assets. Can it
make any difference here, that Rowntree himself held the policy?

COLERIDGE, J.: If a third person had held a policy worth 200*l.*
for a debt of 100*l.*, and the executors, to obtain the 100*l.*, had
claimed, and given a receipt to the Insurance Company for 200*l.*;
would the 200*l.* be assets ?)

The party entitled to the 100*l.* would stand in the situation of a
simple contract creditor, and must give precedence to creditors
of a higher degree, if such came in.

[*714]   (PATTESON, J.: If that were so, *he might say, "I will keep
the policy.")

The defendants, by signing a receipt as executors, have admitted
assets, and made themselves absolutely liable, according to
Childs v. *Monins* (1). An executor, having dealt with property
of the testator as his own, cannot afterwards allege it to be the
testator's, for the purpose of defeating an execution : *Quick* v.
Staines (2): conversely, an executor who has treated his own
property as the testator's cannot afterwards set up his own title
to it against a creditor of the testator. The defendant Rowntree,
in this case, had no legal lien. The policy being deposited with
him, he had merely an equitable lien upon the proceeds. He
cannot set that up against the legal claim of the plaintiff. The
executors here are both liable for the whole sum come to their
hands. If Rowntree has a lien, the other defendant at least
holds by way of retainer only.

(1) 23 R. R. 513 (2 Brod. & B. 460).   (2) 4 R. R. 801 (1 Bos. & P. 293).

Cresswell, with whom was *Granger*, *contrà*, was stopped by the COURT.

LORD DENMAN, Ch. J.:

This is a clear case. Rowntree, having paid Price, and taken the policy as a security, applies to the Insurance Company for the sum of which, on the testator's death, he has become the owner. They refuse to pay it, unless he will sign a receipt as executor; and he does so under protest. He was bound to give some discharge for the purpose of exonerating the office. Then can the other creditors take advantage of the mode in which this was done? I think there is no reason for it either in strict law or in justice. The *word "retain," in the case cited from the Year Books (1), is not to be taken in the strict sense which has been ascribed to it: the meaning must be that the executors, having purchased the property, may keep it.

[*715]

LITTLEDALE, J.:

The policy was legal assets, but subject to a lien in Rowntree. Although the lien was only equitable, he was as much entitled to receive the amount secured to him from the Insurance Company as if he had had an assignment. Then, suppose the party holding the policy as a security had been, not an executor, but a stranger; it would have been assets belonging to the executors, in the hands of a creditor; and, his claim not being equal to the value of the policy, if there had been no dispute about the debt, the creditor and the executor would probably have gone to the insurance office together to claim the amount due on the policy: the Company would most likely have required a discharge from the executor as well as from the creditor; and the creditor would then have had in his hands the sum which had been secured to him, and the executor the residue. Then, what difference does it make that the holder of the policy was an executor, and not a stranger? In either case, the executors could not obtain the value of the policy without the creditor's concurrence. A court of equity would, if it had become necessary, have ordered payment to the creditor; here that has been

(1) Year B. Mich. 20 Hen. VII. f. 2 B. pl. 5; f. 4 A, B. pl. 12, 14.

GLAHOLM
v.
ROWNTREE.

[*716]

done without the intervention of a Court.   It is observed that
the defendants have signed a discharge to the insurance office as
executors; but there is no magic in this.   The legal right is not
altered by their inability to *obtain payment without a receipt in
this form.   The signature was given under a protest; and the
Insurance Company then paid the money.   Can it be said that, to
enforce this lien, the circuitous course of a proceeding in equity
should have been adopted?   The payment was made to Rowntree
in his capacity of executor, and the proceeds of the policy were
assets; but, as they were subject to a lien, the executors could
receive only so much of them as was due after discharging the lien.

PATTESON, J. :

This is an action against two executors, one of whom had the
policy in question deposited with him as security, not merely for
a by-gone debt, but for money paid off on the testator's behalf,
and advanced to him on the credit of this policy.   So much for
the honesty of the proceeding.   Had not the defendant Rowntree
a right to retain that on which he had advanced his money,
against all the world?   It is suggested that the lien was upon
the paper only; not on the produce.   I cannot understand that.
It seems to me impossible to say that holding the policy for a
debt is not having a lien on the produce.   Then is the holder to
lose the benefit of his lien because he is an executor?   It is said
that Rowntree, having no legal assignment (which he could not
get), and having been obliged to obtain the 200*l.* as executor, is
estopped from saying that he received any part of it as pledgee.
Now, at least that does not apply to the other defendant, who
seeks merely to give the creditor the benefit of his lien, and the
estate the benefit of the surplus.   Nor is Rowntree estopped; for
it is clear that the proceeds of the policy, to the extent of the
lien, never were assets.   That is not a new doctrine, but accords

[*717]

with all the cases cited.   It *is a fallacy to treat the .word
"retain," in the case cited from the Year Books (1), as necessarily meaning a retainer out of assets.   The expression means
only *to keep:* for it is said, not merely that, if the executor has
paid off the lien with his money, he shall retain the thing, but,

(1) Year B. Mich. 20 Hen. VII. f. 2 B. pl. 5; f. 4 A, B. pl. 12, 14.

that it shall not be administered ; he is not, therefore, to retain *quâ*
executor.   It would have been so here, if the executors had had
to advance any money for the purpose of redeeming the policy.
There was, however, nothing to pay in this case ; but, because there
had been no assignment, the executors were obliged to go through
certain proceedings.   In those they were merely a conduit pipe as
to the sum secured to Rowntree ; the surplus was clearly assets.

COLERIDGE, J. :

It would be a great disgrace to our law if the form which
Rowntree was bound to go through, at the desire of the Insurance
Company, were conclusive against him as to the whole 200*l.*
Remove that difficulty, and for what are the defendants liable?
Only for that which comes to their hands to distribute when the
sum secured is paid off.   It is the same as if the defendant
Rowntree were divided into two individuals, the creditor and
the executor.
                                            Rule absolute.

MINTER *v.* MOWER.

(6 Adol. & Ellis, 735—745; S. C. 1 N. & P. 595; W. W. & D. 262; 6 L. J.
(N. S.) K. B. 183.)

The specification of a patent described the invention to be of "an
improvement in the construction, making, or manufacturing of chairs,"
and to consist in the application of a self-adjusting leverage to the back
and seat of a chair, whereby the weight on the seat acted as a counterbalance to the pressure against the back, and whereby a person sitting
in the chair might, by pressing against the back, cause it to take any
inclination, and yet might be supported.   In an action for infringing
the patent, it was pleaded that plaintiff was not the inventor ; and that
the specification did not describe the invention ; and it was proved that
a chair had previously been sold, to which a similar leverage was applied,
acting by the pressure in the same way, but having also other machinery,
which prevented the inclination of the back from being shifted except
when a spring was touched by the hand.   The jury found that, without
such other machinery, the chair previously sold would have produced an
equilibrium by the self-adjusting leverage ; that the maker of it was the
inventor of the machine, and found out the principle, but not the practical
purpose to which it was now applied ; and that the plaintiff had discovered
such purpose.

The COURT ordered a nonsuit.

CASE for infringing a patent.   The declaration stated that the
plaintiff, before and at the time of making the letters patent,

MINTER
v.
MOWER.

and of the committing &c., was the true and first inventor of
a certain reclining chair; and thereupon heretofore, to wit 9th
November, 1 Will. IV., by letters patent, dated &c., under the
great seal &c. (profert of the letters patent), after reciting that
the plaintiff had, by his petition, represented "that he had
invented an improvement in the construction, making, or
manufacturing of chairs, which he intended to denominate
Minter's patent reclining chairs; that he was the first and true
inventor thereof, and that the same had never been practised by

[*736] any *other person or persons whomsoever to his knowledge or
belief; " and that he had prayed for letters patent for fourteen
years, &c.; the King did therefore &c. (grant of the privilege in
the usual terms): provided that, if the plaintiff should not
particularly describe and ascertain the nature of the invention,
and in what manner the same was to be performed, by an
instrument in writing under his hand and seal, and cause the
same to be enrolled in Chancery within two calendar months &c.,
the patent should be void. Averment, that the plaintiff did,
within the two months, to wit, &c., by a certain instrument &c.,
enrolled &c., particularly describe &c. Breach, that defendant,
after the making the letters patent, and within the term &c.,
without licence &c., used the invention of the plaintiff, by
making, constructing, vending, and exposing to sale divers, to
wit 100, chairs in imitation of the plaintiff's said invention, 100
other chairs in and to which the said invention was applied by
the defendant in a different part of such chairs than in that part
to which the plaintiff was used and accustomed to put the same
in the chairs made by him under the patent, and 100 other
chairs with certain small and trifling variations and alterations
from the said invention of the plaintiff, and which were intended
by the defendant to imitate and resemble, and did imitate &c.,
the said invention of the plaintiff, in violation &c.

Pleas. 1. Not guilty.

2. That the plaintiff was not the first and true inventor of the
said supposed invention or improvement mentioned in the letters
patent and declaration, and that, at the time of granting the
letters patent, such supposed invention or improvement was not

[*737] a new *invention or improvement as to the public knowledge,

use, or exercise thereof, &c.: conclusion to the country. Issue
thereon.

3. That the said instrument or writing under the plaintiff's
hand and seal, in the declaration mentioned, was and is as
follows, &c. The plea then set out a specification, the material
part of which was in these words. " I, the said George Minter,
do hereby declare that the nature of my said invention, and the
manner in which the same is to be performed, are particularly
described and ascertained by the following description thereof,
reference being had to the drawing hereunto annexed, and to the
figures and letters marked thereon; (that is to say) my invention
of an improvement in the construction, making, or manufacturing
of chairs consists in the application of a self-adjusting leverage
to the back and seat of a chair, whereby the weight on the seat
acts as a counterbalance to the pressure against the back of such
chair, and whereby a person sitting or reclining in such chair
may, by pressing against the back, cause it to take any inclination, and yet, at the same time, the back of such chair shall, in
whatever position it is placed, offer sufficient resistance, and give
proper support to the person so sitting or reclining." The
specification then described the drawings annexed; and, after
some details not necessary to be stated here, proceeded as
follows: " $g\,g$ are two iron plates, affixed by screws to the side
framing of the back of the chair; and it is the application of
these plates, $g\,g$, $h\,h$, by which the object of my invention is
obtained." " Having described the various parts of a chair
constructed according to my invention, I will now describe the
manner of using the same." " In sitting or reclining in a chair
*constructed in the manner above described, a person may have
the back at any inclination: for instance, if he desire that the
inclination should be greater than that shown in the drawing,
all that will be necessary will be to press against the back a of
the chair, when the upper part, or that part which is above the
point of suspension, $f\,f$, will be forced backwards, whilst the
lower part, that is the part which is below the point of suspension, will be raised inwards, and become a support for the loins
of the person sitting or reclining in the chair; and, by this
action, the parts $h\,h$ pass along the curved ends $i\,i$ of the side

[*738]

framing of the seat b, which is thereby raised, by which means
the weight on the seat, by pressing on the parts h h, supports
the back a of the chair in any position. And it will be evident
that, by the passing or advancing of the parts h h along the
curved ends i i, they will approach the weight on the seat b, and
thereby shorten the leverage, and consequently lessen the action
of such weight, whereby the back a may continue to be pressed
into a greater inclination by a decreasing effort or exertion of the
person sitting or reclining in such chair ; and thus will the
leverage, by which the weight on the seat b acts on the back a of
the chair, be continually adjusted by the advancing or receding
of the parts h h, on which the seat b rests ; and, by the seat b so
resting and pressing on those parts h h, the back will always be
supported, and will offer sufficient resistance, and give proper
support to the person sitting or reclining in such chair. If it be
desired to bring the back a into a lesser inclination than that
at which it may at any time be placed, it will only be necessary
for the person sitting or reclining in such chair to relieve the
[*739]   pressure from the back of the *chair, and thus bring the weight
on the seat to act without any counteracting pressure on the
back, which will cause the parts h h to recede back on the curved
ends i i, and thus bring the back a into a lesser inclination.
Having now described the various parts represented in the
drawing, and the manner of their action, I would have it
understood that I lay no claim to the separate parts of a chair
which are already known and in use, neither do I confine
myself to making them in the precise shapes or forms represented. But what I claim as my invention is the application
of a self-adjusting leverage to the back and seat of a chair,
whereby the weight on the seat acts as a counterbalance to
the pressure against the back of such chair, as above described."
The plea then set forth the drawing ; and averred that the
plaintiff did not, within two calendar months &c., enrol &c.,
any instrument &c., except the said instrument &c. : and that
the said instrument &c., did not particularly describe and
ascertain the nature of the said supposed invention or improvement &c., and in what manner the same was to be performed :
verification. Replication, that the said instrument &c., did

particularly describe &c.: conclusion to the country. Issue thereon.

On the trial before Lord Denman, Ch. J., at the London sittings after Trinity Term, 1835, the letters patent and the specification were put in, and appeared to be as above set out. It also appeared that the chair manufactured and sold by the plaintiff corresponded with the description in the patent. It was then proved that the defendant had manufactured and sold chairs, called wedge chairs, acting by a leverage, which adjusted the positions of the back and seat according to the pressure communicated by the person sitting, essentially on the *same principle as that of the plaintiff, with this only difference, that the front part of the seat of the plaintiff's chair was elevated when the back of the chair was thrown back, whereas the seat of the defendant's chair, when the back of it was thrown back, was propelled forward and raised so as to be always in a horizontal plane. The defendant proved that, in 1829, one Browne, who was then his journeyman, had invented a chair which acted on the same principle of a leverage adjusting the positions of the back and seat according to the pressure communicated by the party sitting, but that it had also an additional machinery consisting of a sliding pad on the arm, a spring, and a rack, the effect of which was that the back and seat were retained in any position they had assumed, and that, in order to change the position, it was necessary to suspend the check for the time, which the person sitting effected by his hands, through the machinery of the pad, rack, and spring. The essential difference between Browne's chair and the plaintiff's was, therefore, that in the former the position could not be changed until the person sitting applied his hands to the machinery, but that in the latter the position was changed of itself at every variation of the pressure of the person on the back and seat. Whether the difference made one or the other chair preferable was a point on which the witnesses did not agree. The defendant proved that he had sold Browne's chair before the plaintiff took out his patent. The jury, in answer to questions put to them by the LORD CHIEF JUSTICE, found that Browne's chair, except for the additional machinery, would have operated to produce an

[*740]

equilibrium by a self-adjusting leverage ; that Browne was the inventor of the machine, and found *out the principle, but not the practical purpose to which it is now applied ; and that the plaintiff made that discovery. His Lordship then directed the verdict to be entered for the plaintiff, giving leave to the defendant to move for a nonsuit. In Michaelmas Term, 1835, *Talfourd*, Serjt. obtained a rule accordingly.

Sir J. Campbell, Attorney-General, *Sir F. Pollock*, and *Evans*, showed cause in Hilary Term last (1) :

The validity of the patent itself has been established in *Minter* v. *Wells* (2). There Lord LYNDHURST said (3), " Every invention of a machine necessarily includes the application of some principle, and, in this instance, the application of the principle of a lever to the back and seat of a chair is the machine, the invention of which is claimed by the plaintiff. He has not summed up the extent of his invention, so as to include in it the principle of the lever, but merely the invention of applying it in the manner specified. The claim is not leverage only, but self-adjusting leverage ; nor that only, but the application of it in the manner described." Now the answer given in the present case is, that Browne had invented a chair, on a different construction, the working of which depended on the same principle. But that answer is met by the judgment of Lord LYNDHURST ; for the application of the principle is all that the plaintiff claims, and that is new. It will be contended that the specification goes too far, for that the plaintiff has simply improved Browne's chair, without introducing any fresh machinery or principle. But the invention is entitled an

improvement in the construction, *making, or manufacturing of chairs ; and the essential part of the improvement appears from the specification to be that the chair acts by the mere shifting of the direction of the pressure produced by the weight of a person sitting. That is peculiar to the plaintiff's chair ; for in Browne's chair it was necessary to adjust the machinery by

(1) January 19th, 1837. Before
Lord Denman, Ch. J., Patteson and
Williams, JJ.

(2) 40 R. R. 637 (1 Cr. M. & R,

505 ; 5 Tyr. 163).

(3) See 40 R. R. at p. 638 (5 Tyr.
165).

the hand for every change required. The claim is limited to the precise mode of action. The jury found that Browne had invented the principle of the self-adjusting leverage, but did not know how to apply it: the plaintiff has invented an application, and claims for that only. In *Jones* v. *Pearce* (1) PATTESON, J. laid it down that a patentee was not the less the inventor because another had previously discovered the principle, but had not rendered it public, and had failed to make it answer. So in *Dollond's* case (2) it was held that a patent was not avoided by the discovery having been previously made, but not published. If it be said that no more has been done by the plaintiff than to take away the pad, spring, and rack, from Browne's chair, the answer is that, if, by so doing, he has first discovered an useful application of the principle, he has invented an improvement.

Talfourd, Serjt., and *Godson*, contrà:

The seats of the plaintiff's chair, and of that which the defendant is charged with selling, have different movements. If this variance be material, there is no infringement: if not, the infringement must consist in using what is called the self-adjustment of the leverage; and, in that case, that which *the plaintiff claims was known before, and published; for Browne's chair was actually sold. If this action can be supported, Browne could not sell his own chair; for it would be no defence for him that he had added the machinery by which the movement is stopped. In *Minter* v. *Wells* (3) Lord LYNDHURST said, " Any machine applying a self-adjusting lever to the back and seat of a chair, by which the effect of one counterbalancing the other is produced, would be an infringement of this patent: for the claim is for a self-adjusting lever, as applied to the back and seat of a chair, in whatever shape or form it may be made." In Browne's chair two principles are applied; that of self-adjustment by leverage, and that of checking the movement at will: the plaintiff has taken one of these without the other; but he cannot be

[*743]

(1) First Supplement to Godson on Patents, p. 10.
(2) Cited by BULLER, J. in *Boulton*
v. *Bull*, 3 R. R. at p. 460 (2 H. Bl. 487.)
(3) 5 Tyr. 165.

MINTER
v.
MOWER.

therefore said to have invented the one which he has taken (1).
It is said that the plaintiff claims only an improvement : but
what he claims is an improvement in the manufacture of
chairs by the application of a self-adjusting leverage ; and that
improvement was made before. In *Dollond's* case (2) there had
been no publication at all by the earlier inventor ; in *Jones* v.
Pearce (3) the previous attempts had failed, and the articles
produced had been thrown aside: here there has been an
actual sale. In *Lewis* v. *Davis* (4) a fresh combination of two
known principles was held to be a novelty; but here no such
combination is made.

Cur. adv. vult.

[744]   LORD DENMAN, Ch. J. now delivered the judgment of the COURT:

An action between the same parties has already been decided
by the Court of Exchequer, in which the patent claimed by the
plaintiff was deemed good and valid. But, on the trial in this
Court, an entirely new fact was given in evidence and affirmed
by the verdict of the jury; namely, that a chair very closely
resembling that made by the plaintiff's patent had been made
and sold before that patent was taken out. The words of the
jury were these: "We are of opinion that Browne was the
inventor of the machine, and found out the principle, but not
the practical purpose to which it is now applied. We think that
Minter " (the plaintiff) " made that discovery."

This statement might not be fatal to the plaintiff's title, if his
invention were truly set forth in the specification ; but, the
material issue in this cause being simply whether the plaintiff
did thereby particularly describe and ascertain the nature of the
said invention, we find it needful to examine the terms of it.

Now the patent is taken out for " an improvement in the
construction, making, or manufacturing of chairs : " the method
of making the machine, and the way in which it acts, are then
fully described, without any mention of any of the means
employed in Browne's chair. The specification thus concludes,

(1) See *Hare* v. *Harford*, Godson   487.)
n Patents, 61, *n.* (*k*).
(2) Cited by BULLER, J. in *Boulton*
v. *Bull*, 3 R. R. at p. 460 (2 H. Bl.

(3) First Supplement to Godson on
Patents, p. 10.
(4) 33 R. R. 690 (3 Car. & P. 502).

"What I claim as my invention is the application of a self-adjusting leverage to the back and seat of a chair, whereby the weight on the seat acts as a counterbalance to the pressure against the back of such chair, as above described." Now it was perfectly clear, upon the evidence, that this description applies to Browne's chair, *though that was encumbered with some additional machinery. The specification therefore claimed more than the plaintiff had invented, and would have actually precluded Mr. Browne from continuing to make the same chair that he had made before the patentee's discovery. We are far from thinking that the patentee might not have established his title by showing that a part of Browne's chair could have effected that for which the whole was designed. But his claim is not for an improvement upon Browne's leverage, but for a leverage so described that the description comprehended Browne's. We are therefore of opinion that the patent cannot be sustained: and a nonsuit must be entered.

MINTER
v.
MOWER

[*745]

Rule absolute.

TYSON v. SMITH.

(6 Adol. & Ellis, 745—752; S. C. 1 N. & P. 784, 6 L. J. (N. S.) K. B. 189.)

[THIS case went to the Exchequer Chamber, where the judgment of the King's Bench was affirmed. It is reported in 9 Ad. & El., and will be reprinted in the corresponding volume of the Revised Reports.]

1837.
May 5.

[745]

HIS IMPERIAL MAJESTY DON PEDRO THE SECOND, EMPEROR OF BRAZIL, v. ROBINSON AND OTHERS.

(6 Adol. & Ellis, 801—802; S. C. 1 N. & P. 817; W. W. & D. 278; 5 Dowl. P. C. 522; 6 L. J. (N. S.) K. B. 168.)

1837.
May 8.

[801]

A foreign prince resident abroad, being plaintiff in an action upon a charter-party in this Court, was directed to give security for costs.

W. H. WATSON moved for a rule to show cause why proceedings in this action should not be stayed till security should be given for payment of costs. Affidavit was made that the plaintiff's residence was at Rio Janeiro, and in other parts in the kingdom of Brazil, and that he was usually resident, and

EMPEROR OF
BRAZIL
v.
ROBINSON.
[*802]

now (as was believed) *resided, in the said kingdom. The action was on a charter-party, made for a commercial purpose. The rule was first moved for at chambers, but was referred to the Court. *Watson* contended that the plaintiff, trading as a merchant, ought to be subject to the same regulations as any other person bringing an action.

Martin showed cause in the first instance, and cited *The Duke de Montellano* v. *Christin* (1), where a similar application was made against a foreign ambassador resident in this country, on the ground that, he being a privileged person, the case was the same as if he were beyond sea, or out of the jurisdiction of the Court, there being no remedy for the costs: but the COURT refused a rule, and Lord ELLENBOROUGH observed that, as "an ambassador is the immediate representative of the crowned head, whose servant he is, it would hardly be respectful, in the first instance, to exact such a security, unless there were pregnant reasons for believing it necessary." Here, the application is actually against a crowned head.

LORD DENMAN, Ch. J.:

Lord ELLENBOROUGH did not say that such a rule could not be granted. It did not appear that the ambassador was about to leave the country. Here the plaintiff is out of the country. I think there is great reason for granting the rule.

LITTLEDALE, PATTESON, and COLERIDGE, JJ., concurred.

Rule absolute.

1837.
May 8.

[810]

REX *v.* PARRY.

(6 Adol. & Ellis, 810—823.)

On motion for a *quo warranto* information against a town councillor, founded on a defect in the burgess roll, it is not a valid objection to the relator that he is not a burgess; his interest is sufficient if he be subject to the government of the councillors as an inhabitant.

If the motion be made on the affidavits of three persons, two of whom are not qualified to be relators, the information may nevertheless be

(1) 17 R. R. 418 (5 M. & S. 503).

granted if the third party be unobjectionable as a relator, though his affidavit alone does not show sufficient ground for the information.

Leave to file a *quo warranto* information against an individual corporator, at the instance of a private person, will not be refused merely because the proceeding may or will have the effect of dissolving the corporation.

It is discretionary in the Court to grant or withhold a *quo warranto* information, even where a good objection to the title is shown (1). And, therefore, in a case where the assessors were objected to, as having been assessors of the borough and not for the mayor's ward, and no satisfactory answer was given, the Court refused a rule for an information, on the grounds that no fraud was imputed, that no mischief appeared to have been done, that the prosecution, if successful, would probably dissolve the corporation, and that the prosecutors appeared to have that intention.

In Michaelmas Term, 1836, a rule *nisi* was obtained for exhibiting an information in the nature of a *quo warranto* against John Parry, to show by what authority he claimed to be a councillor of the borough of Hereford; on the grounds, 1. That he was not duly elected by a majority of the burgesses duly enrolled; 2. That there was no regular burgess-roll in existence at the time of his supposed election.

The borough of Hereford is divided, under stat. 5 & 6 Will. IV. c. 76 (2), into three wards, Ledbury ward, Leominster ward, and Monmouth ward, each returning six councillors. In October, 1836, the mayor held a court for the revision of the burgess-lists, and the same were revised by him and two assessors, Peter Warburton and Robert Anderson, who had been elected assessors for the whole of the borough. Assessors had likewise been elected for the respective wards; but the assessors for the mayor's (Ledbury) ward did not attend the revision. The defendant Parry was elected a councillor for Monmouth ward on November 1st, 1836, by the burgesses on the roll made up from the lists so revised.

Two of the affidavits in support of the present application were made by William Pulling and John Roberts, *inhabitant householders and rate-payers of Ledbury and Monmouth wards, entitled, as they stated, to be on the burgess roll. They deposed,

[*811]

(1) The case is cited on this point by Lord BLACKBURN in *Julius* v. *Bishop of Oxford* (H. L. 1880) 5 App. Cas. 214, 246, 49 L. J. Q. B.

577, 591.—R. C.

(2) Repealed by the Municipal Corporations Act, 1882 (45 & 46 Vict. c. 50), s. 5.—R. C.

REX
v.
PARRY.

in substance, to the facts above stated, and, further, that, on the revision, William Henry Cooke, gentleman, on their behalf, warned the mayor and Warburton and Anderson not to proceed without the assessors of the mayor's ward, notwithstanding which they persisted. The affidavits denied that Parry was duly elected, as the persons who voted for him had not been duly enrolled burgesses of Monmouth ward. Mr. Cooke (who was described as of the Inner Temple, and did not appear to be an inhabitant householder or rate-payer, or entitled to be a burgess) also deposed that he had, on behalf of Pulling, Roberts, and one Gwillim, who was entitled to be enrolled a burgess of Leominster ward, protested, at the revision court, against the legality of the proceedings, and required that the assessors of the mayor's ward should be present; and that the town clerk, acting as adviser and clerk of the mayor and assessors at the revision court, had made a minute of the protest.

By an affidavit of the town clerk, in opposition to the rule, it appeared that, before the revision, an opinion of counsel had been taken on the construction of sects. 37 and 43 of stat. 5 & 6 Will. IV. c. 76; that assessors for the whole borough had been chosen, according to such opinion; and that the town clerk, having taken such opinion, had advised the mayor and the assessors chosen for the borough to proceed in revising the lists. That three days' notice was given of the intention to hold the court, and of the persons before whom it would be holden, and no objection was made to the assessors before the above-mentioned protest of Mr. Cooke. That no objection was made

[*812] to the burgesses named in any *of the lists delivered to the town-clerk by the overseers of the several parishes in the borough and its liberties, nor was any claim delivered to the town clerk on behalf of any person in Monmouth ward, nor did the assessors in any manner alter or correct the lists delivered in for Monmouth ward, which were signed by the mayor only, pursuant to sect. 19 of the Act. It further appeared, by this and other affidavits, that Roberts was an unsuccessful candidate at the election of councillors for Monmouth ward on November 1st, 1836, and obtained eighty-eight votes, and that he also voted at that election, and brought up voters; that Cooke had been

busy in promoting the election of Roberts ; and that no objection had been taken to the burgess roll at the Monmouth ward election. That Pulling and Roberts, and Cooke, who was not a burgess, but was in the habit of attending the revision courts as a legal adviser, were active supporters of the political party opposed to that of the majority of the corporation ; that each of them had used expressions (which were stated) showing a desire that the corporation might be dissolved, and a design and expectation of producing that result by means of the present application.

Sir J. Campbell, Attorney-General, *Maule* and *Chilton* showed cause in last Hilary Term (1) :

The two objections stated in the rule resolve themselves into one, that the assessors who revised should have been the assessors for the mayor's ward, and not those elected for the whole borough. In the first place, as to Monmouth ward, for which the defendant was elected, it was immaterial who were the assessors, for there was neither *objection nor claim. The [*813] assessors had nothing to deal with. No objection being made in any of the wards, the mayor had a simple ministerial duty under sect. 18 of the Act, which directs that he " shall retain on the said list the names of all persons to whom no objection shall have been duly made." The assessors, if they had interposed, could not have altered his line of conduct in this respect. And further, by sect. 22, when the burgess lists have been delivered to the town clerk, and by him copied in a book, " every such book " " shall be the burgess roll of the burgesses of such borough entitled to vote " for councillors, &c., at any election between the first of November, in the year in which such roll shall have been made, and the ensuing first of November. The roll, therefore, is conclusive ; and, after it is made up, the preliminary steps taken for the formation of it are not to be enquired into. As to the objection itself ; the Act is certainly obscure. Sect. 18 enacts that the court for revising the burgess lists shall be held by " the mayor and the two assessors hereinafter mentioned, to be chosen in every year by the burgesses of every

(1) January 27th. Before Lord Denman, Ch. J., Williams and Coleridge, JJ.

borough." Sect. 37 enacts that, on the 1st of March in every
year, "the burgesses of every borough shall elect from the
persons qualified to be councillors by a majority of votes,"
"two burgesses, who shall be and be called assessors of such
borough." Then, in sect. 43, a provision is made applying,
not to every borough, but only to those divided into wards,
that the burgesses of each ward shall yearly elect two assessors
"for such ward;" "and the assessors who shall hold the court for
revising the burgess lists with the mayor shall be the assessors
of the mayor's ward." This section appears to conflict with
sect. 18; and the Act does not show which is intended to prevail.

[*814] *The fairer rule appears to be, that assessors chosen for the
whole borough should revise.

But further, the Court will not listen to these relators. If the
objection is good, neither Pulling nor Roberts is entitled to be a
burgess; and a relator cannot be heard if his own title stands on
the same ground with that which he seeks to impeach : *Rex* v.
Bond (1), *Rex* v. *Bracken* (2). Besides, Roberts was a candidate
and voter at the election now impeached, and was supported by
Cooke, who, at that time, was aware of the objection now made.
Such an acquiescence disqualifies a party from applying to
set aside an election: *Rex* v. *Trevenen* (3), *Rex* v. *Parkyn* (4).
Again, it is for the consideration of the Court that the success of
an information, as prayed, would dissolve the corporation: for
the councillors elected in 1836 would all be disqualified; and,
the burgess roll being vitiated, there could be no valid election
of successors for 1837. The fact that an application might have
such a result, was evidently considered by the Court to be a
legitimate ground of rejection in *Rex* v. *Bond* (1) and in the
second case of *Rex* v. *Trevenen* (5). And, lastly, the Court will
look at the motives of parties making such an application as
this: *Rex* v. *Trevenen* (5): and the motives shown in the present
case are a good ground of rejection.

(1) 2 T. R. 767.
(2) Alcock & Napier's Rep. (K. B.
and Exch. Chamber, Irel.) 113;
where *Rex* v. *Cudlipp*, 6 T. R. 503,
and *Rex* v. *Cowell*, 6 Dowl. & Ry.
336, were cited.
(3) 20 R. R. 461 (2 B. & Ald. 339).
(4) 1 B. & Ad. 690.
(5) 21 R. R. 364 (2 B. & Ald. 479).

Sir W. W. Follett and *Whateley, contrà :*

As to the main objection, it would be sufficient ground for the *present rule, to show that the construction of the Act was doubtful. But it is clear that different regulations were intended for a borough divided into wards and for one not so divided.

(LORD DENMAN, Ch. J.: At present, we wish to hear you on the personal objection to the relators.)

It is contended that, if this application ultimately prevails, Pulling and Roberts themselves are not burgesses. But there is no reason that the parties impeaching the election of councillors should be burgesses. A rated inhabitant has an interest in the election of those who are entrusted with power to impose rates. The parties applying here do not come in the character of burgesses. In *Rex* v. *Hodge* (1), where the motion was for a *quo warranto* against a person acting as a chief burgess of Penrhyn, an inhabitant was held a good relator, the government of the town being vested in the mayor and chief burgesses. In *Rex* v. *Bracken* (2) it does not appear that the relator claimed any interest except as a freeman. The objection now suggested would, if valid, have prevailed in the *Sunderland* case, *Rex* v. *White* (3), where the relators contended, in effect, that no member of the corporation had any title.

(LORD DENMAN, Ch. J.: We think it is a complete answer to this objection, that a party applying is an inhabitant, subject to the government of the councillors.)

If it be contended that Roberts would himself be liable to a *quo warranto* if this rule could be granted, the observation, at all events, does not apply to Pulling, who is not shown to have acted as a burgess. Nor can it be objected against him that he concurred in any of the proceedings. The concurrence of the others, therefore, *is immaterial. That the persons applying are of an opposite party in politics to those affected by the application can be no answer. Almost every such motion is

(1) 20 R. R. 464, *n.* (2 B. & Ald. 344, *n.*).   (2) Alcock & Napier's Rep. 113.
(3) 5 Ad. & El. 613.

made under similar circumstances. Nor is it an objection that a *quo warranto* information, if successful, would dissolve the corporation. The Court has often interfered where parties were usurping powers from the Crown, although that result was threatened. In *Rex* v. *Trevenen* (1) the reason which weighed with the Court was, not that the corporation was likely to be dissolved by granting the rule, but that the relator appeared to be put forward by another person who had only an electioneering interest. Although Lord KENYON said, in *Rex* v. *Bond* (2), "If it had appeared that the corporation would be dissolved in consequence of the loss of so considerable a number of its members, that also would have been a good reason for refusing this application," yet that ground was not acted upon there, or in any other case. In *Rex* v. *White* (3) this Court, after more experience of such motions, clearly held that a rule for a *quo warranto* against an individual was not to be refused because it tended, by consequence, to dissolve the corporation; and the case was distinguished from *Rex* v. *The Corporation of Carmarthen* (4), where a private relator applied directly for a *quo warranto* against a whole corporation, and from *Rex* v. *Ogden* (5), where the application was similar, and the persons showing cause expressly disclaimed exercising any corporate powers. If a prosecutor is interested, [*817] and entitled to apply, and shows reasonable grounds in *law, the Court ought not to refuse a rule from any regard to consequences; if the effect of granting a rule would be (as the assumption is here) that the corporation must be dissolved, steps must be taken to obtain a new charter, or some other remedy. As to the time when opposition was first made to the proceedings of the revision court, the protest was made at the proper period; but, if the Act was not complied with in making up the lists, it is immaterial whether there was any protest or notice of objection, or none. It is incorrect to say that, where there are no claims or objections, the assessors have nothing to do; they may still have important duties to

(1) 20 R. R. 461 (2 B. & Ald. 339).   (4) 2 Burr. 869 ; *S. C.* 1 W. Bl.
(2) 2 T. R. 771.   187.
(3) 5 Ad. & El. 613.   (5) 34 R. R. 375 (10 B. & C. 230).

execute, under sect. 18, in expunging names and correcting mistakes and omissions.

Cur. adv. vult.

LORD DENMAN, Ch. J., now delivered the judgment of the COURT:

This was an application for a *quo warranto* against the defendant, to show by what authority he claimed to hold the office of a town-councillor in the city of Hereford. The ground of objection to his title was, that the burgess roll for the Monmouth ward in that city had not been revised pursuant to the provisions of the 5 & 6 Will. IV. c. 76.

This objection was stated in two ways, 1. That the defendant had not been elected by a majority of burgesses duly enrolled. 2. That no burgess roll existed at the time of his election.

It appeared that, although Hereford had been divided into wards, and two assessors duly elected for each ward, yet, instead of the burgess list for the whole city having been revised by the two assessors of the mayor's ward, pursuant to the forty-third section of the Act, two separate *assessors had been elected for the whole city under the thirty-seventh section, and the revision had been made by the mayor with them. If these two had no authority to form part of the court of revision, the court itself was never competently formed; the mayor was sitting alone, when, by the statute, he and two assessors are required to form the court. This objection is of so serious a nature, and the answer appears to us so insufficient, that the rule undoubtedly ought to be made absolute, unless some one of the preliminary or personal objections which were made to it be sustainable. On these the argument mainly turned, and we took time to consider these.

[*818]

The affidavits in support of the rule were made by three persons of the name of Cooke, Roberts, and Pulling. It was objected to Roberts, that he, with a full knowledge of the objection to the burgess list now insisted on, had taken a part in the election in question, by being himself a candidate and voter therein; and to Cooke, that he had also taken an active part as an agent in the election, and, besides, had no such interest as

REX
v.
PARRY.

qualified him to be a relator, being neither burgess nor inhabitant, but only a visitor there on certain occasions. It was not much insisted on that the information could be filed at the relation of either of these persons. But Pulling was put forward as a relator, against whom no objection existed, for he was an inhabitant of the city, subject to its municipal government, and therefore interested in the due election of the council, *Rex* v. *Hodge* (1) ; and although, by his agent Cooke, he had protested at the revision court against the legality of the revision, he had taken no part, nor been present, at the election for councillors.

[819]

In the case of *Rex* v. *Symmons* (2), in which four persons made affidavits in support of a rule for a *quo warranto*, there were valid personal objections against three as relators ; none existed against the fourth ; but it was urged that, as all were acting in concert, no distinction could be made. The Court however made the rule absolute ; the counsel avowing such fourth person to be the relator, and that he would be responsible for the costs. It was there indeed stated that the relator's affidavit "disclosed the whole ground on which the defendant's title was impeached," and this case certainly could not stand on the affidavit of Pulling alone. We do not think that a material circumstance, nor is it relied upon by the Court in the decision cited (3). A relator's case will constantly depend in part on the testimony of those who, from want of interest or their previous conduct, could not be themselves relators. In such cases the Court will ascertain who is the real relator, and that he is sufficient : it will then distinguish between him and those who are merely his witnesses, and will not affect him by their previous acts or declarations, unless he be identified with them in such a way as to disqualify him from being received as a relator.

It was however urged, in showing cause, that, if Parry be not duly elected, it is only because there is no good burgess-list in existence, an objection which not only applies to all the

(1) 20 R. R. 464, *n.* (2 B. & Ald.   (3) And see *Rex* v. *Brame*, 4 Ad. & El.
344, *n.*).   664.

(2) 4 T. R. 223.

councillors elected at the same time, but to all the existing burgesses, and shows that no future valid election can be made to any municipal office in the city. The force of this objection remains to be considered.

It cannot be stated as a proposition of law, or as a settled point of practice in this Court, that leave to file an information will not be granted, merely because the effect may or even will be to dissolve the corporation. That objection was recently made in the case of *Rex* v. *White* (1), and, under the circumstances, properly overruled. The facts of that case, indeed, hardly substantiated the objection; but our brother PATTESON there stated that, where the objection is in itself an individual objection, the circumstance of every member of the corporation being in a similar predicament to the person against whom the motion is made is not a sufficient ground to refuse a *quo warranto*: and we all agree that, in itself and standing alone, it is not.

But the argument at the Bar, in support of the present rule, did not and could not stop short of denying all discretion in this Court as to originating proceedings in *quo warranto*. It was, in effect, asserted that, wherever a reasonable doubt is raised as to the legal validity of a corporate title, we are bound to grant leave to file the information. This proposition, however, is wholly untenable. Every case (and they are most numerous), which has turned upon the interest, motives, or conduct of the relator, proceeds upon the principle of the Court's discretion; however clear in point of law the objection may have been to the party's abstract right to retain his office, yet the Court has again and again refused to look at it or interfere upon one or other of these grounds.

In the case of *Rex* v. *Trevenen* (2) Lord Ch. J. ABBOTT lays down the general rule in accordance with this view, and also incidentally directs its application to a case *like the present. " In the case of individual members of the corporation " " it is wholly within the discretion of this Court to say, whether such an information ought to be granted or refused. The Court,

[820]

[*821]

(1) 1 N. & P. 84; *S. C.* 5 Ad. & El. 613.   (2) 21 R. R. 364 (2 B. & Ald. 479).

undoubtedly, have, in some cases, permitted these informations to be filed, where the effect has been thereby to dissolve the corporation ; but that has been where strong cases have been made out."

Cases much earlier and nearer to the date of the statute o Anne (1) may be found, which not merely lay down the rule, but show that it had grown into the admitted practice of the Court. The cases of *Rex* v. *Dawes* and *Rex* v. *Marten* (2), or the *Winchelsea* cases, as they were called, are very remarkable in this point of view. They were often before the Court and well considered, and may be found in 1 Sir W. Bl. 634, 4 Burr. 1962, 2022, 2120. In these, Lord MANSFIELD treats the discretionary power of the Court, not as a matter disputed or requiring proof, but as a settled principle to be applied ; and in Burr. p. 2123, he states the grounds on which the Court in those cases proceeded in their application of the principle. First—" The light in which the three relators, now informing the Court of this defect of title, appear ; from their behaviour and conduct relative to the subject-matter of their information, previous to their making this motion. Secondly—The light in which the application itself manifestly shows their motives, and the purpose which it is calculated to serve. Thirdly—The consequences of granting the information." After examining the affidavits, with these points in view, [*822] the rules were both discharged, though it appeared *clear that the titles of both the defendants at the times of their election were invalid.

These seem to be grounds safely applicable to the present case. On the one hand, if the rule be made absolute, the dissolution of the corporation may at least be reasonably apprehended ; on the other, it is remarkable that the affidavits in support of the rule impute no corrupt, fraudulent, or indirect motive for the acts complained of as irregular, nor do they allege that they have produced injustice, inconvenience, or even any one result different from what would have followed the fullest compliance with the law as they lay

(1) 9 Ann. c. 20, s. 4.   (2) 1 W. Bl. 634 ; *S. C.* 4 Burr
                                        1962, 2022, 2120.

it down. They do not go the length of suspecting that a single vote has been won or lost, or that the burgess list would have varied in a single name. It appears, moreover, that the town clerk had taken the precaution of procuring, and had *bonâ fide* acted upon, the most eminent legal advice; and, in fact, neither claim nor objection, as regarded the Monmouth ward, was made to the overseer's list. We do not say that the court of revision had therefore no duties to perform: but, in fact, they were not called upon to perform any; and the defective constitution of the court has been, in all respects, an immaterial circumstance.

If these considerations would, under the old law, have been entitled to weight, they lose none from the passing of the recent statute. On the contrary, the difficulties that might attend the reconstruction of corporations once dissolved, and the important functions now vested in the municipal bodies, would rather induce increased circumspection in our proceedings. The inferior officers ought, indeed, to conform with care to the provisions of the law: the wilful departure from them *this Court will visit with severity; and even negligence may   [*823] not always escape animadversion: but our discretion as to the issuing of *quo warranto* informations must be regulated by a regard to all the circumstances which attend the application, and all the consequences likely to follow. Upon the whole, for the reasons stated, we think we act most in accordance with the current of authorities, with the statute of Anne, and with the public interest, in refusing the permission prayed by the present rule.

As there was great irregularity, however, in the appointment of the court of revision, we think that it ought to be discharged without costs.

Rule discharged.

BEVERLEY *v.* The LINCOLN GAS LIGHT and COKE COMPANY (1).

(6 Adol. & Ellis, 829—846; 2 N. & P. 283; W. W. & D. 519; 7 L. J. (N. S.) Q. B. 113.)

A corporation aggregate may be sued in *indebitatus assumpsit* for goods sold and delivered, though the contract be not under seal.

The contract may be implied or express, as in cases of assumpsit against an individual.

The implication may arise from the object of the incorporation, as compared with the subject-matter of the contract.

As in assumpsit against an incorporated gas company for the price of gas meters sold and delivered to the amount of 15*l*.

In the case of corporations aggregate, as in that of individuals, if goods be taken on the terms of their being returned if not approved of, and they be retained an unreasonable time, the party so taking and retaining may be sued for goods sold and delivered.

AssumpsIT for goods sold and delivered, and on an account stated. Plea, *non assumpsit*. Issue thereon.

On the trial before the assessor for the sheriff of Yorkshire, December 8th, 1836, it appeared that the defendants were a corporation (2), and that one of the committee of the Company, named Winter, ordered of the plaintiff six gas meters, in September, 1832, for the Company: that these were delivered, and that the clerk of the Company, in November, 1832, acknowledged the delivery: that one of the meters was used by the Company in January; that, on 23rd April, the Company sent a notice that they would be returned; and that they actually were sent back on 30th May, 1833; but that the plaintiff would not receive them. It appeared also that the terms on which the Company originally received them were that they might be returned if, on trial, they were not approved of. It was objected for the defendants that this evidence did not support the declaration; that a corporation aggregate was not liable in such an action, and that the contract should have been under their seal. The assessor refused to nonsuit, but reserved leave to move;

(1) Referred to by PARKE, B. in *Mayor of Ludlow* v. *Charlton* (1840) 6 M. & W. 815, 818, 10 L. J. C. P. 75. And see *South of Ireland Colliery Co.* v. *Waddle* (C. P. 1868 and Ex. Ch. 1869) L. R. 3 C. P. 463, 4 C. P. 617, 37 L. J. C. P. 211, 38 L. J. C. P. 338. And see Sale of Goods Act, 1893 (56 & 57 Vict. c. 71), sections 3 and 18, Rule 4 (*b*).—R. C.

(2) Incorporated by stat. 9 Geo. IV. c. xxiv. local and personal, public.

and he directed the jury to find for the defendants, if they thought the articles had been returned in a reasonable time; if not, for the plaintiff. The jury found for the plaintiff. In Hilary Term, 1837, *Peacock* obtained a rule *nisi* for a nonsuit. In the same Term (1),

BEVERLEY
v.
THE LINCOLN
GAS LIGHT
AND COKE
COMPANY.

Alexander showed cause:

The first objection is, that this was a conditional contract, and therefore that the declaration upon a sale and delivery is not supported. But a contract, though conditional in its origin, may, if the condition is afterwards performed, be declared upon *simply as an absolute contract. *Bailey* v. *Gouldsmith* (2), is, in this respect, not distinguishable. The principle of that case was expressly upheld in *Bianchi* v. *Nash* (3); and *Brooke* v. *White* (4), *Swancott* v. *Westgarth* (5), and *Harrison* v. *Allen* (6), are to the same effect. The second objection is, that assumpsit for goods sold and delivered cannot be maintained against a corporation aggregate. It must be admitted that no definite rule has been laid down as to the extent to which corporations aggregate can bind themselves without seal. In *The· Dean and Chapter of Rochester* v. *Pierce* (7) it was held that debt would lie for use and occupation by a corporation aggregate, without any demise under seal. In *The Mayor of Stafford* v. *Till* (8) it was decided that a corporation aggregate may maintain assumpsit for use and occupation when their land has been occupied. So in *The Mayor and Burgesses of Carmarthen* v. *Lewis* (9) it was held that a corporation aggregate might maintain assumpsit for use and occupation for standings, market places, sheds, and tolls, on an agreement not under seal. In *The East London Waterworks Company* v. *Bailey* (10), where the directors of an incorporated Company were authorised by Act of Parliament to "make contracts, agreements, and bargains with the workmen, agents, undertakers, and other persons employed or concerned in making,

[*831]

(1) January 28th, 1837. Before Patteson, Williams, and Coleridge, JJ.
(2) Peake, 78.
(3) 1 M. & W. 545; Tyr. & Gr. 916.
(4) 1 Bos. & P. (N. R.) 330.

(5) 4 East, 75.
(6) 2 Bing. 4.
(7) 1 Camp. 466.
(8) 29 R. R. 511 (4 Bing. 75).
(9) 6 Car. & P. 608.
(10) 4 Bing. 283.

[*832]

completing, or continuing the works belonging to the said undertaking," it was held that the Company could not recover in
assumpsit for the non-delivery of certain pipes, which the defendants, by contract not under seal, had agreed to deliver: but
BEST, Ch. J., in his judgment, *admitted that there was an
exception to the general principle in the case "where the acts
done are of daily necessity to the corporation," referring to Bro.
Abr. Corporations and Capacities, pl. 56, and *Horn* v. *Ivy* (1).
It cannot be disputed that the contract here is of that description.   In *The City of London Gas-Light and Coke Company* v.
Nicholls (2) it was held that a Company incorporated for the
supply of gas might maintain assumpsit for such supply, on the
principle (it may be presumed) that the contract was in the
necessary course of business.   In *Smith* v. *The Birmingham Gas
Company* (3) it was held that a corporation aggregate might
appoint an agent to distrain, without seal, and would be liable
in tort for his tortious acts.   The cases on this point are
collected in Com. Dig. Franchises, (F. 13), 2 Bac. Abr. 265.
Corporations, (E), 3 (4), and 6 Vin. Abr. 287, Corporations, (K).
A question similar to the present was raised, but not determined,
in *Dunston* v. *The Imperial Gas Light Company* (5); but Lord
TENTERDEN said, "I wish, however, to be understood as by no
means deciding the question, whether third persons, who may
sell coal or other materials to the Company, or who may be
employed by them as servants or workmen, may or may not
maintain an action against them for remuneration, though the
contract was not under seal.   This is a corporation established
for the purpose of carrying on trade and manufactures, and may,
therefore, differ from others as to its powers of contracting, and
its remedies upon contracts relating to the purposes for which
the Company is formed."   From the language held by the Judges

[*833]

in *Broughton* v. *The Manchester Water Works Company* (6),
where many authorities are collected, the rule seems to be, that
an incorporated Company cannot be sued on its acceptance,
unless there be a power given to it, either expressly, or impliedly

(1) 1 Vent. 47.	(4) 7th ed. 1832.
(2) 2 Car. & P. 365.	(5) 37 R. R. 352 (3 B. & Ad. 125).
(3) 40 R. R. 358 (1 Ad. & El. 526).	(6) 22 R. R. 278 (3 B. & Ald. 1).

from the object of the incorporation, to accept bills.   The   BEVERLEY
question, in such cases, is mainly affected by the Acts for   THE LINCOLN
preserving the monopoly of the Bank of England; that con-   GAS LIGHT
sideration does not arise in the present case; but, the general   COMPANY.
principle of looking to the object of the incorporation applies (1).
And this is strengthened by the language of sect. 36 of the
Company's Act (2).

Peacock, contrà :

The authorities cited sufficiently answer the first objection, as
between individuals.   The question remains, whether the case
of a corporation be within the same principle.   The general
principle undoubtedly is, that a corporation cannot contract
without seal : 2 Bac. Abr. 265, Corporations, (E) 3 (3).   There is
*a distinction between corporations aggregate which have a con-   [*834]
stituted head, as mayor, &c., and those which have none.   The
former class may contract by implication, through their head, in
many cases, without seal ; the latter cannot, even in the case of
ordinary services, as appears from Com. Dig. Franchises, (F 13),
(F 14); 6 Vin. Abr. 291, Corporations, (K), pl. 39; *Ib.* 317
(C. a), pl. 49; *Frevill* v. *Ewebancke* (4).   The reason of this
distinction is that, although the head of a corporation may by his
personal act enter into, or impliedly make, a contract on behalf
of the corporation, if there be circumstances showing that he has

(1) See also *Clarke* v. *The Imperial*   poses of the said Company, as in
Gas Company, 4 B. & Ad. 315.   contracting for and purchasing mes-
    (2) Stat. 9 Geo. IV. c. xxiv. s. 36,   suages, lands," &c., entering into
enacts, "That the committee of direc-   agreements for lighting the city, &c.,
tors for the time being shall or may   of Lincoln; appointing and displacing
have the custody of the common seal   officers, agents, &c., with such salaries,
of the said Company, and shall have   &c., as they shall think proper; order-
full power and authority at any time,"   ing and employing works and work-
to call special general meetings of the   men ; selling articles produced under
Company, " and to direct the affairs   the authority of the Act ; bringing
and business of the said Company   actions, &c., for recovering debts due
(subject to the orders and directions   in respect of such sales; enforcing,
of the said Company made at any   rescinding, &c. contracts touching the
general or special general meeting),   same, subject to the rules, bye-laws,
as well in issuing, receiving, and   &c., to be made by the Company.
laying out and disposing of all sums   (3) 7th ed. 1832.
of money to be issued or received,   (4) 1 Roll. Rep. 82.
laid out or disposed of, for the pur-

BEVERLEY
v.
THE LINCOLN
GAS LIGHT
AND COKE
COMPANY.

power so to do, yet the body cannot show their intention by any but a corporate act, which can be only by the common seal.   A liability may, in such a case, arise from the legal relation of the parties; but then the remedy should be shaped in debt or tort, not in assumpsit.   A servant may be constituted in certain cases, without writing: but then he cannot bring assumpsit for his salary: 6 Vin. Abr. 288, Corporations, (K), pl. 10.   As to the clause of the Act, the words are less strong than those in *East London Waterworks Company* v. *Bailey* (1).   No case has been cited of assumpsit being maintained against a corporation upon an executed contract: the authorities go the length only of show-ing that they may maintain assumpsit; and this because an individual may promise to them either expressly, or impliedly by his acts, without seal, though they cannot contract except under seal.   Thus, *The Dean and Chapter of Rochester* v. *Pierce* (2), *The Mayor of Stafford* v. *Till* (3), *The Mayor and Burgesses of*

[*835]

Carmarthen *v. *Lewis* (4), *The City of London Gas-Light and Coke Company* v. *Nicholls* (5), were cases in which the corpora-tions were plaintiffs.   The act of an individual may raise an implication of a contract with the corporation, as it may create a liability to an action of tort by them; and the breach of such contract may be sued on by the corporation, as well as a breach of duty.   But, against a corporation (except in the case of contract under seal), the remedy must be on the tort or the duty, or in debt.   *Tilson* v. *The Warwick Gas-Light Company* (6), and *Dunston* v. *The Imperial Gas-Light Company* (7), were actions of debt.   In *Murray* v. *The East India Company* (8) the action was assumpsit; but there the Court proceeded on the ground that the authority of the defendants to draw and accept bills was recognised by statute: and, where the plaintiff is indorsee (which was the case as to one of the bills there), no remedy but assumpsit lies against the acceptor for want of privity.   In *Broughton* v. *The Manchester Water Works Company* (9) BAYLEY, J. doubted, independently of the question of the monopoly of the Bank of

(1) 4 Bing. 283.	(6) 28 R. R. 529 (4 B. & C. 962).
(2) 1 Camp. 466.	(7) 37 R. R. 352 (3 B. & Ad. 125).
(3) 29 R. R. 511 (4 Bing. 75).	(8) 24 R. R. 325 (5 B. & Ald. 204).
(4) 6 Car. & P. 608.	(9) 22 R. R. 278 (3 B. & Ald. 1).
(5) 2 Car. & P. 365.	

England, whether the corporation could contract; and BEST, J. expressed himself against the right of action, on the general ground (1), referring to the opinion expressed by the Court of C. B. in *Slark* v. *Highgate Archway Company* (2).

Cur. adv. vult.

PATTESON, J., in this Term (June 6th), delivered the judgment of the COURT:

This was a rule to set aside a verdict for 15*l.* and enter a non-   [836]
suit, which was argued before my brothers Williams, Coleridge, and myself. It appeared that Winter, one of the committee of the Company, had ordered six meters in September, 1832; they were delivered, and their receipt acknowledged by the clerk of the Company in November: one of them was seen in use in January; on the 23rd of April, they were returned as inadequate for the intended purpose; the plaintiff, however, refused to receive them, and brought an action of *indebitatus assumpsit* for goods sold and delivered. Two objections were insisted on: 1st, That the action was misconceived in form, for that the contract was executory only; 2ndly, That, at all events, assumpsit could not be maintained against the defendants, being a corporation aggregate without a head.

As to the first, the jury found, at the trial, that the time of return was unreasonable. Upon the argument in support of this ground of nonsuit, it was not denied that, if the action had been between two individuals, upon this finding of the jury the form of action would have been sustainable. For this, the cases of *Bailey* v. *Gouldsmith* (3), and *Bianchi* v. *Nash* (4), are certainly sufficient authorities. But it was said that those decisions were inapplicable to the case of a corporation; because that could not, at all events, enter into a parol contract for the delivery of goods on sale or return. It seems to us, that this distinction cannot be maintained, even if the facts were sufficient to raise it; for the principle on which the cases cited above, and others, have been *decided, as to the proper form of declaring where the   [*837]
original contract has been executory, but the period of credit has

(1) 3 B. & Ald. 12.   (3) 1 Peake, 78.
(2) 5 Taunt. 792.   (4) 1 M. & W. 545; Tyr. & Gr. 916.

BEVERLEY
v.
THE LINCOLN
GAS LIGHT
AND COKE
COMPANY.

expired, or condition has been performed, is, not that the law alters the mode of declaring on the original contract and states it not according to the fact, but that it conclusively infers that simple contract to pay the price for goods sold and delivered which would arise upon the facts of a sale and delivery without any special circumstances accompanying them. He who seeks to disturb that inference must not content himself with merely showing conditions, or other special provisions, forming part of the contract at the time of its being entered into; he must show them in existence and operation at the time of action brought; if not, they may be struck out of consideration, and the contract treated as originally simple, unconditional, and executed. Now this reasoning will apply equally to a corporation and an individual; and we must now take it that the goods were sold unconditionally, have been delivered, and are in the possession and use of the corporation.

This, therefore, brings us to the second question, which is, Whether an action of assumpsit can be maintained against a corporation aggregate without a head, on an executed parol contract? It is well known that the ancient rule of the common law, that a corporation aggregate could speak and act only by its common seal, has been almost entirely superseded in practice by the Courts of the United States in America (1). The decisions of those Courts, although intrinsically entitled to the highest respect, cannot be cited as direct authority for our proceedings; and there are obvious circumstances *which justify their advancing with a somewhat freer step to the discussion of ancient rules of our common law than would be proper for ourselves. It should be stated, however, that, in coming to the decision alluded to, those Courts have considered themselves, not as altering the law, but as justified by the progress of previous decisions in this country and in America. We, on our part, disclaim entirely the right or the wish to innovate on the law upon any ground of inconvenience, however strongly made out; but, when we have to deal with a rule established in a state of society very different from the present, at a time when

[*838]

(1) 2 Kent's Commentaries, 288—291 (part 4, lect. 33), ed. 3. New York. 1836,

corporations were comparatively few in number, and upon which
it was very early found necessary to engraft many exceptions,
we think we are justified in treating it with some degree of
strictness, and are called upon not to recede from the principle
of any relaxation in it which we find to have been established by
previous decisions. If that principle, in fair reasoning, leads to
a relaxation of the rule for which no prior decision can be found
expressly in point, the mere circumstance of novelty ought not
to deter us ; for it is the principle of every case which is to be
regarded ; and a sound decision is authority for all the legitimate
consequences which it involves.

Several cases have determined that corporations aggregate
may maintain actions on executed parol contracts. In *The Dean
and Chapter of Rochester* v. *Pierce* (1) Lord ELLENBOROUGH first
at Nisi Prius, and this Court afterwards, held that they might
sue in debt for use and occupation of their lands ; and the Court
of Common Pleas, in *The Mayor of Stafford* v. *Till* (2), held the
*same as to assumpsit. This establishes that, where a benefit
has been enjoyed, such as the occupation of their lands, by their
permission, the law will imply a promise to make them compensation, which promise they are capable of accepting, and upon
which they may maintain an action. The action for use and
occupation is established by stat. 11 Geo. II. c. 19, s. 14 ; and,
according to the words of the statute, may be maintained
" where the agreement is not by deed." Some agreement
seems to be implied as the foundation ; though it is well
established that it need not amount to a formal demise, or even
be express. To hold, then, that a corporation is within this
statute, is to hold that it may be a party to an agreement not
under seal, at least for the purpose of suing on it ; and it would
be rather strong to deny, at the same time, that it could be
a party to it for the purpose of being sued on it. Lord ELLEN-
BOROUGH, indeed, says, in *The Dean and Chapter of Rochester*
v. *Pierce* (3), that the action for use and occupation does not
necessarily suppose any demise. " It is enough that the
defendant used and occupied the premises by the permission

[*839]

BEVERLEY
v.
THE LINCOLN
GAS LIGHT
AND COKE
COMPANY.

(1) 1 Camp. 466.
(2) 29 R. R. 511 (4 Bing. 75).

(3) 1 Camp. 467.

BEVERLEY
v.
THE LINCOLN
GAS LIGHT
AND COKE
COMPANY.

[*840]

of the plaintiff; and a *corporation, as well as an individual, may, without deed, permit a person to use and occupy premises of which they are seised." But, call it by whatever name we please, permission or demise, it clearly binds the corporation; the party occupying and paying rent under it acquires rights from the corporation, becomes their tenant from year to year, and can be ejected only by the same means as would be available for an individual landlord. Here, then, the law implies that the corporation has acted as a contracting party, and that too in a contract to the validity of which, for the purposes of this action, the absence of any deed is essential. If, in that case, an express agreement not under seal had been tendered in evidence to prove the terms on which the defendant held, it must have been received; and if, on the face of it, it had appeared that the plaintiffs had come under any conditions precedent to the recovery of rent on their part, such conditions would surely have been binding on them though not under seal; and the non-performance of them would have been an answer to the action. In *The Southwark Bridge Company* v. *Sills* (1) the contract for letting was proved by a series of letters. We agree that the relation between the corporation and the occupier of its land may commence without express contract; that it may, in the first instance, appear to want many of the legal incidents of the relation between landlord and tenant; but add the fact of payment of rent for one year, and acceptance by the corporation, and you add nothing of express contract on the part of the corporation: it has apparently done no more than acquiesce

[*841]

in the receipt *of a certain compensation for the occupation of its land for a year; and yet, by the addition of that fact, the corporation and the occupier are demonstrated to be landlord and tenant. This appears to us to show that in the eye of the law the relation between them commenced in contract, though it wanted at first the evidence from which it might be inferred.

But, if this be a contract to which a corporation may be a party, though not under seal, and any rights resulting from that agreement come to be enforced, may not that form of action be applied which is appropriate to parol agreements? Is it not

(1) 2 Car. & P. 371.

unreasonable to hold that a corporation may make a binding promise, and yet that assumpsit shall not be maintainable against it if the promise be broken ?

If then it be established that, upon the same contract, the remedies are mutual, that, if the corporation may sue its tenant in assumpsit on a parol demise, the tenant may in turn sue it in the same form of action, we do not see how it can be denied that a corporation occupying land may be sued in assumpsit generally.

We may suppose two contracts entered into at the same moment in writings not under seal : by the one, a corporation professes to demise its land to A. B., by the other A. B. demises his land to the corporation ; and enjoyment of the premises is had under both. It would be surely an unsatisfactory state of the law which should compel us to hold that, if the corporation sued A. B. in assumpsit for his rent, A. B. might not set off or sue in the same form for that which was due from the corporation.

We have been thus minute in examining the case of *use and occupation, because it appears to us very fairly to open the principle on which this matter ought to stand. The same point has been ruled in an action for goods sold and delivered. *The City of London Gas-Light and Coke Company* v. *Nicholls* (1) was assumpsit for gas supplied : the objection was taken, that the contract was not under seal : BEST, Ch. J. overruled it at once, saying, " It is quite absurd to say, that there is any necessity for a contract by deed in such a case." If, in that case, a set-off had been pleaded for meters supplied to the Company, could evidence in support of it have been rejected because there was no contract under seal for the supply ? Yet, if it could not, upon what principle can it be maintained that that supply might not have been made the ground of an action of *indebitatus assumpsit ?*

We have not overlooked the technical difficulty which has been alleged upon the form of the declaration, in which a mere promise is stated. Part of our argument has already been addressed to meet it : it seems to us that it rests on no solid

[*842]

(1) 2 Car. & P. 365.

foundation.   When the question is, Whether a particular party can sue or be sued, by a particular writ or count, or be counted against in any particular form?   the true answer is to be found by putting another question, Can he enter into the contract, or bring himself, or be brought, within the special circumstances which form essential parts of the statement in such writ or count?   That this is the principle may be seen conclusively in the history of our forms of action, ancient and modern, given in the third volume of Blackstone's Commentaries.   If, therefore, it be asked, *Whether a corporation can be sued in assumpsit?   we ask, in return, Can it bind itself by a parol contract?   Can it make a promise?   If it can, the former question must be answered in the affirmative.

[*843]

We, therefore, agree with the Court of Common Pleas in the *Mayor of Stafford* v. *Till* (1), that there is no substantial difference in this respect between assumpsit and debt.   Every count, indeed, in debt for goods sold and delivered charges a contract; "the words 'sold and delivered,'" says BULLER, J. in *Emery* v. *Fell* (2), "imply a contract; for there cannot be a sale, unless two parties agree."   *De Grave* v. *The Mayor and Corporation of Monmouth* (3) was debt against a corporation for the price of weights and measures.   It was contended that the action could not be maintained, as a corporation cannot contract unless by some instrument under the common seal.   The delivery had been proved, an examination of the goods at a full meeting of the corporation, and subsequent use of them; the order for them was by the mayor *de facto*, who was afterwards ousted.   Lord TENTERDEN thought the examination was the exercise of an act of ownership, "and that, by so doing, the corporation have recognised the contract."   The verdict passed for the plaintiffs, and was not disturbed.   The recognition of a contract is its adoption—the taking it to be the contract of the party so recognising it; but that assumes it to be a contract which the party was capable of entering into.   Lord TENTERDEN, therefore, must have considered the corporation as capable of contracting for the purchase of goods without a deed.   And in *Dunston* v.

(1) 29 R. R. 511 (4 Bing. 75).   (3) 4 Car. & P. 111.
(2) 2 T. R. 30.

BEVERLEY
v.
THE LINCOLN
GAS LIGHT
AND COKE
COMPANY.

[*844]

The Imperial Gas Light Company (1), where *the plaintiff failed on another ground, he carefully guards himself from being supposed to decide the contrary.

We certainly have not found any decided case in which it has been held that a corporation may be sued in assumpsit on an executed parol contract, a circumstance of great, but not conclusive, weight. For (not to mention that there is no case in which the contrary has been expressly decided upon argument), if it be remembered what the course of the law has been on this subject, we shall find that circumstance not unnatural, and that some deduction must be made from the weight of *dicta* unfavourable to our present view, which may be found here and there in the books upon this subject. At first the rule appears to have been exclusive, as indeed its principle required it to be. A corporation, it was said, being merely a body politic, invisible, subsisting only by supposition of law, could only act or speak by its common seal: the common seal, in the words of Peere Williams, in *Rex* v. *Bigg* (2), was the hand and mouth of the corporation. The rule therefore stood, not upon policy, but on necessity, and was of course equally applicable to small as to great matters; to acts of daily or of rare occurrence; to what regarded personal as well as real property. But this, though true in theory, was intolerable in practice; the very act of affixing the seal, of lifting the hand, or opening the mouth, could only be done by some individual member, in theory quite distinct from the body politic, or by some agent; the management of the corporate property, the daily sustentation of the members, *the performance of the very duties for which the corporation was created, required incessantly that acts should be done, sometimes of daily recurrence, sometimes entirely unforeseen, yet admitting of no delay, sometimes of small importance, or relating to property of little value. The same causes also required that contracts to a small amount should often be entered into. In all these cases, to require the affixing of the common seal was impossible; and therefore, from time to time, as the exigencies of the case have required, exceptions have been admitted to the rule: and what we desire

[*845]

(1) 37 R. R. 352 (3 B. & Ad. 125).   (2) 3 P. Wms. 423.

BEVERLEY
v.
THE LINCOLN
GAS LIGHT
AND COKE
COMPANY.

to draw attention to is this—that these exceptions are not such as the rule might be supposed to have provided for, but are in truth inconsistent with its principle and justified only by necessity. As each exception of this kind was made, it was not unnatural that the rule in all other yet unforeseen cases should receive confirmation, though it would be hardly fair to anticipate thence what the opinion of the Judges would have been if the cases had been presented before them and required their decision.

In the progress, however, of these exceptions, it has been decided that a corporation may sue in assumpsit on an executed parol contract; it has also been decided that it may be sued in debt on a similar contract: the question now arises on the liability to be sued in assumpsit. It appears to us that what has been already decided in principle warrants us in holding that this action is maintainable. It seems clear that, for a matter of such constant requirement to a Gas Company as gas meters, and to so small an amount as 15l., the Company, whether with or without a head, might contract without affixing the common seal: see Bro. Abr., Corporations *and Capacities, pl. 56, *Horn* v. *Ivy* (1); and it is clear that they might have been sued in debt for goods sold and delivered. For the reasons given, we think they are equally liable in assumpsit; and consequently this rule will be discharged.

[*846]

Rule discharged (2).

1838.

[846]

CHURCH *v.* THE IMPERIAL GAS LIGHT AND COKE COMPANY (3).

IN ERROR.

(6 Adol. & Ellis, 846—862; S. C. 3 N. & P. 35; 1 W. W. & H. 137; 7 L. J. (N. S.) Q. B. 118.)

A corporation, created for the purpose of supplying gas, may maintain assumpsit for breach of a contract by the defendant to accept gas from year to year, at 12l. 16s. per annum, the consideration being alleged to be the promise of the plaintiffs to supply it on those terms. Such a

----

(1) 1 Vent. 47.
(2) See the next case.

(3) See last case, and note, p. 626, *ante.*—R. C.

promise by the Company, though not under seal, is valid, and a good consideration.

It makes no difference as to the right of a corporation to sue on a contract entered into by them without seal, whether the contract be executed or executory.

Nor whether the promises be express or implied.

ERROR from the Palace Court of Westminster. The defendants in error declared in assumpsit, in the Palace Court of Westminster, against the plaintiff in error. The declaration commenced thus. "The Imperial Gas Light and Coke Company, the plaintiffs in this suit, by" B. E. W. their attorney, complain &c. There was no averment describing the plaintiffs further (1). The first count charged that the defendant *below, heretofore, to wit &c., bargained for and agreed to take of the plaintiffs, and the plaintiffs, at the request of the defendant, agreed to supply

CHURCH
v.
THE
IMPERIAL
GAS LIGHT
AND COKE
COMPANY.

[*847]

(1) Stat. 1 & 2 Geo. IV. c. cxvii. (local and personal, public), by sect. 1, incorporates "The Imperial Gas Light and Coke Company," by that name, and authorises the Company to make inflammable air, gas, coke, &c.; "and to sell and dispose of the same respectively in such manner as the said Company shall think proper."

Sect. 2 enacts, that the Company shall have full power and authority to supply and light with inflammable air, gas, and carburetted hydrogen, the shops, houses, streets, &c., in the places there named.

Sect. 6 authorises the Company to contract with any commissioners, persons, &c., having the management of the lighting of the said streets, &c., or any persons, &c., willing to contract for the lighting of any streets, &c.

Sect. 71 enacts, that the "directors for the time being shall have the custody of the common seal of the said Company, and shall have full power and authority to use the same for the affairs and concerns of the said Company, and shall have full power and authority to meet and adjourn from time to time, and from

place to place, and also to direct, manage, and transact the affairs and business of the said Company, as well in issuing, laying out, and disposing of all sum and sums of money to be issued or laid out or disposed of for the purposes of the same, as in contracting for and purchasing messuages, lands, tenements, hereditaments, materials, goods, and chattels for the use of the said Company, and entering into contracts for the lighting of any streets, squares," &c., "buildings," &c., "and other parts and places within the limits of this Act, and in ordering, directing, and employing the works and workmen, and selling and disposing of all or any messuages, lands," &c., "and all articles produced as aforesaid, and in making, enforcing, and carrying into effect, all contracts and bargains touching or anywise concerning the same, subject to such orders, bye-laws, rules, and regulations as shall at any time be duly made by the said Company, in restraint, control, or regulation of the powers and authorities by this Act granted."

CHURCH
v.
THE
IMPERIAL
GAS LIGHT
AND COKE
COMPANY.

to him, a certain large quantity of gas, to wit so much gas as
was necessary to furnish two lights for one year, to wit from 21st
July, A.D. 1833, and so on from year to year, at and for the rate
or price of 12l. 16s. per annum, for the said two lights; and the
defendant, in consideration thereof, and that the plaintiffs, at
the said request of the defendant, had then promised the defendant to supply the said gas to him, the defendant, as aforesaid,
then promised the plaintiffs to accept the said gas of and from
the plaintiffs and to pay them for the same, at the rate or price

[*848]   aforesaid, quarterly, at the end of fourteen *days from the end
of each quarter, and to give the plaintiffs not less than three
calendar months' notice of intending to discontinue taking the
said gas, to expire at the end of the then ensuing quarter, or to
pay the plaintiffs the amount of the price of the said gas, at the
rate or price aforesaid, to the end of the said ensuing quarter.
Averments that the plaintiffs always, during the quarter of a
year, namely, from 1st October, 1834, to 31st December, 1834,
were ready and willing, and tendered to supply &c., and
requested the defendant to accept the same as aforesaid; and
that the defendant did not give to the plaintiffs three calendar
months', or any longer, notice, as aforesaid. Breach, that the
defendant did not accept or pay. Second count, for goods and
gas bargained and sold.   Third count, for goods sold and
delivered. Fourth count, on an account stated.

Pleas.   1. *Non assumpsit.*   2. A denial of the plaintiffs'
readiness and tender, &c. A verdict was found for the defendant
on the first issue, as to the third count, and for the plaintiffs on
the rest of the first issue, and on the second issue. The damages
were assessed on the first, second, and fourth counts generally;
and judgment was given in the Palace Court for the said damages
and costs. Upon which error was brought in this Court.

The case was argued in Easter Term, 1837 (1).

*   *   *   *   *

[858]   LORD DENMAN, Ch. J., in Hilary Term, 1838 (January 16th),
delivered the judgment of the COURT:

This was error from a judgment pronounced in the Palace
Court for the defendants in error, who were plaintiffs below in

(1) April 28th. Before Lord Denman, Ch. J., Patteson and Coleridge, JJ.

an action of assumpsit, on the breach of an executory contract
for the supply of gas on the one hand, and acceptance and
payment on the other. The error insisted upon, in argument
before my brothers Patteson, Coleridge, and myself, was that
the plaintiffs, being a corporation, were incapable of suing in
assumpsit on an executory contract: and the distinction was
taken between a contract executory and executed. In support of
this distinction, the case of *East London Water Works Company*
v. *Bailey* (1) was cited as a direct authority. When this case
was argued, this Court had not pronounced its judgment in
that of *Beverley* v. *The Lincoln Gas Light and Coke Company* (2),
in which it determined that assumpsit was maintainable
against a corporation upon an executed contract for goods sold
*and delivered. We do not mention this latter case as directly
in point, but because, having there considered at some length
the principles upon which the law stands as to the powers and
liabilities of corporations in respect of parol contracts, we are
now relieved from some parts of the enquiry which it might
otherwise have been necessary to have gone through.

Assuming it, therefore, to be now established in this Court
that a corporation may sue or be sued in assumpsit upon
executed contracts of a certain kind, among which are included
such as relate to the supply of articles essential to the purposes
for which it is created, the first question will be, whether, as
affecting this point, and in respect of such contracts, there is
any sound distinction between contracts executed or executory.
Now the same contract which is executory to-day may become
executed to-morrow; if the breach of it in its latter state may
be sued for, it can only be on the supposition that the party was
competent to enter into it in its former; and, if the party were
so competent, on what ground can it be said that the peculiar
remedy which the law gives for the enforcement of such a contract may not be used for the purpose? It appears to us a
legal solecism to say that parties are competent by law to enter
into a valid contract in a particular form, and that the appropriate legal remedies for the enforcement or on breach of such a
contract are not available between them. Where the action is

CHURCH
v.
THE
IMPERIAL
GAS LIGHT
AND COKE
COMPANY.

[*859]

(1) 4 Bing. 283. (2) *Ante*, p. 626 (6 Ad. & El. 829).

CHURCH
v.
THE
IMPERIAL
GAS LIGHT
AND COKE
COMPANY.

[*860]

brought for the breach of an executed contract, the evidence
of the contract, if an express one, must be the same as if the
action were brought while it was executory ; an oral or written
agreement, or a series of letters, might be produced to prove the
fact, *and the terms of the contract : could it be contended that
these would be evidence of a valid contract after execution, but
of a wholly inoperative one before? Unless positions such as
these can be maintained, we do not see how to support any
distinction between express executory and executed contracts of
the description now under consideration.

A distinction, however, seems to be intimated, in some cases,
between the express contract of the parties and that which the
law will imply for them from an executed consideration.   And a
validity is attributed to the latter which is denied to the former.
But there is no foundation for this : the difference between
express and implied contracts is merely a difference in the
mode of proof.   On the one hand, a plaintiff, who should sue
on a contract to be implied from certain acts done, must be
nonsuited if those acts were shown to be in compliance with
stipulations antecedently entered into, unless he was prepared
with evidence of all the stipulations.   On the other hand, no
contract can be implied from the acts of parties, or result by
law from benefits received, but such as the same parties were
competent expressly to enter into.   And this is important in the
present argument, because it makes the decisions on implied
contracts authority for our decision upon an express one.   Upon
these grounds we are prepared to decide that the present action
was maintainable.   So far, therefore, as the decision of the
Court of Common Pleas in *East London Water Works Company*
v. *Bailey* (1) proceeded on the distinction between contracts
executed and executory, we are compelled, after consideration,

to express our *opinion that it was wrongly decided.   The case
may be sustained, however, on another ground, consistent with
our previous remarks, and which affords another reason for our
present decision.   The general rule of law is that a corporation
contracts under its common seal : as a general rule, it is only in
that way that a corporation can express its will or do any act.

(1) 4 Bing. 283.

That general rule, however, has from the earliest traceable periods been subject to exceptions, the decisions as to which furnish the principle on which they have been established, and are instances illustrating its application, but are not to be taken as so prescribing in terms the exact limit that a merely circumstantial difference is to exclude from the exception. This principle appears to be convenience amounting almost to necessity. Wherever to hold the rule applicable would occasion very great inconvenience, or tend to defeat the very object for which the corporation was created, the exception has prevailed : hence the retainer by parol of an inferior servant, the doing of acts very frequently recurring, or too insignificant to be worth the trouble of affixing the common seal, are established exceptions ; on the same principle stands the power of accepting bills of exchange, and issuing promissory notes, by Companies incorporated for the purposes of trade, with the rights and liabilities consequent thereon. These principles were, it is evident, present to the attention of the Court of Common Pleas when the case in question was decided ; and they might reasonably have held that a contract with a Water Company for the supply of iron pipes was neither one of so frequent occurrence, or small importance, or so brought within the purpose of the incorporation, that the principle of convenience *above established required it to be taken out of the general rule.

If, however, the present case be tried by the same test, the decision ought to be the other way. On the face of this record, we must understand this Company to have been incorporated for the purpose of supplying individuals willing to contract with them for gas light and coke : and the present appears to have been a contract for the supply of gas for a year, amounting to 12*l.* 16*s.*, and so from year to year. We cannot be ignorant that such contracts must be of frequent and almost daily occurrence ; and to hold that for every one of them, of the same or less amount (for, where the sum is so small, a diminution of half could not vary the principle), it was necessary to affix the common seal, would be so seriously to impede the corporation in fulfilling the very purpose for which it was created, that we think we are bound to hold the case fairly brought within the principle of the established exceptions.

CHURCH
v.
THE
IMPERIAL
GAS LIGHT
AND COKE
COMPANY.

[*862]

41—2

CHURCH
v.
THE
IMPERIAL
GAS LIGHT
AND COKE
COMPANY.

Leaving, therefore, the ancient rule still unbroken in all the instances to which it is fairly applicable, we are of opinion that the present action was well brought; and, consequently, our judgment will be for the defendants in error.

Judgment affirmed.

1837.

[899]

PEARSON, ASSIGNEE OF JAMES GRAHAM, A BANKRUPT, *v.* ANDREW GRAHAM AND OTHERS (1).

(6 Adol. & Ellis, 899—904; S. C. 2 N. & P. 636; 7 L. J. (N. S.) Q. B. 247.)

Defendant, being in the employment of J. in his trade, sold, *bonâ fide*, some goods belonging to J., after J. had committed an act of bankruptcy, of which defendant was ignorant. The sale was more than two months before the commission issued. Defendant acted under a general authority. The assignee brought trover: Held,

1. On a plea of Not guilty, that defendant, having sold under a general authority only, had been guilty of a conversion; and that, if he had any justification, he should have pleaded it specially.

2. On issue joined on a traverse of the assignee's possession, that the plaintiff must recover; no evidence being given that the purchaser was ignorant of the bankruptcy; sects. 81 and 82 of stat. 6 Geo. IV. c. 16 (2) protecting the transfer only where the party dealing with the bankrupt is without notice; and the burthen of proof being here on the defendant who affirmed the sale.

TROVER for hops, laying the possession in the plaintiff as assignee. Andrew Graham pleaded (3), first, Not guilty; secondly, that James Graham was not a bankrupt in manner &c.; thirdly, that the plaintiff was not lawfully possessed in manner &c. Issues on all the pleas. On the trial before Tindal, Ch. J. at the Westmoreland Summer Assizes, 1835, it was proved that James Graham, being a dealer in seeds, committed an act of bankruptcy, 24th July, 1834, by absenting himself. On the following day, Andrew Graham, who had been for some time employed by the bankrupt in his business, sold the hops in question to a person who paid the fair value for them and took them away. It appeared that Andrew had not any express authority from the bankrupt to sell the goods, but took upon himself to sell them

---

(1) Cited and followed in the judgment of MELLISH, L. J., in *Ex parte Schulte, In re Matanlè* (1874) L. R. 9 Ch. 409, 413.—R. C.

(2) See now the Bankruptcy Act,

1883 (46 & 47 Vict. c. 52), s. 49.—R. C.

(3) The other defendants pleaded separately from A. Graham, and the plaintiff demurred.

under his general authority. The commission issued in November, 1834. In answer to separate questions from the LORD CHIEF JUSTICE, the jury found, first, that James Graham absented himself with intent to defeat his creditors; secondly, that Andrew acted under a general authority, and had no notice of the act of bankruptcy at the time of the sale. His Lordship directed a verdict for the plaintiff, giving leave to move for a *nonsuit. In Michaelmas Term, 1835, *Blackburne* obtained a rule *nisi* accordingly. In Easter Term last (1),

PEARSON
v.
GRAHAM.

[*900]

.   *   *   *   *

LORD DENMAN, Ch. J. in this Term (May 31st) delivered the judgment of the COURT. After stating the pleadings and facts, his Lordship said:

[902]

The jury found that the defendant acted under a general authority, and that he did not know of the act of bankruptcy; but no question appears to have been submitted to them as to the knowledge of the purchaser. Upon this state of facts two questions arise: first, whether the defendant did convert the goods at all; and, secondly, if he did, whether the plaintiff, as assignee, was possessed of them, or, in other words, whether any property in them passed to him by the assignment.

As to the first question, it might be very doubtful whether a servant delivering goods by his master's order, could be said to have converted those goods, as against the assignees of his master. *Coles* v. *Wright* (2) rather seems to show that he could not. But, in the present case, the defendant had received no express orders as to *the goods in question, but took upon himself, under a general authority, to sell and deliver them at a time when, as it afterwards turned out, his master had absconded and abandoned all control over his property. This was a sufficient dealing with them to constitute a conversion, unless by any other facts the defendant could show that he was justified in what he did; and then such justification should have been put on the record by way of special plea.

[*903]

The next question therefore arises, viz. whether the property

(1) May 3rd. Before Lord Denman, Ch. J., Littledale, Patteson, and Coleridge, JJ.

(2) 4 Taunt. 198.

PEARSON
v.
GRAHAM.

in these goods passed to the plaintiff, as assignee, under the assignment of the commissioners. Now, assuming that it would pass by relation to the act of bankruptcy, that is, from the 24th of July, still it is contended that the sale is protected and rendered valid by the eighty-first section of stat. 6 Geo. IV. c. 16, and that the plaintiff had, in consequence of that section, no property and no possession actual or constructive.

That section renders valid all conveyances by, and all contracts and other dealings and transactions by and with, any bankrupt, *bonâ fide* made and entered into more than two calendar months before the date and issuing of the commission against him, notwithstanding any prior act of bankruptcy, provided the person so dealing with such bankrupt had not, at the time of such conveyance, contract, dealing, or transaction, notice of any prior act of bankruptcy. In this case the transaction was more than two months before the commission, and the defendant had no notice of a prior act of bankruptcy. But the defendant was not the person dealing with the bankrupt; he was the agent or servant of the bankrupt, and the person dealing with the bankrupt was the purchaser.

[904]

In order, therefore, to render the transaction valid, the jury should have been satisfied that the purchaser had no notice of a prior act of bankruptcy, as to which no question was put, nor, as it should seem, any evidence offered. The *onus* of showing the validity of the sale, in order to raise the question of property or no property in the plaintiff (assuming that it could be so raised), lay with the defendant; and, as he failed in showing the validity, the general rule applies; and the property was in the plaintiff by relation.

A further question arises on the eighty-second section, which provides that all payments really and *bonâ fide* made to a bankrupt before the date and issuing of a commission shall be deemed valid, notwithstanding a prior act of bankruptcy, provided the person so dealing with the bankrupt had not, at the time of such payment to him, notice of any prior act of bankruptcy.

Cash v. *Young* (1) and *Hill* v. *Farnell* (2) are authorities to show that a payment on a ready money purchase is within this section;

(1) 2 B. & C. 413.   (2) 9 B. & C. 45.

but still, as before, the point for the jury is, whether the person paying had notice of an act of bankruptcy, and that point was not submitted to the jury. The former observations, therefore, apply, and the rule for entering a nonsuit must be discharged.

Rule discharged (1).

THE EARL OF EGREMONT *v.* SAUL (2).

(6 Adol. & Ellis, 924—931; S. C. 6 L. J. (N. S.) K. B. 205.)

The grant of a fair "cum omnibus libertatibus et liberis consuetudinibus ad hujusmodi feriam pertinentibus" does not give a right to take tolls.

In an action for tolls at a fair, plaintiff gave evidence of immemorial usage. Defendant, in answer, produced a grant of the fair by Henry III. with the above words. The Judge told the jury that "consuetudines" generally meant tolls, but that, if the context raised a doubt, the expression might be interpreted by usage. It was also a question at the trial whether the charter was the original grant, or only a confirmation, of which some probability appeared. A verdict being given for the plaintiff, this Court granted a new trial, on the ground that the jury, if they believed the charter to be the original grant, would have been misled as to its effect by the above direction.

DEBT for tolls, payable to the plaintiff as owner and proprietor of Wigton fair, in Cumberland, in respect of defendant having bought divers live cattle, to wit ten bullocks, &c., exposed to sale in the fair. Plea, *Nunquam indebitatus.* Issue thereon.

On the trial before Lord Abinger, C. B., at the Carlisle Summer Assizes, 1835, the plaintiff proved the sale of the cattle in the fair, and that, in fact, a payment of *1*d.* for every beast sold in the fair had been immemorially made to the owner of the fair (which owner the plaintiff was shown to be), with some recent instances of resistance to the claim. In answer, the defendant's counsel contended that the exaction of tolls was an usurpation, and that the original grant of the fair contained no grant of tolls; and he put in a charter of 3rd February, 46 Hen. III., whereby the King granted and confirmed (3) to Walter de Wigton a weekly market

---

(1) See *Willis* v. *The Bank of England*, 43 R. R. 282 (4 Ad. & El. 21).

(2) Referred to by CLEASBY, B., in his judgment in *Mayor of Penryn* v.

Best (Ex. Ch. 1878) 3 Ex. D. 292, 295, 48 L. J. Ex. 103, 105.—R. C.

(3) Sciatis nos concessisse et hâc cartâ meâ confirmâsse.

and an annual fair, " cum omnibus libertatibus et liberis consuetudinibus ad hujusmodi mercatum et feriam pertinentibus,"
unless the same should be a nuisance to markets and fairs in the
vicinage.   The proceedings in a *quo warranto* were also put in by
the defendant, for the purpose of showing that the fair had
originated in this grant.   The *quo warranto* was of 20 Edw. I.,
and was against John de Wygeton, to answer by what warrant
he claimed to have a market and fair, and a gallows (*furcas*) and
infangthef.   John de Wygeton made claim to the market and fair
through the charter, which he set out, and the gallows and
infangthef as used by himself and his ancestors from time immemorial.   The jury found that John de Wygeton and his ancestors
had used the liberties aforesaid as claimed from time immemorial;
and the judgment was that he should go without day.   Lord
ABINGER, C. B., in his charge to the jury, said that " consuetudines " was generally used as signifying tolls; but that, if, by
the context in the charter, any doubt were thrown on the meaning,
the expression might be interpreted by usage.   He further pointed
out that, on the *quo warranto*, it had been found that the party

[*926]   had the rights from time immemorial; he *suggested that it was
therefore probable that the charter was merely a confirmation (1);
and he told the jury that, if they thought the evidence sufficient
to show a right antecedent to the charter, the charter itself was
not conclusive against the claim.   Verdict for the plaintiff.   In
Michaelmas Term, 1835, *Cresswell* obtained a rule *nisi* for a new
trial on the ground of misdirection.

Alexander, Armstrong, and *W. H. Watson* showed cause in
Hilary Term last (2) :

The learned Judge merely, in substance, told the jury that
the expression " consuetudines," in this charter, did not necessarily invalidate the evidence of usage.   Unless, therefore, it be
impossible that the word can ever mean tolls, the direction must
be supported.   If the jury had thought that the evidence of

---

(1) It was suggested, on behalf
of the defendant, that the liberties
referred to by the verdict on the
quo warranto, meant only those not

comprised in the charter.
  (2) May 2nd, 1837.   Before Lord
Denman, Ch. J., Littledale, Patteson,
and Coleridge, JJ.

payment was insufficient proof of the right antecedently to the charter, and that the charter was the origin of the right to the fair, they would not have been bound by the direction to find in favour of the right to the tolls on the construction of the charter. But they were entitled to infer a right by earlier grant, and to take the charter to be, as its language warrants, a mere confirmation. Then, as to the meaning of the word " consuetudines." In *Heddy* v. *Wheelhouse* (1) the defendant, in trespass for taking a cow, justified under a charter of Hen. VII. granting an annual fair " cum omnibus libertatibus, et liberis consuetudinibus, ad hujusmodi feriam spectantibus, vel pertinentibus," alleging *that he had distrained for one penny toll; and, on demurrer, the plaintiff had judgment, on the ground that the words gave no toll. But there the charter was not one of confirmation but of original grant; and, unless the words themselves necessarily carried toll, the defendant had no title to it, since his right depended upon the charter alone. Here the charter is, not one of original grant, but of confirmation; and the immemorial payment is strong evidence that the original grant (which may be presumed to have been lost) passed a right to tolls, although the subsequent charter of confirmation (which was produced at the trial) did not specifically notice them. Had there been no evidence of immemorial payment, or had the word "confirmâsse" not appeared in the charter, the cited case would have been in point; but those two circumstances form a distinction. *Holloway* v. *Smith* (2), which decided that " free customs " did not, in a grant of a new fair, imply tolls, is distinguishable on the same grounds. The question arose on demurrer; the claim rested on the words of an original grant, and was unsupported by any usage. In *Brett* v. *Beales* (3) nothing was decided upon the interpretation of " consuetudines," though there was some discussion on the point; and, in *Corporation of Stamford* v. *Pawlett* (4), the point conceded by the counsel for the plaintiffs, and adopted by the CHIEF BARON in giving judgment, carries the law of present case

[*927]

---

(1) Cro. Eliz. 558, 591; *S. C.* Moore, 474.

(2) 2 Str. 1171.

(3) 34 R. R. 499 (Moo. & Mal. 426).

(4) 35 R. R. 675 (1 Cr. & J. 71); *S. C.* affirmed on error in Dom. Pr. 1 Cr. & J. 400; 1 Tyr. 291.

no further than has been already admitted.   But, independently of the effect of usage as evidence of an earlier grant of toll *eo nomine*, it is sufficient to maintain *this verdict if the expression used in the charter *may* mean tolls; for, if it may, the immemorial payment affords abundant evidence that such is its meaning.

In Co. Litt. 58 b it is said, "This word *consuetudo* being derived *a consueto*, properly signifieth a custom;" "but in legal understanding it signifieth also tolls, murage, pontage, paviage, and such like newly granted by the King; and therefore when the King grants such things, the words be, Concessimus, &c. in auxilium villæ prædict' paviand', &c. consuetudines subscriptas, viz. de quolibet sunnagio, &c. And it was an article of the justices in Eyre to enquire de novis consuetudinibus levatis in regno, sive in terrâ, sive in aquâ, et quis eas levavit et ubi; where 'consuetudo' is taken for tolls and such like taxes or charges upon the subject."   The ambiguity, if there be one, is to be interpreted, as the LORD CHIEF BARON directed, by usage.   Thus, in 2 Inst. 282, it is said, "And when any claimed before the justices in Eyre any franchises by an ancient charter, though it had express words for the franchises claimed; or if the words were general, and a continual possession pleaded of the franchises claimed, or if the claim was by old and obscure words, and the party in pleading, expounding them to the Court, and averring continual possession according to that exposition; the entry was ever Inquiratur super possessionem et usum, &c. which I have observed in divers records of those Eyres, agreeable to that old rule, optimus interpres rerum usus."   In *The Mayor of Truro* v. *Reynolds* (1), where, the corporation having proved a prescriptive right to tolls, a charter was relied upon which granted that the burgesses *and inhabitants should be free of tollnet, &c., the COURT held that, if such a charter were ambiguous, contemporary usage ought to have great weight in the exposition of it.   The claim here made by John de Wygeton through the charter may be understood as a claim of confirmation by the charter; he set it out, and left it to its legal effect, either as confirmation or grant.

[*929]

(1) 34 R. R. 713 (8 Bing. 275).

Cresswell and *Wightman, contrà :*

It is conceded on the other side, upon the authority of the cases, that the word "consuetudines" would not, of itself, give the toll. But the LORD CHIEF BARON threw the weight of the evidence arising upon the charter only against the defendant : for he stated that the word was generally used for tolls, but that, if doubt arose on the context, usage might explain the meaning. The jury, therefore, could not but understand that the charter, in itself, assisted the plaintiff's case, and that it lay upon the defendant to meet this. But the word, at the most, proves nothing for the plaintiff: it is often found joined with such words as "custumagia" and "theolonia," as in the charter in *Holcroft* v. *Heel* (1).

(LORD DENMAN, Ch. J. : It is not to be assumed that, in such instances, there is no repetition.)

In the passage cited from Coke upon Littleton, "consuetudines" is joined with the participle "subscriptas," which may justify interpreting the word to mean tolls. It is said that the words "concessisse et confirmasse" show that the charter was one of confirmation, not of grant; but such language is not unusual in instruments of original grant; and the words making void the grant in case the fair, &c., should be a nuisance to the vicinage *would scarcely have occurred if the fair had existed immemorially : and, again, the grant is not of the "consuetudines" belonging to this fair, but to fairs "hujusmodi." The charter shows the origin of what might otherwise have been claimed as immemorial. It is clear that John de Wygeton rested his right to the fair exclusively on the charter; the other liberties were defended upon immemorial usage.

[*930]

(COLERIDGE, J. : The charter is nearer, in point of date, to the time of Magna Charta than to that of the charter which was under discussion in *Heddy* v. *Wheelhouse* (2). What is the meaning of the words "per antiquas et rectas consuetudines" in Magna Charta(3)?)

It there occurs in opposition to the words "toltis malis."

(1) 1 Bos. & P. 402.   Moore, 474.
(2) Cro. Eliz. 558, 591; *S. C.*   (3) Stat. 9 Hen. III. c. 30.

THE EARL OF
EGREMONT
v.
SAUL.

(COLERIDGE, J.: There seems to be no distinction between "consuetudines" and "liberæ consuetudines" (1).

LORD DENMAN, Ch. J.: In the passage cited from Co. Litt. 58 b it is said that the justices in Eyre are to enquire "de novis consuetudinibus levatis." If "consuetudines" meant only tolls customarily taken, would not that be a contradiction?)

Cur. adv. vult.

LORD DENMAN, Ch. J. in this Term (June 3rd) delivered the judgment of the COURT:

[*931]

In this case a charter was put in containing a grant of the fair, by the words "Sciatis nos concessisse et" "confirmàsse;" and the fair was granted "cum omnibus libertatibus et liberis consuetudinibus ad hujusmodi mercatum *et feriam pertinentibus." The jury were told by the learned Judge who tried the cause that these words generally signified tolls; and, upon that direction, a new trial was moved for. On the other hand, it was said that the words might mean tolls in a charter of confirmation, if tolls had existed before; and that the charter would not destroy the evidence of immemorial usage. Certainly there was much probability that the charter might have been one of confirmation. But the effect of the charge seems to have been that, even if the charter were one simply of grant, the words might signify tolls. The jury therefore may, upon that charge, have felt themselves bound to find as they did, though they were of opinion that it was an original grant, and not a confirmation. From the high respect which we feel for the learned Judge, and for his great familiarity with questions of this sort, we thought it right to pause. But we can find no such use of the word. In one passage in Coke (2) those words appear to be considered as signifying toll created newly: but we cannot find any instance in which it has been held that, of themselves, they conferred

(1) Mag. Chart. 9 Hen. III. c. 9. "Civitas London' habeat omnes libertates suas antiquas et consuetudines suas. Præterea, volumus et concedimus quòd omnes civitates aliæ et burgi et villæ et barones de quinque portubus et omnes portus habeant omnes libertates et liberas consuetudines suas."

(2) Co. Litt. 58 b.

toll. On the other hand, in a case in Cro. Eliz. (1), and another
in Strange (2), it is expressly laid down that tolls cannot be so
described in an original grant.   The rule must therefore be
made absolute.   *Rule absolute.*

THE EARL OF
EGREMONT
v.
SAUL.

HITCHCOCK *v.* WAY (3).

(6 Adol. & Ellis, 943—952; S. C. 2 N. & P. 72; W. W. & D. 491; 6 L. J.
(N. S.) K. B. 215.)

1837.
—
[943]

> Where the law is altered by statute, pending an action, the law as it
> existed when the action was commenced must decide the rights of the
> parties, unless the Legislature, by the language used, show a clear intention
> to vary the mutual relation of the parties.

ASSUMPSIT by indorsee against acceptor of a bill of exchange
for 250*l.* Plea, *non assumpsit.* Issue was joined in 1831. On
the trial before Coleridge, J., at the sittings in Middlesex in
Trinity Term, 1836, it appeared that the bill was drawn by
Thomas Hopkinson on the defendant, September 25th, 1830,
payable to Hopkinson at three months, and was accepted by the
defendant in part payment of a wager on a horse-race; and that
Hopkinson indorsed it in payment of a debt, to a party who
indorsed it to the plaintiff also in discharge of a debt, in
September, 1830. It was urged, for the defendant, that the
bill was void by stat. 9 Ann. c. 14, s. 1 (4). For the plaintiff,
stat. 5 & 6 Will. IV. c. 41 (sects. 1, 2) (4) was relied upon.
The learned Judge left the case to the jury, who found that the
bill was accepted for a gambling transaction, but that both the
first indorsee and the plaintiff took it innocently, and were *bona
fide* holders for valuable consideration. A verdict was taken for
the plaintiff for the amount of the bill and interest, and leave
given to move to enter a nonsuit.

[The motion having been argued, the COURT took time for
consideration.]

(1) *Heddy* v. *Wheelhouse*, Cro. Eliz.
558, 591; Moore, 474.

(2) *Holloway* v. *Smith*, 2 Str.
1171.

(3) Referred to as laying down the
general rule, but the particular Act
in question distinguished in *Ansdell*

v. *Ansdell* (1880) 5 P. D. 138, 141,
49 L. J. P. D. & A. 57, 58.—R. C.

(4) See now the Gaming Act, 1845
(8 & 9 Vict. c. 109), s. 18; the S. L. R.
Act, 1874; and the Gaming Act, 1892
(55 & 56 Vict. c. 9).—R. C.

LORD DENMAN, Ch. J., in this Term (June 12th), delivered the judgment of the COURT (1) : After stating the outline of the case, his Lordship proceeded :

On these facts the defendant obtained a rule for entering a nonsuit under stat. 9 Ann. c. 14.   The plaintiff set up stat. 5 & 6 Will. IV. c. 41, s. 1, as an answer.

The action had been brought long before the latter Act passed : the plea of *non assumpsit*, pleaded before the new rules, entitled the defendant to make his present defence.   After issue joined, the Act was passed, repealing that part of the said statute which makes the bill void, and enacting that any bill which, if this Act had not passed, would have been void, " shall be deemed and taken to have been made, drawn," &c., " for an illegal consideration," and the same consequences shall ensue.   The plaintiff argued that this enactment could only receive effect at the time of trial, and the Court was bound to act upon it at that period.   And many cases were cited in which Acts of Parliament repealing and altering the law had been so construed. But they all turned on the peculiar wording of those Acts, which appeared to the Court to compel them to give the law an *ex post facto* operation.   It is enough to say that we find no such words in the 5 & 6 Will. IV. c. 41, and are of opinion in general that the law as it existed when the action was commenced must decide the rights of the *parties in the suit, unless the Legislature expresses a clear intention to vary the relation of litigant parties to each other.

[*952]

In the present case we should have been glad to come to a different conclusion, but think we are not warranted in doing so, but that the rule for a nonsuit must be absolute.

Rule absolute.

(1) Lord Denman, Ch. J., Littledale, Patteson, and Coleridge, JJ.

ARCHER AND OTHERS, EXECUTORS OF THOMAS ARCHER
v. ISAAC MARSH (1).

(6 Adol. & Ellis, 959—968; S. C. 2 N. & P. 562; W. W. & D. 641; 6 L. J.
(N. S.) K. B. 244.)

M. executed a deed reciting that he had entered into treaty with A.
for the disposal of the business of a carrier from London to certain places
in Norfolk and Suffolk, and from those places to London, which M.
carried on and intended relinquishing to A.: that it was thereupon
stipulated that M., his heirs, executors, and administrators, should not
at any time thereafter exercise the trade of a common carrier from &c.
to &c. (as above), and that A. should pay M. a certain sum for the good-
will. After reciting further the actual resignation of the business by
M., and payment of the sum stipulated, M., in consideration of such
payment, covenanted to A., his executors, administrators, and assigns,
that M., his heirs, executors, and administrators, should not take in or
convey any goods or articles whatever from London to the other places
above mentioned, or from them to London, which places were formerly
connected with the said carrying concern, and for the relinquishment of
the carriage to which M. had received the above consideration.

A.'s executors brought covenant on the deed, and alleged as a breach
that M. had taken in and conveyed divers goods and articles from London
to other places above mentioned, which were before the making of the
deed connected &c., and from those places to London, contrary to the
tenor of the deed and of his covenant therein. Held (on objection taken
to the declaration upon demurrer to the plea),

1. That the breach was assigned with sufficient particularity, though
it did not allege that M. conveyed the goods as a common carrier.

2. That, where a party has agreed to forego a business for a consideration, the Court cannot enter into the reasonableness of the restraint as
compared with the consideration; and, therefore, that, although the
restriction here was unlimited as to time, the covenant could not be
pronounced void as operating in undue restraint of trade.

COVENANT on a deed poll. The declaration recited a deed,
which was afterwards set out on *oyer*, and the material parts
of which were as follows.

The deed, dated January 17th, 1814, was executed by Robert
Marsh, the defendant Isaac Marsh, and others, and recited that
the said Robert Marsh and the other parties to the deed (naming
them) did some time since carry on the trade or business of
carriers from London to Cambridge, Norwich, Brandon, Swaffham, Dereham, and various other parts of Norfolk and elsewhere,
under the firm &c., and being desirous of disposing of part of
such concern, they did, in April, 1812, enter into a treaty with

(1) See *Hitchcock* v. *Coker*, p. 522, *ante*, and note there.—R. C.

Thomas Archer of &c., common carrier (the testator), for the disposal of such branch or part of their said business as extended to or from Swaffham, Mundford, Mildenhall, and the several other parishes or *places contiguous or near thereto, or to either of them, to London, or from London to any or either of such towns or parishes as were above specified, or any other parish or place contiguous or near to either of them, and which said towns &c., and the towns and places intended to be included as contiguous &c., were considered as belonging to their trade carried on by them to Swaffham, and known and distinguished by the "Swaffham waggon concern," which waggon concern it was their intention to give up and relinquish to the said Thomas Archer; and upon such treaty it was stipulated that the said Robert Marsh and others should not, or should any or either of them, their, any or either of their heirs, executors or administrators at any time or times thereafter exercise the trade or business of a common carrier or common carriers from any or either of such parishes or places, or parts adjacent thereto, to London, or from London to any or either of such parishes or places, or parts adjacent thereto, and as were formerly considered as belonging to their Swaffham concern; and that, as an equivalent for the good will or profit likely to be derived to the said Thomas Archer from taking such part of their concern or business, the said Thomas Archer should pay unto the said Robert Marsh and others 1*s.* for every firkin of butter to be carried by the waggon of the said Thomas Archer from Swaffham to London, as would have been conveyed by them had they continued to conduct and carry on such branch or part of their said business or concern from that time to the 5th day of April now last past, being one third part of the carriage of such butter; to which terms the said Thomas Archer consented: The deed then stated that the

said Robert Marsh and others had *resigned the said part of the business to Thomas Archer, who had from that time carried it, and still did carry it, on upon his own account: and that an account had been taken of the said third part of the carriage of butter from Swaffham to London, which amounted to 308*l.* 9*s.*; and it then proceeded: Now, therefore, know ye that, in consideration &c. (of 308*l.* 9*s.*, the full payment of which was acknowledged), they the said Robert Marsh, &c., do hereby, for themselves, severally and respectively, and for their several and respective heirs, executors, and administrators, covenant, promise, and agree to and with the said Thomas Archer, his executors, administrators, and assigns, by these presents, in manner following: that is to say, that they the said Robert Marsh, Isaac Marsh, &c. (naming the other parties), their heirs, executors, and administrators, shall not, nor will any or either of them, by themselves or any of themselves, or any of themselves jointly or separately, or in partnership with any other person or persons whomsoever, or by their, any or either of their partners, servants, or agents, take in or convey any goods or articles of any description whatsoever from London to any or either of such parishes or places whatsoever, or any other parish or place contiguous or near thereto, and as were formerly connected with the said Swaffham waggon, and usually carried thereby, or take in or convey any butter, goods, or other articles of any description whatsoever from Swaffham, Mundford, or any or either of such other parishes or places, or any other parish or place contiguous or near thereto, to London, upon any account or pretext whatsoever, which said places were formerly connected with *their said Swaffham concern, and for the relinquishment of the carriage to which they have received the consideration before mentioned.   In witness, &c.

[*962]

The breach assigned in the declaration was, that defendant, after the making of the deed, viz. on &c., and on divers other days &c., hath taken in and conveyed, and still continues to take in and convey, divers goods and articles from London to Swaffham, Mundford and Mildenhall, and to divers other parishes and places contiguous and near thereto, which were, before the making of the said deed, connected with the said Swaffham waggon, and usually carried thereby, to wit &c. (mentioning a number of places in Norfolk and Suffolk, among which was Beachamwell), and hath taken in and conveyed, and still continues &c., divers goods and articles from Swaffham &c., and divers other parishes and places contiguous and near thereto, which were, before the making of the said deed, connected &c., viz. &c., to London, contrary to the tenor and effect

ARCHER   of the said deed poll, and of the covenant of the said defendant
  v.   in that behalf made as aforesaid.
MARSH.

Sixth plea. As to the carrying, &c., goods from Beachamwell
to London, that defendant did not at any time &c. take in or
convey or continue to take in or convey from Beachamwell to
London any other goods or articles than rabbits, and that
rabbits were not, at any time before the making of the deed,
usually carried by the said Swaffham waggon, or connected with
the said Swaffham concern ; and that the carriage of rabbits was
not any part of the branch of the said business mentioned in the
deed to have been resigned to, and, at the time of the making
[*963]   of the said deed, carried on *by, Thomas Archer, or for the
relinquishment of which Robert Marsh, &c., had received the
consideration &c. Verification.

General demurrer and joinder. The ground of demurrer
stated in the margin was, that the defendant was precluded by
his covenant from carrying rabbits as well as other things.
The defendant stated, as the points to be argued on his side,
that the deed precluded him only from carrying such articles
as were theretofore usually carried by the Swaffham waggon
and connected therewith, and that rabbits were admitted by
the demurrer not to be such articles, &c.; that the pleadings
disclosed no consideration for giving up the branch of business
mentioned in the sixth plea, and that the absence of such
consideration was admitted by the demurrer : Also, that the
declaration showed no cause of action, the deed being an agreement in undue restraint of trade ; nor did the declaration show
that the defendant had conveyed any goods as a common carrier.
The demurrer was argued in last Michaelmas Term (1).

[966]   LORD DENMAN, Ch. J. :

I think there is no doubt on any point but the restraint
of trade. We will wait the decision of *Hitchcock* v. *Coker*.

Cur. adv. vult.

(1) November 18th, 1836. Before Lord Denman, Ch. J., Patteson,
Williams, and Coleridge, JJ.

LORD DENMAN, Ch. J. in this Term (June 12th) delivered the judgment of the COURT:

This case arose on a covenant entered into between the plaintiffs and the defendant and others, that the latter, for considerations specified, should relinquish to the former a certain portion of their carrying trade, and abstain from exercising it within certain limits. The breach alleged was, that the defendant had still continued it: and, as the defence rested on the supposed illegality of the agreement as in restraint of trade, which nearly resembled the case of *Hitchcock* v. *Coker* (1), decided in this Court in last Easter Term, and pending in the Court of Error at the time of the argument, it was determined to postpone our judgment till that case should be finally decided.

The particular objection to the agreement, which was common to the present case and that above mentioned, was, that the restraint was much more extensive than was necessary for the full protection of the plaintiff, the purchaser of the good will of the business.

The Court of Error has reversed our judgment, on the principle that the restraint of trade in that case could not be really injurious to the public, and that the parties must act on their view of what restraint may be adequate to the protection of the one, and what advantage a fair compensation for the sacrifice made by the other.

We may observe that our own opinion, when *Hitchcock* v. *Coker* (1) was under discussion, leant much the same way; but we thought ourselves bound by the authority of *Horner* v. *Graves* (2), where the Court of Common Pleas entered into an inquiry into the terms *of the contract between the parties. That case appears to be overruled by the late decision in error. We not only bow to its authority, but think that in this respect it establishes a more correct and much more convenient rule of law. Our judgment must be for the plaintiff.

[*968]

Judgment for the plaintiff.

(1) *Ante*, p. 522.   (2) 33 R. R. 635 (7 Bing. 735).

1837.
May 26.

[29]

BERKLEY v. WATLING, NAVE, AND CRISP.

(7 Adol. & Ellis, 29—39; S. C. 2 N. & P. 178; 6 L. J. (N. S.) K. B. 195.)

Declaration, in assumpsit, stated that defendants W. and N. were
owners of a ship; that, in consideration that plaintiff at their request
shipped goods on board to be delivered to him, W. and N. promised to
deliver: breach, non-delivery. N. pleaded separately, and traversed the
shipment. On the trial, plaintiff produced a bill of lading, signed by
the captain of the ship, transmitted to plaintiff by W., stating the goods
to be shipped by W., to be delivered to plaintiff or his assigns. Proof
also was given to show that plaintiff held the bill for value. W. was the
managing owner:

Held, that N. might produce evidence that the goods were not shipped
in fact, and was not estopped by the bill of lading, supposing such
estoppel to exist in general, inasmuch as the plaintiff could support his
issue only by making W. his agent, and if W. was so, the plaintiff was
cognisant, through him, of the fact.

Quære, whether, generally, a bill of lading be conclusive evidence of
the shipment, as against the ship owner, in favour of a holder of the bill
for value. Semble, per LITTLEDALE, J., that it is not (1).

ASSUMPSIT. The declaration stated that the defendants,
before and at &c., to wit, 29th April, 1835, were owners of
a ship called the *Search*, then lying at Great Yarmouth, and
bound to Newcastle, and that the plaintiff, at their request,
caused to be shipped, in and upon the said ship, then lying
as aforesaid &c., and bound &c., of which John Blyth was
master for the then present voyage, divers goods, to wit 168
quarters of wheat, to be delivered at Newcastle to the plaintiff or
his assigns, he or they paying freight; that defendants, in
consideration &c., promised to deliver the goods at Newcastle,
plaintiff or his assigns paying freight; that afterwards, to wit
1st May, 1835, the ship departed from Yarmouth on the said
voyage, and afterwards, to wit 11th May, 1835, arrived at
Newcastle; but defendants did not deliver, &c.

The defendant Watling pleaded separately *non assumpsit*.
The two other defendants pleaded jointly. 1. *Non assumpsit*.
2. That the plaintiff did not cause the goods to be shipped in
and upon the said vessel. 3. That the defendants did convey,
&c. On these pleas issues were joined.

---

(1) This opinion was acted on by   is now unquestioned law. See also
the Court of Exchequer in *Jessel v.*   *McLean* and *Hope v. Fleming* (H. L.
Bath (1867) L. R. 2 Ex. 267, and   1871) L. R. 2 H. L. Sc. 128.—R. C.

On the trial before Tindal, Ch. J., at the Summer *Assizes for the town and county of Newcastle, 1835, a verdict was found for the plaintiff, subject to the opinion of this Court upon a case, which was substantially as follows :

The plaintiff was a corn factor, residing and carrying on business at Newcastle.   The defendant Watling was, during the years 1833, 1834, and 1835, a merchant residing at Great Yarmouth ; and, during that time, had several dealings with the plaintiff, in the way of consigning from Yarmouth, to the plaintiff at Newcastle, cargoes of corn for sale on commission. The ship *Search* had been engaged occasionally in bringing cargoes of corn from Yarmouth to Newcastle, from Watling to the plaintiff and other merchants and factors in Newcastle during those years : and, at the time of signing the bill of lading after mentioned, the three defendants were the owners of the *Search*, whereof John Blyth was the master, and Watling the managing owner at Yarmouth.

On 2nd May, 1835, the plaintiff received a bill of lading for 168 quarters of wheat, signed by Blyth, then the master of the *Search*, lying at Yarmouth, and bound on a voyage to Newcastle, of which bill of lading the following is an extract.

" Shipped, in good order and well conditioned, by John Watling, in and upon the good ship called the *Search*, whereof John Blyth is master, for this present voyage, and now lying in the port of Great Yarmouth and bound for Newcastle, 168 quarters of wheat, being marked," &c., " and are to be delivered in the like good order and well conditioned at the aforesaid port of New-castle," " unto Mr. John Berkley, or to his assigns, he or they paying freight for the said goods, nine shillings" &c.   *" In witness whereof, the master or purser of the said ship hath affirmed to two bills of lading," &c. Dated Great Yarmouth, 29th April, 1835.

This bill of lading was enclosed in a letter from Watling to the plaintiff, dated Yarmouth, 30th April, 1835, of which the following is an extract : " Anticipating that you can have no objection to the transhipment of the wheat per *Herring* to *Search*, I have done so, and annexed, or rather enclosed, you have the bill of lading. I have suffered more than once by wheat going

to Sunderland, and think you will approve of this arrangement."
" I should like to put 100 qrs. more on board, but you keep me
short of money."

Watling, by a letter dated Yarmouth, 18th April, 1835, had
inclosed a bill of lading for the same 168 quarters of wheat,
signed by the master of a vessel called the *Herring*, of which
letter the following is an extract : " The *Herring* is bound for
Sunderland with some anchors : and I have put 168 quarters of
wheat on board, as per annexed bill of lading, which you will
please insure for 350*l.*, and remit me a similar amount by
return." In answer to which, the plaintiff sent Watling 200*l.*,
as an advance on the wheat mentioned in the bill of lading, by a
letter dated 22nd April, 1835, which Watling received. Subsequently, Watling wrote and sent to the plaintiff a letter, dated
25th April, 1835, in which he acknowledged the receipt of 200*l.*,
observing, however, that it should have been another hundred ;
and added, " I will endeavour to get the *Herring* to go to your
quay." Also a second letter of 27th of April, 1835, in which he
said, " The *Herring* will not go to your quay ; and, as Sunderland
is likely to *prove a losing market, I purpose, with your permission, to reship the wheat into the *Search*, or some other vessel,
and do hope this will meet your approbation. The insurance can
be transferred. Waiting your reply, I remain," &c.

[*32]

On the 2nd of May the plaintiff wrote, and sent to Watling, a
letter of which the following is an extract : " Your wheat I think
will come to a good market, as we have an advance to-day ; you
never had reason to complain of my remittances, but you have
frightened me on many occasions ; and the delay in your shipments, after bill of lading, annoys me. Of course my capital
is limited and not large : the times have not enabled me either
to increase it : but, if you will not deprive me of confidence
in the shipping documents, and dispatch your shipments with
promptitude, I will let you be very little money out in your
consignments to me."

The *Search* afterwards sailed from Yarmouth, and arrived
at Newcastle without the wheat ; in consequence whereof the
plaintiff, by letter dated 20th May, 1835, applied to the defendant
Nave, as follows : " Mr. JAMES NAVE. As one of the owners of

the ship *Search*, I have to require of you the value of 168
quarters of wheat, shipped therein according to bill of lading to
my order, dated the 29th of April, the vessel having arrived here
without the wheat."

An answer, of which the following is an extract, was sent by
defendants' attorneys, dated May 27th : " SIR,—Mr. Nave has
handed to us your letter, to which he has requested us to reply.
As Mr. Watling, who was the ship's husband for the *Search*, has
left the town, we have to request that you will send the bill
of *lading to some one of your correspondents here, in order
that we may have an opportunity of inspecting the same. We
are &c., REYNOLDS AND PALMER."

The plaintiff wrote also on the 20th of May, 1835, to Mr. G.
D. Palmer, owner of the *Herring*, as follows : " SIR,—As owner
of the *Herring*, I have to require of you the value of 168
quarters of wheat, shipped by Mr. J. Watling of Yarmouth,
according to bill of lading transmitted to me, and dated 18th
of April, this vessel not having delivered the same."

The corn, if delivered at Newcastle by the *Search*, would have
been of the value of 360*l*. Watling was, and still is, indebted
to the plaintiff, over and above the 200*l*. advanced as aforesaid,
in the sum of 72*l*. 16*s*. 5*d*.

On the part of the defendants Nave and Crisp, evidence was
offered to show that, although the master signed the bill of lading
for the corn as aforesaid, yet no part of the corn was shipped on
board of the *Search*, as therein expressed. This evidence was
objected to on the part of the plaintiff, but was received, the
question as to its admissibility to be a question in this case. (The
case then stated parol evidence given to the above effect.) If the
COURT should think that the evidence was not admissible, the case
was to be considered as if such evidence had not been stated.

The question for the opinion of the COURT was, whether the
plaintiff was entitled to recover ?

W. H. Watson, for the plaintiff :

The question is, whether, when a bill of lading is handed
over for value, the ship-owner can say that the goods were
not shipped which the bill asserts to have been shipped. In

Howard *v. *Tucker* (1) it was held that, where a bill of lading
had been indorsed over for value, the ship-owners could not deny,
as against the indorsee, that freight had been paid, as stated in
the bill. In *Bates* v. *Todd* (2) TINDAL, Ch. J. held that a bill
of lading was not conclusive as between the actual shipper and
the ship-owner : but here the plaintiff is a holder for value ; and
to admit the evidence would be like admitting proof of want
of original consideration against a *bonâ fide* holder of a bill of
exchange. The effect of the trans-shipment from the *Herring*
to the *Search* can make no difference : it is analogous, merely,
to the substitution of one bill of exchange for another. The
plaintiff, perhaps, acted improperly in writing to the owner of
the *Herring ;* but that cannot prevent his being a holder of the
bill of lading of the *Search* for value. By the bill of lading the
captain admits the shipment and engages to convey. If it be
argued that the captain is agent for the ship-owners only after
the actual shipment, and that he is not authorised to sign the
bill of lading till that has taken place, the answer is, that the
acts of a general agent, exceeding the authority, bind the
principal, though the acts of a particular agent do not : Paley's
Prin. and Ag. 162 (3rd ed.). It is like an indorsement by an agent
who has a general authority to indorse from time to time ; that
binds the principal, though made, in the particular instance, contrary to his order. Now the captain is a general agent. If he sign
a bill of lading for particular goods, he binds the owner : the way

[*35]

to avoid this is to add "contents *unknown :" Abbott on Shipping,
217 (5th ed.). The Court will uphold the negotiability of bills of
lading. It is the constant practice to send them before the goods
arrive : and the receipt of them authorises the factor, by the
common law, to sell them, and, by stat. 6 Geo. IV. c. 94, to
pledge. The transferree of the bill is owner of the goods, to all
intents, as is laid down by BULLER, J. in *Lickbarrow* v. *Mason* (3).

(PATTESON, J. : Is there any instance of an action by a consignee of a bill of lading before the actual delivery of the goods?
With whom is the contract ?)

(1) 35 R. R. 418 (1 B. & Ad. 712).   (3) 1 R. R. 425 (2 T. R. 63 ; 6 East,
(2) 42 R. R. 766 (1 Moo. & Rob. 106).   22, *n.*).

The consignee is the party to enforce the contract against the ship-owners.

(PATTESON, J.: That seems not to be so: in *Moore* v. *Wilson* (1) it was held no variance to describe, in a declaration, the freight as payable by the consignor, though in fact payable by the consignee.)

In *Sargent* v. *Morris* (2), where the goods, by the bill of lading, were to be delivered to the consignor, and, in his name, to the consignee, it was held that an action for damage to the goods should, on the special form of the contract, be brought by the consignor, the consignee being there merely an agent; but, in general, the consignee sues.

(PATTESON, J.: That is after a delivery, which vests the property.)

Perhaps no instance of an action by the consignee before delivery is reported: but the bill of lading always represents the property; and advances are made on it.

(PATTESON, J.: This is assumpsit: what contract is there between the ship-owner and the assignee of the bill of lading? Is there any instance of a mere indorsee suing the ship-owner?)

As to the effect of an acknowledgment made to the party to whom *the goods are transferred, *Hawes* v. *Watson* (3) is an authority for the plaintiff.

[*36]

Wightman, contrà, for the defendants Nave and Crisp:

If the statement in the bill of lading had led to any act changing the situation of the parties, perhaps it might have bound the parties to the bill (4).   But, generally, such an admission is not conclusive: even a receipt is not so: *Graves* v. *Key* (5), *Skaife* v. *Jackson* (6).

(1) 1 R. R. 347 (1 T. R. 659).
(2) 22 R. R. 382 (3 B. & Ald. 277).
(3) 26 R. R. 448 (2 B. & C. 540).
(4) See the judgment in *Pickard*
v. *Sears*, p. 538, *ante* (6 Ad. & El. 474).
(5) 3 B. & Ad. 313.
(6) 3 B. & C. 421.

(LORD DENMAN, Ch. J.: A receipt is not a negotiable instrument.)

The negotiability could not make the bill of lading conclusive, where the situation of the parties was not changed. In *Howard* v. *Tucker* (1) Lord TENTERDEN, at Nisi Prius, pointed out that the indorsees of the bill of lading had probably, in consequence of the statement in it that the freight was paid, received it at a value which they would otherwise have thought inadequate. *Bates* v. *Todd* (2) shows that the bill is not conclusive between the consignor and the ship-owner : if it be not in all cases conclusive, then the question must be, in each instance, as to the effect it has had in changing the situation of parties. There is no instance of an action where there has actually been no shipment; it was suggested hypothetically in the earlier judgment of BULLER, J., in *Lickbarrow* v. *Mason* (3), where it is said that the consignee might sue the captain for his fraud. Here the attempt is to make the innocent ship-owners liable. The advance is made on the bill of lading of the *Herring* : Watling [*37] may be liable *for not sending the corn; but that does not affect the ship-owners. No change in the situation of the parties results from the bill of lading of the *Search*. The argument on the other side would indeed apply with more force against the owners of the *Herring*.

(PATTESON, J.: Suppose the consignor had brought the action, how could the bill of lading be conclusive in his favour ? The fact would be within his own knowledge. Then, how does the present plaintiff become a party, except by making Watling his agent ?)

That objection is conclusive; the defendants are sued only as ship-owners by the party who puts himself in the place of consignor.

W. H. Watson, in reply :

Dutton v. *Solomonson* (4) and *Browne* v. *Hodgson* (5) show that the property would be in the plaintiff immediately on the

(1) 35 R. R. 418 (1 B. & Ad. 712).   (3) 1 R. R. 425 (2 T. R. 75, 76).
(2) 42 R. R. 766 (1 Moo. & Rob.   (4) 7 R. R. 883 (3 Bos. & P. 582).
106).   (5) 2 Camp. 36.

shipping. He held the bill for value. It is scarcely disputed that the owners of the *Herring* would, in the original state of things, have been liable for not delivering. Then the plaintiff, having assented to the substituted contract, loses the right against them, but acquires one against the owners of the *Search*. The negotiability of the bill of lading appears from Abbott on Shipping, 383 (5th ed.).

(LITTLEDALE, J.: But your argument fails in this, that, whatever estoppel may exist generally against ship-owners, here Watling stands in a double capacity: he is agent to the plaintiff.)

He is shipper as well as owner: and the presumption of his performance of the duty of shipping the goods is the stronger. It does not, however, appear that the plaintiff knew Watling to be an owner. It is a case of consignor and consignee, not of principal and agent.

LORD DENMAN, Ch. J. :

[38]

The argument for the plaintiff is that the defendants, Nave and Crisp, are not entitled to disprove the shipment, because the bill of lading, signed by Blyth and transmitted by Watling, asserts the shipment. I think the evidence was admissible. The plaintiff was to prove that he had shipped the goods. This he could do only by proving that Watling was his agent, although the partner of the other two defendants. There is therefore nothing to prevent the defendants, Nave and Crisp, from showing that what the bill of lading asserted to have been done was in fact not done. This view of the case makes it unnecessary for us to determine the point which has been raised as to the extent and consequences of the negotiability.

LITTLEDALE, J.:

I am of the same opinion. The statement in the declaration is that the plaintiff caused the goods to be shipped, which is put in issue by the second plea. Then how does the plaintiff prove his allegation? He puts in a bill of lading, which certainly appears to be signed by the master; but, on the face of it, the goods are shipped by Watling. Then the plaintiff must prove

BERKLEY
v.
WATLING.

Watling to be his agent: by doing so, he supports the allegation. It turns out that in fact the goods were not shipped on board the *Search* at all. But the plaintiff says that the defendants, Nave and Crisp, are estopped from showing this, by the bill of lading signed by their own agent. How are they estopped? Watling knew the fact, and his knowledge is the plaintiff's knowledge. The plaintiff knowing the fact by Watling, his agent, how are the defendants, Nave and Crisp, estopped by what Watling does as their agent? Since, therefore, the plain-

[*39]

tiff, as shipper, is cognizant of the facts, we need *not say how far, on the general question, there is an estoppel. But, in my opinion, the bill of lading is not conclusive.

PATTESON, J.:

This is an action by the consignee in a bill of lading, not an indorsee. That makes a difference; though I recollect no instance of such an action being brought by an indorsee. If any such were brought, the plaintiff would have to state the original contract and the indorsement. Here that is not done. Nor does the declaration state the plaintiff to be consignee of goods shipped by another person, but that he, the plaintiff, caused to be shipped. If he did so, then the party who is shipper on the face of the instrument is the plaintiff's agent. Had the statement been that Watling had caused to be shipped, the case might have assumed a very different aspect. But, as it now stands, is the bill of lading to be conclusive between the plaintiff and the two other defendants? It is impossible so to hold, for the reasons already given by my Lord and my brother LITTLEDALE. This decision will not affect any question which may arise hereafter, as to the conclusiveness of a bill of lading between a ship-owner and an indorsee for value. I should be sorry to destroy the negotiability of the instrument. But the plaintiff is here the shipper in effect, and sues as shipper; and the bill of lading, made out by his agent, is not conclusive between him and the defendants Nave and Crisp.

Judgment for the defendants (1).

(1) Williams, J. was absent.

MECHELEN *v.* ELIZA WALLACE (1).

(7 Adol. & Ellis, 49—57; S. C. 2 N. & P. 224; 6 L. J. (N. S.) K. B. 217.)

1837.
May 6.

[49]

Declaration stated that defendant wished plaintiff to hire of her a house, and furniture for the same, at the rent of &c.; and thereupon, in consideration that plaintiff would take possession of the said house partly furnished, and would, if complete furniture were sent into the said house by defendant in a reasonable time, become tenant to defendant of the said house, with all the said furniture, at the aforesaid rent, and pay the same quarterly from a certain day, to wit &c., defendant promised plaintiff to send into the said house, within a reasonable time after plaintiff's taking possession, all the furniture necessary, &c.:

Held, that the defendant's agreement to send in furniture was an inseparable part of a contract for an interest in lands, and therefore came within stat. 29 Car. II. c. 3, s. 4, which, in the case of such contract, requires the agreement, or a memorandum thereof, to be in writing.

ASSUMPSIT. The declaration stated that whereas before and at the time of the making of the promise &c., the plaintiff was desirous and intended to hire and take as tenant a furnished house and premises suited for the convenient accommodation and reception of the plaintiff and his family, and of divers, to wit &c., female scholars and boarders, in order that a school, consisting of such number of boarders and scholars, might be carried on in and upon such furnished house and premises by the plaintiff's wife; of which desire and intention the defendant, before and at the time &c., had notice: "And whereas, also, the defendant at the same time was possessed of a certain house and premises in part furnished, and was desirous that the plaintiff should take and hire, at a certain rent, viz. 170*l.* per annum, the same house and premises, with the said furniture and all other furniture necessary for the completely furnishing the same for the purpose aforesaid; and thereupon, to wit on the 14th day of May, A.D. 1835, in consideration that the plaintiff, at the request of the defendant, would take possession of the same house and premises so partly furnished as aforesaid, and would, if the furniture necessary for the completely furnishing the said house and premises for the purpose aforesaid should be sent into the said house and premises by the defendant within a reasonable

(1) Commented on and distinguished by LUSH, J. in *Angell v. Duke* (1875) L. R. 10 Q. B. 174, 178, 44 L. J. Q. B. 78, 80.—R. C.

time, become the tenant to the *defendant of the said house and
premises, with all the furniture aforesaid, at the rent aforesaid,
and pay the same rent quarterly, commencing from a certain
day then in that behalf agreed upon, to wit the 25th day of the
said month of May, the defendant promised the plaintiff that she
the defendant would, within a reasonable time after the plaintiff
should have so taken possession of the same house and premises,
send into the said house and premises all the furniture necessary
for the completing of the furnishing of the said house with
furniture, of good quality, and suited for the purpose aforesaid,
to wit " &c. (describing the furniture to be sent in).   The
declaration then stated that plaintiff, relying,· &c., did, on
May 25th, at defendant's request, take possession of the said
house and premises so partly furnished, and remained in possession of the same until the expiration of such reasonable time,
&c., to wit &c. And, although plaintiff would have become
tenant as aforesaid, and paid rent as aforesaid, if defendant
would have sent in such furniture as aforesaid within such
reasonable time as aforesaid ; and although such reasonable time
elapsed long before the commencement of this suit, and plaintiff,
during such reasonable time, to wit &c., requested defendant to
send in such furniture ; and although defendant did, during such
reasonable time, to wit on &c., send into the said house and
premises divers, to wit twenty, articles of furniture ; yet &c.
Breach, that the articles so sent in were not of good quality, nor
suited for the purpose aforesaid ; but on the contrary &c. : and,
further, that defendant did not, within such reasonable time, &c.,
send into the said house and premises all the furniture necessary
to complete the furnishing, &c., but neglected &c., and a great

part, to *wit three fourths of the furniture necessary &c., never
was sent in : by means whereof the said house and premises
were and remained insufficiently furnished and unfit for the
purposes aforesaid, and plaintiff was thereby prevented from
having in the said house and premises such school as aforesaid,
&c. : alleging damage in various other ways.

Second plea, that the promise in the declaration mentioned
was and is part and parcel of a contract made by and between
plaintiff and defendant concerning the said tenement, and the

interest relating to the same, as in the said declaration appears; and that neither the said contract nor any memorandum or note thereof was or is in writing signed by defendant, or any other person thereunto by her lawfully authorised.   Verification.

MECHEL
v.
WALLAO

Demurrer, assigning for cause, among others, that the promise, as it appears by the declaration, is a promise relating only to personal chattels, and that the agreement to take possession of the said house and premises, and further to do as in the declaration is mentioned, is not the contract on which the action is brought, but the consideration of defendant's promise; and such contract, as appears in the declaration, has been performed, and is sufficient as a consideration without writing.   Joinder in demurrer.

John Henderson, for the plaintiff:

The fourth section of the Statute of Frauds, 29 Car. II. c. 3, is not available in this case.   Where there is an entire contract to do several things, some of which are within the statute, it applies to the whole; but here the promise declared upon is separate and single, and relates to personal *chattels only; the statute, therefore, does not take effect.   This distinction is supported by *The Earl of Falmouth* v. *Thomas* (1), where the statute was held to apply, because the land and the other subjects of contract were so incorporated together as to be inseparable.   In *Chater* v. *Beckett* (2), and *Thomas* v. *Williams* (3), where contracts, subject to the statute as to one of the matters promised, were held to be so altogether, the promises within and those not within the statute were indivisible.   And in *Wood* v. *Benson* (4), where those decisions were recognised, it was observed by Lord LYNDHURST, C. B., and BAYLEY, B., that in those cases an entire contract was set out in the declaration, but the proof failed as to a portion of it, by reason of the statute; consequently there was a variance.   In *Mayfield* v. *Wadsley* (5), where there was a contract for the interest in a farm, and for growing crops, and likewise for dead stock, it was held that the

[*52]

(1) 38 R. R. 584 (1 Cr. & M. 89; 3 Tyr. 26).

(2) 4 R. R. 418 (7 T. R. 201).

(3) 34 R. R. 535 (10 B. & C. 664).

(4) 37 R. R. 635 (2 Cr. & J. 94; 2 Tyr. 93).

(5) 3 B. & C. 357.

bargain for dead stock, being distinct from the rest of the
contract, was not affected by the statute. There it was contended (and a like suggestion may be made here) that the agreement for dead stock was subsidiary to the contract for the
interest in land; but the argument did not prevail. In the
present case, however, there is only one subject-matter of
contract in question. The defendant engages to send the
plaintiff furniture for a house. It is immaterial for the present
purpose, whether the furniture was to be supplied for a house or
for a ship. Supposing that the word "contract," in the fourth
section of the statute, means (like "agreement") the considera-

[*53]
tion as well as the promise, *which is rendered doubtful by the
comments on sect. 17 in *Egerton* v. *Mathews* (1), still the plaintiff
here is not seeking to charge the defendant with any "contract
or sale of lands, tenements or hereditaments, or any interest in
or concerning them;" but only with a contract to deliver
furniture. The "agreement," therefore, is not required to be
in writing. It is true that the consideration for the defendant's
contract was the taking of a house by the plaintiff; but that may
have been a good consideration, though the contract for such
taking was not testified by writing so that, according to the
statute, an action could have been brought upon it. The
consideration was executed by the plaintiff's taking possession:
and it is not to be presumed on these pleadings that he did not
sign an agreement for becoming tenant.

(Patteson, J. referred to *Harvey* v. *Grabham* (2), and Lord
Denman, Ch. J. to *Head* v. *Baldrey* (3).)

Maule, contrà :

The enactment in sect. 4 of the Statute of Frauds is, that no
action shall be brought to charge any person upon any contract
or sale of lands, or any interest in or concerning them, unless
the agreement upon which such action shall be brought, or some
memorandum thereof, shall be in writing, &c. It manifestly
treats "agreement" and "contract" as equivalent; and the

(1) 8 R. R. 489 (6 East, 307).　　　(3) 6 Ad. & El. 459.
(2) 5 Ad. & El. 61.

MECHELEN
v.
WALLACE.

question here is, whether the agreement, or contract, upon which it is sought to charge the defendant, be for lands or any interest in or concerning them.   The general rule is, that a contract is entire, and not to be separated ; the cases in which the application of that rule fails are where there are two contracts, *not [*54] one.   That was the ground of decision in *Mayfield* v. *Wadsley* (1). It cannot be said here that there was one contract that the defendant should send in furniture, another that the defendant should become tenant.   In the former case of *Mechelen* v. *Wallace* (2) *it [*55]

---

(1) 3 B. & O. 357.

(2) MECHELEN v. ELIZA WALLACE.

(7 Adol. & Ellis, 54, *n.*—55, *n.* ; S. C.
6 N. & M. 316.)

M. agreed verbally with W.'s agent to take a house of W., furnished, at 170*l.* a year rent, for the house and furniture, payable quarterly, and in advance. The house was furnished only in part, but the agent said that it should be completely furnished ; not, however, specifying any time. M. was let into possession within a month from the above treaty. After the expiration of a quarter, W. distrained for rent, the furniture not having been sent in as promised. M. brought trespass :

Held, that it was a question for the jury whether the agreement to pay rent was absolute, or on condition only of the furniture being sent in : that there was evidence upon which they might find it to have been conditional : and, therefore, that the distress was not justified.

TRESPASS for taking plaintiff's goods. Plea, Not guilty. On the trial before Alderson, B. at the Gloucester Spring Assizes, 1836, it appeared that, the defendant having a house to let, the plaintiff, in May, 1835, entered into a negotiation with one Wood, the defendant's agent, for taking it ; and it was agreed verbally

between Wood and the plaintiff that the latter should rent the house, furnished, and pay, for the house and furniture, 170*l.* a year, by quarterly payments, to be made in advance. At the time of this treaty the house was furnished in part only, but the agent said that it should be furnished completely, in a manner suitable to a lady's school. No time was fixed at which the furnishing was to be completed. The plaintiff entered on the 25th of May. The furniture was never put in. After the plaintiff had entered, a written agreement was tendered for his signature ; but he (by letter to the agent) replied that he declined executing an agreement for a house which was not furnished, complained that furniture had not been sent in, and stated that he had relied upon the honour of Wood for this being performed. In September, 1835, the defendant distrained for 42*l.* 10*s.* The learned Judge left it to the jury to say, whether the payment of rent, as above stated, had been agreed for between the plaintiff and defendant absolutely, or on condition, only, of the house being properly furnished ; and, in the latter case, whether or not the defendant had broken the condition. Verdict for the plaintiff.

Talfourd, Serjt. now moved for a new trial, on the grounds that the jury were misdirected, and that the

1836.
April 16.

[54, *n.*]

MECHELEN
v.
WALLACK.

was expressly held that the undertakings of the respective parties could not be separated. There is one contract, to do several things, a part of which is within the statute. It is not necessary that the breaches alleged should relate to that part. The argument of the defendant's counsel in *Chater* v. *Beckett* (1) (where *Lord Lexington* v. *Clarke* (2) was cited), and the judgments

[*56]

of *Lord KENYON and GROSE, J., who held that an agreement void in part by the statute could not be severed, apply strongly to this case. Supposing here, that the promise to take the house were cancelled, the remaining promise to send in

verdict was against evidence. The agreement for taking the premises and paying 170*l.* rent was a complete bargain; there was a time fixed from which the rent was to run, and the plaintiff had taken actual possession. The stipulation for furnishing, if it rested on any thing more than the honour of Wood (which the plaintiff appears by his letter to have relied upon), could, at most, be only the subject of a cross action. If this were otherwise, the defendant's claim

[*55, n.]

of *rent might be answered as long as a single chair or table was not perfectly completed and sent in. There was no evidence that the agreement for rent was intended to be conditional. *Reguart* v. *Porter* (3) was cited for the plaintiff at the trial; but there the rent was to commence at a future day, and the works engaged for by the landlord were to be done immediately; the performance of these, therefore, might justly be regarded as a condition precedent in point of time. In note (4) to *Pordage* v. *Cole*, 1 Wms. Saund. 320 a, *Mr. Serjt. Williams* lays it down that, "If a day be appointed for payment of money, or part of it, or for doing any other act, and the day is to happen, or may happen, before the thing which is the consideration of the money, or other act, is to be performed, an action may be brought for the money, or for not doing such

other act before performance; for it appears that the party relied upon his remedy, and did not intend to make the performance a condition precedent: and so it is where no time is fixed for performance of that, which is the consideration of the money or other act:" and many authorities are cited.

LORD DENMAN, Ch. J. :

If the performance of the furnishing was not left to the defendant's honour, the stipulation respecting it is part of the agreement. The observation upon it in the letter to Wood is only reproach to him. In my opinion there was evidence that the payment of rent was intended to be conditional; the house to be rented was to be a furnished house and no other.

PATTESON, J. :

I do not see how the contracts for rent and for furnishing can be separated. I think, with my Lord, that there was evidence of the agreement being conditional.

COLERIDGE, J. concurred.

(LITTLEDALE, J. was absent.)

Rule refused.

(1) 4 R. R. 418 (7 T. R. 203).
(2) 2 Vent. 223.
(3) 33 R. R. 537 (7 Bing. 451).

furniture would appear without reason or consideration. *Bird* v.
Higginson (1), where the demise of a messuage without deed
was held void, because coupled with a license to shoot and fish,
is analogous to the present case. *Wood* v. *Benson* (2) is consistent
with the argument for the defendant.

(LORD DENMAN, Ch. J.: It is merely an exemplification of the
doctrine in *Mayfield* v. *Wadsley* (3).)

Carrington v. *Roots* (4) shows that a contract void by the
clause now in question cannot be the ground of an action, even
though such action be not brought expressly to enforce the
contract.

(He was then stopped by the COURT.)

J. Henderson, in reply:

The former case of *Mechelen* v. *Wallace* (5) turned on the
question, whether an actual renting at 170*l*. had commenced;
and it was there decided only that the furnishing was a condition precedent. The question here is, whether the contract
insisted upon in this action, that is, the defendant's promise to
furnish the house, affects an interest in land. The ground of
decision in *Bird* v. *Higginson* (1) was, that the demise was
entire. The argument for the defendant here assumes that
the alleged contract would oblige her, not only to send in furniture, but to let a house. No such obligation is suggested in
the plaintiff's *pleading, or would be established by a judgment   [*57]
in his favour.

(PATTESON, J.: The declaration states that the plaintiff was
to become tenant to the defendant, at a certain rent, the payment
to commence from a day agreed upon.)

The only promise alleged to be made by the defendant, is to
send in furniture.

(1) 2 Ad. & El. 696; affirmed on   2 Tyr. 93).
error, *Bird* v. *Higginson*, 6 Ad. & El.   (3) 3 B. & C. 357.
824.   (4) 2 M. & W. 248.
  (2) 37 R. R. 635 (2 Cr. & J. 94;   (5) *Ante*, p. 673, *n*.

MECHELEN
v.
WALLACE.

MECHELEN
v.
WALLACE.

LORD DENMAN, Ch. J.:

The bare statement of the case on the pleadings shows that the contract in question does relate to an interest in lands. The judgment must be for the defendant.

LITTLEDALE, J.:

The declaration states, as the consideration for the defendant's promise, that the plaintiff was to become tenant to the defendant of the house and furniture together, if certain things should be performed; that is, if the furniture should be sent into the house in reasonable time. It cannot be contended that there was not an agreement for an interest in the land, and, that being so, the defendant's promise came within the statute.

PATTESON, J.:

It is clear that the plaintiff, at any rate, contracted for an interest "in or concerning" "lands, tenements, or hereditaments" (1).

Judgment for the defendant.

1837.
May 30.

[80]

ECKSTEIN AND ANOTHER *v.* REYNOLDS.

(7 Adol. & Ellis, 80—82 ; S. C. 2 N. & P. 256; 6 L. J. (N. S.) K. B. 198.)

Tender, as follows. Defendant's agent told plaintiff that he had called to tender 8*l.* in settlement of defendant's account; plaintiff answered that he would take nothing less than the bill, which defendant's agent produced at the time, amounting to 19*l.* :

Held, that the question whether this tender was conditional or unconditional, was proper to be left to the jury.

DEBT for goods sold and delivered, &c. Pleas, *nunquam indebitatus*, except as to 8*l.*, and, as to that, a tender. On the trial before Lord Denman, Ch. J., at the London sittings after Michaelmas Term, 1835, the defendant, in support of his plea of tender, called a witness, who stated that he had tendered to one of the plaintiffs 8*l.*, saying that he had called to tender 8*l.* in settlement of Reynolds's account; that the plaintiff said he would take nothing less than his bill; and that, at the time of this conversation, the witness produced the bill, which (after

(1) Williams, J. was absent.

deducting for payments allowed by the plaintiff) amounted to   ECKSTEIN
19*l.* 5*s.* 6*d.* The LORD CHIEF JUSTICE left it to the jury whether   *v.*
this was a conditional or an unconditional tender, expressing   REYNOLDS.
his own opinion that it was conditional; but adding that, if the
words "in settlement" merely meant "in payment," the tender
was good, for that this was the meaning of every tender. The
jury found that it was unconditional, and gave a verdict for
the defendant on both issues. In Hilary Term, 1836, *Thesiger*
obtained a rule for a new trial.

   Alexander (with whom was *C. C. Jones*), now showed cause:

   It is true that a tender, under circumstances which, if the
plaintiff accept it, preclude him from proceeding further, is not
valid. Here the plaintiff would not be so precluded. At all
events, the finding of the jury disposes of the question; for, if
any expression *used in a commercial transaction be ambiguous,   [*81]
the jury are to decide upon its meaning: *Clayton* v. *Gregson* (1),
Bold v. *Rayner* (2). If the words used had been "as a settlement," they would have been stronger, though, perhaps, not
conclusively conditional. The fair construction is, that the
money was offered by the defendant, in order to discharge what
he considered to be the debt. But that left the plaintiffs at
perfect liberty to proceed for the residue, if they considered
that more was due. In *Evans* v. *Judkins* (3) the tender was
held bad, because made only upon condition that the plaintiff
would accept it as the balance due. Whether that point was
put to the jury or not, does not appear. In *Read* v. *Goldring* (4)
the party tendering said that he was come "to settle" the
business between the defendant and the plaintiff; and, a verdict
being given for the defendant, the Court refused a rule for
a nonsuit.

   (He was then stopped by the COURT.)

   Turner (with whom was *Thesiger*), *contrà* :

   The plaintiff would have been precluded from proceeding if
he had accepted the tender under these circumstances; and,

(1) 5 Ad. & El. 302 ; 6 N. & M. 694.   (3) 4 Camp. 156.
(2) 1 M. & W. 343 ; Tyr. & Gr. 820.   (4) 14 R. R. 594 (2 M. & S. 86).

ECKSTEIN
v.
REYNOLDS.

therefore, the tender is invalid : *Evans* v. *Judkins* (1), *Mitchell* v. *King* (2), *Strong* v. *Harvey* (3), *Cheminant* v. *Thornton* (4), *Peacock* v. *Dickerson* (5). The words " in settlement " imply that it was to be understood that the dispute was put an end to if the money

[*82]

were accepted. *The jury should have been so instructed. At any rate, the verdict is against the evidence (6).

LORD DENMAN, Ch. J. :

Read v. *Goldring* (7) is like a case which I was going to suggest. Suppose a man should begin by saying, I am come to settle, and should then go on to make an offer of the money, that could not vitiate the tender ; yet, what difference can it make at which part of the conversation the expression occurs? The cases cited by *Mr. Turner* admitted of no ambiguity : here there was enough of ambiguity to make the matter fit for a jury, and they have decided it.

LITTLEDALE, J. :

The question, whether a tender be conditional or unconditional, is not necessarily for the Judge. Some cases are clear, others not : the Judge is not bound to take the decision on himself as a matter of law.

PATTESON, J. concurred.

Rule discharged (8).

1837.
June 1.

[95]

REX *v.* STARKEY.

(7 Adol. & Ellis, 95—108 ; S. C. 2 N. & P. 169 ; W. W. & D. 502 ; 6 L. J. (N. S.) K. B. 202.)

B., being entitled to a market in the manor of K., which was held in the public street on B.'s soil, removed it to another site in K., which site he had demised, without demising the franchise, for a term of years. Per LITTLEDALE, J., the removal was bad, because the lord of the market ought to be owner of the soil in which the market is held.

By all the COURT : The removal was at any rate bad, unless the public

(1) 4 Camp. 156.
(2) 40 R. R. 810 (6 Car. & P. 237).
(3) 3 Bing. 304.
(4) 2 Car. & P. 50.
(5) 2 Car. & P. 51, *n.*
(6) The action was brought in the Palace Court, whence the defendant

removed it by *habeas corpus ;* it was, therefore, contended that the smallness of the damages would be no objection to a new trial on the ground last taken.

(7) 14 R. R. 594 (2 M. & S. 86).
(8) Williams, J. was absent.

had the same privilege in the new market as in the old : and therefore, it appearing that no toll had ever been taken in the old market, but that the lease, after a covenant by the lessees to allow the soil to be used solely for the market, empowered them to impose rents at their discretion for the liberty of selling in the market, the COURT held that the removal was bad, and that the site of the old market, on the King's highway, might be used on market days as it was before the removal.

INDICTMENT for erecting and continuing a stall in a certain street called Church Street, in the parish of Keighley, in York-shire, being the King's common highway for horses, coaches, &c., whereby the highway was obstructed. Second count, like the first, laying the obstruction in a certain other street called Church Green. Plea, Not guilty.

On the trial before Lord Denman, Ch. J., at the York Spring Assizes, 1836, it appeared that a market had been held in the *locus in quo*, which was within the manor of Keighley, till the time of the attempted removal of the market, hereafter men-tioned, by the Earl of Burlington, who was lord of the manor of Keighley, and who claimed under a charter of Edward I. to Henry de Kyghelay, by which the King confirmed and granted to the said H. de K. that he and his heirs for ever might hold a market every week, on the Wednesday, at his manor of Kyghelay, and an annual fair, &c.; and that the aforesaid Henry and his heirs for ever might hold the aforesaid market and fair at his aforesaid manor, with all liberties and free customs to such like market and fair appertaining. The market had been held, and stalls, &c., erected, on the market day, as far back as could be recollected, without any tolls, stallage, or piccage being taken. In 1832, a committee of the inhabitants was formed, under the sanction of the Earl *of Burlington, for erecting a new market-place in another part of the town, within the manor, being land belonging to the Earl. Buildings for the convenience of the market were commenced; and, in 1833, the Earl granted a lease of the intended site to certain of the committee.

[*96]

This lease (1) was an indenture, dated 13th August, 1833, between George Augustus Henry, Earl of Burlington, of the

---

(1) This lease was not produced on the trial, the prosecutor insisting merely on the removal of the market *de facto.* But, on the argument in Banc, it was agreed, at the suggestion of the COURT, that, for the purpose of determining the question finally, the lease should be considered as put in.

first part, and John Greenwood and four others, of the second
part; and it witnessed that the Earl of Burlington (in consideration of the rents, covenants, &c., thereinafter reserved and
contained on the part and behalf of Greenwood, &c., and of the
works, &c., thereinafter stipulated and covenanted to be erected,
&c., by them on the demised premises), in exercise of all powers
and authorities vested in him, or anywise enabling him in that
behalf, did direct, limit, and appoint, grant, demise, lease, and
to farm let, unto John Greenwood, &c., their executors, administrators, and assigns, all that piece or parcel of land situate in &c.,
as the same was then marked and set out for the purpose of
erecting a new market place thereon for the town of Keighley,
measuring &c., and containing &c., and also the right of a road
of the width of &c., from and out of the street called &c., to lead
into the said intended new market place, at the centre part &c.,
" together also with the privileges which the said G. A. H., Earl
of B., may have in obliging persons exposing goods *for sale
openly in any of the different streets in Keighley aforesaid to
remove the same into the said intended new market place so to
be erected as aforesaid ; to have and to hold the said piece or
parcel of ground, right of road, and premises hereby demised or
intended to be, with the appurtenances," to John Greenwood,
&c., their executors, administrators, and assigns, from 24th of
May, 1833, for sixty years, at the yearly rent of 10l. And the
said John Greenwood, &c., for themselves, their heirs, executors,
administrators, and assigns, thereby covenanted with the Earl
of Burlington, and the person or persons to be entitled to the
reversion, to pay the rent, and (immediately, or as soon as
circumstances would allow) to erect and finish a market place
intended to be erected and then begun, " and all requisite con-
veniences for using the said premises as and for a general market
for the town of Keighley," and lay out therein 1,000l. at least,
and also that J. Greenwood, &c., their executors, administrators,
and assigns, " shall and will, at all times hereafter (when the
said market has been completed), appropriate and use the said
premises as and for a general market for the said town and
manor of Keighley, and the buying, selling, and dealing in
marketable commodities in open market, as now used in the

[*97]

open markets held in the said town; and that they, their
executors, administrators, and assigns, shall not nor will, at any
time hereafter, use or employ the said premises for any other
use, purpose, or trade whatsoever, without the previous licence
and consent in writing of the said Earl of Burlington, his heirs,
appointees, or assigns, or such person or persons so for the time
being to be entitled as aforesaid; and also, particularly, that
the said premises shall be open for *public resort and the   [*98]
purpose of such markets, on such days of the week as the said
markets and the fairs of the said town or manor of Keighley are
now held, and any other days or times, weekly or otherwise, as
the said John Greenwood," &c., "their executors, administrators,
and assigns, shall choose so to use the same: during which
periods of open market, all persons shall be at liberty to attend
the same, and enter in and upon the said premises for the
purpose of buying and bartering in the said markets, without
the let, molestation, or hindrance, or necessity of licence first
had and obtained of or by the said J. G.," &c., "their executors,
administrators, and assigns; but, nevertheless, with full power,
liberty, and authority, for them the said" J. G., &c., "their
executors, administrators, and assigns, to make all such orders
and regulations for the maintenance and good management of
the said markets, and the renting of the stalls or other con-
veniences thereof, and imposing rents or other sums as and for
licence and permission of vending, selling, or exposing goods to
sale on the said premises, to deny entrance to the said premises
for any such purpose to all persons not so authorised, and the
exclusive enjoyment of all rents and profits to arise thereby, and
of and from the said premises, as to them the said" J. G., &c.,
"their executors, administrators, and assigns, shall seem meet
and proper." And John Greenwood, &c., for themselves, their
heirs, executors, and administrators, covenanted with the Earl,
his heirs, appointees, and assigns, or the parties entitled to the
reversion, to repair, &c., the new market place and buildings:
and liberty was reserved to the Earl, his heirs, &c., to enter
and view: and power of re-entry, to determine the term on non-
performance of the covenants, to the Earl, his *heirs, &c.; with   [*99]
other covenants and provisoes not material here.

On the 9th of June, 1834, a notice of that date, signed by an
agent of the Earl of Burlington, and also by the steward and two
bailiffs of the Keighley manor court, was read publicly in the old
market place, and on the site of the intended new market, reciting
that the Earl had found it expedient for the public convenience
that the market should be removed, and held in a more convenient place within the manor, and announcing that, on
Wednesday, 25th June then instant, and upon every other market
day following, until other notice should be given, the market
would be held in the new market, and that, after the notice, all
persons who should enter in or upon the public streets for the
purpose of using them as a market overt, or should set down any
cart or carts, or any other thing containing goods for sale, or set
up any stall or table, or erect any stand for the purpose of
exposing goods to sale, in any other place within the manor, and
not in the new market place, would thereby become trespassers,
and liable for any obstruction thereby created, and to such actions
at law as the lord of the manor and owner of the market would
be thereupon entitled to bring. Copies were also posted in the
streets of Keighley.

Another notice, dated 29th January, 1835, signed by the clerk
of the new market, appointed by the lessees, was, by the direction
of the lessees, posted in the streets of Keighley and the neighbourhood, announcing that the new market was toll free, and
that persons frequenting it were subject only to the regulations
and order of the clerk of the market, who would direct in what
[*100]   manner, *and in which place, goods should be therein exposed
for sale.

It appeared that, between the publication of these two notices,
and ever since, a market had in fact been held, on the old market
days, in the new market place, and that, for several weeks, tolls,
whether market tolls or for stallage did not distinctly appear, had
been taken, but that no tolls of any kind had been demanded
after the second notice. On Wednesday, 25th March, 1835, the
defendant put up a stall in the old market place, which was a
public highway, and where it had been customary to set up stalls
in the market in the same way on market days. This was the
obstruction complained of in the indictment. The defendant's

counsel contended that the evidence did not establish a rightful removal of the market. The LORD CHIEF JUSTICE reserved the point, and directed the jury to find for the Crown, if they were of opinion that the Earl of Burlington was lord of the market and manor, and that an obstruction of the public highway in fact existed. Verdict for the Crown. In Easter Term, 1836, *Alexander* obtained a rule *nisi* for entering a verdict for the defendant, on the point reserved.

REX
v.
STARKEY.

Cresswell, Wightman, and *Baines* now showed cause (1) :

The demand of tolls in the new market was not persisted in ; and, if illegal, might be resisted : the question, therefore, is simply whether the lord of the manor, having a right to a market within the manor, might remove the market to a new site within the manor. *Dixon* *v. *Robinson* (2), *Curwen* v. *Salkeld* (3), and *Rex* v. *Cotterill* (4), show decisively that he may ; and that a party persisting in the use of the old market, after the removal, is liable to an action of trespass or to indictment. It is true that the site of the new market is leased for a term : but, if the market had not been removed, and the site of the old market had been leased, the market would have still continued.

[*101]

(LITTLEDALE, J. : Parties frequenting the new market would come there at the risk of being treated as trespassers.)

That objection would go the length of showing that the site of the old market could not be leased without destroying the market. But, in fact, the land is leased for the purposes of the new market only ; and it appears that it is so used. The lessees could not call this a trespass. The land might have been let, excepting the market days : here the exception is of the right to exclude from the market. It will be said that the lease gives to the lessees the power of exacting rent for stalls, and that, therefore, the new market is less free than the old one : but the lord was entitled to exact stallage at any time, even in the old

(1) The case was argued on June 1st and 2nd, and decided on the latter day.
(2) 3 Mod. 107. And see *De Rutzen*
v. *Lloyd*, 5 Ad. & El. 456.
(3) 7 R. R. 510 (3 East, 538).
(4) 1 B. & Ald. 67.

market, in right of the soil; and such a right is not lost by non-user. Thus, if the land be borough-English, the stallage and picage will descend to the youngest son, but the market to the heir at common law: 3 Bac. Abr. 556, Fairs and Markets, (D), note (a), (ed. 7, 1832); *The Mayor of Northampton* v. *Ward* (1). A plea that no payment had been made for stalls from time immemorial would be bad.

[*102]

(LORD DENMAN, Ch. J.: *In 15 Viner's Abridgment, 245, Market, (B), pl. 3, it is said, "the stallage must be certain;" for which reference is made to the argument of the Solicitor-General, *Finch*, in *Rex* v. *Mayor of London* (2), who cites the Year Book, Mich. 9 Hen. VI. f. 45, pl. 28 (3).)

That is true of tolls only, properly so called.

(LITTLEDALE, J.: If the soil can be granted away, and yet the market remain in the grantor, the party using the market might be subject to two actions.)

That would be for two different claims: the division is recognised in the case of the land being borough-English. If the lord had removed to a place which he had not demised, he might have claimed stallage in the new market as well as the old: then what difference can it make, that he has assigned over that property in virtue of which he could have claimed the stallage? Besides, it does not appear that here the lord has reserved the market to himself; the lease passes all his rights; there is, therefore, a mere substitution, during the term, of one lord for another. The lord might have hired land of another for the purpose of holding his market. Again, if the market be less free than before, the person using it may resist the new exaction; and that is the proper way of trying the question. Or he may resist the lord's authority, as owner of the market, on the ground that the lord no longer gives the proper protection and immunities. So he might sell without the limits of the market, if room were not left within them: *Prince* v. *Lewis* (4). But he cannot insist upon the permanence of the market on the old site. Or, if the lord have

---

(1) 2 Str. 1238; *S. C.* 1 Wils. 107.   (3) *Prior of B. in London* v. *Barton.*
(2) 2 Show. 266.   (4) 29 R. R. 265 (5 B. & C. 363).

been guilty of extortion, or have removed to an inconvenient place, the franchise *may be forfeited by him, and revoked by *scire facias:* 8 Bac. Abr. 555, Fairs and Markets, (C) ; per Lord ELLENBOROUGH (1) and ABBOTT, J. (2) in *Rex* v. *Cotterill.*

Alexander and *Bliss* (with whom was *R. C. Hildyard*), *contrà:*

If the prosecutor has failed in establishing a legal removal of the market, the defendant is entitled to an acquittal : *Rex* v. *Smith* (3), *Holcroft* v. *Heel* (4). Now, the removal is not properly made unless the lord was entitled, not only to the place where the market was originally held, but to the place where he proposes to hold it in future. It is conceded that the lord of a market may remove to another place in the manor, &c., within which the market is granted, provided it be to a place which is his own soil, or over which he himself has as full rights as he had in the relinquished site. This is all that *Dixon* v. *Robinson* (5), *Curwen* v. *Salkeld* (6), and *Rex* v. *Cotterill* (7) establish. Here the site of the old market is out of the lord's possession for a term, during which he cannot perform his duty to the parties frequenting the market, or secure their immunities. The latter fact is clear, inasmuch as for several weeks toll was exacted by the lessees of the new site ; and their subsequent waiver could be no protection to parties resisting any future exaction of the same nature. It may be inferred from the language of Lord ELLENBOROUGH in *Curwen* v. *Salkeld* (6), and from that of ABBOTT, Ch. J. in *Prince* v. *Lewis* (8), that the lord cannot *remove to a place not equally convenient, in all respects, with the original site. So in *Mosley* v. *Walker* (9) BAYLEY, J. said, " I take it to be implied in the terms in which a market is granted, that the grantee, if he confine it to particular parts within a town, shall fix it in such parts as will from time to time yield to the public reasonable accommodation ; and that if the place once allotted ceases to give reasonable accommodation, he is bound, if he has land of his own, to appropriate land on which

[*104]

---

(1) 1 B. & Ald. 75.

(2) 1 B. & Ald. 79.

(3) 6 R. R. 842 (4 Esp. 109).

(4) 1 Bos. & P. 400.

(5) 3 Mod. 107.

(6) 7 R. R. 510 (3 East, 538).

(7) 1 B. & Ald. 67.

(8) 29 R. R. 265 (5 B. & C. 363).

(9) 31 R. R. 146 (7 B. & C. 40, 55).

to hold it; or if not, to get land from other people in order that
the market which was originally granted for the benefit of the
public, as well as for the benefit of the grantee, may be effectually
held; and that the public may have the benefit which it was
originally intended they should derive from it." Now, here, the
lease shows, at the utmost, only a right of action in the lessor
if the new market be impeded : but how can this be a good
substitute for the right which the public had, in the old market,
to enforce their own privileges directly ? In fact, the lease
grants to the lessees authority to impose rents, not only on
stalls (which rent probably could not have been imposed in the
old market against the usage, and after the dedication for a long
time) but "for licence and permission of vending, selling, or
exposing goods to sale on the said premises," and to deny
entrance for such purpose to persons not so authorised. That
allows the lessees to exact tolls, properly so called, and to exclude
parties refusing to .pay them. But there are no tolls in the old
market : nor could any be legally claimed there ; for they are
not incident to a market unless expressly given : Com. Dig.

[*105] Market, (F 1), and the charter of *Edward I. does not give
them, nor is any usage shown. Besides, the market not being
leased, the correction of it will be in the original lord, the lessor,
while the market tolls and its soil will, under the lease, be vested
in others. It is said that the public may, if the new market
place be inconvenient, use ground without the limits : but it does
.not appear that there is any such ground which can be used. It
is also said that a *scire facias* would be the appropriate remedy for
the lord's breach of duty: but that point need not be discussed ;
for, the prosecutors, having raised the question by indicting for
a nuisance, are bound in the first instance to establish all those
circumstances upon which the alleged guilt depends. They
must, then, show that the old market place has, by law, ceased
to exist.

(They were then stopped by the COURT.)

LORD DENMAN, Ch. J. :

This is an indictment for an obstruction : and it appears that
the defendant's act would be justifiable, except for the supposed

removal of the market. The question therefore is, whether the market has been so removed as to make that use of the old market, which was proper before the removal, a nuisance. Now the removal is illegal, if the public have been deprived by it of any right. It is unnecessary to go through all the clauses of the lease, or discuss the several points which have been raised as to the rights in the soil and market. There is one clause which makes it impossible for us to say that the market has been well removed. A power is given to the lessees to impose rents, at discretion, for the licence and permission of vending, selling, and exposing to sale. There is no evidence that, in the old market, there was even any *rent for stalls, much less that it was certain, and least of all that there was any payment exacted for exposing to sale. That is so essential an use of the market, that the creation of a discretionary power to exact payments for doing it cannot be sustained. I expected that the clause would end with giving the lessees the same power, as lords during the term, which the lessor had. But here is a discretionary power to impose rents ; and, even as to the stallage, I am not prepared to say that, when that appears to have never been paid, a claim can be made to it by virtue of the ownership of the soil. A market may be beneficial to the grantee, though there be neither tolls nor stallage : it may be useful to him that the public should resort to the place, though without paying. A right to the market, therefore, does not necessarily give the power of exacting tolls. Consequently I am of opinion that the removal is not good ; and that no nuisance has been committed by resorting to the old market, which still exists till a removal has been duly made.

[*106]

LITTLEDALE, J. :

I agree in the construction put by my Lord upon the clause in the lease. But, independently of that point, I own that, if the lord had leased the site, granting to the lessees precisely the same powers which he himself had, I should have said that the market was not well removed. The market must still be held in the soil of the lord. It is true that the soil, if borough-English, would descend one way, and the right to the market

[*107]

another : that is the act of the law ; but the division cannot be made by the act of parties.   When the law creates the difficulty, we must deal with it as well as we can : and the principle of this distinction, *between the act of law and the act of parties, has been recognised from *Wild's* case (1) downwards.   The lord is to have the correction of the market : but how can he have that when he has not the soil ?   It may perhaps be answered that the lease, substantially, gives nothing to the lessees but the correction.   But how can the public know that?   The lessees may indeed be liable to the Earl of Burlington for breach of covenant : but the public can take no advantage of it.   The language of Bayley, J. in *Mosley* v. *Walker* (2) shows that the lord must retain the power over the soil.   I am of opinion, therefore, that the market was not well removed, the soil of the place to which it was removed having been parted with by the owner of the franchise.   The lord could not, in such case, sue for the disturbance of the franchise ; for the consideration which he gives to the public for the market is the correction which he exercises ; and that he cannot exercise where he is not owner as well as lord.

Patteson, J. :

I think, on one short ground, that the market was not well removed.   I take it to be quite clear that, when the lord removes, the new market must be as unrestricted and free as the old one.   It is conceded that, in the old one, no market tolls were exacted from either buyer or seller.   I do not enter into the question, whether the lord could now exact stallage : much less do I say that he could.   But he gives the power to impose a rent in respect of selling : so that the public clearly would not have the same right in the new market as in the old one.   Had

[*108]

*we not seen the lease, we might have had some doubt ; but, on the terms of the lease, there can be none.   If the lease had stopped at the words, " as now used in the open markets held in the said town," it might have been well enough ; but afterwards come the words, " during which periods " &c., where the

(1) 8 Co. Rep. 78 b.   See Co. Litt.   (2) 31 R. R. at p. 155 (7 B. & C.
147 b, 164 b.   55).

exemption from the necessity of licence by the lessees is
expressly confined to the "buying and bartering," and the
licence to sell is made subject to a discretionary rent.

WILLIAMS, J. concurred.

Rule absolute.

TAYLERSON *v.* PETERS AND ANOTHER.

(7 Adol. & Ellis, 110—114 ; S. C. 2 N. & P. 622 ; W. W. & D. 644 ; 1 Jur. 497.)

A tenant of a farm, having remained a few days after the expiration of
his term, and after entry by a new tenant, went away, leaving a cow and
some pigs, but giving no further intimation of a purpose to return, or to
continue holding any part of the farm : Held, that the landlord could
not justify distraining the goods so left for arrears of rent under stat.
8 Ann. c. 14, ss. 6, 7.

TRESPASS for seizing and taking away cattle, goods, and
chattels, of the plaintiff. Plea, the general issue. On the trial
before Lord Denman, Ch. J., at the York Spring Assizes, 1836,
it appeared that the animals in question, a cow and some pigs,
of the value, altogether, *of 17*l*. 16*s*., were taken as a distress
for rent due from the plaintiff for a farm and buildings. The
plaintiff had duly received notice to quit on May 13th, 1835,
when his time of holding expired. The distress was put in
May 22nd. Between May 13th and May 22nd, the plaintiff,
who still remained on the premises, was asked by Welford, the
incoming tenant, whose term had commenced, when he meant
to leave ; he replied that he did not know ; but before the distress he went away, removing part of his property, but leaving
the cow and pigs on the farm. He did not ask Welford's permission to leave them ; nor did he, in going away, state any
thing as to his intentions. No question was specifically left to
the jury as to the giving up of possession by the plaintiff (1).
The new tenant entered, but did not obtain complete possession
before May 22nd. On that day, and before the distress was put
in, he had possession of the whole farm, unless there was a continued possession by the plaintiff as after mentioned. A verdict
was found for the defendant ; but in the next Term a motion was

(1) The principal dispute in the   parties who acted in making the
case was on the authority of the   distress.

TAYLERSON
v.
PETERS.

made (by leave reserved) to enter a verdict for the plaintiff. The only point raised, on which the Court ultimately gave any decision, was, whether the distress, made after the expiration of the term as above stated, was justified by stat. 8 Ann. c. 14, s. 6 (1). A rule *nisi* having been granted,

[112]

Cresswell and *Wightman* now showed cause:

The plaintiff remained in possession of a part of the farm, by keeping his cattle there, down to the time of the distress. If nothing was left to the jury on this point, still the Court will not now assume that the plaintiff had wholly given up possession. It is true that he had removed part of his goods, but some remained. Will the Court say that, if he had merely withdrawn himself, the possession would not have continued? *Nuttall* v. *Staunton* (2) shows that, to render the statute applicable, it is not necessary for the tenant to continue occupying the whole premises, or to hold them adversely. There the tenant held on by the landlord's permission. In *Bearan* v. *Delahay* (3), where the tenant, according to the custom of the country, left his away-going crop in barns upon the farm after the expiration of his term, it was held that (independently of the statute) a distress might be made of the crop so left, the · landlord's right continuing as to that part of the farm which the tenant still occupied.

---

(1) Stat. 8 Ann. c. 14, s. 6. "And whereas tenants *pur auter vie* and lessees for years, or at will, frequently hold over the tenements to them demised, after the determination of such leases: and whereas after the determination of such, or any other leases, no distress can by law be made for any arrears of rent that grew due on such respective leases before the determination thereof; it is hereby further enacted" &c., "that from and after" &c., "it shall and may be lawful, for any person or persons, having any rent in arrear or due upon any lease for life or lives, or for years, or at will, ended

or determined, to distrain for such arrears, after the determination of the said respective leases, in the same manner as they might have done, if such lease or leases had not been ended or determined."

Sect. 7. "Provided, that such distress be made within the space of six calendar months after the determination of such lease, and during the continuance of such landlord's title or interest, and during the possession of the tenant from whom such arrears became due."

(2) 28 R. R. 207 (4 B. & C. 51).
(3) 2 R. R. 696 (1 H. Bl. 5).

Alexander and *W. H. Watson, contrà :*

TAYLE
v.
PETERS

It cannot be said that the old tenant continues to occupy when the new one has taken possession. Whatever possession of the old tenant is relied upon, to justify a distress under the statute, should be exclusive. At all events it should *be in the character of tenant; but that is not kept up by merely leaving behind a few articles of property. In *Beavan* v. *Delahay* (1) and *Nuttall* v. *Staunton* (2) an actual tenancy continued as to part of the premises. Here the attempt is to set up a constructive one. Welford, the incoming tenant, had a right to full possession on May 13th; and it was, substantially, given up to him. He might have brought trespass against the plaintiff for leaving the animals on the farm.

[*113

LORD DENMAN, Ch. J.:

I think there was no possession by the plaintiff at the time of the distress. It might have been different if the cow and pigs had been left with a view of keeping possession, and of maintaining a right in the plaintiff to come back. A small thing, so done, might serve to show a continuing possession. But here it would be unreasonable to construe the facts so. Though the cow and pigs remained till May 22nd, the plaintiff was gone before the distress. The circumstances under which he went do not raise the inference of a continued possession, unless the mere circumstance of his leaving this property behind him be sufficient; and I think it is not.

LITTLEDALE, J.:

I am of the same opinion. The plaintiff's time expired on Old May Day; he is asked by the incoming tenant when he means to leave, and answers that he does not know; and then he goes away, under circumstances which appear to me to show a complete abandonment. I think that the cow and pigs were not left with a view of keeping possession, *but that the plaintiff had determined his possession by leaving the premises without any intention to return.

[*114]

(1) 2 R. R. 696 (1 H. Bl. 5).   (2) 28 R. R. 207 (4 B. & C. 51).

TAYLERSON
  v.
PETERS.

PATTESON, J.:

To bring a case within sect. 7 of the statute of Anne, the continuance of possession may be either tortious or otherwise. In *Nuttall* v. *Staunton* (1) it was by permission. In *Bearan* v. *Delahay* (2) the possession was continued under a custom. But, to make the statute applicable, there must be a keeping as the party's own, to the exclusion of other people. That fact is wanting here.

WILLIAMS, J.:

The facts here negative the inference relied upon. The mere fact of the plaintiff's leaving these cattle does not show a continuance of possession. It was an accidental circumstance, not indicating possession, nor accompanied by a claim of it.

Rule absolute.

———————

1837.
June 3.
———
[136]

SIR FRANCIS BURDETT, BART. *v.* WITHERS (3).

(7 Adol. & Ellis, 136—138; S. C. 2 N. & P. 922; W. W. & D. 444; 6 L. J. (N. S.) K. B. 219; 1 Jur. 514.)

In an action against a tenant on agreement to keep premises in good repair, the state of the premises at the commencement of the tenancy is a relevant fact in regard to the amount of damages.

ASSUMPSIT. The declaration stated that heretofore, to wit 29th September, 1827, defendant became tenant to plaintiff of certain farms, upon the terms, among others, that defendant should, during the tenancy, keep all the premises in good and sufficient repair at his own expense; and, in consideration thereof, defendant promised plaintiff that he would, during the continuance of the tenancy, keep all the premises, &c. (as
[*137] before): that the defendant became tenant, &c.: *breach, that he did not keep, &c., and at the end of the term yielded the premises up in bad repair. Plea, that the plaintiff ought not further, &c., because the defendant brings into Court 5*l.*, and plaintiff has not sustained damages to a greater amount.

(1) 28 R. R. 207 (4 B. & C. 51).
(2) 2 R. R. 696 (1 H. Bl. 5).
(3) See *Payne* v. *Haine* (1847) 16
M. & W. 541, 16 L. J. Ex. 130;

Lister v. *Lane* [1893] 2 Q. B. 212, 62 L. J. Q. B. 583, 69 L. T. 176, C. A. —R. C.

Replication, that the plaintiff has sustained damages to a greater amount. Issue thereon. On the trial before Alderson, B., at the Berkshire Spring Assizes, 1836, the plaintiff produced evidence to show the bad state of the premises at the time of the defendant's quitting. The defendant's counsel cross-examined as to the state of the premises at the time of the defendant's coming into possession : but the learned Judge, being of opinion that this was not relevant to the issue, stopped the cross-examination, and refused to admit evidence for the defendant on this point; and he said, in his charge to the jury, that they must estimate the damages on this issue at the sum which it would cost to put the premises into tenantable repair, without reference to the state in which the defendant found them. Verdict for the plaintiff; damages 162*l.* 10*s.* In Easter Term, 1836, *Cooper* obtained a rule *nisi* for a new trial, citing *Harris* v. *Jones* (1) and *Gutteridge* v. *Munyard* (2).

Ludlow, Serjt. now showed cause :

By the form of the issue the liability is admitted; so that, if the damages exceed 5*l.* by any sum, the Court can only reduce the damages. The cases cited on moving for the rule were discussed in *Stanley* v. *Towgood* (3), where, in an action on a covenant to keep and leave in good *and tenantable repair, [*138] it was held that, although a jury should be allowed to take into consideration whether the house was new or old, the state of repair at the time of the demise was not to be considered. Here the tenant purchased his term by agreeing to keep in good repair : after that, he is not to be allowed to show that the state of the premises was bad, he having made his contract.

Cooper, contrà, was stopped by the COURT.

LORD DENMAN, Ch. J. :

The verdict might have been for the defendant if the evidence had been submitted to the jury. It is very material, with a view both to the event of the suit, and to the amount of

---

(1) 42 R. R. 772 (1 Moo. & Rob. 173).

(2) 1 Moo. & Rob. 334.

(3) 3 Bing. N. C. 4.

damages, to show what the previous state of the premises was. We cannot reduce the damages; for we have no means of forming an estimate.

LITTLEDALE, PATTESON, and WILLIAMS, JJ. concurred.

Rule absolute

———•———

THOMAS WARRE AND OTHERS, EXECUTORS OF JAMES WARRE, *v.* CALVERT, ADMINISTRATOR OF LAYCOCK.

(7 Adol. & Ellis, 143—157; S. C. 2 N. & P. 126; W. W. & D. 528; 6 L. J. (N. S.) K. B. 219; 1 Jur. 450.)

By agreement between plaintiff and S., S. was to perform certain works for plaintiff for a certain sum, and to receive from time to time three-fourths of the cost of the part completed, the first payment to be made after one-eighth was performed, the remaining fourth part to be paid one month after the whole was completed: if S. should fail to perform the work, plaintiff might employ others to perform it, and deduct the expense from the sum payable to S. Defendant entered into a bond, conditioned for performance of the agreement by S.

S., after performing part of the works, abandoned the contract. Plaintiff, at the request of S., and upon new security given by him, had advanced to S., for assisting him in performing the works, a sum exceeding the whole cost of the works performed at the time of the abandonment, but less than the whole contract price. Plaintiff had the works completed at an expense which, added to the cost of the part performed by S., was less than the whole contract price agreed on with S., but which, added to the sum actually advanced to S., exceeded that contract price.

Plaintiff brought an action of debt on the bond, suggesting, as a breach, S.'s non-performance, and the plaintiff's loss thereby. Defendant pleaded *non est factum*. Held,

That plaintiff was entitled to nominal damages only, the loss having arisen, not from the non-performance of S.'s contract, but from plaintiff having advanced more than the contract required. Especially as the sum advanced exceeded, not only the three-fourths, but the whole of the work completed; and as the advances had been made on a fresh negotiation with, and security taken from, S.

Held, also, that this answer could not be pleaded by defendant, but was properly set up, under *non est factum*, to meet plaintiff's evidence of damages.

DEBT on bond of the intestate Laycock, to the testator, James Warre, dated 2nd of November, 1829, for 5,000*l.* Plea, *Non est factum.* Issue thereon.

The plaintiffs suggested breaches, and set forth the condition of the bond: which was, that Robert Streather, his executors,

&c., should observe, perform, &c., all and singular the covenants, promises, &c., mentioned *and contained in a certain instrument in writing, bearing date 29th September, 1829, purporting to be an agreement or contract made with the plaintiffs' testator, Warre, treasurer of the London Dock Company, and on their behalf, by the said Robert Streather, which, on the part and behalf of Streather, his executors or administrators, were to be observed, &c. The suggestion then set out in part the contract in writing (1), which was *stated to be for the performance of

WARRE
v.
CALVERT.

[*144]

[*145]

(1) The whole contract (as afterwards stated in the special case, see p. 698, *post*) was as follows; but the parts in brackets were omitted in the suggestion.

"Articles of agreement and contract, entered into this 29th day of September, 1829, between Robert Streather, of" &c. "of the one part, and James Warre, Esq., treasurer of the London Dock Company, for and on behalf of the said Company, of the other part, as follows; that is to say, the said Robert Streather doth hereby contract, promise, and agree, to and with the said James Warre, as treasurer aforesaid, that he the said Robert Streather shall and will execute and perform, in a substantial and workmanlike manner, the whole of the works required in the formation of an entrance from the river at Shadwell to the Eastern London Dock; that the said works shall be commenced at such period as the Directors of the said Company shall appoint, they giving the said Robert Streather twenty days' previous notice, and the whole be completed within twelve months from such period; the said Robert Streather doth further contract, promise, and agree, to provide at his own expense the whole of the materials, labour, engines, tools, implements, and every other matter or thing which may be required in the formation and completion of the said entrance, and also execute the

whole of the works as laid down and described in the plans numbered 1, 2, 3, 4, 5, 6, 7, 8, 9, 10, 11, and the specification hereunto annexed, and according to the particulars and conditions of this contract, in consideration of being paid the sum of 52,200*l.*, and also of being allowed to appropriate to his own use the materials of the houses and other premises therein referred to. [Such parts of the materials as shall be approved by the engineer to the said Company may be used by the said Robert Streather in the works to be performed under this contract; the remainder are to be removed by him, in conformity with the directions which may be given to him by the said engineer. The said engineer to be the sole judge of the said works, and every part thereof, being executed and performed agreeably to the said plans and specification, and to have the power of rejecting at any time any materials or work which *in his opinion shall not be conformable thereto, and to provide other materials in lieu of those rejected, and employ competent persons to perform the work, if the said Robert Streather shall fail so to do, in which case the cost or amount thereof shall be deducted from the sum so to become due and payable to him under this contract.] The said Directors are to be at liberty to alter the plans, and thereby add to or diminish any part

[*145, *n*.]

certain works by Streather for 52,200*l*., in twelve months from
the commencement, with power to the Directors of the Company
to appoint the time when the works were to be commenced, to
make alterations on certain terms, and to extend the time.

The suggestion then stated that, after the making of the said
instrument and of the bond, viz. 1st December, 1829, the
Directors appointed that the works should be commenced on a
day then to come, viz. 28th December, 1829, whereof they gave
notice to Streather, viz. on &c. : whereupon Streather commenced
the works in pursuance of the contract.   That afterwards, and
before the period of twelve months so limited, &c., had expired,
and in the lifetime of Laycock, viz. on 21st December, 1830, by
[*146] a certain memorandum of agreement under *seal, between
Streather of the first part, one Thomas Warburton and Laycock
of the second part, and James Warre, for and on behalf of the
Company, of the third part, after reciting (amongst other
things) the giving of the bond, and that Streather had, with the
concurrence of Warburton and Laycock, requested of the
Directors an extension of the term for completing the works, it
was declared to be agreed by and between the parties, that
Warre, on behalf of the Company and the Directors thereof, did
consent and agree that Streather should be allowed an additional
term of three months, viz. to 28th March then next, for the
completion of the works : and Laycock thereby agreed that the
extension of time should not in any respect lessen the security,
or prejudice or affect the rights of, the Company under the bond,

of the intended works, without prejudice to or making void this contract,
in which case a proportionate addition
or deduction shall be made to or from
the sum to be paid to the said Robert
Streather, the amount of such addition or deduction to be computed
according to the schedule of prices
contained in the said specification.
[The said James Warre doth hereby
undertake, promise, and agree, for
and on behalf of the said Company,
to pay to the said Robert Streather
the said sum of 52,200*l*. by the following instalments, upon the production,
in each case, of a certificate signed
by the Company's engineer; viz.
three fourths of the cost of the work
certified to have been done every two
months; the first instalment to be
paid whenever the said engineer shall
certify that the portion of the work
performed amounts in value to
one-eighth part of the whole; the
remaining one fourth within one
month after the full completion of
this contract."   Signed by ROBERT
STREATHER.   Then followed the
specification referred to.]

and that Streather should complete the whole of the works, so WARRE
contracted &c., within the said extended term, and that, save v.
and except as to the extension of time thereby granted, such CALVERT.
bond should remain and be in full force &c.

The suggestion then stated that the Directors, whilst Streather
was carrying on the said works, did, under the power reserved
by the contract, from time to time alter the said plans, and
thereby did add to certain parts of the said intended works, and
diminish other parts; and it stated that, upon the balance of
such additions and diminutions, computed according to the
schedule of prices contained in the specification annexed to the
contract, a certain sum, viz. 3,731*l*. 16*s*. 8*d*., became and was
payable to Streather in respect of such additions and diminutions, over and beyond the said contract price of 52,200*l*. : And,
although Streather was allowed to appropriate, and did in fact
appropriate, to his own use the *materials &c., in the suggestion   [*147]
in that behalf referred to, and although the Directors, whilst
Streather was so carrying on the works, did advance and pay to
him divers sums of money, amounting &c., to wit 48,155*l*. 0*s*. 9*d*.,
in respect of the said contract price of 52,200*l*., and of the said
balance of 3,731*l*. 16*s*. 8*d*., and were always ready and willing to
advance and pay him the residue thereof respectively, on due
performance by him of the said contract or agreement, whereof
Streather always had notice, nevertheless, for assigning &c., the
plaintiffs did further suggest and say that Streather did not nor
would execute, complete or perform &c. the whole of the said
works &c., in the said contract or agreement mentioned &c.,
within twelve months from the time of commencement appointed
by the Directors, or within such additional term of three months
as aforesaid, or at any other time whatsoever; but, on the
contrary thereof, at the expiration of the said additional term of
three months, viz. on 28th March, 1831, the said works were
and remained still uncompleted and in great part unperformed
and unexecuted by Streather, and Streather then left and
abandoned the said works so unperformed &c., contrary to his
said contract &c., and the same remained and continued so
unperformed, &c., until the Company were afterwards, viz. on
the day and year aforesaid, and on divers other &c., forced and

WARRE
v.
CALVERT.

obliged to cause and procure, and did in fact cause and procure, the same to be performed, executed, and completed by certain other persons on their behalf, viz. as laid down and described in the plans and specification referred to in the suggestion, and according to the particulars and conditions of the contract. And, in and about so causing and procuring the said works to be

[*148]

performed *&c. as last aforesaid, the Company hath necessarily paid, laid out, and expended divers sums, &c., viz. 20,339l. 7s. 5d., over and beyond the said sum of 48,155l. 0s. 9d., so as afore-said paid and advanced to Streather whilst he was carrying on the said works ; and thereupon and thereby the said Company hath, in the whole, been put to a much greater cost and expense in and about the performance &c. of the said works, than the said several sums of 52,200l. and 3,731l. 16s. 8d., for which the same ought to have been performed &c. by Streather, viz. to the amount of 12,562l. 11s. 6d. over and above those sums : and so the said plaintiffs say that the said Company, by and through the nonperformance and nonfulfilment by the said Robert Streather of the said covenants and agreements matters and things mentioned and contained in the said contract or instru-ment in writing, to be by him performed and fulfilled, have have sustained loss and damage to a large amount, viz. 12,562l. 11s. 6d.

On the trial before Lord Denman, Ch. J., at the London sittings after Hilary Term, 1836, it was contended for the defendant that; upon the facts of the case, the plaintiffs were entitled to nominal damages only. The LORD CHIEF JUSTICE being of that opinion, a verdict was given for 1s. damages, his Lordship suggesting, however, that the question as to damages should be brought before the Court by a special case. In Easter Term, 1836, *Sir F. Pollock* obtained a rule *nisi* for a new trial, with liberty to state a case. A case was afterwards agreed to, in substance as follows.

On the 29th of September, 1829, Streather entered into the contract with the London Dock Company, to execute the works.

[*149]

The case then set out the whole of the contract, as *ante*, p. 695. It provided, among other things, that the work should be paid for by instalments, three fourths of the cost of the work certified to have been done every two months; the first instalment to be paid when it should be certified that one eighth, in value, of the whole, had been performed: the last fourth to be paid within one month after full completion of the contract. If Streather should fail to perform the work, the Company might employ others to do it, and deduct the cost from the sum otherwise payable to him.

On the 2nd November, 1829, Streather entered into the bond mentioned in the pleadings, with the defendant and another as his sureties. The Directors, pursuant to the terms of the contract, appointed that the works should be commenced on 28th December, 1829; and the same were commenced accordingly. They should, therefore, by the terms of the contract, have been completed on 28th December, 1830. Streather having, with the concurrence of his sureties, applied for an extension of the time, the Directors agreed to allow him an additional term of three months, viz. to 28th March, 1831; and, accordingly, the memorandum of agreement under seal in the pleadings mentioned was, on 21st December, 1830, entered into between Streather of the first part, the defendant and his co-surety of the second part, and the late treasurer of the London Dock Company of the third part (see suggestion of breaches, *ante*, p. 696). On the 28th March, 1831 (when the extended time expired), a considerable part of the works remained unfinished; and Streather having become embarrassed in his circumstances, and being unable farther to prosecute the works, his men withdrew on 30th April, 1831. On the 21st of that month, a *commission of bankrupt was issued against him; and the works were ultimately completed by the Company.

[*150]

The plans of the works were from time to time altered by the Directors, pursuant to the power reserved to them by the contract, the result of which alterations was that 3,731*l*. 16*s*. became payable to Streather over and beyond the contract price of 52,200*l*.

Between 18th May, 1830, and 25th March, 1831, inclusive, Streather received from the Company advances or payments to the amount of 48,155*l*. 0*s*. 9*d*. The dates and amounts were set forth in the plaintiffs' particular of demand.

After Streather left the premises, the Company completed the works at an expense (ascertained as far as practicable, according to the scale of prices in Streather's contract) of 18,875*l*. 3*s*. 2*d*. Some materials were left on the premises when Streather quitted them, which the Company used in completing the work, and had to pay for: their value was 1,209*l*. (1). The case added, that they were obliged to pay a part of this sum to Streather's assignees, on the grounds stated in *Crowfoot* v. *The London Dock Company* (2).

The amount of the work done by Streather, at the time when he left the premises, was 36,429*l*. 10*s*.

[After argument:]

[154]   LORD DENMAN, Ch. J.:

I had no doubt at Nisi Prius, and I feel none now. It is perfectly clear that the loss sustained by the Company arises, not from the breach of the contract, but from their having volunteered an advance to the contractor. But the surety has undertaken only to be liable for the damages arising from the breach of contract.

LITTLEDALE, J.:

I am also of opinion that the verdict must be confined to nominal damages. It appears (to use round numbers) that the work actually performed by Streather was of the value of 36,000*l*. The advances, according to the Company's contract with him, were to be three fourths of the cost of the work done, that is, 27,000*l*. They however advanced, not only more than this, but 48,000*l*., being 12,000*l*. more than the value of the work done. Then, through Streather's default, they are obliged to get the work finished by others, which costs them 18,000*l*. more. The money therefore which was payable under the contract to Streather, by way of instalment, added to the sum afterwards paid for the completion of the work, is less than the sum which, if Streather had performed all the contract, they would have had to pay him,

(1) The plaintiffs contended that this sum was not included in the 18,875*l*. 3*s*. 2*d*.; but the COURT were of opinion that it was.

(2) 2 Cr. & M. 637; 4 Tyr. 967.

namely, 55,000*l.* The advances beyond the 27,000*l.* were not made under the contract. It might perhaps be proper for the Company to make advances for the purpose of enabling Streather to fulfil his undertaking; but such advances are not made in terms of the contract. A surety has a right to require that the obligee shall do his duty; and I think that advances *made in this manner by the obligee do not render the surety liable. It is contended that the surety is to see to the performance of his principal's contract; and that is true: but how can he watch the advances made by the other party? Here he may, in fact, have known of the advances: but that does not affect the general rule. The Company should have advanced only what the contract bound them to advance: in the result, the work was completed at an expense below the contract price. Now the assignment of breaches charges that Streather did not perform the contract within the twelve months, nor within the additional term of three months, and that, by reason thereof, the Company were obliged to procure the works to be completed by others, whereby they were damaged. But they have, in fact, sustained no damage at all by this. *Sir F. Pollock* suggests that the defence should have been pleaded; but it could not; performance might be pleaded, or that the obligee was damnified by his own wrong; but this is not a damnification by the wrong of the obligee, but a damnification not arising on the contract. The ground of my judgment is that the advance has been made, not only beyond the 27,000*l.*, but beyond the 36,000*l.* How far the defendant could be made liable in another form is not now in question.

[*155]

PATTESON, J.:

This being an action on a bond, the question is, whether, on the breach suggested, any damages are shown to have been sustained by the non-performance *of the covenant. Whether the alteration of the time takes the case out of the condition of the bond is immaterial; for the plea denies only the execution of the bond, not the breach. It is clear, therefore, that there has been a breach, and that the plaintiffs must have a verdict: and the question is whether there be any damage. It is asked, what

[*156]

would be the use of the bond, if the Company were bound to retain in hand one fourth of the cost of the work performed. The object was, that the Company might have some one to whom they might resort in the event of Streather failing to perform the contract, and of the works being completed by others at a cost exceeding the contract price. That shows why the penalty of the bond is not larger; it was merely to cover such excess, which was not likely to amount to more than 5,000*l.* The argument, therefore, as to the inconsistency of the security with the alleged restriction on the Company fails. Then let us look at the contract. Streather could call for no money till he had performed one eighth of the work; and, after that, as the work went on, he could call for three fourths only of the cost of the work performed. Any further advances were, no doubt, as *Sir Frederick Pollock* urges, made *on* the contract; but they were not made *under* the contract. Even, therefore, if there were no specific agreement, the surety would not be answerable. His liability is for damages accruing from the breach of contract, not from advances by the Company. Still less could he be liable, if the advances were made upon a subsequent negotiation between the Company and Streather, and a fresh security given by the latter. No damage, therefore, has been sustained.

Williams, J.:

[157]   The liability which it was intended to impose upon the surety was for the nonperformance of the contract; but the Company are not aggrieved by the nonperformance of the contract, since the works have been completed at an expense less than the sum which they would have had to pay to Streather. The loss arises from the contract in no sense except that, if there had been no contract at all, there would have been no advance. But the dvance is made, not under the contract, but upon the security of Streather.

Verdict to stand for nominal damages.

WILLIAMS *v.* BYRNE.

(7 Adol. & Ellis, 177—184; S. C. 2 N. & P. 139; W. W. & D. 535; 6 L. J.
(N. S.) K. B. 239; 1 Jur. 578.)

Declaration stated that defendant promised plaintiff to employ him,
as reporter to a newspaper, for a given salary, for one whole year, from
20th May, and so from year to year, to the end of each year commenced
while the plaintiff should be so employed, reckoning each year to commence from 20th May, for so long as plaintiff and defendant should
respectively please: breach, that, after plaintiff had continued in the
employment two years and part of a third, defendant would not continue plaintiff in the employment to the end of the third year, but
discharged him.

Plea, that defendant offered to pay plaintiff a sum of money larger
than plaintiff would have been entitled to if a reasonable notice of determining the agreement had been given, and required plaintiff to quit
immediately, and at the same time gave him a reasonable notice of
defendant's intention, in case the tender was refused, to put an end
to the agreement, to wit at the end of three weeks from 3rd October
instant; that plaintiff refused to accept and quit, whereupon defendant
discharged him at the expiration of the notice, and that defendant was
still ready to pay the sum tendered.   On demurrer,

Held, that the contract alleged in the declaration and confessed in the
plea, was determinable only by notice ending with a current year; and,
therefore, that the plea was no answer.

ASSUMPSIT. The first count of the declaration stated that,
whereas heretofore, to wit 20th May, 1833, in consideration that
plaintiff, at defendant's request, *would enter into his employ in
the capacity of a reporter of the proceedings in the House of
Commons and House of Lords, and would furnish reports of
such proceedings, and other articles, to defendant, for publication
in a newspaper of the defendant, called the *Morning Post*, for
one whole year from a certain day, to wit from the day and year
aforesaid, and so from year to year to the end of each year
commenced whilst the plaintiff should be so employed by the
defendant, and reckoning each year to commence from a certain
day, to wit the 20th of May therein, for so long as the plaintiff
and defendant should respectively please, at and for a certain
salary or wages, to wit at the rate of 5*l.* 5*s.* per week for and
during each session of Parliament, and at the rate, to wit, of
2*l.* 12*s.* 6*d.* per week for and during the remainder of the year,
defendant undertook &c. to employ plaintiff in the capacity
aforesaid, at and for the salary or wages aforesaid, and to
continue him in such employ for one whole year from a certain

[*178]

day, to wit &c., and so from year to year, &c. (following the
consideration to the words "should respectively please"); and,
although plaintiff, confiding &c., did afterwards, to wit on the
day and year first aforesaid, enter into the employ of defendant
in the capacity aforesaid, and on the terms aforesaid, and continued in the employ of defendant in the capacity &c., and did
furnish reports &c. to defendant for the purpose &c., for a long
space of time, to wit two years then next following and also for
part of another year after that time, to wit until 24th October,
1835; and although plaintiff was, on the day and year last aforesaid, and hath always been, ready and willing, and then offered,

[*179]   to continue in the defendant's employ, in the capacity *&c., and
on the terms &c., and to furnish &c. for the remainder of the
last-mentioned year so commenced as aforesaid, yet defendant
did not nor would continue plaintiff in defendant's said employ
till the expiration of the last-mentioned year; but, on the
contrary, during the said last-mentioned year, and before the
expiration thereof, to wit on &c., refused to suffer plaintiff to
continue in defendant's said employ, and wrongfully discharged
him therefrom, without any reasonable or probable cause whatsoever, and hath thence hitherto wholly neglected and refused to
retain or continue plaintiff in his employ for the remainder of
the last-mentioned year so commenced as aforesaid.

Fourth plea to the first count.   That, after the making of the
said promise, and before the said discharge of plaintiff, to wit
5th October, 1835, defendant, being desirous to determine and
put an end to the said agreement and defendant's said employ
of plaintiff in the said capacity, tendered and offered to pay
plaintiff a large sum of money, to wit 18l. 10s., as and for and in
the name of salary and wages, the same being more than the
amount of salary or wages which the plaintiff would be and have
been entitled to if a reasonable and usual notice of determining
the said agreement and employ of plaintiff had been given to
him by defendant, and required plaintiff immediately to quit his,
defendant's, said employ. Averment, that defendant did, at the
same time, give plaintiff a reasonable and usual notice of his,
defendant's, intention, in case of the said tender and requisition
so made by defendant being refused by plaintiff, to determine

and put an end to the said agreement and the said employ WILLIAMS
of plaintiff, to wit at the end of three weeks from 3rd October *v.*
then instant; *that plaintiff refused to accept the said 18*l.* 10*s.*, BYRNE.
or any part thereof, or to quit the said employ; wherefore, at [*180]
the expiration of the said notice, being the said time when
&c., defendant discharged plaintiff, &c., and hath from thence
hitherto refused, and still doth refuse, to employ plaintiff &c.,
as he lawfully &c. Averment, that defendant hath always, from
the time of his tendering the 18*l.* 10*s.*, hitherto been, and still
is, ready and willing to pay plaintiff the said 18*l.* 10*s.* if he will
accept the same for the cause aforesaid; whereof the plaintiff
hath always hitherto had notice. Verification.

Demurrer, assigning for causes that the plea neither traverses,
nor confesses and avoids, the cause of action in the first count;
for that, by the agreement as therein stated, defendant had no
power to put an end to the agreement before the end of the year
commenced, nor to discharge the defendant for the causes alleged
in the plea. Joinder.

W. H. Watson, for the plaintiff:

The declaration shows an express contract for a year, and so
on from year to year, without any stipulation as to the method
of determining it. In *Beeston* v. *Collyer* (1), where a yearly
hiring of a clerk was implied, it was held that the employer
could not turn off the clerk in the middle of a year, and that
there must be reasonable notice; and the case was distinguished
from that of a menial servant. The notice to determine a
contract from year to year must fix the determination at the end
of a current year. In all cases except that of a menial servant,
the *primâ facie* presumption is that the hiring is for a year:
Fawcett v. *Cash* (2). Upon any construction of this contract, [*181]
as stated on the record, there is no power to determine it by
such a notice as that pleaded. The plea, as now framed, does
not confess the contract in the declaration, but relies upon a
supposed qualification of it, which is not on the record.

(He was then stopped by the COURT.)

(1) 29 R. R. 576 (4 Bing. 309).   And see *Turner* v. *Robinson*, 39 R. R.
(2) 39 R. R. 709 (5 B. & Ad. 904).   650 (5 B. & Ad. 789).

Mansel, contrà :

Every contract of hiring must be understood to be determinable upon reasonable notice.   The contract in the declaration is not traversed ; and, therefore, according to the present rules of pleading, it is confessed.   In *Beeston* v. *Collyer* (1) the question of notice was not raised : but BURROUGH, J. said, "Unless reasonable notice be given, or ground for dismissal assigned, the defendant was bound to go on to the end of the year." It would be hard on both parties to interpret the contract without this qualification.   In *Fawcett* v. *Cash* (2) TAUNTON, J. expressly confined his judgment to the case of a dismissal during the first year.

(LITTLEDALE, J. : You are setting up a contract different from that in the declaration.)

The contract in the declaration implies a power to determine on reasonable notice.   It is only from year to year to the end of each year commenced "while the plaintiff should be so employed."   In the case of a tenancy from year to year the contract specifies no notice, nor is it pleaded as a contract subjected to determination by notice ; yet the law imports the power so to determine.   The notice in the case of a menial [*182]   servant takes effect upon *the same principle.   What is a reasonable notice, is, in each case, a question for the jury.

LORD DENMAN, Ch. J. :

I have no doubt upon the case.   The plaintiff states the contract to be for one year from May 20th, and so on from year to year, to the end of each year commenced while the plaintiff should be so employed, reckoning each year to commence at the day named.   This contract the defendant does not deny ; but he answers that, in the third year of the employment, he tendered a sum amounting to what would have been payable if a reasonable notice had been given, and gave a reasonable and usual notice that, if the tender was not accepted, he should discharge the plaintiff.   What is there to show that any part of

(1) 29 R. R. 576 (4 Bing. 309).   And see *Turner* v. *Robinson*, 39 R. R.
(2) 39 R. R. 709 (5 B. & Ad. 904).   650 (5 B. & Ad. 789).

the contract enabled him to do this? If he meant to contend that he had the right to do it, he should have denied the contract set out in the declaration; then the jury would have determined, on the evidence, what the contract was. That must, I take it for granted, have been the question in every case which has occurred: though, in some instances, the nature of the contract is, in fact, so well understood that it is often put as a matter of law. Still it is always a matter of fact, and, being so, should be here stated on the record.

LITTLEDALE, J.:

It appears not to be disputed that the parties were, at any rate, bound to the end of the first year. I think their position was the same in all the subsequent years. Therefore, when any year had commenced, the service was to run on to the end. And this was to continue as long as the parties pleased, that is, till one of them determined the engagement by reasonable notice expiring at the end of the current year. *And that is the case in other contracts; as, for instance, in the hiring of houses, the understood custom in some cases requiring more notice, in others less, before the end of the current year. It is not necessary to decide, whether, if the hiring were subject to be determined by notice at any period, that must be shown by a special plea, or could be proved under *non assumpsit*. The plea speaks of a reasonable and usual notice. But we cannot say that a notice is reasonable which determines the service before the end of the current year. The case of a menial servant is put in illustration: but, even there, I do not know that we could, as matter of law, imply the power to determine the service at any time on a month's notice. It should be on the record; and then, on a traverse, the jury would no doubt so find it. The plea, in this case, as it stands, is no answer to the declaration.

[*183]

PATTESON, J.:

The only question is, What is the legal construction of the contract which the declaration states, and which the plea does not deny? It is argued that the jury are to say what is a reasonable notice. That might be so, if the contract was stated to be determinable on a reasonable notice. But the contract stated in the declaration, and confessed by the plea, is not so. It is an employment for a year, and so on from year to year, the year beginning on a day named. The words, "while the plaintiff should be so employed," are satisfied by a power to put an end to the employment in the way warranted in the contract; that is, if it be put an end to adversely and not by agreement, by a notice expiring with the current year. How long such notice must be, we need not now determine.

[184]   WILLIAMS, J. :

The case is precisely the same as if this had occurred during the first year; for the contract puts each successive year on the same footing as the first. The notice, therefore, should have terminated with the end of the current year. No delinquency on the part of the plaintiff is suggested; but it is attempted to introduce a new term into the contract.

Judgment for the plaintiff.

CLAY v. STEPHENSON AND OTHERS.

(7 Adol. & Ellis, 185—190; S. C. 2 N. & P. 189; W. W. & D. 537; 6 L. J. (N. S.) K. B. 211; 1 Jur. 448.)

A commission to examine witnesses was directed to the Court of Commerce at Hamburgh; and it was ordered by the commission that the examinations should be taken, and that the same should be sent to the Court of King's Bench to be filed of record in the office of the clerk of the rules. The Court of Commerce took the examinations by an act of their own; copies of the minutes of that act, certified by their assistant actuary (whom they had added to the commission for the purpose of keeping the minutes), were transmitted under the seal of the Court of Commerce, with the commission; and that Court certified, by indorsement on the commission, the execution thereof, by referring to the annexed extract of their minutes: Held, that these copies could not be read in evidence, the commission requiring that the examinations actually taken should be transmitted.

ASSUMPSIT for money had and received, for interest, and upon an account stated. Plea, *Non assumpsit*. On the trial before Lord Denman, Ch. J., at the York Spring Assizes, 1836, the plaintiff produced, in support of his case, certain interrogatories

and answers. It appeared that they had been taken under a
commission issued from this Court, directed to the Court of
Commerce at Hamburgh : and the commission contained the
following directions, among others : " That you do take such
their examinations, and reduce them to writing on paper or
parchment ; and, when you shall have so taken them, you are
to send the same without delay to our said Court before us at
Westminster, closed up under the seal of the Chamber of
Commerce at Hamburgh, or under the seals of any two or more
of you distinctly and plainly set together, with the said interrogatories and this writ, to be filed of record in the office of
Charles Short, Esq., the clerk of the rules of the same Court."
The examinations tendered in evidence at the trial had been
transmitted in an envelope sealed with the seal of the Court of
Commerce ; and the same seal was set to the *examinations.   [*186]
The document commenced as follows : (1)

    " HAMBURGH.

  " Court of Commerce.

  " This is an extract of the minutes (2) to which the certificate
indorsed on the commission refers.

          " (Signed)   D. F. WORLEE, Assistant Actuary."

  "On this day, Wednesday the 15th July, 1835, before
Messieurs Georg Gottlieb Friedrick Schmidt, and David
Friedrick Weber, members of the Court of Commerce at Ham-
burgh (who, by an order of the said Court, dated 11th July,
1835, granted at the request of Dr. M. Pohls, on behalf of
Richard Clay, the younger, of Goole, were appointed as

---

(1) The original, in German, was
produced at the trial, with a translation. It appeared that the depositions had been taken in German, and
so sent over ; that the translation was
made in England, and oral evidence
was given at the trial of the correctness of the translation, by the
translators. A question arose, both
at Nisi Prius and in bank, whether
such a translation was admissible
under the precise terms of the commission, which directed that the

translators should be sworn to interpret, transcribe, and engross faithfully, so far forth as they should
be directed by the commissioners to
interpret or engross the depositions ; but the Court did not decide
this question : *Atkins* v. *Palmer*, 4
B. & Ald. 377, was cited as to this
point as well as the point in the text.
  (2) " Protocoll - extract." Some
question arose, both at Nisi Prius
and in bank, whether "minutes"
was the correct translation.

CLAY
v.
STEPHENSON.

commissioners, whilst, by the same order of the Court, Daniel Friedrick Worlee, the assistant actuary, one of the sworn officers of the Court, was added to the commission for the purpose of keeping the minutes), after proper summons appeared," &c. Then followed the name, addition, &c. of the witness (Johann Martin Precht), the entry of the administration of the oath to him, and his answers to the interrogatories; and, at the close of his evidence, the following words were added:

[187]

"Whereupon the witness, after perusal and approbation, signed this declaration; and, after being enjoined to secrecy, he was dismissed.

"(Signed on the minutes.)"   " JOHN MARTIN PRECHT."

"Whereby this minute was closed for to-day, and signed by the commissioners and assistant actuary.

"(Signed on the minutes.)"   " GEORG GOTTLIEB FRIEDK. SCHMIDT, Judge of the Court of Commerce.   DAVID FRIEDRICK WEBER, Judge of the Court of Commerce.   D. F. WORLEE, Assistant Actuary."

The depositions of Langnese were sent in the same way.

At the end of the whole was the following:

"Whereby this act was closed and signed by the commissioners and the assistant actuary. (Signed on the minutes.)" [Names as before.]   "The correctness of this act, and that the same entirely agrees with the original minutes, is hereby attested. (Signed.) (L.S.)   D. F. WORLEE, Assistant Actuary."

The following certificate was indorsed on the back of the original commission, which was returned with the above document, the whole inclosed in an envelope under the seal of the Court:

"The Court of Commerce of the Free and Hanseatic town of Hamburgh certifies the execution of the herein demanded examination of the witnesses Langnese and Precht, by referring to the extract of the minutes annexed herewith.—D. F. WORLEE, Actuary Assistant."

The defendants' counsel objected that this was only a copy, and could not be received as taken under the commission. Several other objections were made to *the admission of the document.

[*188]

The LORD CHIEF JUSTICE received the evidence, giving leave to the defendants to move on all the objections. Verdict for the plaintiff. In Easter Term, 1836, *Wightman* obtained a rule *nisi* for a new trial or nonsuit, on the objection above mentioned, and others, which were also discussed on the argument in bank, but were not decided upon by the Court.

CLAY
v.
STEPHENSON

[After argument, the COURT took time for consideration.]

LORD DENMAN, Ch. J. in this Term, June 8th, delivered the judgment of the COURT : (1)

[190]

We decide this case upon one very short ground. The principal evidence for the plaintiff was comprehended in the depositions taken under the commission. The commission required that, when the examinations were taken, *the same* should be sent. But it is clear that what was sent was not the same as that which was taken under the commission. There has been the intervention of a person professing to be an officer of the foreign Court. Whether he was such an officer or not we ought not to enquire : the very thing which we require ought to be in Court : no copy is admissible.

Rule absolute for a new trial (without costs).

WATTS *v.* FRASER AND ANOTHER.

1837.
June 9.

(7 Adol. & Ellis, 223—233 ; S. C. 2 N. & P. 157 ; W. W. & D. 451 ; 6 L. J.
(N. S.) K. B. 226 ; 1 Jur. 671 ; S. C. at Nisi Prius, 7 Car. & P. 369 ;
1 Moo. & Rob. 449.)

[223]

In an action of libel the defendant may show, in mitigation, that he was provoked to issue the libel by publications of the plaintiff reflecting upon him.

A defendant offering such evidence in mitigation must prove that the libel which he complains of came to his knowledge before he libelled the plaintiff.

CASE. The first count was for a libel in a work called "Fraser's Magazine," ridiculing the plaintiff as editor of a publication called the "Literary Souvenir," and attacking the "Souvenir ;" the second count was for a libel in the same

(1) Lord Denman, Ch. J., Littledale, Patteson, and Williams, JJ.

WATTS
v.
FRASER.

[*224]

Magazine. reflecting on the plaintiff personally.   Plea, Not
guilty. On the trial before Lord Denman, Ch. J., at the sittings
in Middlesex after Michaelmas Term, 1835, it appeared that the
alleged libels were published in 1834 and 1835.   The defendants
proposed to show, in mitigation, that the defendant *Fraser,
before publishing the matter now complained of, had on several
occasions been libelled by the plaintiff in the "Literary Souvenir,"
and in newspapers called the *United Service Gazette* and the
Alfred ; which libels, it was suggested, had provoked those now
in question.   The reception of such evidence was objected to,
but the LORD CHIEF JUSTICE held it admissible (1).   To prove
the plaintiff's connection with the *United Service Gazette,* the
defendants put in a certified copy of an affidavit filed at the
Stamp Office in 1833 pursuant to stat. 38 Geo. III. c. 78, ss. 1,
2, 5 and 9 (2), stating Watts to be a proprietor of that paper.
They also produced, from the British Museum, newspapers
which they proved to have been deposited at the Stamp Office,
under sect. 17, and transmitted from thence to the Museum,
corresponding with the description in the affidavit, and of subsequent dates.   Evidence according to the statute was also given
as to the *Alfred ;* and a witness was called who had printed
the copies sent to the Stamp Office and now produced, and had
signed them with his name, as servant to the plaintiff.   It was
proved that the plaintiff had read to a witness, as his own, an
article in one of the papers which it was now proposed to put
in.   The defendants' counsel then proposed to read, for the
purpose of mitigation, parts of the several papers thus given in
evidence ; but the reading was objected to, and the LORD CHIEF
JUSTICE held the evidence inadmissible (3).   A "Literary Souvenir"
for 1832 was also produced for the same purpose ; and a witness,
in the employ of Messrs. Longmans, *the booksellers, deposed
to his belief that this was one of a number of copies published
by them for the plaintiff ; but he declined to say positively

[*225]

---

(1) *Watts* v. *Fraser,* 1 Moo. & Rob.
449.

(2) Since repealed ; but see now
the Newspaper Libel and Registra-
tion Act, 1881 (44 & 45 Vict. c. 60),
ss. 9—15.—R. C.

(3) Copies of another newspaper,
the *Old England,* were tendered and
rejected, under similar circumstances ;
but no further point arose on this
part of the case.

that the individual copy might not have been still in sheets within a week before the trial. This book also was rejected. The libels for which this action was brought did not refer to any of the alleged libels on the defendant Fraser. A verdict was found for the defendants on the first count, and for the plaintiff on the second, with 150*l.* damages. *Erle*, in the ensuing Term, obtained a rule *nisi* for a new trial, on account of the rejection of evidence.

[After argument, the COURT took time for consideration.]

LORD DENMAN, Ch. J. now delivered the judgment of the COURT (1):

In deciding this case, we must look both to the nature of the proposed evidence and to the object with which it is offered. The object is to show that the defendant was provoked by libels published against him. It is of the essence of such a case that some proof should be given of the libels having come to the defendant's knowledge; if such proof was totally wanting, the defence could not be made available. But the present case hardly came to this point; for I thought that the newspapers could not be received as evidence without proof that some other copy had been issued than that deposited at the Stamp Office, with which it appeared that the defendant could not have been acquainted. And no evidence was given of any duplicate having been published. Then a question is raised, whether or not, in the absence of direct proof, it can be inferred from the printing of one newspaper, which was not circulated, that another exactly corresponding with it was printed, which might meet the defendant's eye. The same question arises as to the book which was offered in evidence. We think that the inference cannot be drawn, and that some evidence should have been given of the publications having actually come abroad. We are not warranted in presuming that the usual numbers of a publication were in fact issued in any particular *instance. One authority, *Baldwin* v. *Elphinston* (2), was cited, where the Court of Exchequer Chamber held that printing must, *primâ facie*, be understood to be a publishing, because the matter must be

WATTS
v.
FRASER.

[232]

[*233]

(1) Lord Denman, Ch. J., Littledale and Patteson, JJ.

(2) 2 W. Bl. 1037.

WATTS
v.
FRASER.

delivered to a compositor and other workmen: but it does not follow, as of course, from a work being printed, that the party sending it forth employed a compositor or other workmen. We cannot, therefore, act upon that case. The rule must be discharged.

Rule discharged.

———————

1837.
June 10.

[235]

DOE d. THOMAS DANIEL, SHERIFF, and AFFLECK, *v.* COULTHRED and BALDREY.

(7 Adol. & Ellis, 235—239; S. C. 2 N. & P. 165; 7 L. J. (N. S.) Q. B. 52.)

In ejectment on the demise of S., evidence is admissible to show that a deceased party, being then in receipt of the rents, executed a deed, charging the land with an annuity, in which he stated S. to be legal owner of the fee, and himself to hold, for the term of his natural life, by permission of S.

EJECTMENT for lands in Suffolk. On the trial before Bolland, B., at the Suffolk Summer Assizes, 1835, the plaintiff relied upon the demise of Sheriff only, who was shown to be heir-at-law of Edmund Affleck, the surviving trustee named in the will of one William Daniel, deceased.

William Daniel, after disposing by the will of certain lands in Essex, devised to the trustees the residue of his freehold messuages, lands, and hereditaments, in Suffolk, to and to the use of the trustees in fee, on trust that they, or the survivor, or the heirs of such survivor, should with all convenient speed sell the same, and apply the money arising from the sale to the payment of debts, funeral expenses, and legacies, and lay out the residue in the purchase of freehold messuages, lands, tenements, and hereditaments, in Essex, and settle and convey the same to such uses and estates, &c., as were previously devised and limited concerning the landed property in Essex before mentioned. The Essex property thus referred to was devised to trustees in fee, *habendum* to them in fee, to the use of William Barker Daniel for life; remainder (after certain
[*236] intermediate *limitations of estates tail which failed for want of issue) to the use of Thomas Daniel in fee. W. Daniel, the testator, died in 1791.

To show that Sheriff was legal owner of the lands which

were the subject of the present action, it was proved that
W. B. Daniel, for many years before and after the year 1813,
was in the receipt of the rents. The plaintiff then offered in
evidence an indenture of 1st October, 1813, executed by W. B.
Daniel, and made between him of the first part, John Watier
of the second part, and James Christie of the third part;
wherein, after reciting the will of William Daniel respecting
the lands thereinafter mentioned, and that the debts and
legacies were duly paid, it was witnessed that W. B. Daniel,
for securing an annuity by him granted to John Watier, party
to the indenture, did grant, bargain, sell, and demise, to James
Christie (as trustee for Watier), among other parcels, eight
acres of land, &c., then in the occupation of John Baker as
tenant thereof to W. B. Daniel; which land, the deed stated,
"was part and parcel of the freehold estate late of the said
William Daniel, as was by his said will directed to be sold, and
held by the said W. B. Daniel for the term of his natural life,
with the concurrence" of the trustees, "or the survivor of them,
or the heirs of such survivor, without proceeding to any such
sale."   It was proved that the land conveyed by this indenture
was the land which was the subject of the present action (1);
and that W. B. Daniel died in 1832. The defendants' counsel
objected *to the receipt of this indenture as evidence; but the   [*237]
learned Judge admitted it, reserving leave to the defendants to
move for a nonsuit. Verdict for the plaintiff. In Michaelmas
Term, 1835, *Storks*, Serjt. obtained a rule for a nonsuit. On a
former day in this Term (2),

Kelly showed cause:

W. B. Daniel, having been shown to be in receipt of the
rents and profits, would appear *primâ facie* to be tenant in
fee. According to his statement in the deed, he was, at law,
merely tenant at will to the trustees, and had only an equitable
life estate. The evidence tendered is, therefore, that of a

(1) Some question arose whether
the defendants, on the evidence, were
not shown to have come into possession through W. B. Daniel; but the
argument ultimately rested only on
the facts mentioned in the text. See
the judgment.

(2) May 29th. Before Lord Denman, Ch. J., Littledale and Patteson,
JJ.

DOE d.
DANIEL
v.
COULTHRED.

declaration by a deceased party, made while in possession, to cut down his own interest; and such evidence is constantly held admissible. The case falls within the principle of *Holloway* v. *Rakes* (1), *Doe* d. *Foster* v. *Williams* (2), *Davies* v. *Pierce* (3), *Peaceable* d. *Uncle* v. *Watson* (4), *Carne* v. *Nicoll* (5), and *Doe* d. *Human* v. *Pettett* (6).

(LORD DENMAN, Ch. J. referred to *Woolway* v. *Rowe* (7).)

Storks, Serjt. and *Gunning*, contrà:

It does not appear that W. B. Daniel had any interest under the will; for no evidence was given of the payment of debts, and the existence of a surplus. His possession is, in fact, in contravention of the trusts in the will. In *Doe* d. *Human* v. *Pettett* (6) ABBOTT, Ch. J. seems to put the decision on the particular circumstances of that case; and his language there shows

[*238]

that there is no stringent *rule to the extent contended for on the other side. If the land mentioned in the annuity deed be not the land mentioned in the devise, the evidence is inadmissible; if it be, the declaration is in favour of W. B. Daniel, and not against him, for he claims a right to charge it with the annuity, which, under the devise, he could not do without a breach of the trust. In *Doe* d. *Human* v. *Pettett* (6) the declaration was strongly against the party making it. In *Outram* v. *Morewood* (8) it was held that declarations by a deceased owner, of receipts of rent, could not affect third parties. In *Woolway* v. *Rowe* (7) the interest of the party who made the declaration was, at that time, the same as the interest of the party, against whom the declaration was proved, at the time of the trial: that is not the case here.

Cur. adv. vult.

LORD DENMAN, Ch. J., now delivered the judgment of the COURT:

The plaintiff's title was derived from the surviving trustee under the will of W. Daniel, empowering them to sell the

(1) Cited by BULLER, J. in *Davies*
v. *Pierce*, 1 R. R. 421 (2 T. R. 55).
(2) 2 Cowp. 621.
(3) 1 R. R. 419 (2 T. R. 53).
(4) 13 R. R. 552 (4 Taunt. 16).

(5) 1 Bing. N. C. 430.
(6) 5 B. & Ald. 223.
(7) 40 R. R. 264 (1 Ad. & El. 114).
(8) 12 R. R. 542 (14 East, 330, n.;
5 T. R. 121).

premises sought by this ejectment, and to purchase, with the
price, other lands which were to be settled on his son W. B.
Daniel for life, with remainders over. The trustees never sold.

Baldrey, one of the defendants, succeeded his father, who
had paid rent as tenant for some years to W. B. Daniel for
many years before. The defendant first named came in
as landlord.

A rule *nisi* for a nonsuit was granted, on the question whether
certain evidence was admissible ; *namely, a deed executed by
W. B. Daniel for raising a sum of money, to be secured by
annuity on these premises, in which the will was recited ; that
the trustees had not sold ; that W. B. Daniel was in possession
by permission of the trustees.

The learned Judge admitted the evidence : we think he was
right, on the principle that, W. B. Daniel being once shown to
be in receipt of the rents and profits, his declaration in the
deed that he held under and by the permission of the lessor
of the plaintiff's ancestor was in derogation of his own apparent
right to be considered as the owner in fee. We cannot look at
the equitable relation in which the parties stood to each other.
The sole question is, in whom the legal estate resides. We
think the admission of the person in receipt of the rent that
he held under another, whether as tenant by sufferance, or as
receiver of the rents, is undoubtedly evidence that he himself
is not the owner of the legal estate. Then there is proof here,
aliundè, that the lessor of the plaintiff had the legal estate
under W. B. Daniel's will ; and it is also proved that the
father of the defendant was in possession in the lifetime of
the testator.

Rule discharged.

REX *v.* The RECTOR and CHURCHWARDENS of BIRMINGHAM.

(7 Adol. & Ellis, 254—260 ; S. C. 1 Jur. 754.)

One of two candidates for the office of churchwarden was elected at
a vestry, and subscribed the declaration of office, but the election was
alleged to have been so improperly conducted that the proceedings were
void. To give the parties impugning the election an opportunity of

DOE d.
DANIEL
v.
COULTHRED.

[*239]

1837
June 10.

[254]

trying its validity, the COURT (considering a *primâ facie* case to be presented) granted a *mandamus*, calling on the rector and churchwardens to
convene a vestry for electing a churchwarden for the remainder of the year.

At an election in vestry, where the right of voting is regulated by
Sturges Bourne's Act (58 Geo. III. c. 69), s. 3 (1), it is no objection to
the proceedings that the chairman directed a poll without first taking a
show of hands : although a show of hands was demanded, and the poll
was not demanded, but was objected to. Per Lord DENMAN, Ch. J. and
LITTLEDALE, J.

A RULE was obtained in this Term, calling upon the rector
and churchwardens of the parish of Birmingham to show cause
why a *mandamus* should not issue commanding them, or such of
them to whom the same should of right belong, to convene a
meeting in vestry of the inhabitants for the election of a churchwarden of the said parish for the remainder of the present year ;
cause to be shown on notice of the rule given to the rector, and
to the churchwardens and overseers, or some of them, and to
James Brown. It appeared, by the affidavits in support of the
rule, that, on Easter Monday last, the rector and parishioners
met in vestry, according to custom, to elect two churchwardens.
The rector took the chair, and, as he was entitled to do,
nominated one churchwarden. Two other persons were then
proposed and seconded as candidates for the remaining office of
churchwarden, which was in the appointment of the parishioners ;
and the rector was called upon (in pursuance of an alleged
custom) to take a show of hands upon the question which
candidate should be appointed. He refused, assigning, as a
reason, that the provisions of stat. 58 Geo. III. c. 69 (1), applied
to this election, and were inconsistent with the proceeding by
show of hands ; and he gave directions for a poll, which was forth-

[*255] with taken, although, as these *affidavits stated, no parishioner
present demanded a poll, and several remonstrated against it.
Votes were given for both candidates ; and the result of the
poll was declared to be in favour of James Brown. The affidavits
went into a detail of circumstances to show that the poll had
been improperly closed ; and that, in other respects, it had been
so unfairly conducted as to render the election void. By the

(1) The clauses as to proceedings   under the Local Government Act,
in vestry are repealed so far as relates   1894 (56 & 57 Vict. c. 73).—R. C.
to parish meetings and parish councils

affidavits in opposition to the rule, it was denied that any custom of taking a show of hands existed (1), although such a practice had prevailed from the year 1831 ; and the rector stated that he had directed a poll at once, to avoid confusion, and because, on a show of hands, it could not be known what voters were entitled to give one or more votes under the statute. Brown subscribed the declaration of office as churchwarden at the usual time.

Sir J. Campbell, Attorney-General, *Sir W. W. Follett*, and *Humfrey*, now showed cause.   *   *   *

Hill and *Amos*, contrà.   *   *   *   [256]

LORD DENMAN, Ch. J. :   [258]

The case which seemed most adverse to this application was *Rex* v. *Shepherd* (2) ; but it appears that the only reason assigned for refusing a *quo warranto* there was, that to claim the office of churchwarden wrongfully was not an usurpation on the rights or prerogatives of the Crown : it was not surmised that the party disputing the claim had another remedy. Nor is there any other in this case, as far as I can see. There is no mode of trying the right by action, because the office is not one of profit. And, if there has been an improper election, it is not desirable that the rates should remain in the hands of those who may have been parties to such wrongful election. Now, *on the facts stated   [*259]
here, I think it very questionable whether the election was a proper one. I do not know what opinion a jury might form ; but there are strong circumstances which make its validity questionable. I do not see any thing in the omission to take a show of hands. A show of hands could be no criterion of the number of votes according to Sturges Bourne's Act, 58 Geo. III. c. 69, although, in cases where each man has one vote, such a mode of voting may sometimes be convenient. However, there are other circumstances here which raise a suspicion that the proceedings were not correct. (His Lordship then commented on other facts of the case not material to this report.) If the

(1) The alleged custom was given up on the argument.
(2) 2 R. R. 416 (4 T. R. 381). See

Rex v. *Daubney*, 1 Bott. 347, pl. 358 (6th ed.) ; *S. C.* 2 Str. 1196.

election is void, there ought to be another; and, if it be not void, still there are circumstances which render it fit that the parties should make a return, and show how it is maintainable; the matter may then be put into a proper train of inquiry. I give this as my opinion, because I do not at present see any other mode of correcting that which may have been an improper proceeding.

LITTLEDALE, J.:

There is a doubt whether these churchwardens were properly elected; and I see no other mode in which we can proceed than to grant the rule for a *mandamus*. In the two cases first cited by the *Attorney-General*, a *quo warranto* lay; here, as in *Rex* v. *Shepherd* (1), it does not.

(*Sir W. W. Follett* referred to *Anthony* v. *Seger* (2), as showing that, in the present case, resort might be had to the Ecclesiastical Court.)

[*260] I do not see my way so clearly to another remedy, as *to say here that a *mandamus* ought not to go. The objections which have been taken to the show of hands are, I think, inapplicable; because, where the number of votes depends on property, a show of hands could not decide any thing. The granting of this *mandamus* may no doubt be attended with difficulties; but I do not, at present, see any other mode of putting the case in the way of investigation than by making this rule absolute.

PATTESON, J.:

I see no distinction between granting a *mandamus* to swear in one of two candidates, who says that, although apparently in a minority, he had a legal majority, and a *mandamus* to elect where an election has taken place, but under circumstances which are said to render it void. If we interfere by *mandamus* for the purpose of putting in the right person, where the wrong has been elected, I think we ought also to interfere in the manner here suggested, where the election is alleged to be void. On principle, I think that the *mandamus* ought to issue (3).

Rule absolute.

(1) 2 B. R. 416 (4 T. R. 381).   (3) Williams, J. was absent.
(2) 1 Hagg. Consist. Rep. 9.

EMMERSON *v.* SALTMARSHE AND OTHERS.

(7 Adol. & Ellis, 266—277; S. C. 2 N. & P. 446; 6 L. J. (N. S.) K. B. 235.)

> Under stat. 23 Hen. VIII. c. 5, s. 3, and a commission framed according to it, a sewer's rate assessed in gross on a township at large is bad, though laid only for defraying the expenses of the commission, and though the rate has been, in previous instances, so assessed, and submitted to by the township in question.

REPLEVIN. The defendants avowed and made cognisance under the authority of the commissioners of sewers. On the trial before Parke, B., at the York Spring Assizes, 1835, a verdict was found for the plaintiff, subject to a case, which, so far as is material to the point decided, was as follows.

The plaintiff was, at the time of making the distress, constable of the township of Elvington; and was and had been, for fourteen years previously, the occupier of about forty-four acres of land in that township. One defendant was bailiff of the other defendants, who are commissioners of sewers, appointed by his Majesty's commission, dated 12th of July, 1833, for Howdenshire and the west parts of the East Riding of Yorkshire, within which Elvington is situate.

The commission, granted under stat. 23 Hen. VIII. c. 5, recited, that the walls, ditches, &c., sewers, &c., bridges, streams, and other defences by the coasts of the sea and marsh grounds in the East Riding, viz. for Howdenshire, &c. (setting out certain limits), by rage of the sea, &c., and by means of the trenches of fresh water descending, &c., were dirupt, lacerate, &c., with other impediments, annoyances, and defaults, specified; and it assigned commissioners, including the defendants, or any six of them, with a quorum of three, to survey the said walls, &c., to cause the annoyances to be corrected, "as also to inquire by the oaths of the honest and lawful men of our said county, place, or places where such defaults or annoyances be, as well within the liberties as without, by whom the truth may the rather be known, through whose default the said hurts and damages have happened, and who hath or holdeth any lands or tenements, or common of pasture, or profit of fishing, or hath or may have any hurt, loss, or disadvantage by any manner of means in the said places, as well near to the said dangers, lets, and impediments, as inhabiting or dwelling thereabouts by the said walls," &c., "and other the said impediments and annoyances; and all those persons, and every of them, to tax, assess, charge, distrain, and punish, as well within the metes, limits, and bounds, of old time accustomed, or otherwise or elsewhere within this our realm, after the quantity of their lands, tenements, and rents, by the number of acres and perches, after the rate of every person's portion, tenure, or profit, or after the quantity of their common of pasture, or profit of fishing, or other commodities there, by such ways and means, and in such manner and form, as to you, or six of you (whereof we will that three of you of the quorum *shall always be three), shall seem most convenient to be ordained and done for redress and reformation to be had in the premises; and also to reform, repair, and amend the aforesaid walls," &c.

[*268]

On 14th December, 1833, a session of sewers was held, at which the Court made an order of that date, "that, for the raising of a fund to pay off and discharge the charges and expenses remaining unpaid, attendant upon, or incurred in, the execution of the commission of sewers for the shire and parts aforesaid, dated " &c., "and also the charges and expenses of the solicitation and suing out of the commission of sewers for the shire and parts aforesaid, dated " &c., "also unpaid, and such subsequent charges and expenses as shall attend and be incident to the execution, or in respect of, the same commissions, the constable and constables of the several townships within the shire and parts aforesaid, in the assessment hereunder written particularly mentioned, do, on or before the first day of March next, pay unto the York city and county banking company, at " &c. "in Howden aforesaid, the several and respective sum and sums of money in such assessment particularly rated, assessed, or imposed upon each and every of the said townships, for the purposes aforesaid." Then followed the assessment, one item of which was "Elvington, 4l."

On 26th April, 1834, at a session of sewers then holden, the commissioners made an order that the constable of Elvington should appear at the next Court, " to show cause why the sum of 4l., rated or assessed upon the said township, by a certain rate" &c., had not been paid pursuant to the order of the Court.

The defendant appeared at the next Court, and refused *to pay; upon which a warrant issued to one of the defendants, as bailiff, signed and sealed by the remaining defendants (all of whom were commissioners), reciting the rate and assessment on the township of Elvington, and that the plaintiff, constable of the township, being an inhabitant and holder of certain lands and tenements within the said township, and a party subject and liable to pay and contribute towards the said rate and assessment, had refused to pay the said sum of 4l., though he had notice of the rate and assessment, and the sum had been demanded of him; and authorising and commanding the bailiff to levy the 4l., with the costs, &c., on the plaintiff's goods by distress.

The earliest commission of sewers for the district in question, preserved amongst the proceedings of the Court, is in 8 Anne; and similar commissions (in the whole fourteen) appear to have been granted from time to time till the commission appointing the present defendants. It also appears by the books of the commissioners that, from 1725 to the present time, rates or assessments have been made by the commissioners acting under the said commissions upon the same townships, and in the same relative proportions, as the assessment of 14th December, 1833, but for different amounts; and that the following payments of rates have been made by or for the township of Elvington. In 1725, Elvington, 1l.; 1728, Elvington, 1l.; 1748, Elvington, 1l.; 1759, Elvington, 1l. 6s. 8d.; 1828, Elvington, 2l.; 1831, Elvington, 4l.: and that the last two payments were made after orders of Court for such payment, and under threat of a distress upon the constable. It also appears from the books and proceedings of the commissioners that an order was made on 22nd of August, 1778, requiring *the attendance of several inhabitants of Elvington, Barmby (1), and other places, at the next court of sewers, to show cause why their assessments had not been paid; and that, by an order of the Court, dated 24th October, 1778, a warrant of distress for levying a rate was issued against the inhabitants of Elvington.

(1) One of the townships named in the present assessment.

From 1725 until the commencement of the present action, no instance, with the above exception, was proved, wherein disobedience to an order upon the constable for the rate laid by the commissioners upon the entire township was followed by a warrant of distress upon his goods : but no account of receipts of the rates from 1778 until the appointment of the present clerk, in 1831, has been kept. And no instance was produced of disobedience by a constable to any order of the commissioners for the payment of a rate, till the occasion of the present distress. (The case then stated certain facts, raising questions as to the jurisdiction of the commissioners, and the benefit received by the township of Elvington and the plaintiff in particular; but the decision of the Court renders it unnecessary to state the facts or arguments on these points.)

If the Court should be of opinion that the distress was illegal, the verdict for the plaintiff was to stand : otherwise, a verdict to be entered for the defendants.

The case was argued on a former day in this Term (1).

Alexander, for the plaintiff:

The distress is not justified by the rate, which is bad, as being assessed on a whole township. By stat. 23 Hen. VIII. c. 5, s. 3, with which the commission corresponds, the parties subjected to the *powers of the commissioners are the persons deriving benefit, or guilty of default : that can apply only to individuals. No other rule can be a fair one. The authorities collected in 2 Phil. Ev. 443 (2), and in Woolrych's Law of Waters and of Sewers, 395, are strongly in favour of the plaintiff on this point. In *The Case of the Isle of Ely* (3) it was resolved that a tax in gross upon a town is not warranted by the commission, but should be upon every owner or possessor of lands, &c. Mr. Fraser, in note (E) upon that case, has collected several authorities. A passage there extracted from Lord Ellesmere's Observations appears to show that Lord Ellesmere considered a rate on a township to be good, because, upon emergency, the commissioners could not wait " till every acre or perch be by survey divided and

[*271]

(1) Friday, May 26th. Before
Lord Denman, Ch. J., Littledale
and Patteson, JJ.

(2) 7th ed.
(3) 10 Co. Rep. 141 a.

numbered :" Lord Chancellor Egerton's Observations on the
Lord Coke's Reports, pp. 13, 14. But this, at the utmost, can
justify such a rate only in cases of emergency; and, indeed,
before the emergency occurs, the commissioners ought to be
sufficiently acquainted with the property to be able to lay the
rate properly on the individuals. So, by the Charter of Romney
Marsh, cited in Callis on Sewers, 122, the tax is to be laid on the
individuals. The first editor of Callis also cites *Hetley* v. *Boyer* (1),
and *Custodes, &c.* v. *The Inhabitants of Owtwell* (2). These cases
show the rate on the township to be bad. They are cited, with
most of the old authorities, in 19 Vin. Ab. 418, Sewers, (B). In
Bow v. *Smith* (3) it was admitted that an assessment on all the
lands, " from such a place to such a place in the level," was bad.
There, indeed, Lord Chancellor MACCLESFIELD said that it was
*not necessary to name the owners, but that the particular lands
should be assessed ; here even that is not done. In *Masters* v.
Scroggs (4) this COURT laid down that " it ought to appear that the
party assessed receives, or is likely to receive, a benefit." In
the Appendix to Callis, No. viii., p. 352 (5), there is a precedent
of a rate and assessment, where the whole is laid on the individual
occupiers. It is true, that Callis, p. 128, after mentioning some
authorities against rating a township, contends that such a rate
is good : but the current of authorities is the other way. Here,
too, the individual has been distrained upon for the tax laid on
the whole township. Callis suggests that, if a party not liable
at all be distrained on, he may bring trespass ; and that, if he be
liable at all, he may give in the names of the other parties liable
and crave of the commissioners to make a law that all may contribute. He also observes that the township may apportion
among themselves. The suggestion of such circuitous remedies
shows the badness of the principle.

[*272]

Cresswell, contrà :

It is admitted, on the other side, that the authority of Callis is
in favour of a rate on the township. In this particular instance,

(1) Cro. Jac. 336.
(2) Style, 178.
(3) 9 Mod. 94 : *S. C.* 2 Eq. Ca. Ab.
206.

(4) 3 M. & S. 447. See *Soady* v.
Wilson, 42 R. R. 379 (3 Ad. & El.
248).
(5) 4th (Broderip's) ed.

EMMERSON
v.
SALT-
MARSHE.

the rate is laid to defray the expense of the commission ; therefore the necessity of apportioning according to the benefit received
does not arise ; the proportions must be invariable ; and it is like
the acre rate which was held to be good in *The Case of the Level
of Hull* (1). In *The Case of the Isle of Ely* (2) the rate was laid
for making a new river, which it was held the commissioners

[*273]

could *not do. It was, indeed, also resolved that a rate on a
township was bad. But the argument on that point is not given ;
and it may have applied to the particular case only. Callis states
that, in *The Case of Sir Philip Conisby* (3), tried before Lord Coke
the year after he had reported *The Case of the Isle of Ely* (2), an
assessment laid generally on a township was treated as good.
Callis's doctrine is adopted in Com. Dig. Sewers (E 2). The
passage from Lord Ellesmere's Observations, referred to on the
other side, is an authority to the same effect. And the resolutions
in *The Case of the Isle of Ely* (2) were disapproved of by the Privy
Council, whose decision is reported in Moore, 824. *Hetley* v.
Boyer (4) was the case of a fine set upon a village and ordered to
be levied on an individual, which is very different from a rate like
the present. Even in the case of amercements, townships have
been charged generally: Callis, p. 124, cites an instance from
Doctor and Student, fol. 74 (5), and refers to the Statute of
Winchester, 13 Edw. I. stat. 2, c. 2, making hundreds liable for
the escape of felons. It is true that here the individual is distrained upon for the whole; but his remedy is to call on the commissioners to apportion. Having laid the rate on the township, they
summoned him, being one landholder, to show why payment was
not made. He did not answer, as he might have done, that others
were liable with him : *non constat*, therefore, that he is not the
only party in the township liable. Besides, it seems from *Soady*

[*274]

v. *Wilson* (6) that, in an action of *trespass against the commissioners, the Court will not inquire into the *quantum* of benefit.

Alexander, in reply:

It is very doubtful whether an acre rate could be laid :

(1) 2 Str. 1127.   (4) Cro. Jac. 336.
(2) 10 Co. Rep. 141 a.   (5) Dial. 2, c. 9.
(3) Call. Sew. 128.   (6) 42 R. R. 379 (3 Ad. & El. 248).

Commissioners of Sewers v. *Newburg* (1). But, in that case, the particular lands receiving benefit would be designated. As to the argument, that the plaintiff, on being summoned, might have pointed out the proportions in which other occupiers in the township are liable, that would throw upon an occupier, under the penalty of distress, the duty which belongs to the commissioners.

(PATTESON, J. referred to 37 Assis. fol. 218 A., pl. 10, and 38 Assis. fol. 225 A., pl. 15, cited in Call. Sew. 123.)

It does not appear that either of those was the case of a sewers' rate.

Cur. adv. vult.

LORD DENMAN, Ch. J. now delivered the judgment of the COURT:

The question in this case is, whether a rate or assessment can be made by the commissioners of sewers upon a whole township. And it will be proper, in the first instance, to advert to the commission of sewers itself, to see the powers of the commissioners.

They are to inquire by the oaths of the honest and lawful men of the county, (His Lordship then read the commission, as set out at p. 721, *ante,* to the words "to be had in the premises ").

Now, such being the effect of the commission, in *The Case of the Isle of Ely* (2) it is stated to be clearly resolved *that the tax generally of a several sum in gross upon a town is not warranted by the commission of sewers, but it ought to be particular, according to the express words, upon every owner or possessor of lands, tenements, and rents, &c. That indeed was a case of a new river: but still the fourth resolution of Lord Coke and the two Judges, to whom the decree of the commissioners of sewers was referred, must be considered as authority.

In Moore, 824, at a meeting of a board of the Privy Council, a full report upon the authority of the commissioners of sewers was made by Lord Chief Justice POPHAM; "that they cannot lay a tax or rate upon any hundreds, towns, or the inhabitants thereof in general, but upon the first presentment and judgment

[*275]

(1) 3 Keb. 827.   (2) 10 Co. Rep. 141 a.

to charge every man in particular according to the quantity of his land or common " (1).

The same rule was laid down in *Hetley* v. *Boyer* (2). So also in the case of *Custodes, &c.* v. *The Inhabitants of Outwell* (3). Several other cases will be found collected in Viner's Abridgement, tit. Sewers, and in Comyns's Digest, tit. Sewers : and reference is made to several cases in Fraser's edition of Coke's Reports, in *The Case of the Isle of Ely* (4).

Callis, however, in page 122 and the following pages, says that a rate or assessment may be made on a town generally, and that the persons who are liable may afterwards apportion it among themselves ; though he *also says, in another place, that the co mmissioners may, in the first instance, assess the particular individuals ; and he cites a number of instances to prove his proposition. The cases he cites appear to be amercements on towns or other districts ; but which are not circumstanced as assessments made by commissioners of sewers, where their duty is prescribed by the commission itself.

[*276]

Comyns, indeed, in his Digest, tit. Sewers (E. 2), says that an assessment may be charged in general upon such a town, who may afterwards apportion it among themselves ; but the only authority he cites for that is Callis. And Comyns afterwards says that an assessment upon a town in general, if it be not afterwards apportioned, is not good.

And it does not appear that there is any other direct authority for the validity of the assessment upon an entire township but what is derived from Callis. And we think that the other several authorities outweigh his.

The Case of the Level of Hull (5) was cited in support of the assessment: but that appears to be an assessment of 9*d.* an acre on 1,312 acres ; and we therefore may suppose that the commissioners had considered what lands were liable ; and the question there appears to have been, whether it should have been

(1) See p. 729, *post*; and Moore, 828.
(2) Cro. Jac. 336.
(3) Style, 178, Mich. 1649. *Hetley* v. *Boyer* was decided, Hil. 11 Jac. 1 (1614), between the decision in *The Case of the Isle of Ely* (Mich. 7 Jac. 1, 1609), and the resolution of the Privy Council, Moore, 824 (November, 1616), and appears to be one of the cases referred to by that resolution.
(4) Note (E) to 10 Co. Rep. 143 a.
(5) 2 Str. 1127.

upon the occupiers ; but, supposing it did support Callis, it could not, in our opinion, be a sufficient answer to the other authorities.

It has been said that this is the course which has been pursued ever since the year 1725. That may be; and perhaps it may, upon the whole, have been found more *convenient to let the landowners settle the proportions among themselves, so as not to trouble the commissioners to fix the proportions, unless there should be a necessity. This course of practice, however, cannot vary the law of the case: and, upon the whole, we are of opinion that the general assessment cannot be supported; and that there must be

[*277]

Judgment for the plaintiff.

[The following addition to the judgment is made by the desire of the learned Judges.

The COURT inadvertently cited the case from Moore, 824, in support of this judgment; but, though the words in Moore are the same as in the present judgment, yet in the case in Moore the COURT express their disapprobation of those propositions. But, though this case was thus cited inadvertently as an authority in favour of the plaintiff, it makes no difference in the judgment of this COURT on the whole case; as they do not concur in the disapprobation expressed in the report in Moore.]

REX v. JOHN GANN COUSINS.
REX v. TWELVE OTHER PERSONS, SEVERALLY.

(7 Adol. & Ellis, 285—287; S. C. 2 N. & P. 164; 6 Dowl. P. C. 3.)

1837.
June 12.

[285]

Several *quo warranto* informations having been filed on the same grounds, for exercising the office of alderman of the same corporation, one was tried, a verdict found for the Crown, and a rule *nisi* granted for a new trial, or to enter a verdict for the defendant. A rule *nisi* was then obtained for a stay of proceedings in the other informations pending the above application.

The COURT discharged the rule, the prosecutor undertaking to proceed with only one other information till further order. But they refused to direct that either party should be bound by the result of such one proceeding.

RULES were obtained on a former day of the Term in the above cases, calling upon the prosecutor to show cause why all proceedings in the several prosecutions, on information in the

nature of *quo warranto*, should not be stayed until the determination of another rule now pending in this Court, in the case of a
like information against Thomas Brightwell. The last mentioned
information, for claiming to be an alderman of the city of Norwich,
was tried at the Norfolk Spring Assizes in this year, and a
verdict found for the Crown. A rule was obtained in the last
Easter Term to show cause why a verdict should not be entered
for the defendant, or a new trial had ; which was the depending

[*286] *rule above mentioned. The grounds upon which the rule for
that information had been granted were, that the defendant was
not duly elected ; that he was not proposed separately to the
councillors ; that the persons proposed as aldermen were proposed
jointly and not separately ; and that no separate proposal was
made, or vote come to, as to the election of the defendant. The
rules against Cousins and twelve other parties, to which the
present applications related, were granted on the same day
(November 24th, 1836) on which the rule was made absolute
against Brightwell, and at the instance of the same relator,
Henry Rogers ; the informations were likewise for claiming the
office of alderman of Norwich ; and the grounds stated in applying
for the informations respectively were the same as in *Brightwell's*
case, with the addition, only, that the individual was proposed
and elected jointly with a list of himself and others together,
and not otherwise. In support of the present application, it
was stated that the parties now applying did not show cause
against the rules as to them, having no other cause to show than
that already submitted by Brightwell, and the rules were therefore made absolute ; and that the affidavits used in obtaining
the rule against Brightwell were in all material respects the
same as those used against the several parties now applying.
It was further stated that Rogers was preparing to exhibit
informations, in pursuance of the rules granted, against all the
present applicants, and that (as was believed) there were no
other questions to be tried on those informations than were in
issue upon that filed against Brightwell. On the rules now
coming on for determination, it was suggested that the prosecutor
should try one more information, the result of which should
decide the rest.

Sir W. W. Follett and *Kelly* showed cause, and stated that
the prosecutor was willing, on the rule being discharged, to proceed with a single information ; but that if the cases were to be
consolidated, the defendants only, and not the prosecutor, must
be bound by the result; and they cited *Doyle* v. *Anderson* (1) as
an analogous case.

Sir J. Campbell, Attorney-General, *contrà*, denied the
analogy between these prosecutions and actions on a policy of
insurance, and insisted that, if the prosecutor was not bound by
the event of one case, the defendants must claim the like liberty.

LORD DENMAN, Ch. J. :

The prosecutor is willing to proceed at present with only one
case. I should be glad that that were final ; but I do not find
that it has been usual to make a rule for such a purpose. The
defendants certainly obtain an advantage by the suspension of
all the cases but one. The only rule we can make is, that the
prosecutor shall, at present, try only a single information : but
we order nothing as to any party being bound by the result.

LITTLEDALE, PATTESON, and WILLIAMS, JJ. concurred.

It was ordered, that the rule *nisi* for staying proceedings, as
above-mentioned, should be now discharged, " the prosecutor
hereby undertaking to file an information in one of these prosecutions only, and to proceed to trial in such one information
only, until the further order of this Court."

IN THE EXCHEQUER CHAMBER.

(ERROR FROM THE KING'S BENCH.)

ALSTON, CLERK, *v.* ATLAY.

(7 Adol. & Ellis, 289—312 ; S. C. 2 N. & P. 492; W. W. & D. 662; 7 L. J.
(N. S.) Ex. 392.)

Plaintiff, being incumbent of the living of C., which was under the
annual value of 8*l.*, accepted the living of O., with cure of souls. Afterwards, the patron of C. sold the advowson to L. ; and L. presented a
clerk, who was instituted and inducted, and subscribed the Articles:
Held, that the living, as against the patron, was void by plaintiff's

(1) 40 R. R. 381 ; and see note there.—R. C.

RXX
v.
COUSINS.
[287]

1837.
June 13.
[289]

acceptance of O., and disannexed from the advowson; that, consequently, it did not pass by the sale; that L.'s presentee was not incumbent; and that plaintiff, not having been ousted *de facto*, might sue for the tithes.

And that it made no difference, as to this, whether the patron of C., or his vendee, knew or did not know of plaintiff's acceptance of O.

By the Court of Exchequer Chamber, reversing the judgment of the Court of K. B.

DEBT for treble value of tithes not set out, under stat. 2 & 3 Edw. VI. c. 13, s. 1 (1). The declaration (of 29th February, 1834) stated that the plaintiff, before and at &c., was, and still is, rector of the parish of Cowsby in the county of York, and proprietor of the tithes of corn, &c., yearly arising on land occupied by the defendant during all the time &c.; and that defendant, to wit on 1st January, 1832, and on divers other days &c., at &c., reaped certain corn then growing upon the said land, the tithe of which said corn then belonged to plaintiff, and of right ought to have been set out and paid to him as such rector and proprietor as aforesaid, &c. Averment, that defendant, after the said reaping, and before the commencement of this suit, took and carried the said corn from the land, the tenth part of the said corn not having been separated &c., or agreement made &c., contrary to the form of the statute. (There were other counts not material here.)

Plea, *Non debet :* and issue thereon. On the trial before [*290] Parke, B., at the Yorkshire Spring Assizes, 1835, *a verdict was found for the plaintiff for the treble value of the tithe, subject to the opinion of this Court on the following case.

The rectory of Cowsby is a benefice under the value of 8*l.* in the King's books ; and the plaintiff was instituted and inducted into it in 1816, and duly subscribed and read the Articles. The defendant, who was a farmer in Cowsby, paid his tithe regularly to the plaintiff, as rector, down to Michaelmas, 1832 ; but did not pay to the plaintiff, or set out, the tithes accruing subsequently (including those which are the subject of this action), in consequence of the same being claimed by the Reverend George Wray.

In 1829 the plaintiff was instituted and inducted into the rectory of Odell, in the county of Bedford, being distant 100

(1) Repealed S. L. R. Act, 1887.

miles from the said rectory of Cowsby, upon the presentation of
his brother, and subscribed and read the Articles. Odell is a
benefice with cure of souls of higher value than 8*l.* in the King's
books. In 1831 Justinian Alston, the brother of the plaintiff,
who was owner of the manor of Cowsby, and of an estate there,
and patron of the rectory of Cowsby, sold the manor and estate,
and the advowson, right of patronage and presentation of and to
the rectory or parish church of Cowsby, to George Lloyd, and
the same were conveyed to him by indentures bearing date 27th
and 28th November, 1831. In 1832 Lloyd, thinking that the
rectory of Cowsby had become voidable in consequence of the
acceptance by the plaintiff of the rectory of Odell, and that he,
Lloyd, had then a right to present a clerk to the rectory of
Cowsby, presented the Reverend George Wray to such rectory;
and, in pursuance of such presentment, George Wray was
instituted and inducted *into such rectory, and read and   [*291]
subscribed the Articles.

Either party, with the consent of the Court, was to be at
liberty to turn the case into a special verdict.

The case was argued in the Court of King's Bench on
Friday, June 3rd, 1836, by *Wightman* for the plaintiff and
Tomlinson for the defendant.

[The COURT having given judgment for the defendant,]

Leave was obtained to turn the case into a special verdict.   [296]
The verdict corresponded precisely with the special case; and judgment thereon was entered in the King's Bench for the defendant.

Error being brought in the Exchequer Chamber on the judgment of the Court of King's Bench, the case was argued on
Wednesday, May 10th, 1837, before Tindal, Ch. J., Bosanquet
and Coltman, JJ., Bolland, Parke, and Gurney, Barons.

*   *   *   *   *

Cur. adv. vult.

TINDAL, Ch. J., now delivered the judgment of the COURT: ⌊ 303

(After stating the pleadings and the special verdict, his
Lordship proceeded as follows.) It is to be observed that this
special verdict does not find that the plaintiff was presented to

ALSTON
v.
ATLAY.

the living of Cowsby by his brother Justinian; nor that he was presented to that of Odell by the same brother; nor that the patron had knowledge of the institution or induction of the plaintiff to the second living, at the time he conveyed the advowson *to Mr. Lloyd. The questions, therefore, which arise on this record are two; first, whether, after an incumbent of a benefice under value has accepted and been instituted and inducted to another benefice with cure of souls, the right of presentation, which accrues thereby to the patron, be assignable by law to another? and, secondly, whether the want of knowledge on the part of the patron of the fact of cession, at the time of such transfer, causes any difference? That the advowson itself was assignable there is no doubt; but, if the right of presentation was not, under these circumstances, assignable, then it follows that Mr. Lloyd had no right to present his clerk, and that the plaintiff in error, not having been deprived, and no new clerk having been presented, is still the incumbent, and still legally entitled to the tithes: 2 Roll. Abr. 361, pl. 6 (1); Watson's Clerg. L. ch. 2, pp. 7, 8; Com. Dig. Esglise, (N. 5); and the concluding part of the judgment in *Halton* v. *Core* (2).

[*304]

And, upon a careful consideration of the authorities, we are compelled to come to the conclusion that the judgment of the Court of King's Bench is erroneous.

There is no question but that, if a benefice be actually void, by the death of an incumbent, by his resignation, or by cession, under 21 Hen. VIII. c. 13, or by deprivation (*Leak* v. *The Bishop of Coventry* (3)), the right to present upon that avoidance is not capable of being transferred, either alone, or with the entire advowson: it is a personal right or interest, severed from the advowson and vested in the person of him who was patron at the time; a chose in action, which is not *assignable, and which is designated in the books by a great variety of names, all indicating its personal and unalienable quality. (See those collected in *Mirehouse* v. *Rennell* (4)).

[*305]

(1) Presentment, L.
(2) 35 R. R. 373 (1 B. & Ad. 559).
(3) Cro. Eliz. 811.

(4) 36 R. R. 139, 179 (1 Cl & Fin. 527; 8 Bing. 518).

The question then is, whether the right to present, caused by the cession in this case, was a chattel disannexed from the advowson, and vested in the person of Mr. Justinian Alston, before the transfer to Mr. Lloyd, or not? If it was, it could not be assigned.

There is no doubt but that this right of presentation accrued by the canon law, namely, by the Fourth Council of Lateran; but it is equally clear, that this canon has been recognised in this country, and has become a part of the common law of the land (*Holland's* case (1), *Digby's* case (2), *Evans* v. *Ascough* (3)). The point to be decided is, What is the nature of the right given by that canon to the patron? Is it an immediate right of presentation in the then patron, when he chooses to exercise it, without doing any thing previously to avoid the interest of the then incumbent; or is it only a right to avoid that interest, by some act, and then to present; or to avoid it by the act of presentation only, *per se*, such interest of the incumbent being valid, and the church full, as to the patron, in the meantime? If the former be the true answer, then we conceive such right is, like every other vested and complete right of presentation, a personal thing, and incapable of transfer. If the latter, then it is probable that the right would pass with the advowson to the new patron.

Now, although the books use some variety of expression on this subject (in some cases the benefice being said to be "void;" in others, "void as to the patron for his benefit;" in some, "to be void at his election;" and in others, but of a comparatively recent date, "to be voidable"), yet in none is it intimated that the patron has not an immediate right to present, as to a void church, without doing any further act in order to make such presentation valid. And the substance of the authorities is, that he has a complete right to present upon the cession, by institution to the second benefice, but does not lose his right by lapse, till sentence of deprivation and notice by the Bishop, from which time the six months begin to run.

[306]

(1) 4 Co. Rep. 75 a; *S. C. as Armiger* v. *Holland*, Moore, 542; Cro. Eliz. 601.

(2) 4 Co. Rep. 78 b.

(3) Latch, 243.

ALSTON
v.
ATLAY.

It may be advisable to take a short review of these authorities.

The Fourth Council of Lateran is to this effect: "Quicunque receperit aliquod beneficium curam habens animarum annexam, si priùs tale beneficium habebat, eo sit, ipso jure, privatus; et si fortè illud retinere contenderit, etiam alio spolietur. Is quoque ad quem prioris spectat donatio, illud post receptionem alterius liberè conferat, cui meritò viderit conferendum " (1).

The fair construction of the words of this canon is, that, upon acceptance of the second benefice, the clerk should be deprived of the first, by the law itself, "*jure ipso*," without any actual sentence of deprivation; and the patron may then freely present a clerk without any other act to be done, as on a deprivation. The constitution itself (it will be seen afterwards) operates in the

[*307]

nature of a general sentence of deprivation. And that *this is the true construction of the canon is confirmed by many authorities. One of the earliest cases on this subject is *Holland's* case (2), in which the COURT held the benefice to be " void," not " by the common law, but by the constitution of the Pope, of which avoidance the patron might take notice if he would, and might present if he would without any deprivation; but because the avoidance accrued by the ecclesiastical law, no lapse incurred without notice, as upon deprivation or resignation, and yet the patron might present, and take upon him notice if he would; so that for the benefit of the patron the church is void," " but not for his disadvantage." In the report of the same case in Moore (3), the first benefice is said to be "void" "by the common law," "without sentence declaratory, at the election of the patron;" which really means the same thing, and is so explained by the context, "that he may, if he will, present without notice." There is no intimation, in this or any other case, that any act of the patron is necessary to avoid the benefice before presentation. In the report in Croke (4), the first benefice is said to be "void by the order of the common law." In *Digby's* case (5) POPHAM, Ch. J., and the whole COURT, state that

---

(1) Note (a) to 2 Gibson's Codex, p. 904, tit. xxxvii. ch. 1 (2nd ed.).

(2) 4 Co. Rep. 75 a.

(3) *Armiger* v. *Holland*, Moore, 542.

(4) *Armiger* v. *Holland*, Cro. Eliz. 601.

(5) 4 Co. Rep. 79 b.

the first is void by institution to the second, without deprivation or sentence declaratory; yet no lapse shall incur, unless notice be given to the patron, no more than if the church became void by resignation or deprivation; and yet the patron may take notice if he will, and present according to the said constitution. In *Rex* v. *The Archbishop of Canterbury* (1) the church is said to be "void. But not so that *the lapse incurred." So in Fitzh. N. B. 34, the first benefice is said to be "void." In *Edes* v. *The Bishop of Oxford* (2) it is also said to be "void." In *Winchcombe* v. *Bishop of Winchester* (3) it is said, "a thing may be void or not void, at the election of him whom it concerns, as in *Holland's* case." "The patron of the first church may take it as void, and present presently, or may leave it as full till sentence of deprivation." It is remarkable that there the church is not said to be full. In the case in Sir William Jones (reported also in Croke), *Rex* v. *Priest* (4), the law is laid down to the like effect as in *Holland* (5) and *Digby's* (6) cases, and a very clear explanation given of the Council of Lateran. It is said to have been held, first, by the greater part of the justices, that before the statute of 21 Hen. VIII. the first church was void, and the patron could present, if he would, without sentence declaratory, by the said constitution of Lateran; for the words are, *ipso jure sit privatus*, and do not mention any sentence of deprivation; by the same canon, a church shall be void, without sentence, if one be consecrated bishop, so for the same reason, and by the same words, the first benefice shall be void by the taking of the second benefice; if a party resign, or be deprived by a particular sentence for crime, the church shall be void, and *à multò fortiori*, the constitution (which is a general sentence of deprivation, as is said 10 Edw. III. 2 (7)) will make an avoidance; but true it is that, in the said case, the patron is not bound *to take notice of it, being an ecclesiastical constitution, so, upon a particular

ALSTON
v.
ATLAY.

[*308]

[*309]

(1) Hetley, 125.
(2) Vaughan, 21.
(3) Hob. 166 (5th ed.).
(4) 1 Jones, 337; *S. C.* as *Rex* v. *The Archbishop of Canterbury* and *Pryst*, Cro. Car. 356.
(5) 4 Co. Rep. 75 a; *S. C.* as *Armiger*

v. *Holland*, Moore, 542; Cro. Eliz. 601.
(6) 4 Co. Rep. 79 b.
(7) The reference seems to be to *Rex* v. *The Bishop of Norwich*, Year B. Hil. 10 Edw. III. pl. 3, fol. 1 A.

deprivation or resignation, notice ought to be given to the patron, otherwise no lapse; yet there is an avoidance. And it was agreed on the other part, according to the said cases, that the patron can present, if he will, without notice or sentence declaratory; and that could not be, unless the church was void before the presentation, for the form of presentation is, " ad ecclesiam jam vacantem," which presupposes vacancy before the presentation.

In *Rex* v. *Bishop of London* (1) it was resolved by all the four Judges that, where the first living was under value, the acceptance of a second was an avoidance by the canon law, *ipso jure*, without any deprivation, so that the patron could present, if he wished, without any sentence of deprivation; and, the church being once void, as to the patron to present, a dispensation by the Archbishop afterwards came too late, and could not restore the clerk to his benefice; and Jones says it seemed to him clearly that, by the institution and induction to the second benefice, the first being under value, the first benefice was void, as well as if it was above value; but the difference in the last case is, that the patron must take notice at his peril, for it is void by the Act of Parliament, and the words are, it shall be void as if the incumbent were dead; and, if he does not present in six months, the living will lapse. But in the first case there was no lapse, and the patron might present. And he also gave his opinion, that, if the Bishop gave notice to the patron of the taking of the second benefice, if he do not

[*310] present within six months, there *would be a lapse, as upon deprivation or resignation; and, if the benefice was not void, but there ought to be a deprivation, then the presentment and institution upon that would be a void institution; which is not so, for the first institution and incumbency is made void by taking the second benefice.

And the case of *Leak* v. *The Bishop of Coventry* (2) has a very important bearing upon the question now under discussion, for it is a direct authority that, where the Bishop, after deprivation, but without giving notice of such deprivation, collated, and the patron afterwards grants the advowson in fee, and the clerk

(1) 1 (Wm.) Jones, 404.   (2) Cro. Eliz. 811.

collated by the Bishop dies, the grantee of the advowson cannot bring a *quare impedit* : and the reason given is that, when the original patron had right to present upon the deprivation, as in his turn, although the collation by the Bishop, without notice, was not good, nor ousted him, but that he always might have presented, and ousted the incumbent by his bringing a *quare impedit*, yet it is but a thing in action, and when he hath granted the advowson over, the grantee cannot have this thing in action.

It is only in more modern times, we believe, that the benefice is said to be " voidable." In 2 Gibson's Codex, 906, in a note (1), it is said to be " voidable ; " but that word is used as an explanation of the former part of the note. In the very modern cases of *Betham* v. *Gregg* (2), and *Apperley* v. *Bishop of Hereford* (3), the word " voidable " is used. In *Halton* v. *Cove* (4) the *word " voidable " is coupled with the words " perhaps actually void." We do not, however, understand that, by the use of this word " voidable," it is intended that any previous step is necessary before the patron presents ; for there is no authority whatever for such a position. It means merely that, if the patron does not elect to present, the incumbent may hold the living : it does not mean that the living is full as against the patron, in the mean time.

[*311]

It cannot well be that the living is full as relates to the patron, and that the presentation itself determines the interest of the clerk ; because it is clear that the presentation must be when the church is already void, and proceeds upon that assumption. An authority for this position has been before cited ; and Lord Coke, in *Harris* v. *Austen* (5), citing *Smale's* case, 17 Edw. III. 59 (6), distinctly says, the church ought to be void before he can present ; for, if the church be voidable, no presentation can be made. *Rud* v. *The Bishop of Lincoln* (7) is another authority that the right to present implies that the church is then void.

The result of all these authorities is that, upon institution

(1) Vol. 2, tit. xxxvii. ch. 1, note (z) (2nd ed.).
(2) 38 R. R. 449 (10 Bing. 352, 359).
(3) 9 Bing. 686.

(4) 35 R. R. 373 (1 B. & Ad. 558).
(5) 1 Roll. Rep. 213.
(6) Year B. Mich. 17 Edw. III. f. 59 B. pl. 59.
(7) Hutton, 66.

ALSTON
v.
ATLAY.

to the second living, the first is void as to the patron, but not so as to incur a lapse without sentence of deprivation and notice by the ordinary, or, at least, until notice by the ordinary ; and, if void as to him, he cannot deal with the fallen right of presentation at all : it is a personal inalienable right.

The second question, whether the want of a notice of the cession makes any difference, is readily disposed of. If the right to the fallen presentation be a personal *right, disannexed from the advowson, it is clear that want of knowledge of the vacancy by the patron cannot alter the quality of that right : it cannot make a personal thing real : it will not reannex it to the advowson, any more than want of notice of rent being in arrear (which bears the closest analogy to the subject-matter under consideration) would enable the vendor of a reversion to transfer the rent in arrear with the reversion. The only point of view in which it could be important is with reference to the rights of the grantee of the advowson, as against the grantor, arising out of their contract.

For these reasons we are all of opinion that the judgment of the Court of King's Bench should be reversed.

[*312]

Judgment reversed.

————•————

(ERROR FROM THE KING'S BENCH.)

1837.
June 13.
——
[313]

WRIGHT *v.* DOE D. SANDFORD TATHAM.

(7 Adol. & Ellis, 313—408; S. C. 2 N. & P. 305; 7 L. J. (N. S.) Ex. 340.)

[THE judgment of the Exchequer Chamber in this case, where the Judges, on an equal division of opinion, affirmed the judgment of the King's Bench, was affirmed by the House of Lords in 1838. The case will be reported at that stage in the Revised Reports, from 5 Cl. & Fin. 670.]

IN THE QUEEN'S BENCH.

TAYLOR *v.* DEVEY AND GRAHAM.

(7 Adol. & Ellis, 409—416; S. C. 2 N. & P. 469; W. W. & D. 646; 1 Jur.
892; 7 L. J. (N. S.) M. C. 11.)

1837.
Nov. 25.
─
[409]

Plea, to trespass for breaking and entering plaintiff's dwelling-house,
that the house was in the parish of B., in which there was an immemorial
custom for all the parishioners to go through the house, upon their
perambulations of the parish boundaries, on the Thursday in Rogation
week, every third year; and justification under the custom. Issue being
joined on a traverse of the custom, and a verdict found for the defendants: Held, on motion for judgment *non obstante veredicto*, that it could
not be assumed, on this plea, that the house stood on the boundary; and
that the custom was therefore bad, as pleaded.

Entries in the parish books, recording the fact that the perambulations
had taken a particular line, would not be evidence upon such an issue.

TRESPASS for breaking and entering the plaintiff's dwelling-
house, making a disturbance there, and continuing, &c., and
breaking doors and locks, &c. Plea, *that the said dwelling-   [*410]
house now is, and at the said times when &c. was, and from
time whereof &c. hath been, situate within, and parcel of, the
parish of St. Bridget, otherwise St. Bride, in the city of London:
that, from time whereof &c., there hath been, and at the said
times when &c. there was, and now is, within the parish of
St. B., a certain ancient and laudable custom there used and
approved, that is to say, that, during all the time aforesaid,
it hath been, and still ·is, lawful for all and every the
parishioners, for the time being, of the parish of St. B., to
go through the said dwelling-house in which &c., upon their
perambulations of the boundaries of the parish of St. B., upon
Thursday in Rogation week in every third year: and that, from
time whereof &c., the parishioners, for the time being, of the
parish of St. B. have used and been accustomed, in the exercise
of the custom aforesaid, to go through the said dwelling-house
in which &c., upon their perambulations of the boundaries of the
parish of St. B., upon Thursday in Rogation week in every third
year; wherefore the said defendants, being then and there two
parishioners of the parish of St. B., on Thursday in Rogation
week, in the year 1833 aforesaid (being then and there a third
year), in the exercise of the custom aforesaid, went through the

said dwelling-house in which &c., upon the perambulation by the parishioners of the said parish of St. B. of the boundaries of the same parish, using the said custom there for that purpose and on the occasion aforesaid, as they lawfully might for the cause aforesaid : and, in order &c. (justification under the custom). The replication traversed the custom ; and the defendant joined issue on the traverse.

[411]   On the trial before Lord Denman, Ch. J., at the London sittings after Michaelmas Term, 1885, a verdict was found for the defendants.   In Hilary Term, 1886, *Cresswell* obtained a rule *nisi* for judgment *non obstante veredicto*, on the ground that the plea, if it did not allege that the house was on the boundary of the parish, was no justification ; or for a new trial, on the ground that the plea, if taken to allege that fact, was not proved ; and also on the ground of a supposed misdirection (as to which see the judgment).

Sir J. Campbell, Attorney-General, *Barstow*, and *G. T. White*, in Trinity Term last (1), showed cause :

First : the plea does not allege that the plaintiff's house is on the boundary ; nor, in fact, is it so.   But the justification is nevertheless valid.   In *Goodday* v. *Michell* (2) a similar justification was pleaded by way of prescription, and held ill, because it should have been pleaded as a custom which is done here.   One reason of this was that parishioners cannot release.   And the COURT considered the defence substantially good ; ANDERSON, Ch. J. saying, "it is not to be doubted, but that parishioners may well justify the going over any man's land in their perambulation, according to their usage, and to abate all nuisances in their way."   The case is cited to the same point in 16 Vin. Abr. 307, Perambulation, pl. 5.   Such a custom would be useless, if maintainable only when the *locus in quo* is on the boundary : a boundary is a line upon
[*412]   which the perambulating party cannot all go.   Very *frequently too the line cannot be followed, on account of natural obstacles.

(LORD DENMAN, Ch. J. : Must you not show the necessity for a deviation, in your plea ?)

(1) May 30th, 1837.   Before Lord Denman, Ch. J., Littledale, Patteson, and Williams, JJ.

(2) Cro. Eliz. 441 ; *S. C.* Owen, 71 ; Co. Ent. 650 b, 651 b, Trespas, pl. 5.

It is enough that a custom, if proved in fact, may have had a legal origin : the actual origin need not be shown : *Pain* v. *Patrick* (1). Here the custom may have originated in the assent of the owner; especially if he held the land all the way up to the boundary, for he may have obstructed the way along the boundary, and have opened the other way as a compensation. Circumstances causing a necessary deviation may have ceased to exist : yet that would not make the custom bad, if once good. *Fitch* v. *Rawling* (2) shows that inhabitants may have a custom to play on the close of an individual : HEATH, J. there said that the lord might have made the grant before the time of memory. The custom often is for parishioners to meet within the parish at the vestry room, and to proceed thence to the boundary : a part of their route must then be not along the boundary. Besides, a perambulation often is for the purpose of ascertaining the boundary ; a part of it, therefore, must be performed on what is not the line ; and here the plea is that the act was done upon the perambulation. (They then argued on the supposed misdirection.)

Cresswell and *W. H. Watson, contrà :*

In *Goodday* v. *Michell* (3) the plea failed ; and there is no authority in favour of the custom, except an extra-judicial *dictum.* And, even as to that, it does not appear that the perambulation supposed was not one performed exclusively *along the boundary. A custom authorising the whole parish to pass, without necessity, every third year, through an individual's house cannot be supported : neither is the custom made good by its being laid on a particular day only : *Reynolds' case* (4). Customs which incroach upon individual rights are good only from necessity ; as to turn a plough upon a neighbour's land, to use the sea-shore for fishing, and other similar rights, some of which are alluded to in *Blundell* v. *Catterall* (5). Thus, if a deviation from the boundary were made necessary by

[*413]

(1) 3 Mod. 289. See pp. 293, 294.
(2) 3 R. R. 425 (2 H. Bl. 393).
(3) Cro. Eliz. 441 ; *S. C.* Owen, 71 ; Co. Ent. 650 b, 651 b, Trespas, pl. 5.
(4) Moore, 916.
(5) 24 R. R. 353 (5 B. & Ald. 268). And see *Blewett* v. *Tregonning*, 42 R. R. 463 (3 Ad. & El. p. 569, &c.).

TAYLOR
v.
DEVEY.

its passing through a pond, the deviation would become illegal if the pond were dried up. A deviation into a waste might not be illegal: but, if the waste became private property, and a house were built on it, a deviation through the house would be illegal. It is said that a perambulation may be for the purpose of ascertaining the boundary: but the custom is lawful only for the purpose of recording the boundary. (They then argued on the supposed misdirection.)

Cur. adv. vult.

LORD DENMAN, Ch. J., in this Term (November 25th), delivered the judgment of the COURT:

In the course of trying the existence of a custom for all the parishioners of St. Bride's, on their annual perambulation of the parish bounds, to go through the plaintiff's house, though not in the line of the parish boundary, the plaintiff's counsel observed to the jury that the defendants had given no evidence of the contents of parochial books on the subject, nor any [*414] evidence of *reputation (1). In summing up, I observed on this statement, and am supposed to have said that such evidence would have been inadmissible. A rule *nisi* has been obtained, on the ground that herein I misdirected the jury, because the existence of a public right of this nature may be proved by reputation.

We agree that, if a Judge misleads a jury on any question of law, the losing party is entitled to a new trial: for the jury must be supposed to adopt the law as expounded to them, and their verdict may have proceeded on the erroneous direction: nor can any calculation be permitted of the extent to which the error may have operated.

But I am by no means clear that the observation was made in the manner supposed. My attention was not called to it at the time of the summing up; and I took no note of what I said in that particular. On the contrary, recalling what passed as accurately as I now can, I am rather inclined to believe that the evidence, which I thought would have been inadmissible,

---

(1) On this point, Stark. Ev. part I. s. 34 (p. 54, 1st ed.; see vol. i. p. 156. 2nd ed.), and *Ireland* v. *Powell*, Peake on Ev. ch. 1, p. 16 (5th ed.), were referred to. See *Rex* v. *Antrobus*, 2 Ad. & El. 794, 795.

was that of entries in parish books recording the fact that the
perambulations had taken a particular line. We all think that
this would have been correct: and even a careful reporter
might have confounded this opinion with that which was justly
considered erroneous.

On this ground, therefore, no sufficient case for granting a
new trial is made out. But the learned counsel for the plaintiff
moved to enter judgment for him notwithstanding the plea
found for the defendant, arguing that a custom to pass through
a particular *house within a parish, upon the perambulation of
the boundaries, is bad in law, unless such house is upon the
boundary line, so that the perambulation cannot be made
without passing through the house.

The plea, indeed, stated that the defendants went through the
plaintiff's house upon the perambulation of the boundaries,
"using the said custom there," which expressions might import
that the house was in the boundary line. If this construction
was admissible, the plaintiff would be entitled to a new trial,
and ultimately to a verdict, because the plea, so understood,
was disproved. But the construction cannot be adopted, the
plea only averring the house to be within the parish, and the
custom to be that it is lawful for all and every the parishioners
to go through it upon their perambulation of the boundaries.
The question, therefore, is whether the custom so laid is valid
in law.

The right to perambulate parochial boundaries, to enter
private property for that purpose, and to remove obstructions
that might prevent this from being done, cannot be disputed.
It prevails, as a notorious custom, in all parts of England, is
recorded by all our text writers, and has been confirmed by high
judicial sanction. Lord Ch. J. ANDERSON, and the whole Court
of Common Pleas, assert the custom and the right in the most
unqualified manner in *Goodday* v. *Michell* (1), the pleadings in
which are to be found in Coke's Entries, 651 b. That case,
indeed, appears to be the only decision in the books on the
subject of parish perambulations. There the justification
failed; but the defect was in the mode of pleading; for the

(1) Cro. Eliz. 441; *S. C.* Owen, 71; Co. Ent. 650 b, 651 b, Trespas, pl. 5.

[*415]

defendant's right was thought *to be placed on prescription, and not on custom ; and, besides, the bar did not embrace all the trespasses laid in the declaration.   These material faults, being pointed out and adjudged fatal, superseded the necessity for examining the plea more minutely, and enquiring whether the custom was well laid.   It claims a prescriptive right to enter plaintiff's close exactly in the same manner as the defendant in this action justifies under the custom for all and every the parishioners upon the perambulation of the boundaries to enter plaintiff's house, which is averred to be within the parish.   Now it is obvious that the right to perambulate boundaries cannot confer a right to enter any house in the parish, however remote from the boundaries, and though not required to be entered for any purpose connected with the perambulation : and it seems to follow that a custom on that occasion to enter a particular house, which is neither upon the boundary line nor in any manner wanted in the course of the perambulation, cannot be supported.

On principle, therefore, the custom laid is bad in law ; and the authority of the case, as to the form of pleading, cannot go for much, as the plea was set aside for two fatal faults in other respects.   The report contains several references to the Year Books, and one to Fitzherbert's Natura Brevium (1), none of which have any bearing on this objection.   The Book of Entries (p. 158) is also quoted ; but neither in that page, nor in any other, is light thrown upon it.

For the reasons given, we think ourselves bound to give our judgment for the plaintiff.

Rule absolute for judgment non obstante veredicto.

(1) Fitz. N. B. 185 B.

POWELL, HUGHES, AND PROTHERO, *v.* REES,

ADMINISTRATRIX OF JOHN REES (1).

(7 Adol. & Ellis, 426—430; S. C. 2 N. & P. 571; W. W. & D. 680; 8 L. J.
(N. S.) Q. B. 47.)

> An administrator is liable to an action for money had and received by
> the intestate, for coal tortiously taken by him from the plaintiff's land,
> if the intestate has sold it and received the money.
> And this, although no direct evidence be given of the actual sum
> received on the sale, if the jury believe the fact of the sale.
> And, where part has been raised more than six months before the
> intestate's death, and part within six months, the plaintiff may bring
> trespass, under stat. 3 & 4 Will. IV. c. 42, s. 2, for so much as was raised
> within the six months, and also money had and received for so much as
> was raised before; the acts being distinct, and therefore the two actions
> not incompatible.

ASSUMPSIT for money had and received by the intestate to the
use of the plaintiffs, and on an account stated between the
intestate and the plaintiffs; with promise by the intestate.
Plea, *non assumpsit;* with another plea not material here.

On the trial, before Coleridge, J., at the last Monmouthshire
Assizes, the facts (so far as material to the point here reported)
were as follows. The intestate had been lessee under the plaintiffs of certain coal mines; the minerals under three closes had
been excepted from the demise, but he had worked them, brought
the coals to the market, and received the produce. The plaintiffs had sued the defendant in trespass, after the intestate's
death, and recovered damages for the coals abstracted within the
six months next preceding that event, availing themselves of
the remedy given by stat. 3 & 4 Will. IV. c. 42, s. 2. The
present action was brought to recover damages for the proceeds
of the sales of coals by the intestate from under the excepted
closes, for the period antecedent to the six months before
mentioned (2). No direct evidence of the amount obtained by
the intestate for the coals was given. It appeared that they

---

(1) See similar point considered
on principles of equity in *Garth* v.
Cotton (1753) 1 Dickens, 183; and
Phillips v. *Homfray* (1883) 24 Ch. Div.
439, 52 L. J. Ch. 833 (affirmed on
technical grounds, 11 App. Cas. 466),
where judicial opinion is evenly
divided; and the Scotch case of
Davidson v. *Tulloch* (H. L. 1860)
3 Macq. 795, 1 Paterson, 930.—R. C.

(2) The facts, thus far, are stated
as in the judgment delivered by the
LORD CHIEF JUSTICE on the present
motion.

had been mixed with coals taken from the mines demised, and all sold together. The plaintiffs relied on the evidence of surveyors, as to the quantity of coal which *had been excavated. The defendant's counsel objected that the action did not survive against the administratrix under these circumstances; and that, at any rate, the action of trespass which had been brought was inconsistent with the present action. The learned Judge reserved leave to the defendant to move for a nonsuit; and the plaintiff had a verdict for the sum which the jury considered to be the value of the coal taken, deducting for the expense of raising and conveying it to market.

Talfourd, Serjt. now moved according to the leave reserved:

The first question is, whether, generally, money had and received can be maintained against an administrator upon such a tort committed by the intestate, or whether it be a personal action which expires with the person. It is true that, in many instances of tort, the party injured is permitted to waive the tort, and to proceed for the money obtained by the tort-feasor, affirming his act. This point is discussed in *Hambly* v. *Trott* (1). But here there was no evidence of the actual price (2), which seems necessary to the action for money had and received: *Harvey* v. *Archbold* (3). Again, this was, substantially, an action for an injury to the freehold: and it has never been held that such injuries can be treated as contracts. The statute 3 & 4 Will. IV. c. 42, s. 2, seems to show that the Legislature considered trespass to be the only remedy; otherwise the provision there would have been unnecessary. Secondly, the

[*428]   plaintiffs, by proceeding under the statute, have *elected to treat the act of the intestate as a trespass. They cannot now waive the tort; and, if not, they cannot bring the action for money had and received, which assumes that the act of the tort-feasor is affirmed.

Cur. adv. vult.

(1) 1 Cowp. 371.
(2) The motion was also made on the ground of the absence of direct

evidence of any sale; but the COURT held that the jury might infer it.
(3) 3 B. & C. 626.

LORD DENMAN, Ch. J., in this Term (November 9th), delivered
the judgment of the COURT:

In this case, we disposed of one ground, on which a rule for
entering a nonsuit was sought to be obtained, upon the hearing.
It remains to decide upon another, which arose under the
following circumstances. (His Lordship then stated the facts,
as at p. 747, *ante*.)

It was objected, in the first place, generally, that no such
action was maintainable; that the foundation of it was a tort,
the remedy for which died with the person; and that the
doctrine of waiving the tort and suing upon a contract implied
by law, could not be extended to a case in which no remedy by
action in tort existed to be waived. We were pressed, too, by
the remark that such an action was of the first impression, and
by the inference to be drawn from the language of the section
above mentioned, and from the remedy there given. If,
however, the legal principles upon which the action is maintainable are clear, these considerations ought not to prevail.
In the present case, the money which has been produced by
the sale of that which had been wrongfully severed from the
plaintiffs' estate, and converted into chattels, is traced into the
pocket of the intestate: it cannot be doubted that an action for
money had and received would have been maintainable against
him for that money. His personal estate has come to the
hands of the defendant, by so much increased; and *we cannot   [*429]
see any grounds why the same action is not to be maintained
against her who represents him in respect of that estate.

In the case of *Hambly* v. *Trott* (1) Lord MANSFIELD very fully
considers this subject, and lays down the distinctions which
arise, as to the surviving of remedies, upon the cause of action,
and the form of action. He observes (2) that there "is a fundamental distinction. If it is a sort of injury by which the
offender acquires no gain to himself at the expense of the
sufferer, as beating or imprisoning a man, &c., there, the
person injured has only a reparation for the *delictum* in
damages to be assessed by a jury. But where, besides the

(1) 1 Cowp. 371.   (2) 1 Cowp. 376.

POWELL
v.
REES.

crime, property is acquired which benefits the testator, there an action for the value of the property shall survive against the executor.   As for instance, the executor shall not be chargeable for the injury done by his testator in cutting down another man's trees, but for the benefit arising to his testator for the value or sale of the trees he shall."   The former part of this example illustrates the operation of the recent statute : in the latter, which is the present case, it was not needed.

But it was pressed on us, secondly, that, at all events, this action was not maintainable after recourse had been had to the statute first referred to ; for that the plaintiffs, having elected to proceed for damages for the trespass in part, could not split it and sue in contract for the other part.   The conduct of the plaintiffs may have been vexatious ; but that furnishes no legal answer to this action, because, in truth, the intestate was guilty of a series of trespasses, and not of one single

[*430] wrongful act.   *The plaintiffs, therefore, have only pursued different remedies for different injuries : they might indeed have recovered a compensation for all under the present form of proceeding, but they were not bound to do so.

Upon the whole there must be no rule.

Rule refused.

———•———

1837.
Nov. 8.
———

[454]

BRICKELL *v.* HULSE, BART. (1).

(7 Adol. & Ellis, 454—458 ; S. C. 2 N. & P. 426 ; 7 L. J. (N. S.) Q. B. 18.)

If a party, on motion before a Judge, use the affidavit of another person, such affidavit is, on any subsequent occasion, admissible as evidence against him who so used it.   Even on a trial when the person who swore the affidavit is present in Court and is not called.

TROVER for horses, goods, chattels, &c.   The defendant paid 20*l.* into Court, and pleaded that the plaintiff had sustained no further damages, which the plaintiff traversed.   Issue thereon.

[*455] On the trial before *Tindal, Ch. J., at the last Hampshire Assizes, it appeared that the goods in question had been seized under a writ of execution against the plaintiff, the defendant being sheriff.   Other writs of execution had also issued against the plaintiff.

(1) Cited and followed by DEN-   (1877) 47 L. J. Q. B. 144, 145.—
MAN, J. in *Campbell* v. *Rothwell*   R. C.

The conversion relied upon consisted of certain acts done by one James White. To connect White with the defendant, the plaintiff proved that, in June, 1836, after Trinity Term, the defendant applied to a Judge at Chambers to extend the time for returning the writs, in order that an application might be made in Term time under the Interpleader Act, 1 & 2 Will. IV. c. 58; that the time was extended accordingly; and that on the application at Chambers the defendant had put in an affidavit of James White, now produced, and from which it appeared that White had seized the goods as officer to the defendant, and had been in possession of them. White was in Court at the time of the trial. The evidence was objected to, but received. Verdict for the plaintiff.

Erle now moved for a new trial (1):

The depositions of a party who may be produced cannot be given in evidence. The fact, that the defendant had himself used the affidavit on a former occasion, does not take the case out of this rule; it has been decided that depositions used by a party in an equity suit cannot afterwards be produced against him on a trial, if the person making them might be called; *Rushworth* v. *Countess of Pembroke* (2), 2 Phil. Ev. 577 (3). There was no proof, independent of the affidavit, that White was the defendant's agent: the affidavit cannot therefore be received *as the declaration of an agent.

[*456]

(LORD DENMAN, Ch. J.: In the class of cases mentioned in the note to 1 Stark. Ev. 264 (4) the party sought to put in depositions which he had himself made use of.)

The defendant ought to have had an opportunity of cross-examining White.

(COLERIDGE, J.: He might have called White.)

Not without releasing him. The depositions could be evidence only if the witness could not be produced, and if the suit was

---

(1) He also moved for a nonsuit, on a point not material here.
(2) Hardres, 472.
(3) 8th ed.
(4) 2nd ed.

between the parties to the former proceeding: *Fry* v. *Wood* (1),
Benson v. *Olive* (2), *Lutterell* v. *Reynell* (3).   Here the plaintiff
cannot be called a party to what took place on the application
being made to the Judge at Chambers.   The Court will not lay
down, as a general rule, that every affidavit which a party uses
becomes, as against him, an admission on all future occasions.

LORD DENMAN, Ch. J.:

It is very important that this question should not be left
subject to doubt.   There can, I think, be no question but that
a statement which a party produces on his own behalf, whether
on oath or not, becomes evidence against him.   There is nothing
to distinguish it from a statement made by the party himself.
Rushworth v. *The Countess of Pembroke* (4) at first seems opposed
to this view ; for there the defendant was not permitted to use
any of the depositions made in an equity suit, where the plaintiff had been defendant.   That decision, however, was founded
on the nature of the proceedings in equity.   A party who uses
such depositions does not know, beforehand, what they are (5):
[*457]   if he did, such cases would stand on the same footing as *the
present.   He can only refer to what he expects will be produced:
it is like the case of a witness called at Nisi Prius, whose
evidence does not bind the party calling him.   It is quite
different from a case where a party produces, as part of his own
statement, an affidavit of which he knows the contents.

PATTESON, J. :

The statement in the affidavit was used by this defendant for
the purpose of staying proceedings.   Supposing the party
swearing it had been in fact an officer who merely used the
defendant's name, the defendant is identified with him as far
as this question is concerned.   When a party, for any purpose,
produces a document containing certain statements, such statements are, as against him, evidence of the facts which they
contain.

(1) 1 Atk. 445.
(2) 2 Str. 920.
(3) 1 Mod. 284.
(4) Hard. 472.

(5) This appears to have been a
misapprehension as to the practice of
the Court of Chancery. See Taylor
on Evidence, § 438.—R. C.

WILLIAMS, J.:

Suppose this had been the statement of the sheriff himself: then it would clearly be evidence against him. It would be unimportant whether or not the measure which he wished to adopt would avail him: the question would only be, What was the statement of facts on which he claimed relief? That such a statement is made on oath cannot affect the case.

COLERIDGE, J.:

This is a very clear case when we attend to the facts. On one side, the defendant makes an application to a Judge, and arms himself with a statement, which he makes his own, and uses. That is clearly evidence against him afterwards of the facts in the statement. The statement may be of more or less avail: and it may be matter of remark that the person making the affidavit is present and is not called. But *that is not the question here. As to the depositions in Equity, they stand on the same footing with *virâ voce* evidence given in a court of law. A man does not make all that is said by a witness whom he calls evidence against himself hereafter. In Chancery, the depositions are sealed up from the time of their being taken until publication passes. That is like the case of a party calling a witness, whose evidence he does not hear till it is given. The present is the case of a party using a statement which he has seen before he uses it, and which is neither the more nor the less admissible for being made upon oath.

[*458]

Rule refused.

REG. *v.* GEORGE WATTS.

(7 Adol. & Ellis, 461—471; S. C. 2 N. & P. 367; 7 L. J. (N. S.)
M. C. 72.)

1837.
Nov. 8.

[461]

Appeal lies against the accounts of an assistant overseer, unless there be any limitation, in the warrant of appointment, which prevents his being accountable to the parish.

And where, in a case stated on appeal against such accounts, the Sessions find that the assistant executed all the duties of an overseer, this Court will intend that the warrant was before the justices in Sessions, and was not limited as above mentioned.

The appeal against an overseer's account, under stat. 17 Geo. II. c. 38,

s. 4, must be made to the next practicable Sessions after the account is published; that is, after it has been deposited with the churchwardens and overseers for public inspection, and the fact of depositing *bonâ fide* made known.

ON appeal against the account of George Watts, assistant over-seer of the poor of the parish of Slimbridge, in the county of Gloucester, entitled, " An account of the disbursements of George Watts, assistant overseer from April 6th, 1834, to April 6th, 1835," and containing, among other things, the following items :—

	£	s.	d.
Paid six months pay for maintenance of the poor, as per contract, 29*l.*	174	0	0
Paid six months pay for maintenance of the poor, as per contract, 39*l.*	234	0	0

[462]

The Court ordered the said items to be struck out of the account, subject to the opinion of this Court upon the following case.

The said George Watts was assistant overseer of the poor for the parish of Slimbridge, from the 6th of April, 1834, to the 6th of April, 1835, and executed all the duties of an overseer of the poor. On the 2nd of April, 1835, at a vestry meeting duly held, the said account of the said George Watts was examined and allowed by James Cornock and John French, churchwardens, George Greening, overseer, William Ludlow, James Smith, and John Bailey ; and on the next day, being Friday the 3rd of the same month, the account was submitted to two justices of the peace for the county, at a special sessions holden at Wotton-under-Edge, for that purpose, and was by such justices signed and allowed. George Watts did not, however, deliver over his said account until the 8th of May following, when he delivered it in vestry to the churchwardens and the person who had been appointed assistant overseer to succeed him. An affidavit of the appellant (who was a rated inhabitant of the said parish), sworn in Court, was put in ; and, after objection by the counsel for the respondents to its admissibility, was received by the Court. By this affidavit it appeared that the appellant had no actual knowledge of the account until the 23rd of April, 1835. The Easter Sessions for the county, if they had been held accord-ing to the ordinary course, would have commenced on Tuesday

the 7th of April; but, in consequence of the Assizes, they were
held on Tuesday the 14th of April, by an order made pursuant
to stat. 4 & *5 Will. IV. c. 47.   By the rules of the Quarter
Sessions for the said county, notice of trial of an appeal must
be given on or before the Tuesday in the week preceding the
Sessions; and, consequently, the last day for giving such notice
for the said Easter Sessions was Tuesday the 7th of April.   No
notice of Appeal against the account was given for, nor was any
appeal entered at, the said Easter Sessions: but notice was duly
given for the Trinity Sessions holden in the month of June
following.   The questions for the opinion of the Court, were:
—First, Whether, upon the evidence, the appeal was brought
in due time?   Secondly, Whether an appeal lies against the
account of an assistant overseer?

[After argument, the COURT took time for consideration.]

LORD DENMAN, Ch. J., in this Term (November 25th), delivered
the judgment of the COURT:

Our opinion is asked by the Sessions on three points.
1. Whether appeal lies against the account of an assistant
*overseer?   2. Whether the notice of appeal was given in due
time?   3. Whether the appellant's affidavit was properly received
by the Sessions to prove at what time he became acquainted
with the allowance of the account by two justices of the peace?

On the first point, we see no reason to doubt that an assistant
overseer's account may be the subject of an appeal.   He is not
the servant of the churchwardens and overseers of the parish,
but of the vestry, from whom he directly receives his authority;
an authority which may indeed be limited by the warrant of
appointment, but which does not appear to have been limited in
the present case.

The second point may admit of some difference of opinion,
but seems capable of being decided on principles of reason and
convenience.   Some cases have held that the time of allowance
by the justices of the peace is that from which the time for
giving notice must be calculated: *Rex* v. *Coode* (1), *Rex* v. *The*

REG.
v.
WATTS.
[*463]

[468]

[*469]

(1) 1 Bott, 307, pl. 290, 6th ed.;   *field*, 1 Bott, 310, pl. 291; *S. C.* Cald.
S. C. Cald. 464.   See *Rex* v. *Mickle-*   507.

48—2

Justices of Worcestershire (1). The language of some others may be thought to import that every parishioner's right to appeal is kept alive as long as he is personally ignorant of the fact of such allowance. A strict adherence to either of these rules might obviously produce injustice; nor do we think that the cases, when fairly considered with reference to their circumstances, lay down either the one or the other : on the contrary, the Court must, on those occasions, have had the words of the statute 17 Geo. II. c. 38 [s. 4], in their contemplation, which gave [*470] the right of appeal to the party grieved, "giving *reasonable notice," to the next General or Quarter Sessions of the Peace.

The Sessions have therefore to adjudge what notice is reasonable, which must depend on their usual practice. Still the word "next" applied to the Sessions requires an interpretation Next to what period ? Not to the period of examination by the vestry before allowance, because the justices of the peace, upon their investigation and before allowance, may have struck out every item to which parishioners feel an objection: not to the allowance itself, because it may be unknown to all the parties interested : nor to the fact of knowledge by any one disposed to appeal, because that would lead to an inconvenient enquiry into the particular knowledge of individuals, and might keep the officer's account subject to appeal indefinitely. The only other period, to which recourse can be had for this purpose, is that when the parish had the opportunity of knowing the contents of the account. Thus in *Rex* v. *Thackwell* (2) the time for giving notice was held to be properly reckoned from the time when the account was allowed and published. We think it may be correctly described as published at the time when it is deposited (according to the first section of 17 Geo. II. c. 38) with the churchwardens and overseers for public inspection, and the fact of depositing *bonâ fide* made known.

In the present instance, the Sessions have found that this was done on the 8th of May. Therefore the June Sessions, when the appeal was lodged, were the next Sessions; and the notice was in due time. This makes it immaterial to enquire whether [*471] the appellant's affidavit *of the time when he knew of the account

(1) 17 R. R. 397 (5 M. & S. 457).   (2) 4 B. & C. 62; 6 Dowl. & Ry. 61.

was properly admitted, because the enquiry was completely
immaterial, The Court was consequently justified in entering
on the merits of the appeal; and, having disallowed certain items,
the rule for setting aside their judgment must be discharged.

Order of Sessions confirmed.

REG. *v.* BLISS.

(7 Adol. & Ellis, 550—556 ; S. C. 2 N. & P. 464 ; W. W. & D. 624 ; 7 L. J.
(N. S.) Q. B. 4.)

> The question in a cause being, whether a particular road, admitted to
> exist, was public or private, evidence was offered that a person, since
> deceased, had planted a willow on a spot adjoining the road, on ground
> of which he was a tenant, saying, at the same time, that he planted it to
> show where the boundary of the road was when he was a boy :
>
> Held, that such declaration was not evidence, either as showing repu-
> tation, as a statement accompanying an act, or as the admission of an
> occupier against his own interest.

INDICTMENT for obstructing a public highway. Plea, Not
guilty. On the trial before Gaselee, J., at the Suffolk Spring
Assizes, 1836, a principal question was, whether the way
obstructed was public or private. A witness for the prosecution
stated that one Ramplin, a publican, who was dead at the time
of the trial, had planted a willow thirty years ago on a meadow
of which he was tenant and occupier, and over which the way
in question now ran. The counsel for the prosecution then
asked "what Ramplin said, when he planted the willow, about
his planting it ? " The question was objected to, but admitted
by the learned Judge, and the witness answered that Ramplin
said he planted it to show where the boundary of the road was
when he was a boy. The willow had remained ever since.
The jury found that the way was public, and a verdict was taken
for the Crown. In the ensuing Term, a rule *nisi* was obtained
for a new trial, on the ground that the above evidence ought not
to have been admitted.

B. Andrews and *Byles* now showed cause :

First, Ramplin's statement was receivable as the declaration
of a tenant against his own interest (1). By admitting that a

(1) See *Doe* d. *Daniel* v. *Coulthred*, *ante*, p. 714 (7 Ad. & El. 235).

public road passed over the land he abridged his own rights in it.   The acts of tenants in such cases have been held legitimate evidence, their interests being the same as those of the rever-

[*551]

sioners, though, in *Daniel* v. *North* (1) a distinction was drawn as to window-lights established, with the tenant's acquiescence, in opposite premises.   LE BLANC, J., said there, "It is true, that presumptions are sometimes made against the owners of land, during the possession and by the acquiescence of their tenants, as in the instances alluded to of rights of way and of common; but that happens, because the tenant suffers an immediate and palpable injury to his own possession, and therefore is presumed to be upon the alert to guard the rights of his landlord as well as his own, and to make common cause with him; but the same cannot be said of lights put out by the neighbours of the tenant, in which he may probably take no concern, as he may have no immediate interest at stake."

(WILLIAMS, J.: If the lights in such a case would be a nuisance to the reversioner, it does not appear why they would not be so to the tenant.

PATTESON, J.: I should think the establishing of such lights would hurt his feelings as well as those of the landlord.

LORD DENMAN, Ch. J.: And, on the other hand, the use of a path might be beneficial to the tenant during his term; as, for instance, if the tenant kept a public-house to which it led.)

Secondly, the evidence offered was not mere evidence of reputation; the planting of the willow was an act done by the tenant, and his words were a declaration accompanying the act, and showing his intention in doing it.   The evidence on this point was not tradition of a particular fact, which has been held inadmissible, 1 Phil. on Ev. 258, part 1, c. 13, s. 2 (2); but, so far as it could be said to relate to a particular fact, it was proof

[*552]

of the thing done, with its accompanying circumstances, on *the oath of an eye and ear witness.   Thirdly, if the evidence went

---

(1) 11 East, 372.   (2) 8th ed.   The 7th edition was
                                     cited in the argument.

no further than the statement of a deceased person that such a
portion of land was the highway, it falls within the common
rule as to evidence of reputation.

(LORD DENMAN, Ch. J.: It is a question with me whether
Ramplin's was a statement of reputation. He does not assert
that he has heard old people say what was the public road; but
he plants a tree, and asserts that the boundary of the road is at
that point. It is the mere allegation of a fact by the individual.

COLERIDGE, J.: In the usual course, it is first proved that
there is a way running in a certain direction, and evidence is
then given of its being public. Can the mere existence of a way
be proved by reputation? The words ascribed to Ramplin do
not amount to a statement that the road was public.)

Whatever he said on the subject was evidence. It was as if he
had been alive and stated it in Court.

(PATTESON, J.: In that case he might have been asked what
repairs he had seen done upon it; but anything that he might
have said formerly on that subject would not be evidence after
his death.)

The evidence was at least admissible, whether it might ultimately
be considered as showing a public or only a private right: and
the natural import of his expression, under all the circumstances,
was that the road was public.

(COLERIDGE, J.: You make the evidence admissible or not
according to the interpretation which a jury might give the
words. Can that ever be?)

The Judge must decide when the evidence is offered, and desire
the jury, in summing up, to give it weight or not, according to
their construction of it.

(LORD DENMAN, Ch. J.: Suppose Ramplin had said, "When I
was a boy, a hedge ran in this direction, bounding the highway,"
*that would have been more satisfactory than the evidence
offered here; but would such proof be admissible?)   [*553]

It would; or even evidence of Ramplin's saying that he had

heard so. The statement offered was, in truth, evidence on the question whether the road was public or private. It can be represented as evidence of a particular fact only by confining the effect of Ramplin's words to the spot where he planted the tree. But those words give a character to the whole surface over which the alleged road lies. If he said that the point at which the tree stood was public road, he clearly meant to say the same of any square yard forming part of the way in question.

Kelly, contrà, was stopped by the COURT.

LORD DENMAN, Ch. J. :

The question in this case was, whether the road obstructed was or was not a public highway. To prove that it was so, a witness was called whose statement was calculated to make a great impression on the jury. He stated that Ramplin, a former occupier of the meadow over which the road ran had planted a willow, and, in doing so, said that he planted it to show where the boundary of the road was when he was a boy. And it is inferred, from the circumstances, that Ramplin meant to speak of the road as having been public. I think the evidence was not admissible. It is not every declaration accompanying an act that is receivable in evidence : if it were so, persons would be enabled to dispose of the rights of others in the most unjust manner. The facts that Ramplin planted a willow on the spot, and that persons kept within the line pointed out by it, would have been evidence ; but a declaration to show that the party planted it with a particular motive is not *so. Then, is the declaration evidence as made against the party's interest ? If we held that it was, we should get rid of the authority of *Daniel* v. *North* (1), where it was held that a tenant cannot, merely by his own admission, bind the landlord.   It is true that the landlord and tenant here may have had the same interest ; but so they possibly may in any case : they might in *Daniel* v. *North* (1). Neither was the evidence admissible as showing reputation. Any statement from a person since deceased is to be received with caution. Lord ELLENBOROUGH, in a leading case on this subject (2), allowed,

[*554]

(1) 11 East, 372.   (2) Probably *Weeks* v. *Sparke*, 14 R. R. 546 (1 M. & S. 679).

with great reluctance, the admissibility of reputation as evidence. But here the deceased party is reported to have said that the boundary of the road was at a particular spot; that is, that he knew it to be so from what he had himself observed, and not from reputation. I think, therefore, that the rule ought to be absolute.

PATTESON, J.:

In looking at this evidence as proof of reputation, we must consider what is the issue. If the question had been of boundary merely, the statement of the deceased person would have been receivable; but evidence of reputation as to boundary is not let in where the question is whether a road be public or private. If evidence of user had been offered, it would have been very different; and proof of declarations that the line of road in question had always been used as public would have been admissible. It was agreed here that the alleged road was a road of some sort; the evidence was not necessary as to that; and the reputation which it was attempted to introduce was of a particular fact. *Then it was said that the declaration might be proved as accompanying an act; but whether it accompanied the act, as explanatory of it, is equivocal; and, at any rate, the declaration signified nothing in this case, the question being not of boundary, but as to the character of the road, whether public or private. The mere fact of the tree being placed there could not, I think, be relevant, unless as introductory to other matters. Then was the declaration of Ramplin admissible as contrary to his interest? He was only an occupier under some one else. To say that he could bind his landlord in the manner supposed, so as to give the public a right against him, would be overturning *Daniel* v. *North* (1), *Wood* v. *Veal* (2), and other authorities. If the long acquiescence of a tenant cannot bind the landlord, his declaration can neither bind him, nor be evidence at all against his right.

[*555]

WILLIAMS, J.:

There is no doubt that evidence of reputation is admissible where the question to which it applies is merely whether the

(1) 11 East, 372.   (2) 24 R. R. 454 (5 B. & Ald. 454).

REG.
v.
BLISS.

road be public or not. In *Ireland* v. *Powell* (1), the question being whether a turnpike stood within the limits of a town, CHAMBRE, J. admitted evidence of reputation that the town extended to a certain point, and allowed it to be proved that old people, since dead, had declared that to be the boundary, but not that those people had said that there formerly were houses where none any longer stood; observing that that was evidence of a particular fact, and not of reputation. The statement offered in evidence here is very like the declarations so rejected.

[*556]

It is not reputation, *in the proper sense. Declarations accompanying acts are a wide field of evidence, and to be carefully watched. The declaration here had no connection with the act done; and the doing of the act cannot make such a declaration evidence.

COLERIDGE, J.:

It is a rule that evidence of reputation must be confined to general matters, and not touch particular facts. To try whether the declaration here was admissible according to that rule, let it be severed from the fact of planting which took place at the same time. Then it stands that Ramplin said he planted the tree for a certain purpose; namely, to show the boundary. That is a particular fact; and evidence given of it is like proof of old persons having been heard to say that a stone was put down at a certain spot, or that boys were whipped, or cakes distributed, at a particular place, as the boundary; which statements would not be admissible.

Rule absolute.

1837.
Nov. 21.

[565]

ARKWRIGHT v. CANTRELL.

(7 Adol. & Ellis, 565—580; S. C. 2 N. & P. 582; W. W. & D. 686; 7 L. J. (N. S.) Q. B. 63; 2 Jur. 11).

By the custom of a lordship in a lead-mining district, there was an officer called a barmaster, appointed by the lord to see that the duties of lot and cope, &c., were properly accounted for to the lord; to be indifferent and to do justice between miner and miner, and miner and adventurer, and the miner and the lord; to apportion veins of ore newly discovered between the discoverer and other adventurers, and the lord;

(1) Peake on Evidence, 16 (5th ed.).

to enforce proper working of the veins; to keep a dish by which all the
ore was to be measured; to punish small depredations, and to collect
fines. In case of certain defaults, he was himself liable to fines, payable
to the lord of the field or his farmer. Certain disputes within the lordship were tried at a customary court called the Barmote Court, before
the deputy stewards and a jury who were summoned by the barmaster,
or his deputy, on precept from the deputy steward. The summoning
officer selected them at his discretion.

The lord granted, by indenture, to A. for years, in consideration of a
certain fine and rent, all the mines in the district, with the duties of lot
and cope, and also, for the same term, the office called the barmastership,
with all profits, &c., thereto belonging, at a rent, with a proviso for
re-entry, if the grantee should make a deputation of the office without
license, or without having such deputation enrolled:

Held, that the grant, as to the barmastership, was void, because the
grantee took an interest, as lessee or farmer, incompatible with the
duties of barmaster.

That the grant was not void as giving incompatible offices, the lease
not conferring an office.

And that, on an issue whether or not A. was barmaster at a certain
time, the verdict, on the above facts, ought to be entered in the negative.

DEBT. The declaration stated that, whereas our sovereign lord
the now King, long before and at the time of the committing
of the grievance by the defendant hereinafter mentioned, and
before and at the time of the holding of the Barmote Court
hereinafter mentioned, was, and from thence hitherto hath been
and still is, lord of the King's Field in the soke and wapentake
of Wirksworth in the county of Derby; and he and all those
whose estate he hath and had of and in the said lordship of the
King's Field with the appurtenances, from time whereof &c.,
have had and held, and have been accustomed to have and hold,
and of right ought &c., and still of right ought &c., within the
soke and wapentake aforesaid, a certain customary court, viz.
the Great Barmote Court, held before his and their steward for
the time being, or his deputy, every year twice in the year, that
is to say &c. (naming the times), amongst other things to
determine questions *arising within the said lordship of and   [*566
concerning the mines, groves, shafts, or mears of ground within
the said lordship, according to the customs of the said lordship,
as belonging and appertaining to the said lordship; and that,
at the said Barmote Courts, so held at the times aforesaid,
a jury of twenty-four honest and able men, duly summoned and
sworn according to the customs of the said lordship, during a l

ARKWRIGHT
v.
CANTRELL.

the time whereof &c., have enquired, and have been used and accustomed to enquire, of, at such Court, such matters and things as have happened within the said lordship which belonged to the said Court to determine, concerning the mines, groves, shafts, or mears of ground within the said lordship, and have been used and accustomed, during all the time aforesaid, to make such orders and awards touching such matters and things as should be reasonable, according to the custom of the said lordship; and that within the said lordship there now is, and from time whereof &c. there hath been, a certain ancient and laudable custom of the said lordship, there used and approved of, for determining questions arising within the said lordship, of and concerning the mines, groves, shafts, or mears of ground within the said lordship; viz. that, if any miner or other person do keep lawful possession of any grove, shaft, or mear of ground within the said lordship, according to the custom of the said lordship, and if any other person or persons, by day or by night, cast in or fill up such grove, shaft, or mear of ground, however the same shall be wrought, every such person so offending therein shall forfeit for such offence 10l., the one-half to the lord of the field or farmer, and the other half to the barmaster

[*567]

or steward, and shall pay the party *so much as will make good the work again: The count then stated that heretofore, viz. on March 20th, 1834, one Job Bunting, then being a miner of and in certain mines within the said lordship and jurisdiction of the said Court, did keep lawful possession, according to the custom of the said lordship, of a certain shaft at a certain mine within the lordship aforesaid and jurisdiction of the said Court, and thereupon, whilst the said J. B. so kept &c., the defendant wilfully, unlawfully, maliciously, and against the will of the said J. B., and contrary to the customs of the said lordship and the laws of this realm, cast in and filled up the said shaft, to the great injury of the said shaft and mine, and damage of the said J. B., viz. to the injury of the said shaft and damage of the said J. B. of 20l., within the lordship and jurisdiction aforesaid, and to the injury of the rights of others the miners within the lordship and jurisdiction aforesaid; and that afterwards, viz. April 7th, 1834, at a great Barmote Court of the lordship

aforesaid, duly held at the Moot Hall in Wirksworth aforesaid, ARKWRIGHT
within the said lordship and jurisdiction, within &c. (one of the *v.*
periods for holding courts), viz. &c., before William Eaton CANTRELL.
Mousley, then and still being the deputy to one Charles Clarke,
then and still being steward of our said lord the King of the
said court of the said lordship, upon the oaths of &c. (naming
twenty-four), honest, able, and lawful men, duly summoned,
sworn, and charged, according to the custom of the said lordship,
to enquire of, order, and award all such things as belonged to
the said jury to enquire of, order and award, the said jury at
the said Court so held as aforesaid, on the day and year last
aforesaid, duly enquired of and concerning the casting in and
*filling up of the said shaft by the said defendant as aforesaid,   [*568]
and thereupon the said jury did order and say that the said
defendant should, amongst other things, pay the sum of 10*l.*,
the one half to the lord of the field or farmer, and the other
half to the barmaster or steward, according to the custom in
that behalf : averment, that, at the time of the committing of
the said grievance by the defendant, and at the time of the
holding of the court, and of the making of the said order for
the payment of the said sum of money, and from thence hitherto,
the plaintiff was, and from thence hitherto hath been, and still
is, the barmaster: whereby an action hath accrued to the
plaintiff, as such barmaster as aforesaid, to demand and have of
and from the defendant the sum of 5*l.*, being one half of the
said sum of 10*l.* so ordered to be paid by the defendant as aforesaid, and being the said sum of 5*l.* above demanded : yet the
said defendant has not paid &c.

There were several pleas ; the sixth, which is the only one
requiring particular mention, was : That the plaintiff was not,
at the time of the holding of the Court, and of the making of
the order for payment of the said sum of money as in the
declaration alleged, the barmaster of the said Court in manner
and form &c. Conclusion to the country. Issue thereon.

On the trial before Lord Abinger, C. B., at the Derbyshire
Spring Assizes, 1836, the plaintiff, in support of his case on the
above issue, put in an indenture of lease under the seal of the
Duchy of Lancaster, dated November 17th, 1827, from the King

ARKWRIGHT   to Richard Arkwright, the plaintiff, whereby, after certain
v.   recitals, his Majesty, in consideration that R. A. had surrendered
CANTRELL.   a former *grant, dated in 1808, and had paid 5,750*l*. by way
[*569]   of fine, and for other considerations, did grant and demise to
             R. A. all those mines of lead, with their appurtenances, within
             the soke and wapentake of Wirksworth, with the duties of lead
             ore called the lot and cope within the said soke and wapentake,
             parcel of his Majesty's Duchy of Lancaster in the said county of
             Derby, habendum to R. A., his executors, administrators, and
             assigns, from March 25th then last past for thirty-one years
             thence next ensuing, at a yearly rent of 226*l*. for the first seven
             years, and 296*l*. for the residue of the term ; and his Majesty
             did also, for the considerations aforesaid, " grant and demise
             unto the said Richard Arkwright all that the office called the
             bearmastership, otherwise the barmastership, otherwise " &c.,
             " within the soke and wapentake of Wirksworth aforesaid in the
             said county of Derby, parcel of the possessions of the said Duchy
             of Lancaster, with all profits, commodities, and advantages to
             the said office belonging, or in anywise incident or appertaining :
             to have and to hold the said office called &c., " and all and
             singular other the premises hereby last granted and demised or
             mentioned or intended so to be, with their and every of their
             appurtenances, and every part and parcel thereof, unto the said
             Richard Arkwright, his executors, administrators, and assigns,
             from the said 25th day of March last past, for and during and
             until the full end and term of thirty-one years from thence next
             ensuing," &c., " yielding and paying therefore in every year,
             during the said term of thirty-one years hereby thereof granted,
             unto the King's Majesty, his heirs and successors, the rent
             or sum of 4*l*.," &c. ; and Arkwright, for himself, his heirs and
[*570]   assigns, covenanted to pay the several rents, and to *account for
             profits arising or received by him under these presents.   Proviso
             for re-entry on the premises demised in case of breaches of
             covenant, or if the executors, administrators, or assigns of R. A.
             " shall assign or transfer the premises hereby demised, or any
             part thereof respectively, unto any person or persons whatsoever,
             without licence under the seal of the said Duchy for that purpose
             first had and obtained, or grant any deputation or appointment

of the office of barmaster for the said soke or wapentake, or
for any of the liberties within the same, without the licence and
approbation of the Chancellor or Vice-Chancellor of the said
Duchy for the time being by writing under their hands for that
purpose first had and obtained ; or in case the said R. A.,
his executors, administrators, or assigns shall neglect or refuse
to cause these presents, and every such assignment, deputation,
or appointment which shall or may at any time or times
hereafter be made of these presents, or of the premises hereby
demised, or any part thereof, or of the said office of barmaster,
with any such licence as aforesaid, to be inrolled before the
auditor of the said Duchy for the time being, or his deputy,
within six months next ensuing the respective dates thereof, and
also, within the time aforesaid, to cause every such assignment,
deputation, or appointment as aforesaid to be docquetted, or
a minute thereof entered in the office of the clerk of the council
of the said Duchy for the time being, containing the dates of,
and parties' names to, every such assignment, deputation, or
appointment respectively, and a description of the premises
assigned, and the purport of such deputation and appointment."

The following evidence was given as to the barmaster's
*duties, by the deputy steward : "The duties of the barmaster
are to see that the ore is properly measured, and the duties
properly accounted for to the Crown, and to do justice between
miner and miner, and miner and adventurer, and between the
miner and the lord, and to see that the customs are properly
observed. If there should be any dispute between the lessees of
the Crown and the miner as to the proper quantity, I apprehend
the twenty-four " (jurymen) " are to decide."

A book was also referred to as authority on this subject, by consent of parties at the trial, called "The Miner's Guide, or Complete
Miner," by William Hardy, 2nd edition, published at Birmingham
in 1762, containing, among other things, "The articles and customs
for the High Peak Hundred, in the King's Field, in Derbyshire."
Immediately under that title were the following paragraphs :

    " Wirksworth wapentake.

" At the great Court-Barmote, for the lead mines held at
Wirksworth, for the soke and wapentake of Wirksworth, in

ARKWRIGHT
r.
CANTRELL.

[*571]

ARKWRIGHT   the county of Derby, the 10th of October, in the year of our
   v.
CANTRELL.   Lord 1665.

" The inquisition of the late great inquest, taken upon oaths
of " &c. (names of twenty-four jurors).

" Article 1.

" We say, upon our oath, That by the ancient custom of the
mines, within the soke and wapentake of Wirksworth, the miners
and merchants at first chose themselves an officer called a barmaster, to be an indifferent person betwixt the lord of the field
or farmer and the miners and betwixt the miners and merchants ;

[*572]   *which barmaster, upon finding any new rake or vein, did, upon
notice given by the miner, deliver to the first finder two meares
of ground in the same vein, each meare in a rake or pipe work
containing twenty-nine yards in length, and in a flat work
fourteen yards square ; the which two meares of ground the
miner is to have, one for his diligence in finding the vein, and
the other for mineral right ; paying the barmaster, or his
deputy, one dish of his first ore therein gotten : And then the
barmaster or his deputy is to deliver to the lord of the field
or farmer one meare of ground in a new vein, at either end of
the aforesaid two meares half a meare of ground, and then
every one, in such rake or vein, one meare or more, according
to their taking.

" Observation on Article 1.

" The barmasters were first chosen by the miners and
merchants, but are since chosen by his Majesty's farmers of
the mineral duties ; and all other barmasters are chosen by the
lords, or their farmers of the mineral duties, in all mineral fields
in the county of Derby, where barmasters act, and are removable
at the direction of those who put them into office.   The branches
of a barmaster's office, according to the oath he acts under,
are many."

Then followed other articles (referred to in the present argument), the substance of which was as follows : Art. 2. We say,
if any miner or other set on any old work, the barmaster or his
deputy is to deliver him but one meare of ground, for which he
is to pay one dish of his first ore therein gotten, and the lord or

farmer to have no half meare.   Art. 9. The barmaster or his
deputy *ought to walk the mines once a week at least, and
where he sees a meare of ground, which, to his knowledge, is
lawfully possessed, to stand unwrought three weeks together,
and might be wrought, not being hindered by water, &c., then,
if he can conveniently, he should give notice to the parties
neglecting ; and, (after certain other proceedings which are
pointed out, then) in case of continued neglect, the barmaster
or his deputy may lawfully set another man to work on such
meare.   The barmaster, if he neglect his duty herein, shall
forfeit 5*s.* to the lord of the field or farmer.   Art. 17. No person
ought to keep any counterfeit dish or measure for ore, but every
one to buy and sell by the barmaster's lawful dish, and no other
be used or had ; every buyer offending herein to forfeit 40*s.* to
the lord or farmer, and the sellers to forfeit their ore, &c.
Art. 18. Provision for measuring the ore of poor miners, if the
barmaster or deputy neglect after warning.   Art. 19. The barmaster or his deputy shall see that measure be indifferently
made between the buyer and seller ; and the buyer not to touch
the dish, &c., on pain to forfeit 10*s.*   Art. 20. After the ore is
measured, the merchant, buyer, or miner carrying it away doth
pay to the lord or farmer cope, being 6*d.* for every load of ore,
nine dishes to the load, for which cope the miners, &c., have
liberty to carry away the ore, and dispose of it to whom they
please, without disturbance, &c.   Art. 48. Power to the barmaster to punish (in the stocks or otherwise) persons feloniously
taking away ore or other materials from any groove, shaft, &c.,
if below a certain value.   Art. 53. That the barmaster, or his
deputy, or the steward, ought to levy and collect all fines and
forfeitures due by the custom of the mine ; and, where any
person is not able or willing to discharge the forfeiture *or fine,
then the barmaster or his deputy shall (for every such offence)
punish such person in the stocks, &c. ; but, in case the barmaster or his deputy, or the steward, do not henceforth levy and
collect all fines and forfeitures due by the custom of the mine,
nor punish such offenders in the stocks as are fit to be punished,
they shall forfeit for every such neglect 5*s.* to the lord of the
field or farmer.

ARKWRIGHT
v.
CANTRELL.

The Great Barmote Court of the soke and wapentake of Wirksworth was holden, as mentioned in the declaration, before the deputy steward of the said Court, in the usual manner, on the Monday before Easter, 1834, the plaintiff being then, as he alleged in this cause, the barmaster.   The deputy steward, when about to hold a Court, issues a precept to one of the deputy barmasters, of whom there were five at the time in question, to give notice of holding a Court; and such deputy barmaster directs a jury of twenty-four miners to attend.   By the custom, if twenty-four do not attend, the deficiency may be supplied *de circumstantibus*.   The principal deputy barmaster of the Wirksworth district gave evidence on the present trial, as follows. "The barmaster appoints me, and I am sworn in by the steward. I received directions from Mr. Mousley" (the deputy steward) "to summon the jury of the Barmote, in April, 1834.   The jury are not summoned, but I give verbal notice to such persons as I think to be most intelligent in mining matters.   I have been deputy since 1831, but have assisted my father for twenty-five years.   I sign myself barmaster in my books; the others are called deputies; they are not appointed by me, neither do they act under my authority, but under the authority of the lessee of the Crown."

[*575]

On the above evidence it was contended, on the defendant's *part, first, that the grant of November, 1827, did not convey the barmastership, but only the right of appointing to that office; secondly, that, if it conveyed the barmastership, the grant was void, as making the officer judge in matters affecting his own interest as lessee.   The LORD CHIEF BARON reserved leave to move to enter a nonsuit or a verdict for the defendant. A verdict having been found for the plaintiff, *Hill*, in the ensuing Term, moved according to the leave reserved; and a rule *nisi* was granted.

> *Sir J. Campbell*, Attorney-General, *Balguy*, and *Clarke*, now showed cause:

The deed of 1827 is a lease of the mines with the duties of lot and cope, and a grant of the office of barmaster.   There is no analogy between such grant and the sale of an advowson or right of appointing ; the office itself is granted in terms. The right

to appoint a deputy implies that the party has the office in himself. It is contended that the office of barmaster is void, because incompatible with the rights conferred by the lease, which are also put on the footing of an office. But, if that were so, they, and not the barmastership, would be void, because, where incompatible offices are granted, the first becomes null: Com. Dig. Officer, (B. 6) : note [22] to *Rex* v. *Godwin* (1) ; and it is necessary for carrying on the affairs of the district that there should be a barmaster, but not that the lot and cope should be leased. The grants, however, are not incompatible. The barmaster sees that there is a proper render of duties to the Crown ; there he acts, not judicially, but as a mere agent. He *does not settle disputes between the Crown and the miner : those, if they arise, are determined by a jury.

[*576]

(COLERIDGE, J. : He summons whom he pleases on the jury.)

In that he acts ministerially : he decides nothing. The deputy steward presides in the Barmote Court ; and, if the jury were not impartially returned, there can be no doubt (though it was not expressly stated in evidence) that he would dismiss them and issue a new precept.

(LORD DENMAN, Ch. J. : If that were so, who would summon the new jury ?

COLERIDGE, J. : The same barmaster would summon the next jury.)

But, further, the barmaster does not act by his own hand ; he appoints deputies, as the King deputes judicial officers to act between him and his subjects, and as the lord of a manor appoints a steward.

(LORD DENMAN, Ch. J. : If there is an objection to the barmaster's exercising the functions of his office, is there any authority for saying that he can remove it by appointing a deputy ?

(1) 1 Doug. 398. It is said there that, where incompatible offices are taken, the acceptance of the higher vacates the other.

COLERIDGE, J. : There is no express provision for his making a deputy : the grant only states what shall be done if he makes a deputy without licence.)

It is in the nature of his office that he should appoint one ; and, if he has power, and ought, to do so, it is to be supposed he will. In fact, there has always been such an appointment.

(PATTESON, J. : Nothing in the grant obliges him to make it.)

If he is interested, and therefore cannot properly exercise the office himself, he must appoint a deputy.

Hill, contrà :

The union of the barmastership with the interest of lessee is not shown to be immemorial ; the evidence, at any rate, traces it only as far as 1803, the date of the grant recited in that of 1827.   The plaintiff was not legally barmaster ; he had, at most, but the power of making a deputy.   If the subject of grant *was the office itself, then, as it concerns the administration of justice, it was, by stat. 5 & 6 Edw. VI. c. 16, s. 2, not saleable.

[*577]

(COLERIDGE, J. : If the office of deputy barmaster was judicial, could the Crown grant a power of appointing to it for years ?

LORD DENMAN, Ch. J. cited *Sir George Reynel's* case (1).)

The argument against a junction of the barmastership with the interest of a lessee is strengthened by the book of articles and customs for the High Peak hundred, referred to, by consent of both parties, on the trial.   The duties there prescribed require an impartial dealing by the barmaster between the miner and the farmer.   But this requisite cannot be properly fulfilled where the barmaster is himself the farmer.

(Here he referred to the articles and observation cited, *ante,* pp. 767—769.   He was then stopped by the COURT.)

LORD DENMAN, Ch. J.:

I think it is clear that the two subjects of grant are incompatible.   The office of barmaster is an office of trust and

(1) 9 Co. Rep. 96 b.

confidence, in which there are personal duties to be performed
independent of a jury. The objection arising from that circumstance is, in my opinion, incapable of being cured by the
barmaster's appointment of a deputy to do that which he is
unable to perform himself. This is clear from the articles which
Mr. Hill has read. The barmaster is to do acts of measuring,
and to perform various duties between the merchant and miner,
and the farmer: but the lease gives him the produce of the
mines as farmer, while it also appoints him barmaster. An
office may, indeed, continue full, though the party be appointed
to another incompatible office; and on this ground it might be
contended here, that the verdict was rightly found *for the
plaintiff. But the office of barmaster in the present case was void,
because the plaintiff, when he accepted it, became also, as lessee,
directly interested in violating that confidence, the maintaining
of which is essential to a discharge of the barmaster's duties.

ARKWRIGHT
v.
CANTRELL.

[*578]

PATTESON, J.:

When we see the duties which are to be performed by the
barmaster, according to the articles referred to, it is quite clear
that the plaintiff could not discharge them, being also farmer;
and therefore that, being farmer, he could not be appointed barmaster. I do not say that his acceptance of that office vacated
the other part of the grant, because the lease of mines was not
an office: and, besides, it does not always follow, when a party
holding an office accepts one incompatible with it, that the first
is therefore vacant. Thus, in *Rex* v. *Patteson* (1), it was held
that an alderman, justice of the peace, accepting the office of
treasurer to the county of the city of which he was justice, did
not thereby vacate his former office, because for that purpose
there should have been an amotion, or a resignation accepted;
and this, although it was agreed that the offices of justice and
of treasurer were incompatible. But the situation of a farmer
renders it impossible that he should discharge the duties of a
barmaster. By the articles cited, the barmaster should be
a person indifferent between the miner and the farmer; the
farmer himself cannot be so. Then it is said that he may act

(1) 38 R. R. 191 (4 B. & Ad. 9).

ARKWRIGHT
v.
CANTRELL.

by deputy; but it is the first time I have heard that the incompatibility of offices can be got rid of by appointing a deputy for one, especially where it is not obligatory on the party to appoint. It is a novel argument, that a person who,

[*579]

at the time *of appointment, cannot himself execute the office may cure the defect by making a deputy. The grant, however, merely contains a certain provision, *if* the grantee shall appoint a deputy without licence and enrolment. By the articles referred to, the barmaster or his deputy is, in several instances, made answerable to the farmer. Could the deputy barmaster account with his principal as farmer? The interests which the same party would have as barmaster and as farmer are so inconsistent that, supposing a deputy appointed, the offices are still incompatible.

WILLIAMS, J.:

The doctrine as to acceptance of inconsistent offices does not apply, because the taking of lot and cope is a benefit only, not an office. But the party having that benefit would, as barmaster, be called upon to perform conflicting and inconsistent duties, and is therefore incapable of holding the office.

COLERIDGE, J.:

The interest which the plaintiff takes as lessee makes him incompetent to the office of barmaster. That is the ground on which I rest my judgment. The barmaster would have to decide upon conflicting interests of the miner and the lord of the field; and the deputy would be as the barmaster, and the lessee as the lord. The barmaster is appointed by the lord, and has to appoint the jury who are to decide disputes between miners and the lord or farmer. No difficulty arises here from any evidence of long custom; and, even if that had been proved, the custom would not be maintainable. In *Wood* v. *Lovatt* (1), where the

[*580]

plaintiff had been amerced in the *court leet for a private injury to the lord, and a custom was pleaded for presenting and amercing at the leet for injuries to the lord, it was held that, where the injury was private, the custom was no justification. It was indeed decided, in *Rex* v. *Joliffe* (2), that a custom

(1) 6 T. R. 511.   (2) 26 R. R. 264 (2 B. & C. 54).

for the steward to nominate the jury to serve on the court leet ARKWRIGHT
was good; but that decision was grounded on the particular CANTRELL.
nature of courts leet. On the principle of *Wood* v. *Lovatt* (1),
I think that, where the lord's private interest is concerned, he
cannot authorise a person, who represents himself, to decide
between himself and others in matters affecting that interest.
This is not the case of a party holding two incompatible offices,
or of an office sold contrary to stat. 5 & 6 Edw. VI. c. 16: the
party here is disqualified by the interest which he takes under
the lord. The rule must therefore be absolute.

> *Rule absolute to enter a verdict for the defendant on
> the issue upon the sixth plea.*

MARY CAROLINE EVANS *v.* TAYLOR (2).

1838.
Jan. 11.

[617]

(7 Adol. & Ellis, 617—627; S. C. 3 N. & P. 174; 7 L. J. (N. S.) Q. B. 73.)

On a question as to the boundary of a manor, formerly, but no longer,
part of the Duchy of Lancaster, a document of the time of Elizabeth
(when the manor belonged to the Duchy) was offered in evidence. It
was produced from the Duchy office, and purported to be a survey of
the manor, taken by J. W., deputy of the surveyor-general of the Duchy,
by authority of letters of deputation to J. W., by the oaths and presentment of such of the tenants of the manor whose names were subscribed.
The names of twenty persons followed, described as "jurors at the Court
of Survey:" and it was added, that they, being examined, did present
&c. Then came a statement of the boundaries, a list of tenants and
rents, and a presentment of the demesnes, of customs, of injuries suggested, and of some other particulars. No authority for taking the
survey was proved, except as above-mentioned:

Held, that the document was not admissible, either as a survey
appearing to be taken by the proper officer, agreeably to the statute
Extenta Manerii, 4 Edw. I. stat. 1, or as furnishing evidence of
reputation.

TRESPASS. The first count was for breaking and entering the
plaintiff's closes covered with water, and taking and converting
fish, to wit, lamperns, &c. *The second count was for trespasses
on the plaintiff's several fishery; the third for trespasses on her
free fishery; the fourth for taking away and converting dead

[*618]

(1) 6 T. R. 511.
(2) Cp. and dist. *Smith* v. *Earl
Brownlow* (1870) L. R. 9 Eq. 241, 21

L. T. 739; *Evans* v. *Merthyr Tydfil
Urban Council* [1899] 1 Ch. 241, 68
L. J. Ch. 175, 79 L. T. 578, C. A.

fish of the plaintiff. The defendant pleaded, 1. Not guilty, generally ; 2. To the first count, that the closes were part of the river Severn, and that the *locus in quo* was, and from time &c. had been, part of a public navigable river in which the tide flowed and reflowed, and that every subject of the realm, at the times when &c., had the liberty of fishing in that part of the same river, called the Severn ; 3. A like plea to the first count, alleging the closes to be part of an arm of the sea ; 4. As to one of the closes mentioned in the first count, and the taking, &c., lamperns therein, a prescriptive right in the defendant and his predecessors, occupiers of a certain messuage, &c., to fish in the said close for lamperns. The plaintiff, by her replication, traversed the prescriptive right, and, as to the closes in which public rights were claimed, she prescribed for a sole and several fishery in those closes as being within and parcel of the manor of Minsterworth, of which she was seised in fee. The defendant traversed the alleged rights of the plaintiff; and issues were joined on the several traverses.

On the trial before Lord Denman, Ch. J., at the Gloucester Summer Assizes, 1835, the plaintiff, to prove that the *locus in quo* was within the boundary of the manor, called as a witness the deputy record keeper in the Duchy of Lancaster office, who produced, from that office, a document bearing date 25th October, 33 Eliz. A.D. 1591, at which time the manor of Minsterworth was parcel of the Duchy.

It was headed, " Manor of Minsterworth, Gloucestershire. A survey thereof taken the 25th day of October, *in the thirty-third year " &c., " by John Worth, gentleman, deputy unto Sir John Poyntz, Knight, General Surveyor of the Duchy of Lancaster lying on the south parts, by the authority aforesaid (1), performed by the oaths and presentment of such of the tenants

[*619]

(1) The survey was bound up in a volume with others, and the first survey in the volume had a similar heading (*mutatis mutandis*) to that set forth above, except that, in place of the words " by the authority aforesaid, performed, by the oaths," were the following ; " by virtue of letters of deputation unto the said John Worth made, dated " &c., " by the commandment of the Honourable Sir Thomas Heneadge, Knight Chancellor of the said Duchy as also by oaths," &c. The intermediate surveys all referred to the " authority aforesaid."

of the said manor, as hereafter follows," viz.   Then followed a
list of twenty names, in the margin of which was written "The
names of the jurors at the Court of Survey."   And after the
names was written, "Who, being examined, do, for the circuit
and boundary of the said manor, present: That the boundary
of the said manor beginneth" &c. (setting out the limits):
"Without which circuit and boundary aforesaid there lieth" &c.
(mentioning some outlying lands and premises, and the tenants
of them): "Within which circuit and boundary of the said
manor, and within the circuit of the recited premises, all waifs,
strays, felons' goods," &c., "and all other things incident to a
royalty do belong unto her Majesty."   Then followed lists of
the "supposed freeholders," and of the customary tenants, with
their holdings; an entry of "certain rents due to her Majesty"
by the tenants and inhabitants of the manor; a presentment of
the demesnes; a statement of customs (as to commons, officers
of the manor, &c.); and a presentment of "injury suggested"
by reason of certain irregularities.   In this part of the survey
it was presented "That the fishing of the river Severn, from
*Crewell Cross to Woodleys Bridge, doth belong unto her Majesty,   [*620]
which is used and enjoyed by the tenants and inhabitants of the
said manor under the yearly rent aforesaid, between which
boundaries of the said river divers of the tenants and inhabitants
of Elmore do fish, where by right they ought not; which is to
the great prejudice and hindrance of the tenants of the said
manor, because they rent it as aforesaid; the names of which
tenants and inhabitants are as follows," &c.   The survey closed
with a statement of the total amounts of different rents.

It was proved that an order had been made by the Queen for
payment of the surveyor-general's expenses in making the above
survey.   The manor, with all waters, fisheries, &c., was granted
away from the Crown by James I.

The LORD CHIEF JUSTICE thought the survey inadmissible,
there being no proof of any authority under which it was made.
The plaintiff's counsel argued that it was at least evidence of
reputation; but his Lordship refused to admit the document.
A verdict having been found for the defendant, *Talfourd*, Serjt.,
in Michaelmas Term, 1835, obtained a rule *nisi* for a new trial,

EVANS
v.
TAYLOR.

on the ground (among others) of the rejection of evidence. He cited, in moving, *Nicholls* v. *Parker* (1), *Freeman* v. *Phillipps* (2), *Crease* v. *Barrett* (3), and *Drinkwater* v. *Porter* (4). In Hilary Term, 1837 (5),

Ludlow, Serjt. and *R. V. Richards* showed cause:

[*621]

First, as to the manner of introducing the survey: it was *merely proved to have come from the Duchy office, without any more particular evidence as to the custody, or the documents with which it was associated. The extent of Crown lands, admitted in *Rowe* v. *Brenton* (6), was introduced by much fuller preliminary evidence. Next, such a document as this may be evidence as between the Crown and a subject, and yet not be so as between private persons. And, further, no commission or other authority is shown for taking this survey: it has the character of a mere voluntary enquiry made by a proprietor into the condition of his own estate. And, at all events, if the officers of the Crown could enquire into the existence of a fishery as part of the possessions of the Duchy, and the value of such fishery, they could not authoritatively lay down its boundary.

Talfourd, Serjt., *Shepherd*, and *Lumley, contrà*:

The survey was part of a series of documents relating to the possessions of the Duchy, produced from the Duchy office, a place publicly known, and where such an instrument ought to be found if genuine; it was brought into Court by the proper officer; and there is no ground for the distinction suggested between cases where the Crown is a party and those where the dispute is between private persons.

(LORD DENMAN, Ch. J.: I believe that distinction has never hitherto been taken. I do not think that we are at all impressed with the argument as to the custody, or as to the transfer of this manor from the Crown to a private person.)

(1) 12 R. R. 542 (14 East, 331).
(2) 16 R. R. 524 (4 M. & S. 486).
(3) 40 R. R. 779 (1 Cr. M. & R. 919; 5 Tyr. 458).
(4) 7 Car. & P. 181.

(5) January 17th. Before Lord Denman, Ch. J., Williams and Coleridge, JJ.

(6) 32 R. R. 524 (8 B. & C. 737).

Then as to the survey itself. It was made by the Crown; it related to a matter of public concern; and the officer taking it appears to have been one whose duty it was to conduct such an *enquiry into the possessions of the Duchy. It would have been against his duty to do it without authority. This was the line of argument pursued by BAYLEY, J. in *Rowe* v. *Brenton* (1), on the question whether the extent of the manor of Tewington was admissible in evidence, no statement appearing upon it of the authority under which it was taken, and no commission for taking it being produced. BAYLEY, J. there appears to have relied upon the circumstance that the extent appeared to have been taken conformably to the statute Extenta Manerii (2). The survey here follows very nearly the order prescribed by the statute, and may therefore be presumed to have been made in pursuance of it. Lord TENTERDEN said of the extent just mentioned, in *Rowe* v. *Brenton* (3), "The only ground of argument against its reception is, that it does not appear to be taken under any warrant from the King or any competent authority; but considering the nature of the instrument itself, and the statute that requires such things to be done, and the place in which it is found, we must presume that it was not taken without proper authority. I do not know that that authority need be given by any letters-patent or any instrument; I do not know that the King might not, verbally, or by one of the superior officers, have directed it to be taken: we must presume that it was taken by a competent authority." In *The Vicar of Kellington* v. *The Master and Fellows of Trinity College* (4), a survey of ecclesiastical possessions, taken in 1568, and produced from the First Fruits office, was held admissible without proof of the authority under which it was made; and PARKER, C. B. said, "These surveys have always been allowed as proper evidence, *and to be read, notwithstanding the commissions under which they were taken be lost." But, further, the present survey was at all events evidence of reputation, being the declaration of persons who at the time were tenants of the manor. The answers of

EVANS
v.
TAYLOR.

[*62!]

[*623]

(1) 32 R. R. 524 (8 B. & C. 749; 3 Man. & Ry. 169).
(2) Stat. 4 Edw. I. stat. 1.

(3) 32 R. R. 524 (8 B. & C. 748, 749; 3 Man. & Ry. 169).
(4) 1 Wils. 170.

EVANS
v.
TAYLOR.

tenants of the manor at an assession court were admitted in *Rowe* v. *Brenton* (1). In *Crease* v. *Barrett* (2) the answers of conventionary tenants of the manor were held admissible as evidence of reputation coming from persons connected with the place and subject-matter to which the alleged custom related. The declarations of a deceased lord as to boundary were held there to have been properly rejected as evidence of reputation; but that was because they did not relate to the boundary of the manor, but to that of the lord's own waste.

(COLERIDGE, J.: The declaration, being, in substance, that his boundary came up to a certain point, might be for, rather than against, his own interest.)

Supposing, here, that the persons whose names are affixed to the survey were merely ten or twenty of the tenants assembled without authority, still their report is the declaration of neighbouring persons, having a concern in the subject-matter, that an exclusive right belonged to the Crown in a public navigable river. If reputation is evidence to affirm public rights, it is evidence to narrow . them: this was ruled in *Drinkwater* v. *Porter* (3).

Cur. adv. vult.

LORD DENMAN, Ch. J., in this Term, January 19th, delivered the judgment of the COURT as follows:

[*624]   On the trial of this cause before me at Gloucester, I *rejected a document tendered in evidence, as to the admissibility of which we have entertained considerable doubt. It was the survey of the manor of Minsterworth, parcel of the possessions of the Duchy of Lancaster, made by a person named " deputy to Sir J. Poyntz," surveyor, appointed by Queen Elizabeth, on the finding of certain tenants of the manor at a court of survey. The evidence was tendered to show what were the boundaries of the manor. The action was in trespass on plaintiff's close covered with water, on her free fishery, and on her several fishery, with a count for trespass in carrying away plaintiff's

(1) 32 R. R. 524 (8 B. & C. 765).   919; 5 Tyr. 458).
(2) 40 R. R. 779 (1 Cr. M. & R.   (3) 7 Car. & P. 181.

fish. Besides the general issue, defendant placed several justifications on the record; but the only one on which the trial proceeded was, that defendant and all those who held his messuage and tenements (abutting on the *locus in quo*), for sixty years, had and enjoyed the privilege of fishing for lamperns in the *locus in quo*. The replication (1) stated that the plaintiff, as lady of the manor of Minsterworth, and all those &c., have enjoyed from time beyond memory the sole and several privilege of fishing on the close, which was the river Severn, at that spot. This right being traversed, it was necessary to show that the *locus in quo* was in the manor of Minsterworth ; and the survey was tendered for the purpose of proving it.

On the argument before us the admissibility of this document was mainly rested on the authority of *Rowe* v. *Brenton* (2), where the Court admitted a document purporting to be an extent of the manor of Tewington, *temp. Edw. III., by the steward of the King's land on this side Trent.   They decided that the statute applied to the possessions of the Duchy, as well as those of the Crown. Whether the statute authorised more than one survey to be made was not argued ; but, assuming that this ought to be done from time to time, the Court very reasonably inferred from the form and contents of the document that it was an act of official duty prescribed by that statute.   The question turned there wholly on the right of the conventionary tenants of lands in certain manors belonging to the Duchy to minerals there found.   The document stated the privileges enjoyed by such tenants. Now the eighth section of the statute 4 Edw. I. (stat. 1) directs enquiry to be made of freeholders' services, value, and rent, whether they follow the county court, and what heriots are payable to the lord : and the ninth section directs enquiry also "of customary tenants, that is to wit, how many there be, and how much land every one of them holdeth ; what works and customs he doth, and what the works and customs of every tenant be worth yearly, and how much rent of assize be paid yearly besides the works and customs, and which of them may be taxed at the will of the lord, and which not."   The

[*625]

(1) The replication, as to this plea,   as pleaded. See p. 775, *ante*.
merely traversed the prescriptive right   (2) 32 R. R. 524 (8 B. & C. 747).

EVANS
v.
TAYLOR.

Court, considering that this document conveyed direct information on the very point in issue, and might, on the grounds above
stated, have been in exact conformity with the aforesaid statute,
were surely well warranted in holding the instrument authentic
and legitimate.

It is, however, remarkable that this statute, Extenta Manerii,
does not contain the word "manor," though no doubt that
species of property is within it; but it gives no power to define
boundaries of manors.

[626]   The report, then, of the deputy surveyor, that the tenants of
a particular manor had at a court of survey found its boundaries, is a statement which they were not authorised by this
statute to make, nor he to receive; and the contents of this
document do not bring it within the description of proceeding
enjoined by this statute. If this be so (and I may observe that
Rowe v. *Brenton* (1) was never mentioned at Nisi Prius), we must
now examine the argument which was then pressed on my consideration. It was contended that, though the proceeding of
Sir John Poyntz might have no legal authority, yet the reported
declaration of the tenants of the manor must be considered good
evidence as showing the reputation of that time in respect of its
boundaries; *Freeman* v. *Phillipps* (2) and *Crease* v. *Barrett* (3)
were cited to this effect. But in the former case there had been
an actual suit in the Exchequer: depositions then taken of
persons representing the same interest as that of plaintiff
Freeman were produced. The only presumption then, that
the Court had to make, was that these were real parties to
the suit, and that they made the depositions actually sworn to
in their names. In the latter case no doubt existed that similar
depositions, made by conventionary tenants in answer to interrogatories, were the real statements of parties actually interested
in a pending proceeding, though the nature of it (owing to the
loss of the commission) could not be ascertained. A similar
presumption of verity in the proceedings was the only thing here
required to make the depositions good evidence. The present
case is entirely different; for the deputy surveyor of the Duchy

(1) 32 R. R. 524 (8 B. & C. 737).   (3) 40 R. R. 779 (1 Cr. M. & R.
(2) 16 R. R. 524 (4 M. & S. 486).   919; 5 Tyr. 458).

does *not appear to have had any authority to institute the
enquiry; and, stripped of this authority, he has not merely no
right to make any kind of return, but the presumption that he
did make it falls to the ground.   The paper may have been
written by any clerk idling in the office, from his own imagina-
nation, or compiled possibly by some interested person in
furtherance of a sinister object of his own.   From these
considerations, it appears that the document was no evidence
for any purpose.   *Rule discharged.*

PRINCE *v.* SAMO.

(7 Adol. & Ellis, 627—635; S. C. 3 N. & P. 139; W. W. & D. 132; 7 L. J.
(N. S.) Q. B. 123; 2 Jur. 323.)

A witness, who has been cross-examined as to what plaintiff said in a
particular conversation, cannot, on that ground, be re-examined as to
other assertions, made by the plaintiff in the same conversation, but not
connected with the assertions to which the cross-examination related;
although the assertions, as to which it is proposed to re-examine, be
connected with the subject-matter of the present suit.

CASE for a malicious arrest for 60*l.*   Plea, Not guilty.

On the trial before Lord Denman, Ch. J., at the Middlesex
sittings after Trinity Term, 1836, it appeared that, in the action
in which the defendant arrested the plaintiff, the defendant's
claim had been 60*l.* for money lent; that the plaintiff had
resisted the claim on the ground that the advance was a gift and
not a loan; that the verdict had been in his favour, and that he
had had judgment thereupon.   In the present action, a witness
for the plaintiff, his attorney, stated, on cross-examination, that
the now plaintiff, after the first action, had indicted a witness,
who appeared for the defendant on the first trial, for perjury at
that trial; that the now plaintiff had been a witness on the trial
of that indictment, and had then stated, on his cross-examination, that he had been remanded by the Court for the Relief of
Insolvent Debtors.   The counsel for the *plaintiff, on the
re-examination of this witness, proposed to ask him whether
the plaintiff had not also, on the trial of the indictment, sworn
that the advance now in question was a gift, and not a loan.   The
question was objected to; and the LORD CHIEF JUSTICE ruled

that it could not be put.   Verdict for the defendant.   In
Michaelmas Term, 1886, *Sir F. Pollock* obtained a rule to show
cause why the verdict should not be set aside, and a new
trial had.

> *Sir W. W. Follett* and *Chandless*, showed cause in
> Michaelmas Term last (1) :

The question rejected did not arise out of the cross-examination.   It will be argued that this case falls within the supposed
rule, that the whole of a conversation may be given in evidence,
if any part of it be so given.   But the rule is not so general.
There may, in the case of a written document, be a difficulty in
separating matter connected with that which is insisted on by
the party producing such document from the matter not so
connected, because the whole document, not a part of it, is
laid before the jury: but in the case of parol evidence, a
witness should be stopped as soon as he proceeds to state what
is not material.   The principle upon which one part of a conversation is admitted when another has been proved is, that
otherwise some qualification or explanation of the part received
in evidence might be excluded.   That principle stops short of
making the whole conversation admissible, whether or not
connected with the part proved.

[*629]
(PATTESON, J. referred to 1 Stark. Ev. 180, ed. 2 : "Where a
witness has been cross-examined as to a conversation *with the
adverse party in the suit, whether criminal or civil, the counsel
for that party has a right to lay before the Court the whole
which was said by his client in the same conversation ; not only
so much as may explain or qualify the matter introduced by the
previous examination, but even matter not properly connected
with the part introduced upon the previous examination, provided
only that it relate to the subject-matter of the suit ; because it
would not be just to take part of a conversation as evidence
against a party, without giving him at the same time the benefit
of the entire residue of what he said on the same occasion.")

(1) November 21st, 1837. Before Lord Denman, Ch. J., Patteson,
Williams, and Coleridge, JJ.

That is laid down exclusively on the authority of a *dictum* of
Abbott, Ch. J. in *The Queen's* case (1).   It will be found that
this *dictum* was extra-judicial, the questions propounded by the
House of Lords relating to the declarations of a third party ;
and the Judges confine the doctrine respecting these to matter
showing the signification of the words and declarations previously
given in evidence, and the motive for uttering them : and the
distinction between the two cases cannot be supported.   But
even the *dictum* is limited to the subject-matter of the suit : here
the matter proposed to be given in evidence related to a previous
suit.   There were, in fact, two different conversations.   Except
from the subject-matter, it would be impossible to lay down a
test as to what did or did not form part of a single conversation.
Every thing that passes while the parties conversing remain in
each other's company cannot necessarily belong to the same
conversation ; as, for instance, where two parties make a long
journey together in the same carriage.

[630]

Sir F. Pollock and *Ball, contrà :*

It is impossible to resist this rule, except upon arguments
which would show that a part of a letter may be read without
reading the whole.   Indeed the separation of a written document
into distinct subject matters is much easier than such a process
in the case of oral conversation (2).   It is true that in Chancery
a party of whose answer a portion has been read is not entitled
to insist upon every thing contained in the answer being taken
as proved : but, at law, the whole must be read if a part be read ;
Lynch v. *Clerke* (3), *Earl of Bath* v. *Bathersea* (4), where it is said
that "it is like examination of witnesses."

(Coleridge, J. : Has the question ever been decided as to
depositions ?)

No express decision has been found.   This comes within the
analogy of an admission, as to which the following rule is laid
down in 1 Phil. Ev. 110 (ed. 7) (5) : " It is scarcely necessary to

---

(1) 22 R. R. 673, 674 (2 Brod. & B.   (3) 3 Salk. 154.
297, 298).   (4) 5 Mod. 9.   And see 1 Stark.
(2) See *Catt* v. *Huward*, 23 R. R.   Ev. 286, 287 (2nd ed.).
751, 3 Stark. 6.   (5) See 1 Phil. Ev. 357 (8th ed.).

PRINCE
v.
SAMO.

observe, that the whole of an admission must be taken together, in order to show distinctly the full meaning and sense of the party.   Thus, if a person, in making an admission against his own interest, refers to a written paper, without which the admission is not complete, the contents of the paper ought to be shown, before the statement can be used as evidence against the party.   Or, if a person says, ' that he did owe a debt, but that he had paid it,' such an admission would not be received as evidence to prove the debt, without being also evidence of the payment.   What he has said in his own favour may perhaps weigh very little with the jury, while his admission against himself may be conclusive ; however, it is reasonable, that if any

[*631]

part of his statement *is admitted in evidence, the whole should be admitted."   In *Thomson* v. *Austen* (1) ABBOTT, Ch. J. said, " It is at all times a dangerous thing to admit a portion only of a conversation in evidence, because one part taken by itself may bear a very different construction, and have a very different tendency, to what would be produced if the whole were heard ; for one part of a conversation will frequently serve to qualify and to explain the other."

(They then contended that the matter referred to by the question was in fact connected with the matter previously received in evidence ; but the COURT intimated that, from the course taken at the trial, and in moving for the rule, this line of argument was not open to them.)

Cur. adv. vult.

LORD DENMAN, Ch. J., in this Term (January 29th), delivered the judgment of the COURT :

This was an action for malicious arrest on a false suggestion that money was lent by defendant to plaintiff, when it had been in fact given.   The plaintiff called his attorney as a witness ; he happened to have been present at the trial of a prosecution for perjury instituted by the plaintiff against a witness in the action wherein he had been arrested.   The defendant's counsel inquired of him, in cross-examination, whether the plaintiff had not, on the trial for perjury, stated that he himself had been insolvent

(1) 2 Dowl. & Ry. 358.

repeatedly, and remanded by the Court. This question was not objected to. On his re-examination the same witness was asked whether plaintiff had not also, on that occasion, given an account of the circumstances *out of which the arrest had arisen, and what that account was, for the purpose of laying before the jury proof that the arrest was without cause, and malicious, of both which facts there were scarcely any, if any, evidence whatever. This question, expressly confined to that purpose, was whether plaintiff did not say, in the course of his examination, that the money was given, and not lent. To this question the defendant's counsel objected, not on account of its leading form, but because the defendant's having proved one detached expression that fell from the plaintiff when a witness does not make the whole of what he then said evidence in his own favour. My opinion was that the witness might be asked as to every thing said by the plaintiff, when he appeared on the trial of the indictment, that could in any way qualify or explain the statement as to which he had been cross-examined, but that he had no right to add any independent history of transactions wholly unconnected with it.

That a witness's statement of some one thing said by him, though drawn out by a cross-examination, does not permit the opposite party to add to it all that he may have uttered on the same occasion, was in effect decided by seven out of eight Júdges whose opinion was taken by the House of Lords in the progress of the bill of Pains and Penalties against her Majesty Queen Caroline (1). Lord TENTERDEN, in delivering that opinion, said, " I think the counsel has a right, upon re-examination, to ask all questions, which may be proper to draw forth an explanation of the sense and meaning of the expressions used by the witness on cross-examination, if *they be in themselves doubtful, and, also, of the motive, by which the witness was induced to use those expressions ; but, I think, he has no right to go further, and to introduce matter new in itself, and not suited to the purpose of explaining either the expressions or the motives of the witness." And, "as many things may pass in one and the same conversation " which do not relate to either, the learned

(1) 22 R. R. at p. 673 (2 Brod. & B. 297).

PRINCE
v.
SAMO.

[*632]

[*633]

CHIEF JUSTICE declared the opinion of the Judges, that the witness could not be re-examined even to the extent of all that might have passed relating to his becoming a witness, to which the statement proved had reference.

Lord WYNFORD, then Mr. Justice BEST, it is true, dissented (1) from this doctrine, and thought that the whole matter that passed in the same conversation was made admissible by the adversary's introduction of any part. But he rested his dissent on the propriety of giving a witness a full opportunity of self-vindication, which, in truth, the opinion of the seven Judges already secured for him; and he also lamented that the prevailing rules of evidence were too narrow, and thus proved that he rather thought it a good opportunity to extend them, than was contented to abide by them.

Lords ELDON and REDESDALE are also reported, in the Parliamentary Debates (2), to have intimated their disagreement from the opinion of the seven Judges. They however acted upon it; and the extreme caution with which the former learned Lord framed and often remodelled the question to be proposed to the Judges can hardly be reconciled with the doctrine that the whole [*634] *of what passed at the conversation referred to was for that reason admissible.

Upon the whole, we think it must be taken as settled that proof of a detached statement made by a witness at a former time does not authorise proof by the party calling that witness of all that he said at the same time, but only of so much as can be in some way connected with the statement proved.

But, in the present case, the statement did not proceed from a witness, but from a party to the suit; and the opinion delivered by Lord TENTERDEN is not only confined to the former case, but is expressly said by him not to apply in the latter. His language is accurately cited by Mr. Starkie (Evidence, vol. i. 180, ed. 2), from 2 B. & B. 297. (His Lordship here read the passage cited *ante*, p. 784.)

We forbear from entering into a detailed examination of the doctrine here laid down. We have considered it repeatedly with

(1) See 2 Hansard's Parl. Deb. New Series, p. 1302.

(2) 2 Hansard's Parl. Deb. New Series, pp. 1309, 1310.

the utmost care and with all the diffidence inspired by such an
authority; but we cannot assent to it. We will merely observe
that it was not introduced as an answer to any question proposed
by the House of Lords, and may therefore be strictly regarded
as extra-judicial; that it was not necessary as a reason for the
answer to the question that was proposed; that it was not in
terms adopted by Lord ELDON, or any of the other Judges who
concurred; that it was expressly denied by Lords REDESDALE
and WYNFORD; and that it does not rest on any previous
authority. We ought to add that, in our opinion, the reason of
the thing would rather go to exclude the statements of a party
making declarations which cannot be disinterested.

Nothing would be more easy than to find or imagine *examples   [*635]
of the extreme injustice that might result from allowing such
statements to be received. But none can be stronger than the
actual case. Because the plaintiff was shown to have said that
he was insolvent, he would have been allowed, without any
reference to his own insolvency, to prove by his discourse at the
same period every averment in his declaration, with every
circumstance likely to excite prejudice and odium. And, if this
were evidence, the jury would be bound to consider, and might
give full effect to it, and thus award large damages for an injury
of which no particle of proof could be found but the plaintiff's
own assertion.

We are of opinion that the line was correctly drawn at the
trial; and this rule must be discharged.

Rule discharged.

DOE D. WILLIAM HODGSON CADOGAN v. DAVID EWART.

1838.

[636]

(7 Adol. & Ellis, 636—670; S. C. 3 N. & P. 197; 7 L. J. (N. S.) Q. B. 177.)

A testator devised personalty to trustees, to pay debts, and invest the
surplus, and to receive the interest, and pay it to his wife during her life
and widowhood, and afterwards to apply the interest, or a sufficient part,
to the maintenance of his daughter I., until she should attain the age
of twenty-five, and then to pay and assign the principal and unapplied
interest to her; but, in case she should happen to die before attaining
that age, leaving lawful issue, then in trust to pay the same to such
issue, share and share alike, if more than one, as soon as they should

respectively attain twenty-one, and to pay the interest towards their maintenance in the meantime ; but, in case I. should happen to die under twenty-five, and without leaving lawful issue, testator bequeathed the whole surplus of the personalty to W. and D., share and share alike.

By the same will, he devised to D. an annuity of 200*l.* for life, charged on his land, to be paid by the above- mentioned trustees; and he devised to the same trustees (one of whom was W.), and the survivors and survivor, and the heirs of the survivor, all his lands, charged with the annuity, and with so much of his debts, legacies, and funeral expenses, as the residue of the personalty would not extend to, in trust to receive the rents, issues, &c., and apply them to the use of testator's wife, during her life and widowhood, and afterwards to apply the rents, &c., to the maintenance of I. until she should attain the age of twenty-five, and afterwards in trust for I. and her heirs; but, in case it should happen that I. died without leaving lawful issue, then testator devised the lands to W. and D. in fee, as ténants in common. The will also empowered the trustees, in order to pay debts, &c., in case the residue of the personalty should be insufficient, to sell any part of the lands, and to grant, alien, and convey the same lands, or any part thereof, in fee simple.

The testator's wife died in his lifetime; I. survived the testator, and attained the age of twenty-one, but died under twenty-five, leaving no issue.

The personalty not being sufficient to pay the debts, the trustees sold part of the land.

Held, 1. That the trustees took a legal fee simple in all the land, such estate being requisite for the purposes of the trusts.

2. That, on the testator's death, I. took a vested equitable estate tail, and W. and D. took equitable remainders. And, therefore,

3. That I., by suffering a recovery in which the trustees did not join, created no legal estate; but that the equitable remainders of W. and D. were barred.

EJECTMENT for lands in Cumberland. Issue having been joined, the facts were stated, by consent of parties, for the opinion of this Court, in a case, which was substantially as follows :

Richard Hodgson, by his will, dated 18th January, 1828, [*637] devised (1) unto Jane Dalston Hodgson and her *assigns, during

---

(1) The will commenced with bequests of personalty; and the Court directed that the whole should be considered as part of the case. The bequests of personalty were substantially as follows. The testator, after bequeathing household furniture and other personal chattels to his wife Mary Hodgson, gave the residue of his personal estate to trustees (the same persons as the trustees of the realty), in trust to apply it in pay-

ment of his debts, and then to invest the surplus, in their own names, in securities at interest, and to receive the interest, and pay and apply it for the use and benefit of his wife for life, in case she should so long continue his widow; and afterwards to apply the interest, or a sufficient part thereof, towards the maintenance and support of his daughter Isabella, until she should attain the age of twenty-five, and, as soon as she

her natural life, one yearly annuity or rent charge of 200*l*., to be issuing and payable out of all such messuages, lands, tenements, and real estate (except his estate at Fauld) as he might be possessed of at the time of his decease, to be paid, by the trustees after named, to her by half-yearly payments. And he devised to his sister Jane Hodgson the dwelling-house, &c., then in her occupation, situate at Fauld, in the parish of Burgh by Sands, during her natural life, for her own residence only. And he devised to John Forster, therein described, and to the lessor of the plaintiff William Hodgson Cadogan (by his then name of William Hodgson), and Joshua Anderson, and the survivors and survivor of them, and the heirs of such survivor, all his messuages, lands, and tenements situate at Moorhouse, Orton, and Burgh, in the said county of Cumberland, and all other his real estate whatsoever and wheresoever, subject to the life estate of his *sister Jane Hodgson in his real estate at Fauld, and charged with the payment of the said annuity or rent charge, and also with so much of his just debts, legacies, funeral expenses, and costs of proving his will, as the residue of his personal estate and effects thereinbefore mentioned would not extend unto, upon the several trusts, and to and for the several uses, ends, intents, and purposes following, that is to say: Upon trust to receive the rents and issues thereof, and to pay and apply the same from time to time, as and when the same should be received, unto the only proper use and behoof of the testator's wife Mary, during her life, in case she should so long continue his widow; and, from and after her decease or marrying again, which should first happen, then " upon trust to apply the said rents, issues, and profits towards the maintenance and

[*638]

should attain that age, to pay and assign the principal and unapplied interest to her; but, in case she should happen to die before attaining the age of twenty-five, leaving lawful issue, then in trust to pay the same to such issue, share and share alike, if more than one, as soon as they should respectively attain their ages of twenty-one years, and to pay the interest towards their maintenance, education, and support in the mean time. But, in case his said daughter should happen to die under that age, and without leaving lawful issue, then he gave and bequeathed the whole of such surplus of his personal estate and effects unto Major William Hodgson (one of the trustees), and the testator's natural daughter Jane Dalston Hodgson, in equal shares, share and share alike.

support of my said daughter Isabella, until she shall attain the
age of twenty-five years ; and, from and after her attaining that
age, then upon trust, as to my real estate, subject and charged
as aforesaid, for my said daughter Isabella, her heirs and
assigns, for ever ; and I give and devise the same to her
accordingly: but, in case it should happen that my said daughter
Isabella depart this life without leaving issue lawfully begotten,
then I give and devise the said messuages, lands, tenements, and
real estate, unto the said Major William Hodgson and the said
Jane Dalston Hodgson, their heirs and assigns, for ever, as
tenants in common." And the will provided that, if the said
J. D. H. should, by virtue of the limitations thereinbefore contained and hereinbefore set forth, become entitled to any part of
the said testator's said real estates, the annuity of 200*l.* therein-

[*639] before given to her should cease. And the testator *ordained
that the trustees, for the performance of his will, and in order to
raise money for the payment of his just debts, funeral expenses,
and legacies, should and might, with all convenient speed after
his decease, in case the said residue of his personal estate should
be insufficient for that purpose, bargain, and sell, and alien in
fee simple, any part of his said freehold messuages, lands, and
tenements before mentioned ; for the doing, executing, and
perfect finishing whereof, he gave to his trustees, and the
survivors, &c., and the heirs, &c., full power and absolute
authority to grant, alien, bargain, sell, convey and assure the
same premises, or any part thereof, to any person or persons and
their heirs for ever in fee simple, by all and every such lawful
ways and means in the law as to his said trustees, or the survivors
or survivor of them, or the heirs of such survivor, or to his or
their counsel, should seem fit and necessary. And the testator
authorised the trustees, and the survivors, &c., and the heirs,
&c., to give receipts for purchase-monies, and did commit the
management of the estates and fortunes of his said daughter to
his said trustees and executors until she should attain the age of
twenty-five years : and he appointed the said trustees executors
of his will.

The testator died 21st May, 1830, leaving his said daughter
Isabella his heiress at law ; and the will was duly proved.

Mary, the wife of the testator, died in his lifetime. The personal
estate not being sufficient for the payment of his debts, the
trustees, in pursuance of the power or direction in that behalf,
sold part of the real estate, including the premises devised to the
testator's sister Jane Hodgson for her life.

By indentures of lease and release, bearing date respectively
*25th and 26th January, 1832, the release being made between
the said Isabella Hodgson (who had then attained the age of
twenty-one years), of the first part, William Higley, gentleman,
of the second part, and George Saul, gentleman, of the third
part, for barring and extinguishing all estates tail of her the
said Isabella Hodgson, of and in the hereditaments devised by
the said will, and not sold as aforesaid, and the remainders and
reversions thereon expectant or depending, and for assuring and
limiting the same hereditaments in the manner in the said
indenture of release and hereinafter mentioned, Isabella Hodgson
conveyed to William Higley, his heirs and assigns, all those the
messuages or tenements, &c., and premises thereinbefore referred
to, and by the said will of Richard Hodgson devised to or in
trust for the said Isabella Hodgson, her heirs and assigns, and
not sold by the trustees as aforesaid, to hold the same, with the
appurtenances, unto and to the use of the said William Higley,
his heirs and assigns, for ever, to the intent that he might be
immediate tenant of the actual freehold of the said hereditaments
and premises, so that one or more good and perfect common
recovery or recoveries, with double voucher, might be had and
suffered of the same; in which recovery or recoveries George
Saul was to be demandant, William Higley tenant, and Isabella
Hodgson vouchee, who was to vouch over the common vouchee.
And it was thereby declared that the said recovery, and all other
recoveries whatsoever, of the said hereditaments (so far as
Isabella Hodgson lawfully or rightfully might direct the uses
thereof), should operate and enure to the only proper use and
behoof of Isabella Hodgson, her heirs and assigns, for ever.

In pursuance of the said indentures, a common recovery was,
in Hilary Term, 2 Will. IV., duly had and suffered of the said
hereditaments and premises.

By indentures of lease and release, bearing date respectively

Doe d.
CADOGAN
v.
EWART.

[*640]

[641]

9th and 10th August, 1833, the release being made between Isabella Hodgson, of the first part, the defendant David Ewart, of the second part, John Forster and Simon Ewart, of the third part, and George Saul and Silas Saul, of the fourth part, in consideration of the marriage then intended and afterwards solemnised between Isabella Hodgson and the defendant, Isabella Hodgson, with the privity and approbation of the defendant, did convey to John Forster and Simon Ewart, and their heirs, the capital and other messuages, &c., therein mentioned and described (being the hereditaments devised by the will of Richard Hodgson, and not sold as aforesaid), with the appurtenances, to hold the same unto John Forster and Simon Ewart, and their heirs, to the use (from and after the solemnisation of the marriage) of John Forster and Simon Ewart, and their heirs and assigns, during the joint lives of Isabella Hodgson and the defendant, upon the trusts in the now stating indenture of release declared ; and, from and after the decease of Isabella Hodgson, or of the defendant, which should first happen, to the use of the survivor of them, and his or her assigns, for the term of his or her life, without impeachment of waste; remainder to the use of John Forster and Simon Ewart, and their heirs, &c. (to support contingent remainders); remainder to the use of the children or issue of the marriage, as the said Isabella Hodgson should by will appoint; and, in default of such appointment, to the use, &c. (certain estates limited in favour of the children *of the marriage) ; and, in default of all issue of Isabella Hodgson by the defendant, to the use of Isabella Hodgson, her heirs and assigns, for ever.

[*642]

By indenture, dated 9th November, 1833, made between the defendant and Isabella his then wife (formerly the said Isabella Hodgson), of the one part, and John Forster and Simon Ewart of the other part, the said defendant covenanted and agreed that he and the said Isabella his wife (she thereby consenting) should and would, in or as of the then Michaelmas term, acknowledge and levy unto the said John Forster and Simon Ewart, and the heirs of one of them, one or more fine or fines *sur conuzance de droit come ceo* &c. of the hereditaments comprised in the said indenture of settlement, with their appurtenances: and it was thereby agreed that such fine or fines, and all other fines, conveyances and assurances of the same hereditaments, should operate and enure to confirm all the uses and trusts in the said indenture of settlement of 10th August, 1833, contained, anterior to the limitation to the use of Isabella, then the wife of the said defendant, her heirs and assigns, and all the powers contained in the same indenture, and to assure the same hereditaments (subject as aforesaid) to such uses, upon such trusts, and for such intents and purposes, as the said Isabella Ewart, by her last will or testament in writing, or any codicil or codicils thereto, to be by her (notwithstanding her coverture, and whether covert or sole) signed and published, in the presence of and attested by three or more witnesses, should direct, limit, or appoint; and, in default of such direction, limitation, or appointment, and so far as any such direction, limitation, or appointment *should not extend, to the use of Isabella Ewart, her heirs and assigns, for ever.

[*643]

In pursuance of the lastly mentioned indenture a fine was, in or as of Michaelmas Term, 8 Will. IV., duly levied of the said hereditaments, and proclamations made thereon.

Isabella Ewart, by her last will and testament, or testamentary writing, dated 7th January, 1834, signed &c. (in conformity with the power), in exercise of, and after reciting, the power given to her by the indenture of 9th November, 1833, and the fine levied in pursuance thereof, and of every or any other power or authority enabling her in that behalf, did direct, limit, and appoint, that the several hereditaments situate at Moorhouse, &c., and all other the hereditaments of her the said Isabella Ewart, situate at or near Moorhouse aforesaid, or elsewhere in Cumberland, should, subject to such, if any, of the uses and trusts anterior to the power of appointment so given or reserved to her, as under or by virtue of the said indenture of 9th November, 1833, and fine, were then subsisting, or should take effect, be and remain unto and to the use of her husband David Ewart, his heirs and assigns; and she did accordingly give and devise the same hereditaments unto and to the use of the defendant, his heirs and assigns, for ever.

Isabella Ewart died in January, 1834, under the age of

twenty-five years, without leaving any issue of her body, but leaving her husband, the defendant, her surviving.

It was contended, for the defendant, that either the trustees under the will of Richard Hodgson took the legal estate in fee simple absolutely, and that the gift over to the lessor of the plaintiff and Jane Dalston Hodgson, in case of the death, without [*644] leaving issue, of *the testator's daughter Isabella, was to be construed as meaning on an indefinite failure of issue, and consequently that she was equitable tenant in tail; or that (the testator's wife having died in his lifetime) the trustees took an estate only for so many years as the said Isabella should be under twenty-five, which was a chattel interest, and that the devise to her operated as an immediate gift to her of the legal estate of freehold for an estate tail: Or, if the trustees took an estate of freehold until Isabella attained the age of twenty-five years, the defect occasioned by their not concurring in making a tenant to the præcipe for the recovery suffered by her before her marriage was cured by stat. 3 & 4 Will. IV. c. 74, s. 11, which provides " that no common recovery already suffered " " shall be invalid in consequence of any person in whom an estate at law was outstanding having omitted to make the tenant to the writ of entry or other writ for suffering such recovery, provided the person who was the owner of or had power to dispose of, an estate in possession, not being less than an estate for a life or lives in the whole of the rents and profits of the lands in which such estate at law was outstanding, or the ultimate surplus of such rents and profits after payment of any charges thereout, and whether any surplus after payment of such charges shall actually remain or not, shall, within the time limited for making the tenant to the writ for suffering such recovery, have conveyed or disposed of such estate in possession to the tenant to such writ; " and that, consequently, the defendant's late wife, by the said recovery, acquired either the legal or the equitable fee-simple; and, she having died without issue, the defendant, [*645] *under and by virtue of the fine levied by him and his wife, and the declaration of the uses thereof, and of her said will, had acquired such fee simple in the hereditaments the subject of the present action.

It was contended, for the lessor of the plaintiff, that either the trustees under the will of Richard Hodgson took an estate of freehold in the devised hereditaments until his daughter Isabella attained the age of twenty-five years, with a power, only, to sell for the payment of debts and legacies, and, consequently, the recovery suffered by her was ineffectual to bar her estate tail (if any), by reason that the trustees did not join in making a tenant to the *præcipe* in that recovery, in which case the limitation over to the lessor of the plaintiff and Jane Dalston Hodgson, upon the death of the testator's daughter Isabella, had taken effect; or else that the said Isabella took an estate in fee simple in the devised hereditaments, subject to an executory devise over to the lessor of the plaintiff and Jane Dalston Hodgson, in the event of the said Isabella dying without issue under the age of twenty-five, or without leaving issue at the time of her death, although such death might take place after that age, and, consequently, that the recovery suffered by her was ineffectual to bar or destroy the remainder or estate by the said testator's will limited to the lessor of the plaintiff and the said Jane Dalston Hodgson, as tenants in common in fee simple.

The question for the opinion of the Court was, whether the lessor of the plaintiff was entitled to recover in this action a moiety under the devise to him and the said Jane Dalston Hodgson, as tenants in common in fee simple, of such of the hereditaments devised by the *said will of Richard Hodgson, as were not sold by the trustees of his will.

[*646]

If the Court should be of that opinion, then the defendant agreed that judgment should be entered against him by confession, immediately after the decision of this case, or otherwise, as the Court should think fit; and, if the Court should be of opinion that the lessor of the plaintiff was not entitled to recover such moiety in this action, then he agreed that judgment should be entered against him of *nolle prosequi*, immediately after the decision of this case, or otherwise, as the said Court might think fit.

The case was argued in Easter Term last, by *Sir W. W. Follett* for the plaintiff, and *Sir F. Pollock* for the defendant.

1838.

Cur. adv. vult.

Doe d.
CADOGAN
v.
EWART.

Lord Denman, Ch. J. in this Term (January 31st) delivered the judgment of the Court (1):

After stating the nature of the action, the terms of the devise of the realty by Richard Hodgson, and the other principal facts, with the points put for the respective parties in the case, his Lordship proceeded as follows.

There are two principal questions in this case.

First, whether Isabella Hodgson, the daughter of the testator, [*647] took an estate in fee with an executory devise *over to Major William Hodgson and Jane Dalston Hodgson, or whether she took a vested estate tail with remainder over to the same persons? If she took an estate in fee with an executory devise over, then the plaintiff (who is now called Cadogan, but in the will called Hodgson), who is one of the persons named in the devise over, is entitled to recover, because the recovery suffered by Isabella Hodgson could not bar the executory devise over.

But, if Isabella Hodgson took a vested estate tail with remainder over, then the second question will arise, whether the recovery suffered by her be a valid recovery sufficient to bar the remainder over?

On the first question, the words of the will, which give the estate to the testator's daughter, Isabella Hodgson, her heirs and assigns for ever, *primâ facie* import a devise in fee simple; and then the words which follow, " but, in case it should happen that my said daughter Isabella depart this life without leaving issue lawfully begotten, then I give the said messuages, lands, tenements, and real estate, unto the said Major William Hodgson and the said Jane Dalston Hodgson, their heirs and assigns, for ever, as tenants in common," would, according to the common and ordinary idiom and construction of the English language, independent of any technical rules which have been applied to the construction of legal instruments, imply that the devise over was to take place in the event of Isabella dying without issue which should be living at the time of her death (2).

(1) April 25th, 1837. Before Lord Denman, Ch. J., Littledale, Patteson, and Coleridge, JJ.

(2) See the construction on this point settled (as to wills coming into operation in and after the year 1838) by the 29th section of the Wills Act, 1837 (1 Vict. c. 26), as stated by Lord Denman at p. 812 below.—R. C.

But the law has prescribed certain limits for the validity of executory devises ; and one of them is, that the contingency upon which an estate of this sort is *permitted to take effect, shall happen within a short space of time, as a life or lives in being, and some few years, now settled at twenty-one years and the period of gestation ; otherwise it would be in a testator's power to limit an estate unalienable for generations to come, a power which the law denies.   And therefore, where an executory devise is limited to take effect after an indefinite failure of issue, the limitation over is void.

Under this rule, if the limitation be to take effect after a dying without heirs or without issue generally, that is considered to be an indefinite failure of issue, and therefore void. And the same rule holds in the limitation of a term or other personal estate, that a disposition to take effect after failure of the heirs of the body or dying without issue generally, without other restriction, is too remote ; for the law will no more admit of a perpetuity in one sort of estate or species of property than in another.

But, with regard to executory devises of terms for years or other personal estates, the Courts have for a very considerable time very much inclined to lay hold of any words in the will to tie up the generality of the expression, dying without issue, and confine it to dying without issue living at the time of the person's decease.   There are a great variety of cases, not necessary to be referred to, illustrating this position ; and we may say, without any doubt, that the words of the present will would, if the question arose upon a term for years or other personal estate, now be held to mean a dying without issue living at the death of the daughter Isabella.

But, though the Courts, in the case of personal estates, generally incline to pay attention to any circumstance *or expression in the will that seems to afford a ground for construing a limitation after dying without issue to be a dying without issue living at the death of the party, in order to support the devise over, yet in the case of real estate it seems the construction is generally otherwise ; and the reason given is, that the interest of the heir is concerned, who is said to be always favoured in our law.

In *Target* v. *Gaunt* (1) the expression dying without issue is recognised as having two senses : first, a vulgar sense, and that is, dying without leaving issue at the time of the death ; secondly, a legal sense, and that is, whenever there is a failure of issue : and that there is a great diversity betwixt the devise of a freehold estate for life, and, if A. dies without issue, then to B., and a devise of a term in the same words.

The case of *Forth* v. *Chapman* (2) establishes this distinction. There the testator gave the residue of his real and personal estate to two nephews, W. G. and W. G., and, if either of them should depart this life and leave no issue of their respective bodies, then he gave the said [leasehold] premises to other persons ; upon which the question arose, whether the limitation over of the leasehold premises was void as too remote ? The Master of the Rolls, Sir JOSEPH JEKYLL, was of opinion that the devise over was void, and said that, if the words had been, if A. or B. should die without issue, the remainder over, this plainly would have been void, and exactly like the case of *Love* v. *Windham* (3). And then he goes on to say "there

[*650]

is no diversity betwixt a *devise of a term to one for life, and if he die without issue, remainder over, and a devise thereof to one for life, with such remainder, if he die leaving no issue ; for both these devises seem equally relative to the failure of issue at any time after the testator's death." Afterwards, in Trinity Term, 1720, this case coming on before Lord PARKER on an appeal, his Lordship reversed the decree, and said, that, "if I devise a term to A., and if A. die without leaving issue, remainder over, in the vulgar and natural sense this must be intended if A. die without leaving issue at his death, and then the devise over is good ; that, the word 'die' being the last antecedent, the words 'without leaving' issue must refer to that." Lord PARKER also observed, "that by this will the devise was of a freehold as well as a leasehold estate to William Gore, and, if he or Walter died leaving no issue, then to the children of his brother and sister, in which case it was more

(1) 1 P. Wms. 432 ; *S. C.* 1 Eq.
Ca. Abr. 193, pl. 11 ; Gilb. Rep. Eq.
149 ; 10 Mod. 402.

(2) 1 P. Wms. 663.

(3) 1 Sid. 450 ; *S. C.* 1 Vént. 79 ;
1 Mod. 50.

difficult to conceive how the same words, in the same will, at the same time, should be taken in two different senses. As to the freehold, the construction should be, if William or Walter died without issue generally, by which there might be at any time a failure of issue; and, with respect to the leasehold, that the same words should be intended to signify their dying without leaving issue at their death. However," the LORD CHANCELLOR said, "it might be reasonable enough to take the same words, as to the different estates, in different senses, and as if repeated by two several clauses." Mr. Peere Williams, in a note on this case, says that by the will, as it is stated above, from the registrar's books, in the statement of the case at the Rolls, and on the appeal, the limitation over was expressly restrained to the leasehold; but in Lord Macclesfield's *notes that word is omitted, and the devise over is general: but in *Sheffield* v. *Lord Orrery* (1) Lord HARDWICKE says that Mr. Williams is mistaken in this note; "for, upon looking into the case, it appears that both freehold and leasehold were devised by the same words; but probably the limitation of the real was overlooked, and so omitted by the register."

The words in that case are in effect the same as in the present; the words there being, if the nephews should die and leave no issue of their respective bodies; and, in the present case, if it should happen that my daughter "depart this life without leaving issue lawfully begotten." It will be to be considered how far the case of *Forth* v. *Chapman* (2) has been recognized or impugned in other cases.

In *Sheffield* v. *Lord Orrery* (3), before cited, Lord HARDWICKE recognises the doctrine of Lord MACCLESFIELD in *Forth* v. *Chapman* (2), that the same words may have different constructions to effectuate the intention of the party.

In *Walter* v. *Drew* (4), where the will was that, if W. W., the son of the testator, should happen to die and leave no issue of his body lawfully begotten, then, after the death of W., he gave and bequeathed all his lands of inheritance to his son Richard and his heirs, it was held that W. took an estate tail by

[*651]

DOE d.
CADOGAN
v.
EWART.

(1) 3 Atk. 288.   (3) 3 Atk. 282.
(2) 1 P. Wms. 663.   (4) 1 Com. Rep. 372.

implication, which was barred by the recovery; and that the
limitation over was a remainder, and not an executory devise.
The authority of that case is also confirmed by Lord HARDWICKE
in *Southby* v. *Stonehouse* (1), where, in page 616, *he says, "The
only objection to this construction is, that this will not construe
the words according to her expression in the former clause, but
puts a different construction upon the same words in two different
events.   Now that that may be done, there are authorities, and
in a much stronger case, viz. *Forth* v. *Chapman* (2); where the
greatest difficulty in the way of Lord MACCLESFIELD was, that
the freehold and leasehold were devised by the same words: and
yet he held, those words were to receive a construction according to the subject-matter."   And he again repeats what he had
done in *Sheffield* v. *Lord Orrery* (3), that there was a mistake in
Mr. Williams's note, as to the limitation in *Forth* v. *Chapman* (2),
for that he, Lord HARDWICKE, was counsel in the cause.

In *Denn* d. *Geering* v. *Shenton* (4), the devise was to Samuel
Shenton and the heirs of his body and their heirs for ever,
chargeable with the payment of 8*l*. a year; but, in case the said
Shenton should "die without leaving issue of his body, then I
give " the said devised premises to William G. and his heirs for
ever.   Lord MANSFIELD asked *Mr. Cowper* if he had any case to
show, where, upon a limitation of lands upon a dying without
issue, these words had been confined to a dying without issue
living at the time of the death.   The distinction is taken
"between a devise of lands and personal estate: in the latter
case, the words are taken in their vulgar sense; that is, dying
·without leaving issue at the time of his death.   In the former,
they are taken in a legal sense; and that is, whenever there is a
failure of issue."   Lord MANSFIELD said, "the question is,

whether the *grandson took an estate tail, or an estate in fee?
Now the devise is to Samuel Shenton, and the heirs of his body,
and their heirs for ever; but the words 'their heirs for ever,'
are qualified by the subsequent words, 'in case he shall die
without leaving issue,' which clearly show it to be an estate tail;
and then, the testator gives it over to the lessor of the plaintiff;"

(1) 2 Ves. Sen. 611.   (3) 3 Atk. 288.
(2) 1 P. Wms. 663.   (4) 1 Cowp. 410.

and he adds, " it is too clear to admit of a doubt." There the words were " without leaving issue."

In *Goodtitle* d. *Peake* v. *Pegden* (1), which was the devise of a chattel interest, Lord KENYON relies upon the case of *Forth* v. *Chapman* (2), without any objection.

In the case of *Daintry* v. *Daintry* (3), Lord KENYON recognizes the case of *Forth* v. *Chapman* (2).

In *Tenny* d. *Agar* v. *Agar* (4) the devise was to the devisor's son John Agar, and his right heirs for ever, on condition of paying certain sums to his daughter ; " and, in case my said son and daughter both happen to die without leaving any child or issue," then he devised the reversion and inheritance to his cousin Richard, and his right heirs for ever. John Agar suffered a recovery ; and the question was, whether he took an estate tail, or whether there was a valid executory devise to Richard ? The COURT held that John Agar, the son, took an estate tail, which was well barred by the recovery ; and Mr. Justice LE BLANC said there was no case where the words " die without leaving issue," simply, have been adjudged to mean " without leaving issue at the time of the death : " and he added, " in *Porter* v. *Bradley* (5) there were also the words behind him."

In *Dansey* v. *Griffiths* (6) Richard Dansey devised his estates [654] to his eldest son, Dansey Richard Dansey, and his heirs for ever ; but, if it should so happen that his eldest son should die and leave no issue, then he devised his estates to his son W. Dansey and his heirs ; and, if he should die without issue, then to his son E. C. Dansey ; and, in the like case, to his son, G. H. D. ; and, in the like case to his son J. D. ; and, in failure of issue from him, to the eldest surviving son of his sister Mary and his heirs. The testator died, leaving his eldest son surviving him : and the question sent by the MASTER OF THE ROLLS was, what estate the eldest son took. And the Court certified their opinion that the eldest son, D. R. Dansey, took an estate tail under the will.

There is also the case of *Doe* d. *Ellis* v. *Ellis* (7). The testator

(1) 1 R. R. 606 (2 T. R. 720).
(2) 1 P. Wms. 663.
(3) 3 R. R. 179 (6 T. R. 307).
(4) 12 East, 253.

(5) 1 R. R. 675 (3 T. R. 143).
(6) 16 R. R. 383 (4 M. & S. 61).
(7) 9 East, 382.

devised to his eldest son Joseph, his heirs and assigns for ever,
the estate in question; but, in case his son Joseph should die
without issue, he devised the same to the child or children with
which his wife was *enseint*, his or her heirs and assigns for ever;
and it was held that Joseph took an estate tail.

There is also the case of *Brice* v. *Smith* (1), which was referred
to by Lord ELLENBOROUGH in *Doe* d. *Ellis* v. *Ellis* (2).   There
the testator devised the premises to his son Philip and his heirs
for ever, and other estates to other sons and their heirs; and
then he adds, "in case any of my said children" "shall die
without issue, then I give the estate of him or them so dying
unto his or their right heirs for ever:" held an estate tail.

And also *Roe* v. *Scott* in Mr. Fearne's manuscripts, and which
[*655]   is published in the notes of Butler's edition (3): *there the
testator devised certain lands to his son James, and his heirs
and assigns for ever; and other lands to his son John, and his
heirs and assigns for ever; and other lands to his son Thomas,
and his heirs and assigns for ever: and, if either of his sons
should depart this life without issue of him so dying, then to the
survivor; and, if they should all die without such issue, then to
his daughters and their heirs and assigns for ever: held an estate
tail in Thomas.

But none of those three last cases have the words "leaving
issue;" and it is beyond all doubt that, if a man devised in such
manner as in these three cases, the words, "if he die without
issue," in legal construction mean an indefinite failure of issue:
and the same words also without more words, even in personal
estates, import an indefinite failure of issue.

In opposition to these cases are *Porter* v. *Bradley* (4) and *Roe*
d. *Sheers* v. *Jeffery* (5), both decided in this Court while Lord
KENYON was Chief Justice, and which are particularly entitled to
attention from the very great knowledge which that learned Lord
possessed upon all matters relating to real property.

In the case of *Porter* v. *Bradley* (4) the testator devised to his
son Philip Dobin, his heirs and assigns for ever, all that

(1) Willes, 1.   9th ed.
(2) 9 East, 382.   (4) 1 R. R. 675 (3 T. R. 143).
(3) Fearne's Cont. Rem. 473, n. (s),   (5) 7 T. R. 589.

messuage, &c.; "but my will is that in case my said son Philip
Dobin shall happen to die leaving no issue behind him, then my
said wife" "shall receive and take the rents, issues, and profits"
during her widowhood; "and after her decease," "I give and
devise the same, for want of issue" "as aforesaid, unto my son
James Dobin, his heirs and assigns for ever;" "but in case
*my son James Dobin shall happen to die before my son Philip,
and the said Philip shall not leave any issue of his body begotten,
then my will is, that my said lands shall be sold, and equally
divided between my six daughters" "and their issues." One
question was, what estate Philip Dobin took under the will of his
father? Lord KENYON, after stating the words of the devise,
says, "The first question that arises in this case is, whether this
is an estate tail or in fee? The first part of the devise to Philip
Dobin *primâ facie* carries a fee; for it is to him, his heirs, and
assigns for ever: but it is clear that those words may be
restrained by subsequent ones so as to carry only an estate tail.
And a long string of cases may be cited in order to show that
where an estate is limited to a man and his heirs for ever, and,
if he die without leaving heirs, then to his brother, or to any
person who may be his heir, those words shall not have their full
legal operation, but shall be restrained to heirs of a particular
kind, namely, heirs of the body. If the subsequent part of this
devise had been 'and in case he shall die without heirs, then
over,' it would have given to P. Dobin an estate tail, which he
might have barred by the recovery. But here the words are
'but in case he shall happen to die, leaving no issue behind
him;' which makes a very material difference, and brings it
within the case of *Pells* v. *Brown* (1) which is the foundation, and
as it were the Magna Charta of this branch of the law. This
question arose soon after executory devises were first taken notice
of, which was in the reign of Queen Elizabeth. And that doctrine
has never been since doubted by the courts of law. *But the
defendant's counsel has attempted to distinguish this case from
that of *Pells* v. *Brown* (1); because there the words are 'If Thomas
(the first devisee) died without issue, living William his brother:'
but it is to be observed that there are words in this case" (*Porter*

(1) Cro. Jac. 590.

[*656]

[*657]

Doe d.
CADOGAN
v.
EWART.

v. *Bradley*) " equivalent to those, namely, ' If P. Dobin shall die,
leaving no issue behind him.'   If indeed only the first words
' leaving no issue ' had been used, they, according to the opinion
of Lord MACCLESFIELD in *Forth* v. *Chapman* (1), must be restrained
to leaving issue at the time of his death.   But it is contended,
that rule is confined to chattel interests only : " yet " it would be
very strange if these words had a different meaning when applied
to real and personal property.   If such a distinction existed in the
law, it certainly would not agree with the rule *lex plus laudatur
quando ratione probatur:* but it is not founded in law.   And
there are even additional words in this case, ' leaving no issue
behind him ; ' which necessarily import that the testator meant
at the time of his son's death.   The subsequent parts of the will
also convey the same idea : " and then he states the other parts
of the will.   The Court of King's Bench certified to the Court of
Chancery that Philip Dobin took an estate in fee simple in the
premises above devised to him : but, as Philip died without issue
living at the time of his death, they were of opinion that the
further disposition made by the testator in that event was good
by way of executory devise.

In *Roe d. Sheers* v. *Jeffery* (2) the testator devised the premises in question to his wife for life ; after her decease, to his
daughter for life ; after her decease, to *his grandson and his
heirs for ever ; but, in case his grandson should depart this life
and leave no issue, then that the premises should be and return
unto the three daughters of W. and M. Friswell, or the survivor
or survivors of them, to be equally divided betwixt them, share
and share alike.   The question was, whether the grandson took
an estate tail, or an estate in fee with an executory devise over.
Lord KENYON made the same remark as in *Porter* v. *Bradley* (3),
" That the very same words in the same clause in a will, should
receive one construction as applied to one species of property,
and another construction as applied to another," not being
" reconcileable with reason : " but he added, " that if it had
become a settled rule of property, it might be dangerous to
overturn it."   The case stood over ; and Lord KENYON, in giving

[*658]

(1) 1 P. Wms. 663.   (3) 1 R. R. 675 (3 T. R. 143).
(2) 7 T. R. 589.

the judgment of the Court, said that, in looking through the
whole of the will, the Court had no doubt but that " the testator
meant that the dying without issue, was confined to a failure of
issue at the death of the first taker ; for the persons to whom it
is given over were then in existence, and life estates are only
given to them ; " and that there was no doubt about the testator's
intention.   And it was held that the devise over was a good
executory devise.

In *Doe* d. *Barnfield* v. *Wetton* (1) the testator devised the premises in question to his wife for her life, and, after her death,
his freehold and leasehold premises to Francis Barnfield, his
heirs, executors, and administrators, upon trust to permit his
son John to take the rents and profits for his life ; and, after his
*death, upon trust for all the sons and daughters of his son   [*659]
John and their heirs ; and, after the death of his wife, he
devised his copyhold premises to his daughter Susannah, her
heirs and assigns for ever : but, if his daughter should happen
to die leaving no child or children, lawful issue of her body,
living at the time of her death, then he devised the premises to
Francis Barnfield and his heirs, upon trust &c.   It was held to
be an executory devise ; and it seems quite clear it must be so ;
because the dying without issue was limited to the life of
Susannah, the daughter, and therefore fell within the case of
Pells v. *Brown* (2) and other similar cases.

In the case of *Crooke* v. *De Vandes* (3) Lord ELDON thus
expresses himself, in page 203.   " When I read the case of *Porter*
v. *Bradley* (4), speaking with all due deference to the learned
Judge, who expressed that *dictum*, it appeared to me, that it
went to shake settled rules to their very foundation.   I had heard
the case of *Forth* v. *Chapman* (5) cited for years, and repeatedly
by Lord KENYON himself, as not to be shaken.   I never knew it
shaken ; and if *Porter* v. *Bradley* (4) has not since been disturbed
in the Court of King's Bench, upon the principle, expressed by
Lord ALVANLEY in *Campbell* v. *Campbell* (6), against shaking
settled rules, I will not add to the authority of that *dictum*."

(1) 2 Bos. & P. 324.   (4) 3 T. R. 143.
(2) Cro. Jac. 590.   (5) 1 P. Wms. 663.
(3) 9 Ves. 197.   (6) 4 Br. C. C. 18.

[*660]

In *Elton* v. *Eason* (1) Sir WILLIAM GRANT, the Master of the Rolls, thus begins his judgment: "There is no reason why the same words may not be differently construed, when they apply to different descriptions of property, *governed by different rules." And, in another part, he says "the case of *Crooke* v. *De Vandes* (2), in which the LORD CHANCELLOR expresses his opinion very strongly in favour of the distinction in *Forth* v. *Chapman* (3) (and Lord HARDWICKE has repeatedly recognised it) appears to be just as strong as this."

After these remarks of Lord ELDON and Sir WILLIAM GRANT, we cannot consider the case of *Porter* v. *Bradley* (4) to have overturned the case of *Forth* v. *Chapman* (3), and the more so, as, since that case, there have been the two cases of *Tenny* d. *Agar* v. *Agar* (5), and *Dansey* v. *Griffiths* (6), in this Court, above cited, directly the other way. And, if the case of *Porter* v. *Bradley* (4) be supportable at all, it can only be on the ground of the words "behind him" being introduced after the words "leaving no issue"; and which distinction is observed upon by Mr. Justice LE BLANC in his judgment in *Tenny* d. *Agar* v. *Agar* (5). And, with regard to *Roe* d. *Sheers* v. *Jeffery* (7), that case, if supportable at all, can only be so on the ground of the devise over being of life estates. In *Barlow* v. *Salter* (8) Sir WILLIAM GRANT says that in *Roe* d. *Sheers* v. *Jeffery* (7) the devise over was only of life estates, and on that ground Lord KENYON compared it to *Pells* v. *Brown* (9).

We have made these remarks, as applicable to the words of the will, as we do not think that there are any parts of it which show any intention to be inferred different from what the words import in their general legal signification; and, upon the whole,

[*661]

we come to the conclusion *that, as the case originally stood, the daughter Isabella took an estate tail. If indeed the words of the will had been, "but in case it should happen that my said daughter Isabella depart this life before she shall attain the age

---

(1) 12 R. R. 142 (19 Ves. 77).   (6) 16 R. R. 383 (4 M. & S. 61).
(2) 9 Ves. 197.   (7) 7 T. R. 589.
(3) 1 P. Wms. 663.   (8) 17 Ves. 483.
(4) 3 T. R. 143.   (9) Cro. Jac. 590.
(5) 12 East, 253,

of twenty-five years, and without leaving issue lawfully begotten," the addition of the words "before she shall attain the age of twenty-five years, and" might have varied the case; and it might be contended that these words would make it a dying without leaving issue living at the time of the death before twenty-five. However, there are not any similar words in the will, and the former part of the will does not import them; for, though Isabella is not to enter into the receipt of the rents and profits till she attains the age of twenty-five years, yet the devise over is not to depend at all upon her dying under that age, but on her leaving issue. And it is not necessary to consider the cases referred to in the argument on that point. When the age to which a person is to attain, and the dying without issue, are to form the basis of the devise over, sometimes the word "and" is mentioned, and at other times the word "or," and the reasoning is formed upon those words: but here is the total absence of one of the branches.

So far we have commented upon the will as originally set out in the case. But the Court, when this case was first begun to be argued, directed the whole will to be introduced into and to form part of the case. And by the will, as fully set out, after bequeathing his household furniture, &c., to his wife, he gives the residue &c. (his Lordship here read the bequests of the personalty (1)). It will be seen by that, the testator makes *a provision as to his daughter dying under twenty-five years of age, and without leaving issue; which shows that he knew what would be the effect of those words; and, therefore, from his silence when he comes to the limitation of the real estate, where no such words or any words of similar import are introduced, it seems to follow that he did not mean that they should be taken into consideration; and that the words must speak for themselves, according to their general legal import. And, therefore, the objection to the same words being construed into two different senses, as to the real and personal estate, does not apply to the present will.

It has been argued in one of the former cases, *Dansey* v.

[*662]

_____
(1) *Ante*, p. 790.

Griffiths (1), that in *Forth* v. *Chapman* (2), and most of the other cases cited as to this point, where the subsequent words on which the remainder over was limited were held to give an estate tail to the first taker, the estate was limited to the first taker indefinitely, and not by words of inheritance. But, notwithstanding that, the COURT held in the case that the first taker had an estate tail : and in several of the cases above cited there were words of inheritance in the estate of the first taker : and the Courts have never gone upon any distinction of that sort.

And, upon the whole, we come to the conclusion that the daughter Isabella took an estate tail (3).

[663]

Then, assuming that Isabella took an estate tail, another question is, whether the estate tail be vested in her before she attains the age of twenty-five years.

In *Boraston's* case (4) the testator devised to Thomas Amery and his wife the premises in question for eight years, and after the said term to remain to his executors until Hugh Boraston should attain his age of twenty-one years, "and the mesne profits to be employed by my executors towards the performance of this my last will; " and, when the said Hugh shall attain the age of twenty-one years, " then I will that he shall enjoy " the premises " to him and to his heirs for ever." Hugh Boraston died at the age of nine years. The COURT said (5) the case at Bar was no other in effect, but that a man devises his lands to his executors for the payment of his debts, until his son shall have come to his full age of twenty-one years, remainder to his son in fee : " for although these are adverbs of time, ' when,' &c. ' and then,' &c. yet they do not amount to make any thing precede the settling of the remainder, no more than in the common case."

(1) 16 R. R. 383 (4 M. & S. 64).
(2) 1 P. Wms. 663.
(3) On this point, the following authorities were cited in argument, besides those mentioned in the judgment : *Pleydell* v. *Pleydell*, 1 P. Wms. 748; *Donn* v. *Penny*, 13 R. R. 255 (19 Ves. 545; 1 Mer. 20); *Wilkinson* v. *South*, 7 T. R. 555 ; *Price* v. *Hunt*, Pollexf. 645; *Eastman* v. *Baker*, 9 R. R. 728 (1 Taunt. 174); *Glover* v. *Monckton*, 28 R. R. 559 (3 Bing. 13); *Read* v. *Snell*, 2 Atk. 646; 2 Powell on Devises, 205, 3rd (Jarman's) ed. ; *Murray* v. *Addenbrook*, 28 R. R. 144 (4 Russ. 407); *Bradshaw* v. *Skilbeck*, 42 R. R. 581 (2 Bing. N. C. 182).
(4) 3 Co. Rep. 19 a.
(5) Fol. 21 a.

In *Mansfield* v. *Dugard* (1) the testator devised to his wife till
his son should attain the age of twenty-one years, and, when his
son should attain the age of twenty-one years, then to his son
and his heirs: his son died at the age of thirteen years; and it
was held that the wife's estate determined at his decease, and
that the remainder vested in the son upon the testator's death,
and did not expect the contingency of his attaining twenty-one
years.

In *Goodtitle* d. *Hayward* v. *Whitby* (2) the testator *devised
the premises in question to trustees and their heirs, in trust to
lay out the rents and profits for the maintenance of his nephews
during their minorities, and, when and as they should attain
their ages of twenty-one years, to remain to them and their heirs.
It was held that the nephews took the fee immediately.

In *Denn* d. *Satterthwaite* v. *Satterthwaite* (3) Clement Satterthwaite devised the premises to William Satterthwaite his fourth
son, for the use of William Satterthwaite, the son of the said
William, for his maintenance and education, till he attained the
age of twenty-one years; after which he devised the same to
William Satterthwaite, the grandson, and his heirs. The Court
was clear that William, the father, was only in the nature of a
guardian to William, his son, and that the fee simple vested
instantly in William, the son.

In *Doe* d. *Wheedon* v. *Lea* (4) the testator devised the premises
to Thomas Lea and Edward Johnston, their heirs and assigns,
to hold them to them and their heirs until Michael Lea, then an
infant of thirteen years of age, should attain the age of twenty-
four years, on condition that they should, out of the rents and
profits, during all that time, keep the buildings in repair; also
he devised to the said Michael Lea, his heirs and assigns for
ever, when and so soon as he should attain his age of twenty-
four years, the premises in question, and directed the trustees
to surrender the premises accordingly. Michael Lea attained
the age of twenty-one years, but died under the age of twenty-
four years. Lord KENYON said, "The only question is, whether,
in the event of Michael Lea dying before he attained his age of

(1) 1 Eq. Ca. Abr. 195, pl. 4.   (3) 1 W. Bl. 519.
(2) 1 Burr. 228.   (4) 1 B. R. 631 (3 T. R. 41).

twenty-four, *this was a vested interest in him, descendible to his heir-at-law." "And I conceive that there can be no doubt on this question. It has been argued, that it depended on a condition precedent, and that not having happened, that the estate never vested in Michael Lea." "The only case cited in support of it is that of *Brownsword* v. *E lwards* (1) : but it must be remembered that the words there are very different from the present. There it was ' if he should attain the age of twenty-one : ' but the words in this case only denote the time when the beneficial interest was to accrue." The other two Judges in Court, Mr. Justice ASHHURST and Mr. Justice GROSE, gave their opinions to the same effect.

There is also on this point the case of *Doe* d. *Morris* v. *Underdown* (2).

We think these cases quite sufficient to show that the estate tail of Isabella was vested on the death of the testator, her mother having died in his lifetime (3).

We may here observe that this may perhaps be the last time of the question, as to the effect of dying without issue, being agitated : for, by the Act 7 Will. IV. & 1 Vict. c. 26, s. 29, which takes effect at the beginning of this year, all these expressions of " die without issue," or " die without leaving issue," or any other words which may import a failure of issue, shall be construed to mean a want or failure of issue in the lifetime of the party ; and therefore the fifty-seven cases alluded to by Lord ELLEN-BOROUGH, in *Doe* d. *Ellis* v. *Ellis* (4), as having been mentioned

by Lord THURLOW in *Pigge* v. *Bensley* (5), as having occurred on this head, as well as several others since that time, may be considered as out of our reports, except as to wills made before the present year.

The second question is, assuming Isabella to have a vested estate tail, whether the recovery suffered by her was sufficient to bar the estate tail : and, to do that, it is necessary to consider what estate the trustees took under the will. This Court had

(1) 2 Ves. Sen. 243.
(2) Willes, 293.
(3) On this point, *Driver* d. *Frank* v. *Frank*, 15 R. R. 385 (3 M. & S. 25), was cited in argument, besides

the authorities mentioned in the judgment.
(4) 9 East, 386.
(5) 1 Br. C. C. 190.

occasion, a short time ago, to consider the question, what estate
trustees took under a will, in the case of *Doe* d. *Shelley* v.
Edlin(1); in which they adopted the rule laid down by Mr.
Justice BAYLEY and Mr. Justice HOLROYD in *Doe* d. *Player* v.
Nicholls (2), where Mr. Justice BAYLEY says, that "It may be
laid down as a general rule, that where an estate is devised to
trustees for particular purposes, the legal estate is vested in
them as long as the execution of the trust requires it, and no
longer, and therefore, as soon as the trusts are satisfied, it will
vest in the person beneficially entitled to it." And Mr. Justice
HOLROYD, in the same case, says that "A trust estate is not to
continue beyond the period required by the purposes of the
trust." But the COURT goes on (3) to say that, "if the rules
above mentioned, as laid down by these Judges, be confined so
as to say that the trustees originally take only that quantity of
interest which the purposes of the trust require as far as is
expressed by the words used in the instrument itself, or by the
apparent intention of the maker of the instrument consistent
with the language of it, then I *admit the rule to be correct.
But if it be meant to apply to all cases in general where the
trusts are no longer capable of being carried into effect, but yet
the instrument, by the legal construction of it, already gave an
estate which might continue for a longer period than that during
which the objects of the trust had an actual existence, then that
in my mind will admit of a different consideration. I admit
that, for a great number of years past, the Courts have held
that trustees take that quantity of interest which the purposes
of the trust require ; and the question is, not whether the maker
of the instrument has used words of limitation or expressions
adequate to convey an estate of inheritance, but whether the
exigencies of the trust require a fee, or can be satisfied by a less
estate." We acquiesce in what the COURT there said ; and we
will now consider what estate the trustees took under the will,
as qualified by the rule laid down in that case.

The first thing to notice is the interest they took before
Isabella attained her age of twenty-five years : that was only an

DOE d.
CADOGAN
v.
EWART.

[*667]

---

(1) 43 R. R. 432 (4 Ad. & El. 582).   (3) *Doe* d. *Shelley* v. *Edlin*, 43
(2) 25 R. R. 398 (1 B. & C. 336).   R. R. 437 (4 Ad. & El. 589).

estate for years, determinable upon her attaining that age or
dying before ; and that was not a freehold, but a term of years ;
and it would not prevent Isabella from suffering a recovery, as
she had the first immediate estate of freehold; and as the devise
to her gave her the legal estate as far as the mere devise to her
went, that would be a legal recovery.   Another trust, imposed
upon the trustees by the will, is to pay the rents and profits of
the estate to the wife of the testator for her life, or during her
widowhood : that would give them a freehold interest in the
estate ; but, as she died in the lifetime of the testator, it never
took effect.   And, as the duration of their estate for that purpose

[*668] is limited *by the will, it would fall within the general rule that,
the object ceasing, the estate of the trustees ceases also.   We
do not enter into any consideration, whether the words in the
will would give the legal estate to the trustees ; but, if it did not,
the wife of the testator would have had the legal estate ; but, the
estate being gone altogether, it is no objection to the recovery.
The next thing is the annuity to Jane Dalston Hodgson.   If an
annuity be left charged upon the real estate, and the estate be
devised to trustees, that alone does not give the legal estate to
the trustees ; but, if they are directed to pay the annuity, then
they have the legal estate for that purpose.   This is fully
illustrated by Lord ALVANLEY in *Kenrick* v. *Lord W. Beauclerk* (1),
as to payment of debts ; and annuities stand upon the same
footing.   And then, inasmuch as the will directs the trustees to
pay the annuity, there appears to be an estate of freehold in the
trustees which precedes the estate of Isabella the daughter, and
consequently would prevent her suffering a valid recovery.   The
next trust to be noticed is, that the trustees are to sell to pay
debts, in case of deficiency of the personal estate.   It appears
from the case there was such deficiency ; consequently, the
trustees had an estate in fee to enable them to sell : and they
have, in fact, sold part of the estates accordingly : and I presume
(though it is not so stated in the case) that they have sold
enough to pay the debts, and that, therefore, there does not
remain any thing more to be done by them in that respect.
Then a question arises, whether, as the objects of that part of

(1) 6 R. R. 746 (3 Bos. & P. 175).

the trust have been performed, there was any estate remaining
in the trustees *which had been created for the purposes of this
trust; and, therefore, it might appear, according to the case of
Doe d. *Player* v. *Nicholls* (1), that, the object of the trust being
performed, the estate of the trustees in fee-simple should cease
also: but, inasmuch as the power of the trustees as to this arose
upon a contingency, and that contingency has happened, they
had a full power to sell any part of the premises: and then, as
the will does not confine their power to sell so much as should
be sufficient to pay the debts, and also as there is no devise over
of such parts as should remain unsold, we are of opinion that
the trustees retained the fee-simple created by the will in the
whole of the estates of the testator, according to the qualification
of the rule in *Doe* d. *Shelley* v. *Edlin* (2).

It is true that the beginning of the language of the power to
sell says " any part " of the estate, and does not say the "whole"
or any part; but the latter part of the power says " the same
premises or any part thereof; " and we think the legal effect of
this, taken altogether, is to extend the power over the whole.
The case of *Warter* v. *Hutchinson* (3) was, in some respects, the
same, as to the limitations, as the present; and, though there
was a devise in fee to the trustees, this Court held they only took
a chattel interest; but the limitations were very complicated,
and we consider the decision as having turned on the particular
circumstances, and not on the general point of the trustees taking
the fee.   And we do not think that case sufficient to vary what
we *consider the general principle, so as to give a chattel interest   [*670]
only to the trustees.

Then, as the trustees, in our opinion, have a general fee simple
in the whole of the estate, it is to be considered how that affects
the recovery; and, upon that, we think such fee simple absorbs
the freehold which they had for the payment of the annuity to
Jane Dalston Hodgson. though not as a regular merger, and that
the case is to be considered as upon the estate in fee being in the
trustees; and, upon that, that they have the legal estate in fee.

(1) 25 R. R. 398 (1 B. & C. 336).   and see *Warter* v. *Hutchinson*, 23 R. R.
(2) 43 R. R. 432 (4 Ad. & El. 582).   457 (2 Brod. & B. 349).
(3) 25 R. R. 551 (1 B. & C. 721);

And Isabella has an equitable estate in tail; and therefore she may suffer an equitable recovery, which will have the effect of barring all equitable remainders over, though it would not bar legal remainders.

Then, is the remainder to the lessor of the plaintiff and Jane Dalston Hodgson a legal or an equitable remainder? We are of opinion that it is an equitable remainder. It is of the same quality in that respect as the estate to Isabella; and the trustees have the legal estate; and therefore the remainder over is barred.

We are of opinion, therefore, that the lessor of the plaintiff is not entitled to recover; and the judgment will be entered as agreed in the case.

Nolle prosequi entered.

1838.

*[698]

RICHARDS *v.* FRY (1).

(7 Adol. & Ellis, 698—707; S. C. 3 N. & P. 67; W. W. & D. 116; 7 L. J.
(N. S.) Q. B. 68; 2 Jur. 641.)

Trespass for chasing and detaining cattle. Plea, that defendant was possessed of a messuage, &c., and that he and all occupiers thereof for the time being, for thirty years' next before the time when, &c., had of right had, and been used, &c., to have common of pasture in the *locus in quo*, that the cattle were depasturing, &c., to the disturbance of such right of common, and that defendant distrained, &c.

On special demurrer, for that the right was not claimed to have been used, &c., thirty years before the commencement of the suit: Held,

1. That, as a plea under stat. 2 & 3 Will. IV. c. 71, the plea was bad, for not claiming the right either so, or as used, &c., thirty years before the commencement of some suit. As to which latter averment, *quære.*

2. That the plea could not be construed as claiming right of common simply by virtue of possession, assuming that, if so construed, it would have been good.

TRESPASS. The declaration charged that defendant, on &c., broke and entered plaintiff's closes (described by names, abuttals, &c.), did damage there, and drove plaintiff's sheep, ewes, and lambs, &c., then depasturing and being in and upon the said closes of plaintiff, from and off the said closes to places at a distance from plaintiff's said closes, and kept and detained the said sheep, &c., and afterwards drove them to other places still more distant, &c.

(1) Cited in the judgment of the   13 Q. B. D. 304, 306, 53 L. J. Q. B.
Court of Appeal delivered by LIND-   430, 432.—R. C.
LEY, L. J., in *Hollins* v. *Verney* (1884)

Pleas. 1. Not guilty. 2. That the closes in which &c. were   RICHARDS
not plaintiff's. 3. As to the driving and chasing the sheep, &c.,   *v.*
elsewhere than in the said closes of plaintiff, and as to the keep-   FRY.
ing and detaining the same, that, before and at the times respectively in the declaration mentioned, defendant was, and still is,
in the lawful possession, and the occupier, of a certain messuage
and lands, with the appurtenances, to wit situate and being
in &c.; and that defendant, and all the occupiers for the time
being of the said messuage, &c., for thirty years next before the
said several times when &c., have actually as of right had, and
have been used and accustomed to have, and of right ought &c.,
and defendant then and still of right ought &c., for himself and
themselves, his and their tenants and farmers, occupiers of the
said messuage, &c., common of pasture in, upon, *and throughout   [*699]
a certain place and lands in the county &c., to wit in the parish
&c., to wit called &c., for all his and their commonable cattle,
levant and *couchant* in and upon the said messuage &c., every
year, and at all times of the year, as to the said messuage, &c.,
belonging and appertaining : and, because the said sheep, &c.,
were, before and at the time of the commencement of the trespasses in the introduction to this plea mentioned, in and upon
the said place and lands in this plea aforesaid, and whereon
defendant is hereinbefore mentioned to have been and to be
entitled to common of pasture as aforesaid, depasturing, destroying the grass, &c.: justification, that defendant took them
depasturing and doing damage so that defendant could not enjoy
his common in so ample a manner as he ought; and that defendant was driving them to a pound, but released them at
plaintiff's request.

Demurrer to the third plea, assigning for causes, that it does
not appear by the plea for how many years next before the
commencement of this suit defendant and the occupiers for the
time being of the said messuage, &c., or defendant, have actually
of right had, or have been used and accustomed to have, the
common of pasture as in that plea mentioned. Joinder in
demurrer. The case was argued in Michaelmas Term last (1).

(1) November 10th, 1837. Before Lord Denman, Ch. J., Patteson,
Williams, and Coleridge, JJ.

RICHARDS   *Ogle*, for the plaintiff:
  v.
FRY.   First, the thirty years should have been laid next before the
commencement of the suit, or, (according to *Jones* v. *Price* (1))
simply, before. By sect. 1 of stat. 2 & 3 Will. IV. c. 71, no
claim by prescription to right of common, &c., where the "right,
[*700]   *profit, or benefit shall have been actually taken and enjoyed by
any person claiming right thereto without interruption for the
full period of thirty years," shall be defeated by showing only
that it was first taken at some time prior to such period. That
period, by sect. 4, is "the period next before some suit or action
wherein the claim or matter to which such period may relate
shall have been or shall be brought into question." These words
have never been understood to relate to the period as measured
back from the trespass, in any of the cases from *Bright* v.
Walker (2) to the present time. In *The Monmouthshire Canal
Company* v. *Harford* (3) the fourteenth plea laid the period as
twenty years ·next before the commencement of the suit, and
before either of the times when &c. In *Tickle* v. *Brown* (4) the
period was laid as forty years next before the commencement of
the suit. In *Wright* v. *Williams* (5) the plea was in the same
form; and, on demurrer, it was objected that the period should
have been laid as forty years before the time when &c. ; but the
plea was held good. It may be said that these authorities,
although they show that the period may be so laid, do not prove
the mode here used to be incorrect. But both forms cannot
be good.

(PATTESON, J. : Why not? Thirty years before the trespass
must, *à fortiori*, be thirty years before the suit.)

Suppose a trespass committed in 1800. A party now suing for
that might, unless the Statute of Limitations were pleaded,
recover. But could it be meant that, if there had been a sub-
[*701]   sequent cesser and abandonment of the *right, a party should
still be entitled to avail himself of such right, because it had been

(1) 3 Bing. N. C. 52.   614; 5 Tyr. 68).
(2) 40 R. R. 536 (1 Cr. M. & R.   (4) 4 Ad. & El. 369.
211; 4 Tyr. 502).   (5) 1 M. & W. 77; Tyr. & Gr. 375.
(3) 40 R. R. 648 (1 Cr. M. & R.

exercised for a period of thirty years before such abandonment
or cesser?

(PATTESON, J.: The Legislature never meant to meet such a
case: they left it to the Statute of Limitations.)

Secondly, the plea should have stated the right to have been
enjoyed without interruption.   Thirdly, the declaration charged
a series of acts, all of which are trespasses; the plea answers it
only as to driving the sheep, after they were driven from the
plaintiff's closes, and detaining them; it admits, for the purposes
of that plea, that the defendant, before doing so, broke and
entered the plaintiff's closes, and drove the sheep thence.   Now
the defendant cannot avail himself of his own wrong; he had no
right to drive the sheep from the plaintiff's closes to a place
where he, the defendant, had common. and then to distrain them.
(On the second objection he cited PARKE, B. in *Bright* v. *Walker* (1),
Tickle v. *Brown* (2), *Beasley* v. *Clarke* (3); but the COURT decided
on the first objection only.)

> *Montague Smith, contrà:*

As to the first objection.   The point on the Prescription Act
does not arise.   This is a transitory action for damage to personal
chattels; and the defendant, justifying his act as done in defence
of his right of common, which is infringed, is in the same
position as a plaintiff in trespass *quare clausum fregit:* he may,
therefore, rely on the naked possession as against the plaintiff,
a wrong doer; and the allegation of thirty years' enjoyment is
surplusage.   It lies on the plaintiff here, as on the defendant in
an *action of trespass, to set out his title specially.   This appears
from an *Anonymous* (4) case in Salkeld.   The *dictum* there has
since been disputed; but the principle of the decision, which is
all that is material here, was upheld in *Taylor* v. *Eastwood* (5);
and the authority is cited to the same effect in Com. Dig. Pleader

[*702]

(1) 40 R. R. 536 (1 Cr. M. & R.   705).
219; 4 Tyr. 509).
(2) 43 R. R. 358 (4 Ad. & El. 369).   (4) 2 Salk. 643.
(3) 42 R. R. 704 (2 Bing. N. C.   (5) 1 East, 212.

(C 41), and in note (1) to *Stennel* v. *Hogg* (1) and note (2) to *Mellor* v. *Spateman* (2).

(PATTESON, J.: You say it is as if you had sued for disturbance of common.)

Bright v. *Walker* (3) since the statute, and *Atkinson* v. *Teesdale* (4) before the statute, show that it is enough to declare on the possession. Further, this is a good plea under the statute. The material question is the right of the party at the time of the trespass. The intention of the statute was to get rid of the difficulty which formerly existed in proving a prescription. Sect. 5 prescribes a mode of pleading in lieu of the allegation of time immemorial. Now the prescription must have related, under the former state of law, to the time of the Act; for it was an allegation of right under which the defendant justified. Sect. 4 relates only to the mode of proof when the fact of enjoyment is challenged: it does not appear to be incorporated in sect. 5. If sect. 4 be literally applied to the form of the plea, the allegation must be of an enjoyment for thirty years next before *any* suit in which the claim has been questioned.

(PATTESON, J.: Suppose a defendant plead thirty years' enjoyment before the commencement of the suit, and fail upon a traverse of such enjoyment; and, ten years after, a second action be *brought: can he set up a thirty years' enjoyment before such second action?)

[*703]

That appears to be a necessary result of a literal interpretation of the statute; which shows that such interpretation is erroneous. Indeed, it is not necessary that the right should be brought into question in this suit: the possession might alone be traversed. Suppose, after the alleged trespass, the defendant had released his right of common: he could not then plead in the form contended for on the other side: yet the statute could not intend that he should be precluded by this from justifying under the

(1) 1 Wms. Saund. 221.   (3) 40 R. R. 536 (1 Cr. M. & R.
(2) 1 Wms. Saund. 346 e. And   211; 4 Tyr. 502).
see *Ibid*. 346, *n*. (2).   (4) 3 Wils. 278.

right which he had at the time of the trespass. The utmost that
Wright v. *Williams* (1) shows is that a plea alleging the enjoyment forty years before the commencement of the action is not
demurrable. If sect. 4 were imperative as to the form of pleading, it would be necessary to plead "next before;" but the
contrary was decided in *Jones* v. *Price* (2), where TINDAL, Ch. J.
said that the fourth section "is nothing but an exposition of
the proof required to establish the right. It is a mere question of evidence." (On the second objection, he cited *Bright* v.
Walker (3); and, on the third, note (1) to *Potter* v. *North* (4),
and *Mattravers* v. *Fosset* (5).)

Ogle, in reply:

As to the first objection. The plea is of a prescription under
the statute : it cannot be construed as a simple justification under
possession. But, if it could, it would be bad. It is clear law that
a right of common upon a mere possession cannot be pleaded in
answer to an action of trespass, though it is otherwise *as to the
declaration. No distinction can be drawn, as to this, between
trespass *quare clausum fregit* and trespass for taking cattle. As
to the statute, most of the difficulties suggested on the other side
were brought before the Court in *Wright* v. *Williams* (6). If the
act complained of was committed twenty years before the commencement of the suit, and a thirty years' enjoyment before such
commencement is shown, that is the very case upon which the
statute intended to found a prescriptive right. But, if, before the
action, though after the trespass, the right has been interrupted,
there the prescriptive right, to be tried in the action, can no longer
be shown within the meaning of the statute.   *Cur. adv. vult.*

[*704]

LORD DENMAN, Ch. J., in this Term (January 18th), delivered the
judgment of the COURT. After stating the pleadings, and
the demurrer, his Lordship proceeded as follows :

The objection arises upon statute 2 & 3 Will. IV. c. 71,
sections 1, 4, and 5. The defendant's counsel, however,

(1) 1 M. & W. 77; Tyr. & Gr. 375.   (4) 1 Wms. Saund. 347.
(2) 3 Bing. N. C. 52.   (5) 3 Wils. 295.
(3) 40 R. R. 536 (1 Cr. M. & R.   (6) 1 M. & W. 77; Tyr. & Gr. 375.
211; 4 Tyr. 502).

RICHARDS
v.
FRY.

endeavoured to avoid the objection by arguing that this plea may be supported at common law, without any reference to that statute; that it is, in substance, an allegation that the defendant is possessed of a messuage and lands, by reason whereof he is entitled to right of common, and that he drove away the plaintiff's sheep which were disturbing that right; and that such allegation is sufficient in a plea to a transitory action for chasing sheep, without claiming the right of common by prescription in a que

[*705] estate, inasmuch as that right is in this case *only inducement or conveyance.   He relies on the cases which establish that such an allegation is sufficient in a declaration for disturbance of common, and on the analogy to a plea justifying the taking of cattle damage feasant, in which it is sufficient to allege the defendant's possession of the place where the cattle are taken. We have not found any case in which the principle established in those cases, viz. that, as against a wrong doer, it is sufficient to allege possession, has been applied to a plea stating a right of common.   A note of Mr. Serjeant Williams in the case of *Mellor* v. *Spateman* (1) was referred to, in which he so lays down the rule in these words, "Indeed, where the right of common is only inducement or conveyance, it is held sufficient for the defendant to allege that he is possessed ; as where the justification is, an escape of the cattle from a common to the close in which, &c. through defect of a fence, which the plaintiff is bound to repair, or an escape from the defendant's own close; " but the authority he cites, viz. *Faldo* v. *Ridge* (2), supports only the latter part of the sentence.

The point may be doubtful; but we think that we are not called upon to determine it: for, on attentively considering this plea, we cannot treat it as averring only possession of a right of common, but are satisfied that it avers a right of common in a que estate, substituting for time immemorial thirty years under the late statute.   *Dorne* v. *Cashford* (3) is an express authority to show that a bad averment of a right in a que estate in a declara-

[*706] tion cannot be treated as an averment of possession *only,

(1) Note (2) to *Mellor* v. *Spateman*,   (3) 1 Salk. 363; *S. C.* 1 Com. Rep.
1 Wms. Saund. 346.   44.
(2) Yelv. 74.

though such an averment, properly framed, would have been
sufficient in the case.

We come, therefore, to the principal objection; viz., that the thirty years are laid "next before the said times when, &c." instead of "next before the commencement of this suit."

The first section of stat. 2 & 3 Will. IV. c. 71, enacts that no claim to right of common which shall have been actually enjoyed by any person claiming right thereto without interruption for the full period of thirty years, shall be defeated by showing only that it was first taken at a prior time. The fourth section enacts that the thirty years shall be deemed and taken to be the period next before some suit or action wherein the claim shall be brought into question. The fifth section enacts that, in all pleadings in trespass, it shall be sufficient to allege the enjoyment of common as of right by the occupiers of the tenement in respect whereof the same is claimed, for and during such of the periods mentioned in the Act as may be applicable to the case, and without claiming in the name or right of the owner of the fee as is now usually done.

Taking these sections together, it seems quite clear that the averment of enjoyment for thirty years next before the times when &c. is not in conformity with the Act. The period mentioned in the Act is plainly thirty years next before some suit or action in which the claim shall be brought into question. Generally speaking, that would be next before the commencement of the suit in which the pleading takes place; at all events, it is not ' next before the times when &c.

But we were pressed with absurdities and inconveniences which, it is supposed, would arise from such construction *of the Act;   [*707] and on the other hand difficulties of the same nature were pointed out, to which we should give occasion by holding the plea to be good.

These absurdities and inconveniences were urged to the Court of Exchequer in the case of *Wright* v. *Williams* (1), in which the averment was "next before the commencement of this suit;" but that Court held the averment to be correct; and the decision is directly in point; for we cannot think, as was suggested at

(1) 1 M. & W. 77; Tyr. & Gr. 375.

the Bar, that both modes of averment are correct, and either may be adopted at the option of the pleader. The periods in the two averments are certainly quite different: and the evidence requisite to support them manifestly not the same. We shall not attempt to obviate the difficulties which have been suggested; but, adhering to the express words of the statute, and to the decision in *Wright* v. *Williams* (1), with which we fully agree, we hold that the only correct averment is, "next before the commencement of this" (or possibly some other) "suit."

We do not feel that the case of *Jones* v. *Price* (2) at all militates against this decision: that case merely establishes that the averment of "thirty years before the commencement of the suit" means "thirty years next before the commencement of the suit;" in other terms, that the omission of the word "next" does not alter the sense.

Other objections were taken by the counsel for the plaintiff to the plea in question, which it becomes unnecessary for us to notice.

For the reasons stated, we think that the plea is bad, and that judgment must be given for the plaintiff.

Judgment for the plaintiff.

REG. *v.* THE DIRECTORS OF THE POOR OF THE PARISH OF ST. PANCRAS.

(7 Adol. & Ellis, 750—755.)

By the Foundling Hospital Act, stat. 13 Geo. II. c. 29, the hospital is incorporated by the name of The Governors and Guardians of the Hospital for the maintenance and education of exposed and deserted young children; and has power to purchase lands, and erect or purchase buildings for such maintenance, &c.; and the lands, &c., shall be rated as in 1739; the corporation may receive, &c., as many children as they think fit; any person may bring children to be received by them in case the corporation think proper; no parochial officer is to prevent persons from so doing, nor to exercise any parochial authority in the hospital; and no settlement is gained by being received, maintained, educated, or employed therein; and the corporation has power to make bye-laws.

Held, first, that the hospital is not extra-parochial.

Secondly, that this power to receive children is discretionary.

Therefore, where a woman left a parcel containing a child at the hospital, but went away before the contents were ascertained, and was

(1) 1 M. & W. 77; Tyr. & Gr. 375.   (2) 3 Bing. N. C. 52.

REG.
v.
THE
DIRECTORS
OF THE POOR
OF ST.
PANCRAS.

not again found, and the governors, acting in conformity with their rules, refused to receive it : Held, that on such a refusal (found as a fact by the jury, on trial of a *mandamus*, under the Judge's direction) the parish of St. Pancras, within the ambit of which the hospital is, was bound to maintain the child as casual poor.

MANDAMUS to the directors of the poor of the parish of St. Pancras. The inducement suggested that, by stat. 59 Geo. III. c. xxxix. (local and personal, public), " for establishing a select vestry in the parish of St. Pancras, in the county of Middlesex, and for *other purposes relating thereto," it was enacted that, from and after the appointment of directors as in the said Act was mentioned, the said directors and their successors should exercise the powers of overseers of the poor, electing nominal overseers (with additional regulations set out in the *mandamus*) ; that the defendants had duly nominated two such overseers ; and that a certain male child, aged about two years, on or about 11th May last, was found exposed and destitute within the said parish ; that it was and is the duty of the directors to receive into the workhouse of the said parish, or to provide for the necessary relief and support of, the said child ; and that due notice was given to the directors and nominal overseers, and the said directors were required to provide for the necessary relief and support of the said child ; yet the directors, not regarding their duty in that behalf, had refused and neglected, and still do refuse and neglect, to receive into the workhouse of the said parish, or otherwise to provide for the necessary relief and support of, the said child, &c., to the damage of the said child and of one Hannah Robins. The writ then required the defendants to receive into the said workhouse, or otherwise provide for the necessary relief and support of, the child, now living with Hannah Robins, or show cause &c.

Return. That the child was not found exposed and destitute within the said parish, as in the writ alleged, and that it was not the duty of the directors to receive &c., or provide &c.

The relator traversed both the allegations of the return.

The issue was tried before Coleridge, J. at the Middlesex sittings after last Michaelmas Term ; when the *following facts appeared. On the morning of May 11th, 1837, a woman rang the bell at the gate of the Foundling Hospital, and, on the

[*751]

[*752]

REG.
v.
THE
DIRECTORS
OF THE POOR
OF ST.
PANCRAS.

porter's opening the gate, delivered to him a basket directed to
the governor of the Foundling.   The porter took the basket to the
lodge, and almost immediately discovered that it contained the
child in question.   In the mean time, the woman had gone away,
and she was not again found.   The hospital lies within the
ambit of the parish of St. Pancras, and is merely separated from
it by the wall enclosing the premises.   By order of the secretary
of the hospital the child was taken to St. Pancras workhouse ;
but the directors refused to take it in ; and the hospital had
maintained the child ever since.   The stat. 13 Geo. II. c. 29,
was referred to, which recites shortly the effect of the charter of
the hospital ; but the charter itself was not produced.   It
appeared in evidence that, by the regulations of the hospital,
no child was received except upon the petition of the mother,
and upon her personally appearing before the governors, unless
the governors should specially order otherwise ; and that these
steps had not been taken in the present case.   The learned
Judge directed the jury to find for the Crown, unless they were
of opinion that the hospital had received the child ; and he
stated that this was a mixed question of law and fact ; and that,
in his opinion, the hospital had not received the child.   The
jury found for the Crown ; and his Lordship gave leave to the
defendants to move for a verdict to be entered for them.

Sir W. W. Follett now moved for such verdict, or for a
new trial on the ground of misdirection :

[*753]   This child *was not casual poor within the parish.   In the
first place, it was not deserted, for the hospital were bound to
provide for it ; and, secondly, the desertion at any rate did not
take place within the parish, for the hospital must be considered
extra-parochial.   Stat. 13 Geo. II. c. 29, s. 1, recites that, in
compassion to the many infants which are liable to be exposed
to perish in the streets, the hospital has been incorporated by
the name of The Governors and Guardians of the Hospital for
the maintenance and education of exposed and deserted young
children.   From this it would appear that the governors were
not meant to have any option as to the receipt of children left
with them, so far as their funds extended.   By the same section

REG.
v.
THE
DIRECTORS
OF THE POOR
OF ST.
PANCRAS.

they are empowered to purchase lands, and erect or convert buildings, " to be an hospital or hospitals for the reception of such poor and exposed children, in such manner as to the said corporation shall seem meet." It is true that sect. 5 enacts that it shall be lawful for the corporation to receive, maintain, and educate, " all or as many children as they shall think fit ; " and for every person whatsoever to bring children to the hospital, " to the end that such child or children may be received, maintained, and educated by the said corporation therein, in case they shall think proper to receive the same ; " and sect. 11 gives the corporation power to make bye-laws : but it is inconsistent with the principle of the institution, as shown by the words before cited, to assume that this gives them the power of arbitrary rejection, except so far as their funds are inadequate to the maintenance of the children left with them. Then sect. 2 provides that the houses and lands, purchased and hired for the purposes of the hospital, shall not be rated beyond the amount of the rates paid in 1739 : sect. 5 provides *that no church-   [*754] warden, overseer, or other person, shall stop or molest any person bringing a child to the hospital ; and, by sect. 6, no parish officer is to have any power or authority in the hospital, " nor shall have any authority to enquire concerning the birth or settlement of any such child or children, who shall be therein maintained and educated, or to place them out apprentices, or to do any other act, matter, or thing whatsoever, within such hospital," &c., except to collect taxes. The parochial authorities have, therefore, no power of preventing desertion, or of taking any measures within the hospital. And further, by sect. 7, no settlement is gained by being received, maintained, educated, or employed within the hospital. The hospital is therefore extra-parochial ; and the child did not, by being deserted within it, become chargeable to the parish.

Lord Denman, Ch. J. :

I think that what was done at the trial was perfectly correct ; and that no other course could have been pursued. The maintenance of the child, as casual poor, was upon the parish, unless the burden was thrown elsewhere. No doubt the Legislature might so have framed the statute as to relieve the parish; but it has not done so.   It is clear that the hospital did not receive the child, that it is bound to maintain such children only as it does receive, and that it has a power to reject.   I do not conceive that the result of this case is likely to be of extensive importance; for, if the porter had refused to take in the basket, no doubt could have arisen; and circumstances like the present must be of very rare occurrence.

LITTLEDALE, J.:

[*755]

The child was not brought into the Foundling Hospital within the rules.   And the hospital *is within the parish: for, if the buildings were pulled down, the site would unquestionably be parochial.

WILLIAMS, J.:

There is no provision making the hospital extra-parochial; and, as to the other point, the statute shows as strongly as possible that the Hospital is not bound to maintain children, except where it has adopted them by some intentional and voluntary act.

COLERIDGE, J.:

It is perfectly clear that the hospital is not extra-parochial. There seems to have been a bargain, when the Act passed, by which the hospital was bound to pay a certain rate.   Had it been required that the hospital should be extra-parochial, this would probably have been objected to on the part of the parish. The bargain, as made, turns out to be a bad one for the parish. The Act does not apply; and the hardship supposed to arise from the exclusion of the parochial authorities cannot occur, because it is only by an adoption of a child that the hospital can withdraw it from their superintendance.   And, as to this adoption, they have a choice, as the language of sect. 5 shows. The only question, therefore, is whether they did receive the child; and clearly they did not.

Rule refused.

REG. v. THE INHABITANTS OF WYE (1).

(7 Adol. & Ellis, 761—772; S. C. 3 N. & P. 6; 7 L. J. (N. S.) M. C. 18.)

D. and E. were removed, by an order describing them as man and wife, with their six children, named in the order of removal, to W. The order was appealed against. Pending the appeal, the parish officers of W. instituted a suit in the Spiritual Court, to dissolve the marriage as incestuous. After this, the order was confirmed; and, subsequently, the Spiritual Court decreed the marriage incestuous, and void from the beginning to all intents and purposes. Pauper was born of the supposed marriage, before the order, but he was not named in it, and he was unemancipated, and had gained no settlement, when the order was made :

Held, that the confirmation of the order, under these circumstances, was not conclusive proof of a derivative settlement of the pauper in W., on appeal against an order removing the pauper to W. after the decree of the Spiritual Court, but that, on such appeal, W. might show, by the decree, that, since the first order, the marriage had become void *ab initio*, and the pauper illegitimate.

On appeal against an order of justices, removing William Shrubsole from the parish of Doddington to the parish of Wye, both in Kent, the Sessions confirmed the order, subject to the opinion of this Court on the following case.

David Shrubsole, whose settlement was in Wye, was married [762] to Elizabeth Fenn, whose settlement was in Kennington, on 24th May, 1818. By her he had issue William, the pauper, and several other children, all born during the marriage, in the parish of Eastling. David Shrubsole continued to reside in Eastling, with his wife and family, from the day of his marriage until June, 1833, and, during this period, he frequently received relief from the parish of Wye.

By an order of justices, dated June 6th, 1833, he was removed from Eastling to Wye, together with his wife and six children therein named, by the description of David Shrubsole and Elizabeth his wife, and their six children (naming them); the pauper William was not named in the said order; but he was then unemancipated, and had gained no settlement in his own right. The churchwardens and overseers of Wye, at the July Sessions, 1833, entered and respited an appeal, which was further

(1) Referred to in the judgment of Bowen, L. J., in *De Mora* v. *Concha* (1885) 29 Ch. Div. 268, 301, 54

L. J. Ch. 532, 538. See *S. C.* in H. L. *Concha* v. *Concha* (1886) 11 App. Cas. 541, 56 L. J. Ch. 257.—R. C.

REG.
v.
THE INHABI-
TANTS OF
WYE.

respited at the Michaelmas Sessions, 1833 ; and the order was confirmed at the Epiphany Sessions, December 1st, 1833.

Before the confirmation of this order, the churchwardens of Wye had commenced a suit in the Arches Court of Canterbury, for the purpose of annulling the marriage between David Shrubsole and his wife; and, on 1st May, 1834, the sentence of that Court (a copy of which formed part of the case (1)) was pronounced, by which the said marriage was dissolved, " as having been absolutely null and void from the beginning, to all intents and purposes in law whatsoever."

[*763]   The Sessions, on the present appeal, were of opinion *that the order of removal from Eastling to Wye, having been confirmed on appeal, was conclusive of the pauper's derivative settlement in Wye from David Shrubsole, his father.   The question for the opinion of this Court was, whether, in consequence of the dissolution of the marriage by sentence of the Arches Court, pronounced subsequently to the date of the order confirmed, for the removal of David Shrubsole and Elizabeth his wife to Wye, the settlement of the pauper is in Eastling, the place of his birth, or in Wye.

[After argument, the COURT took time for consideration.]

[768]   LORD DENMAN, Ch. J. now delivered the judgment of the COURT (2) :

In this case the pauper's father and mother, as man and wife, with their six children, were removed by an order, naming them,
[*769]   and dated in June, 1833, from Eastling *to Wye: an appeal was entered, and respited at the following July Sessions ; and, after another respite, the order was confirmed at the Epiphany Sessions, December 31st, 1833.   Pending this appeal, and before the confirmation of the order, the churchwardens of Wye had instituted proceedings in the Ecclesiastical Court to annul the marriage between the father and mother as incestuous; and, on the 1st May, 1834, by a decree of that Court, the marriage was for this reason dissolved, " as having been absolutely null and void from

(1) By which it appeared that the ground of the dissolution was, that Elizabeth was the daughter of David's brother.

(2) Lord Denman, Ch. J., Patteson, Williams, and Coleridge, JJ.

the beginning, to all intents and purposes in law whatsoever."
At the date of the order the pauper was alive, but was not named
in it, nor removed by it : he was born during the existence of the
marriage, and, at that date, was unemancipated, and without any
acquired settlement. He was now, by the order at present in
question, removed to Wye ; and the only point which we have to
consider is, whether the first-named order, with proof that the
pauper was born during the existence of the marriage, conclusively proves a derivative settlement for him in the parish
of Wye. Our opinion is that it does not.

The judgment of the Court of Quarter Sessions upon the
former appeal decided directly the settlement of the persons
included in the order ; and, this being a judgment *in rem*, was
conclusive, not only between the parties, but against all the
world.   In order to arrive at this judgment, as to so much of it
as affected the wife and children, it was necessary for the Court,
and within its competence, to examine into and determine both
the fact and legality of the marriage.   And, although, the last
mentioned matter being only incidentally within the cognisance
of a temporal Court, it might have seemed, according to the
judgment delivered by DE GREY, Ch. J. *in the House of Lords,   [*770]
on the *Trial of the Duchess of Kingston* (1), that the order was
no evidence with regard to it in any future proceeding, yet
numerous cases have decided that orders of removal, unappealed
against or confirmed on appeal, are, not only evidence, but conclusive, as to all the facts mentioned in them, and which are
necessary steps to the decision.   Marriage and the legitimacy of
children are among the facts as to which this rule has been
upheld ; and it has been extended to the case of a child
emancipated at the date of the order : *Rex* v. *Catterall* (2), and
even to that of children unborn at the time : *Rex* v. *Woodchester* (3) and *Rex* v. *St. Mary, Lambeth* (4).   These, and many
other cases, have formed a class which has settled the practice
at Quarter Sessions ; and it is so especially desirable, with regard
to this branch of the law, to avoid all uncertainty and all subtle

(1) 20 Howell's St. Tr. 538, *n.*   1172.
(2) 6 M. & S. 83.   (4) 6 T. R. 615.
(3) Burr. S. C. 191 ; *S. C.* 2 Str.

distinctions, that we should upon no account think ourselves justified in throwing any doubt upon these decisions.

The principle, however, on which these cases mainly proceed is a perfectly sound one ; that a matter once examined into and decided by a competent tribunal shall not be reagitated, and in effect shown to have been decided erroneously, upon new evidence which either could or could not have been, but in fact was not, produced upon the former hearing.   And, accordingly, it is observable that, in all the cases where the conclusive effect of the former order has been disputed, it has been the object of the party tendering the rejected evidence to procure a contrary decision upon the same state of facts, by throwing new light upon them.   Thus, for *example, in *Rex* v. *Woodchester* (1) and *Rex* v. *St. Mary, Lambeth* (2), the marriages were in fact equally void at the respective dates of the prior orders as of the later ; but the evidence failed to prove them so.   If the new and better evidence had been admitted on the second appeals, the effect must have been, not indeed to destroy the legal effect of the former adjudications on the points decided, *i.e.* the settlements of the parties actually removed, but, by showing them to have been erroneously decided, to take away their effect upon settlements derivative from the former ; and the Courts have rightly said, the opportunity for this is past.

[*771]

But, in the case now before the Court, a new state of facts has arisen since the former decision.   An incestuous marriage, until avoided by the sentence of the Court Christian, is voidable only, and remains valid to all civil purposes.   The judgment of the Court of Quarter Sessions, having passed before the sentence pronounced, was therefore correct in fact and in law; no alteration of the evidence consistent with the state of facts then actually subsisting ought to have made any difference in it.   Had the incest *de facto* been ever so clearly made out, still the marriage must have been held valid, the children legitimate, and all the civil consequences as to the settlement of the wife and children named in the order must have followed.   Whatever, therefore, has been decided upon the then existing state of facts remains unimpeached.

(1) Burr. S. C. 191 ; *S. C.* 2 Str. 1172.   (2) 6 T. R. 615.

But the settlement of the pauper now comes in question for the first time: and it is admitted that he has no settlement in Wye except upon proof that he is the *legitimate son of his father. The former order, with proof of the date of his birth, is no doubt *primâ facie* evidence of his legitimacy: but suppose the appellants had tendered evidence that his father had been absent in America for a year before his birth, while the mother was in England, in order to show him a bastard, can it be doubted that such evidence would have been receivable? It would have contravened no fact found, or matter decided, by the former order; it would merely have cut the link which connected, *primâ facie*, his settlement with that found by the former order. It does not appear to us that the evidence tendered in the present case differs at all in principle from that just supposed. The appellants admit the former case rightly decided, that the settlement was as there found, and the marriage then valid; but they say the decree of the Ecclesiastical Court shows that the pauper is, and always was, a bastard. Whatever be the conclusiveness of a former order on the facts found by it, it cannot in point of time extend beyond its date: it conclusively shows the state of facts then existing, and declares the law that results from it; but what is so shown conclusively then may not continue; a change of circumstances may occur, to which the former finding is inapplicable.

We are of opinion, therefore, that, consistently with all the former decisions', and desiring in no way to break in upon them, the Sessions were wrong in refusing the evidence tendered; that the respondents did not by their proof make out conclusively a derivative settlement in Wye; and, consequently, that the orders must be quashed.   *Orders quashed.*

PUGH *v.* GRIFFITH.

(7 Adol. & Ellis, 827—841; S. C. 3 N. & P. 187; 7 L. J. (N. S.) Q. B. 169.)

1888.
Jan. 19.

[827]

1. Trespass for breaking and spoiling a lock, bolt and staple appertaining and fixed to the outer door of plaintiff's dwelling house, and wherewith the same was fastened. Plea, that a *fi. fa.* issued against plaintiff, and was delivered to defendant, being sheriff, by virtue whereof defendant, then lawfully being in a room of the dwelling house occupied

PUGH
v.
GRIFFITH.

by D. as tenant to plaintiff, peaceably entered into the residue of the dwelling house through the door communicating between the room and the residue, the same being then open, to take in execution plaintiff's goods then in the dwelling house, and did take them; and because the outer door was shut and fastened with the lock, bolt, and staple, so that defendant could not carry away the goods or execute the writ without opening the outer door, nor open the door without breaking the lock, &c., and because neither plaintiff nor any other on his behalf was in the dwelling house so that defendant could request plaintiff or such other to open the outer door, defendant, for the purposes aforesaid, did open the outer door, and, in so doing, did necessarily break, &c., the locks, &c., doing no unnecessary damage.

Held, on demurrer, that the plea was good, though it was not shown how the defendant entered into the house, nor who fastened the outer door; and that it sufficiently appeared that there was no other way of getting out.

2. Where the declaration complained of breaking and opening divers doors of plaintiff's dwelling house, and breaking to pieces their locks, &c., and the plaintiff then new assigned that he brought his action for defendant's breaking the outer door of the house; and then new assigned again that he brought his action for defendant's breaking, &c., the locks, &c., belonging to the outer door, and wherewith it was fastened: Held, that the second new assignment was not bad, inasmuch as, under the complaint of breaking the outer door, plaintiff might give evidence of breaking the locks, &c.; and that the second new assignment and the plea to it raised the question whether the sheriff, under the circumstances in the plea, might break open the outer door, as if the declaration had been merely for breaking the lock, &c., of the outer door.

TRESPASS. The declaration charged that defendant, on 1st October, 1835, and on divers other days and times between &c., with force and arms &c., broke and entered a dwelling house of plaintiff, situate, &c., and made a great noise, &c., and stayed and continued therein, making such noise, &c., for a long &c., and forced and broke open, broke to pieces and damaged, divers, to wit ten, doors of plaintiff, of and belonging to the said dwelling house, and broke to pieces, damaged, and spoiled divers, to wit, twenty locks, twenty bolts, twenty staples, and twenty hinges, of and belonging to the said doors respectively, and wherewith the same were then fastened, and of great value, &c., and also, during the time aforesaid, to wit on &c., seized and took divers goods and chattels, to wit &c., of plaintiff, and carried away and converted &c.

[828]   Plea 1. As to coming with force and arms, &c., and whatever else is against the peace &c., and as to seizing, taking, carrying away, and converting &c. (a part of the goods). Not guilty.

Plea 2. As to the residue, that heretofore, and before any of   PUGH
the said times when &c., Robert Jones sued out in the Court   *v.*
of Exchequer a writ of *fi. fa.*, directed to the sheriff of Mont-   GRIFFITH.
gomeryshire, to levy of the goods and chattels of plaintiff
55*l.* 1*s.* 4*d.*, indorsed to levy the whole and 7*s.* for costs, &c.,
which was delivered to defendant, being then, and thence until
and at and after the times when &c., sheriff of Montgomeryshire,
to be executed ; by virtue of which writ, afterwards, and before the
return of the said writ, to wit at the said time when &c. in the
declaration first mentioned, defendant then lawfully being in a
certain room in and parcel of the said dwelling house in which
&c., and which said room then was occupied by one Elizabeth
Davies as tenant thereof to the plaintiff, defendant, so being
such sheriff as aforesaid, peaceably and quietly entered into the
residue of the said dwelling house in which &c., through the door
communicating between the said room so occupied by the said
Elizabeth Davies and the residue of the said dwelling house in
which &c., the same being then open, in order to seize and take
in execution the said goods and chattels of plaintiff in the
introductory part of this plea referred to, the same then being
in the said dwelling house in which &c., for the purpose of
levying the said monies so directed to be levied by the said
writ and the said indorsement so made thereon as aforesaid, and
did, at the said times when &c., seize and take in execution the
said last mentioned goods and chattels, and, by sale thereof, levy
a certain *sum of money, to wit &c., part and parcel of the   [*829]
damages &c., and, in so doing. and because certain doors of and
belonging to the said dwelling house in which &c., at the said
time when &c., were shut, locked, and fastened with the said
locks, bolts, staples, and hinges in the said declaration mentioned,
so that defendant, so being in the said dwelling house in which
&c., could not seize, take, and carry away the goods and chattels
aforesaid, to levy the monies aforesaid, or execute the said writ,
without forcing and breaking open the said doors, defendant,
while he so continued in the said house as aforesaid, at the said
time when &c., and for the purpose aforesaid, did force and
break open the said doors, and, in so doing, did necessarily a
little break and damage the same, and also a little break to pieces,

damage, and spoil the said locks, bolts, staples and hinges of
and belonging to the said doors respectively, doing no unnecessary
damage to the plaintiff in that behalf; and also, in the said
execution of the said writ, defendant, so being such sheriff, did
necessarily and unavoidably make a little noise, &c., and stay,
&c., for the space of time in the declaration mentioned, as he
lawfully &c., which are the said &c.

The plaintiff joined issue on the first plea; and, as to the
second, replied that he brought his action, not for the trespasses
in the second plea mentioned and attempted to be justified, but
for that defendant, on the said several days and times &c., with
force and arms, &c., broke and entered the outer door of the
said dwelling house in the declaration mentioned, and also broke
and entered the said dwelling house, and made the said noise, &c.,
therein in the declaration mentioned, and stayed and continued
&c., making the said noise, &c., *on other and different occasions,
and at other and different times, and in other and different parts
of the said dwelling house in the declaration mentioned than in
the second plea mentioned, and therein attempted to be justified,
in manner and form as the said plaintiff hath above thereof in
his declaration in that behalf complained against defendant;
which said several trespasses above newly assigned are other and
different trespasses &c.   Verification.

[*830]

Plea to the new assignment. As to all except breaking the
outer door of the said dwelling house, in which &c., and entering the same, as in the new assignment &c., Not guilty. As to
breaking the outer door &c., and entering, &c. as in the new
assignment is alleged, &c., that, the said *fieri facias* having so
issued, and having been so delivered to defendant, so being
sheriff &c., and defendant having peaceably and quietly entered
into the said dwelling house in which &c., to seize and take in
execution the goods and chattels of plaintiff in the second plea
mentioned, in the manner and for the purpose therein also mentioned, defendant, at the said times when &c., did seize and take
in execution the said goods and chattels as in that plea is alleged,
under and by virtue of the said writ; and, because the outer
door of and belonging to the said dwelling house in which &c.,
at the said time when &c. in the said new assignment mentioned,

was shut and fastened, so that defendant, so being in the said dwelling house &c. as aforesaid, and having so seized &c. as aforesaid, could not take and carry away the goods and chattels aforesaid in order to levy the monies directed to be levied by the said writ and indorsement, or execute the said writ, without opening the said outer door, and because neither plaintiff *nor [*831] any other person on his behalf was in the said dwelling house at the same time when &c., so that defendant could request plaintiff or such other person to open the said outer door, defendant, so being in the said house at the said time when &c., for the purpose last aforesaid, did open the said outer door, and, in so doing, did necessarily and unavoidably a little break the same, doing no unnecessary damage &c. ; and defendant did then take and carry away the said goods and chattels for the purpose aforesaid, and in order to levy &c. ; and, in so doing, defendant did necessarily and unavoidably go out of and re-enter the said dwelling house by the outer door thereof, the said outer door being open at the time of such re-entry, in order to take and carry away the said goods and chattels for the purpose aforesaid, and as he lawfully &c., which are the same supposed trespasses &c.

The plaintiff joined issue on the traverse ; and, as to the second plea to the new assignment, new assigned again, that he brought his action, not for the trespasses in the introductory part of the second plea to the said new assignment mentioned &c., but for that defendant, on the several days and times in the declaration and in the said new assignment in that behalf mentioned, with force and arms, &c., broke to pieces, damaged, and spoiled the locks, bolts, staples, and hinges in the declaration mentioned, which said locks, bolts, staples and hinges were appertaining, belonging, and fixed to the said outer door of the said dwelling house in the declaration and in the said new assignment mentioned, and wherewith the same was fastened, in manner and form as plaintiff hath above thereof in his declaration &c. complained, which said several trespasses lastly new assigned *are [*832] other and different trespasses than the said trespasses in the said second plea to the said new assignment mentioned, &c.

To this second new assignment, the defendant pleaded, first, Not guilty ; secondly, as to breaking &c., one lock, one bolt, and

PUGH
v.
GRIFFITH.

one staple, parcel of the locks, bolts, and staples in the said last new assignment mentioned, and as is therein alleged, that, the said *fieri facias* having so issued, and been so delivered to defendant, being sheriff, as in the said second plea is mentioned, and defendant having peaceably and quietly entered into the said dwelling house in which &c., to seize and take in execution the goods and chattels of plaintiff in the second plea mentioned, in the manner and for the purpose therein also mentioned, defendant, at the said times when &c., did seize the said goods and chattels, as in that plea is alleged, under and by virtue of the said writ; and, because the outer door of and belonging to the said dwelling house in which &c., at the said time when &c., in the last new assignment mentioned, was shut and fastened with the said one lock, one bolt, and one staple, in the introductory part of this plea mentioned, so that defendant, so being in the said dwelling house in which &c., and having so seized &c. the said goods and chattels as aforesaid, could not take and carry away the said goods and chattels in order to levy or execute the said writ, without opening the said outer door, nor could defendant, upon that occasion open the said outer door so being fastened as aforesaid, for the purpose last aforesaid, without a little breaking, &c., the said last mentioned lock, bolt, and staple, and because neither plaintiff nor any other person on his behalf

[*833]

was in the said dwelling house at the said *time when &c. so that defendant could request plaintiff or such other person to open the said outer door, defendant, so being in the said house as aforesaid, at the said time when &c., and for the purpose last aforesaid, did open the said outer door, and, in so doing, did necessarily and unavoidably a little break, &c., the said last mentioned lock, bolt, and staple, then appertaining and belonging to the said outer door, and wherewith the same was so fastened as aforesaid, doing no unnecessary damage &c., and as he lawfully, &c., which are the said supposed trespasses &c., and whereof plaintiff hath above by his said last new assignment complained &c.

The plaintiff joined issue on the traverse; and, as to the rest of the plea, demurred, assigning for cause that defendant acknowledged the breaking to pieces, &c., one lock, one bolt, and one

staple, appertaining, belonging, and fixed to the outer door of
the dwelling house of plaintiff, and wherewith the same was
fastened, as in the declaration and in the second new assignment
alleged, and attempted to justify the same breaking, &c., under
the execution of a writ of *fieri facias* directed to the sheriff, &c.
Joinder in demurrer.

PUGH
r.
GRIFFITH.

[After argument, the COURT took time for consideration.]

LORD DENMAN, Ch. J., in this Term (January 31st), delivered the
    judgment of the Court (1).   After going through the pleadings
    his Lordship said :

[837]

Upon this state of the pleading, it appears that the defendant,
in his plea to the declaration, has justified breaking and entering
the house, and seizing the goods, under a writ of *fieri fac as*. He
does not allege in the plea that the outer door was open, which
is generally necessary ; but he says that he was lawfully in a part
of the house in the occupation of a lodger ; and, if the communication between the part of the house occupied by the lodger and
the rest of the house should be in the nature of an outer door for
the protection of the plaintiff's house, there is an averment in the
plea that the communication between the two was open, and
therefore the entry into the part occupied by the plaintiff was
authorised. The plaintiff, in answer to this, says the matters
justified in the plea are not what he complains of ; but he says he
brought his action, not for that, but for breaking the outer door,
and entering the house on other occasions, and at other times,
and in different parts of the house. The defendant's answer to
this new assignment is what has been already stated ; *that, in
order to take the goods out of the house, it was necessary to open
the outer door ; and, as neither the plaintiff nor any body on his
behalf was there, so as a request could be made to them, he
opened it. The plaintiff, in answer, says, by another new assignment, that he did not bring his action for that, but for breaking
the locks, bolts, staples, and hinges of the outer door.

[*838]

It is to be observed that, in the first new assignment, the
plaintiff says nothing about the locks, bolts, staples, and hinges ;

    (1) Lord Denman, Ch. J., Littledale, Williams, and Coleridge, JJ.

and, as the plaintiff has in that new assignment confined his complaint to breaking the outer door, and breaking and entering the house, he cannot carry his second new assignment beyond the first new assignment. A question may at first appear to arise, whether this second new assignment is not bad altogether : but we think not, because, under the complaint of breaking the outer door, the plaintiff might give evidence of breaking the locks, &c., fixed to and part of the door.

Then the defendant, in answer to this, pleads as before stated : so that the general question, whether a sheriff who has seized goods under a *fieri facias* has a right to break an outer door to take them out of the house, when there is nobody of whom to request that the door may be opened, would not appear to arise ; for the plaintiff, by his second new assignment, abandons that complaint: and the only question on this record would now appear to be, whether he has a right to break the lock, bolt, and staple of the outer door to take out the goods. But, though the plaintiff has abandoned the general complaint of breaking the outer door of the house, yet, under the objection he makes as to breaking the lock, bolt and staple, he may contend that the
[*839]   sheriff had no *right to break the outer door ; and, though he has abandoned the general breaking open the door, he has not admitted, in the pleadings, as he might have been held to do if he had pleaded over in answer to the defendant's pleading : but here his pleading over is that the defendant has not given any answer to what the plaintiff means to complain of, and that he has mistaken the nature of the plaintiff's complaint, and that it ought to be considered in the same light as if there was a *nolle prosequi* as to the whole of the trespasses except breaking the lock, bolt, and staple of the outer door ; and, as to that, we think that he may stand in the same situation as if his declaration had been originally confined to the mere act of breaking the lock, bolt, and staple of an outer door of the house.

It appears to us that, on the allegations on this record which are not denied, the sheriff had a right to break open the outer door, and to break the lock, bolt, and staple affixed to it. The sheriff shows a lawful entry into the house, and a lawful seizure of the goods ; and, in his plea to the first new assignment, he says that he could not take the goods out of the house without opening the outer door; the particular door therefore is identified, so that it cannot be said there were any other doors, or any other mode of getting the goods out. Then what was the sheriff to do? The goods could not be kept for ever in the house; and neither the plaintiff, nor any body else, was there so that he could request them to open the door, and there was nothing else to be done but to open it himself; and he says that he did no unnecessary damage; and then, as to the complaint of breaking the lock, bolt, and staple, that he could not open the outer door without breaking, *damaging, and spoiling them; and as to that also he alleges the absence of the plaintiff and every other person to whom he could make a request; and therefore, as to that also, which is now the only cause of complaint, he appears to be justified as a matter of necessity in order to get the goods out to execute the writ. It may be said that he locked the door himself; and, if so, he could not justify the breaking the lock, &c., to pieces. If he had done so, it might be further new assigned, or replied in some way or other; but, in pleading a justification, we do not think it necessary to aver that the trespass complained of was not occasioned by his own default. The case of *White* v. *Whitshire* (1) was trespass for breaking and entering plaintiff's house: justification under a *fieri facias*; and that, after entry to take the goods in execution, the plaintiff shut the door upon the bailiffs, and imprisoned them; then the defendant broke open the doors, and broke the locks to rescue the bailiffs. The COURT said that, though the sheriff cannot break open a house to make execution by a *fieri facias*, yet, when the door is open, and he enters and is disturbed in his execution by the parties who are within the house, he may break into the house and rescue his bailiffs, and so take execution. In that case, the breaking into the house was justified, because the plaintiff himself had occasioned the necessity of it; but it does not follow that there may not be other occasions where the outer door may be broken.

Several cases were cited, as to the duties and powers of sheriffs; but they do not so nearly apply to the point raised on

[*840]

(1) Palm. 52; S. C. 2 Roll. Rep. 137; Cro. Jac. 555.

this record as to make it necessary to comment *upon them. Some of them seem to require that a demand should be made by the sheriff in particular cases; but the necessity of a demand in the present case is obviated, because there was nobody on whom a demand could be made.

Upon the whole of the case, we are of opinion that there should be judgment for the defendant.

Judgment for defendant.

REG. *v.* GUEST AND OTHERS (1).

(7 Adol. & Ellis, 951—956; S. C. 2 N. & P. 663; W. W. & D. 651; 7 L. J. (N. S.) M. C. 38.)

> In a rate laid upon buildings to which machinery is attached for the purpose of manufacture, the real property ought to be as-essed according to its actual value as combined with the machinery, without considering whether the machinery be real or personal property, and liable, or not, to distress or seizure under a *fi. fa.*, or whether it would go to the heir or executor, or, at the expiration of a lease, to the landlord or tenant.

ON appeal against a rate made for the relief of the poor of the parish of Merthyr Tydvil, Glamorganshire, the following case was submitted to this Court by the Sessions:

The appellants are the lessees and occupiers of the Dowlais iron works in the said parish, and, as connected with these works, they are also the lessees and occupiers of certain iron mines and coal mines. (The case then stated a point on which an objection was taken and the Sessions made an amendment, and which was not referred to this Court.) The appellants further objected to the amount of the rate upon their iron works, because several engines and other machinery used for working the iron mines mentioned in the rate, and also the several engines and other machinery used *in the process of manufacturing iron from the iron stone, were, as the appellants alleged, not fixed to the freehold so as to be regarded in law as real property rateable to the relief of the poor, and it was proved that personal property was not charged to the poor-rate in the parish. The mode of erecting such engines and machinery was

[*952]

---

(1) Cited in judgments: *Laing* v. *Bishopwearmouth* (1878) 3 Q. B. D. 299, 305, 47 L. J. M. C. 41, 44; *Tyne*   *Boiler Works* v. *Longbenton Overseers* (1886) 18 Q. B. Div. 81, 89, 56 L. J. M. C. 8, 11.—R. C.

proved to be as follows.   The soil is first excavated to a certain depth for the purpose of laying down foundation walls of strong masonry.   Into the walls, when built, are introduced balk and other strong timber which are covered and secured by means of bolts and other contrivances to and by an iron platform.   Upon this platform are placed frames made of wood and iron, which frames are inserted into the walls of the buildings in which the engine and machinery are enclosed ; these frames then serve as the foundations of the engines and machinery, which are attached to the frames by means of cotterels or keys and jibs in such a manner as to be tightened, or slackened, or altogether removed, at pleasure.   Such removal may be effected from and out of the buildings which enclose them without injury either to the engines or machinery or to the buildings or the soil, and without displacing any part thereof.   The machinery thus described is referred to in amount of value in the schedule No. 2 of the rate, as thereunto annexed.   The iron mines occupied by the appellants are situate in the parish of Merthyr Tydvil, and within a short distance from the works, the engines and the machinery comprised in the rate.   As to such of the engines as are applicable to the working of the iron mines, whether such engines are fixed to the freehold or not, the Sessions allowed the objection and amended the rate accordingly ; and no question is raised as to such amendment.

The Sessions, with the amendments before mentioned, confirmed the rate, subject to the opinion of this Court.

[953]

The schedule referred to consisted of several columns.   The first was headed "Landlords," and contained the names of the Marquis of Bute, and Messrs. Guest, Lewis & Co.   The second was headed "Persons rated," and contained the names of Messrs. Guest, Lewis & Co.   The third specified the "Property assessed," fixed, and moveable.   Among the articles of the first description were blast furnaces, casting-houses, foundry, blast-engines, &c.   Of the latter, blast-engines, furnaces, engines for rolling, "machinery" (described generally as such), &c.   The fourth and fifth columns, headed "Schedule No. 1" and "Schedule No. 2," stated the values of the two descriptions of property respectively.

The question for this Court was stated to be, whether the appellants are liable to be rated for the various properties referred to in the schedule No. 2 of the rate before set forth, or whether the rate is unequal in respect of the appellants being rated for them.   If the Court should be of opinion that the properties charged in schedule 2 ought not to be charged, the rate was to be amended accordingly.   The case was argued in Hilary Term, 1837 (1).

Maule and *John Evans*, in support of the order of Sessions :

The articles in schedule 2 were properly taken into account in the rate.   On a question as to rating, if the article is practically connected with the real property, and forms a part of the means of enjoying *it, the Court will not inquire with nicety whether it would fall within any of the cases which have arisen between heir and executor or landlord and tenant, or upon the subject of reputed ownership.   The principle is that, where real property derives an increased annual value from a personal chattel annexed to it, the rate must be calculated on such increased value : 1 Nol. P. L. 81—84 (4th edit.), and *Rex* v. *St. Nicholas, Gloucester* (2), and other cases cited in those pages.   The present case is stronger than those, as to the connection of the machinery with the real property.   In some of those instances the building and the annexed property were demised together ; but, with reference to the poor law, that circumstance creates no distinction.   It would be absurd to say that, in rating a house built for the purpose of working machinery, the overseers should assess the building as a shell, denuding it of that for the sake of which it exists.   Nor can it reasonably be contended that, if the machinery be rateable, but there is a portion which might be subtracted without damage, a deduction should be made for so much.

[*954]

Sir J. Campbell, Attorney-General, *E. V. Williams*, and
Powell, *contra* :

The rate here is on buildings and machinery ; but part of the machinery is personal property, and therefore ought not to be

(1) January 25th.   Before Lord   (2) Cald. 262; S. C. note (a) to
Denman, Ch. J., Williams and   *Rex* v. *Hogg*, 1 B. R. 375 (1 T. R.
Coleridge, JJ.   723).

assessed in a parish where no other personal property is rated. The articles which, the appellants contend, have been improperly rated, are removable, and would go to the executor, not the heir, might be taken in execution, and would be the subject of trover. Messrs. Guest & Co. have not *the freehold; they are lessees, and may remove these articles at the end of their term. In *Rex* v. *St. Nicholas, Gloucester* (1), the subject of rate was a "machine-house;" and it was assessed more highly on account of the increased value of the house, derived from a weighing-machine. Here the appellants are rated for buildings, and for machinery, part of which is personal property. The light in which such property would be considered in an action between outgoing and incoming tenants, in a case of settlement, or on a question of reputed ownership, appears from *Davis* v. *Jones* (2), *Rex* v. *Otley* (3), *Horn* v. *Baker* (4), *Storer* v. *Hunter* (5), *Clark* v. *Crownshaw* (6), *Coombs* v. *Beaumont* (7). The law as to fixed machinery is summed up by Lord LYNDHURST, C. B., in *Trappes* v. *Harter* (8).

(COLERIDGE, J. mentioned *Wansbrough* v. *Maton* (9).)

The COURT desired to see the original rate.

Cur. adv. vult.

The rate-book having been submitted to the Court in Easter Term, 1837,

LORD DENMAN, Ch. J. now delivered judgment as follows:

This was an appeal against a rate on the ground that many articles of machinery employed by the appellant in his manufacture were personal property, and not subject to be rated. The Sessions proposed numerous *questions to us (10); but we did not think their statement so full as it might have been, and we desired to see a copy of the rate, in the hope that we might be

Rⁱᵍ.
v.
GUEST.

[*955]

[*956]

(1) Cald. 262.
(2) 20 R. R. 396 (2 B. & Ald. 165).
(3) 35 R. R. 258 (1 B. & Ad. 161).
(4) 9 R. R. 541 (9 East, 215).
(5) 3 B. & C. 368.
(6) 3 B. & Ad. 804.
(7) 39 R. R. 400 (5 B. & Ad. 72).

(8) 2 Cr. & M. 153; 3 Tyr. 603.
(9) 43 R. R. 510 (4 Ad. & El. 884).

(10) A case, with many questions, had been sent up; but it was afterwards reduced to the form in which the present report gives it.

REG.
v.
GUEST.

enabled, from the description there given, to specify the articles that ought to be included.   In this we are disappointed, and can only direct that the rate should finally stand on the general principle which we have lately had occasion to lay down (1), that real property ought to be rated according to its actual value, as combined with the machinery attached to it, without considering whether the machinery be real or personal property, so as to be liable to distress or seizure under a *fieri facias*, or whether it would descend to the heir or executor, or belong, at the expiration of a lease, to landlord or tenant.

Rate to stand accordingly.

(1) See *Rex* v. *The Birmingham and Staffordshire Gas Light Company*, p. 572, *ante* (6 Ad. & El. 634).

INDEX.

END OF VOL. XLV.

BRADBURY, AGNEW, & CO. LD., PRINTERS, LONDON AND TONBRIDGE.

Lightning Source UK Ltd.
Milton Keynes UK
UKHW010616030119

334852UK00010B/964/P